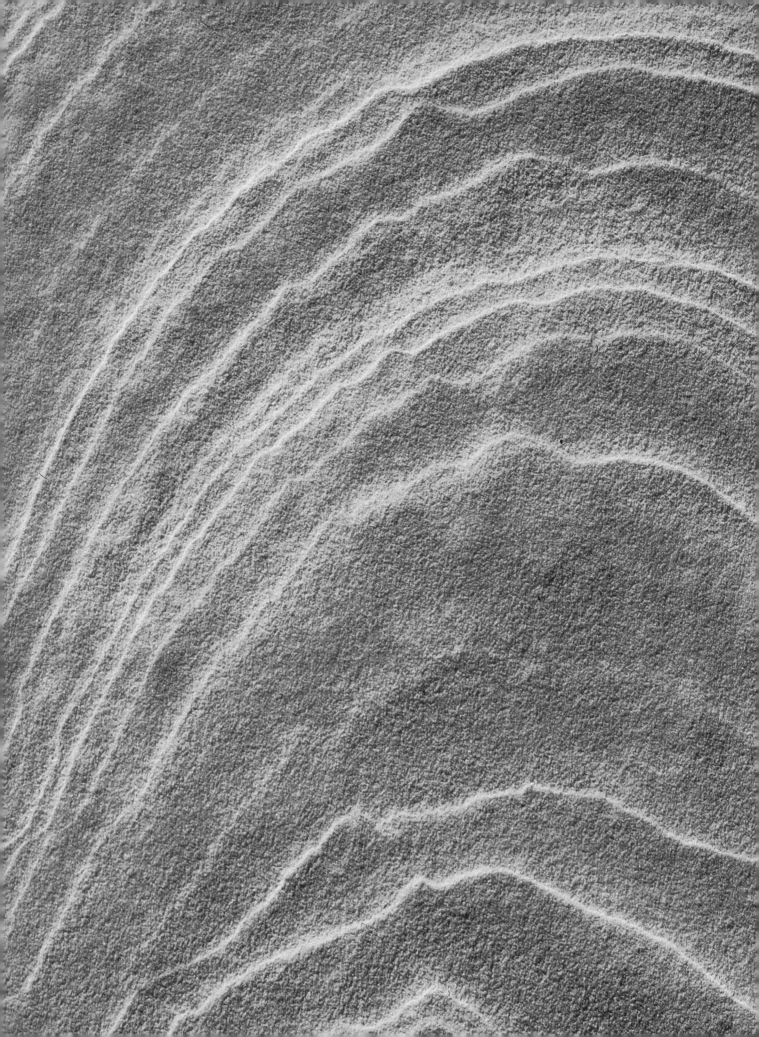

HARCOURT
Science

Harcourt School Publishers

Orlando • Boston • Dallas • Chicago • San Diego

www.harcourtschool.com

Cover Image: This reptile is a veiled chameleon *(Chamaelo calyptratus)*. They are often raised and sold as pets. In the wild, they live in trees on the humid parts of the Arabian penisula.

Printed in the United States of America

ISBN 0-15-311207-7

3 4 5 6 7 8 9 10 032 2002 2001 2000

Authors

Marjorie Slavick Frank
Former Adjunct Faculty Member at Hunter, Brooklyn, and Manhattan Colleges
New York, New York

Robert M. Jones
Professor of Education
University of Houston-Clear Lake
Houston, Texas

Gerald H. Krockover
Professor of Earth and Atmospheric Science Education
School Mathematics and Science Center
Purdue University
West Lafayette, Indiana

Mozell P. Lang
Science Education Consultant
Michigan Department of Education
Lansing, Michigan

Joyce C. McLeod
Visiting Professor
Rollins College
Winter Park, Florida

Carol J. Valenta
Vice President—Education, Exhibits, and Programs
St. Louis Science Center
St. Louis, Missouri

Barry A. Van Deman
Science Program Director
Arlington, Virginia

UNIT A

LIFE SCIENCE
A World of Living Things

UNIT B

LIFE SCIENCE
Looking at Ecosystems

E A R T H   S C I E N C E

Earth's Surface

UNIT D

EARTH SCIENCE

Patterns on Earth and In Space

UNIT E

PHYSICAL SCIENCE
Matter and Energy

UNIT F

PHYSICAL SCIENCE
Forces and Motion

Using Science Process Skills

When scientists try to find an answer to a question or do an experiment, they use thinking tools called the process skills. You use many of the process skills whenever you speak, listen, read, write, or think. Think about how these students used process skills to help them answer questions and do experiments.

Matthew is spending the day at the beach. He finds seashells. He carefully **observes** the shells and **compares** their shapes and their colors. He **classifies** them into groups according to their shapes.

Try This Observe, compare, and classify objects that interest you, such as rocks or leaves.

Talk About It How did Matthew use the skills of observing and comparing to classify his shells into groups?

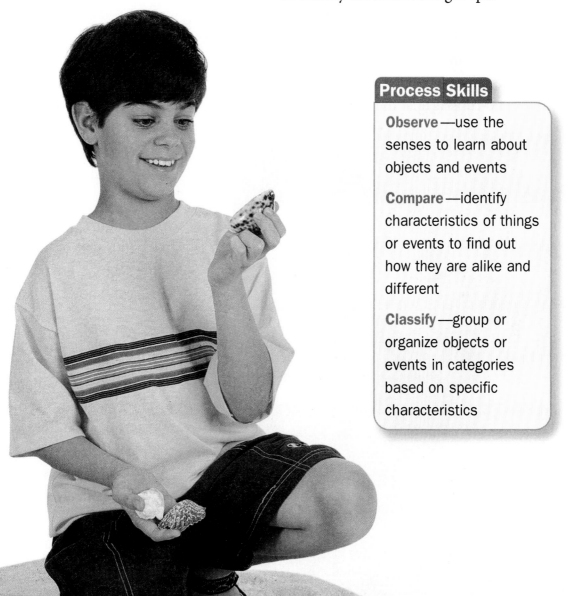

Process Skills

Observe—use the senses to learn about objects and events

Compare—identify characteristics of things or events to find out how they are alike and different

Classify—group or organize objects or events in categories based on specific characteristics

Ling wanted to find out whether sand rubbing against rocks would cause pieces of the rock to flake off. He collected three rocks, measured their masses, and then put them in a jar with sand and water. He shook the rocks every day for a week. At the end of the week he **measured** and **recorded** the mass of the rocks and the mass of the sand and the container. He **interpreted** his data and **concluded** that rocks are broken down when sand rubs against them.

Try This Use a thermometer to measure the temperature inside and outside your classroom at the same time each day for a week. Record, display, and interpret your data to find the average indoor and outdoor temperatures for the week.

Talk About It How does displaying your data in charts, tables, and graphs help you interpret it?

Process Skills

Measure — compare an attribute of an object, such as mass, length, or capacity, to a unit of measure such as gram, centimeter, or liter.
Gather, Record, Display, or Interpret Data
- gather data by making observations which are used to make inferences or predictions
- record data by writing down the observations
- display data by making tables, charts, or graphs
- interpret data by drawing conclusions about what the data shows

Caitlin wanted to know how the light switch in her bedroom worked. She decided to **use a model** to see how the electrical wires in the wall and the switch worked to turn the light on and off. She used batteries, wires, a flashlight bulb, a bulb holder, thumbtacks, and a paper clip to build her model. She **predicted** that the bulb, the wires, and the batteries had to be connected to make the bulb light. She **inferred** that the paper clip switch interrupted the flow of electricity to turn off the light. Caitlin's model verified her prediction and her inference.

Try This Make a model to show how you can light more than one bulb.

Talk About It How does using a model help you understand how electricity works to light a bulb?

Process Skills

Use a model — make a representation to explain an idea, an object, or an event, such as how something works

Predict — form an idea of an expected outcome based on observations or experience

Infer — use logical reasoning to explain events and make conclusions based on observations

Kendra wants to know which brand of paper towel absorbs the most water. She **planned and conducted a simple investigation** to find out. She chose three brands of paper towels. She poured one liter of water into each of three beakers. She put a towel from each of the three brands in a beaker for 10 seconds. She pulled the towel out of the water and let it drain back into the beaker for 5 seconds. She then measured the amount of water left in the beaker.

She **controlled variables** in her experiment by making sure each beaker contained exactly the same amount of water and that she timed each step in her experiment exactly. Based on the results of this test, she was able to tell her Dad which brand of paper towel was the most absorbent.

Try This Plan and conduct an investigation to compare different brands of a product or service that you and your family use. Identify the variables that you will control.

Talk About It Why is it important to identify and control the variables in an investigation?

Process Skills

Plan and conduct simple investigations — identify and perform the steps necessary to find the answer to a question using appropriate tools and recording and analyzing data collected

Control variables — identify and control factors that affect the outcome of an experiment so that only one variable is affected in a test

You will have many opportunities to practice and apply these and other process skills in *Harcourt Science.* An exciting year of science discoveries lies ahead!

Safety in Science

Doing investigations in science can be fun, but you need to be sure you do them safely. Here are some rules to follow.

1. Think ahead. Study the steps of the investigation so you know what to expect. If you have any questions, ask your teacher. Be sure you understand any safety symbols that are shown.

2. Be neat. Keep your work area clean. If you have long hair, pull it back so it doesn't get in the way. Roll or push up long sleeves to keep them away from your experiment.

3. Oops! If you should spill or break something, or get cut, tell your teacher right away.

4. Watch your eyes. Wear safety goggles anytime you are directed to do so. If you get anything in your eyes, tell your teacher right away.

5. Yuck! Never eat or drink anything during a science activity unless you are told to do so by your teacher.

6. Don't get shocked. Be especially careful if an electric appliance is used. Be sure that electric cords are in a safe place where you can't trip over them. Don't ever pull a plug out of an outlet by pulling on the cord.

7. Keep it clean. Always clean up when you have finished. Put everything away and wipe your work area. Wash your hands.

In some activities you will see these symbols. They are signs for what you need to act safely.

Be especially careful.

Wear safety goggles.

Be careful with sharp objects.

Don't get burned.

Protect your clothes.

Protect your hands with mitts.

Be careful with electricity.

A World of
Living Things

UNIT A

LIFE SCIENCE

A World of Living Things

Unit Project

Animal Observer

Design and make an animal feeder. Your feeder could be either for birds or for squirrels. Decide what kinds of food to provide. After you have built your feeder, use binoculars to observe it from a distance. Take notes about the animals at the feeder. You might also take photographs or draw sketches of the animals that visit your feeder and the foods they eat. Classify the birds or other animals you see. Make a bar graph to show the data you collect.

Chapter 1

Classifying Living Things

Have you ever noticed how some living things have the same kinds of parts? A cat and a dog each have fur, four legs, and a tail. An ant and a cockroach each have six legs. Scientists look at the similarities among living things and put them into groups.

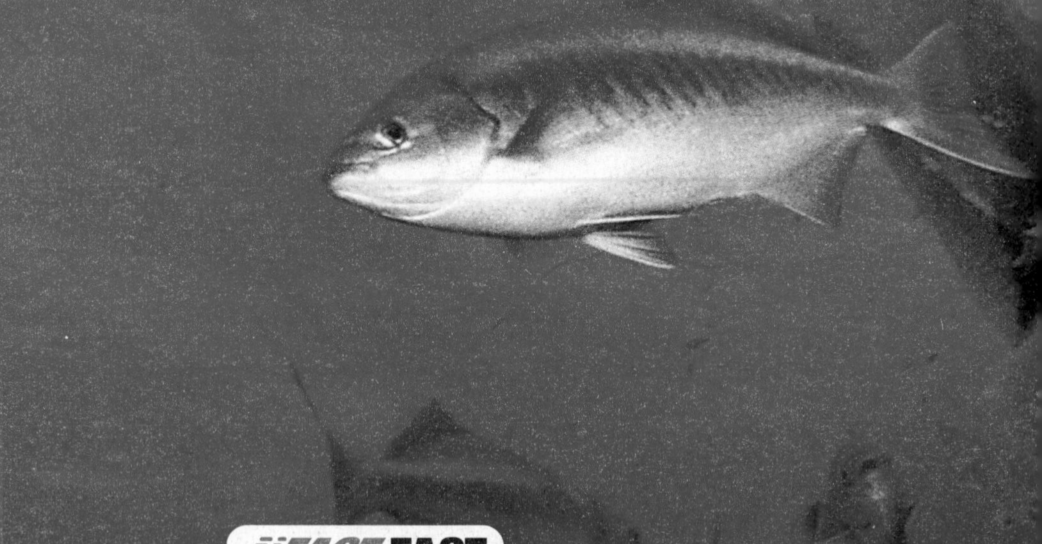

Vocabulary Preview

classification
kingdom
moneran
protist
fungi
genus
species
vertebrates
mammals
reptiles
amphibians
invertebrates
arthropods
mollusks
vascular plants
nonvascular plants

FAST FACT

A kelp may look like a plant, but it's not. The leaf and stem parts of a kelp are different from those of plants. Instead, kelps belong to the protist kingdom. Other protists include microscopic amoebas and paramecia.

A duckbill platypus looks like a mixed-up animal. You might think it's a bird because it has a bill and lays eggs. But scientists say it's a mammal like a dog or cat because it has fur and produces milk for its young.

This Ithaca bog beetle was in an insect collection at Cornell University in Ithaca, New York, for 85 years before anyone realized it had no scientific name. Scientists think there are many more living things to be classified and named. Many haven't even been discovered yet.

Numbers of Living Things

Type of Living Thing	Number of Known Species, or Kinds
Insects	750,000
Fish	25,000
Orchids	20,000

A3

How Do Scientists Classify Living Things?

In this lesson, you can . . .

 INVESTIGATE ways to group nonliving objects.

 LEARN ABOUT classification.

 LINK to math, writing, art, and technology.

◄ This sun bear is a type of animal called a mammal. What other types of animals can you name?

INVESTIGATE

Classifying Shoes

Activity Purpose You've probably looked for a certain book in a library. Imagine how hard it would be to find a book in a library full of books if they were not grouped by topic. In this activity you will practice **classifying** some familiar items.

Materials
- shoes
- newspaper or paper towels

Activity Procedure

1. Take off one shoe and put it with your classmates' shoes. If you put the shoes on a desk or table, cover it first with newspaper or paper towels. (Picture A)

2. Find a way to **classify** the shoes. Begin by finding two or three large groups of shoes that are alike. Write a description of each group. (Picture B)

3. **Classify** the large groups of shoes into smaller and smaller groups. Each smaller group should be alike in some way.

Picture A

Picture B

4 Write a description of each smaller group.

5 Stop classifying when you have sorted all the shoes into groups with two or fewer members.

Draw Conclusions

1. What features did you use to **classify** the shoes?

2. **Compare** your classification system with a classmate's system. How are your systems alike? How are they different?

3. **Scientists at Work** Scientists **classify** living things to show how living things are alike. Why might it be important for scientists to agree on a set of rules for classifying living things?

Investigate Further **Classify** other groups of things such as toys, cars, or pictures of animals. Write a brief explanation of your classification system.

Process Skill Tip

When you **classify** things, you put them into groups based on how they are alike. Things that are not similar are in different groups. Things that have similar characteristics form a group.

Classification

Grouping Living Things

If you were asked to go to the grocery store to buy fresh peaches, how would you find them? You know how your grocery store is set up, so you would probably go to the produce department and find the fruit section. There you would look for peaches. If a store decided to put some fruit with the cereal and some with the meat, finding peaches would be much more difficult.

Like grocery shoppers, scientists need to be able to find things easily. Just as you did with shoes in the investigation, scientists look at living things and identify their characteristics. They then group together living things that have similar features. This act of grouping things by using a set of rules is called **classification** (klas•uh•fih•KAY•shuhn).

✔ **How do scientists group living things?**

FIND OUT

- why scientists group living things
- the names of the five largest groups of living things

VOCABULARY

classification
kingdom
moneran
protist
fungi
genus
species

The living things shown in the forest scene and in the smaller photos belong to different groups.

Bacterium

Water strider

Paramecium

The Five Kingdoms

Kingdom	Important Characteristics	Examples
Animals	Many-celled, feed on other living things	Monkeys, birds, frogs, fish, spiders
Plants	Many-celled, make their own food	Trees, flowers, grasses, ferns, mosses
Fungi	Most many-celled, absorb food from other living things or dead things such as logs	Mushrooms, yeasts, molds
Protists	Most one-celled, make their own food or feed on other living things	Algae, amoebas, diatoms
Monerans	One-celled, no cell nuclei, some make their own food, some feed on other living things	Bacteria

Grouping by Similarities and Differences

Scientists classify for many reasons. Classifying living things makes it easier to find and share information about them. When scientists discover a new living thing, classification can show how the new living thing relates to others that are already classified.

All living things can be classified into one of five kingdoms. A **kingdom** (KING•duhm) is the largest group into which living things can be classified. Every member of a kingdom has some characteristics that are the same as those of other members. For example, the bacterium shown on page A6 is a moneran. Every member of the **moneran** (muh•NIR•uhn) kingdom is only one cell.

The cell has no nucleus (NOO•klee•uhs), or control center.

Compare the bacterium to the paramecium on page A6. Paramecia are protists. Most members of the **protist** (PROHT•ist) kingdom are also only one cell. However, each cell does have a nucleus.

Fungi make up a third kingdom. **Fungi** (FUHN•jy) have nuclei, and most are many-celled. They look like plants, but they can't make their own food as plants do. You have eaten fungi if you've ever eaten mushrooms.

Plants and animals make up the other two kingdoms. Every day you see members of these two kingdoms such as grass, flowers, cats, and dogs.

✔ **How are monerans and protists the same? How are they different?**

Forming Smaller Groups

Classification doesn't stop at the kingdom level. Scientists studied the living things in each kingdom to see how they are alike and how they are different. They used characteristics to make smaller and smaller groups, and they gave each smaller group a name. The most specific classification groups have only one type of living thing. The chart below shows how brown bears can be classified by using this method.

Most living things have a common name such as *brown bear.* But common names may be different in different places. It's important to have names that scientists everywhere recognize. For this reason, scientists name animals with the labels of the two smallest classification groups. The name of the second smallest group, the **genus** (JEE•nuhs), is joined with the name of the smallest group, the **species** (SPEE•sheez). For example, the scientific name for a house cat is *Felis domesticus,* and a brown bear is called *Ursus arctos.*

✔ **How do scientists form smaller groups of living things?**

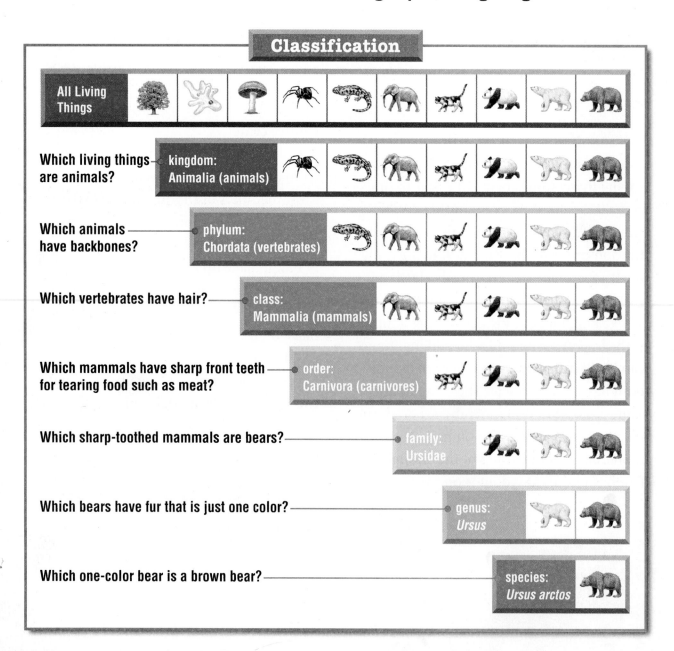

Classification

All Living Things									

Which living things are animals? — **kingdom: Animalia (animals)**

Which animals have backbones? — **phylum: Chordata (vertebrates)**

Which vertebrates have hair? — **class: Mammalia (mammals)**

Which mammals have sharp front teeth for tearing food such as meat? — **order: Carnivora (carnivores)**

Which sharp-toothed mammals are bears? — **family: Ursidae**

Which bears have fur that is just one color? — **genus: Ursus**

Which one-color bear is a brown bear? — **species: Ursus arctos**

▲ This grizzly bear cub's scientific name is *Ursus* (genus) *arctos* (species).

Summary

Scientists organize living things to make studying and discussing them easier. Scientists classify all living things into five kingdoms—monerans, protists, fungi, plants, and animals. The five kingdoms are divided into smaller groups.

Review

1. Why do scientists organize information about living things?
2. What are the five kingdoms of living things?
3. How do scientists name each type of living thing?
4. **Critical Thinking** There are probably millions of living things that scientists haven't discovered yet. If scientists were to find a living thing that didn't fit into any of the five kingdoms, what would they need to do?
5. **Test Prep** Which kingdom contains one-celled living things without nuclei?
   A plants   C fungi
   B monerans   D protists

LINKS

MATH LINK

Graphing Suppose you have found a cave in which animals—three snakes, six bats, and a bear—are living. To report your discovery to your classmates, make a bar graph showing the types and numbers of animals in the cave.

WRITING LINK

Informative Writing—Description Suppose you've discovered a new species of living thing. For your teacher, write two or three paragraphs to describe how you found it, what its characteristics are, and how you decided on its name.

ART LINK

Designing Labels Think about how you could improve the organization of your books, games, or CDs. Classify them and then design picture labels for each group. Put the labels on your books, games, or CDs so that you can more easily find the ones you want.

TECHNOLOGY LINK

To learn more about some bears, watch *China Panda* on the **Harcourt Science Newsroom Video**.

Building a Model Backbone

Activity Purpose Animals are classified into two very large groups. Animals in one of these groups all have a backbone that protects the spinal cord and helps support the body. In this investigation you will **build a model** backbone.

Materials
- chenille stem
- wagon-wheel pasta, uncooked
- candy gelatin rings

Activity Procedure

1 Bend one end of the chenille stem. Thread six pieces of wagon-wheel pasta onto the stem. Push the pasta down to the bend in the stem. Bend the stem above the pasta to hold the pasta in place.

2 Bend and twist the stem. What do you see and hear?

3 Take all the pasta off the chenille stem except one. Thread a candy gelatin ring onto the stem, and push it down. (Picture A)

◀ Birds have backbones. Worms don't. That is a major reason why these two living things belong to different animal groups.

How Are Animals Classified?

In this lesson, you can . . .

 INVESTIGATE a model of a backbone.

 LEARN ABOUT animal classification.

 LINK to math, writing, health, and technology.

Picture A

Picture B

4 Add pasta and rings until the stem is almost full. Bend the stem above the pasta and rings to hold them in place. (Picture B)

5 Bend and twist the stem. What do you see and hear?

6 Draw pictures of the model backbones you made. **Compare** your models with those shown in the picture on page A25.

Draw Conclusions

1. A real backbone is made of bones called vertebrae (VER•tuh•bree) and soft discs that surround the spinal cord. What does each part of your final model stand for?

2. How is your final model like a real backbone?

3. Study your final model again. What do the soft discs do?

4. **Scientists at Work** Scientists **use models** to study how things work. Would a piece of dry, uncooked spaghetti work better than a chenille stem to stand for the spinal cord in your model? Explain your answer.

Investigate Further Think of other materials you could use to **make a model** of a backbone. Plan and make the model. Does it show how a real backbone works better than the model you made in the investigation? Explain.

Process Skill Tip

Some objects are too big, too small, or too far away to observe directly. You can't observe your backbone directly because it is inside your body. But you can **make a model** to learn more about it.

Animal Classification

Animals with a Backbone

You are probably familiar with many members of the animal kingdom. An animal is a living thing made up of many cells that have nuclei. Animals can't make their own food. They must eat other living things to survive. Scientists divide the animal kingdom into two large groups. One group of animals has backbones. The other group does not.

Animals that have a backbone are called **vertebrates** (VER•tuh•brits). The large group of vertebrates is divided into several smaller groups. **Mammals** (MAM•uhlz) have hair and produce milk for their young. Cats and dogs are mammals that you may have as pets. Lizards, snakes, and turtles are reptiles. **Reptiles** (REP•tylz) have dry, scaly skin. **Amphibians** (am•FIB•ee•uhnz) have moist skin and no scales. Most of them begin life in water, but they live on land as adults. Frogs, toads, and newts are amphibians. Other groups of vertebrates include birds and fish.

Most vertebrates have sharp senses and large brains. These characteristics help them survive in their surroundings.

✔ **What makes vertebrates different from other animals?**

Mongoose

Frog

◀ A mongoose and a frog are both vertebrates. What characteristic do they share with a snake?

Snake skeleton

Crab

Snail

Tortoiseshell beetle

Sea sponge

Crabs, snails, sea sponges, and beetles are invertebrates. None of these animals has a backbone.

Animals Without a Backbone

Animals without a backbone are called **invertebrates** (in•VER•tuh•brits). There are many more types of invertebrates than types of vertebrates. Most invertebrates are smaller than vertebrates.

Arthropods (AR•throh•pahdz) are invertebrates with legs that have several joints. Their bodies have two or more parts, and they often have shells that protect them. There are several groups of arthropods. Insects make up the largest group. Adult insects, such as beetles and bees, have six legs. Spiders aren't insects. They and other arthropods, such as mites, crabs, and scorpions, have eight legs.

Mollusks (MAHL•uhsks) are invertebrates that may or may not have a hard outer shell. Snails, clams, and squids are mollusks.

Invertebrates also include several groups of worms. Worms have no shells, legs, or eyes. Earthworms, tapeworms, and flatworms belong to different groups of invertebrates.

✔ **What characteristic do all invertebrates have in common?**

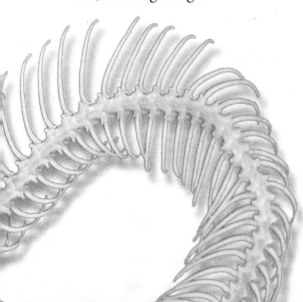

Only a small part of all the animals in the world have a backbone. ▶

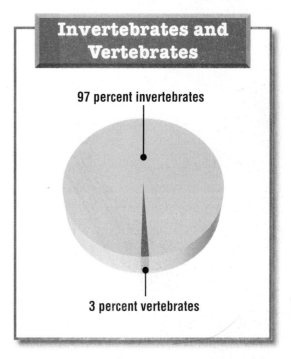

Invertebrates and Vertebrates

97 percent invertebrates

3 percent vertebrates

Body Parts for Jumping

Frogs and grasshoppers are in different animal groups. Both animals are known for their ability to jump. Their back legs are different, but they work in much the same way.

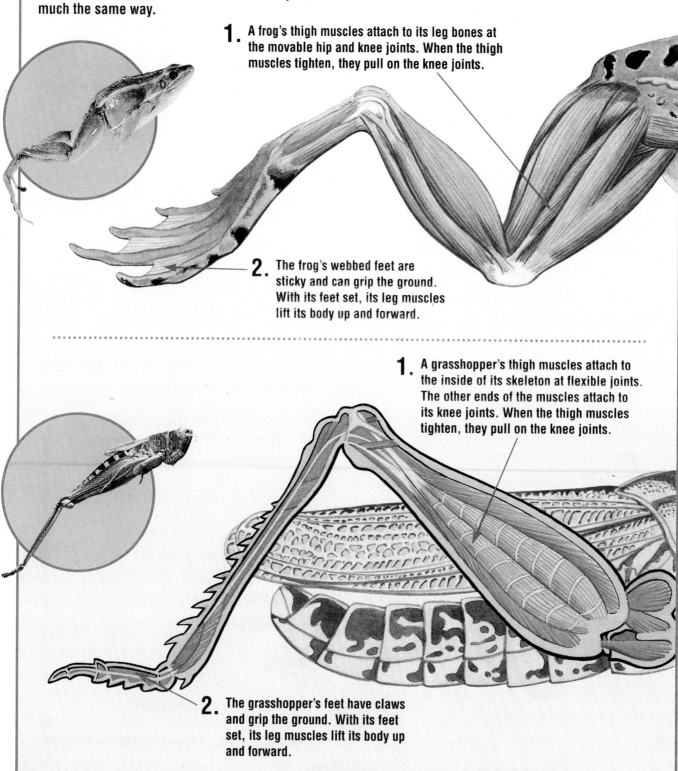

1. A frog's thigh muscles attach to its leg bones at the movable hip and knee joints. When the thigh muscles tighten, they pull on the knee joints.

2. The frog's webbed feet are sticky and can grip the ground. With its feet set, its leg muscles lift its body up and forward.

1. A grasshopper's thigh muscles attach to the inside of its skeleton at flexible joints. The other ends of the muscles attach to its knee joints. When the thigh muscles tighten, they pull on the knee joints.

2. The grasshopper's feet have claws and grip the ground. With its feet set, its leg muscles lift its body up and forward.

A Closer Look at Animals

Not all animals have a backbone, but almost all animals have skeletons and muscles that work together to allow the animals to move. The skeletons of vertebrates are made up of bones that support their bodies from the inside. Muscles attach to the bones at movable joints.

Most invertebrates have skeletons that form hard outer coverings. These skeletons are made of a material much like human fingernails. Muscles attach on the inside of these coverings at flexible joints.

✓ **Where do muscles attach to the skeletons of animals?**

Summary

Vertebrates, such as mammals, reptiles, amphibians, birds, and fish, have backbones. Invertebrate animals, such as arthropods, mollusks, and worms, do not have backbones.

Review

1. Which group of vertebrates begins life in water and later lives on land?
2. How is a spider different from an insect?
3. How are the skeletons of vertebrates and invertebrates different?
4. **Critical Thinking** How might having sharp senses and large brains help vertebrates survive?
5. **Test Prep** Which animals are **NOT** vertebrates?
   - **A** reptiles
   - **B** mammals
   - **C** amphibians
   - **D** arthropods

LINKS

MATH LINK

Graphing Vertebrate skeletons are made up of bones. The adult human spine has 33 bones. Find out how many bones the spine of five other vertebrates have. Make a bar graph to show what you learn.

WRITING LINK

Informative Writing—Explanation
You've learned that skeletons support animals' bodies and help them move. Skeletons also protect animals' organs. Would you prefer to have a hard outer shell or the skeleton you have now? Write a paragraph to explain your answer to a classmate.

HEALTH LINK

Prevention Calcium helps build strong bones. Eating calcium-rich foods prevents bone problems as you get older. Find out which foods are rich in calcium. Then make a chart to post in your kitchen at home.

TECHNOLOGY LINK

To learn more about types of vertebrates and invertebrates visit this Internet site.
www.scilinks.org/harcourt

How Are Plants Classified?

In this lesson, you can . . .

INVESTIGATE
plant stems.

LEARN ABOUT
plant classification.

LINK to math,
writing, literature, and
technology.

INVESTIGATE

Plant Stems

Activity Purpose You have learned that animals can be classified by whether they have a backbone. Plants also can be classified by their parts. One of those parts is the stem. In this investigation you will **observe** a stem, or stalk, of celery to help you **infer** what stems do.

Materials

- fresh celery stalk with leaves
- plastic knife
- two containers
- water
- red food coloring
- blue food coloring
- paper towels
- hand lens

Activity Procedure

1. Use the plastic knife to trim the end off the celery stalk. Split the celery from the middle of the stalk to the bottom. Do not cut the stalk completely in half. (Picture A)

2. Make a chart like the one here.

Time	Observations

▼ These flowers and mosses are two different types of plants. They move water in different ways.

Picture A

Picture B

3 Half-fill each container with water. Add 15 drops of red food coloring to one container. Add 15 drops of blue food coloring to the other container.

4 With the containers side by side, place one part of the celery stalk in each container of colored water. You may need to prop the stalk up so the containers don't tip over. (Picture B)

5 **Observe** the celery every 15 minutes for an hour. **Record** your observations on your chart.

6 After you have completed your chart, put a paper towel on your desk. Take the celery out of the water. Cut about 2 cm off the bottom of the stalk. Use the hand lens to **observe** the pieces of stalk and the freshly cut end of the stalk.

Draw Conclusions

1. Where did the water travel? How do you know?

2. How did the water travel? How do you know?

3. **Scientists at Work** Scientists **infer** what happens in nature by making careful observations. Based on this investigation, what can you infer about the importance of stems?

Investigate Further How could you change a white carnation into a flower with two colors? Draw and write an explanation of your answer.

Process Skill Tip

When you **infer**, you use what you observe to explain what happened. Inferring is like using clues to solve a mystery. Observing carefully, like finding good clues, can help you infer correctly.

Plant Classification

Plants with Tubes

FIND OUT

• how the plant kingdom is divided

• members of each main group of plants

VOCABULARY

vascular plant
nonvascular plant

All plants are members of the plant kingdom. Plants have many cells, and their cells have nuclei. Unlike animals, plants do not need to eat other living things to survive. Instead, they make their own food. Scientists divide the plant kingdom into two main groups. One group of plants has tubes. The other group does not.

Vascular (VAS•kyuh•ler) **plants** have tubes. These tubes can be found in roots, stems, and leaves. Water and nutrients enter a plant through the roots. The tubes in the roots then carry this mixture to the stems. You observed some stem tubes in the investigation. Tubes in stems carry the water and nutrients to tubes in a plant's leaves. A different set of tubes carries the food the leaves make to the other parts of the plant. Some food tubes run from the leaves to the roots.

Ferns are a type of vascular plant. The tubes of fern stems form a network. They often split apart and rejoin. Cells that make up the tubes are stiff. This helps provide support for the fern as its stems grow.

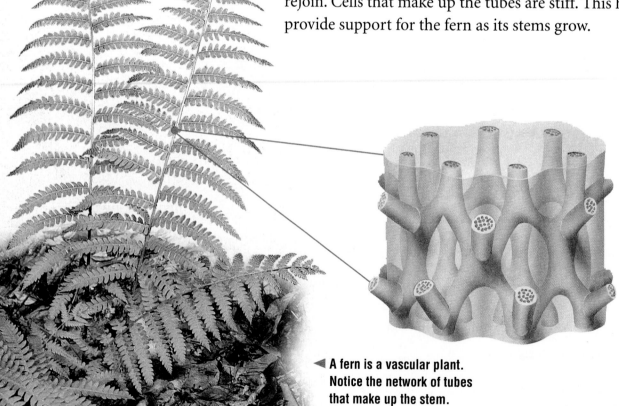

◄ A fern is a vascular plant. Notice the network of tubes that make up the stem.

A18

Sapwood

Growth ring

Heartwood

Bark

Trees are another type of vascular plant. The stems of trees contain cells that are woody, or very hard. Some large bushes also have woody stems. The largest woody stem of a tree is called the trunk. Look at the detailed picture of the tree trunk. The center of the trunk is made of hard, dead cells called heartwood. Around the heartwood are rings of sapwood. The living tubes that carry water and food are in the sapwood around the heartwood. Each year, a new set of tubes is formed, adding a growth ring of sapwood around the trunk. The outside layer of the trunk is called the bark. The bark is made up of dead cells that protect the living sapwood layer.

There are many other types of vascular plants. Any plant that has flowers or cones is a vascular plant.

✔ **What is carried by the tubes of vascular plants?**

The giant sequoia is a conifer. Conifers (KAHN•uh•ferz) are vascular plants that produce cones. As new sapwood is added each year, a new growth ring forms in the trunk. ▶

Plants Without Tubes

Have you ever seen something that looked like green carpet growing on stones and walkways? If so, you probably saw moss. Moss is a nonvascular plant. **Nonvascular** (nahn•VAS•kyuh•ler) **plants** don't have tubes. Water must soak into the plants and pass slowly from cell to cell. Food made in the plants must travel with the water from cell to cell. For this reason, nonvascular plants live in damp places and don't grow to be large or tall.

Mosses are often the first plants to grow on bare rock. Their rootlike structures help break down the rock into soil. When the mosses die, their dead bodies help to enrich the soil, making it more fertile. Nonvascular plants need fertile, moist soil in which to grow.

Nonvascular plants have no roots, stems, or leaves. The lobes, or rounded parts, of the liverwort may look like leaves, but they are not true leaves because they have no tubes.

✔ **How does water travel through a nonvascular plant?**

Enlarged, these liverworts look like small palm trees with leafy bases. However, liverworts have no tubes. So, they can have no true stems or leaves. ▶

▲ Moss grows in shady, damp places.

▲ These plants are liverworts. Liverworts grow in damp places.

Summary

Scientists have classified plants into two main groups. Vascular plants, such as ferns and trees, have tubes. Because they have tubes to carry water and nutrients, vascular plants can grow quite tall.

Nonvascular plants, such as mosses, do not have tubes. These plants take in water from their environment. So they need to live in a moist place, and they do not grow to be very large.

Review

1. What are the two main groups of plants?

2. Where are the tubes of vascular plants found?

3. Because nonvascular plants do not have tubes, in what kind of place do they need to grow?

4. **Critical Thinking** What probably would happen to a plant if its main stem were crushed or broken?

5. **Test Prep** Which of these is an example of a nonvascular plant?
   - **A** conifer
   - **B** fern
   - **C** moss
   - **D** flower

LINKS

MATH LINK

Nature's Weather Record The width of a tree ring depends on the amount of rainfall the tree received that year. Wide rings form in rainy years. Narrow rings form in dry years. Examine a tree stump or the end of a log. Count the sapwood rings, and then measure the width of each ring. Make a line graph or a bar graph to show what you see. What can you infer from your graph?

WRITING LINK

Informative Writing—Description Gather several types of plants, and examine their characteristics. Write clues describing each plant. Your clues can be about color, smell, height, size, plant's use, or they may tell where it was found. Read your clues to your classmates, and see if they can guess your plant.

LITERATURE LINK

Sugaring Time Would you like to learn how maple syrup is made from sap that flows through the tubes in maple trees? Read *Sugaring Time* by Kathryn Lasky.

TECHNOLOGY LINK

Visit the Harcourt Learning Site for related links, activities, and resources.
www.harcourtschool.com

WELCOME TO
THE
LEARNING
SITE

NAMING Living Things

People have classified living things for a long time. Cave people probably sorted animals into groups such as those that were good to eat and those that were likely to eat you. Classification is an important first step in the study of almost anything.

The history of classification shows how ideas in science can change through time. As scientists learn more, they change their ideas about how things work. For example, the first recorded classification system for living things that we know about was developed by Aristotle. Aristotle was a philosopher, teacher, and scientist in ancient Greece. In about 350 B.C. he classified living things into two large groups—plants and animals. He divided animals by how they looked, how they behaved, and where they lived. He divided plants by their size and shape. He said that the three main divisions of the plant kingdom were trees, shrubs, and herbs (small plants such as grasses).

A New System

Aristotle's system didn't work for all plants and animals. However, it was used for more than 2000 years. In 1753, Carolus Linnaeus published the system that is the basis for the system we use today. Linnaeus, like Aristotle, divided living things into two kingdoms. However, for more exact sorting, he then broke the kingdoms into many smaller groups. The smallest group is the *species.* Today, scientists use genus and species names to identify living things.

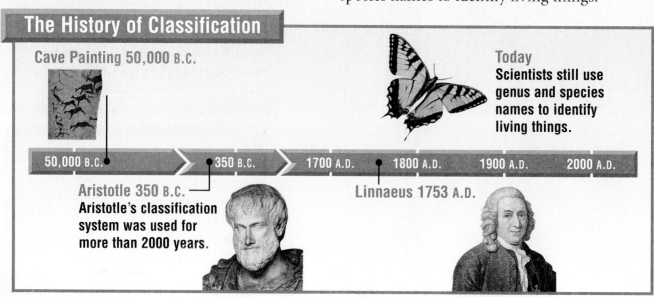

The History of Classification

Cave Painting 50,000 B.C.

Today
Scientists still use genus and species names to identify living things.

50,000 B.C.   350 B.C.   1700 A.D.   1800 A.D.   1900 A.D.   2000 A.D.

Aristotle 350 B.C.
Aristotle's classification system was used for more than 2000 years.

Linnaeus 1753 A.D.

Which Cat?

Genus and species names are important because they help scientists and other people talk about exactly the same organisms. For example, people use different names for one kind of large cat—*puma, panther,* and *mountain lion.* However, a scientist uses only the name *Felis concolor.* That way you know exactly which type of cat he or she is talking about.

As microscopes and other instruments for the study of living things became better, people began to realize that there were probably more than two kingdoms. Fungi were the first organisms classified as a new kingdom. After a lot of study, living things were divided into five different kingdoms. Some scientists now suggest that there may be as many as seven kingdoms.

As we learn more, our ideas about how living things are related change. As those ideas change, the way we classify the world of living things also changes. Each change in classification system is a direct result of more study and better understanding of the relationships of living things.

Think About It

1. Linnaeus classified living things. Give examples of two other classification systems and what they classify.

2. How have changes in technology affected the classfication of living things?

In different parts of the United States, both of these animals are called gophers. The scientific name of each helps you know to which animal a scientist is referring.

Gopherus polyphemus (gopher tortoise)

Marmota monax (gopher or woodchuck)

Ynes Enriquetta Julietta Mexia

BOTANICAL EXPLORER

Ynes Mexia spent the last 13 years of her life, from 1925 to 1938, collecting plant specimens outside the United States. She was the daughter of an agent for the Mexican government, so she knew other languages and understood other cultures. This helped her when she traveled. She visited many places, including Mexico, Alaska, Brazil, Ecuador, Argentina, Bolivia, and Peru. During her trips she discovered almost 50 new plant species.

While living in San Francisco, she traveled with the local Sierra Club. She took classes in natural science at the University of California and became interested in botany(BHAT•uhn•ee). She took a class on flowering plants, and it changed her life.

The botany class led to her first collecting trip, with botanist Roxanna S. Ferris. The trip was cut short when Mexia fell from a cliff. She broke several ribs and injured her hand. But before her fall, she had already collected 500 species of plants. One new species was named in Mexia's honor.

Nearly all Mexia's trips were to tropical countries. Because of the humid climates, it was

difficult to dry and preserve plant samples. Alice Eastwood, a noted botanist, taught Mexia how to collect and preserve plants. Later, Mexia was proud to tell Eastwood that she had been able to preserve every specimen she collected!

Mexia's samples went to important museums, such as the Field Museum in Chicago and the Gray Herbarium (her•BAIR•ee•uhm) at Harvard University. During 13 years she collected 137,600 plant specimens.

THINK ABOUT IT

1. Do you think it is easier to collect and preserve plants now? Why?

2. How do you think collecting plants helps scientists understand more about plant classification?

Bracken fern

Backbone Construction

How do backbones give vertebrates flexible support?

Materials

- construction paper
- tape
- scissors
- books

Procedure

1. Roll the paper into a tube about 5 cm across. Tape all along the edge.

2. Stand the tube on one end. Will the tube hold up a pair of scissors? A book? More than one book?

3. Squeeze the tube gently to make an oval. Make slits about 2 cm apart all down the tube. Cut the slits from each side almost to the middle.

4. Experiment to see how much weight the tube will now hold up.

Draw Conclusions

What happened each time the tube gave way? How did the cuts change the tube?

Plants and Water

How do leaves give off water?

Materials

- pencil
- water
- marker
- scissors
- piece of thin cardboard
- leaf with a long stem
- modeling clay
- 2 clear plastic cups

Procedure

1. Carefully use the pencil to poke a hole in the center of the cardboard. Then push the leaf stem through the hole.

Use the clay to close up the hole around the stem. Be careful not to pinch the stem.

2. Fill one cup about $\frac{2}{3}$ full with water. Mark the water line with the marker.

3. Snip off about 1 cm from the stem end. Place the cut stem into the water, resting the cardboard on the rim of the cup. Place the empty cup over the leaf. Set the cups in the sun.

4. After a few hours, observe both cups and the stem. Record your observations.

Draw Conclusions

What can you infer from your observations?

Chapter ① Review and Test Preparation

Vocabulary Review

Use the terms below to complete the sentences. The page numbers in ( ) tell you where to look in the chapter if you need help.

classification (A6)
kingdom (A7)
monerans (A7)
protists (A7)
fungi (A7)
genus (A8)
species (A8)
vertebrate (A12)
mammal (A12)
reptile (A12)
amphibian (A12)
invertebrate (A13)
arthropods (A13)
mollusks (A13)
vascular plants (A18)
nonvascular plants (A20)

1. The largest group into which scientists classify living things is a ____.

2. An animal that does not have a backbone is an ____.

3. Plants are either ____ or ____, depending on the presence of tubes.

4. ____ and ____ are the smallest groups into which living things are classified.

5. ____, ____, ____, birds, and fish are groups of vertebrates.

6. The two kingdoms of microscopic living things are ____ and ____.

7. An animal with a backbone is a ____.

8. ____ and ____ are invertebrates that often have hard outer shells.

9. Scientists use ____ to organize living things.

10. ____ have many cells with nuclei and absorb food from other living things.

Connect Concepts

Use the terms in the Word Bank to complete the concept map.

animals
classification
fungi
genus
kingdoms
monerans
plants
protists
species

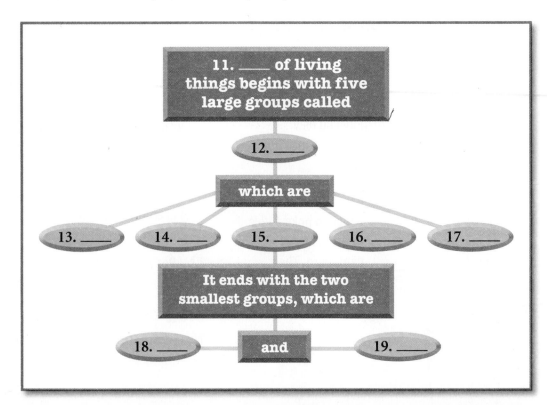

11. ____ of living things begins with five large groups called

12. ____

which are

13. ____   14. ____   15. ____   16. ____   17. ____

It ends with the two smallest groups, which are

18. ____   and   19. ____

Check Understanding

Write the letter of the best choice.

20. Which of the following is a type of moneran?

    A algae   **C** fish

    B bacteria   **D** mushroom

21. Which characteristic makes vertebrates different from invertebrates?

    F Vertebrates have a backbone.

    G Vertebrates do not have a backbone.

    H Vertebrates are monerans.

    J Invertebrates have a backbone.

22. In a nonvascular plant, water travels —

    A through the roots

    B through the sapwood

    C from cell to cell

    D through the flowers

23. Which part of a vascular plant has tubes for carrying water and food?

    F leaves   **H** bark

    G heartwood   **J** seeds

24. Which of the following is **NOT** a kingdom?

    A fungi   **C** plants

    B animals   **D** vertebrates

25. Where do muscles attach to the skeletons of invertebrates?

    F at flexible shell joints

    G at the backbone

    H where bones meet

    J at movable bone joints

26. Which of the following vertebrates have hair and give milk for their young?

    A reptiles   **C** amphibians

    B mammals   **D** birds

27. What makes a moneran different from a protist?

    F A moneran has no nucleus.

    G A moneran has a backbone.

    H A moneran has tubes.

    J A moneran has jointed legs.

Critical Thinking

28. Why is it important that scientists share what they learn from their research?

29. A dog has a backbone and fur. To which kingdom and to which two smaller groups does it belong?

Process Skills Review

30. Which three items would you **classify** in one group? Explain your answer.

    shoelace, stop sign, button, zipper

31. Which would make the better **model** for showing how water is carried inside a tree? Explain your answer.

    a frozen-treat stick and paper

    a cardboard tube and a rubber hose

32. Think about your observations of the feet of ducks and chickens. Which animals would you **infer** are the better swimmers? Explain your answer.

Performance Assessment

Sorting Scheme

Work with a group to make rules for classifying items in your desks or in your classroom. Sort the items into several "kingdoms." Then sort the members of each kingdom into as many smaller groups as you can.

Animal Growth and Adaptations

Try to think of as many kinds of animals as you can. You can probably think of a lot, and there are thousands more—all different from each other. But all animals have something in common. They all have adaptations that help them live and grow.

Vocabulary Preview

environment
climate
oxygen
shelter
metamorphosis
adaptation
camouflage
mimicry
instinct
migration
hibernation

FAST FACT

Ostriches are the largest birds in the world. Their strong legs help them run up to 64 km/hr (40 mi/hr). They can also use their legs to kick animals that may threaten them.

Fast Animals

Animal	Speed in km/hr (mi/hr)
Peregrine falcon	320 (200)
Cheetah	110 (70)
Hummingbird	97 (60)
Jack rabbit	72 (45)
Dolphin	40 (25)

The male seahorse gives birth! The female seahorse lays eggs in the male's pouch, and he carries them until they are born.

Scientists think that the Aldabra tortoises live longer than any other animals. It's been hard to tell because the tortoises have outlived many of the people studying them. Scientists estimate that these tortoises may live longer than 100 years!

What Are the Basic Needs of Animals?

In this lesson, you can . . .

INVESTIGATE animal needs.

LEARN ABOUT how animals meet their needs.

LINK to math, writing, social studies, and technology.

◀ This tiger hunts for food in tall grasses and tropical wetlands. Food is a basic need of animals.

Basic Needs of Mealworms

Activity Purpose Have you ever had a pet or watched animals in a zoo? Then you know that an animal has needs. Animals meet their needs in different ways. In this investigation you will make observations to help you **infer** what those needs are.

Materials

- bran meal
- spoon
- 3 shallow dishes
- plastic shoe box
- flake cereal
- water
- 10 cm square of poster board
- mealworms

Activity Procedure

1. Make a chart like the one on the next page to **record** your observations and measurements.

2. **Measure** two spoonfuls of bran meal. Put them into a shallow dish. Put it at one end of the shoe box. Count 20 flakes of cereal. Put them into another shallow dish. Put this dish at the other end of the shoe box. Put a little water in the last shallow dish. Put it in the center of the shoe box.

3. Fold about 1 cm down on opposite sides of the poster board. It should stand up like a small table. (Picture A) Put it next to the water container. (Picture B)

Mealworm Observations

Condition	Location	Size and Appearance	Food Measurements	Other
One hour in dark				
Overnight in dark				
Bright sunlight				

4 Put the mealworms in the shoe box next to, but NOT in, the water. Put the lid on the box. Then put the shoe box in a dark place for an hour. Be careful not to spill anything.

5 Take the box to a dimly lit area. Open the lid, and **observe** the contents. Try to find the mealworms. **Record** your observations. Put the lid back on.

6 Put the box in a dark place overnight. Again, take the box to a dimly lit area. **Observe** the contents of the box. **Record** your observations. **Measure** the bran meal and count the cereal flakes. Record your measurements.

7 Put the box into bright sunshine for a few minutes. Does anything change? What can you **infer** from the location of the mealworms?

Picture A

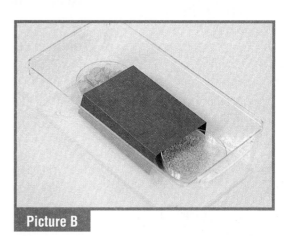
Picture B

Draw Conclusions

1. What happened to the mealworms?

2. What happened to the food? Why?

3. **Scientists at Work** Scientists learn by **observing.** What can you **infer** about animal needs by observing the mealworms?

Investigate Further How could you find out which food the mealworms liked best? Plan an investigation. Decide what question you would like to answer and what equipment you will need.

Process Skill Tip

Observations and inferences are different. When you **observe**, you use your senses and then record information from your senses. When you **infer**, you use what you have observed to form an opinion called an inference.

How Animals Meet Their Needs

Where Animals Meet Their Needs

Wild-animal parks are home to many kinds of animals. All the animals in these parks have some basic needs in common. You learned in the investigation that animals have basic needs for food, water, and a place to live. As you read on, you will find that animals have other needs, too.

In planning a wild-animal park, scientists include an environment for each type of animal. An **environment** (en•VY•ruhn•muhnt) is everything that surrounds and affects an animal, including living and nonliving things. All an animal's basic needs can be met in its environment.

For a wild-animal park, scientists first study each animal's natural environment and observe how the animal meets its needs. Then they can plan a similar environment for the park.

✔ **What makes up an animal's environment?**

FIND OUT

- five basic needs all animals have
- how some animals meet each need

VOCABULARY

environment
climate
oxygen
shelter
metamorphosis

A vulture finds its food in the desert. ▼

This desert area in Arizona is dry and has little vegetation.

When the sun is too hot, this tortoise lies in the shade or under the sand. ▶

Kangaroo rat ▶

A32

The Need for the Right Climate

People plan and build the environments in wild-animal parks. But most environments aren't made by people. Most environments are natural.

Deserts are natural land environments. In a desert, the climate is dry all year. **Climate** is the average temperature and rainfall of an area over many years. Even though deserts get very little rainfall, many plants and animals can live there.

A desert has vultures, foxes, snakes, tortoises, kangaroo rats, and other small animals. Vultures live in nests in cacti, bushes, or small trees. Kangaroo rats and foxes live in burrows in the ground.

Tortoises and kangaroo rats feed on leaves, fruits, and seeds of desert plants. Vultures, snakes, and foxes feed on other animals. Because there is little rainfall, there are few streams or lakes from which to drink. Desert animals get much of their water from the food they eat.

Different animals meet their needs in a tropical rain forest. There, the climate is wet and warm year-round. Monkeys and hummingbirds live in the trees. Jaguars, a type of large cat, hunt along the forest floor.

✔ **How are the climates of a desert and a tropical rain forest alike? How are they different?**

▲ Ocean mammals, such as this whale, come to the water's surface to breathe.

The Need for Oxygen

Animals need **oxygen**, one of the many gases in air. Many land animals get oxygen by breathing air into their lungs. Ocean mammals, such as whales and dolphins, come to the water's surface to breathe air into their lungs.

Most fish get oxygen from the water around them. Fish and many other ocean animals have body parts called gills. As water moves over the gills, the oxygen in the water passes into the fish's blood.

✔ **Where do fish get the oxygen they need?**

▲ Brown bears eat both plants and animals. This bear is trying to catch a salmon.

The Need for Food

In any environment, an animal needs energy to live and grow. For example, a hummingbird needs energy to beat its wings 70 times per second so it can fly near a flower and drink the nectar. A cheetah needs energy to run fast so it can catch its prey. Like all animals, hummingbirds and cheetahs get the energy they need from the food they eat.

All animals need food, but different animals eat different kinds of food. If you visit the plains of Africa, you may see zebras grazing on grasses, rhinos feeding on low shrubs, and giraffes nibbling leaves on the high branches of trees. Like most animals in the world, these African animals are plant eaters. Some animals, however, are meat eaters. Living among the zebras and rhinos are meat-eating lions, wild dogs, and leopards. Still other animals eat both plants and animals.

✔ **Why do animals need food?**

◀ Giraffes feed mostly on leaves high on acacia (uh•KAY•shuh) trees.

This chameleon (kuh•MEEL•yuhn) eats insects. ▶

The Need for Water

Animals also need water. They lose water by sweating, panting, or other means. That water must be replaced. Most animals replace the lost water by drinking from ponds, lakes, streams, and puddles.

Deserts, however, usually don't have bodies of water or even damp soil. Desert animals must get water in other ways. Kangaroo rats eat seeds that provide them with some water. Also, their bodies are adapted to produce water as their food is digested and used. Kangaroo rats hardly ever need to drink.

✔ **Where do animals get the water they need?**

Desert fox

Gray fox

Arctic fox

▲ Each type of fox finds shelter in its environment.

▲ These African elephants drink at watering holes to get the water they need.

The Need for Shelter

Most animals need shelter in their environment. A **shelter** is a place where an animal is protected from other animals or from the weather.

Foxes find or dig shelters in their environment. A gray fox may climb a tree to find a hollow place to hide in. An arctic fox may dig into the snow for shelter during a blizzard. Desert foxes dig connecting tunnels under the sand to protect themselves from the desert heat.

Rocks, logs, leaves—almost anything in an environment—can be a shelter for an animal. A rock may shelter a snake from the desert heat. A woodpile may shelter a field mouse from a summer storm. A rotting log on the forest floor may shelter dozens of different insects.

✔ **How does weather affect animals' needs for shelter?**

Animals and Their Young

Animals of all species need to have young. Without having young, all of a species would soon die and disappear. The young grow, become adults, and produce young of their own. Animals grow and develop in many different ways.

Insects such as butterflies lay hundreds of eggs. The eggs hatch into wormlike larvae called caterpillars. As a caterpillar grows, it *molts,* or sheds its outer skin, several times. The last time a caterpillar molts, it seals itself inside a tough shell, or *chrysalis* (KRIS•uh•lis). Inside the chrysalis the caterpillar's body slowly changes. Finally an adult butterfly breaks out of the chrysalis. This process of change from an egg to an adult butterfly is called **metamorphosis** (met•uh•MAWR•fuh•sis). Almost all insects, invertebrates that live in water, and amphibians go through some kind of metamorphosis.

Animals such as birds, fish, reptiles, and mammals do not go through metamorphosis. Instead, the young are born or hatched looking much like their parents.

Most mammals have just a few young at a time. Mammals care for their young until the young are old enough to live on their own. A koala gives birth before the young koala is fully developed. The newborn koala crawls into its mother's pouch, where it is fed and protected for six months. It then spends another six months riding on its mother's back before it is old enough to meet its own needs.

✔ **Why would an animal that has only a few young take care of them for months after birth?**

◄ **Butterfly metamorphosis**

4. Adult

3. Chrysalis (pupa)

2. Caterpillar (larva)

1. Egg

This baby penguin is asking for food from its mother. ▼

▲ A young koala spends six months in its mother's pouch and six months holding on to its mother's back before it can live on its own.

Summary

Animals have some basic needs in common. These include the need for the right climate and for oxygen, food, water, and shelter. Animals of a species must reproduce in order for the species to survive. Each type of animal meets its needs in its own way.

Review

1. What is an environment?
2. What five basic needs do animals have?
3. Why do animals produce young?
4. **Critical Thinking** Choose an animal and describe the shelter it needs.
5. **Test Prep** Which of the following is **NOT** a need of animals?
   A food
   B oxygen
   C clothing
   D shelter

LINKS

MATH LINK

How Many Animals? Suppose you are to report on how many animals you can find in a wooded area near your home. You count 12 snakes, 8 chipmunks, 15 squirrels, and 20 birds. Find the total number of mammals and nonmammals.

WRITING LINK

Informative Writing—Report Choose an animal, and investigate its environment and how it meets its needs. List some questions you want to answer about your animal. Use library resources, encyclopedias, or the Internet to find your answers. Then write an article for your school newspaper to report your findings.

SOCIAL STUDIES LINK

Human Shelters People build many kinds of homes. The building materials and shapes of the homes are different in different environments. Investigate one kind of home in a certain climate of the world. Explain how the climate affects the building materials and the shape of the home.

TECHNOLOGY LINK

Learn more about young animals by visiting the Smithsonian Institution Internet site.
www.si.edu/harcourt/science

Smithsonian Institution®

How Do Animals' Body Parts Help Them Meet Their Needs?

In this lesson, you can . . .

 INVESTIGATE how the shape of a bird's beak is related to the food it eats.

 LEARN ABOUT animal adaptations, including different body parts.

 LINK to math, writing, and technology.

 **INVESTIGATE**

Bird Beaks and Food

Activity Purpose Different birds have different types of beaks. A hummingbird's beak is long and straight. A hawk's beak is short and hooked. The tools in this investigation stand for beaks of different sizes and shapes. You will **use a model** to find what kind of "beak" works best for picking up and "eating" different foods.

Materials

- chopsticks or 2 blunt pencils
- pliers
- clothespin
- spoon
- forceps
- plastic worms

- cooked spaghetti
- cooked rice
- raisins
- birdseed
- peanuts in shells
- water in a cup
- small paper plates

▼ In what ways are these pictures of chopsticks and this bird's beak alike?

A38

Activity Procedure

Bird Food and Beak Observations

Food	Best Tool (Beak)	Observations

1. Make a chart like the one above.

2. Put the tools on one side of the desk. Think of the tools as bird beaks. For example, the pliers might be a short, thick beak.

3. Put the rest of the materials on the other side of the desk. They stand for bird foods.

4. Put one type of food at a time in the middle of the desk. Try picking up the food with each beak. (Picture A)

5. Test all of the beaks with all of the foods. See which beak works best for which food. **Record** your observations in your chart.

Picture A

Draw Conclusions

1. Which kind of beak is best for picking up each food? Which is best for crushing seeds?

2. By **observing** the shape of a bird's beak, what can you **infer** about the food the bird eats?

3. **Scientists at Work** Scientists often **use models** to help them test ideas. How did using models help you test ideas about bird beaks?

Investigate Further Find a book about birds. Identify real birds that have beaks like the tools you used in this investigation. Make a booklet describing each beak type and how birds use it to gather and eat food. Include your own pictures of the beaks and of the matching foods each beak can best gather and eat.

Process Skill Tip

Observing many kinds of real birds would be difficult to do in your classroom. **Using models** of birds' beaks makes it easier to infer how real beaks work.

Animal Adaptations: Body Parts

FIND OUT

- ways birds are adapted to meet their needs

- other types of animal adaptations

VOCABULARY

adaptation
camouflage
mimicry

A Closer Look at Bird Beaks

Finches on the Galápagos Islands in the Pacific Ocean look very much alike. However, their beaks are different in size and shape. Scientists observed and recorded information about where the finches lived, the shapes of their beaks, and their food sources. Scientists noted that some finches eat seeds, others eat fruit, and still others eat insects.

Scientists used the evidence they gathered just as you did in the investigation. They inferred that the differences in the finches' beaks are adaptations to the kinds of foods the finches eat. An **adaptation** is a body part or behavior that helps an animal meet its needs in its environment. The scientists saw that the seed eaters have thick, heavy beaks. The fruit eaters have short, stubby beaks. The insect eaters have sharp, pointed beaks.

✓ **How does having a thick, heavy beak help a bird eat seeds?**

The house finch uses its short, stubby beak to eat fruit. ▼

▲ The European goldfinch eats insects with its sharp, pointed beak.

A Darwin's finch uses its thick, heavy beak to crack open large seeds. ▼

▲ An osprey's talons (TAL•uhnz), or claws, are adapted for catching and carrying its prey.

Other Bird Adaptations

Like finches, all other birds have beaks that help them get food from their environment. Birds also have many other adaptations that help them live. These include the size of an owl's eyes and the shape of a hawk's claws. Although birds have the same basic needs, they have different adaptations that help them meet their needs in different ways.

Feathers keep birds warm and dry and help them fly. Feathers are very light, and they give a bird's body a smooth surface over which air flows easily. Another adaptation for flying is hollow bones. A bird's bones are filled with air pockets. These make a bird especially light.

But not all birds fly. Some flightless birds have adaptations for running. The ostrich's long legs and two-toed feet allow it to run at speeds up to 64 kilometers (about 40 mi) per hour. Some water birds don't fly or run. Penguins are the largest group of flightless water birds. As you can see in the picture, their bodies have adaptations for moving in water. Almost everything about a bird's body, from its beak to its feet, is an adaptation that helps it meet its needs.

✓ **How do strong claws help a hawk meet its need for food?**

Penguins use their wings as flippers and their feet for steering. They can swim underwater as fast as 35 kilometers (about 22 mi) per hour. That's about the fastest you can pedal a bicycle. ▶

Body Coverings

Every animal's body covering is an adaptation that helps the animal survive. You have learned that feathers protect birds and help them fly. The fur or hair that covers most mammals helps keep them warm. Some mammals have sharp hairs that are adaptations for protection. Others have whiskers—stiff hairs that have adapted as sense organs. Many fish are covered with scales. The scales help protect the fish from disease and from other animals that live in the water. A reptile's scales protect it from injury and from drying out. The scales on a snake overlap to form a smooth covering that helps the snake move.

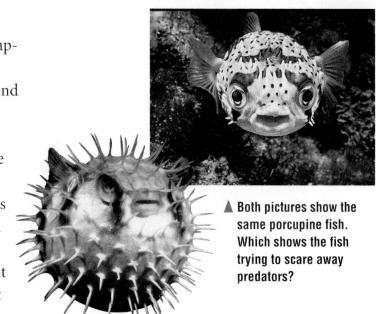

▲ Both pictures show the same porcupine fish. Which shows the fish trying to scare away predators?

✔ **What are three different kinds of body coverings?**

◄ The hairs of a polar bear's thick fur are actually clear, not white. They allow light to get to the bear's dark skin, helping the bear stay warm in the cold Arctic climate.

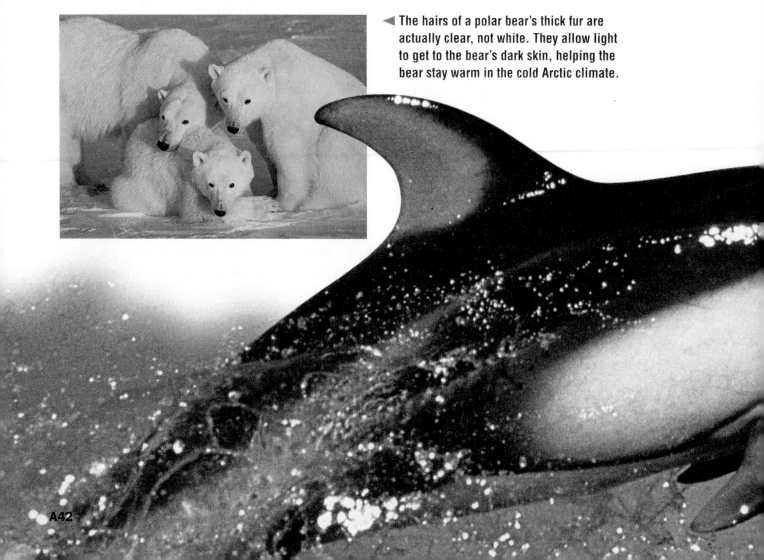

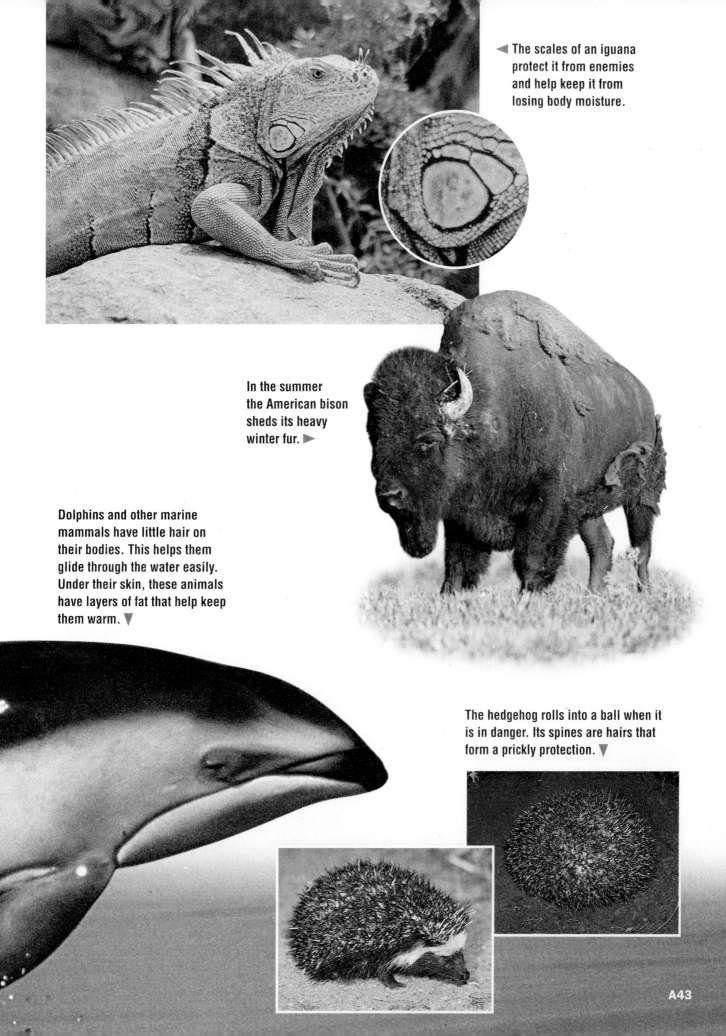

◄ The scales of an iguana protect it from enemies and help keep it from losing body moisture.

In the summer the American bison sheds its heavy winter fur. ▶

Dolphins and other marine mammals have little hair on their bodies. This helps them glide through the water easily. Under their skin, these animals have layers of fat that help keep them warm. ▼

The hedgehog rolls into a ball when it is in danger. Its spines are hairs that form a prickly protection. ▼

Color and Shape

The snowshoe hare is white in winter and brown in summer. Its changing fur color makes the hare difficult for other animals to hunt because the hare blends in with its environment. The hare's color is an example of camouflage. **Camouflage** (KAM•uh•flahzh) is an animal's color or pattern that helps it blend in with its surroundings. Camouflage is an adaptation that helps an animal hide.

Many animals have body coverings and shapes that are camouflage. For example, a tiger's fur is striped. The stripes help the tiger blend in with the light and shadows of the tall grass in its environment. Toads—with their bumpy, brownish skin—look like pebbles on the forest floor. A chameleon's color changes to match its surroundings. The dark skin on an alligator's back makes it blend into the swamps where it lives.

▲ A chameleon's skin can change color in minutes. This form of camouflage enables the chameleon to blend in with the tree in which it waits for food.

Mimicry (MIM•ik•ree) is an adaptation in which an animal looks very much like another animal or an object. The viceroy butterfly is a good example of mimicry. It looks like the monarch butterfly, which tastes bad to birds. Birds often mistake the viceroy for a monarch and leave it alone. The walking stick is another example of mimicry. The walking stick, an insect, would be easy for birds to catch and eat. But because it looks so much like a twig, birds often overlook it.

✔ **How is a viceroy butterfly a mimic?**

▲ The body covering of a snowshoe hare is brown during the summer. In winter a thick coat of white fur covers the hare's body.

Summary

Animals have adaptations, which enable them to meet their needs. Adaptations include body coverings and the shapes, sizes, and colors of body parts.

Review

1. List three bird adaptations.
2. Choose an animal. What needs of the animal can be met by its body covering?
3. Choose an animal you know about. Give three examples of how its adaptations help it meet its needs.
4. **Critical Thinking** How are mimicry and camouflage different? How are they alike?
5. **Test Prep** Which adaptation would best help a hawk catch a mouse?

   A talons
   B camouflage
   C hollow bones
   D feathers

Why do you think this insect is called a walking stick? ▶

LINKS

MATH LINK

Accurate Drawings Choose a bird to research. Draw a life-size picture of the bird viewed from the side. Use a ruler to help you make accurate measurements. Paint or color the bird to show what it looks like. Cut out the bird, and compare it to the birds your classmates drew. Decide how to order the birds by size.

WRITING LINK

Informative Writing—Explanation
Choose an animal to "interview." Write a list of questions you could ask the animal. Include questions about how it meets its basic needs and which of its adaptations are especially helpful. Research the animal to find answers to your questions. Using your interview notes, write an article for your school newspaper explaining how the animal meets its needs.

TECHNOLOGY LINK

Learn more about reptile body adaptations by visiting the Smithsonian Institution Internet site.
www.si.edu/harcourt/science

 Smithsonian Institution

How Do Animals' Behaviors Help Them Meet Their Needs?

In this lesson, you can . . .

INVESTIGATE a behavior of some butterflies that helps them survive.

LEARN ABOUT other animal behaviors that are adaptations.

LINK to math, writing, social studies, and technology.

INVESTIGATE

Monarch Butterfly Travel

Activity Purpose Monarch butterflies cannot live through cold winters. From observations, scientists know that the butterflies travel south for the winter. To discover where the butterflies go and the paths they take to get there, scientists have tagged some of the butterflies. The tags let the scientists track the butterflies as they fly between their summer and winter homes. In this investigation you will learn where the butterflies go during the cold winter months.

Materials
- outline map of North America
- 2 pencils of different colors

Activity Procedure

1. Label the directions north, south, east, and west on your map.

2. During the summer many monarch butterflies live in two general areas. Some live in the northeastern United States and around the shores of the Great Lakes. Others live along the southwestern coast of Canada and in the states of Washington and Oregon. Locate these two large general areas on your map. Shade each area a different color. (Picture A)

◄ **Monarch butterfly**

Picture A

Picture B

3 At summer's end large groups of monarchs gather and travel south for the winter. Most of those east of the Rocky Mountains fly to the mountains of central Mexico. But some of these butterflies make their way to Florida. Butterflies west of the Rocky Mountains fly to sites along the California coast. All these areas have trees where the butterflies can rest, temperatures that are cool yet above freezing, and water to drink. Find these areas on your map. Shade each winter area the same color as the matching summer area. Then use the right color to draw the most direct route from north to south over land. (Picture B)

Draw Conclusions

1. **Compare** the climate where the monarch butterflies spend the summer with the climate where they spend the winter.

2. What can you **infer** about how the behavior of the butterflies helps them meet their needs?

3. **Scientists at Work** Scientists use maps and graphs to **communicate** data and ideas visually. How does making a map of butterfly movements help you understand where monarchs travel?

Investigate Further Many kinds of birds, fish, and mammals travel to different places when the seasons change. Research the travel route of one of these animals. Use a map to show the route.

Process Skill Tip

Sometimes the best way to **communicate** what you have learned is to use a graphic, a visual display such as a map, rather than words.

Animal Adaptations: Behaviors

FIND OUT

- some instincts that help animals meet their needs
- two examples of learned behavior

VOCABULARY

instinct
migration
hibernation

Instincts

In the investigation, you learned that monarch butterflies fly south for the winter. They go to places where they have the food and climate they need to survive. Their *behavior*, or action, of flying south is not something they have learned. It is an instinct. An **instinct** (IN•stingkt) is a behavior that an animal begins life with. Instincts are adaptations that help animals meet their needs.

✔ **What instinct do monarch butterflies have?**

Migration

Like the monarch butterfly, some other animals travel long distances to meet their needs. For example, female Atlantic green turtles go to Ascension Island in the South Atlantic Ocean to lay their eggs. They bury the eggs in the sand on the beach. After hatching, the young turtles move toward the ocean. Then they swim toward feeding areas along the coast of Brazil, more than 1000 kilometers (about 620 mi) away. When the female turtles become adults, they return to Ascension Island to lay their eggs. The turtles do not learn from other turtles where the feeding areas are or how to get to Ascension Island. They know by instinct where to go. Scientists hypothesize that the turtles are able to use Earth's magnetic field to guide them as they swim.

The Atlantic green turtle's instinct for travel to Ascension Island is an example of migration. **Migration** (my•GRAY•shuhn) is the movement of a group of one type of animal from one region to another and back again. It is a behavioral adaptation.

Many birds migrate to environments where there is food and a good climate. For instance, the pectoral sandpiper travels from northern Canada to southern South America each fall. These birds return to Canada in the spring when the weather in Canada warms up.

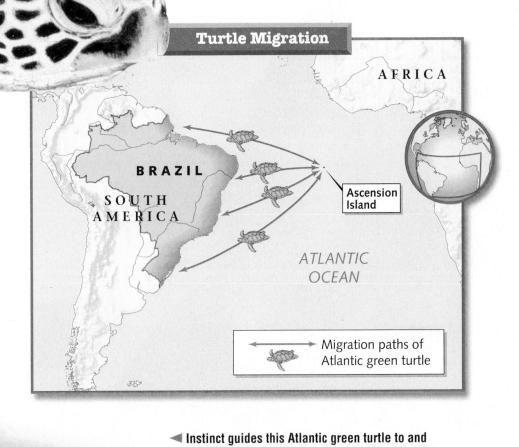

Turtle Migration

AFRICA

BRAZIL

SOUTH AMERICA

Ascension Island

ATLANTIC OCEAN

Migration paths of Atlantic green turtle

◄ Instinct guides this Atlantic green turtle to and from nesting grounds on Ascension Island.

Some animals have an instinct to migrate to places where their young can survive. Gray whales spend the summer in areas where they can find food easily—near the North Pole. In the winter they migrate to the warm waters off Mexico, where they give birth to their young.

Pacific salmon also migrate before producing their young. Salmon hatch from eggs in rivers and streams. Then they swim to the ocean, where they spend most of their lives. When these salmon are ready to produce young of their own, they migrate to the same stream where they hatched.

✔ **Name some animals that migrate.**

▲ These birds migrate each year. In the fall, they fly south. In the spring, they return to the north to lay their eggs and raise their young.

▼ Pacific salmon attempt to leap over whatever is in their way as they travel upstream to the place where they were hatched.

Hibernation

Not all animals have the instinct to migrate as winter brings colder temperatures and a lack of food. Instead, some animals adapt to these changes by hibernating. **Hibernation** (hy•ber•NAY•shuhn) is a period when an animal goes into a long, deep "sleep." An animal prepares to hibernate by eating extra food and finding shelter. During hibernation the animal's body temperature drops and its breathing rate and heartbeat rate fall. As a result, the animal needs little or no food. The energy it does need comes from fat stored in its body.

The ground squirrel is an animal that hibernates. As winter approaches, the squirrel goes into an underground nest. Within a

▲ Many North American bats hibernate in caves or rocky places.

few hours, its body temperature drops to 15°C (about 59°F), and its heartbeat rate and breathing rate fall. Before long, the squirrel is taking only about four breaths per minute.

✔ **How does an animal's body change during hibernation?**

THE INSIDE STORY

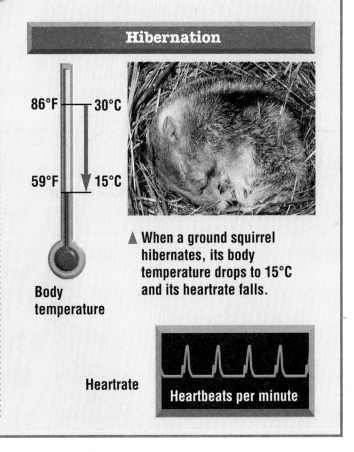

Normal	Hibernation
▲ A ground squirrel prepares to hibernate by eating extra food and building a nest.	▲ When a ground squirrel hibernates, its body temperature drops to 15°C and its heartrate falls.

86°F — 30°C

Body temperature

Heartbeats per minute

Heartrate

86°F — 30°C

59°F — 15°C

Body temperature

Heartrate

Heartbeats per minute

Learned Behaviors

Some animal behaviors are not instincts. They are learned. For instance, adult tigers are excellent hunters, but tigers aren't born knowing how to hunt. Tiger cubs learn to hunt by watching their mothers hunt and by playing with other tiger cubs.

Chimpanzees, too, learn many behaviors that help them survive. Chimps use sounds to communicate with one another. A loud call is a warning. A soft grunt is a happy sound. Young chimps learn the meanings of the sounds by observing the adults in their environment. Observation also helps a young chimp learn how to build a leafy nest for sleeping and how to use a stone to crack open a nut.

The chimpanzee's loud cry warns other chimps of possible dangers. ▼

Some animals are difficult to study, so we know less about them. For example, the humpback whale makes sounds that can be heard for many kilometers under water. Scientists think that males might use these "songs" to attract females or to tell other males to stay away. But is the act of singing an instinct? Or does a whale learn a song by listening to the songs of other whales? Scientists are trying to find out.

✔ **What animals do you know of that can learn behaviors?**

This mother cheetah will teach her cubs to hunt. ▶

▲ Humpback whales make sounds that can be heard many kilometers away under water.

Summary

Animals behave in ways that enable them to meet their needs. The behaviors are adaptations to their environments. Some of the behaviors are instincts. Others are learned.

Review

1. How is an instinct different from a learned behavior? Give an example of each.

2. What is migration? How does migration help an animal meet its needs? Give an example.

3. What is hibernation? How does hibernation help an animal meet its needs? Give an example.

4. **Critical Thinking** Suppose a dog barks when a stranger comes close to its home. Suppose it also barks when asked to speak. Which behavior is probably learned? Which is instinct? Explain your answers.

5. **Test Prep** An animal's body temperature drops for a long period when it is —
   A migrating
   B sleeping
   C hibernating
   D hunting

LINKS

MATH LINK

Measurement Use a globe and a map to measure the migration path of monarch butterflies from Minneapolis, Minnesota, to Mexico City. How is measuring different on the globe and on the map?

WRITING LINK

Narrative Writing—Personal Story Suppose you are an animal that migrates in the spring and fall. Tell what kind of animal you are, where you live in the summer, and where you spend the winter. For your teacher, make a log of the things you might do and see as you travel.

SOCIAL STUDIES LINK

Migration Barriers Study the needs and migration behaviors of deer. Think of ways that people might make it difficult for deer to migrate. Make a large drawing showing the deer's migration routes and any barriers that may be built or caused by people living nearby. Explain your drawing in writing.

TECHNOLOGY LINK

To learn more about instincts, watch the video *Monarch Migration* on the **Harcourt Science Newsroom Video.**

ROBOT
Roaches and Ants

Scientists are finding new uses for insects—both real insects and mechanical ones.

Roaches for Research

Most people think of roaches as pests, and they want to get rid of them. But scientists in Japan are raising these insects. Hundreds of roaches are grown in plastic bins in a laboratory at Tokyo University. Because the American cockroach is harder to kill and bigger than other species, the scientists have chosen it for their experiments.

For some of the roaches, surgery is done to take off their wings and antennae. Then the roaches are fitted with tiny backpacks, weighing about 3 grams ($\frac{1}{10}$ oz). Cockroaches can

Cockroach wearing a control backpack

carry up to 20 times their own weight, and the backpacks are only about twice a roach's weight. Each backpack has tiny wires that guide the roach. Electricity from the wires makes the roach jump forward or backward or turn left or right.

Small Is Beautiful

Japanese scientists hope to use these specially equipped insects as tiny explorers. For example, with a microcamera added to the pack, a roach might crawl through rubble. It could be guided to search for people trapped during a fire or an earthquake. The roaches also could go into other places that are too small or dangerous for people.

There are still problems for scientists to solve. Although the roaches may live for several months, they may stop responding to the electricity. Also, scientists are still studying the nervous systems of roaches to decide on the best places to attach the wires.

Ant Attack!

If you don't like the idea of a living robot roach, what about artificial ants? At the Massachusetts Institute of Technology, scientists are building microrobots. Each tiny robot is only about the size of a walnut. But it has 17 different *sensors,* devices for observing its environment.

The robot ants are being programmed to mimic, or act like, real members of an ant colony. They can hunt for food, pass messages to one another, and play games such as tag and follow the leader. The designers of the ants hope that the robots someday will help doctors. They might also just help with simple tasks around the home.

In England, another group of researchers is also trying to make robots that mimic ants. They hope to use the robots to inspect bundles of wire inside telephone cables. The ants could find which sections of cable are used least. Then system managers could route calls to those sections. This would avoid overuse of some phone lines.

With this kind of microtechnology, we may someday think of roaches and ants as friends, not pests!

Think About It

1. What insects or insect behaviors do you know about that might be useful for technology?

2. How would it be useful for robot roaches to look for survivors of earthquakes or fires?

WEB LINK:
For Science and Technology updates, visit the Harcourt Internet site. www.harcourtschool.com

Careers   Entomologist

What They Do
Entomologists study the ecology, life cycles, and behavior of the more than $1\frac{1}{2}$ million species of insects. Most entomologists work for state agriculture  departments, universities, or industry. Some study how to protect crops and other materials from insect damage. Others study how to protect helpful insect species.

Education and Training   Most entomologists have a college degree in entomology or biology. Many have a Ph.D. in entomology.

Jane Goodall

ANIMAL BEHAVIORIST

"Chimpanzees have given me so much. The long hours spent with them in the forest have enriched my life beyond measure. What I have learned from them has shaped my understanding of human behavior, of our place in nature."

Probably the most famous animal behaviorist of all time, Jane Goodall has spent most of her life studying wild chimpanzees. She set up her camp in the Gombe Stream Game Preserve in Tanzania in 1960. Over the next 35 years, Dr. Goodall and her team of researchers made important observations of chimpanzee behavior and ecology. One of her most important discoveries was that chimpanzees can make and use tools. Before this discovery, people believed that only humans could make tools.

At first Dr. Goodall had trouble finding wild chimpanzees to study. The animals were very shy and tended to avoid people.

When she did spot a family group, she had to observe them from a distance, with binoculars. After more than a year, the chimps got used to her presence. Then she could observe them up close. In time, Dr. Goodall was able to distinguish individual chimpanzee personalities and gave each chimp a name. She gave chimps within each family group names that started with the same letter.

Today Dr. Goodall travels around the world giving lectures about her experiences at Gombe. She also speaks to school groups about "Roots and Shoots," an environmental education program for young people.

THINK ABOUT IT

1. Why was finding out that chimpanzees can make tools an important discovery?

2. Why do you think it took Dr. Goodall so long to get close to the chimps?

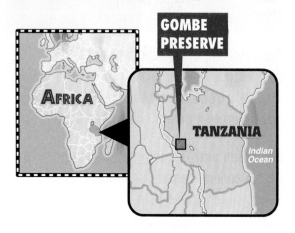

GOMBE PRESERVE

AFRICA

TANZANIA

Indian Ocean

Building a Bird's Nest

How do birds construct their nests?

Materials

- large paper plate
- small branches, twigs, leaves
- string or yarn
- purchased feathers (optional)
- mud

Procedure

1. Build a bird's nest on a plate. Place your branches, twigs, leaves, string, and feathers in a way that makes the nest a sturdy shelter. Use the mud like glue.

2. Share your building methods with a classmate.

Draw Conclusions

Was it easy or hard to build a sturdy nest? What body parts and behaviors do you think help birds build their nests?

Earthworm Instincts

What is an earthworm instinct for keeping safe?

Materials

- black paper
- white paper
- scissors
- tape
- baking pan, 9 in. × 13 in.
- water
- earthworm

Procedure

1. Cut black paper to fit the bottom of one half of the baking pan. Cut white paper to fit the other half. Line the bottom of the pan with the pieces of paper.

2. Tape a black paper lid over the black-paper half of the pan to make a "cave."

3. Moisten the paper in the bottom of the pan. Put the pan in a well-lighted place. Put an earthworm on the white side of the pan.

4. Observe the earthworm for 5 minutes. Record your observations.

5. Repeat Steps 3 and 4 two more times.

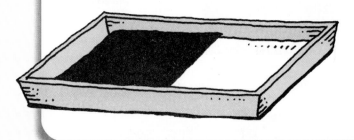

Draw Conclusions

Why do you think the earthworm moved as it did? How do you think its movement is related to instinct?

Chapter ② Review and Test Preparation

Vocabulary Review

Use the terms below to complete the sentences. The page numbers in ( ) tell you where to look in the chapter if you need help.

environment (A32)   **camouflage** (A44)

climate (A33)   **mimicry** (A44)

oxygen (A33)   **instinct** (A48)

shelter (A35)   **migration** (A49)

metamorphosis (A36)   **hibernation** (A51)

adaptation (A40)

1. The body changes that a butterfly goes through as it grows from an egg into an adult are called ____.

2. An adaptation in which an animal looks like an object or another animal is ____.

3. A place such as a burrow where an animal can protect itself is a ____.

4. A body part or behavior that enables an animal to meet its needs is called an ____.

5. The average temperature and rainfall of an area make up ____.

6. ____ enables an animal to blend in with its surroundings.

7. A period when an animal goes into a long, deep sleep is called ____.

8. A behavior such as migration that an animal does not have to learn is an ____.

9. The movement of a group of one type of animal from one region to another is ____.

10. Everything that surrounds and affects an animal is its ____.

11. Some animals meet their need for ____ by breathing.

Connect Concepts

Use the Word Bank to complete the graphic organizer below.

camouflage
food
instincts
learned
needs
oxygen
shelter
water

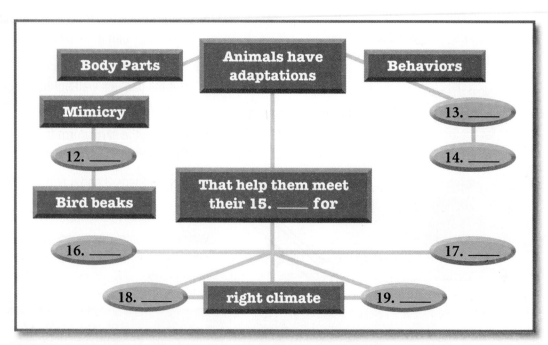

Check Understanding

Write the letter of the best choice.

20. When a winter storm is coming, animals often look for —

  A drinking water

  B a partner

  C shelter

  D an open area

21. A bird's hollow bones help the bird _____ more easily.

  F fly   **H** hop

  G heal   **J** eat

22. When preparing to hibernate, animals must —

  A grow a thinner coat

  B lose weight

  C eat extra food

  D breathe faster

Use the photos below to answer Questions 23–24.

23. What process is shown here?

24. Explain the changes going on.

Critical Thinking

25. Rabbits have large ears. Infer how this adaptation helps rabbits meet their needs.

26. Because humans can think, they can adapt to new environments by making things or changing behaviors. Describe how your life would change if you moved to a place where the climate was very different from where you live now.

Process Skills Review

27. How did you use your observations of the mealworms in Lesson 1 to **infer** about animals' needs?

28. **Compare** tools and birds' beaks.

29. Which is more useful for **communicating** information about migration routes—a data table or a map? Explain your answer.

Performance Assessment

Animal Plan

Work with a partner. Design and make a model of an animal that has adaptations for living in a desert. Explain how these adaptations would help the animal meet its needs.

Chapter 3

Plant Growth and Adaptations

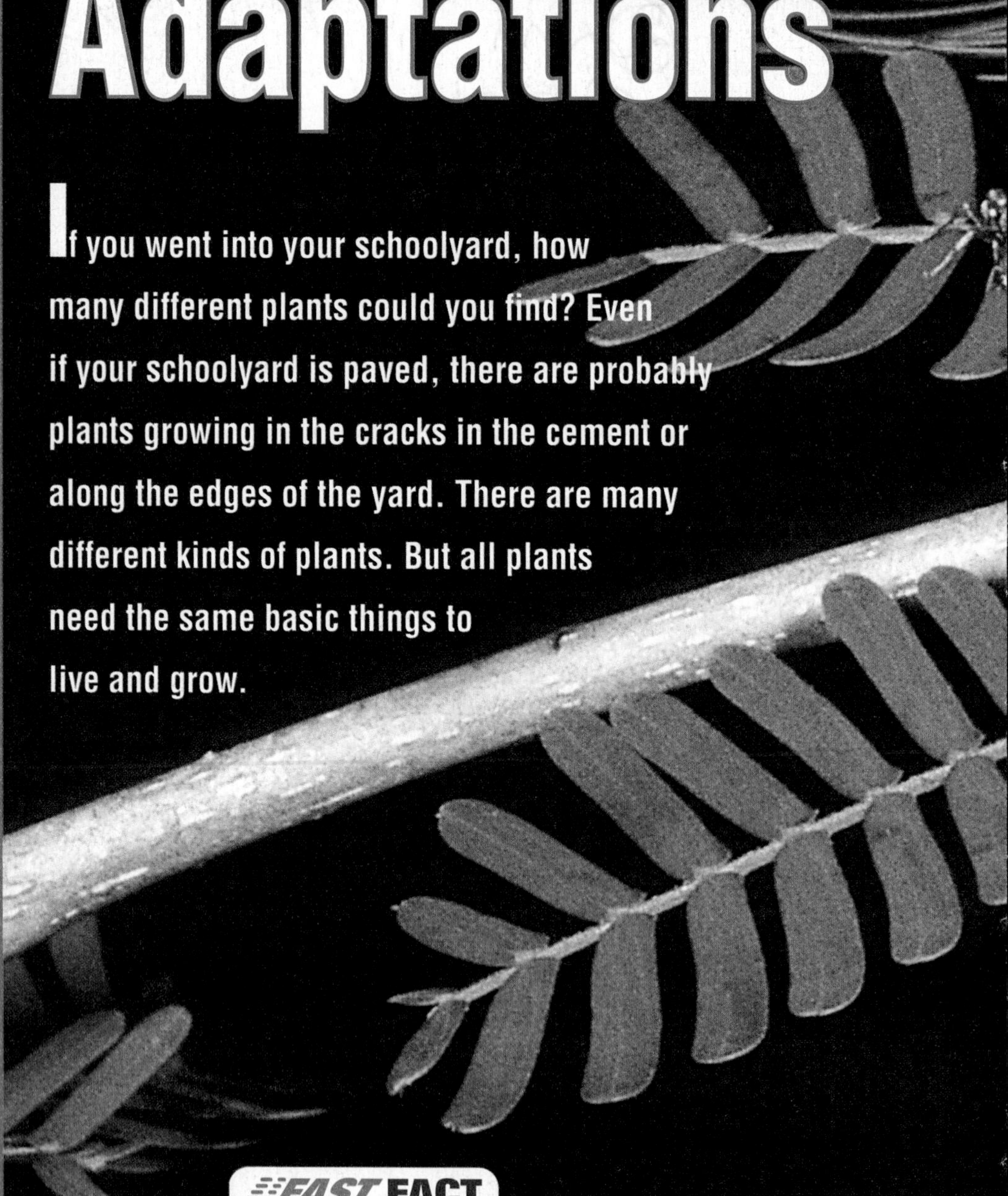

If you went into your schoolyard, how many different plants could you find? Even if your schoolyard is paved, there are probably plants growing in the cracks in the cement or along the edges of the yard. There are many different kinds of plants. But all plants need the same basic things to live and grow.

Vocabulary Preview

carbon dioxide
nutrient
photosynthesis
symmetry
transpiration
taproot
fibrous root
germinate
spore
tuber

FAST FACT

Some living things work together. Ants defend the bullhorn acacia from other insects, mammals, and even other plants. In return, the plant provides food for the ants!

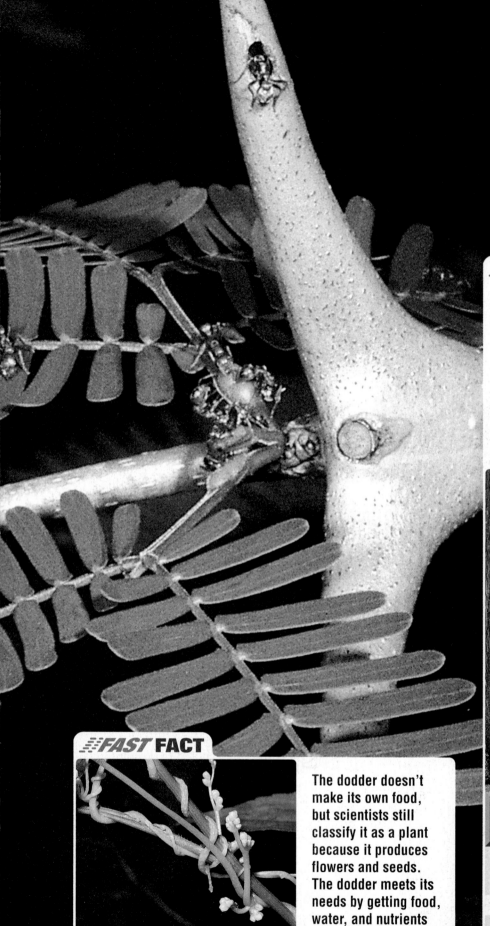

Some of the oldest known living things are trees. Plants that live for a long time have adaptations that help protect them from dangers in the environment. The thick, spongy bark of the giant sequoia protects it from being damaged by insects. The insects eat the bark instead of the inner wood.

How Long Some Plants Live

Plant	Oldest Individual Known
Bristlecone pine	5,000 years
Giant sequoia	2,500 years
Saguaro cactus	200 years

The dodder doesn't make its own food, but scientists still classify it as a plant because it produces flowers and seeds. The dodder meets its needs by getting food, water, and nutrients from other plants.

A61

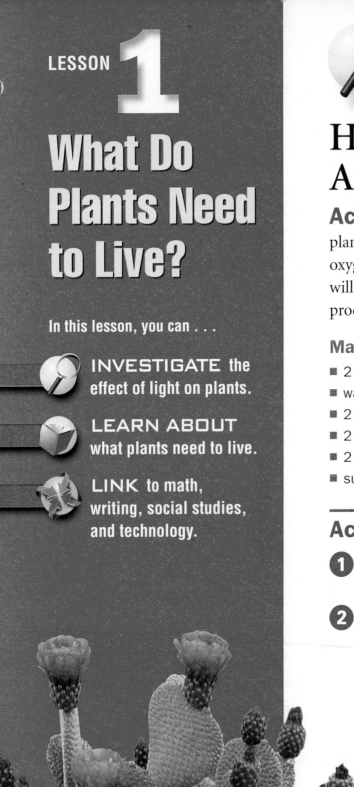

LESSON 1

What Do Plants Need to Live?

In this lesson, you can . . .

INVESTIGATE the effect of light on plants.

LEARN ABOUT what plants need to live.

LINK to math, writing, social studies, and technology.

How Light Affects Plants

Activity Purpose Did you know that as plants make food for themselves, they also make the oxygen that keeps you alive? In this investigation, you will **control variables** to see how sunlight affects this process.

Materials

- 2 large plastic containers
- water
- 2 pieces of elodea
- 2 clear funnels
- 2 test tubes
- sunlight or desk lamp

Activity Procedure

1 Fill one container about $\frac{2}{3}$ full of water. Place one piece of elodea in the water.

2 Turn a funnel wide side down, and place it in the water over the elodea. There should be enough water in the container so that the small end of the funnel is just below the water. (Picture A)

◀ All plants need water. This cactus has adaptations that allow it to live in areas that have little water.

Picture A

Picture B

3 Fill a test tube with water. Cover the end with your thumb and turn the tube upside down. Place the test tube over the end of the funnel. Allow as little water as possible to escape from the tube. (Picture B)

4 Repeat Steps 1–3 using the second container, funnel, piece of elodea, and test tube.

5 Set one container of elodea in sunlight or under a desk lamp. Set the other in a dark place such as a closet.

6 After several hours, **observe** the contents of each container.

Draw Conclusions

1. **Compare** the two test tubes. What do you **observe**?

2. One test tube is now filled partly with a gas. What can you **infer** about where the gas came from?

3. **Scientists at Work** Scientists **control variables** to learn what effect each condition has on the outcome of an experiment. What one variable did you change in this investigation? Which variables were the same in both containers?

Investigate Further How fast can a plant make oxygen? Repeat the procedure for the plant placed in light, but use a graduate instead of a test tube. **Measure** the amount of air in the graduate every 15 minutes for 2 hours. **Record** your findings. Make a line graph to show how fast the plant produced oxygen.

Life Support for Plants

Basic Needs

FIND OUT

- four basic needs of plants
- how plants make food

VOCABULARY

carbon dioxide
nutrient
photosynthesis

Plants are living things. They have many of the same needs as animals. They use energy from food to grow. They use gases from the air. They need water and the right climate. But there is one big difference between plants and animals—plants can make their own food.

To live, a plant needs four things from its environment—air, nutrients, water, and light. Air provides a plant with **carbon dioxide** (KAR•buhn dy•AHKS•yd), a gas breathed out by animals. There is plenty of this gas in the air. Soil provides most plants with needed nutrients. **Nutrients** (NOO•tree•uhnts) are substances, such as minerals, that all living things need to grow. A plant gets water from rain. Some of the water is taken in by the plant's leaves. Most of the water, however, is taken in by roots, which get it from rain-soaked soil. A plant can get enough light if it is not too shaded. Though some plants do well in shade, no plant can live in total darkness.

In the investigation, you saw that light affects how a plant gives off oxygen. Oxygen is given off as plants make food. Light provides the energy for the food-making process.

✔ **What four things do plants need to live?**

▼ These flowers are healthy. They are growing in clean air. They also are receiving plenty of water, nutrients from the soil, and sunlight.

Making Food

A plant makes its own food by a process that is called **photosynthesis** (foht•oh•SIN•thuh•sis). *Photo* means "light" and *synthesis* means "putting together." Photosynthesis takes place in a plant's leaves. Light is trapped by chlorophyll, the material that makes a leaf green. The energy from the light starts the food-making process. Without light, plants would not get the food they need to live and grow.

Carbon dioxide and water are the two main materials that the plant combines to make food. The food made is sugar. The leaves take in carbon dioxide, and the roots take in water. The water travels up tubes in the stem to the leaves. The leaves then use the energy from light to put together the carbon dioxide and water to make sugar. Oxygen is a waste product of photosynthesis. It is given off by the leaves.

✔ **What does a plant need to carry out photosynthesis?**

Photosynthesis

This is a close-up view of the bottom of a leaf. Tiny holes like this take in carbon dioxide and give off oxygen. ▼

Chlorophyll in leaves traps the energy from light. The energy helps combine carbon dioxide with water to make sugar as food for the plant.

Tubes in leaves get water from the roots. Different tubes carry food to the rest of the plant.

The leaves take in carbon dioxide gas from the air.

The leaves give off oxygen.

The roots take in water from the soil, and tubes in the stem carry water to the leaves.

Photo

Diagram

The waterlily's leaves float on the water's surface to take in sunlight. Its roots are in the soil at the bottom of the pond. ▶

Adaptations for Different Environments

Plants live all over Earth's surface. Like animals, plants have adaptations that help them live in different climates and conditions.

Most of the plants that you've seen live on land. Some plants, however, have adaptations that allow them to live in water. For example, waterlilies live in some ponds and lakes. They grow from soil below the water. Sunlight filters through the water to reach the young waterlily. The plant's stems grow toward the surface, taking along the leaves, which are rolled up like tubes. At the surface

◀ Vines can cling to almost anything to reach sunlight.

the leaves unroll to form flat pads. They are then ready to take in sunlight and carbon dioxide. The roots take in water and nutrients from the muddy bottom. The long stems move the materials back and forth between the leaves and the roots. In this way, all the waterlily's needs are met.

Vines have a different type of stem adaptation that helps them meet their needs. Vines often grow on forest floors, where the light is dim. To reach sunlight, vines have long stems with adaptations for clinging to other objects for support. These adaptations help vines climb fences, walls, rocks, and even other plants.

Plants in the desert have adaptations for living with little water. Just as a plant can't live without light, it can't live without water. Desert soil is dry and hard. It may be months, even years, between rain showers in some deserts. Cacti have roots that grow near the surface of the ground where they can collect any rainwater quickly. They also have thick stems in which they store water to use during dry periods.

✔ **How do stems that are adapted for climbing help vines meet their needs?**

▲ This barrel cactus has a thick stem that stores water.

Summary

Plants need air, nutrients, water, and light to live. Their leaves make food through photosynthesis. Plants have adaptations to help them meet their needs in different settings.

Review

1. What are the four things that plants need to live?

2. What provides the energy for photosynthesis to take place?

3. What adaptations do cacti have for life in the desert?

4. **Critical Thinking** What would happen if there were no carbon dioxide in the air?

5. **Test Prep** Which of the following provides most plants with nutrients?
   A air
   B water
   C soil
   D sunlight

LINKS

MATH LINK

Using Graphs Keep track of the heights of two plants that are given different amounts of water for two weeks. Use *Graph Links* or another computer graphing program to make a bar graph to show how water amounts affected the plants.

WRITING LINK

Informative Writing—Compare and Contrast For a younger child, compare ways that plants live in the wild and in homes. Describe how plants in both places meet their needs. In what ways do they meet their needs differently?

SOCIAL STUDIES LINK

History A plant conservatory (kuhn•SER•vuh•tawr•ee) is a building where unusual plants are grown and displayed. Use library reference materials to find out more about conservatories. Choose a conservatory, and write a short report about when and why it was built. Include in your report pictures of plants found in the conservatory.

TECHNOLOGY LINK

Learn more about growing conditions for plants by viewing *Bloomin' Business* on the **Harcourt Science Newsroom Video.**

LESSON 2

How Do Leaves, Stems, and Roots Help Plants Live?

In this lesson, you can . . .

 INVESTIGATE how plants "breathe."

 LEARN ABOUT different parts of plants.

 LINK to math, writing, art, and technology.

INVESTIGATE

How Plants "Breathe"

Activity Purpose It sounds strange to say that plants "breathe." But they do. They need to exchange gases as animals do. In this investigation you will look for evidence that a plant breathes through its leaves.

Materials

- leafy potted plant
- petroleum jelly
- 2 clear plastic bags
- twist ties

Activity Procedure

1 Make a chart like the one below.

2 Put a thin layer of petroleum jelly on both the top and bottom surfaces of a leaf on the plant. (Picture A)

3 Put a plastic bag over the leaf. Gently tie the bag closed. Do this just below the place where the leaf attaches to the stem. (Picture B)

Plant Leaf	Observations
Leaf with petroleum jelly	
Leaf with no petroleum jelly	

◀ Wild orchids grow in many parts of the world. Where are the roots, stems, and leaves on this orchid?

Picture A

Picture B

4. Put a plastic bag over a second leaf and seal it. Do not put any petroleum jelly on this leaf.

5. Put the plant in a place that gets plenty of light, and water it normally.

6. After two days, **observe** the two leaves. **Record** your observations on your chart.

Draw Conclusions

1. **Compare** the two plastic bags. What do you **observe**?

2. What can you **infer** from what you **observed** in this investigation?

3. **Scientists at Work** Scientists often **compare** objects or events. Comparing allows the scientists to see the effects of the variables they control. Compare the leaves you used in this investigation. What can you **infer** about the effect of the petroleum jelly?

Investigate Further Find out where gases are exchanged in a leaf. This time, coat the top side of one leaf and the bottom side of another leaf. Tie a plastic bag over each leaf. What do you **observe**? What can you **infer**?

The Functions of Plant Parts

FIND OUT

- how leaves, stems, and roots help plants live
- unusual adaptations plants have

VOCABULARY

symmetry
transpiration
taproot
fibrous root

Leaves

The leaves of different plants can be very different in shape and size. All leaves, however, work to help plants live. There are two main types of leaves—needles and broad leaves. Most conifers, trees such as pine and spruce, and many cacti have needles. Needle-shaped leaves help prevent water loss. Most other plants have broad leaves. Broad leaves are wide and flat. Beech, oak, and maple trees have broad leaves. So do rosebushes and English ivy.

An interesting characteristic of most leaves is that they have symmetry. An object that has **symmetry** (SIM•uh•tree) can be divided into two parts that look the same. Each half of a leaf is a mirror image of the other.

You already know that leaves carry on photosynthesis. In the investigation, you saw that moisture forms as a leaf "breathes." The water that formed inside the uncoated leaf's bag was caused by transpiration. **Transpiration** (tran•spuh•RAY•shuhn) is the giving off of water by plant parts. As the sun heats a leaf, it causes water to become a gas called water vapor. The waxy surface of most leaves keeps water from escaping, but water vapor can escape from tiny holes in the leaves. These are the same holes where gases are exchanged during breathing.

✔ **What is transpiration?**

— Lemon

— Eastern hemlock

— White mulberry

◀ The leaves of lemon and white mulberry trees are broad. Eastern hemlock trees have leaves shaped like flat needles.

Stems

Stems support plants and give them shape. They also contain tubes that move water and minerals from the roots and take food from the leaves to all parts of the plant. Stems also store water and food.

Many plant stems, such as those of garden flowers, are soft and flexible, or easy to bend. They have a thin, waxy covering that protects them. Most plants with this kind of stem are small and live for only one growing season. When the next season starts, they must grow again from seeds or from the plant's roots.

Other plants have stiff, woody stems. Woody stems are hard and thick. They have a layer of bark that protects them. Each year, woody stems grow thicker and sometimes taller. Plants with these tough stems can live many years. Trees and shrubs have woody stems.

✔ **Which type of plant usually grows for only one season?**

▲ The manzanita has a woody stem.

The Texas bluebonnet has a flexible stem. ▶

▲ A long, thick taproot firmly holds a dandelion in the ground. The taproot reaches deep into the ground.

Shallow-growing fibrous roots hold this marigold in the soil. ▶

Roots

Roots form the third main part of vascular plants—plants that have tubes. Most roots are underground and hold plants in the soil. Roots also take in water and nutrients that plants need for photosynthesis. Some roots store food made by leaves.

Roots have adaptations to help plants meet their needs. Some plants have taproots. A **taproot** is one main root that goes deep into the soil. If you have ever tried to pull up a dandelion, you know how well taproots hold plants in place. Smaller roots branch off from the taproot. Tiny root hairs that take in water and nutrients grow from the taproot.

A plant with **fibrous** (FY•bruhs) **roots** has many roots of the same size. Fibrous roots grow long but not deep. The fibrous roots also have root hairs that take in water and nutrients from the soil. Grass has fibrous roots.

✔ **Cacti have roots that are close to the surface of the soil. Which type of roots are they?**

Unusual Adaptations

You may have read science-fiction stories about human-eating plants. Plants don't really eat humans, but some of them do eat meat. Some plants that grow in poor soils have leaf adaptations that let them trap and eat insects. Such plants still make their own food. Insects just provide needed nutrients that may be missing in the soil.

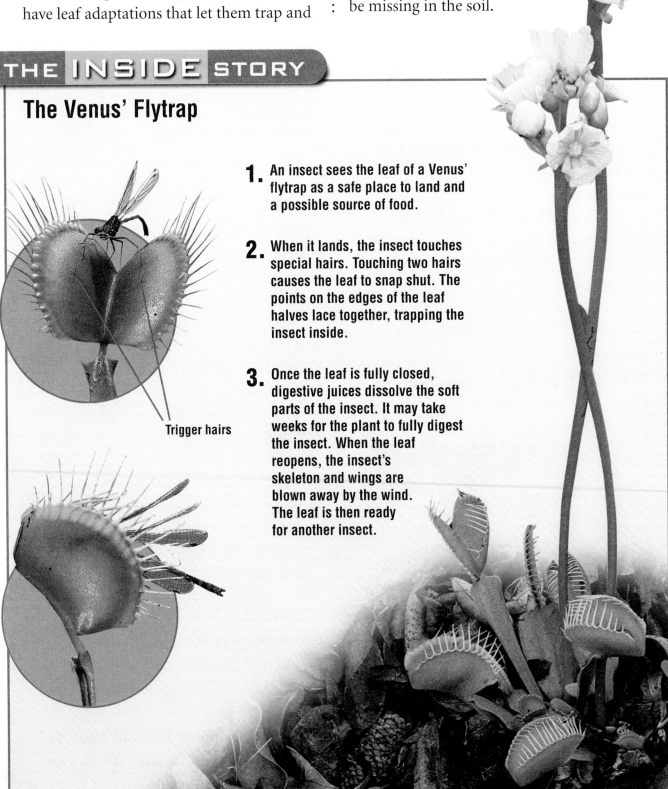

The Venus' Flytrap

Trigger hairs

1. An insect sees the leaf of a Venus' flytrap as a safe place to land and a possible source of food.

2. When it lands, the insect touches special hairs. Touching two hairs causes the leaf to snap shut. The points on the edges of the leaf halves lace together, trapping the insect inside.

3. Once the leaf is fully closed, digestive juices dissolve the soft parts of the insect. It may take weeks for the plant to fully digest the insect. When the leaf reopens, the insect's skeleton and wings are blown away by the wind. The leaf is then ready for another insect.

Some meat-eating plants have a smell that attracts their prey. Insects that land on them become trapped by a sticky surface or fall into a pool of liquid and drown. Then the plant's digestive juices dissolve the insect. Sundews and cobra lilies catch their prey in these ways. Other meat-eating plants have active traps with parts that move. The pictures on the facing page show how a Venus' flytrap works.

✓ **How do adaptations for trapping insects help some plants meet their needs?**

Summary

Plants have leaf, stem, and root adaptations that help them meet their needs. Some plants have parts that trap and digest insects to get needed nutrients.

Review

1. What are the two types of leaves? What is one unusual leaf adaptation?
2. What is the main difference between the two types of stems?
3. Which parts of roots take in nutrients for a plant?
4. **Critical Thinking** Moisture from leaves is produced by transpiration. Why can you use the presence of moisture as evidence that a plant is exchanging gases, or "breathing"?
5. **Test Prep** An insect is to a meat-eating plant as a _____ is to a human.
   A helper
   B drink of water
   C candy bar
   D vitamin pill

LINKS

MATH LINK

Sorting Leaves Collect leaves of different shapes and sizes. Make a Venn diagram by overlapping two circles made of yarn. Place leaves in your diagram by ways they are alike and ways they are different.

WRITING LINK

Narrative Writing—Story Science fiction writers often take an ordinary fact of nature and exaggerate it. Making a Venus' flytrap into a human-eating plant is an example. Think of a plant adaptation that interests you. Exaggerate the facts, and write a short story for a classmate.

ART LINK

Symmetry Get a broad leaf from a tree. Cut the leaf in half along the large vein that runs down the middle. Stand a mirror on edge along the cut side of a leaf half. When you look in the mirror, does the leaf appear whole? Tape your leaf part down on white paper. Carefully draw an identical but opposite side to make the leaf look whole.

TECHNOLOGY LINK

Learn more about garden plants from all over the world by visiting the National Museum of Natural History Internet site.
www.si.edu/harcourt/science

 Smithsonian Institution®

How Do Plants Reproduce?

In this lesson, you can . . .

 INVESTIGATE how plants grow from seeds.

 LEARN ABOUT plant life cycles.

 LINK to math, writing, social studies, and technology.

INVESTIGATE

Seedling Growth

Activity Purpose It's not often that you can see a seed start to grow into a plant. This process is usually hidden by soil until the tiny stem grows above the ground. In this investigation, you will **observe, measure,** and **compare** the growth of two types of seeds.

Materials

- 2 paper towels
- small, clear jar or cup
- alfalfa seed
- bean seed
- water
- hand lens
- yarn
- ruler

Activity Procedure

1 Fold a paper towel, and place it around the inside of the jar.

2 Make the second paper towel into a ball, and place it inside the jar to fill the space.

3 Place the alfalfa seed about 3 cm from the top of the jar, between the paper-towel lining and the jar's side. You should be able to see the seed through the jar.

4 Place the bean seed in a similar position on the other side of the jar. (Picture A)

5 Pour water into the jar to soak the towels completely.

6 Set the jar in a sunny place, and leave it there for five days. Be sure to keep the paper towels moist.

◀ New raspberry bushes can grow from seeds. The seeds are inside the berries.

Picture A

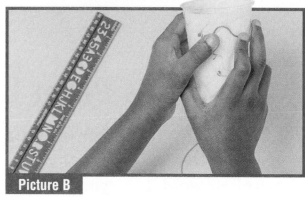

Picture B

Seed Growth				
	Alfalfa		Bean	
	Size	Other Observations	Size	Other Observations
Day 1				
Day 2				

7 Make a chart like the one above.

8 Use the hand lens to **observe** the seeds daily for five days. **Measure** the growth of the roots and shoots with the yarn. Use the ruler to measure the yarn. **Record** your observations on your chart. (Picture B)

Draw Conclusions

1. What plant parts grew from each seed?

2. **Compare** the growth of the roots and shoots from the two seeds. Did they grow to be the same size? Did they grow at the same rate?

3. **Scientists at Work** Scientists take a lot of care to **measure** objects the same way each time. Think about how you measured the plants. How do you know your measurements were accurate?

Investigate Further The bean and alfalfa seedlings will continue to grow after the first five days. Plant each of the seedlings in soil. Give the seeds the same amounts of water and light. Continue **observing** and **recording** information about your plants for a month. Make a drawing of your plants each week. Identify and label the parts of the plants.

Plant Life Cycles

Plants from Seeds

FIND OUT

• ways plants reproduce

• how seeds are spread

VOCABULARY

germinate
spore
tuber

Have you ever planted seeds in a garden? Seeds form in the cones of conifers. Seeds also form in the flowers of flowering plants. When a flower dries up and falls away, fruit forms around the young seeds. The fruit protects the seeds. Inside each seed is a tiny plant and the food it needs to start growing.

Seeds are the first part in a flowering plant's life cycle. To begin to grow, seeds need warmth, water, and air. Most seeds don't get what they need, so they don't grow. When a seed has its needs met, it **germinates** (jer•muh•NAYTS), or sprouts. Seedlings that sprout in soil may keep growing. They grow to become adult, or mature, plants. The mature plants form flowers.

Animals such as bees, birds, and bats feed on nectar, a sweet liquid in the flowers. This spreads pollen and helps flowers form seeds.

✔ **What do most seeds need to begin to grow?**

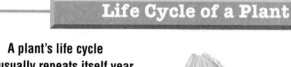
Life Cycle of a Plant

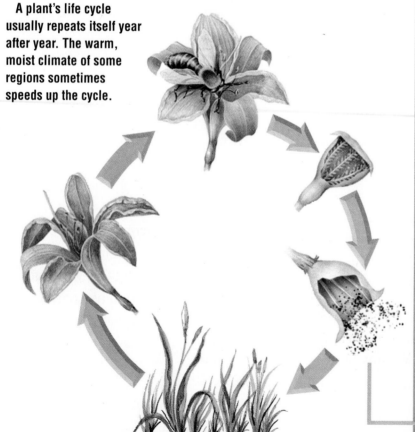

A plant's life cycle usually repeats itself year after year. The warm, moist climate of some regions sometimes speeds up the cycle.

Birds carry seeds in their beaks and on their feathers. ▼

The Spread of Seeds

Fruit falling to the ground is just one way seeds get to the soil. Animals play a role, too. For example, birds eat the fruit from plants. The seeds pass through their bodies and end up far away from the parent plants. Squirrels gather and eat nuts such as walnuts. When there are many walnuts, squirrels bury some to be eaten later. In the spring a few walnuts that were forgotten germinate and become young trees.

Wind and water also spread seeds. Dandelion seeds are light. The fruit is the fluffy part. When the seeds are ready, the wind carries the fluffy fruit away. Large seeds such as those from coconut and mangrove trees can float in water to shores far away from the parent plants.

Some seeds, such as those of beggar's-lice, stick to things. Animals that brush against these plants carry away the seeds in their fur. In the same way, humans carry the seeds on their clothing.

✔ **Describe a seed that can be carried by the wind.**

Seeds of beggar's-lice have tiny hooks that stick to fur, hair, and clothing. ▼

Milkweed seeds are carried away by wind. ▼

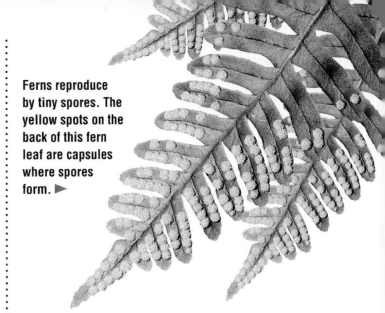

Ferns reproduce by tiny spores. The yellow spots on the back of this fern leaf are capsules where spores form. ▶

Plants from Spores

Not all plants have flowers that form fruits and seeds. Some plants grow from spores. **Spores** (SPOHRZ) are tiny cells. Spores are much smaller than seeds. In fact, most spores are made of only one cell and can be seen only with a microscope.

Spores are like seeds in some ways. Like seeds, spores contain food. And some spores have thick walls that allow them to stay inactive for months. They can be carried by wind, water, and animals.

Spores grow in capsules, or small cases. You may have seen ferns with tiny brown or yellow dots on the underside of their leaves. The dots are capsules and the spores are inside.

When spores are mature, the capsules dry up and open. Spores are then released into the air where they scatter. Spores germinate if they land where conditions are good. But the tiny plants that begin to grow are not complete. Adult plants form only after two different parts of these tiny plants join. Mature spore-making plants grow from the joined parts.

✔ **How are spores spread?**

New Plants from Old

Growing plants from seeds and spores can take a long time. Some plants have adaptations that let them make new plants in other ways.

A spider plant sends out buds on a type of stem called a runner. Buds are immature, or young, plant shoots. When these buds touch the ground, they form roots and begin to grow.

Tulips grow from bulbs. A bulb is a kind of bud that grows underground. Bulbs can be split into pieces. Each piece can grow into a new plant. You may have helped someone plant bulbs in the fall to have flowers the next spring.

Some plants grow from a piece of stem put in water. Many people who grow plants indoors start new ones by cutting off a branch of the stem. Then they trim off lower leaves and put that piece in water. New roots grow from it. The new stem with roots is planted in soil.

People have come up with ways to join two or more different plants to make a new plant. The process is called *grafting*. To graft plants, people attach a cut stem of one plant to a slice in the stem of another plant. The joined stem uses the roots of the other plant to get water and nutrients.

Grafting is used to make a new plant with the good characteristics of each plant. For example, branches of different apple trees can be joined to the trunk of another tree. The tree then grows apples that have more desirable flavors and sizes.

The spider plant sends out runners with buds attached. ▼

Three different branches were grafted to one trunk. That is why this small tree has three different colors of flowers. ▶

Potato tubers develop "eyes," each of which can make a new plant. ▶

Potatoes are **tubers** (TOO•berz), or swollen underground stems. Tubers are often dug up to eat. They also can be cut into pieces and planted. Each piece of a potato that has a bud, or "eye," can make a new plant.

✓ **What process ends with a "new and improved" plant?**

Summary

Plants reproduce by seeds and spores. Many plants can also grow from buds, bulbs, tubers, and stem pieces. Seeds are spread by falling fruit, animals, wind, and water.

Review

1. What must both seeds and spores do before they begin to grow in soil?

2. What are two ways that animals help spread seeds?

3. Spider plants, tulips, and potatoes can grow from seeds. How are their other ways of reproducing alike?

4. **Critical Thinking** If you had a leafy plant with damaged roots, how might you start a new plant?

5. **Test Prep** Which part of a flowering plant protects seeds?

   A flowers

   B fruit

   C capsules

   D birds

LINKS

MATH LINK

Using Fractions Wrap 10 bean seeds and 10 corn seeds in a moist paper towel. Seal them in a plastic bag for a week. What fraction of each seed group sprouts? Why might this information be important to a gardener?

WRITING LINK

Expressive Writing—Poem Haiku is a form of Japanese poetry. Haiku are often written about a season, such as fall. Write a haiku for a family member about what plants are like during your favorite season.

SOCIAL STUDIES LINK

Grains Around the World All grains are seeds. Many grains are important food sources. Find out which grains are eaten in different parts of the world. Use a world map to show which grains are grown in different areas of the world.

TECHNOLOGY LINK

Learn more about growing plants under different conditions—on a computer screen! Try *Do You Have a Green Thumb?* on **Harcourt Science Explorations CD-ROM.**

Superveggies

Researchers have found ways to make eating your vegetables more appealing.

Why Improve Vegetables?

"No dessert until you've finished your vegetables!" If you've ever heard those words, there's good news for you! Researchers at Texas A&M University are working on superveggies. These vegetables are better-tasting

BetaSweet carrots

than many well-known vegetables. They also have more of some nutrients. So people who eat only a few vegetables will still get plenty of nutrients. Superveggies also may prevent or fight diseases such as cancer and heart disease. Many different vegetables are being tested. They include onions, potatoes, peppers, corn, broccoli, cabbage, tomatoes, leeks, and Brussels sprouts.

A Sweet Success

A big success story is the BetaSweet carrot. It is sweeter and crisper than regular carrots, and its color is maroon! It has extra beta carotene (BAYT•uh KAIR•uh•teen), which your body changes to vitamin A. Eating just one-third of a BetaSweet carrot would meet your daily need for beta carotene.

Dr. Leonard M. Pike is the scientist who is heading research at the Vegetable Improvement Center at Texas A&M. He first got the idea for a maroon carrot in 1989. He saw carrots grown from Brazilian seeds. These carrots had maroon patches mixed in with the carrots' normal orange color. He began trying to design a carrot that had more flavor and nutrition.

New Veggies on the Horizon

Another new veggie to watch for is a cucumber that's orange inside! This special cucumber tastes like other cucumbers. But like BetaSweets, it also gives you a higher level of vitamin A.

How would you like a rose-colored onion with a mild flavor? These onions are meant to be eaten raw. Cooking destroys some of the important nutrients that make them look and taste different.

Researchers are also working on types of peppers that will have more vitamin C than an orange. Specially marked bell peppers and chili peppers may be in grocery stores soon. So be sure to "eat your superveggies"!

Think About It

1. If you could ask scientists to improve the nutrition, flavor, or color of certain fruits or vegetables, which ones would you choose?

2. One third of a BetaSweet carrot gives you all of one nutrient you need for a day. In the future, people might need less of all foods to get all needed nutrients. Do you think people will eat less food?

WEB LINK:
For Science and Technology updates, visit the Harcourt Internet site.
www.harcourtschool.com

Careers   Genetic Engineer

What They Do   A genetic engineer in agriculture works with plants to make them stronger or more healthful. For example, a genetic engineer might find a gene that helps a plant live for a while without water. That gene might be put into other plants to make them stronger, too. Genetic engineers also work with animals.

Education and Training   People who want to be genetic engineers study biology in college. They must learn about cell division and DNA. Most get advanced college degrees in genetics and plant or animal sciences.

Mary Agnes Meara Chase

BOTANIST

"If it were not for grasses, the world would never have been civilized."

Agnes Chase devoted her life to the study of grasses. She worked as a botanist (BAH•tuhn•ist), a scientist who studies plants, for the United States Department of Agriculture (USDA). She collected and described over 10,000 species of grasses. Early in her career, Chase made sketches of plants. She also helped write a book called *The Manual of Grasses.*

To a botanist, grasses include more than what grows in a front yard or at a park. Grasses also include grains such as rice, wheat, oats, rye, hay, and corn. Sorghum, bamboo, and sugar cane are also grasses. All these grasses are food for animals and for people. They provide building material and sugar. They also build up the land and prevent soil erosion. At the USDA, Chase helped scientists experiment with crops. The scientists wanted to develop nutritious plants that also resisted disease.

Chase often traveled to collect plants. She visited Europe twice and traveled to Mexico and Puerto Rico to study grasses and get samples. After she retired, Chase went to Venezuela

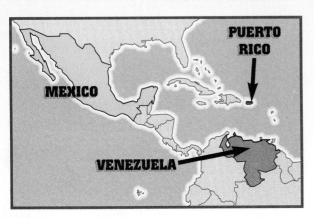

because its government asked for her help in collecting and studying grasses. While there, she encouraged students from South America to come to the United States to study. Some of the students who did come lived at her home in Washington, D.C.

Chase wrote over 70 different books and magazine articles. She kept on working, without pay, after she retired. She was in charge of the National Herbarium at the Smithsonian Institution. She eventually donated her personal collection to the Smithsonian Institution.

THINK ABOUT IT

1. What grasses do you eat regularly?
2. What features of grasses make them useful to people?

Plant Colors

What dyes do plants contain?

Materials

- dry yellow onion skins
- dry red onion skins
- pot
- water
- hot plate
- white cotton cloth
- string
- oven mitt

Procedure

1. An adult will boil each color of onion skins in water for about 20 minutes.

2. Tightly tie the cotton cloth into bunches with the string. Leave a length of string that you can use to hold the cloth.

3. Using an oven mitt, hold the string and put the cloth into one of the pots of hot onion water for about 5 minutes. Let the cloth cool. Then unwrap it and let it dry.

Draw Conclusions

What color did the cloth turn? Compare your cloth to one that was dyed with different colored onion skins. Why are the cloths different?

Identifying Trees

How can you identify trees?

Materials

- 3 zip-top bags, each containing leaves, bark, and seeds from a different type of tree
- paper
- colored pencils

Procedure

1. Observe the contents of each plastic bag.

2. For each bag, make a page that someone else could use to identify the tree without seeing the bag. Include any sketches or descriptions you think are important.

Draw Conclusions

What plant parts are in the bags? What other tree parts could be used to identify a tree? Compare your pages to the key or guidebook your teacher gives you. Try to name each tree.

Chapter 3 Review and Test Preparation

Vocabulary Review

Use the terms below to complete the sentences. The page numbers in ( ) tell you where to look in the chapter if you need help.

carbon dioxide (A64)   **taproot** (A71)

nutrient (A64)   **fibrous roots** (A71)

photosynthesis (A65)   **germinate** (A76)

symmetry (A70)   **spores** (A77)

transpiration (A70)   **tuber** (A79)

1. Water loss due to evaporation is ____.

2. Carrots have a ____, a single main root that grows deep into the soil.

3. *Sprout* is another word for ____.

4. Animals breathe out a gas called ____.

5. A substance a plant needs in order to grow is a ____.

6. The way a plant makes food is ____.

7. A root system that has many roots of the same size is made up of ____.

8. Potatoes have a swollen underground stem called a ____.

9. Tiny reproductive cells of ferns are ____.

10. An object with ____ can be divided into two or more parts that look the same.

Connect Concepts

Use the terms in the Word Bank to complete the concept map.

carbon dioxide   **fibrous roots**

nutrients   **photosynthesis**

taproots

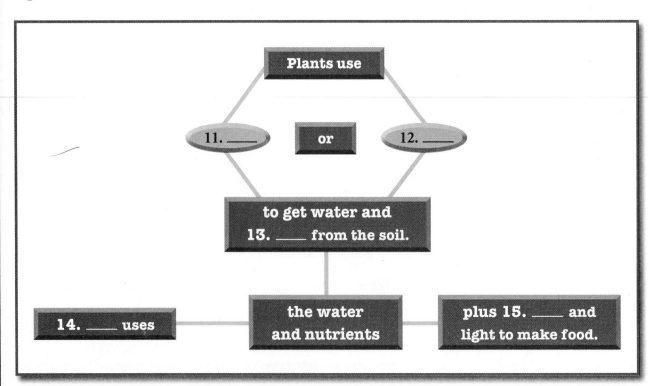

Plants use

11. ____   or   12. ____

to get water and 13. ____ from the soil.

14. ____ uses

the water and nutrients

plus 15. ____ and light to make food.

Check Understanding

Write the letter of the best choice.

16. A plant with a thick stem for storing water would probably grow in the —

  A ocean   **C** forest

  B mountains   **D** desert

17. Transpiration by plants could help form —

  F carbon dioxide

  G symmetry

  H rain clouds

  J oxygen

18. A seed eaten by a bird —

  A cannot grow

  B will probably make the bird sick

  C may become several seeds

  D may germinate far from where it was eaten

19. Which process can end with a "new and improved" plant?

  F grafting

  G cutting up tubers

  H placing cuttings in water

  J splitting apart bulbs

20. Which of the following terms does **NOT** belong with the others?

  A seed   **C** spore

  B flower   **D** fruit

Critical Thinking

21. Why do you think photosynthesis is one of the most important processes on Earth?

22. The fact that plants have many ways to spread seeds can cause problems for gardeners. Why is this?

Process Skills Review

23. You want to find out if a certain plant grows best in a hot, warm, or cool climate. What **variables** should you **control?** What variable will you **test?**

24. You want to buy a new pair of shoes. What are three shoe features you could **compare?**

25. You need to **measure** how fast a friend can run 25 meters. What two measuring instruments would you need?

Performance Assessment

Arctic Plant

The Arctic is very cold. The water and soil there are frozen most of the year, and the growing season is very short. Design and draw a plant that could live in the Arctic. Label the adaptations your plant has that help it live in this harsh climate. How would it reproduce?

Human Body Systems

Your body is made up of many different parts that work together. Think about all the parts you are using right now. Your eyes are sending messages to your brain. Your lungs are moving gases, your heart is pumping blood, and your muscles are keeping you sitting straight in your chair. You may also be digesting your breakfast or lunch! You probably didn't realize you were so busy!

Vocabulary Preview

cell
tissue
organ
cardiac muscle
smooth muscle
striated muscle
lungs
capillary
heart
artery
vein
brain
neuron
nerve
spinal cord
esophagus
stomach
intestine

FAST FACT

You don't have the same body you had a few weeks ago. Each day, your body replaces millions of cells that have worn out. Some cells are replaced every couple of days. Other cells must last your entire lifetime.

When Cells Are Replaced	
Stomach cells	2–3 days
Skin cells	19–34 days
Red blood cells	120 days
Brain cells	Never

Your intestines are tubes inside your abdomen. They're about twice as long as you are tall. Think about coiling a heavy rope that long inside of you!

These red blood cells are shown magnified about 25,000 times.

You may have a whale of an appetite, but you don't have a whale's stomach. Your stomach holds about $1\frac{1}{2}$ L. A right whale's stomach holds 760 L!

How Do the Skeletal and Muscular Systems Work?

In this lesson, you can . . .

 INVESTIGATE types of muscle tissue.

 LEARN ABOUT the skeletal and muscular systems.

 LINK to math, writing, technology, and other areas.

INVESTIGATE

Muscle Tissues

Activity Purpose The muscles you probably know most about are the ones you use to play or do work. There are also muscle types that you may not know you use, such as those in the digestive system and the heart. In this investigation you will **observe** and **compare** three types of muscles.

Materials

- Microslide Viewer
- Slide A—skeletal muscle tissue
- Slide B—smooth muscle tissue
- Slide C—heart muscle tissue

Skeletal muscle

▲ Slide A

Smooth muscle

▲ Slide B

◄ This boy uses the muscles in his leg to kick the soccer ball.

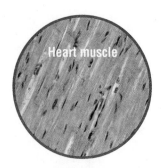
Heart muscle

▲ Slide C

Activity Procedure

Type of Muscle	Observations	Ways Like Other Types of Muscle	Ways Different from Other Types of Muscle
Slide A			
Slide B			
Slide C			

1 Make a chart like the one shown.

2 Use the Microslide Viewer to carefully **observe** the muscle tissue on microslide 1 or the picture of Slide A on page A88. (Picture A)

3 Take notes to describe the way the tissue looks. What shapes do you see? Are there any colors or patterns?

4 **Record** your observations on your chart.

5 Repeat Steps 2–4 for microslides 2 and 3, or Slides B and C on page A88.

Picture A

Draw Conclusions

1. Describe each type of muscle tissue.

2. How do the tissues look the same? How do they look different?

3. **Scientists at Work** Many scientists use microscopes in their work. What does a microscope do that makes it possible to **observe** and **compare** muscle tissues?

Investigate Further If you have access to a microscope, use one to **observe** prepared slides of different kinds of tissue. See page R4 for help in using a microscope. Cells from different kinds of tissue in your body look different. Find pictures of other kinds of tissue, such as nerve tissue, bone tissue, and blood tissue. **Compare** these tissues to the muscle tissues you looked at.

Process Skill Tip

Observing and comparing are two skills you often use together. To **observe**, you may need to use a tool, such as a microscope. Comparing uses information gained from observations. When you **compare**, you look for ways things are alike and ways things are different.

The Skeletal and Muscular Systems

Structures of the Body

FIND OUT

- the basic parts that make up the whole body
- how the skeletal and muscular systems work

VOCABULARY

cell
tissue
organ
cardiac muscle
smooth muscle
striated muscle

The body is like a wonderful machine that needs very little help to keep running smoothly. When it does go wrong, it often can repair itself. The more the body is used, the stronger it gets. Have you ever wondered how this "machine" is put together?

Your body is made up of the basic building blocks of life—**cells**. Every cell in your body has a certain job. There are many types of cells, including bone cells, muscle cells, blood cells, and nerve cells.

Cells of the same type work together to form **tissue**. Bone cells make up bone tissue. Muscle cells make up muscle tissue.

Tissues of different kinds work together in **organs**. Organs are body parts that do special jobs. Bone tissue and other tissues form organs called bones. Muscle tissue and other tissues form organs called muscles.

Groups of organs that work together form *systems*. Your body has many systems. Bones working together make up the skeletal system. Muscles working together make up the muscular system.

✔ **What are organs made up of?**

Bone cells form bone tissue. ▼

Bone tissues form bones, one of the organs in the body. ▶

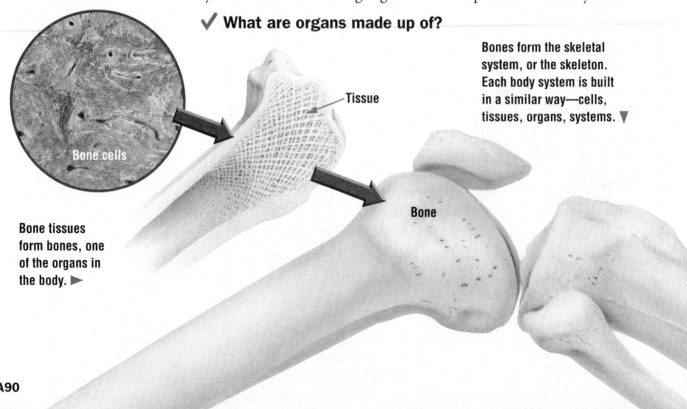

Bone cells

Tissue

Bone

Bones form the skeletal system, or the skeleton. Each body system is built in a similar way—cells, tissues, organs, systems. ▼

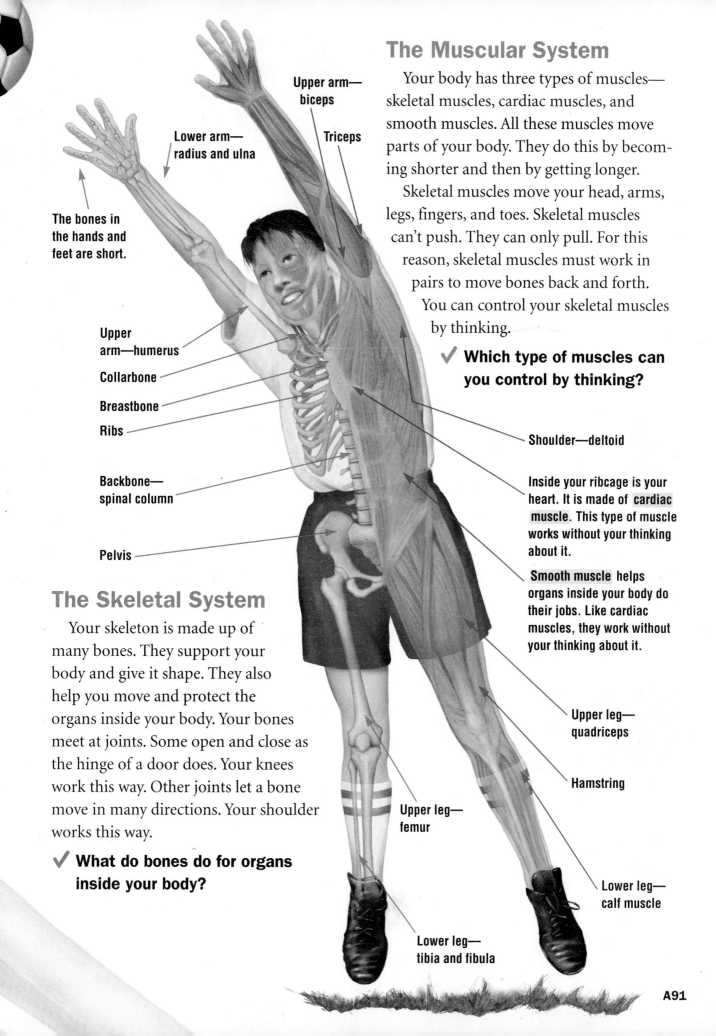

The Muscular System

Your body has three types of muscles—skeletal muscles, cardiac muscles, and smooth muscles. All these muscles move parts of your body. They do this by becoming shorter and then by getting longer.

Skeletal muscles move your head, arms, legs, fingers, and toes. Skeletal muscles can't push. They can only pull. For this reason, skeletal muscles must work in pairs to move bones back and forth. You can control your skeletal muscles by thinking.

✔ **Which type of muscles can you control by thinking?**

Upper arm—biceps

Triceps

Lower arm—radius and ulna

The bones in the hands and feet are short.

Upper arm—humerus

Collarbone

Breastbone

Ribs

Backbone—spinal column

Pelvis

Shoulder—deltoid

Inside your ribcage is your heart. It is made of cardiac muscle. This type of muscle works without your thinking about it.

Smooth muscle helps organs inside your body do their jobs. Like cardiac muscles, they work without your thinking about it.

Upper leg—quadriceps

Hamstring

Upper leg—femur

Lower leg—calf muscle

Lower leg—tibia and fibula

The Skeletal System

Your skeleton is made up of many bones. They support your body and give it shape. They also help you move and protect the organs inside your body. Your bones meet at joints. Some open and close as the hinge of a door does. Your knees work this way. Other joints let a bone move in many directions. Your shoulder works this way.

✔ **What do bones do for organs inside your body?**

A Closer Look at Muscles

As you saw in the investigation skeletal muscles have light and dark stripes. They are called **striated** (STRY•ayt•uhd) **muscles**. The stripes are patterns made by the working parts of the muscle cells. The fibers in a skeletal muscle can be up to 30 centimeters (12 in.) long. Some muscles have more than 2000 fibers packed tightly together.

Smooth muscle does not have stripes. It is found in the walls of organs such as the stomach, intestines, blood vessels, and bladder. Smooth muscle works by squeezing and relaxing slowly and smoothly. Its fibers are shorter than the fibers in skeletal muscle.

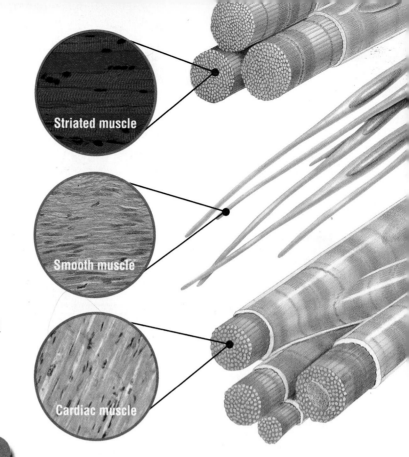

Striated muscle

Smooth muscle

Cardiac muscle

THE INSIDE STORY

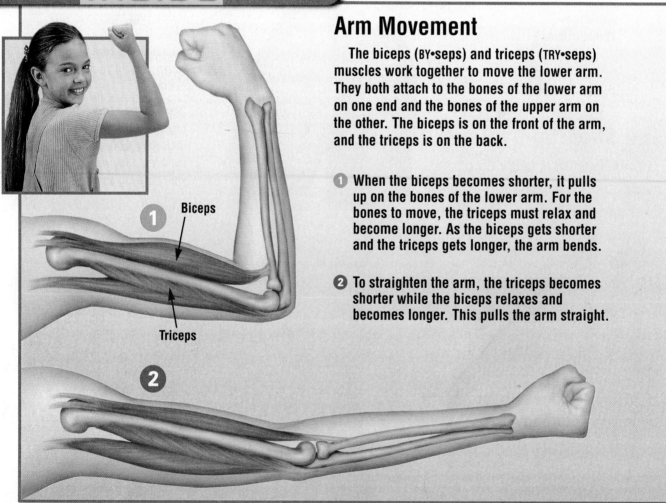

Biceps

Triceps

1

2

Arm Movement

The biceps (BY•seps) and triceps (TRY•seps) muscles work together to move the lower arm. They both attach to the bones of the lower arm on one end and the bones of the upper arm on the other. The biceps is on the front of the arm, and the triceps is on the back.

1 When the biceps becomes shorter, it pulls up on the bones of the lower arm. For the bones to move, the triceps must relax and become longer. As the biceps gets shorter and the triceps gets longer, the arm bends.

2 To straighten the arm, the triceps becomes shorter while the biceps relaxes and becomes longer. This pulls the arm straight.

◄ Muscles are made up of muscle fibers bundled together.

Cardiac muscle has stripes, but not as many as skeletal muscle. Cardiac muscle makes up the walls of the heart. Although cardiac muscle squeezes and relaxes without stopping, it never gets tired.

✔ **Which type of muscle doesn't have stripes?**

Summary

The body is made up of basic parts called cells. Cells make up tissues, tissues make up organs, and organs make up body systems. The skeletal and muscular systems work together to help the body move.

Review

1. What are the basic building blocks of life?
2. How do the skeletal and muscular systems work to move the body?
3. Which type of muscle works without ever stopping?
4. **Critical Thinking** Why is it good that people don't have to think about smooth muscles doing their jobs?
5. **Test Prep** _____ move bones in different directions.
   A Muscle pairs
   B Smooth muscles
   C Cardiac muscles
   D Cells

LINKS

MATH LINK

Calculating with Heartbeats Count the number of times your heart beats in one minute. This is your heart rate. Use this number to figure about how many times your heart beats in an hour and in a day.

WRITING LINK

Narrative Writing—Story Suppose you take a long hike. Write a story from the point of view of the muscles you would use. Describe for another classmate what it is like to walk and climb.

LITERATURE LINK

Let's Exercise Exercise is important for muscles and bones. Learn about exercise by reading *Staying Healthy: Let's Exercise* by Alice B. McGinty.

HEALTH LINK

Nutrition Find out what kinds of foods are important for building strong bones and muscles. Which ones would you like to try? Prepare a menu of meals and snacks for a day. Include foods that help build strong bones.

TECHNOLOGY LINK

Learn more about ways to keep your bones healthy by viewing *Bone Health* on the **Harcourt Science Newsroom Video.**

CNN
Turner
Le@rning

A93

How Do the Respiratory and Circulatory Systems Work?

In this lesson, you can . . .

 INVESTIGATE breathing rates.

 LEARN ABOUT the respiratory and circulatory systems.

 LINK to math, writing, and technology.

 **INVESTIGATE**

Breathing Rates

Activity Purpose Your breathing rate when you are active is different from the rate when you are sitting quietly. It may change even as you walk across the classroom or down the street. In this investigation you will **measure** your breathing rate after you do three different activities.

Materials

■ stopwatch, timer, or clock with second hand

Activity Procedure

1 Make a chart like the one on the next page.

2 While you are sitting, count the number of times you breathe out in one minute. **Record** the number on your chart.

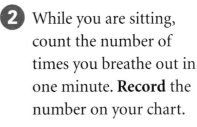

◀ Swimming is healthful exercise for both the respiratory and circulatory systems.

3 Stand up and march in place for one minute. Raise your knees as high as you can. As soon as you stop marching, begin to count the number of times you breathe out. Count your breaths for one minute. **Record** the number of breaths on your chart.

4 Rest for a few minutes, and then run in place for one minute. As soon as you stop running, begin to count the number of times you breathe out. Count your breaths for one minute. **Record** the number on your chart. (Picture A)

5 Make a bar graph to show how your breathing changed for each activity.

Picture A

Activity	Number of Breaths
Sitting	
After marching for 1 minute	
After running for 1 minute	

Draw Conclusions

1. Which activity needed the fewest breaths? Which needed the most breaths?

2. What can you **infer** about breathing from what happened in this investigation?

3. **Scientists at Work** Scientists don't usually **measure** something just once. What could you do to be sure your breathing rate measurements were correct?

Investigate Further Does your breathing rate increase if you exercise longer? March in place for two minutes, and then count your breaths. Run in place for two minutes, and then count your breaths. Add two new rows to your chart and **record** the numbers.

Process Skill Tip

Measuring should be repeated. Scientists often measure more than once to be sure their measurements are correct. They compare the sets of measurements to look for patterns and possible mistakes.

The Respiratory and Circulatory Systems

The Respiratory System

Your body's cells need oxygen to work. When you breathe in, you take in oxygen your cells need. As your cells do work, they give off carbon dioxide. When you breathe out, you get rid of carbon dioxide that cells give off.

You saw in the investigation that your breathing rate goes up as your body works harder. That's because as muscles do more work, they need more oxygen. They also give off more carbon dioxide. You breathe in and out faster to bring in more oxygen and to get rid of more carbon dioxide.

The main organs of the respiratory system are the **lungs**. Air enters your body through your nose and mouth. It goes down your *trachea* (TRAY•kee•uh) to your lungs. As you breathe in, your chest gets bigger and your lungs fill with air.

Your trachea divides to form a system of tubes in your lungs. These tubes look like the branches of a tree. The branches get smaller and smaller until they end in air sacs. All around the air sacs are tiny blood vessels called **capillaries** (KAP•uh•lair•ees). The walls of the air sacs and the capillaries are very thin. Oxygen passes easily through these walls, moving from the air sacs into blood in the capillaries. Carbon dioxide passes the other way, from blood in capillaries into the air in the air sacs.

✓ **What are the main organs of the respiratory system?**

FIND OUT

- what breathing does for the body
- why blood is important to the body's cells

VOCABULARY

lungs
capillary
heart
artery
vein

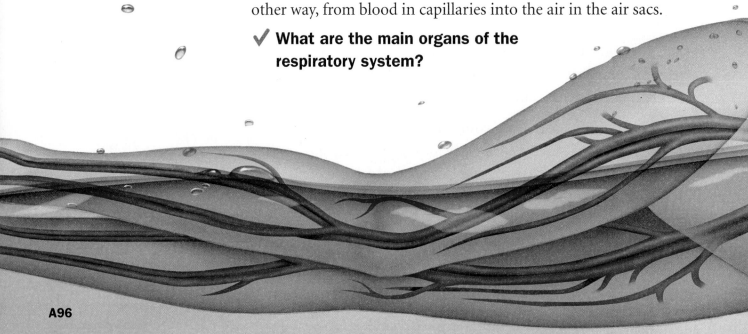

The Circulatory System

The capillaries around the air sacs in your lungs are part of your circulatory system. Your circulatory system includes your heart and all of your blood vessels, the tubes blood flows through. The job of the circulatory system is to take blood to all of your body's cells.

The **heart** is the muscle that pumps blood through your blood vessels to all parts of your body. It is only as big as your fist. It is very strong and works all the time, resting only between beats.

Blood leaves the heart through blood vessels called **arteries**. Arteries branch out to all parts of your body. They become smaller and smaller until they become tiny capillaries.

The capillaries carry blood to every cell in your body. There, oxygen passes from the blood into the cells. Carbon dioxide passes from cells into the blood. Capillaries

Capillaries

Artery

Vein

Blood leaves the heart through arteries. Arteries branch to become capillaries. Then blood returns to the heart through veins.

then become veins. **Veins** are the large blood vessels that return the blood to your heart.

✔ **Which part of the circulatory system pumps blood to all body parts?**

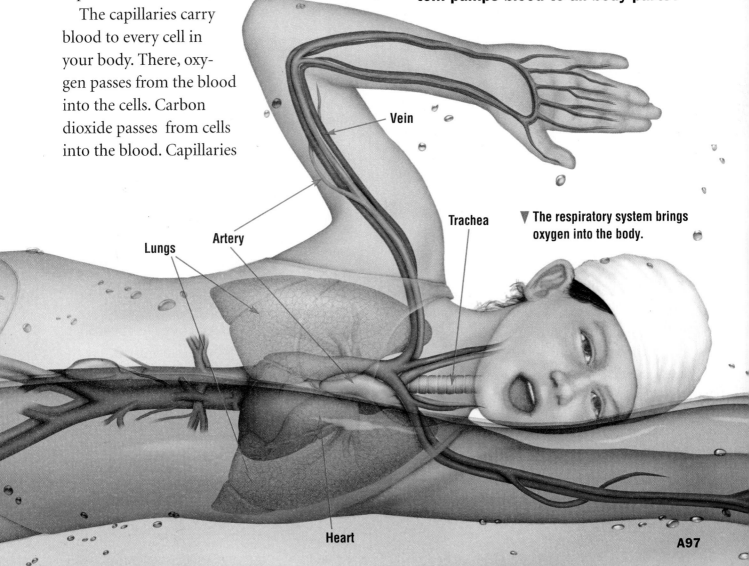

Vein

Trachea

Artery

Lungs

▼ **The respiratory system brings oxygen into the body.**

Heart

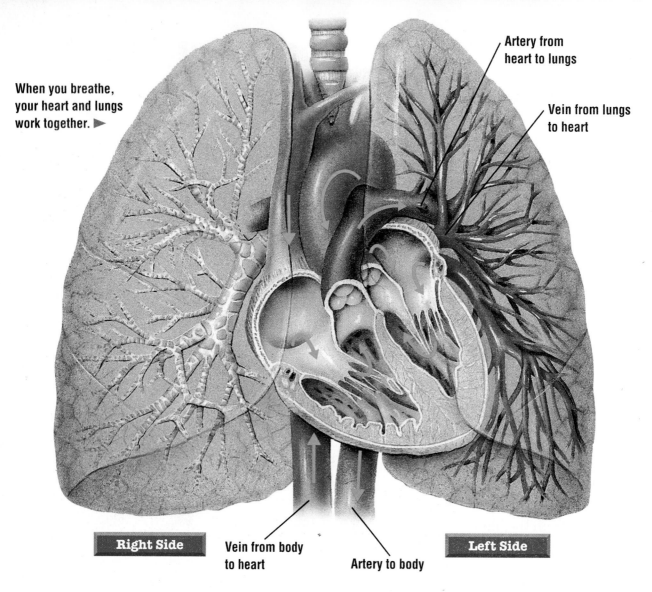

When you breathe, your heart and lungs work together. ▶

Artery from heart to lungs

Vein from lungs to heart

Right Side

Vein from body to heart

Artery to body

Left Side

The Heart and Lungs Work Together

The heart and lungs work together to bring oxygen into your body and to take away carbon dioxide. Each time you breathe in, the blood in your lungs gets fresh oxygen. This blood then travels to the heart, which pumps it to other parts of the body.

The heart has four sections called *chambers.* Each chamber acts as a pump. The chambers keep blood that enters the heart from mixing with blood that leaves the heart. The chambers are connected by openings. Each opening is covered by a valve that opens in only one direction. Each valve closes when its chamber is full.

Blood follows a one-way path through the heart. Blood from the lungs enters the top left chamber. The muscles of the chamber then shorten. This makes the space smaller, forcing the blood out. The only place it can go is into the lower left chamber.

This chamber is the main pump. It pushes blood through the whole body. When this chamber is full, it pushes the blood out of the heart and into the body's largest artery. The blood goes to all of the body, carrying oxygen to cells and picking up carbon dioxide. Then it returns to the heart.

Blood returning to the heart goes into the top right chamber. The muscles of this chamber force the blood into the chamber below.

The lower right chamber pumps the blood to the lungs. Here carbon dioxide leaves the blood and more oxygen enters. The blood is ready for another trip to the heart. It will be pumped around the body once again.

✔ **What makes blood follow a one-way path through the heart?**

Summary

Lungs are the organs the body uses to breathe. Breathing trades carbon dioxide, a waste cells give off, for oxygen, which cells need. Blood carries gases to and from cells through blood vessels. The heart pumps blood through the body.

Review

1. Why is it easy for gases to pass between air sacs and blood?

2. Which blood vessels take blood away from the heart?

3. Which blood vessels in the lungs help your body take in and give off gases?

4. **Critical Thinking** What do you think would happen if blood entering the heart mixed with blood leaving the heart?

5. **Test Prep** Which is a waste product of cells?

   A blood

   B water

   C oxygen

   D carbon dioxide

LINKS

MATH LINK

Interpret Data Knowing your target heart rate helps you exercise at a safe and healthful level. When you exercise, keep your heart rate between the maximum and minimum rates.

Exercise Heart Rate

Age	Minimum	Maximum
8	127	180
9	$126\frac{1}{2}$	179
10	126	$178\frac{1}{2}$
11	125	178

Do you think a 13-year-old would have a higher or lower maximum exercise heart rate than an 11-year-old? Why?

WRITING LINK

Expressive Writing—Song Lyrics Write a funny song for a younger student. Tell about a molecule of oxygen that enters the lungs. Explain what happens when it refuses to go to just any cell because it wants only to visit the big toe.

TECHNOLOGY LINK

Learn more about keeping heart beats regular by visiting the Smithsonian Institution Internet site.
www.si.edu/harcourt/science

 Smithsonian Institution®

How Do the Nervous and Digestive Systems Work?

In this lesson, you can . . .

INVESTIGATE the sense of touch.

LEARN ABOUT the nervous and digestive systems.

LINK to math, writing, health, and technology.

INVESTIGATE

The Sense of Touch

Activity Purpose To protect itself, the body must notice things that touch it. Some parts of the body have a better sense of touch than others. In this investigation you will first **predict** which of three areas of your body is the most sensitive to touch. Then you will **compare** how sensitive the areas are.

Materials

- index card
- ruler
- 8 toothpicks
- tape
- blindfold (optional)

Activity Procedure

1. Make a copy of the chart on the next page.

2. Look at the areas of the body listed on the chart. **Predict** which one has the best sense of touch. Write your prediction on the chart. Explain your choice.

3. Measure a space 1 cm wide on one edge of the index card. Mark each end of the space, and write the distance between the marks. Tape a toothpick to each mark so that one end of each toothpick sticks out about 1 cm past the edge of the card. Make sure the toothpicks point straight out from the edge of the card.

◀ This baseball catcher needs alert senses to catch the ball.

	Prediction: Distance Between Toothpicks When Two Toothpicks First Felt		
	Palm	Lower Arm	Upper Arm
Prediction			
Actual			

4 Repeat Step 3 for the other three sides of the index card. However, use spaces 2 cm, 5 cm, and 8 cm wide, one for each side.

5 Have a partner test your sense of touch. Ask him or her to lightly touch one body area listed on the chart with the toothpicks on each edge of the index card. Begin with the 1-cm side, and then use each side in turn with 2 cm apart, 5 cm apart, and 8 cm apart. Don't watch as your partner does this. (Picture A)

Picture A

6 For each area, tell your partner when you first feel two separate toothpicks touching your skin. Have your partner write the distance between these toothpicks on the chart.

7 Switch roles and test your partner.

Draw Conclusions

1. Which of the body parts felt the two toothpicks the shortest distance apart?

2. Based on this test, which of these body parts would you **infer** has the best sense of touch? Explain.

3. **Scientists at Work** Using what you observed in this investigation, which part of your body do you **predict** to be more sensitive, your fingertip or the back of your neck?

Investigate Further Have your partner use the toothpicks to test your fingertip and the back of your neck to check the **prediction** you just made.

The Nervous and Digestive Systems

The Nervous System

FIND OUT

- how the nervous system controls all the body's systems

- what the digestive system does for the body

VOCABULARY

brain
neuron
nerve
spinal cord
esophagus
stomach
small intestine
large intestine

None of your body systems could work without the help of your nervous system. It controls all parts of your body. Your nervous system is always receiving messages from your body and sending out responses.

Your **brain** is the control center of your nervous system. It and all other parts of the system are made up of nerve cells, or **neurons** (NOO•rahns). The brain uses information it gets from your body to direct how each body system works.

Your brain gets a lot of information from the sense organs in your head—your eyes, ears, tongue, and nose. Your brain also gets information from other parts of your body. In the investigation, you tested the sense of touch in different parts of your arm. Your brain told you what you felt.

Your body has **nerves**, or groups of neurons, that pass along information. The sense organs in your head have nerves that connect directly to your brain. Your spinal cord connects the nerves in the rest of your body to your brain. Your **spinal** (SPY•nuhl) **cord** is a tube of nerves that runs through your spine, or backbone.

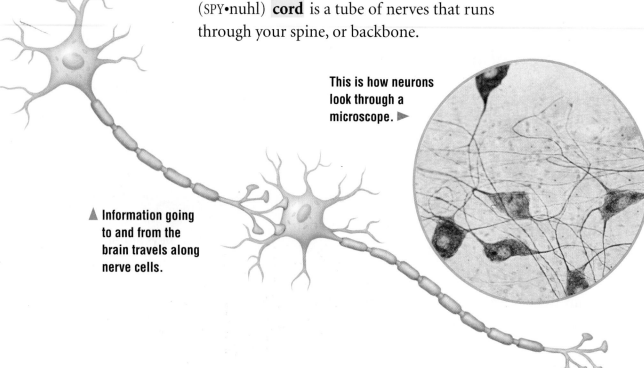

This is how neurons look through a microscope. ▶

▲ Information going to and from the brain travels along nerve cells.

Information from your body goes up your spinal cord to your brain. Your brain acts on the information and sends a message back. For example, if you are at bat in a baseball game, your eyes watch the ball. They send information to your brain about the speed and direction of the ball. In less than a second, your brain decides whether or not to swing at the pitch.

If you decide to swing, your brain will send information down your spinal cord to nerves in your arms. The message will tell your arm muscles when and how hard to swing. If you hit the ball, your brain will tell your leg muscles to run. The more you practice, the better your brain will get at telling your muscles just how to hit the ball.

✔ **Which body part tells a batter whether or not to swing at a ball?**

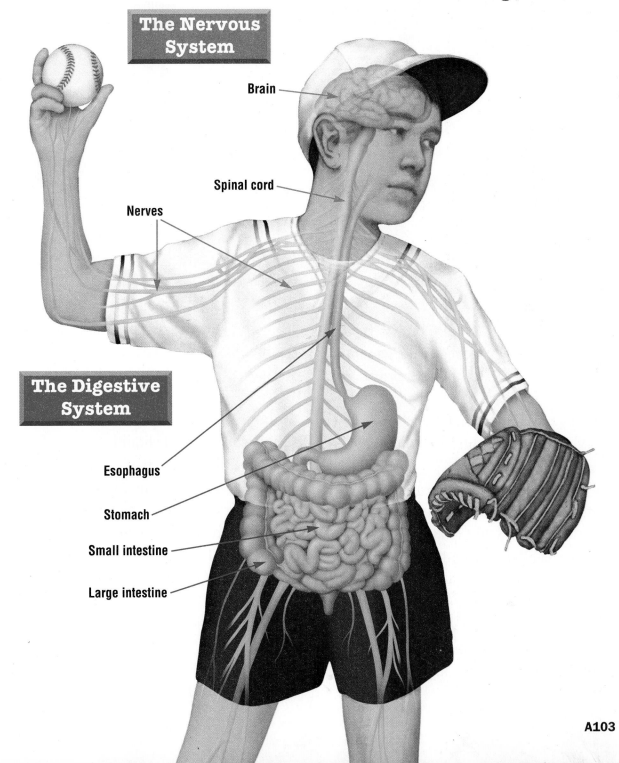

The Nervous System

Brain

Spinal cord

Nerves

The Digestive System

Esophagus

Stomach

Small intestine

Large intestine

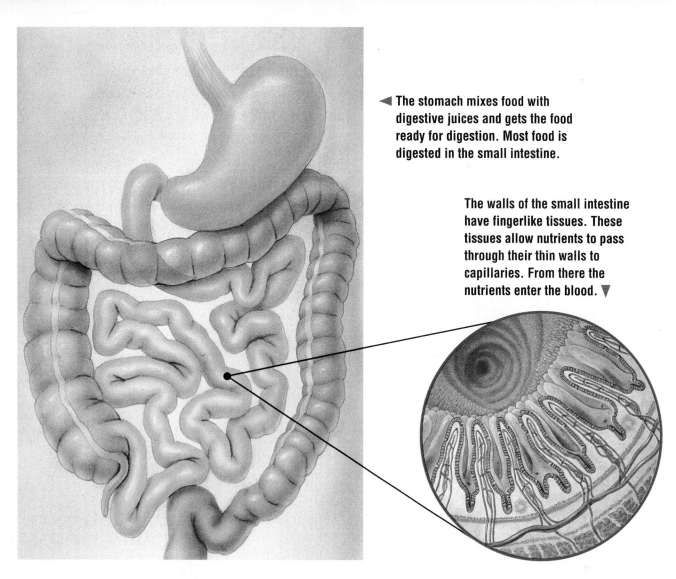

The stomach mixes food with digestive juices and gets the food ready for digestion. Most food is digested in the small intestine.

The walls of the small intestine have fingerlike tissues. These tissues allow nutrients to pass through their thin walls to capillaries. From there the nutrients enter the blood. ▼

The Digestive System

The digestive system also does an important job for the whole body. It provides nutrients to all the body's systems. It does this by breaking down, or digesting, the food you eat into nutrients your body's cells can use.

Digestion begins in your mouth. When you chew, your teeth grind up food into smaller pieces. Saliva (suh•LY•vuh) softens the food and begins to digest it.

After you swallow, the food enters your **esophagus** (ih•SOF•uh•guhs), a tube that connects your mouth with your stomach. The actions of smooth muscles in your esophagus move the food down to your stomach.

The **stomach** is a bag made up of smooth muscles. The stomach muscles squeeze the food and mix it with digestive juices. The juices digest some parts of the food. The food is mixed and squeezed until it becomes mostly liquid.

The liquid food then passes into the **small intestine** (ihn•TES•tuhn), a long tube of muscle. Different digestive juices are added, and other parts of the food are digested. The small intestine does more than any part of the digestive system to digest food.

The nutrients from the digested food pass through the walls of the small intestine into capillaries. Blood carries these nutrients to the body's cells.

The last part of the digestive system is the **large intestine**. Most food that reaches the large intestine can't be broken down any more. The large intestine removes water from this food. What is left of the food travels through the large intestine until it passes out of the body.

✓ **What part of the digestive system does the most to digest food?**

Summary

The brain sends messages to and from all parts of the body through the spinal cord and nerves. It controls the way all other body systems work. The digestive system breaks down food to provide nutrients for all the body's cells. The blood carries these nutrients to every cell in the body.

Review

1. How does the brain connect with other parts of the body?

2. What gives information to the brain?

3. Where does digestion begin?

4. **Critical Thinking** Why would not chewing food enough make it harder for the digestive system to do its job?

5. **Test Prep** Which part of the digestive system makes food mostly liquid?
   A stomach
   B esophagus
   C small intestine
   D large intestine

LINKS

MATH LINK

Calculator Challenge Nerves can send messages back and forth at the amazing speed of 430 kilometers per hour. Find two things that travel faster than nerve messages and two that travel more slowly. Make a bar graph to show and compare all five speeds.

WRITING LINK

Informative Writing—Explanation You have seen how the nervous system controls your muscles. Write a paragraph for your school newspaper. Explain what your nervous system does when you score a point in your favorite sport.

HEALTH LINK

Nutrition Read about the Food Guide Pyramid on pages R12–R13 of the Health Handbook. Make your own model of the pyramid. Draw or cut out pictures of foods for each food group. Glue them to your model.

TECHNOLOGY LINK

Visit The Harcourt Learning Site for related links, activities, and resources.

WELCOME TO
THE
LEARNING
SITE

Skin Adhesive

Almost everyone is badly cut at some time and has to get the cut stitched closed in an emergency room. Now, researchers are trying to make such stitches a thing of the past!

This cut is being glued closed with skin adhesive.

Super Surgical Glue

Stitches are used 86 million times a year all over the world. Doctors predict that half of the cuts will soon be repaired by skin adhesive (ad•HEE•siv), or artificial glue. It is like other "super" glues. But it is made to stick together living layers of skin!

Now, This Won't Hurt!

There are lots of good reasons to use this product. It takes less time than stitches. Doctors simply squeeze it out of a tube, much like rolling on lip gloss. Stitching a cut takes an average of $12\frac{1}{2}$ minutes. Using adhesive takes only about $3\frac{1}{2}$ minutes.

Stitched wounds are three times as likely to become infected as are wounds closed by adhesive. And adhesive stretches with the skin, so cuts don't break open when the patient stretches or moves. The skin adhesive comes off with dead skin cells. As a result, no visit to the doctor is needed to remove it, unlike stitches. Best of all, applying skin adhesive doesn't hurt, so skin doesn't have to be "numbed" first. For these reasons, the adhesive is comfortable for the patient and easier for the doctor. An added bonus is that it usually costs less than stitches.

Still to Come

Other companies are working to make adhesives for other medical work. One company has made an adhesive that also kills germs. Scientist are working to find adhesives to glue bone grafts, to close spinal fluid leaks, and to seal holes in the digestive tract. A spray adhesive may be used for burns. The adhesive would protect tender new skin as the new skin grows.

Don't Try This at Home!

CAUTION If you have a cut or wound, do *not* try to glue it closed. Get help from an adult. Surgical adhesives are **NOT** just like the glues at school or home. Only surgical adhesives are for use on skin.

Think About It

1. Why would a spray type of skin adhesive be helpful for burn patients?
2. What other medical uses can you think of for skin adhesives? Are there nonmedical ways they might be used?

WEB LINK:
For Science and Technology updates, visit the Harcourt Internet site.
www.harcourtschool.com

Careers   Surgical Nurse

What They Do
Surgical nurses help patients before, during, and after surgery. They may help the surgeon during an operation. They also may stay with a patient in the recovery room after surgery.

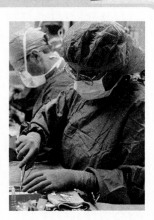

Education and Training   Many nurses have college degrees in nursing. Some learn in programs offered through hospitals. Some take two-year community college programs. Surgical nurses must take courses in surgical nursing. They must also study and train during their career. All nursing programs require practice on the job. All states require nurses to pass a national exam.

Rosalyn Sussman Yalow

MEDICAL PHYSICIST

"You won't all win Nobel Prizes, but the important thing is that you set goals for yourself and then live up to them."

Dr. Rosalyn Yalow knows about setting goals. By the time she was a teenager, she knew she wanted to have a career in science, marry, and raise a family. At that time, it was unusual for a woman to plan to have both a career and a family.

Yalow valued education and was especially good at math. She attended Hunter College and the University of Illinois at Urbana-Champaign.

While at the University of Illinois, Yalow became interested in radioactive particles. These are given off when atoms break apart. Yalow later set up a laboratory in what had been a janitor's closet at the Veteran's Administration Hospital in the Bronx. Dr. Solomon Berson became her research partner. They worked together for over 20 years.

Berson and Yalow found that radioactive particles could help measure antibodies in the blood. They could also detect the level of certain hormones. Their method is called radioimmuno-assay (ray•dee•oh•im•yoo•noh•AS•ay), or RIA. It takes only a small amount of blood. This was important because earlier methods required almost a cup of blood! RIA measures very pre-cisely. It can detect amounts as small as one billionth of a gram. This precision helps doctors diagnose and treat many different diseases.

Dr. Berson died in 1972, and Yalow continued her work with a new research partner. Yalow was the first woman to receive the Albert Lasker Basic Medical Research Award. In 1977 she received the Nobel Prize for Medicine and Physiology.

THINK ABOUT IT

1. How are science and detective work alike?
2. Why is it sometimes helpful for scientists to work together on a large project?

RIA test equipment

Muscle Model

How does the biceps muscle work?

Materials

- 2 boards (about 5 cm × 25 cm)
- duct tape
- scissors
- long balloon
- string

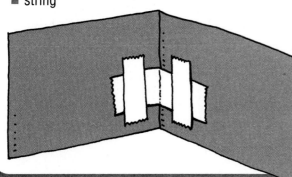

Procedure

1. Place the boards end to end. Use duct tape to make a hinge connecting the boards.
2. Blow up the balloon about one-fourth full.
3. Using the string, tie the two ends of the balloon to the outside ends of the boards.
4. Open and close the model you made.
5. Record your observations.

Draw Conclusions

Explain how this model is like the biceps muscle and the upper and lower bones of the arm.

Reaction Time

How does practice affect the nervous system?

Materials

- meterstick

Procedure

1. Work with a partner. Put your forearm flat on your desktop with your hand extending over the edge.

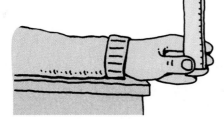

2. Have your partner hold the meterstick above your hand so that the zero mark is between your index finger and your thumb.
3. Have your partner drop the meterstick without giving you any warning. Catch the meterstick as quickly as you can.
4. Record the number that was between your fingers when you caught the stick. This is the distance the meterstick fell before you caught it.
5. Repeat the test ten times. Record the distance the stick fell each time.

Draw Conclusions

Make a line graph of your results. Did your reaction times change? In what way?

Vocabulary Review

Use the terms below to complete the sentences. The page numbers in ( ) tell you where to look in the chapter if you need help.

cell (A90)

veins (A97)

tissue (A90)

brain (A102)

organ (A90)

neurons (A102)

cardiac muscle (A91)

nerves (A102)

smooth muscle (A91)

arteries (A97)

spinal cord (A102)

striated muscle (A92)

esophagus (A104)

lungs (A96)

stomach (A104)

capillaries (A96)

small intestine (A104)

heart (A97)

large intestine (A104)

1. Two long tubes of muscle that lead from the stomach and help absorb food are the ____ and the ____.

2. Your ____ is a bag made up of muscles that churns food.

3. Three main parts of your nervous system are the ____, ____, and ____.

4. From your heart, blood first flows away through ____ to the body, then through ____, and back to the heart through ____.

5. Your ____ is the organ that pumps blood.

6. The ____ is the major building block of life.

7. The ____ are the main organs of the respiratory system.

8. The cells that form nerves are ____.

9. A group of cells of the same type is a ____.

10. The ____ connects your mouth to your stomach.

11. An ____ is made up of different tissues that work together to do a certain job in the body.

12. The three types of muscles in your body are ____, or heart muscle; ____; and ____.

Connect Concepts

Use concepts from the chapter to complete the concept map.

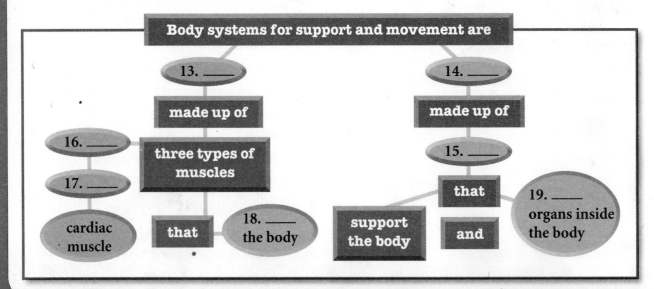

Check Understanding

Write the letter of the best choice.

20. Leg muscles that you use when you lift a box are —
    A smooth muscles
    B striated muscles
    C cardiac muscles
    D heart muscles

21. The brain is an _____ that is part of your nervous system.
    F organ
    G leg
    H cell
    J system

22. When you exercise, your body needs more _____, so you breathe faster.
    A oxygen
    B water
    C carbon dioxide
    D speed

23. When blood passes through _____, it exchanges oxygen and carbon dioxide.
    F arteries
    G veins
    H the heart
    J capillaries

24. Which body system tells you when to reach for and catch a falling book?
    A muscular
    B skeletal
    C nervous
    D respiratory

Critical Thinking

25. Why isn't the heart made up of smooth muscles like other organs inside your body?

26. Which body system would smoking cigarettes affect most directly? Explain.

27. How might a serious injury to your spinal cord affect the rest of your body?

Process Skills Review

28. What features would you look for if you wanted to **compare** bones in the human body?

29. How would you **measure** the number of times students dropped pencils during class?

30. To **predict** who would win a race, what would you want to know?

Performance Assessment

Digestion Model

With a partner, make a small model or a poster showing how your digestive system would digest an apple.

Unit Project Wrap Up

Here are some ideas for ways to wrap up your unit project.

Write a Project Guide

Make a guide to tell others what you learned about the animals that visited your feeder. Explain how you built your feeder, so someone else could build one, too!

Display at a Science Fair

Make a display about your project for a school science fair. Prepare a written report describing the procedure you used and your results. On a poster, display the data you collected. You can also display photographs and sketches of the animals that visited your feeder.

Make a Video Presentation

Ask someone to videotape you as you describe the results of your project. Show your videotape to others for review.

Investigate Further

How could you make your project better? What other questions do you have about animals? Plan ways to find answers to your questions. Use the Science Handbook on pages R2-R9 for help.

Looking at Ecosystems

UNIT
B

Looking at Ecosystems

Unit Project

Ecosystem Model

Make your classroom into a model of an ecosystem that you choose. From art materials, make examples of plants and animals that would live in the ecosystem. Display these along with the nonliving things present in your ecosystem. Use yarn to connect the living and nonliving things that interact. Attach labels to describe how they interact.

1

Ecosystems

Did you ever stop to think why living things live where they do? A maple tree wouldn't grow well in a desert. An elephant probably wouldn't survive in the Arctic. All living things have adaptations to meet their needs in areas where they are found. If the areas change, some living things may find it hard to survive.

Vocabulary Preview

system
stability
ecosystem
population
community
habitat
niche
producer
consumer
decomposer
climate
diversity
salinity

FAST FACT

Some living things stay in a small area. A pine tree doesn't move at all during its lifetime. A mouse stays close to its nest. Wolves and caribou (KAIR•uh•boo) may travel hundreds of kilometers to find food and shelter.

How Far Living Things Travel

Living Thing	Distance Traveled	
Pine tree	0 m	(0 ft)
Mouse	60 m	(200 ft)
Wolf	520 km	(320 mi)
Caribou	1600 km	(1000 mi)

Bridges disturb living things in the areas where they are built. But they also can help. These cliff swallows have turned a bridge into a home. The bridge shelters their mud nests from rain. And like a cliff, the bridge is high in the air.

You can tell a fish's age by looking at its scales. The process is much like counting rings to figure out how old a tree is!

Caribou travel great distances to find lichens (LY•kuhnz) to eat.

What Are Systems?

In this lesson, you can . . .

 INVESTIGATE how parts of a system interact.

 LEARN ABOUT characteristics of systems.

 LINK to math, writing, technology, and other areas.

 **INVESTIGATE**

How Parts of a System Interact

Activity Purpose The plants, soil, air, light, and water in nature are parts of a system. In this investigation you will **make a model** that includes all these parts. You will see how the parts interact, or affect each other.

Materials

- 2 empty 2-L soda bottles
- scissors
- gravel
- sand
- soil
- 6 small plants
- spray bottle containing water
- clear plastic wrap
- rubber bands

 CAUTION

Activity Procedure

1 **CAUTION** **Be careful when using scissors.** Cut the tops off the 2-L bottles.

2 Pour a layer of gravel in the bottom of each bottle. Cover this with a layer of sand.

3 Add a layer of soil to each bottle, and plant three plants in each bottle. (Picture A)

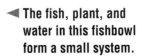

◀ The fish, plant, and water in this fishbowl form a small system.

Picture A

Picture B

4 Spray the plants and the soil with water. Cover the tops of the bottles with plastic wrap. You may need to use the rubber bands to hold the plastic wrap in place. You have now made two examples of a system called a *terrarium* (tuh•RAIR•ee•uhm). (Picture B)

5 Put one terrarium in a sunny spot. Put the other in a dark closet or cabinet.

6 After three days, **observe** each terrarium and **record** what you see.

Draw Conclusions

1. Which part of the system was missing from one of the terrariums?

2. What did you **observe** about the two systems?

3. **Scientists at Work** Scientists learn how different things interact by putting them together to form a system. What did your **model** show you about the interactions among plants, soil, air, light, and water?

Investigate Further **Hypothesize** what would happen if a terrarium had no water. Make another terrarium, but this time don't add any water. Put the terrarium in a sunny spot, and **observe** it after three days. What has happened?

Process Skill Tip

A **model** can help you understand something that is complicated. However, a model can show only some important parts of a complicated system or process.

Characteristics of Systems

System Parts

FIND OUT

- what makes up a system
- how a system gains stability

VOCABULARY

system
stability

You and your friends have probably run through a sprinkler on a hot summer day. The cold water splashed on your skin and cooled you off. You may have slipped and slid on wet grass. Although you may not think of it in this way, you, the grass, and the sprinkler were part of a system. A **system** is a group of parts that work together as a unit. You made a simple system when you built your terrariums. A system also has cycles and processes that interact, or affect each other.

Everything in a yard, including the house, plants, people, animals, hose, sprinkler, and water, is part of a system. The people, plants, and animals are the living parts of the system. The rest of the things in a yard are the nonliving parts of the system. Both the living and nonliving things play important roles in keeping the yard system working right.

The edges of the yard system are easy to see. It is easy to say what is inside and what is outside the system. The edges of many natural systems aren't as easy to see. Often, scientists must decide where the edges of a natural system will be for the purposes of their studies. For example, a scientist might choose to study one tree, a group of trees, or a whole forest.

✔ **What are the living parts of a yard system?**

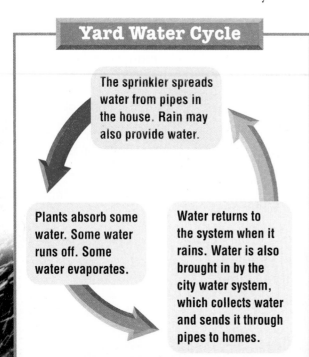

Yard Water Cycle

The sprinkler spreads water from pipes in the house. Rain may also provide water.

Plants absorb some water. Some water runs off. Some water evaporates.

Water returns to the system when it rains. Water is also brought in by the city water system, which collects water and sends it through pipes to homes.

Interactions

The parts of a system interact with other parts of the system. You turn on a faucet to get water. The hose carries the water to a sprinkler that sprays the water. You use the water to cool your body. The grass uses the water to grow. You walk on the grass.

Most systems also interact with the outside. The yard system is an open system because it takes in things called *inputs* from outside the system. Energy from the sun is one input. Water is also an important input. The water may come in the form of rain or from the city's water supply.

Open systems also let things out. *Outputs* are things that leave a system. One output from the yard system is water. Some of the water in the yard runs off into the street. Some evaporates into the air.

The opposite of an open system is a closed system. A closed system has no inputs

▲ This diagram shows some parts of a typical yard system.

or outputs. Very few systems are really closed. Most have some connection to the outside.

✔ **What two features do open systems have?**

A yard forms a simple system that has many parts. ▼

B7

Stability and Change

All systems follow patterns of changes. You sometimes must look carefully to see these patterns because they occur over time. In a yard the cycle of periods of sunshine and periods of shade each day is a pattern. The cycle of being wet and being dry is another pattern. Patterns show a kind of stability. **Stability** (stuh•BIL•uh•tee) means that over time the changes in a system cancel each other out. For example, if something is added, it is later taken out. The system stays in balance.

▲ The yard changes as the seasons change. In fall and winter, the plants stop growing or die. In spring and summer, they grow.

Stability is important because almost all natural systems have it. The yard system has stability. The sun shines in part of the yard each morning. In the afternoon that part is shady. The grass may dry out after a few days without rain, but eventually it gets water from rain or from a sprinkler.

✔ **What is stability?**

◀ Grass grows as it gets water and sunlight. This change is canceled out by the person who cuts the grass. The length of the grass is stable. It is always about the same.

▲ Because the pattern of change is repeated every year, you know that every spring plants will again begin to grow.

Summary

A system is made up of parts that interact. Open systems take in inputs and give off outputs. Patterns and cycles in systems show stability. A system has stability when the changes in it cancel each other out.

Review

1. Describe two ways in which the parts of a yard system interact.
2. How are inputs and outputs of a system alike?
3. What patterns show that a yard system is stable?
4. **Critical Thinking** How do areas of sunshine follow a pattern in a yard that has trees?
5. **Test Prep** A system that is in balance is said to have —
   A openness
   B stability
   C input
   D output

LINKS

MATH LINK

Graphing Use library resources to find your area's average temperature for each month. Make a bar graph to show what you found. Will the pattern repeat? Explain your answer.

WRITING LINK

Narrative Writing—Story The sun is the source of energy for almost all systems that include living things. Write a story called "What If the Sun Suddenly Got Dimmer?" for your friends to read. Tell what would happen to systems of living things on Earth.

HEALTH LINK

Body Systems Make a chart of a body system. Label the parts of the system. Describe what they do and how they interact.

LITERATURE LINK

Disappearing Lake Read *Disappearing Lake—Nature's Magic in Denali National Park* by Debbie S. Miller. Write a paragraph telling about one of the cycles described in the book.

TECHNOLOGY LINK

Learn more about natural systems and stability by visiting this Internet site.
www.scilinks.org/harcourt

What Makes Up an Ecosystem?

In this lesson, you can . . .

 INVESTIGATE an ecosystem.

 LEARN ABOUT living and nonliving parts of ecosystems.

 LINK to math, writing, art, and technology.

Frogs are often seen near water ecosystems. ▽

 **INVESTIGATE**

An Ecosystem

Activity Purpose Ecosystems are all around you. A back yard is an ecosystem. Ecosystems are in your school's playground and walkways. A vacant lot is an ecosystem. An ecosystem can be found any-where plants and animals interact with the world around them. In this investigation you will **observe** an ecosystem at your school to discover what lives there.

Materials

- meterstick
- chalk
- stakes
- string
- hand lens
- hand trowel

Activity Procedure

1 Use the meterstick to **measure** a square area that is 1 m long and 1 m wide. It can be on grass, bare dirt, or the cracked concrete of a wall or sidewalk. Mark the edges of the square with the chalk or with the stakes and string. (Picture A)

2 **Observe** your study area. Look for plants and animals that live there. Use the hand lens. **Record** all the living things you see. Describe any signs that other living things have been there.

3 *In soil or grass,* use the trowel to turn over a small area of soil. Look for insects or other liv-ing things. (Picture B) **Count** and **record** any living things you find. Then **classify** them. Be sure to fill in the holes you dig in your area.

Picture A

Picture B

4 *In concrete or brick areas,* **observe** areas along the sides of the concrete or bricks that may contain soil and places for plants to grow. **Count** and **record** the number of each type of living thing you find. Then **classify** each.

5 **Communicate** your results to your class. Describe your study area. Identify the living things you found.

Draw Conclusions

1. What living things did you find in your study area? Which kind of living thing was most common in your area?

2. How was your study area different from those of other student groups?

3. **Scientists at Work** Scientists often **observe** an ecosystem at different times of the day and in different seasons. This is because different animals can be seen at different times. **Predict** the different animals you might see if you observed your study area at different times of the day or at different times of the year.

Investigate Further Choose an area that is like the area you **observed**. Repeat the investigation. What was the same? What was different? Why were there differences?

Process Skill Tip

When you **observe** an area that includes living things, you need to be aware at all times. Some living things appear only for a short time. Others may never appear when you are there but may leave signs that they were there.

Parts of Ecosystems

Living Parts of Ecosystems

FIND OUT

- the basic parts of an ecosystem
- how the living things in ecosystems are organized

VOCABULARY

ecosystem
population
community

The next time you walk in your neighborhood, stop to look and listen for living things. At first, there may seem to be no living things around you. But if you observe closely, you'll discover them. Even in cities, groups of plants and animals find places to live. Groups of living things and the environment they live in make up an **ecosystem** (EK•oh•sis•tuhm). All living things in an ecosystem can meet their basic needs there.

Some ecosystems have only a few living things. For example, insects and small plants are probably the only easy to see things that live in a concrete parking lot environment. They live in cracks or along the sides of the lot. Other ecosystems, such as those of forests, ponds, and streams, have many living things. That's because these environments have more space, food, and shelter. Many types of plants and animals can easily meet their needs in these environments.

✔ **What must a plant or animal be able to do to live in a certain ecosystem?**

The plants and animals shown here live in a kind of water ecosystem called an estuary (EHS•tyoo•ehr•ee). Here they interact with each other and with the nonliving things in their environment such as water, soil, and sunlight.

◀ Red mangrove tree

Shrimp

Great blue heron

Populations

A group of the same species living in the same place at the same time is a **population** (pahp•yoo•LAY•shuhn). A forest may have several populations of different kinds of trees. Trout may be one of several populations of fish in a stream. Deer may form a population among other animals in a meadow.

Populations live in environments to which they are adapted. Some environments are difficult to live in. The organisms that live there must have unusual adaptations to survive. For example, an estuary forms where fresh water from a river flows into salt water of an ocean. Sometimes estuary water has a lot of salt. Sometimes it has only a little. Most trees and plants cannot live in water that changes in this way. Mangrove (MAN•grohv) trees, however, have roots and leaves that get rid of salt. This adaptation allows them to grow in salt water or in fresh water.

Scientists usually name ecosystems such as estuaries after the main population of plants that live there. Estuaries that have mostly mangrove trees are called mangrove swamps. A *swamp* is an area that is sometimes or always covered in shallow water.

✔ **How is the mangrove tree different from most other trees?**

A population of mangrove trees gives populations of gray snapper fish and egrets a place to live. ▶

Egrets

Gray snapper

Communities

In most ecosystems, plants of the main population are where other organisms interact. Mangrove tree branches hang over the water and attract insects looking for food and shelter. Schools, or groups, of archerfish may live among the roots of mangrove trees. Archerfish can shoot a jet of water up to $1\frac{1}{2}$ meters (about 5 ft) above the water, knocking insects off branches. The fish then eat the insects that fall into the water. A flock of lesser blue herons may feed in or near the shallow water at the roots of the trees. There they find fish, frogs, and other small animals to eat.

All these animals and plants live together and interact with one another in many ways. A **community** (kuh•MYOO•nuh•tee) is made up of all the populations that live in the same area. The plants and animals that live together depend on one another to survive. The animals in a community eat plants and other animals in the community.

THE INSIDE STORY

The Formation of a Mangrove Swamp

Each spring hundreds of mangrove flowers blossom and form fruit. Inside each fruit is a seed.

About two months after the fruit forms, the seed inside grows roots and stems. It becomes a seedling. While it is still attached to the tree, the seedling becomes able to live in salt water. This gets it ready to safely fall from the tree into the soil or salt water below.

One seedling may float thousands of miles. When its base touches ground, it begins to put out roots. If the temperature and soil are right, the seedling takes root. Over time, it grows into a mature tree.

A mangrove's spear-shaped seedling is 15 to 30 centimeters (about 6 to 12 in.) long. The seed stores nutrients to keep it alive after it falls from the parent tree. Some seedlings fall like darts and land directly in soil. Others land in water and float to a new place to grow. ▼

The plants need animals to carry away seeds and to add nutrients to the soil. Sometimes communities provide shelter. The tangled mangrove roots shelter many small fish. The fish swim and reproduce among the roots.

✔ **In what ways are the living things in a community important to one another?**

▲ Underwater mangrove roots provide a place for fish and other animals such as sponges, oysters, and shrimp to find food and shelter.

This mangrove sapling, or young tree, will grow several centimeters a year. The branching roots above the ground grow in the sapling's third or fourth year. The tree will grow to be 15 to 30 meters (about 50 to 100 ft) tall. ▼

In about 25 years, this sapling and others from the parent tree will form a small population of mangrove trees. The roots trap soil and dead plants and animals. They shelter fish and other animals. ▼

Nonliving Parts of an Ecosystem

The nonliving parts of an ecosystem are just as important as the living parts. The main nonliving parts of an ecosystem include sunlight, soil, air, water, and temperature. These nonliving parts interact with one another. For example, water sometimes moves soil from place to place.

The nonliving parts also interact with the living parts of the ecosystem. Salt water is a nonliving part of a mangrove swamp ecosystem. Only certain plants can live in salt water. Because of this, salt affects the ecosystem.

✔ **What are the main nonliving parts of an ecosystem?**

▲ Tall grasses and wildflowers grow in the sunlit mountain meadow. Small plants and saplings grow at the forest edge. Only a few plants grow among the trees in the forest.

Grasses and bushes can grow along the stream where there is water and plenty of light. Pine trees grow where the soil is drier. Few other plants grow in the shade under the trees. ▼

Summary

An ecosystem is made up of groups of living things and their environment. An ecosystem may include plants and animals, and nonliving parts such as sunlight, soil, air, water, and temperature. Organisms of the same species form populations. A community is made up of populations of different species in an ecosystem.

Review

1. Why do some ecosystems include many living things?
2. Is a row of bean plants in a garden a population or a community? Explain.
3. What nonliving part of the mangrove swamp limits the kinds of plants that can live there?
4. **Critical Thinking** Contrast a population with a community.
5. **Test Prep** What might an ecosystem that has mostly pine or spruce trees be called?

   A mountain forest
   B evergreen forest
   C deep woods
   D green woods

LINKS

MATH LINK

Line Graph Make a line graph showing population changes in a small meadow ecosystem over a period of three years. How are the numbers of birds and grasshoppers related? Why might this happen?

	1996	1997	1998
grasshoppers	500	280	350
birds	80	120	100
mice	120	100	125
snakes	18	10	12
hawk	1	2	1

WRITING LINK

Informative Writing—Description Suppose you are a scout ant in a backyard ecosystem. Describe the populations and community you find during one day.

ART LINK

Art in Nature Make a collage of three different ecosystems. Label the ecosystems and the main living things in each ecosystem.

TECHNOLOGY LINK

Visit the Harcourt Learning Site for related links, activities, and resources.
www.harcourtschool.com

What Are Habitats and Niches?

In this lesson, you can . . .

 INVESTIGATE the homes and roles of living things.

 LEARN ABOUT living things in ecosystems.

 LINK to math, writing, social studies, and technology.

INVESTIGATE

The Homes and Roles of Living Things

Activity Purpose You have learned what some animals eat, how they act, and where they live. In this investigation you will use what you know. You'll also find out more about animals' homes and their roles, or the things they do in their communities. For example, the role of some animals is to eat other animals. The role of other animals is to eat only plants.

Materials
- index cards
- crayons or markers
- reference books about animals

Activity Procedure

1. Each member of your group should choose five different animals.

2. Draw a picture of each of your animals on a separate index card. (Picture A)

◀ A spider's web is its home. The spider also uses the web to trap insects for food.

Picture A

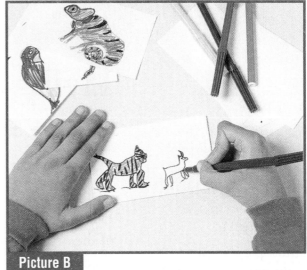

Picture B

3 Using five more cards, draw the homes of your animals or show them in their roles. (Picture B) Look up information about your animals in reference books if you need help.

4 Gather all the cards. Mix up the cards, and place them face down. Take turns playing Concentration®. Turn over two cards at a time until you find a pair that shows an animal and its home or role. Explain how the two cards match. Play until all the matches have been made.

Draw Conclusions

1. What new animals did you learn about as you played the game?

2. Which was easier to identify, an animal's home or its role? Explain your answer.

3. **Scientists at Work** Scientists often make **inferences** based on things they have **observed** and their past experiences. What inferences did you make as you tried to explain how two cards matched?

Investigate Further Choose an animal card, and think of another animal that may have the same home or role. If the animals live in the same community, will they try to eat the same food or use the same places for shelter? Will the new animal keep the animal on the card from meeting its needs?

Process Skill Tip

When you **infer**, you try to explain what has happened based on things you have **observed** or that you already know. An inference is a possible explanation for an observation.

Living Things in Ecosystems

FIND OUT

- examples of habitats and niches in ecosystems

- how plants and animals interact and change their environments

VOCABULARY

habitat
niche
producer
consumer
decomposer

Many organisms live in the pine forest. Each meets its needs by living in a different part of the forest. ▼

Homes for Living Things

In the investigation, you saw places that are homes to animals. Plants and fungi have homes, too. These homes meet the needs of the organisms living there. An environment that meets the needs of an organism is called its **habitat** (HAB•ih•tat). The habitats of some organisms are whole ecosystems. This is often true for birds that can fly from place to place. The habitats of other organisms may be just small parts of ecosystems. For example, fungi may grow only in certain areas of a forest floor.

Some habitats overlap, or take up some of the same space. When they do, similar organisms may compete, or try to get the same food or space. For example, two species of fish living in the same pond may compete for the same insects as food. Organisms that are very different may not need to compete. Even though birds and caterpillars live in the same habitat, they meet their needs in different ways.

✔ **When might living things have to compete?**

Roles

Although caterpillars don't often compete with birds, they must avoid the birds around them. That's because some birds eat caterpillars. Part of the birds' **niche** (NICH), or role, in their habitat is to eat insects.

An organism's niche includes all the ways it meets its basic needs—how it gets shelter, how it produces young, and how it gets food and water. What an organism eats is an important part of its niche. What a living thing eats affects the populations around it.

The sun is the main source of energy for *all* living things. Animals don't get energy directly from the sun. Many eat plants, however, which use sunlight to make food. Animals that don't eat plants still depend on the energy of sunlight. They eat animals that eat plants.

When scientists describe the way energy moves through ecosystems, they use the term *food chains*. Food chains connect and overlap to form food webs. A *food web* shows where many types of living things in a community get food.

Food chains have three levels. Green plants and some protists and monerans are **producers** (proh•DOOS•erz) in food chains, because they produce their own food. Consumers make up the next level of a food chain. **Consumers** (kuhn•SOOM•erz) eat other living things for energy. The last level is made up of decomposers. **Decomposers** (dee•kuhm•POHZ•erz) feed on the wastes of plants and animals or on their remains after they die. They return nutrients to the soil for plants to use as the cycle begins again.

✔ **What are the three levels of every food chain?**

These diagrams show two food chains. One is in a freshwater ecosystem, and one is in a forest edge ecosystem. Identify the producers, consumers, and decomposers in each food chain.

Algae are protists that use the energy of the sun to make food.

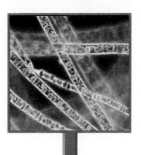

Blueberry bushes grow in sunny areas at the edge of a forest.

Snails eat the algae, using the energy from the algae to live and grow.

To get the energy they need, bears eat berries, insects, and many other plants and animals.

When a snail dies, fungi and other organisms break down the snail's body.

Bacteria in soil decompose the wastes produced by the bear. When broken down, the wastes add nutrients to the soil.

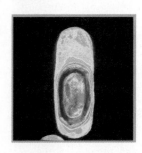

Causes of Change

As organisms meet their needs, they affect their environments. Usually the changes they cause are small and help keep an ecosystem stable.

Some changes affect other organisms. As animals eat plants or other animals, they reduce the number of organisms in their habitat. For example, there are many insects in a bird's habitat. When a bird eats insects, it helps keep the number of insects from getting too large. This helps keep the bird's habitat and the whole ecosystem healthy and stable. But when there are too many birds eating insects, they reduce the insect population quickly. In time, there will not

▲ Lichens slowly break down rock. Rain washes minerals from the rock into the soil. These added nutrients help improve the soil in a habitat.

be enough for the birds to eat. Some birds will leave the area or die, and fewer young birds will be born. This brings the ecosystem back into balance.

Some changes caused by organisms affect the nonliving parts of an ecosystem. Worms and lichens make the soil of their habitats better. Some natural changes, however, can be unwanted by people. Prairie dogs are thought to harm rangeland. Their holes are dangerous for grazing cattle and sheep. Over time, most changes in nature balance out. No harm is done and stability is kept.

✔ **What can happen if too many insect-eating birds live in a habitat?**

Prairie dogs live underground in colonies. They dig tunnels to connect parts of the colony. Prairie dogs eat mostly grasses. ▶

◀ Although prairie dog holes are dangerous for cattle, prairie dogs improve a habitat by digging and mixing soil.

▲ Gypsy moth caterpillars eat the leaves of trees. They sometimes eat so many leaves that the trees die. This not only damages the caterpillars' habitat, but also affects other animals in a forest ecosystem.

Summary

An environment that meets the needs of an organism is called its habitat. An organism's niche is its role within the habitat. As organisms in an ecosystem carry out their roles, they can affect both living and non-living parts of the ecosystem.

Review

1. What happens when two similar animals share a habitat?

2. What type of organism breaks down the remains of dead plants and animals?

3. How can one organism help control the population of another organism?

4. **Critical Thinking** What could happen to an ecosystem that had mice if cats were added to it?

5. **Test Prep** Which of the following is a producer?

   A fox   **C** fungus

   B chicken   **D** grass

LINKS

MATH LINK

Sampling and Estimating Suppose that in 5 minutes you counted 5 grasshoppers on a square meter of your yard. Assume that these insects are spread out evenly in your yard. Estimate the number of grasshoppers on the whole yard if its area is 40 square meters.

WRITING LINK

Informative Writing—Report Your city plans to cut down a forest to make room for a new shopping mall. The city wants you to find out what organisms would be affected by cutting down the forest. Find out which organisms make up a forest ecosystem. Then classify the organisms by their habitats and niches, and prepare a report for the mayor.

SOCIAL STUDIES LINK

State Symbols Each of the 50 states has different environments for wildlife. Each state government chooses a bird, a flower, and a tree to represent the state. Make simple maps of your state and of two neighboring states. Find out the wildlife symbols of the states. On the maps, draw and label the symbols.

TECHNOLOGY LINK

Learn more about animals in a marine ecosystem by viewing *Tide Pool* on the **Harcourt Science Newsroom Video.**

What Are Tropical Rain Forests and Coral Reefs?

In this lesson, you can . . .

INVESTIGATE a coral reef.

LEARN ABOUT tropical ecosystems.

LINK to math, writing, literature, and technology.

INVESTIGATE

A Coral Reef

Activity Purpose One of the most interesting ecosystems is a coral reef. With its many different plants and animals, it looks like a colorful underwater garden. In this investigation you will make a diorama of a coral reef and identify its parts.

Materials

- box
- blue paint or
  blue construction paper
- paintbrushes
- glue or tape
- scissors
- modeling clay
- fishing line
- thumbtacks
- chenille stems
- construction paper
- plastic wrap

Activity Procedure

1. Look through the lesson, and use library resources to find pictures of reef organisms and their habitats.

2. Plan a diorama that uses the materials your teacher provides. Try to find the best material for each living and nonliving thing you will show.

◀ This moray eel hides in the reef, looking for a small fish for its next meal.

Picture A

Picture B

3 Follow your plan. Keep in mind colors, sizes, and the best use of space. (Picture A)

4 Label the organisms in your diorama. (Picture B)

Draw Conclusions

1. What organisms did you include in your diorama?

2. Tell three things you learned while building your diorama.

3. **Scientists at Work** When scientists build a **model** of an organism that is very small, they may make it hundreds of times bigger. If you tried to build your diorama to scale, you may have found it hard to show the very smallest organisms. How could you show large models of the tiniest organisms and still build your diorama to scale?

Investigate Further A diorama can show only part of the picture. Write a paragraph or two describing other organisms that could live near your reef scene.

Process Skill Tip

A diorama is a three-dimensional (3-D) **model**. To be realistic, its parts should be built to scale. For example, some models are 10 times smaller than the real organisms they stand for. An animal that is actually 10 cm long would be 1 cm long in such a model. An animal that is really 1 cm long would be shown as 1 mm long.

B25

Tropical Ecosystems

Tropical Rain Forests

Tropical rain forests grow along the equator, an area that has a lot of rainfall and high temperatures all year. The **climate** (KLY•muht), or average weather over a long time, allows many plants to grow well.

Rain-forest trees grow tall and form a canopy (KAN•uh•pee), or roof. Their leaves shelter the area below, blocking most of the sunlight. Vines grow up the trunks of trees to reach the light. Many plants and animals live high in the canopy. There they can use the sunlight and open space.

The forest floor is home to plants that grow well in shade. Plants that need lots of light make a thick ground cover only where a tree has fallen. The fallen tree makes an opening in the canopy.

Rotting plant material covers much of the rain-forest floor. Decomposers are always at work there. When you think of the many organisms living among the trees, the floor seems unimportant. The rain forest, however, depends on decomposing and

FIND OUT

- how tropical rain forests and coral reefs are alike

- what the resources of reefs and rain forests are and why they are important

VOCABULARY

climate
diversity
salinity

Located near the equator, tropical rain forests are some of the wettest land ecosystems on Earth. Daily temperatures can range from 20°C (68°F) to 34°C (about 93°F). ▼

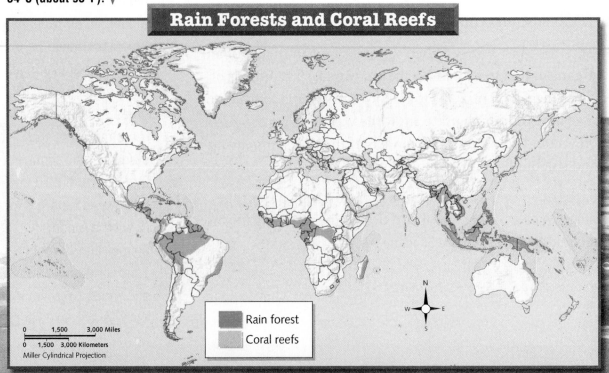

Rain Forests and Coral Reefs

0   1,500   3,000 Miles
0   1,500   3,000 Kilometers
Miller Cylindrical Projection

■ Rain forest
■ Coral reefs

Morpho butterfly

Capuchin

Toucan

Anaconda

Rain-forest orchid

Capybara

recycling of nutrients. Most of this recycling takes place in the forest floor.

A rain forest has a great **diversity** (duh•VER•suh•tee), or variety, of plants and animals. In fact, a rain forest has more species of plants and animals than any other ecosystem on Earth.

Near the tops of trees, there are habitats for thousands of species. Mammals such as spider monkeys and lemurs (LEE•merz) play on sturdy tree limbs. Toucans, macaws (muh•KAWZ), and other colorful birds nest in the branches. Butterflies fly around, drinking nectar from orchids that grow on tree branches. Mosses and ferns cling to tree branches.

✓ **What makes a tropical rain forest different from any other ecosystem?**

River turtle

Giant river otter

Tiger centipede

Caiman

Piranha

Coral Reefs

Coral reefs are a lot like rain forests, only under water. These ecosystems are also located in tropical climates near the equator. Such areas have plenty of sunlight. The sea water is clean and warm all year long. The water's **salinity** (suh•LIN•uh•tee), or the amount of salt in it, is constant. All these conditions are needed for a coral reef to grow.

Coral reefs look like colorful landscapes of cliffs and canyons. They are made up of the rocky skeletons of many tiny animals called *corals*. Corals live in colonies. One colony may look like a big, fan-shaped leaf. Another may look more like a giant brain.

Coral colonies are made up of tiny soft-bodied animals called polyps (PAHL•ips), which are no bigger than your thumb. A young colony of them may have only a few polyps. Older colonies may have millions of polyps.

Coral polyps build limestone skeletons around their bodies by taking calcium out of sea water. Flower-like tentacles, or arms, reach out from the skeletons. The tentacles trap small plants and animals. Prey is stung and then pulled into the coral's mouth. Coral polyps also can get nutrients from algae that live inside their skeletons.

When a polyp dies, its skeleton is left. Another polyp then moves in and adds more limestone. A coral reef can grow like this for many years. Some old reefs cover many square kilometers.

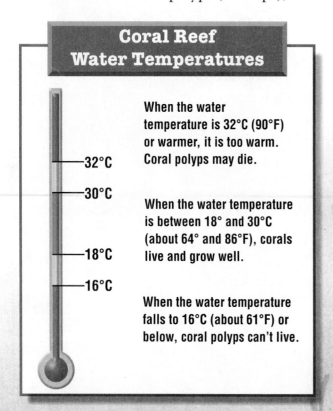

Coral Reef Water Temperatures

When the water temperature is 32°C (90°F) or warmer, it is too warm. Coral polyps may die.

—32°C

—30°C

When the water temperature is between 18° and 30°C (about 64° and 86°F), corals live and grow well.

—18°C

—16°C

When the water temperature falls to 16°C (about 61°F) or below, coral polyps can't live.

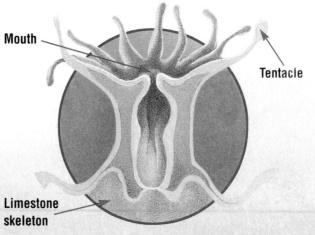

Mouth

Tentacle

Limestone skeleton

▲ A polyp and algae need each other to survive. The polyp gets food and oxygen from the algae. The polyp gives the algae carbon dioxide.

Parrotfish

Sea urchin

Giant clam

The many branches, holes, and layers of the reef offer places for animals to rest. Cracks provide places to hide. Thousands of species are known to live among coral reefs.

Many of the creatures of coral reefs are easy to see. Brightly colored angelfish and striped butterfly fish guard their home areas. Sea horses hold on to the reef by their tails. Other creatures are harder to see. Flat flounders lay hidden on the sandy ocean floor around the reef. Hungry scorpion fish blend in with the colorful coral. Each animal has its habitat and niche in the coral reef ecosystem.

✔ **How does a coral polyp build its skeleton?**

▼ Diatoms (DY•uh•tomz) are plantlike protists that have hard outer body coverings.

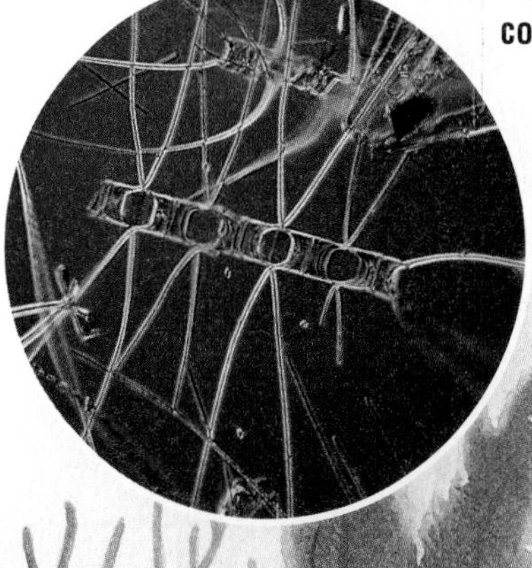

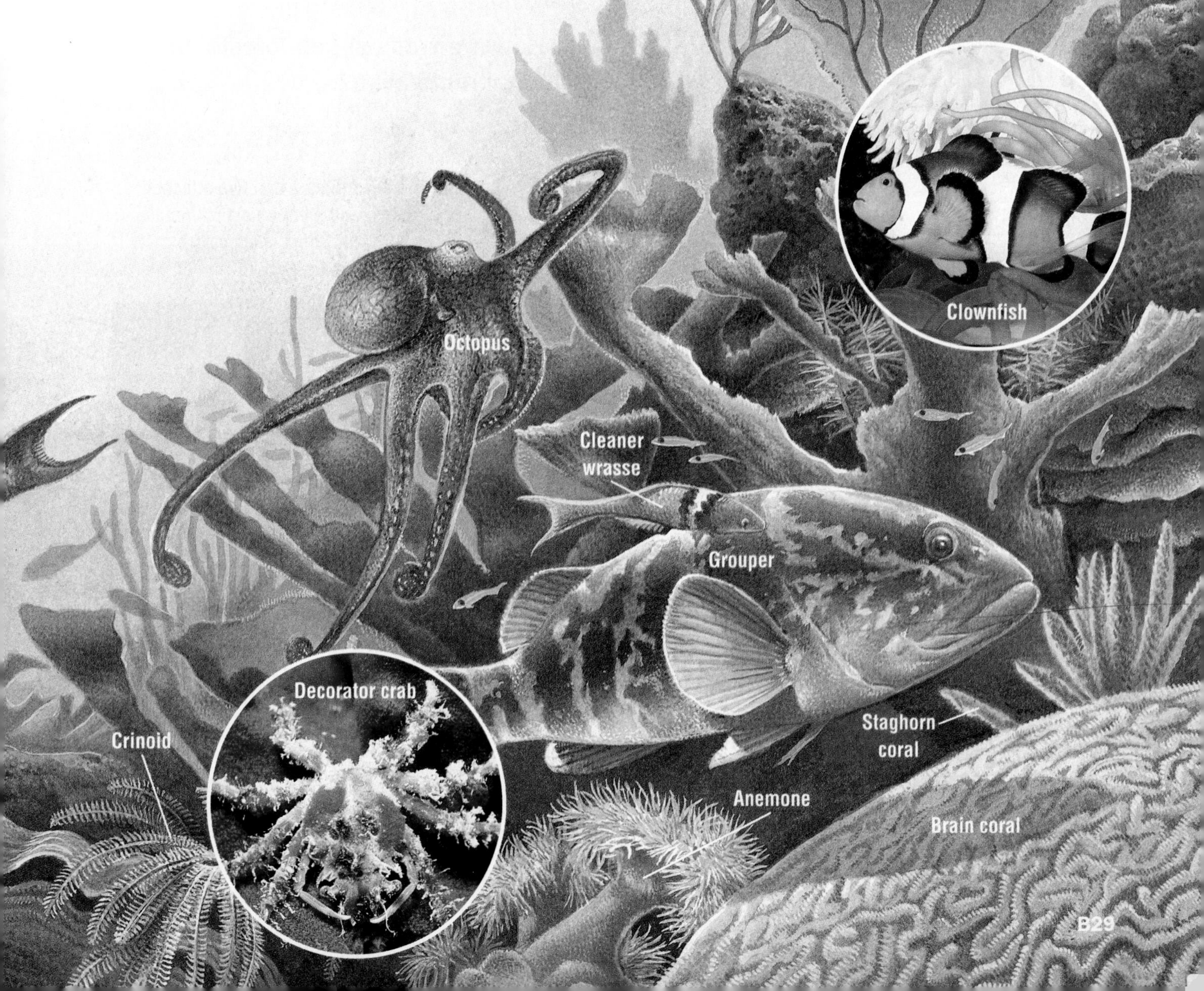

Sea fan

Clownfish

Octopus

Cleaner wrasse

Grouper

Decorator crab

Crinoid

Staghorn coral

Anemone

Brain coral

Resources from the Tropics

Both tropical rain forests and coral reefs are treasure chests of life. Each is home to thousands of species of organisms, many of which are found nowhere else on Earth. From these organisms come hundreds of different products that people need and use.

Wood is one important rain-forest resource. Rain forests provide about 20 percent of the wood used in industry around the world. They also are an important source of foods, including fruits, nuts, and spices. As much as 80 percent of the world's food comes from plants found in tropical rain forests. Raw materials to make furniture, cooking oils, waxes, and dyes also come from rain forests. No rain-forest products are more important than medicines being made from rain-forest plants. And new medicines are still being discovered.

Resources from coral reefs are not as widely used. Some coral is used to make jewelry and other ornaments. Some sponges that grow in the reefs have many uses. Stores that sell tropical fish are full of animals that came from coral reefs. Some people keep these animals in tanks as a hobby.

✓ **How are tropical rain forests and coral reefs alike?**

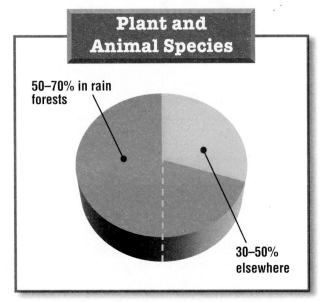

Plant and Animal Species

50–70% in rain forests

30–50% elsewhere

▲ Of all the world's plant and animal species, 50 to 70 percent can be found in tropical rain forests.

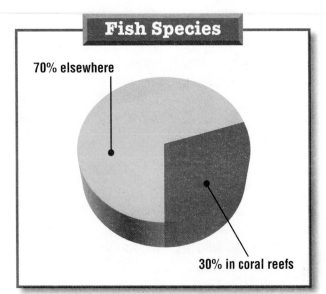

Fish Species

70% elsewhere

30% in coral reefs

▲ Coral reefs provide habitats for 30 percent of all fish species.

Sponges are sea animals that live attached to rocks, plants, and other objects beneath the water's surface. Some sponges are harvested and sold. ▼

Living sponge

Harvested sponge

▲ Liana vines are used to make curare (kyoo•RAH•ray), a drug. Resources from rain forests are used to produce about one out of every four medicines made today.

Summary

Tropical rain forests and coral reefs are ecosystems that provide habitats for a large variety of plants and animals. They both provide resources found nowhere else on Earth.

Review

1. Where do most plants and animals live in a tropical rain forest?

2. Why is the salinity of salt water important for a living coral reef?

3. What are three resources from tropical rain forests?

4. **Critical Thinking** Why is it important to protect tropical rain forests and coral reefs?

5. **Test Prep** The floor of a tropical rain forest is covered with —
   A grasses
   B dead plant material
   C blooming flowers
   D animals

LINKS

MATH LINK

Graphing Use a computer program such as *Graph Links* to make a bar graph that compares the amount of rainfall each year in a rain forest, a desert, and your hometown.

WRITING LINK

Informative Writing—Compare and Contrast Suppose that you have just returned from exploring a tropical rain forest and a coral reef. For a school newspaper, write a story called "A Day in the Life of a Coral Reef and a Rain Forest." Make an outline of your story. List which features you will compare and contrast. The outline also should tell which creatures you will show, photos you will need, and so on.

LITERATURE LINK

At Home in the Rain Forest Read *At Home in the Rain Forest* by Diane Willow. Take an exciting journey through the layers of a rain forest, from its treetops to the forest floor.

TECHNOLOGY LINK

Learn more about the parts of a coral reef ecosystem by exploring *Coral Reefs— A Visit to the Deep* on the **Harcourt Science Explorations CD-ROM.**

Computer Models of ECOSYSTEMS

What would happen to a marsh ecosystem if 24 alligators were released in it? What would happen to a pond ecosystem if all the lily pads died? Scientists are using computers to help answer questions like these.

Virtual Reality

Have you ever played a video game with scenes in it that looked almost real? That kind of game is a kind of computer model. It helped you understand what a real place might be like. Currently, scientists are using computers to make models of ecosystems. To make an ecosystem model, scientists first collect a lot of data about the ecosystem. For example, they measure animal populations, plant populations, growth rates, fire, rain, disease, and climate. Then they put the data into a computer program.

When the program runs, "life" in the ecosystem happens in fast-forward motion.

This ecologist is collecting data from a seashore ecosystem.

Scientist using a computer model.

Watching a wetland age in a model is much faster than waiting for real-life changes. The computer predicts how the ecosystem will change over time. It tells scientists how many plants and animals will grow and how populations will affect each other.

Predicting the Future

Suppose a scientist wants to know what a certain wetland ecosystem will look like after 100 years. When the model is complete, the computer could predict how the wetland will look 10, 20, 50, or 100 years from now. For example, it could show the population of each kind of animal and plant. It could tell how much water is in the wetland. It might even tell how many herons are eating the fish.

Changing the Future

Once scientists have a good model of an ecosystem, they can experiment using just the model. They might add 24 alligators or remove all the lily pads. The computer will tell them whether the alligators take over or whether the frogs leave.

The better the data that scientists use, the more they can learn from computer models. Scientists might even make a good model of something as big and complicated as a forest during a fire.

Think About It

1. How could computer models help scientists during a drought?
2. How could computer models help city planners decide where to place a shopping mall?

WEB LINK:
For Science and Technology updates, visit the Harcourt Internet site.
www.harcourtschool.com

Careers   Computer Programmer

What They Do
Computer programmers write step-by-step instructions for computers. The instructions tell computers what to do with the information that is given to them.

Computers are used in almost all areas of life today, including science, medicine, business, and communication. Programmers work in all these areas and others.

Education and Training   Most programmers are college graduates. They have taken courses in math, computer science, and business. Data processing and classes in modeling are also good choices for study.

Henry Chandler Cowles
ECOLOGIST

"By burying the past, the dune offers to plant life a world for conquest . . . . The advance of a dune makes all things new."

Dr. Henry Chandler Cowles loved the Indiana Dunes on the southern shore of Lake Michigan. He studied and wrote about them while studying botany (the science of plants) at the University of Chicago. The papers he wrote helped create a new field of study, *ecology* (ee•KAHL•uh•jee). Cowles said the job of an ecologist was to discover the relationships between plants and their environment.

Cowles looked for such relationships at the Indiana Dunes. He studied the dunes' distance from the lake, their types of soil, and when seeds and spores germinated on the dunes. He compared the Indiana Dunes to the dunes at Cape Cod and to other dunes. Between 1897 and 1931, he took thousands of photographs of the dunes and of the Midwestern plains.

Cowles's photographs show that plant communities are always changing as the environment changes. He hypothesized that ecosystems were never twice alike. For example, a 1910 photo shows a cottonwood tree on top of a dune. One year later, sand had buried the tree.

The University of Chicago has kept Cowles's photographs for a long time. Many of them have been made into slides.

After Cowles stopped teaching, the photographs were stored in the university's library. The National Park Service sometimes studies them before restoring sections of a park. The slides are now being cleaned and repaired as part of a Library of Congress project.

THINK ABOUT IT

1. Henry Chandler Cowles took photographs as part of his research. How might a scientist record his or her research today?
2. Why do you think scientists would want to restore Cowles's old photographs?

View from Indiana Dunes

Down at the Roots

What roles does grass play in an ecosystem?

Materials
- trowel or small shovel
- hand lens
- white paper

Procedure

1 Dig out a small plug of grass, about the size of your palm. Include all the roots.
CAUTION Get permission from an adult before you dig.

2 Put the grass sample on a clean piece of white paper. Observe the grass and roots with a hand lens. Record your observations.

3 Choose three blades of grass. Measure the lengths of each root and blade. Record your measurements.

Draw Conclusions

How do the lengths of the blades and roots compare? What roles can you infer grass roots and blades play in an ecosystem? How do you know?

Personal Food Chain

What is the original energy source for the foods you eat?

Materials
- 2 large sheets of paper
- pencil

Procedure

1 On one sheet of paper, list foods a person might eat during three meals. Draw a picture

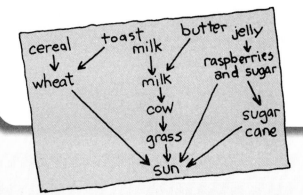

of a person at the top of the other sheet of paper.

2 Draw three arrows beneath your picture, and list the foods eaten at each meal. Leave plenty of space below each food item.

3 Draw an arrow beneath each food item, and identify where each got its energy when it was living.

Draw Conclusions

What is the original source of energy for all the foods the person ate?

Vocabulary Review

Use the terms below to complete the sentences. The page numbers in ( ) tell you where to look in the chapter if you need help.

system (B6)
stability (B8)
ecosystem (B12)
population (B13)
community (B14)
habitat (B20)
niche (B21)

producer (B21)
consumer (B21)
decomposer (B21)
climate (B26)
diversity (B27)
salinity (B28)

1. All the populations that live in the same place make up a ____.

2. An organism's role in its ____, or home, is called its ____.

3. A group of parts that work as a unit is called a ____.

4. A bear is an example of a ____, or an animal that eats plants or other animals.

5. Coral reefs are affected by the ____, or saltiness, of ocean water.

6. ____ is reached when the changes in a system are balanced.

7. A carrot plant is an example of a ____, one of the levels in a food chain.

8. Populations and the environment in which they interact form an ____.

9. All the coral polyps living in a reef form a ____ of polyps.

10. Rain forests and coral reefs are important because they have great variety, or ____, of living things.

11. A fungus is an example of a ____, the last level in a food chain.

12. ____ is the average weather over a long time.

Connect Concepts

Use the terms in the Word Bank to complete the graphic organizer.

ecosystems
producers
population
consumers
community
decomposers

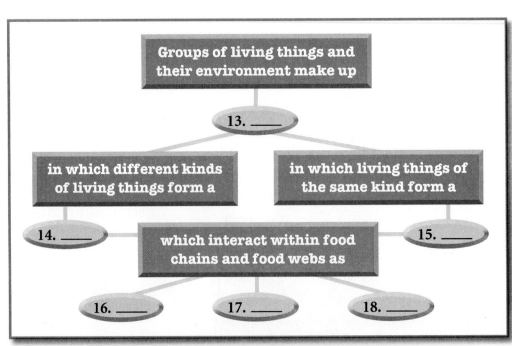

Groups of living things and their environment make up

13. ____

in which different kinds of living things form a

in which living things of the same kind form a

14. ____

15. ____

which interact within food chains and food webs as

16. ____   17. ____   18. ____

Check Understanding

Write the letter of the best choice.

19. Which of these is **NOT** a system?

A grass, soil, water sprinkler

B sun, algae, snails, fungi

C grass, shrubs, trees

D coral, clown fish, salt water, bacteria

20. Which of these are consumers in a coral reef ecosystem?

F algae   **H** monkeys

G clown fish   **J** bacteria

21. For an insect, the space under a rock is likely its —

A population   **C** food source

B niche   **D** habitat

22. A rain forest and all the organisms that live there are —

F a population **H** a community

G an ecosystem **J** a habitat

23. Robins, earthworms, and grass live in a yard. These three groups make up a —

A species   **C** community

B habitat   **D** population

Critical Thinking

24. Explain how rain and water that runs off help maintain the stability of a yard.

25. In a meadow ecosystem, rabbits eat only plants. They eat plants faster than the plants can grow back. What must happen to bring the ecosystem into balance?

Process Skills Review

26. Suppose you put all your favorite plants in a terrarium. You include a cactus, a violet, and a grass plant. **Predict** what will happen. Explain your answer.

27. Suppose that last night during a rainstorm you heard something turn over a trash can. When you turned on the light, you saw an animal run through the mud and briefly get caught in your fence. What experiences and clues could you use to **infer** the identity of the animal?

28. Suppose you knew that an animal lived only in trees and was very slow-moving. **Infer** which of the following it might feed on. Explain how you made your choice.

mice   grass   caterpillars

snakes   leaves   birds

29. If you wanted to show the colors and markings of two animals, would it be better to draw pictures of them or **model** them in clay? What if you needed to show their body shapes as well?

Performance Assessment

Model Ecosystem

Make a poster or diagram that illustrates an ecosystem of a lost land somewhere on Earth. The poster should show living and nonliving things. Add labels to identify the parts of the ecosystem you drew. Then write about a population living there, its habitat and niche, and how the climate affects its food sources.

Chapter 2

Vocabulary Preview

- weathering
- erosion
- humus
- fertile
- soil conservation
- contour plowing
- strip cropping
- terracing

Soil—A Natural Resource

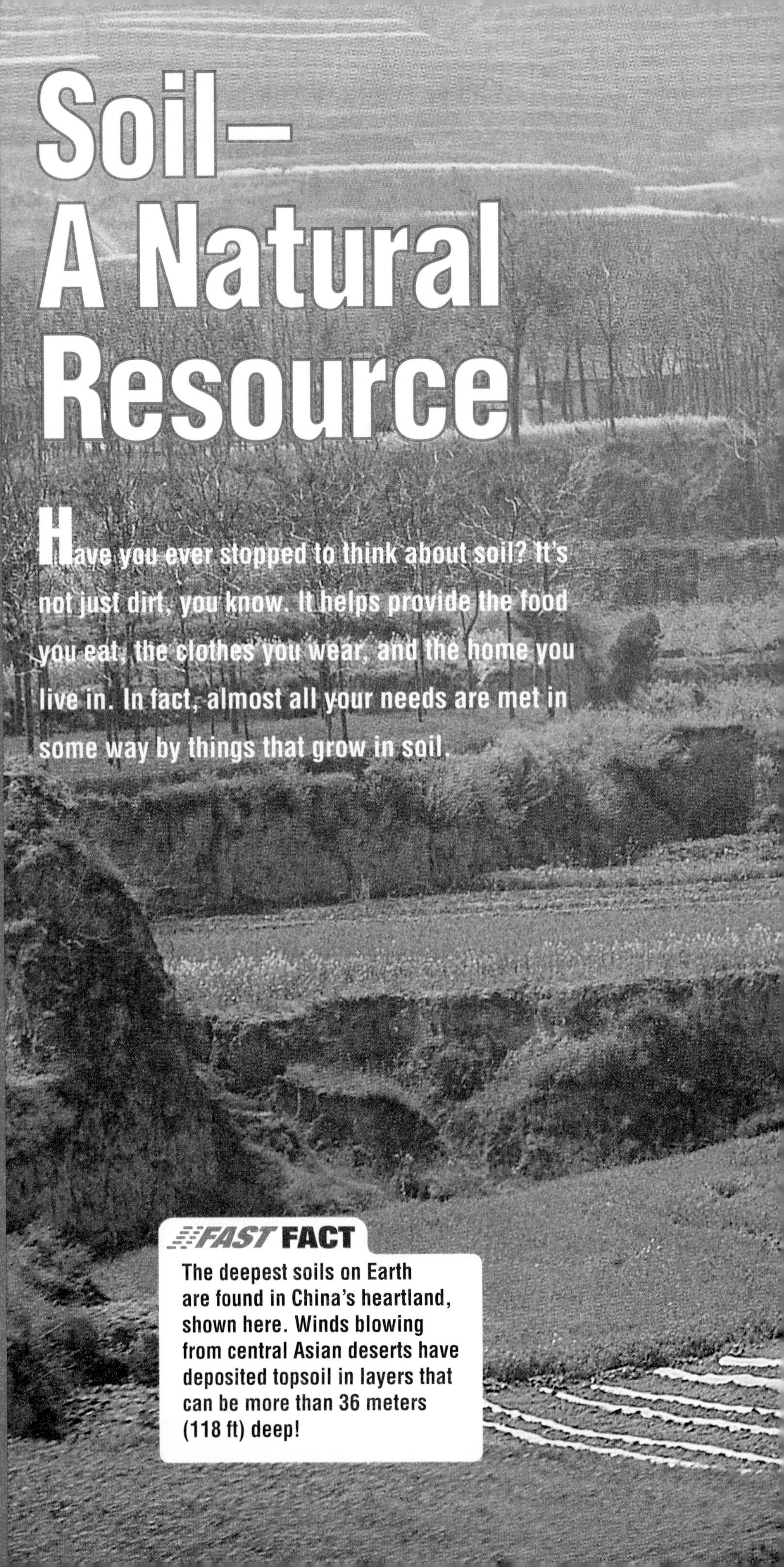

Have you ever stopped to think about soil? It's not just dirt, you know. It helps provide the food you eat, the clothes you wear, and the home you live in. In fact, almost all your needs are met in some way by things that grow in soil.

FAST FACT

The deepest soils on Earth are found in China's heartland, shown here. Winds blowing from central Asian deserts have deposited topsoil in layers that can be more than 36 meters (118 ft) deep!

A square meter of soil might look like just a lot of dirt. But if you dig, you'll find thousands of living things in the soil.

Springtails

Things Living in Soil

Animal	Average Number in a Square Meter
Earthworms	100
Slugs and snails	100
Millipedes	500
Springtails	10,000

FAST FACT

Humans aren't the only animals that grow crops. Attini ants plant and care for fungus gardens. The fungi provide the colony with all its food.

LESSON 1

How Does Soil Form?

In this lesson, you can . . .

 INVESTIGATE the layers of soil.

 LEARN ABOUT soil formation.

 LINK to math, writing, art, and technology.

Soil Layers

Activity Purpose Have you ever taken time to look at soil? You may be surprised to know that soil is actually a mixture of different-sized particles. In this investigation you will **observe** soil to see its parts as it settles in water.

Materials
- newspaper
- soil sample
- hand lens
- wide-mouth glass or plastic jar with lid
- water

Activity Procedure

1. Cover your work surface with newspaper.

2. Examine the soil sample with a hand lens. Look for differences in the particles that make up soil. **Record** your **observations**.

3. Add soil to the jar until it is about one-third full.

◄ Soil has formed in the crack of this rock. The soil gives the tree a place to grow.

Picture A

Picture B

4 Add water until the jar is almost full. (Picture A)

5 Tightly screw the lid onto the jar. Shake the jar for at least 15 seconds to mix the soil and water well.

6 Let the jar sit overnight.

7 **Observe** the soil and water in the jar. Use the hand lens to observe each soil part in the jar more closely. (Picture B) **Record** your observations.

Draw Conclusions

1. How did mixing and shaking change the soil?

2. **Compare** your **observations** of the soil before shaking and after settling. In which observation could you see soil parts more easily? Explain your answer.

3. **Scientists at Work** Scientists often use instruments, or tools, to **observe** details. How did the hand lens help you in this investigation?

Investigate Further Soil particles can be classified by size into four groups. The groups, in order from largest to smallest, are gravel, sand, silt, and clay. Look again at the layers in the jar. Which layer contains which particle? Draw a picture of the layers, and label them.

Soil Formation

The Importance of Soil

FIND OUT

• why soil is important

• how soil forms

VOCABULARY

weathering
erosion
humus

Think about the foods you've eaten and the objects you've used today. Maybe you had breakfast at a wooden table. You may have eaten toast and a banana. For lunch perhaps you had a glass of milk and an egg salad or bologna sandwich. Maybe you wore cotton jeans to school. You probably sat at a desk and wrote on paper.

Soil is needed to provide these things and other things you use every day. Fruits and vegetables grow in soil. Meat, milk, and eggs come from animals, of course. The animals, however, eat corn, wheat, and other plants that grow in soil. Houses, desks, and paper are made from wood. Wood comes from trees, which grow in soil. Cotton and other clothing materials come from plants that grow in soil. Because you buy many of these things in stores, it is easy to forget that they depend on soil.

✔ **What are some foods that depend on soil?**

This dairy cow feeds on grass and hay, which grow in soil. ▼

The wheat that grows in this rich farmland soil may become part of your favorite bread or breakfast cereal. ▼

Soil Begins with Rock

The processes that form soil occur all the time, little by little. Most of the soil you see today has been forming for thousands of years.

Weathering (WETH•er•ing) is the process that breaks up rocks. As the outsides of rocks warm and cool, they expand, or become larger, and contract, or become smaller. You don't notice these changes in size. But they are big enough over time to crack rocks. The cracks become larger and larger. Bits of rock break off. Water gets into the cracks. When the water freezes, it expands. This forces the rock to break up even faster.

Weathering and erosion work together to form soil. **Erosion** (ee•ROH•zhuhn) is the process by which wind and moving water carry away bits of rock and other material. These bits of rock are dropped in another area, where they may build up.

✔ **What is the difference between weathering and erosion?**

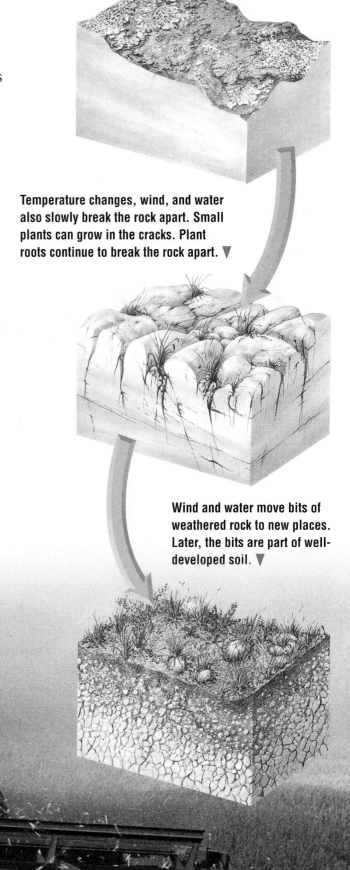

Lichens (LYK•uhnz), or tiny plantlike living things, grow on the outsides of rocks. They slowly break down rock to get nutrients. ▼

Temperature changes, wind, and water also slowly break the rock apart. Small plants can grow in the cracks. Plant roots continue to break the rock apart. ▼

Wind and water move bits of weathered rock to new places. Later, the bits are part of well-developed soil. ▼

Soil Forms Layers

In the investigation, you saw that soil forms layers when it settles in water. The layers form by the size of the particles. If you dug a hole in the ground, you would also see layers. As in the investigation, the particles in the top layers are smaller than those in the bottom layers. The three main layers of soil are topsoil, subsoil, and bedrock, sometimes called parent rock.

Topsoil is the top layer of soil. In most places it is only a few centimeters thick. Topsoil contains rotting plant and animal materials called **humus** (HYOO•muhs). It also contains bits of rock that come from the weathering of rocks above ground.

The second layer is called subsoil. It is made up mostly of small rocks. Subsoil forms as larger rocks are broken up. Because subsoil is near the surface, temperature changes help weather the rocks in this layer.

In fact, most weathering of rock takes place in this layer and the layer below. Tree roots also break up rocks in these layers.

The bottom layer, bedrock, is mostly solid rock. Cracks slowly widen and break up the top parts of the bedrock. Bits of rock break off. Over time, these rock bits become part of the upper layers of soil.

✔ **Where does most rock weathering happen?**

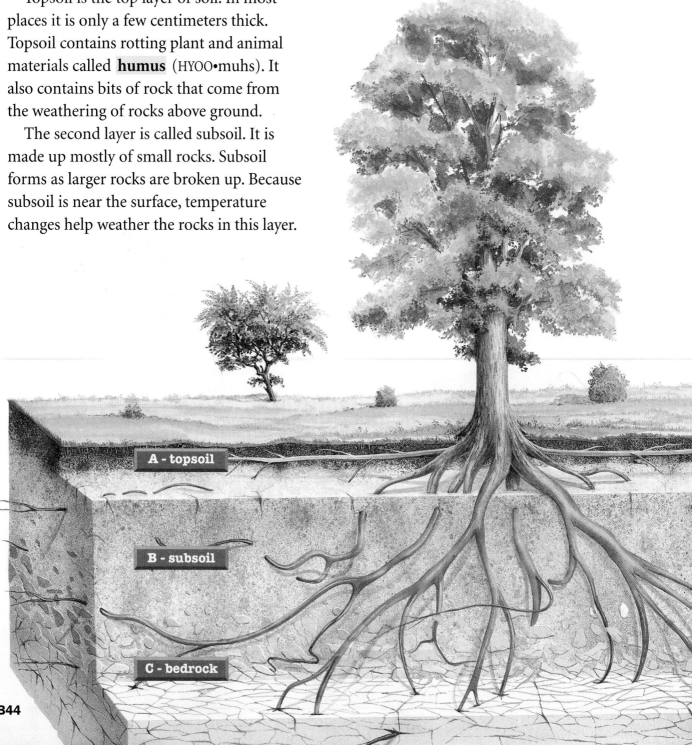

A - topsoil

B - subsoil

C - bedrock

Summary

Most products that we need, such as food, clothing, and building materials, depend on soil. Soil forms by the weathering and erosion of rocks. In weathering, plants and changes in weather cause rocks to break apart. In erosion, wind and moving water carry bits of rock to new places.

Review

1. Explain how a wool sweater depends on soil.
2. How does water freezing in a crack in a rock help break the rock apart?
3. What are the three layers of soil?
4. **Critical Thinking** Effects of weather, such as temperature changes, are greater on the surface than in deeper layers of soil. Why then does most weathering take place in the deeper layers?
5. **Test Prep** Which layer of soil contains the most dead plant and animal materials?

   A bedrock   C parent rock
   B subsoil   D topsoil

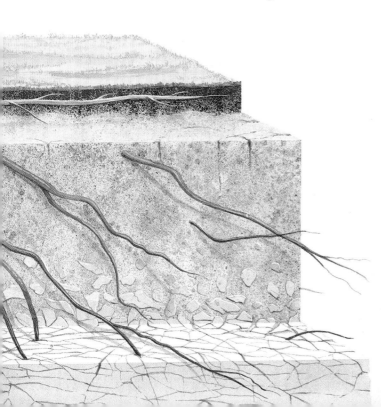

LINKS

MATH LINK

Graphing On your own, make a water and soil sample like the one in the investigation. Shake the container and then allow the soil parts to settle. Measure each layer with a metric ruler. Then make a bar graph to show how thick each layer is.

WRITING LINK

Expressive Writing — Poem Write a poem for a classmate describing how a tree root helps weather rocks to make soil. Begin your poem by describing how the tree seed comes to the spot where it sprouts and grows.

ART LINK

Clay Different kinds of clay are used to make dishes, pottery, sculpture, and other objects. Use the library to learn more about how artists use clay. Make a poster that shows sources of clay. For each source, include a picture of an artwork made of that clay.

TECHNOLOGY LINK

Learn more about how humus forms by visiting the National Museum of Natural History Internet site.

www.si.edu/harcourt/science

 Smithsonian Institution®

What Are Some Properties of Soil?

In this lesson, you can . . .

 INVESTIGATE the ability of soils to hold water.

 LEARN ABOUT soil properties.

 LINK to math, writing, health, and technology.

◄ This terrarium is a habitat for plants. Its soil helps plants meet their needs for water and nutrients.

 **INVESTIGATE**

The Ability of Soils to Hold Water

Activity Purpose Plants take in water mainly through their roots. Some plants need soil that holds plenty of water. Others need well-drained soil, which lets more water pass through it. In this investigation you will **control variables** to find out how well different soil types hold water.

Materials

- 3 clear plastic cups
- wax pencil
- metric ruler
- 2 large coffee filters
- 2 rubber bands
- $\frac{3}{4}$ cup potting soil
- measuring cup
- $\frac{1}{4}$ cup sand
- stir stick or spoon
- water
- stopwatch or watch with second hand

Activity Procedure

1 Make a chart like the one shown on the next page.

2 On each cup, mark lines 1 cm, 2 cm, 3 cm, and 4 cm from the bottom. Label one cup *Potting Soil,* label another cup *Sandy Soil,* and label the last cup *Water.*

3 Put a coffee filter over the top of the potting-soil cup. With your fingertips, push it about halfway into the cup. Fold the filter edge over the rim of the cup. Use a rubber band to hold the filter on the cup.

4 Repeat Step 3 for the sandy-soil cup. (Picture A)

Soil Types and Water Drainage

	Potting Soil	Sandy Soil
Time of first drop		
Time of last drop		
Amount of water drained		

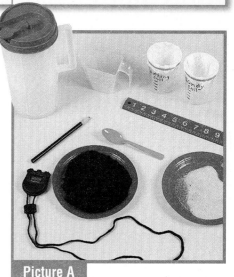

Picture A

5 Pour $\frac{1}{2}$ cup of potting soil into the coffee filter of the potting-soil cup.

6 Pour the sand into the remaining potting soil. Stir it well to make sandy soil. Pour $\frac{1}{2}$ cup of sandy soil into the coffee filter of the sandy-soil cup.

7 **Predict** whether sandy soil or potting soil will drain water faster. **Record** your prediction.

8 Fill the water cup up to the 4-cm mark. Pour the water into the potting-soil cup. As you start to pour, have a partner start the stopwatch. (Picture B) **Record** the time when water begins dripping through the filter. Also record the time when the water stops dripping. Then record the amount of water in the bottom of the cup.

9 Repeat Step 8 for the sandy soil.

Draw Conclusions

1. Which soil type held water longer? Was your prediction correct?

2. Which soil type do you **infer** would be better for planting a cactus? Why?

3. **Scientists at Work** When scientists **control variables**, they can find out the effect of one change. List the variables in this experiment. Which variable was changed? Which variables stayed the same?

Investigate Further Repeat this activity for several soil types. You can use soils you can buy, soil from your yard, or your own soil mixes. How did the different types hold water?

Picture B

Process Skill Tip

When you **control variables** in an experiment, you change only one condition and keep all other conditions the same.

Soil Properties

Soil as a Habitat

FIND OUT

- what properties make soil good for supporting life
- how soil can be improved

VOCABULARY

fertile

Before studying soil, you may have thought that all soil was much alike. Scientists have classified more than 70,000 soil types around the world. The amounts of humus, clay, silt, and sand in a soil determine the soil type. Each soil type helps meet the needs of the living things that depend on it.

Soil is an important nonliving part of ecosystems. The plants and animals that live in a soil meet their needs by using the soil around them. Remember the basic needs of living things. Soil must provide most of these needs for organisms that live in it. Soil with lots of humus provides plenty of nutrients for plants. Loosely packed soil has spaces between the particles. These spaces fill with water and air. Plants and animals in the soil use the water and air to meet their needs.

✔ **How does soil help living things meet their needs?**

Plants and animals that need little water can live in dry, sandy desert soil. ▼

Good farm soil has lots of humus. Such soil helps many kinds of plants and animals meet their needs. ▼

Rain-forest soil is mostly clay. It supports many kinds of life. That is because nutrients are always being recycled quickly. ▼

Water Absorption

Soil types differ in how well they hold water. In the investigation, you saw that potting soil absorbs, or takes in, more water than sandy soil. Potting soil contains a lot of humus. Clay soil absorbs more water than sandy soil but the water is hard for plants to use.

The ability of soil to absorb water affects how much water plants and animals have during dry periods. It also determines how much water runs off during rainstorms or as snow melts.

✓ **Which soil type best absorbs water?**

▲ Soil that contains a lot of humus absorbs water like a sponge. This water is then available to the plants that live in the soil. Only a little water runs off. Also, the plant roots make spaces where water can run into soil.

▲ Packed, dry clay soil with few plants causes a lot of runoff. It blocks water almost as well as brick or tile. Wet clay soil holds water so well that it is difficult for plants to get the water they need.

Sandy soil is usually light in color but can be any color. It is the coarsest form of soil. Sandy soil does not stick together well when wet. ▶

Soil rich in humus is dark in color because it has a lot of decaying plant and animal matter. It feels spongy and crumbles easily. ▶

Various minerals in clay give it color. For example, iron makes it red. Particles of clay are very fine. When wet, clay becomes sticky. ▶

Color and Texture

Two other properties of soil are color and texture. *Color* refers to the way a soil looks. *Texture* refers to the way the soil feels.

A soil's color tells a lot about the soil. It shows the presence of certain minerals or other substances. For example, red soil contains a lot of iron. Black soil contains a lot of humus. Color can also tell you how warm a soil will get. Dark soil is warmed a lot by the sun. Light-colored soil reflects more sunlight and is warmed less.

Texture describes the size of the particles that make up soil. Soil textures range from coarse to fine. A coarse soil is made up of large grains, like sand, which feel rough. A fine soil is made of dust or other powdery substances and feels smooth. Fine soil may feel sticky when wet.

✓ **Which property of soil can you discover by feeling the soil?**

◄ Fertilizers can add nutrients to soil.

◄ Adding sand to soil makes water flow through it more easily.

◄ Adding lime makes water dissolve nutrients more slowly. This can give plants time to absorb nutrients before they are washed away.

Soil Richness

A soil that can grow a lot of plants is said to be **fertile** (FERT•uhl). Fertile soil is rich in nutrients and provides the right conditions for plants to grow.

A soil can be made more fertile by changing it or adding to it. Fertilizers (FUHRT•uhl•eye•zerz) are products that make soil richer. Most fertilizers add decaying plant matter or minerals.

Farmers and soil scientists have found that soil containing an even mixture of sand, clay, and humus is best for growing most plants. Soil with this mixture absorbs just the right amount of water. It also provides enough nutrients. People can add a missing part to make a poor soil better.

Water dissolves nutrients in soil. Sometimes nutrients dissolve so quickly that they are washed away before plants can use them. Adding lime to the soil slows down the rate at which minerals dissolve. Less often, water dissolves nutrients too slowly. Adding sulfur to the soil increases the rate at which water dissolves nutrients.

✔ **What products make soil richer?**

This farmer is spraying the soil with ammonia. The ammonia adds nitrogen to the soil, helping the soil grow more plants. ▼

▲ You can help recycle soil nutrients by making a compost pile. Raked leaves and grass clippings will rot to form a rich humus. You can add the humus back to the soil.

Summary

Soil is important because it is a habitat for plants and animals. Soil properties such as color and texture, fertility, and ability to hold water make some soil types better than others for growing plants. Most soil can be improved by adding fertilizers, missing soil parts, or other minerals.

Review

1. Where are air and water found in soil?

2. Why is a soil's texture important in determining how the soil absorbs water?

3. What combination of soil parts is best for growing most plants?

4. **Critical Thinking** You start a vegetable garden and find that most of the soil is clay. What can you add to make the garden's soil better?

5. **Test Prep** Which of these soil parts has the largest particles?

   A silt

   B clay

   C humus

   D sand

  # LINKS

 ## MATH LINK

Soil Temperature The temperature of soil affects how plants sprout and grow. Measure the temperature of soil outside that has been in direct sunlight for an hour. Then measure the temperature of soil that has been in shade for an hour. Find the difference between the two. Why do you think seeds are more likely to sprout in a warm place?

 ## WRITING LINK

Informative Writing — How-To Find out which plants grow best in the soil types in your area. Make a gardening guide for students your age. Include in your guide a description of each soil type and pictures of the plants that grow in it.

 ## HEALTH LINK

Good Nutrition Fresh fruits and vegetables are often rich in nutrients that they take from the soil. Find out which foods are rich in minerals and what the minerals are. Make a chart of your findings.

TECHNOLOGY LINK

Visit the Harcourt Learning Site for related links, activities, and resources.

www.harcourtschool.com

WELCOME TO THE LEARNING SITE

What Are Some Ways to Conserve Soil?

In this lesson, you can . . .

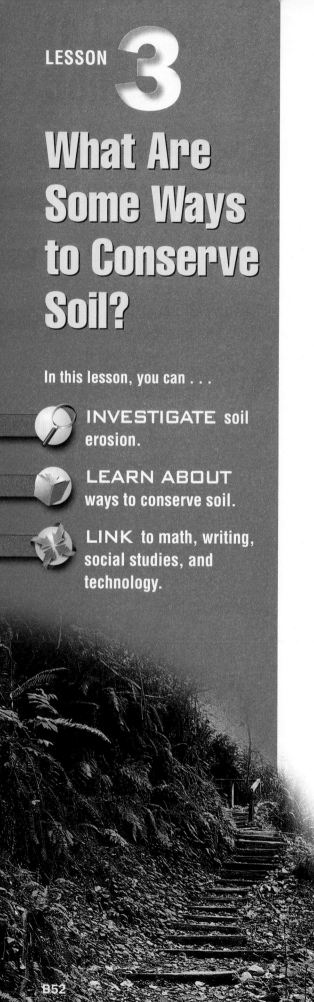

INVESTIGATE soil erosion.

LEARN ABOUT ways to conserve soil.

LINK to math, writing, social studies, and technology.

INVESTIGATE

Soil Erosion

Activity Purpose Sometimes there is more rain than the soil can hold. The extra water runs off. Runoff water can cause soil erosion, especially on hills. Because soil takes so long to form, it is important to keep it in place. In this investigation you will **build models** of two ways to plow a hill. You will compare the amounts of soil eroded in the two models.

Materials

- masking tape
- 2 wide-mouth jars
- flat board about 15 cm long
- sandy soil
- metric ruler
- craft stick
- roller-type paint tray
- plastic cup
- water
- watering can

Activity Procedure

1. Place a piece of masking tape on each jar. Label one jar *Down Rows*. Label the other *Across Rows*.

2. Cover the board with damp soil to a depth of about 2 cm.

3. Make rows that run down the board by pressing the craft stick into the soil. Make the rows about 2 cm apart. (Picture A)

4. Place the board in the paint tray. One end of the board should be slightly higher than the other end.

◀ The boards along this path hold soil in place. They prevent the soil from crumbling or from being washed away.

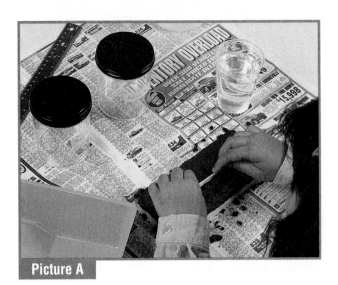

Picture A

Picture B

5 Put 2 cups of water into the watering can. Hold the can about 10 cm above the tray. Sprinkle the soil with water until the can is empty. (Picture B)

6 Carefully remove the board and set it aside. Pour the runoff from the paint tray into the *Down Rows* jar.

7 Smooth out the soil on the board. Add soil to make the depth about 2 cm. Make fresh rows in the soil, only this time make rows that run across the board.

8 Repeat Steps 4–6, but pour the runoff water into the *Across Rows* jar.

9 Allow the soil in both jars to settle for 30 minutes.

Draw Conclusions

1. **Observe** the material in each jar. Which jar has more runoff? Which jar has more soil?

2. Which model showed the better way to keep soil from eroding?

3. **Scientists at Work** Scientists **compare** results of tests to find the best answer. What did you compare in this activity?

Investigate Further See how covering soil affects the amount of runoff and soil erosion. Repeat the experiment, but this time cover the soil with shredded newspaper. Use different jars to collect runoff. Which material had the least runoff? Use your data to **draw a conclusion** about how soil cover affects the amount of runoff and soil erosion.

Process Skill Tip

When you **compare** things, you observe them to see how they are alike and how they are different. It is important to observe all the things in the same way. Otherwise, you may miss important differences. Or you may see false differences because you observed in different ways.

Soil Conservation

Soil Loss

FIND OUT

- how soil and nutrients from soil can be lost

- ways to protect soil

VOCABULARY

soil conservation
contour plowing
strip cropping
terracing

Soil changes all the time. Weathering breaks up rock to form new soil. Erosion by wind and water moves soil from place to place. Because of these and other changes, some places gain soil. Other places lose soil.

Erosion most affects soil without a covering of plants. Farmlands and construction sites usually have lots of such bare soil. The soil soaks up some rainwater. During heavy rains, however, too much rain falls at one time to be soaked up. Water begins to run off. Runoff carries soil to a stream. The stream then drains into larger and larger rivers.

Eroded soil can be deposited anywhere along streams and rivers. However, much of the soil is carried downstream until a river enters the ocean. As the river flows into the ocean, it slows down. Eroded soil is deposited to form new land called a *delta*. As long as soil flows with the river, the delta grows farther and farther out into the ocean. The delta gets rich topsoil from the land the river flows through. But the land upriver loses soil.

In the United States, about half of the land is used for agriculture. ▼

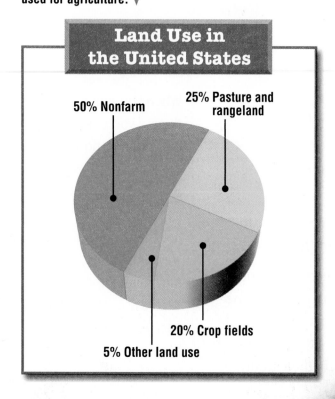

Land Use in the United States

50% Nonfarm

25% Pasture and rangeland

20% Crop fields

5% Other land use

The Mississippi River delta stretches 121 km (about 75 mi) farther into the Gulf of Mexico than it did 100 years ago. ▼

You can see evidence of water erosion. Runoff can dig deep gullies. This usually happens on steep hills. With each heavy rainfall, runoff makes the gullies wider and deeper.

Sometimes deposited soil blocks rivers or streams. There may be flooding, or a new flow path may result.

Land can also lose soil by wind erosion. Plants cover and protect soil. When people clear land to plant fields or build homes, they take away trees and other plants. Then there are no roots to hold soil and no plants to shelter soil from wind and rain. When the wind blows, it picks up dry topsoil and carries it away.

✔ **What happens to soil in a river when it enters the ocean?**

One of these two rivers contains more eroded soil. Notice the different colors of water where they join. ▼

▲ This gully was formed as runoff water rushed to a lower area.

▲ When land cleared for farming is dry, wind can carry soil away.

B55

Controlling Soil Loss

Soil conservation (kahn•ser•VAY•shuhn) is saving soil. Farmers work hard to protect their valuable soil. One way farmers have found to control soil loss is to plow and plant around a hill rather than up and down the hill. Plowing around a hill is called **contour** (KAHN•toor) **plowing**. In the investigation, you saw reasons that contour plowing is good. The rows catch runoff and slow it down. They keep it from flowing quickly downhill.

Farmers also use strip cropping to save soil. In **strip cropping** one or more crops are planted between rows of other crops. For example, alfalfa is sometimes planted between rows of corn. The corn slows down the wind, which could erode soil that isn't covered. The roots of both plants help hold the soil in place.

A farming method used on steep hillsides is terracing. In **terracing** (TER•uhs•ing) a steep hill is cut to form broad, flat areas at different heights. A terraced hillside looks like a huge stairway. The steps

▲ Contour plowing protects soil on gentle, rolling hillsides.

▲ Strip cropping protects soil by planting strips of short and tall plants side by side. The tall plants help slow down the wind. The short plants provide good cover for the soil.

◄ Terracing changes a steep hillside into a series of flat steps. Crops are grown on the steps.

allow farmers to grow crops on hillsides that would otherwise have been too steep. The steps slow down water as it rushes down the hill.

Builders of roads, especially highways, look for ways to protect roadsides from erosion. Roads through mountains may have roadside terracing. Often trees, grass, and other plants are put along roads to reduce erosion.

Gardeners also want to conserve soil. At homes and in city parks, gardeners plant lawns and gardens that look good and protect the soil.

✔ **What are three farming methods that save soil?**

THE INSIDE STORY

Landscaping to Control Soil Loss

Like farmland, a hillside garden can easily lose soil. A gardener must plan carefully and use several ways to control erosion. Using more than one way protects the garden and adds interest.

1 The roots of plants, such as these ornamental grasses, help hold soil in place.

2 Stones can be set in ways that slow the flow of water.

3 A retaining wall holds soil in place, keeping it from being washed away.

Controlling Nutrient Loss

Erosion is not the only way soil becomes less rich. Overuse and misuse can take nutrients from soil. Growing the same crop in a field year after year can take important minerals from the soil. For example, if a farmer planted just corn in a field for several years, the corn would use most of the nitrogen (NY•truh•jehn) in the soil. Eventually, there would not be enough nitrogen to grow corn.

Not every plant uses the same nutrients. Some plants even add nutrients to the soil. Farmers have found that if they plant a different crop in a field every year, they can control nutrient loss. This is called crop rotation. Chemical fertilizers can replace lost nutrients, but chemicals that run off can harm nearby ponds and streams. Crop rotation helps replace nutrients without using as much of these chemicals.

✓ **How can planting the same crop year after year harm the soil?**

▲ The next year, the farmer plants soybeans. Soybeans add nitrogen to the soil.

One spring a farmer plants corn in a field. The corn takes nitrogen from the soil. ▶

Some Important Soil Nutrients	
Nutrient	**How the Nutrient Helps Plants**
Nitrogen	Helps make up the green matter that absorbs the sun's energy
Phosphorus (FAHS•fuh•ruhs)	Helps plants change the sun's energy into food energy
Potassium (poh•TAS•ee•uhm)	Helps a plant keep the right amount of water in its stems, roots, and leaves
Calcium (KAL•see•uhm)	Helps allow water and gases to pass through plant cells
Magnesium (mag•NEE•zee•uhm)	Helps a plant use the food it makes

▲ In the fall, after the soybeans have been harvested, the farmer plants winter wheat. The field "rests" during the late summer and fall after the wheat is harvested. The dead plant parts decay and add nutrients to the soil.

Summary

Soil can be lost to wind and water erosion. Farmers use soil conservation techniques such as contour plowing, strip cropping, terracing, and crop rotation to reduce these problems. Nutrients in soil can be lost if the same crop is planted year after year.

Review

1. In what ways is soil always changing?

2. What are two things gardeners and road builders hope to do?

3. How does crop rotation keep soil from losing nutrients?

4. **Critical Thinking** If farmers didn't try to save soil, what could happen?

5. **Test Prep** Which way of planting can reduce water erosion on a steep hillside?

    A strip cropping   **C** contour plowing

    B terracing   **D** crop rotation

LINKS

MATH LINK

Calculating Soil Loss Suppose topsoil is 1 m deep. It is eroded at a rate of 5 cm a year. How long will the topsoil last? If new strip cropping reduces erosion by half, how long will topsoil last?

WRITING LINK

Informative Writing—How-To Suppose you are in charge of helping the people in an area practice soil conservation. The area could include a construction site, a golf course being built, or a farm. Write a handout that tells ways people could change habits to conserve soil.

SOCIAL STUDIES LINK

Dust Bowl More than 70 years ago, dust clouds blew across many states. People had to wear scarves to keep grit out of their eyes and mouths. Investigate the Dust Bowl years to see the lessons people learned about misusing the land.

TECHNOLOGY LINK

Learn more about ways farmers control erosion by viewing *African Soil Erosion* on the **Harcourt Science Newsroom Video.**

CNN
Turner Le@rning

SOIL ENRICHMENT

People who grow a garden in the same place year after year quickly learn an important fact of soil science—plants take nutrients from the soil. For plants to grow well the next year, the nutrients must be put back in some way.

Ancient Soil Practices

People in China learned about putting nutrients back into soil hundreds of years ago. For more than 4000 years, some farms in China have been replanted every year. Chinese farmers kept their farmland fertile by adding organic material to the soil. One way they did this was by growing a crop of *legumes* (LEG•yoomz). Legumes include beans, soybeans, clover, alfalfa, and peanuts. These plants are rich in nitrogen, an impor-

tant soil nutrient. Farmers harvested the legumes and mixed them with rich soil from near a river. Then they spread this mixture over their fields.

The ancient Roman and Greek farmers added natural fertilizers to the soil, too. They also buried human and animal bones. Bones add nitrogen and potassium to the soil. Many other cultures also have used bones to enrich the soil. Even today you can find bags of bone meal, or ground-up animal bones, in garden supply stores.

Enhancing Soil in the Americas

Some Native Americans enriched their soil by burying fish with their corn seeds. Western Apache families each had several small farms. They would plant only some

The History of Soil Enrichment

Chinese 2,000 B.C.
Chinese use legumes to enrich soil. Romans and Greeks use natural fertilizers including bones.

Carver 1800s
George Washington Carver experiments with plants and soil.

| 2,000 B.C. | 300-900 A.D. | 1600 A.D. | 1700 A.D. | 1800 A.D. |

Mayans 300-900 A.D.
Mayan culture cuts and burns forest to provide farmland.

Americans 1600s
Native Americans teach colonists planting methods.

of the farms each year. Grasses and weeds grew on the unused farmland. These plants were a source of nutrients the next time crops were planted.

Modern Methods—Mix of Old and New

In the United States during the late 1800s, many farmers had soil problems. Planting the same crop, such as cotton, every year was taking nutrients from the soil. But, farmers couldn't afford to leave some fields unplanted each year. George Washington Carver did experiments with plants to solve these problems. Carver came up with a plan of *rotating crops* in the same field. His idea was to plant a crop of cotton one year and a crop of peanuts, a kind of legume, the next year.

Carver also recommended *composting* (KAHM•pohst•ing), which is now popular again. To make compost, people mix leaves, grass clippings, kitchen scraps, paper, and wood chips together. As the leaves and other materials rot, they form rich organic material that can be used to improve soil. If materials aren't composted,

they usually take up space in landfills. So composting is a wise way to reuse resources.

Fertilizers are materials that enrich soil. The United States produces a lot of chemical fertilizers. These are either artificial substances or substances taken out of mineral resources. Fertilizers are made to replace nitrogen, phosphorus, and potassium—the three substances most often missing from soil. Nitrogen fertilizers, for example, usually add some form of ammonia to the soil.

All these ways of improving the soil were developed because people know soil is a valuable resource. As the needs of the world increase, scientists keep looking for new ways to improve soil and to grow more and better crops.

Think About It

1. What are two ways to add needed nitrogen to soil?
2. How are the nonartificial ways of enriching soil alike?

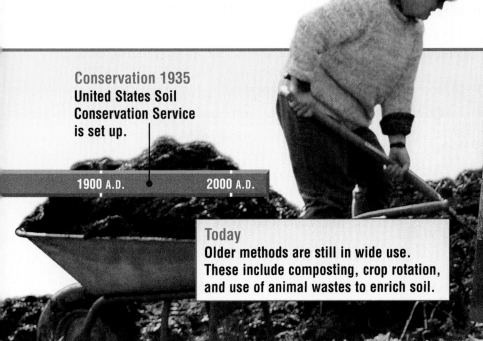

Conservation 1935
United States Soil Conservation Service is set up.

1900 A.D.   2000 A.D.

Today
Older methods are still in wide use. These include composting, crop rotation, and use of animal wastes to enrich soil.

BONE MEAL
5-11-0
NET WEIGHT 4 LBS. (1.8 kg)

Ignacio Rodriguez-Iturbe

HYDROLOGIST

"I always tell my students that to do good research it is necessary to be able to dream."

Dr. Ignacio Rodriguez-Iturbe thinks his ability to dream came from his father. "To see far and to see well, one needs the eyes of the heart," his father would tell him. Ignacio Rodriguez-Iturbe has applied the "eyes of the heart" to his scientific work.

Dr. Ignacio Rodriguez-Iturbe is from Venezuela, and has taught there and at the Massachusetts Institute of Technology. He now teaches at the Princeton Environmental Institute. In 1998 he received the Robert E. Horton Medal from the American Geophysical Union.

Like all hydrologists (hy•DRAHL•uh•jists), Rodriguez-Iturbe studies water. Some hydrologists look for sources of fresh water. Others study water pollution and floods. Rodriguez-Iturbe studies how water moves through river systems, soil, and underground rock. He hopes to understand how this part of nature works. With that understanding, he can solve the problems of flooding or of wells that are drying up.

Rodriguez-Iturbe enjoys working on scientific problems with his students. He has even been known to call a student late at night to discuss research ideas. The people he has been able to work with throughout the years are important to him. He has had friends and co-workers in both Venezuela and the United States who share his interest in water.

THINK ABOUT IT

1. How would it be helpful to have friends and co-workers who share your research interests?
2. What kinds of things about water might a hydrologist study?

Observing Soil Textures

How can you describe soils by their texture?

Materials

- 3 paper towels
- topsoil
- sandy soil
- clay soil
- 3 index cards
- hand lens
- water
- dropper

Procedure

1. Spread each soil type on a separate paper towel. Write the name of each soil type on a different index card.

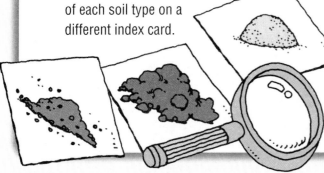

2. Observe each soil sample with the hand lens. Describe each soil type on the index card for that sample.

3. Hold some of one sample in your hand, and add five drops of water to the soil. Then squeeze and work the soil for a few seconds. On the index card for that soil type, describe the texture of the soil.

4. Repeat Step 3 for the other two soil samples. **CAUTION** Be sure to wash your hands after handling soil.

Draw Conclusions

Which of these soil types do you think would work best for a houseplant? A cactus?

Soils as Life Support

How well do soil types support plant growth?

Materials

- 4 small flowerpots with saucers
- potting soil, clay, sand, sphagnum peat moss
- 4 small plants of the same type and size
- water
- spoon

Procedure

1. Fill each pot half way with a different soil.

2. Put a plant in each pot. Add more soil if needed. Give each plant the same amount of water. Put the pots in a sunny spot.

3. Test each pot for dryness daily. To do this, insert a spoon into the soil and then remove it. If little soil clings to it, add water.

4. Keep a daily log. Record when the plants received water. Also record general observations about the plants. Describe how each plant looks.

Draw Conclusions

After two weeks, compare the plants. How well did each soil type meet the needs of its plant?

Vocabulary Review

Use the terms below to complete the sentences. The page numbers in ( ) tell you where to look in the chapter if you need help.

weathering (B43)

erosion (B43)

humus (B44)

fertile (B50)

soil conservation (B56)

contour plowing (B56)

strip cropping (B56)

terracing (B56)

1. The movement of bits of rock or soil by wind and water is called ____.

2. Planting a crop between rows of another crop is ____.

3. Plowing around a hill is ____.

4. Cutting broad, flat areas in the sides of a steep mountain to grow crops is called ____.

5. The natural process of breaking down rock is ____.

6. Soil that is ____ is capable of growing a lot of plants.

7. ____ means saving of soil.

8. The soil part ____ is made up of rotting plant and animal materials.

Connect Concepts

Use the terms in the Word Bank to complete the concept map.

crop rotation   contour plowing   erosion

fertile   soil conservation   terracing

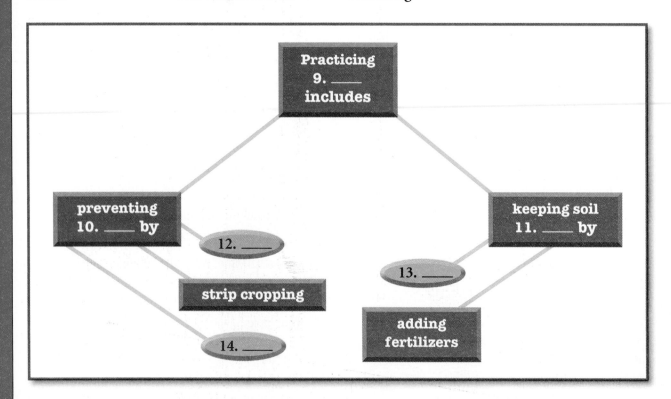

Practicing
9. ____
includes

preventing
10. ____ by

keeping soil
11. ____ by

12. ____

13. ____

strip cropping

adding fertilizers

14. ____

Check Understanding

Write the letter of the best choice.

15. The soil layer that is affected the most by erosion is —

    A topsoil   C bedrock

    B subsoil   D parent rock

16. When the temperature is high during the day and cold at night, rocks are likely to —

    F expand   H crack

    G contract   J harden

17. Cotton, which is grown to make clothing, depends mostly on _____ to grow.

    A topsoil   C bedrock

    B subsoil   D parent rock

18. _____ becomes richer as dead plants decay.

    F Topsoil   H Bedrock

    G Subsoil   J Parent rock

19. Terracing a hillside can slow —

    A weathering   C erosion

    B absorption   D soil formation

20. The soil at the top of a hill has a lot of the smallest type of soil particle. The soil is made up mostly of —

    F bedrock   H humus

    G sand   J clay

21. Tree roots reach down into the middle layer of soil, breaking up the rocks there. This soil layer is called —

    A bedrock   C subsoil

    B topsoil   D parent rock

Critical Thinking

22. You are planning a vegetable garden. You want your first year's harvest to be good. Name two important properties you want your soil to have. Tell how you could improve these soil properties.

23. You have two fields. One is on a gently sloping hillside, and the other is on flat ground. Tell what you would do to reduce soil erosion on each field.

Process Skills Review

24. You **observe** soil that is light in color and that doesn't hold together well when wet. What kind of soil is it likely to be? How well would it take up water?

25. You want to set up an experiment to compare the texture of soil types when they are wet. What are two **variables** you need to control?

26. How could you **compare** the runoff and erosion from two types of terracing?

Performance Assessment

Landscape Plan

Draw a plan for landscaping the schoolyard. Think of ways to make it look good and to prevent erosion. Include areas for games and sports you like to play. Label the parts of your design that are important for erosion control.

Protecting Ecosystems

What would you do if you were living in a cold climate and your furnace didn't work? You might put on more clothes or find another way to heat your home. Or you might just move! Living things in nature face similar problems if their environments change. In this chapter you'll find out how people help protect ecosystems from harmful changes.

Vocabulary Preview

succession
reclamation
conservation
preservation

FAST FACT

Black-footed ferrets are the only type of ferret still living in the wild. Changes in the environment have reduced the population of ferrets to the point that they have been placed on the endangered species list. The ferret shown on page B67 is being released to help increase the number of wild ferrets. Because ferrets can get the flu from people, the man is wearing a surgical face mask.

FAST FACT

Would you believe that this welcome mat is made from ground-up tires? Recycling protects ecosystems by using some of the 250 million automobile tires discarded each year in the United States. The recycled tires are kept out of landfills.

FAST FACT

Causes of Species Endangerment

Cause	Percent of Endangered Species Affected
Habitat loss	88 %
Competition with other species	46 %
Pollution	20 %
Hunting	14 %
Disease	2 %

FAST FACT

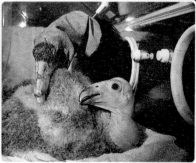

Sometimes endangered animals are raised in zoos and then released into the wild. To make sure this California condor chick can survive without human care, it is being fed with a hand puppet that looks like its mother!

What Kinds of Changes Occur in Ecosystems?

In this lesson, you can . . .

 INVESTIGATE how a pond changes over time.

 LEARN ABOUT ways ecosystems change.

 LINK to math, writing, technology, and other areas.

INVESTIGATE

Changes in a Pond

Activity Purpose Think of ways you have changed as you have grown older. You changed as you grew from an infant to a toddler and from a toddler to a child. All things change over time, including bodies of water. In this investigation you will **make a model** of a pond that forms in a low area of rock. You will change your pond. Then you will use the data you collect to **infer** changes that would happen in a real pond.

Materials
- aluminum foil pan
- water
- metric ruler
- plastic green plants
- aquarium gravel

Activity Procedure

1 Copy the chart shown on page B69. **Make a model** of a pond that has formed in a low spot on exposed rock. Fill the pan half-full of water.

2 **Measure** and **record** the distance across the water's surface. (Picture A) Try to "plant" a few plants near the sides of your pond. Record your **observations.**

3 **Predict** what will happen to the pond if you add gravel and then plants.

◀ Fires do not cause the end of life in a forest. Often, they make room for different kinds of life.

Investigation Step	Measurement of Water's Surface	Observations
Step 2		
Step 4		
Step 5		

4️⃣ Slowly add gravel to your model pond. (Picture B) The gravel stands for soil that has washed into the pond during 200 years. In a real pond more soil builds up around the edges than in the middle. Put more gravel around the edges of the pond than in the middle. **Measure** and **record** the distance across the water's surface. Again "plant" several plants near the sides of the pond. Record your **observations.**

5️⃣ Add more gravel and plants until you can no longer see the water's surface. This represents several hundred years of adding soil. **Record** your **observations** of what was once a pond.

Picture A

Draw Conclusions

1. Describe how your pond changed over time.

2. As a pond changes, how might the living things in it change? Explain your answer.

3. **Scientists at Work** When you **observed** your pond model, you **collected data.** What does your data tell you about how a natural pond changes over time?

Investigate Further Ponds go through *stages,* or steps, as they get older. Draw a picture showing four stages of a pond. Label the stages *new pond, old pond, marsh,* and *meadow.*

Picture B

Process Skill Tip

Data is another word for information. **Collecting data** can be observing, measuring, counting, or even taking photos. It is important to collect data in an organized way.

Ecosystem Changes

Slow Changes

FIND OUT

- how ecosystems change
- how changes affect ecosystems

VOCABULARY

succession

An ecosystem usually has *stability*, or balance. There are many changes occurring all the time, but they cancel each other out. For example, organisms live, die, and decompose, returning the materials they were made of to the soil. New plants grow and use the materials. Water evaporates from a pond, but rain adds more water. Because these changes balance each other, they do not cause the overall ecosystem to change.

Over time, however, changes in climate, rate of erosion, and populations can cause big changes in an ecosystem. New communities can form within it. **Succession** (suhk•SESH•uhn) is the process that gradually changes an existing ecosystem into another ecosystem.

Succession can change an area that has little life into one that has many living things. For example, during Earth's ice ages, widespread glaciers scooped large holes in rock. When the climate got warmer, the ice melted. Water was left in the holes, forming ponds. As in the investigation, at first the ponds had no soil, and no plants grew in them.

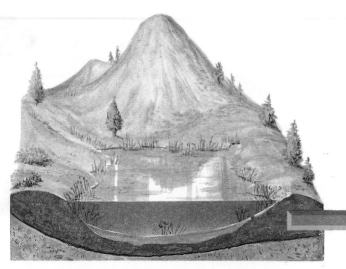

▲ When this pond first formed, nothing lived in it. As soil dropped to the bottom and wind blew seeds and spores into the pond, many organisms began to live there.

▲ Over time, more soil was washed into the pond. It became shallower and narrower.

The first organisms that grew near the ponds were mosses and lichens (LY•kuhns). They grew on the rocks and began breaking down the rocks, forming soil. Some soil was washed into the ponds by heavy rains. The bottom of the ponds became muddy. Wind blew seeds and spores of many living things into the ponds. Bacteria and algae need few nutrients, so they began to grow first.

As these living things grew and died, they increased the amount of nutrients in the ponds. The added nutrients allowed other plants, such as water lilies, to grow there. Insects began to live in the ponds. Frogs soon came to eat the insects.

Dead plants and animals settled to the bottom of the ponds and began to fill them up. The ponds became marshes with cattails and other populations of marsh plants and animals.

Over time, communities of other kinds of plant and animal life replaced the marsh communities. Grassy meadows formed as soil filled in the marshes. Finally, a forest grew where the ponds used to be.

▲ Farming and grazing livestock on the dry grasslands of Africa may change the ecosystem so that it supports much less plant and animal life.

Succession doesn't have to stop with the forest. Climate changes that happen slowly can make it easier for some types of trees to grow than for others. Fires, floods, and other changes that happen quickly can kill many trees at once.

✓ **What allows more and more organisms to live in an ecosystem?**

▲ As organisms died, their remains and more soil continued to fill up the pond until a marsh formed.

▲ Recycling of dead plants and animals, along with added soil, completely filled up the marsh. It became a meadow.

Rapid Changes

Ecosystems can also change quickly. Sometimes one event can cause huge changes in an ecosystem.

Powerful storms can destroy habitats and many living things. A hurricane can be hundreds of kilometers wide and have winds as fast as 121 kilometers (75 mi) per hour or more. Strong winds flatten homes, trees, and other plants. Heavy rains and huge waves flood coastal areas, changing the ecosystems in those areas.

Strong thunderstorms with heavy rains can affect areas away from the coast. The runoff from these storms speeds up erosion. Flooding may occur where the rain falls and in areas through which the waters drain.

▲ Flooding happens when runoff from heavy rain overfills streams. The water overflows and covers low areas.

Thunderstorms can produce tornadoes, the most violent of all storms. A tornado can have wind speeds of 320 kilometers (about 200 mi) per hour. These strong winds destroy almost all they touch.

Forest fires also cause rapid change in ecosystems. Lightning causes some fires. Careless people also cause fires. Fires burn trees and other plants and force wildlife to leave. The animals that lived in the forest must find other places to live until the forest grows back.

▲ Hurricanes can flatten trees and damage buildings in coastal areas. Hurricanes usually weaken when the storm moves over land, but high winds and heavy rains still can cause much damage.

Yellowstone National Park was covered mostly with forest before 1988. That summer, large fires burned for almost four months. More than 3200 square kilometers (about 800,000 acres) of forest burned. ▼

Some volcanoes erupt with an explosion. They shoot out clouds of ash that can travel hundreds of kilometers. Areas near the volcano are affected most by the explosion, ash, and lava. ▶

Plants and animals will live and grow again in an ecosystem after the rapid changes of fires and storms. Even after a volcano covers an area with ash and new rock, plants and then animals return to the area. Succession happens more quickly in areas that have living things nearby. But even if the first seeds and spores must be blown great distances by the wind, the process is the same.

✓ **What can cause rapid changes in an ecosystem?**

▲ Mosses, grasses, and small flowers are among the first plants to grow in empty land. It takes only a few years for plant growth and other weathering processes to break up the ash and lava. Larger plants then can grow there.

Many seeds survive a forest fire. The cones of some pine trees release seeds only after the heat of a fire. Young plants get more sunlight and grow well because trees are gone. ▶

Humans and Rapid Changes

People cause some rapid changes such as those that result from fires. Some rapid changes also put people in danger. Homes and businesses can be damaged by forest fires, floods, and storms. To help keep people safe, governments set up systems to watch for dangers and to warn people.

Forest fires are a threat in dry periods. During seasons when forest fires occur, lookouts watch forests carefully. If they see smoke, firefighters are called. People in the path of the fire are warned. They may be *evacuated* (ee•VAK•yoo•ay•tuhd), or sent to a safe place.

Hurricanes form at sea and usually travel for days before reaching land. Weather satellites and airplanes track these storms. Radio and TV announcements warn people to move to safety as a hurricane nears.

Severe thunderstorms and tornadoes can form quickly. Radar detects these storms. When the storms approach, radio and TV programs are interrupted to warn people to take shelter. Sirens also sound, warning people that a storm is near.

✔ **How do people try to protect themselves from the forces that cause rapid ecosystem changes?**

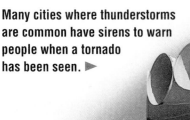
Many cities where thunderstorms are common have sirens to warn people when a tornado has been seen. ▶

Some people choose to live in dangerous areas such as near an inactive volcano. They depend on early warnings to give them time to escape an eruption.

▲ A hillside brush fire spread so quickly that there was no time to move these cars to safety.

Summary

Ecosystems can change slowly through the process of succession. Changes can happen slowly due to changes in climate or in communities of living things. Rapid changes can result from storms and other natural events such as fires, floods, and volcanic eruptions. Even when ecosystems are destroyed, they can recover over time.

Review

1. How does a pond change over time to a forest?

2. What is one cause of rapid ecosystem changes that can result from peoples' actions?

3. How do people try to stay safe during rapid changes in ecosystems?

4. **Critical Thinking** Why might an ecosystem that is damaged by fire be able to recover fairly quickly?

5. **Test Prep** Which of these are most likely to be the first plants in a new ecosystem that has few nutrients?

   A trees   C flowers

   B mosses   D shrubs

LINKS

MATH LINK

Rainfall Adds Up Suppose a hurricane drops 12 cm (about 5 in.) of rain on a town every half-hour. How much rain will fall if the storm lasts 2 hours?

WRITING LINK

Informative Writing—Request Many rapid changes in an ecosystem can have terrible effects on the people living within it. Write a letter to the Federal Emergency Management Administration (FEMA). Find out emergency weather procedures for your area.

LITERATURE LINK

Forest Fire! Read *Forest Fire!* by Mary Ann Fraser. You can journey through a forest fire with animals as they escape and adjust to the changes in the forest.

HEALTH LINK

Floods and Disease Floodwaters can contain harmful organisms. Find out some health hazards caused by flooding. Share your findings with the class.

TECHNOLOGY LINK

Learn more about changes to marine ecosystems by visiting the National Museum of History Internet site.
www.si.edu/harcourt/science

Smithsonian Institution®

How Do People Change Ecosystems?

In this lesson, you can . . .

INVESTIGATE how filtering removes some kinds of water pollution.

LEARN ABOUT ways people change ecosystems.

LINK to math, writing, technology, and other areas.

 **INVESTIGATE**

Cleaning Up Pond Pollution

Activity Purpose The air, land, and water in an ecosystem can become polluted. Pollution affects living things that use these resources. Scientists are looking for ways to clean up polluted environments. In this investigation you will **compare** polluted and filtered water to **observe** how filtering removes some kinds of water pollution.

Materials

- 6 cups and 3 lids
- wax pencil
- water
- safety goggles
- plastic gloves
- 3 coffee filters
- 3 rubber bands
- pollutants
    food coloring, 10 drops
    bits of paper
    vegetable oil, 10 drops
    small pieces of bread
    green dishwashing
        detergent, 10 drops
    carpet fibers

CAUTION

Activity Procedure

1. Label one cup *Pollutant 1,* a second cup *Pollutant 2,* and a third *Pollutant 3.*

2. Label one of the other three cups *Filtered pollutant 1,* the second *Filtered pollutant 2,* and the third *Filtered pollutant 3.* You should now have three pairs of cups. (Picture A)

3. Fill each of the three pollutant cups half-full of water. **CAUTION** **Put on the safety goggles and plastic gloves.** Put two different pollutants in each cup. Put the lids on tightly, and shake each cup well.

◄ This sea otter was rescued from an oil spill. Both the rescue and the oil spill show ways people affect ecosystems.

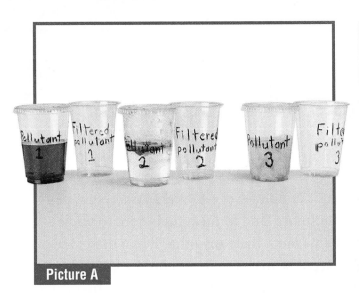

Picture A

Picture B

4. **Observe** one of the cups that contain polluted water. **Record** what you see.

5. Push a clean coffee filter halfway into the *Filtered pollutant 1* cup. Put a rubber band around the top of the cup to hold the filter in place. Pour about half of the *Pollutant 1* water into the filter. (Picture B)

6. When the water has drained, **compare** the filtered water with the polluted water. **Record** your observations.

7. Repeat Steps 4–6 for the other two cups of polluted water.

Draw Conclusions

1. How were the mixtures you filtered alike?

2. Which pollutants were filtered out?

3. **Scientists at Work** Scientists **compare** samples to find the smallest differences. How did the polluted water containing oil look compared to the filtered water? How did the filtered detergent mixture compare to the mixture before it was filtered?

Investigate Further Sand is sometimes used as a filter to clean water for drinking. Fill a cup with water. Add a spoonful of flour or baby powder. Stir well. Plug the end of a funnel with one or two cotton balls. Fill the funnel half-full of clean sand. Put the funnel into a jar. Pour the mixture of water and powder into the funnel. **Observe** the filtered water. How well did the sand work? How do you know?

> **Process Skill Tip**
>
> When you observe, sometimes you must **compare** one sample with another to see small differences.

Humans and Ecosystems

FIND OUT

- **how people affect ecosystems**
- **examples of ecosystem changes that people cause**

VOCABULARY

reclamation

Damage to Ecosystems

For thousands of years, the world's human population grew slowly. Now, however, it doubles every 40 years. As a result, people are using more and more land to meet their needs. People affect Earth's ecosystems more than any other living thing does. Most animals help keep a balance in ecosystems. People, however, can both upset the natural balance and help keep it.

Every day, chemicals are used to build and manufacture things, to kill insects, and to fertilize crops and lawns. Builders clear away trees and plants to make room for growing cities. Trees are cut down and used to build homes or make paper. All these changes harm habitats in ecosystems.

Some chemicals used in factories leak into nearby streams and rivers. Runoff water washes away chemicals used on farms and lawns. These chemicals can end up in ponds, lakes, or rivers, where they can harm or kill water plants and fish. You may remember that all of an ecosystem can be affected even if just one part is taken away.

▲ Wastes that drain into water habitats can poison fish and other wildlife. Scientists think that human wastes in water led to the disease that killed these fish.

▲ Clear-cutting, or cutting down all the trees in an area, is slowly destroying the rain forests. If it continues in the same way, by the year 2030 all the rain forests could be gone.

People's need for lumber and space has led to the decline of forests. More than half the world's rain forests have been cut down. As these areas are lost, so are the many species of plants and animals that live there.

The destruction of rain forests affects other ecosystems. After trees are cut down, the forest soil washes into rivers and out to sea. Some soil drops onto coral reefs, killing the animals there.

Water and oxygen from rain-forest trees are important to ecosystems around the world. Rain-forest trees soak up water and then slowly release it into the atmosphere. The water helps form clouds and rain. These trees also release large amounts of oxygen. When rain forests are destroyed, these processes no longer happen.

✓ **How can the loss of the rain forests affect other ecosystems?**

Bulldozers clear land to prepare it for building. People build roads, homes, and factories on cleared land.

Repair of Ecosystems

People can find ways to lower human effects on ecosystems. For example, dams are built on rivers to generate electricity. But a dam can keep salmon from swimming up the river to lay their eggs. To help the salmon, people build fish ladders around dams.

In other areas, people find ways to repair ecosystems. When mines are dug and land is cleared to get resources, the land is damaged. Often it can no longer be used as it was before. In these areas, people now

▲ Fish ladders are like artificial river rapids. Salmon jump from one level up to the next. The ladder lets them get over the dam so they can reach their home stream to lay eggs.

THE INSIDE STORY

Strip-Mine Reclamation

People need resources such as coal and copper. Open pit or strip mines are often the best way to obtain these resources.

However, in a strip mine, the top layers of soil are taken away to get out coal or other minerals. This leaves big pits that can lead to erosion and mudslides. Rain can wash chemicals from mine wastes into streams. These changes affect the habitats of many living things.

A used-up strip mine is a scar on the land. In the past, no repairs were made to the ecosystem. Today the United States and many other countries have laws that require mining companies to reclaim the land.

1. Companies that dig strip mines today must save the soil that is removed during mining.

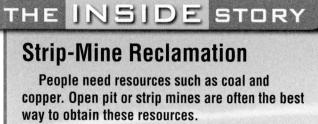

practice **reclamation** (rek•luh•MAY•shuhn), or repairing some of the damage to an ecosystem.

It isn't easy, or even possible, to change a damaged ecosystem back to the way it was. In some cases the area may be used for something completely different. For example, some lands that once had railroad tracks on them are made into hiking and biking trails. Natural habitats near the trails are sometimes protected from development.

✓ **What problems can mining cause?**

▲ Replanting trees helps maintain a forest ecosystem. It also helps make sure there will be paper and lumber in the future.

2. When the mine is used up, the saved soil is used to refill part of the pit. More soil is added.

3. Trees, flowers, and grass are planted to control erosion. Other plants and animals return over time.

Adding to Ecosystems

People also improve and take care of ecosystems. Governments make parks in towns and nearby countrysides. People who own homes set up wildflower gardens and ponds in their yards. These additions make new habitats for living things.

Ecosystem protection and improvement happens in urban areas and in remote, or distant, areas around the world. In Africa, the governments of Uganda, Zaire, and Rwanda passed laws to stop logging and building in certain areas of rain forest. The areas form corridors, or strips of forest, that connect parts of the rain forest. Animals such as mountain gorillas can move safely from one forest area to another along these corridors.

In some places, people harvest coral to sell as souvenirs. This has damaged many coral reefs. Some governments passed laws to stop this. To help replace the damaged reefs, oil rigs that are no longer used are sunk. The rigs give corals a place to build. Slowly, other animals move in. The sunken rigs provide a place for coral and other organisms to live.

Bit by bit, these efforts are helping preserve ecosystems, both for the present and for the future.

✔ **How can people help make habitats for wildlife in their neighborhoods?**

▲ This osprey nest platform was made to replace natural nesting areas that are no longer available.

Planting one tree can provide a habitat for hundreds of animals some day. ▼

▲ People are building this flow control device to help preserve a natural wetland in Florida.

Summary

Ecosystems can be damaged when people use chemicals and clear land to meet human needs. People also can help repair or reclaim damaged ecosystems and help build new ones.

Review

1. How can chemicals used by farms and factories poison nearby waterways?

2. What are two ways people try to repair ecosystems?

3. How do people reuse land that once had railroad tracks on it?

4. **Critical Thinking** If all the rain forests were cut down, how would that affect people?

5. **Test Prep** About how much of Earth's rain forests have already been destroyed?

   A one-quarter

   B one-third

   C one-half

   D two-thirds

LINKS

MATH LINK

Measuring Growth Use historical maps to compare the area your home town took up 50 years ago to its area now. How has the area changed? How do you think any changes affected nearby ecosystems? Draw a simple map to organize and evaluate your information.

WRITING LINK

Informative Writing—Description Write a paragraph for a younger child. Describe an effect people have had on an ecosystem. Include ways plants and animals were affected.

HEALTH LINK

Farming Without Chemicals Some gardeners and farmers grow food without using poisonous chemicals. Find out about organic farming, as this practice is called. Make an oral report to the class. Tell one way organic gardeners control an insect pest and one way they add a nutrient to soil.

TECHNOLOGY LINK

Learn more about positive ecosystem changes by viewing *Artificial Reef* on the **Harcourt Science Newsroom Video.**

What Is Conservation?

In this lesson, you can . . .

 INVESTIGATE ways to save our national parks.

 LEARN ABOUT how to conserve resources.

 LINK to math, writing, technology, and other areas.

 **INVESTIGATE**

Using Our National Parks

Activity Purpose Each year thousands of people visit national parks in the United States. People can bring trash, noise, and other pollution into the parks. There are many opinions about how to balance the needs of park visitors and the needs of the park's living things. For example, a souvenir-shop owner might have a different opinion than a park ranger. In this investigation you and your classmates will discuss different opinions. Then you will decide how to use a national park.

Materials

■ 7 index cards
■ yarn
■ tape recorder or video camera (optional)

Activity Procedure

1 Work with six other students. Each member of your group should role-play one of the following people:

Ten-year-old park visitor
Scientist who studies park plants
Adult park visitor
Park ranger
Souvenir-shop owner
Local member of Congress
Reporter

2 Use the index cards and yarn to make a name tag for each group member. Use the names on the list in Step 1.

◀ After something is used, it doesn't have to be thrown away. This cowboy sculpture is made of car parts, garden hose, and other materials that many people would have thrown away.

3 Below are some questions about protecting national parks. Think about how the person you are role-playing views each question. Discuss the questions with your group. Work to agree on ways to help national parks. (Picture A)

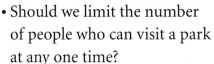
Picture A

- Should we limit the number of people who can visit a park at any one time?
- Should we make people park their cars outside the parks and have them use buses or trains instead?
- Should we reduce the number of restaurants, snack bars, shops, and gas stations in the parks?
- Should we limit activities that harm living things in the parks, such as hiking off marked trails?
- Should we spend more money to study how to preserve national parks?
- Should we provide money to educate people about the value of national parks and about ways to keep parks healthy?

4 Use a tape recorder or a video camera to record the discussion. Review the tape to make detailed notes.

Draw Conclusions

1. Based on your discussion, **record** one or more ways to protect our national parks. Everyone in the group should agree to each way. Give reasons to support each idea.

2. To make your final decision, did anyone have to give up something that he or she wanted? If so, what?

3. **Scientists at Work** Scientists **communicate** with one another to find out new ideas. Were you respectful of one another's ideas and opinions? Did too many people try to talk at once? How could your group communicate better?

Investigate Further Make a list of the solutions your group agreed to. Find out if any of the national parks have made or plan to make these changes.

Process Skill Tip

Communication is giving and receiving information. Sometimes the information is in the form of an opinion. To discuss opinions in a reasonable and fair way, everyone must be open to hearing what everyone else has to say.

Resource Conservation

Wise Use

People don't harm or change ecosystems on purpose. Ecosystems are changed as people use resources to help them meet their needs. For example, trees are cut down to provide furniture, paper, wood for buildings, and other things people need. Wetlands are drained to provide dry land for homes and towns. One way to do less harm to ecosystems is to use less of the natural resources they contain. The careful management and wise use of these natural resources are known as **conservation** (kahn•ser•VAY•shuhn).

Sometimes conservation is needed because a resource in an ecosystem has become scarce. For example, during periods of dry weather, communities may find that there is a shortage of clean water. Members of the community must find ways to use less water. Temporary laws must be passed to restrict when people can water their lawns or gardens. People may need to conserve water during activities such as bathing, brushing teeth, and washing clothes. The chart on this page shows ways people can change their personal habits and use less water.

Even when people conserve, they still use a lot of resources. After many items are used, they often are thrown away as trash. Important resources are thrown away with the trash. Finding ways to reduce the amount of trash helps save not only resources but whole ecosystems.

FIND OUT

- ways people can save natural resources
- how governments help protect ecosystems

VOCABULARY

conservation
preservation

Small changes in personal habits can add up to big savings of water. These changes saved almost half the water normally used for these tasks. ▶

Liters

600

317

0

without conservation   with conservation

Water Conservation Measures	
Habit Changed	**Water Saved**
Shower 5 minutes instead of 10 minutes.	95 L (25 gal)
Turn off tap while brushing teeth. Run water only to rinse.	24 L (9 gal)
Turn off tap while soaping hands instead of letting water run.	15 L (4 gal)
Run dishwasher on short cycle instead of full cycle.	24 L (9 gal)
Wash clothes using short cycle rather than full cycle.	125 L (33 gal)

▲ The bottom of a plastic soda bottle makes a perfect pot for a small plant.

Using products that have less packaging, or wrapping, reduces the amount of trash. For example, choose one large carton of juice instead of many small ones. Or choose an unwrapped bottle instead of a bottle in a box that is wrapped in plastic.

Recycling also reduces trash. People separate paper, glass, aluminum, and plastic from their trash. Companies use these materials to make new products. For example, glass is sorted by color, melted, and then made into new bottles.

Reusing products or their packaging is another way to help reduce the amount of trash. People can use old shopping bags to line trash cans or use empty plastic containers for storage. Reducing, reusing, and recycling can go a long way to conserve natural resources.

✔ **What is conservation?**

Aluminum cans are used over and over again to make new cans. ▼

This symbol is on most products that can be recycled. ▶

Materials that are thrown away can be reused in many projects. ▶

Protected Ecosystems

Some ecosystems are protected from change by limits on their use. The protection of an area is called **preservation** (prez•er•VAY•shuhn). Governments help preserve ecosystems by making laws and setting up protected areas. Some of these areas are made into national parks and national forests.

The United States has 54 national parks. In the investigation, you saw that not everyone agrees on how the parks should be used. Park rangers and park workers teach visitors about natural features of the parks. Park rangers also help keep living things in the parks safe.

To help watch the effects of people on ecosystems, the United States government set up the Environmental Protection Agency (EPA). EPA employees make sure people and businesses obey laws that protect the environment.

✔ **How does preservation help an ecosystem?**

▲ In protected national forests certain trees may be tagged to show they can be cut down, or logged. Cutting only tagged trees helps keep the forest healthy.

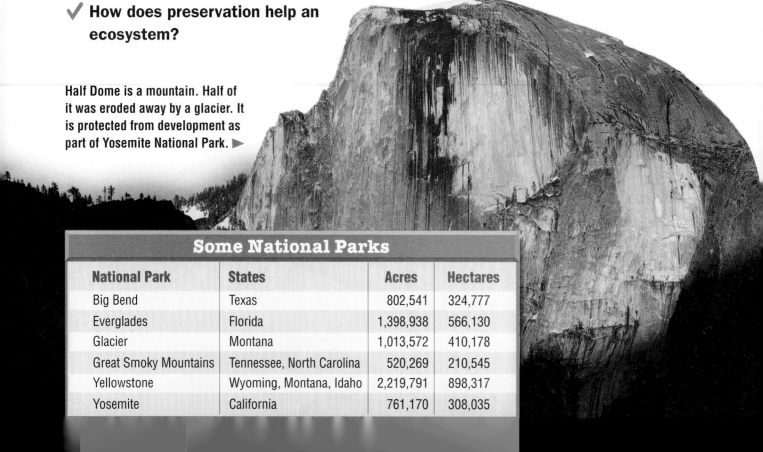

Half Dome is a mountain. Half of it was eroded away by a glacier. It is protected from development as part of Yosemite National Park. ▶

Some National Parks			
National Park	**States**	**Acres**	**Hectares**
Big Bend	Texas	802,541	324,777
Everglades	Florida	1,398,938	566,130
Glacier	Montana	1,013,572	410,178
Great Smoky Mountains	Tennessee, North Carolina	520,269	210,545
Yellowstone	Wyoming, Montana, Idaho	2,219,791	898,317
Yosemite	California	761,170	308,035

▲ This EPA inspector tests water for chemicals that could harm the environment or its inhabitants, including people.

Summary

People can conserve natural resources by reducing their use, and by recycling and reusing materials. Governments help conserve by setting up protected areas, laws, and agencies that preserve the environment.

Review

1. What are three ways you can use less water?

2. What are three materials that can be recycled?

3. How has government helped protect the environment?

4. **Critical Thinking** How does using a shoe box to store letters and pictures help protect the environment?

5. **Test Prep** Protecting an area by making it a park is a form of —

   A conservation

   B preservation

   C reservation

   D reclamation

LINKS

MATH LINK

Conservation Suppose a person used just 75 fewer gallons of water each day for one month. How much water would that person save? What are some ways the water might be conserved?

WRITING LINK

Informative Writing—Explanation Suppose you can send letters to students living 50 years in the past and 50 years in the future. What good and bad things would you explain to the students in each time period about conservation and the environment today? Plan and write the letters.

SOCIAL STUDIES LINK

National Parks Select a national park, and prepare a report. Find out where it is located, when it was established, and how large it is. Describe some of its natural or scientific features.

TECHNOLOGY LINK

Learn more about conservation and other chapter topics by visiting this Internet site.

www.scilinks.org/harcourt

Healing the ENVIRONMENT with Plants

Most people believe that planting a tree is a good thing. Trees give shade and decorate the land. Their roots prevent soil erosion. Now some trees are being useful in a new way. They are cleaning up toxic waste in land and water.

Phytoremediation

A process called *phytoremediation* (FYT•oh•rih•mee•dee•ay•shuhn) is the use of plants to heal the environment. Dr. Ilya Raskin of Rutgers University first used this term. For many years, people have used plants to change ecosystems. For example, trees and grasses have been used to help dry up swamps. Removing harmful substances from soil or water is a *new* use. Scientists have found that plants can absorb many harmful substances from soil. These include metals, pesticides, explosives, and crude oil.

A stand of poplar trees in the wild

The Popular Poplar

Yellow poplars are fast-growing trees. They grow about 4 meters (15 ft) taller each year. Poplars can take in a large amount of water. One poplar tree can take in 95–113 liters (25–30 gal) of liquid per day.

Poplars can help soil that has been harmed by toxic, or poisonous, chemicals. The roots of the poplar tree take in the chemicals. The chemicals are broken down within the tree. Some of the materials are released into the air in less toxic forms. Some stay in the tree. When the tree becomes filled up with hazardous materials, it can be cut down and burned safely. The ashes that are left take up little space.

One other way to clean up toxic soil is to scrape it away and put it in a landfill. Nothing can grow on this land afterward. But poplars put nutrients back into the soil. After some time the soil can be used again. Planting trees is also less expensive than some other ways to clean up water or soil.

Testing, Testing

Scientists have shown that poplar trees "work" in a laboratory. They are finding out how well they work in a natural setting. One big test for poplar phytoremediation is taking place in southern Oregon. In 1984 a truck carrying a toxic substance had an accident. For more than 13 years, people tried to clean up the poisoned water in the area. Finally, scientists planted 800 poplar trees there. Poplars are also being used to clean up toxic areas in Iowa, Utah, and Maryland.

Unanswered Questions

Scientists still are trying to learn if the wastes released by the trees pollute the air. Also, scientists want to know if the trees add harmful materials to the food chain. For example, what happens when small animals eat the leaves of the trees? One group of scientists found what may be good news: Insects that normally eat poplars would *not* eat the trees that take in harmful chemicals.

Other plants also are being tested for use in phytoremediation. These include grasses, juniper trees, clover, and duckweed. Some day we may know about many plants that remove poisons from ecosystems.

Think About It

1. What might be some of the problems of phytoremediation?
2. What other benefit might there be from planting large numbers of trees at a cleanup site?

WEB LINK:
For Science and Technology updates, visit the Harcourt Internet site.
www.harcourtschool.com

Careers — Bioremediation Specialist

What They Do Bioremediation specialists may do experiments on plants in a laboratory. They may work with soil scientists, chemists, and other scientists to solve pollution problems. Bioremediation specialists may also work in polluted areas, advising people who run businesses or farms.

Education and Training People who do this kind of work have a college degree in botany or another science field.

Ruth Patrick

LIMNOLOGIST

"I couldn't believe the world in there . . . a whole world of little animals that only I knew about."

These words describe Dr. Ruth Patrick's first experience as a small child looking into her father's microscope. Frank Patrick gave his daughter her first microscope when she was seven years old. He encouraged both Ruth and her sister to study science. Ruth and her father both liked to study diatoms, single-celled organisms that live in ponds, lakes, and rivers. She became a limnologist (lim•NAHL•uh•jist), a scientist who studies freshwater lakes and streams.

After receiving a college degree, Patrick went on to study at the University of Virginia. While there, she studied the Dismal Swamp. She then moved to Philadelphia with her husband. This was during the Depression, when jobs were hard to find, especially for women. She volunteered at the Academy of Natural Sciences. She remained there for her entire career but didn't get paid for the first ten years! She also taught college courses and wrote books and articles.

Dr. Patrick put together teams of people to study rivers, lakes, and streams. Some people on a team looked for harmful substances in the water. Others studied fish and water animals. Some scientists on a team studied only snails, clams, insects, or algae. Often businesses or the government invited a team to spend about ten days studying the water in an area.

The work of Ruth Patrick and her teams helped businesses avoid harming freshwater resources. She was among the first scientists to study many parts of an environment at once. She helped to make water resources cleaner and safer.

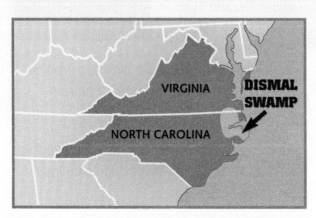

THINK ABOUT IT

1. Ruth Patrick has spoken out to protect rivers. What are the parts of nature that you care deeply about and would like to protect?
2. Why do you think Patrick used large teams of scientists to study water?

Water Quality

How does water quality vary?

Materials

- 4 small, clear plastic jars with lids
- plastic gloves
- masking tape
- permanent marker

Procedure

1. With an adult's help, carefully collect a jarful of water from four different natural sources.

CAUTION Wear gloves to collect the samples. Do not drink water from natural sources. Be sure to wash your hands.

2. On each jar, put a label that tells where it was collected. Describe each ecosystem.

3. Observe the samples. Are there any unusual colors or smells? Shake each sample. Does it foam? How long does the foam last?

Draw Conclusions

Which water appears to be the cleanest? How do you know? What can you infer about water quality and the overall health of each ecosystem?

Making Paper

How can recycled newspapers be made into new paper?

Materials

- 2 plastic tubs
- water
- old newspaper
- measuring cup
- blender
- wooden spoon
- clean cotton cloths
- wire screen
- plastic wrap
- several heavy books

Procedure

1. Fill a tub about one-third full of water. Add a section of newspaper that has been cut into strips. Soak it for a day.

2. Put two cups of wet paper into the blender. Add six cups of water. Tightly put the lid on the blender. Blend until the mixture looks like runny oatmeal. Pour it into the clean tub.

3. Repeat Step 2 until the clean tub is about one-fourth full. Mix the material.

4. Lay a cloth on a flat waterproof surface. Slide the wire screen under the wet paper. Then pick up the screen. Press the wet newspaper to squeeze out any extra water.

5. Carefully flip the screen onto the cloth. Press it down firmly. Remove the screen.

6. Lay another cloth on top of the mixture. Cover the cloth with plastic wrap, and stack the books on the wrap.

7. After several hours, remove the books and cloth and let the paper dry.

Draw Conclusions

How does your paper compare with new paper?

Chapter 3 Review and Test Preparation

Vocabulary Review

Use the terms below to complete the sentences. The page numbers in ( ) tell you where to look in the chapter if you need help.

succession (B70) **conservation** (B86)
reclamation (B81) **preservation** (B88)

1. The United States government helped in the ____ of ecosystems by setting aside national parks.

2. When the community in an ecosystem changes over time, the process is known as ____.

3. The ____ of a strip mine can make a new habitat for wildlife.

4. When people use resources wisely, they are practicing ____.

Connect Concepts

Use the terms in the Word Bank to fill in the chart. It summarizes what happens as a pond changes into a forest through the process of succession.

cattails   marsh   nutrients   soil
forest   meadow   pond   stable
grasses   mosses   small plants   trees
lichens

Pond Succession		
Stages of Pond Succession	**Plant Life**	**Changes to the Ecosystem**
5. _____	9.–10. ____ and ____ grow on rock around the pond.	16. ____ is washed into the pond.
	11. ____ grow in soil that builds up on the bottom of the pond.	17. Bacteria and algae are blown or washed into the pond, increasing the amount of ____ in the pond.
6. _____	12. ____ grow in the shallow water of the marsh.	Soil continues to fill in the pond.
7. _____	13. ____ cover the areas where the pond was.	Seeds of bushes and trees are blown into the area and begin to grow.
8. _____	14.–15. ____ grow and form a ____.	18. The ecosystem is ____ unless the trees are cut.

Check Understanding

Write the letter of the best choice.

19. If a hurricane were to destroy the habitat for plants along the coast, new plants would grow. This process is called —
    A erosion
    B conservation
    C plantation
    D succession

20. As plants and animals die in a marsh, their remains add to the marsh's —
    F air   H meadow
    G nutrients   J populations

21. A new aluminum can made from used cans is an example of —
    A recycling   C reusing
    B reducing   D repairing

22. Where would you probably find a lake that is protected by law from any fishing?
    F a national park
    G private land
    H a farm field
    J a recreation area

23. Which of the following is an example of water conservation?
    A watering the plants
    B mowing the lawn
    C turning off the lights
    D taking short showers

24. Damage can result to nearby water ecosystems if factory pipes carrying _____ leak into a stream.
    F waste oxygen
    G carbon dioxide
    H poisonous chemicals
    J drinking water

Critical Thinking

25. Why do you think governments help protect the environment?

26. A strip mine from which all the minerals have been removed cannot be returned to its natural state. Instead, the land is reshaped for different uses. A pond, trees, and pathways are added. How could people use this reclaimed area?

Process Skills Review

27. You are driving with your family through a national forest. You find a place that has several marked trees standing and other marked trees that have been cut down. From these observations, what can you **infer** is happening?

28. In the second investigation, you found that filters removed the suds from water containing detergent but did not remove the detergent itself. If you shook the sample of polluted water again, how do you think it would **compare** to your first observations? Why?

29. How can you **communicate** to your family ways to recycle?

Performance Assessment

Conserve It!

Work with a partner. Together, brainstorm ways to conserve resources in your classroom. Make a plan for your classroom for conserving resources and reducing waste by recycling and reusing materials. Write down your plan.

Unit Project Wrap Up

Here are some ideas for ways to wrap up your unit project.

Publish a Guide
Write a travel guide to your ecosystem. Add illustrations, maps, charts, and graphs to help communicate the information you've gathered.

Make a Display
Display drawings, photographs, and small models of ecosystems in your state. Describe how the ecosystems are different from each other.

Write a Story
Choose one animal that lives in your ecosystem. Write a story about how the animal uses living and nonliving things to survive in its environment.

Investigate Further
How could you make your project better? What other questions do you have about ecosystems? Plan ways to find answers to your questions. Use the Science Handbook on pages R2-R9 for help.

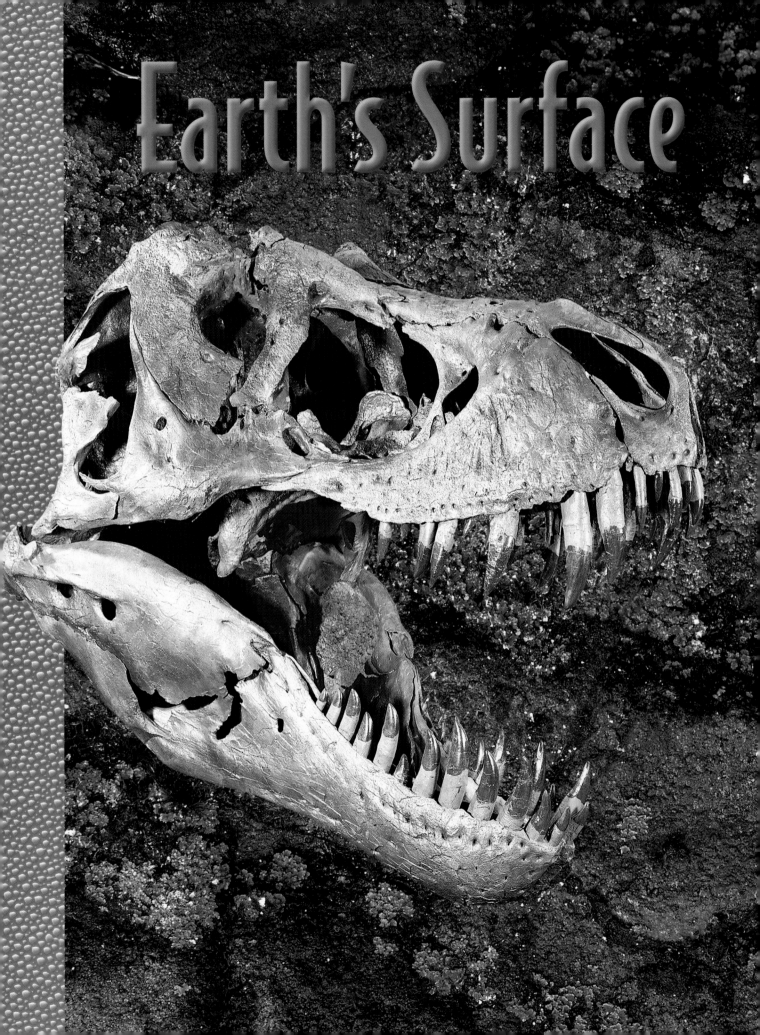

Earth's Surface

UNIT C

Earth's Surface

Unit Project

Earth-Sample Collection

Collect samples of rocks, minerals, and fossils in your area. Record where you find each sample. Plan ways to sort, identify, and label the samples in your collection. Use reference materials to make notes about your samples. Find out what the samples show about the geology of your community.

Chapter 1

Earthquakes and Volcanoes

Earth is a planet that is always changing. When Earth's crust moves, earthquakes occur and volcanoes erupt. While both can be dangerous and scary, they are also natural Earth processes that have shaped the surface of our world.

Vocabulary Preview

crust
mantle
core
plates
earthquake
fault
focus
epicenter
seismograph
volcano
magma
lava
vent
magma chamber
crater

⫶⫶FAST FACT

One day in 1943 the volcano Paricutín appeared in a farmer's field in Mexico. Six days later it was 150 meters (500 ft) high and still growing! Eventually it covered an entire town including this building!

LESSON **1**

What Are the Layers of the Earth?

In this lesson, you can . . .

 INVESTIGATE the layers of the Earth.

 LEARN ABOUT how huge pieces of Earth's crust and mantle act on each other.

 LINK to math, writing, literature, and technology.

The Layers of the Earth

Activity Purpose Have you ever wondered what the inside of Earth looks like? It is not possible to cut Earth in half, but scientists know that our planet is made up of several layers. In this investigation you will **measure** how thick the parts of an apple are. Then you will compare them with Earth's layers.

Materials
- half of an apple
- metric ruler

Activity Procedure

1 **Observe** the apple half carefully. Draw a picture of this piece of the apple. Show its layers. (Picture A)

2 A thin peel covers the outside of the apple. Use the ruler to **measure** the thickness of the peel. **Record** your measurement on your drawing.

3 The thick, white part that you eat is the middle of the apple. **Measure** the thickness of this layer. **Record** your measurement on your drawing. (Picture B)

◀ Giant slabs, or pieces, of Earth's crust and mantle collided, or hit each other, to produce the spectacular Himalaya (him•uh•LAY•uh) Mountains.

Picture A

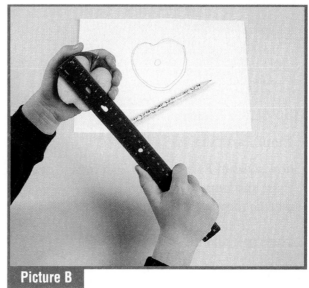

Picture B

4 Deep inside the apple is the core. **Measure** the core, starting at the center of the apple. **Record** your measurement on your drawing.

5 Like the apple, Earth has three layers. The crust is Earth's outside layer. The mantle is the thick, middle layer of Earth. Deep inside Earth is the core. Work with a partner to explain which parts of the apple are like the core, mantle, and crust of Earth.

Draw Conclusions

1. **Use numbers** to **compare** the layers of the apple. Which layer is the thinnest?

2. Which of Earth's layers is most like the apple peel? Explain your answer.

3. **Scientists at Work** Scientists use many kinds of tools to **measure** objects and their characteristics. How did using a ruler help you describe the apple's layers?

Investigate Further Use a small gum ball, modeling clay, and colored plastic wrap to make a cut-away model of Earth's layers. Which material will you use to stand for the core? Which material should you use to stand for the crust? For the mantle?

Process Skill Tip

Scientists use tools such as rulers, scales, and balances to make measurements. You can **measure** using standard units. The numbers you get from measuring can be more useful than words for talking about an object.

Earth's Structure

Earth's Layers

Earth is made up of three layers. As you learned in the investigation, these layers are the crust, the mantle, and the core.

Earth's **crust** is the layer we can walk on. The crust includes the rock of the ocean floor and large areas of land called continents (KAHN•tuh•nuhnts). Asia is the largest continent, followed by Africa, North America, South America, Antarctica, Europe, and Australia. The United States is on the continent of North America.

Below the crust is the **mantle** (MAN•tuhl). It is the thickest layer of the planet. Most of the mantle is solid rock. Some of this layer, though, is partly melted. This partly melted rock flows slowly like a very thick liquid.

Deep inside Earth is the **core** (KOHR). The core is a dense ball made mostly of two metals, iron and nickel.

✔ **What are Earth's layers?**

FIND OUT

- about Earth's layers
- how slabs of Earth's crust and upper mantle move

VOCABULARY

crust
mantle
core
plate

We live on Earth's crust. The crust under the continents is much thicker than the crust under the oceans. ▼

Inside the Earth

Earth's core can be divided into two layers. The *inner core* is a solid ball made mostly of iron and nickel. It is the hottest layer of Earth. It may be as hot as the surface of the sun. Earth's *outer core* is a pool of hot, liquid metal.

Parts of Earth's *mantle* are solid rock. Other parts of this thick layer are partly melted and can flow like a very thick liquid.

Earth's *crust* is the outer layer of the planet. The crust is made of rocks and soil. You live on Earth's crust. Crust also forms the ocean floors.

✔ **Which of Earth's layers is the thickest?**

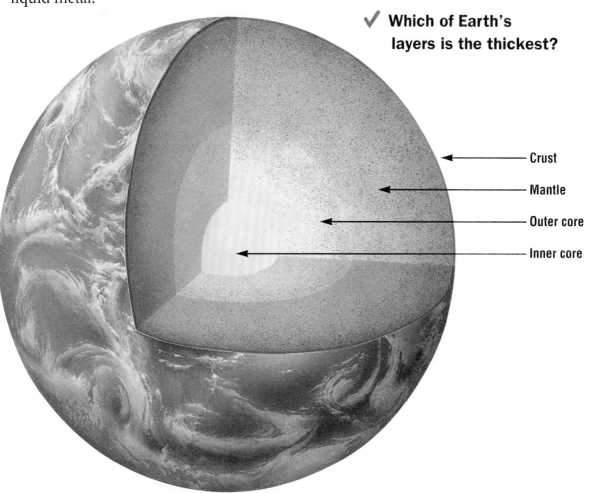

- Crust
- Mantle
- Outer core
- Inner core

Thickness of Earth's Layers

Inner Core 1216 kilometers (about 750 mi)

Outer Core 2270 kilometers (about 1410 mi)

Mantle 2885 kilometers (about 1790 mi)

Crust 5–70 kilometers (about 3–43 mi)

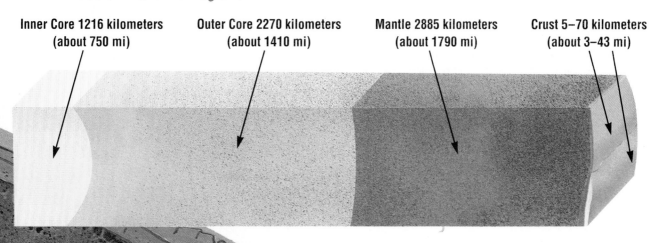

How Plates Move

Earth's crust and upper mantle are broken into continent-sized slabs called **plates**. Plates move very slowly across Earth's surface on a thin layer of partly melted mantle. Most plates move only a few centimeters a year, or about the same length your fingernails grow each year. Plates can move away from each other, toward each other, or past each other.

Look at the top picture on the right. It shows two plates moving away from each other. This type of plate motion usually happens on ocean floors. New ocean-floor crust forms where the plates move apart. A long chain of mountains called the Mid-Atlantic Ridge runs along the ocean floor in the middle of the Atlantic Ocean. It formed where two plates of Earth's crust are moving apart.

The middle picture shows plates moving toward each other. Mountains form when plates come together. Sometimes one plate is pushed below the other plate. This can form volcanoes. At other times the plates meet like cars in a slow-motion, head-on crash. The material on the plates wrinkles and forms high mountains. The Himalaya Mountains of Asia formed in this way. Because the plates are still moving, the mountains continue to grow a little taller each year.

The bottom picture shows plates moving past each other. The rocks along the crack between the plates stick and then move suddenly. This can cause earthquakes. This kind of plate movement happens along the San Andreas fault in California.

✓ **What are three ways plates move?**

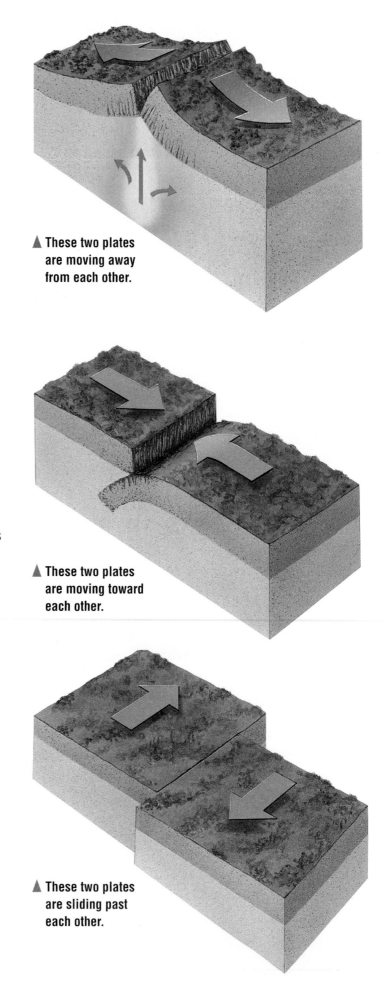

▲ These two plates are moving away from each other.

▲ These two plates are moving toward each other.

▲ These two plates are sliding past each other.

▲ Iceland is slowly being split into two pieces. A large crack, or rift, is forming as two of Earth's plates move away from each other.

Summary

Earth is made up of three layers. The crust is the outer layer of Earth. The mantle is the middle layer. The inner layer of Earth is the core. Earth's crust and upper mantle are broken into giant plates that move very slowly.

Review

1. What are the three layers of Earth?
2. Which layers of Earth make up plates?
3. Describe the three ways plates can move.
4. **Critical Thinking** Why do you think volcanoes may form when one plate is pushed under another?
5. **Test Prep** On which of Earth's layers are the continents?
   - **A** crust
   - **B** mantle
   - **C** outer core
   - **D** ocean floor

LINKS

MATH LINK

Rate of Plate Movement If two of Earth's plates that are touching one another are moving apart at a rate of 3 cm per year, how long will it take for the plates to be 12 cm apart?

WRITING LINK

Expressive Writing—Poem Write a poem for a younger child using the letters in the word *Earth*. Begin the first line of the poem with a word that starts with *E*. Start the second line of the poem using the letter *A*, and so on. Include facts about Earth's layers in your poem.

LITERATURE LINK

The Magic School Bus Inside the Earth What if you were taking a trip to the center of the Earth? Compare and contrast each layer of the planet. Now read *The Magic School Bus Inside the Earth* by Joanna Cole. How does Ms. Frizzle's trip compare to yours?

TECHNOLOGY LINK

Learn more about Earth's plates by visiting the Smithsonian National Air and Space Museum Internet site.
www.si.edu/harcourt/science

 Smithsonian Institution®

What Causes Earthquakes?

In this lesson, you can . . .

 INVESTIGATE the shaking of Earth caused by moving plates.

 LEARN ABOUT why earthquakes occur.

 LINK to math, writing, technology, and other areas.

INVESTIGATE

Earthquakes

Activity Purpose What happens when you snap your fingers? First, you put your middle finger against your thumb. As you press your finger and thumb together and try to move one past the other, they stick for a moment. When the fingers come apart, your middle finger hits your palm. This causes the air to vibrate, or shake. You hear a snap. In this investigation you will **make a model** of something like a finger snap. You'll show how Earth's plates sometimes stick and then move past each other, making Earth's crust vibrate.

Materials

- 3-in. × 5-in. self-stick note
- small plastic cup
- water

Activity Procedure

1. Stick the self-stick note to a table. Be sure that about 1 in. of the short side of the self-stick note is hanging over the edge of the table. (Picture A) Also make sure the self-stick note is firmly stuck in place.

◄ An earthquake can destroy a city in seconds.

Picture A

Picture B

2 Fill the cup $\frac{1}{4}$ full with water. Place the cup on the center part of the self-stick note that is on the table.

3 Carefully and firmly pull the self-stick note straight out from under the cup. (Picture B) The sticky part of the note will stop you from easily pulling it all the way out. **Observe** what happens to the water.

Draw Conclusions

1. How is snapping your fingers like the movement of the self-stick note?

2. What did you **observe** about the water in the cup when you pulled on the self-stick note?

3. **Scientists at Work** Scientists often **infer** things based on their observations. What can you infer might happen when plates are moving past one another if the pressure between the plates is suddenly changed?

Investigate Further Use two 3-in. × 5-in. self-stick notes to model two plates sticking. Bend the notes so that the sticky parts face each other. Touch the sticky parts together and slide one note past the other. How does the shape of the note papers change? How do they move?

Earthquakes and How They Are Measured

How Earthquakes Occur

In the investigation, you made a model of an earthquake. An **earthquake** (ERTH•kwayk) is a vibration, or shaking, of Earth's crust. Most earthquakes occur along faults. A **fault** in the crust is a break along which rocks move. Rocks on either side of a fault can move up and down, side to side, or both.

Many earthquakes happen where plates are moving past each other. Sometimes the rocks along a fault get stuck and don't move for a while. But the plates are still moving and causing pressure on the rocks. When the pressure builds up enough, the rocks break and the plates move suddenly. This releases, or sets free, the built-up energy in the form of vibrations that move through Earth's crust. You made a model of this sticking and slipping in the investigation. When the self-stick note that stood for the rocks moved, you saw the released energy cause vibrations in the water in the cup.

FIND OUT

• what causes earthquakes

• how earthquakes are measured

VOCABULARY

earthquake
fault
focus
epicenter
seismograph

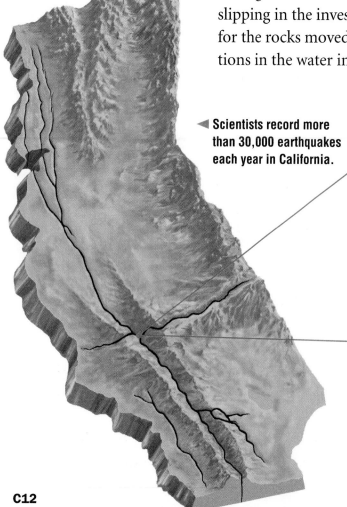

◄ Scientists record more than 30,000 earthquakes each year in California.

▲ The San Andreas fault is two plates sliding past each other. This fault runs through most of California and is about 1000 kilometers (610 mi) long.

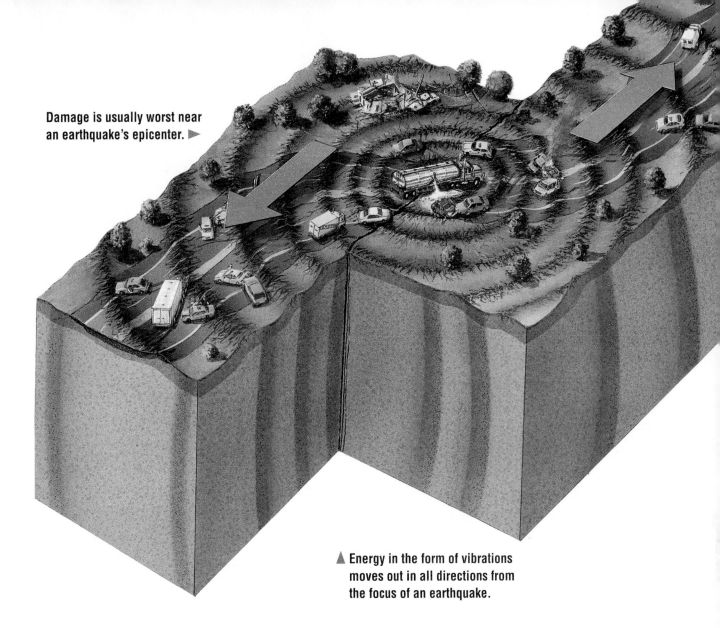

Damage is usually worst near an earthquake's epicenter. ▶

▲ Energy in the form of vibrations moves out in all directions from the focus of an earthquake.

The picture above shows two plates sliding past each other. These two plates had been stuck, but they recently moved, and an earthquake occurred. The point underground where the movement first took place is called the **focus** (FOH•kuhs). When rocks slip at the focus, energy moves out in all directions through the rock around it. Damage from the vibrations caused by this release of energy is usually centered around the epicenter. The **epicenter** (EP•ih•sent•er) is the point on the surface that is right above the focus.

Earthquakes such as the one in the picture happen often along the San Andreas fault. Dozens of major earthquakes have occurred along this well-known fault. In 1906 an earthquake caused fires that burned down most of the city of San Francisco. The 1989 Loma Prieta (LOH•muh pree•AY•tuh) earthquake postponed the third game of the World Series. That earthquake caused about $6 billion in damage. In 1994 the Northridge earthquake caused parts of the crust in Los Angeles to move 20 centimeters (about 8 in.). More than 3000 homes were destroyed. Ten highway bridges and seven concrete parking garages fell down. The total damage was more than $20 billion.

✔ **What causes an earthquake?**

How Earthquakes Are Measured

You saw in the investigation how the water rippled as the self-stick note was pulled from under the cup. The ripples, or waves, traveled through the water. In the same way, the energy from an earthquake travels as waves through the Earth. Scientists can measure this energy in different ways.

A **seismograph** (SYZ•muh•graf) is an instrument that records earthquake waves. A seismograph has two main parts: a pen and a paper-covered rotating drum. As the drum turns, the pen marks a line. When an earthquake happens, the line gets jagged. The more jagged the line, the stronger the earthquake is.

Scientists also use numbers to measure earthquakes. The Mercalli (muhr•KAH•lee) scale measures the movement and damage that an earthquake causes. The scale uses Roman numerals from I to XII. An earthquake measuring III on this scale makes

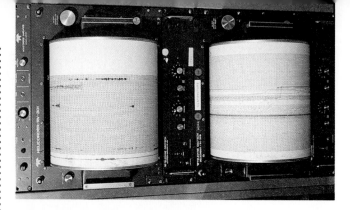

▲ Earthquake watching stations usually have many seismographs like this one.

hanging objects swing back and forth. An earthquake measuring X on this scale causes brick buildings to crumble.

You are probably more familiar with the Richter (RIK•tuhr) scale. This scale uses the numbers 1 through 9 to measure the energy an earthquake releases. An earthquake measuring 3.0 on the Richter scale releases 30 times the amount of energy as an earthquake measuring 2.0. It releases 900 times the energy of an earthquake measuring 1.0.

✔ **What are two scales that scientists use to measure earthquakes?**

Mercalli Scale

The stronger the earthquake, the bigger the waves recorded on a seismograph.

Mercalli scale III: A hanging lamp swings. (about Richter scale 2.0)

Mercalli scale V: Bricks or plaster may fall. (about Richter scale 4.0 to 5.0)

Mercalli scale VII: Brick structures are damaged. (about Richter scale 6.0)

Summary

A fault in Earth's crust is a break along which rocks move. An earthquake is the vibrations produced when energy builds up and is quickly released along a fault. Scientists use the Mercalli scale and the Richter scale to measure earthquake intensity.

Review

1. What causes an earthquake?
2. What is a fault?
3. How do scientists measure the damage caused by an earthquake?
4. **Critical Thinking** Why are there so many earthquakes in California?
5. **Test Prep** What is the point below Earth's surface where an earthquake begins?
   - **A** epicenter
   - **B** focus
   - **C** fault
   - **D** core

Mercalli scale X: Buildings are severely damaged. (about Richter scale 7.0)

LINKS

MATH LINK

Earthquake Time Line Research some of the most damaging earthquakes in history. Make a time line showing the order in which they occurred. Include the Richter scale value if it is available.

WRITING LINK

Expressive Writing — Friendly Letter Suppose you have survived an earthquake. For a younger student, write a letter that describes what causes an earthquake or how an earthquake affects buildings. Use at least three of the terms from this lesson.

HEALTH LINK

Earthquake Safety Use library references to find out how to stay safe during an earthquake. Make a poster that shows what you found.

DRAMA LINK

Earthquakes in Movies Find a movie or play about an earthquake or a prediction of an earthquake. Describe how such events affect the characters.

TECHNOLOGY LINK

To learn more about predicting earthquake damage watch *Quake Liquid Soils* on the **Harcourt Science Newsroom Video.**

How Do Volcanoes Form?

In this lesson, you can . . .

 INVESTIGATE how a volcano erupts.

 LEARN ABOUT how volcanoes form.

 LINK to math, writing, social studies, and technology.

◄ Some volcanoes look like fountains when they shoot molten rock into the air.

 **INVESTIGATE**

Volcanic Eruptions

Activity Purpose Have you ever had a balloon pop because you filled it with too much air? If so, you now know that balloons can stand only a certain amount of pressure before they pop. In this investigation you will **make a model** that shows what happens when pressure builds up in a volcano.

Materials

- 1-L plastic bottle
- small piece of modeling clay
- aluminum pie plate
- puffed rice cereal or tiny pieces of plastic foam
- funnel
- air pump

Activity Procedure

1. Ask your teacher to make a hole near the bottom of the bottle. Use the clay to stick the bottom of the bottle to the pie plate. (Picture A)

2. Use the funnel to fill the bottle $\frac{1}{4}$ full with the rice cereal or foam.

Picture A

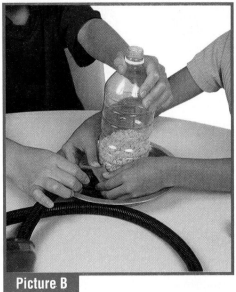

Picture B

3 Attach the air pump to the hole in the bottle. Put a piece of clay around the hole to seal it. (Picture B)

4 Pump air into the bottle. **Observe** what happens.

Draw Conclusions

1. What happened to the cereal when you pumped air into the bottle?

2. How could you make more cereal shoot out of the bottle?

3. **Scientists at Work** Scientists often **make a model** to help them understand things that happen in nature. How is the bottle used to model an erupting volcano?

Investigate Further Some volcanoes have steep sides. Others have gently sloping sides. Use some fine sand and some gravel to **make a model** of each of these two kinds of volcanoes. Make a pile of sand. Do the same with the gravel. Which model has steeper sides? How are the sand and gravel piles like volcanoes? How are they unlike volcanoes?

> **Process Skill Tip**
>
> When it is too difficult or impossible to observe something, scientists sometimes **make a model**. This helps them better understand the way things work.

Volcanoes

How Volcanoes Form

VOCABULARY

volcano
magma
lava
vent
magma chamber
crater

A **volcano** is a mountain that forms when red-hot melted rock flows through a crack onto the earth's surface. Melted rock inside Earth is called **magma** (MAG•muh). Melted rock that reaches Earth's surface is called **lava** (LAH•vuh).

Some volcanoes form in the ocean where plates are moving away from each other. As the plates move apart, magma slowly rises toward the surface from deep in the mantle. When the magma gets to the surface, it cools and hardens to form new ocean floor.

Other volcanoes form where plates are moving toward each other. When a plate made of ocean crust collides with, or hits, one made of continental crust, the plate made of ocean crust is forced down into the mantle. There it partly melts. The magma rises toward the surface through a rocky tube called a **vent** to form volcanic mountains. The volcanic mountains in the Andes in South America and in the Cascade Range in the northwestern United States formed this way.

Some volcanoes form when a plate moves over a hot spot in the mantle. Fountains of hot rock punch through the crust to form volcanoes. The volcanic islands of Hawai'i formed this way.

✓ **What are three ways volcanoes form?**

When plates collide, one plate may be forced down into the mantle. Deep inside Earth, the plate material melts to form magma. ▼

Magma rises to Earth's surface through volcanoes. ▶

C18

Types of Volcanoes

Not every volcano erupts in the same way. Some shoot runny lava high in the air. Others ooze lava like soft-serve ice cream coming out of a machine. Part of what erupts from some other volcanoes is lava chunks that have already hardened into rock. Each type of eruption forms a different type of mountain.

Shield volcanoes are large mountains with gentle slopes. They form from runny lava. Many of the volcanoes in Hawai'i are shield volcanoes. One of the largest is Mauna Loa on the main island of Hawai'i. Mauna Loa rises 9000 meters (about 30,000 ft) from the ocean floor.

Cinder cone volcanoes are small volcanoes made of hardened lava chunks called cinders. Cinder cones have steep sides. They are usually less than 300 meters (about 1000 ft) tall.

Composite (kahm•PAHZ•it) *volcanoes* are medium-sized mountains. They are made up of layers of lava that alternate with layers of cinders. These mountains have steep peaks and gently sloping sides. Mount Fuji (FOO•jee) in Japan, Mount Pelée (PEH•lay) on the island of Martinque (mahr•tuh•NEEK), and Mount Vesuvius (veh•SOO•vee•uhs) in Italy are composite volcanoes.

✔ **Why don't all volcanic mountains look the same?**

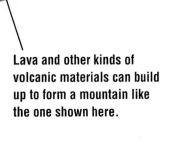

Magma rises toward the surface through a rocky tube called a vent.

Lava and other kinds of volcanic materials can build up to form a mountain like the one shown here.

A **magma chamber** is an underground pool that holds hot magma.

Volcanoes Build

You have learned that some volcanoes form where slabs of Earth's crust and upper mantle are moving away from each other. Where this happens, magma flows from the magma chamber toward the crust. When it reaches the crust, the magma flows through a large crack in the ocean floor. As it cools and hardens, new ocean floor forms.

Volcanic eruptions also form new crust on continents. The mountains discussed on page C19 are examples of land added to the continents.

Crater Lake, which is shown on this page, is also an example of how volcanoes add to Earth's landscape. This landform is what is left of an eruption in southern Oregon about 7000 years ago.

Although volcanic eruptions are often harmful, they can have good effects on the land around them. The soil around an active volcano often has minerals that help crops

THE INSIDE STORY

The Formation of Crater Lake

A large basin, or crater (KRAY•ter), formed at the top of the volcano when it fell in on itself after the eruption. Over time, this basin filled with rainwater to form a lake. Crater Lake is about 10 kilometers (about 6 mi) in diameter and nearly 600 meters (almost 2000 ft) deep.

2. The eruption was so powerful that it left the magma chamber below the volcano almost empty. Later, a much smaller eruption formed an island called Wizard Island.

1. Seven thousand years ago, Mount Mazama, the volcano that became Crater Lake, exploded with violent force.

grow. As volcanic rock is changed by water flowing over it, minerals are added to the soil. For example, many types of plants grow in the soils surrounding the slopes of Mount Vesuvius in Italy. Fruits and vegetables grow well in the soils near the bottom of the mountain. Hardwood trees grow well in soils on the slopes that formed from the lava.

✓ **Name two ways volcanoes build the land.**

In 1707 Mount Fuji in Honshu, Japan, erupted. The eruption sent out about a cubic kilometer of dust, ash, and rock. ▼

3. The top of the mountain fell into the empty magma chamber, leaving a crater.

4. Long after the volcano erupted, rainwater filled the crater to form a large lake. Today, Crater Lake is one of Oregon's most popular places. It is the United States's fifth oldest national park.

▲ The volcanoes in Hawai'i erupt quietly but often blanket the ground with lava.

▲ Volcanoes have destroyed property by spraying ash over houses and other buildings.

Volcanoes Destroy

The lava and gases that erupt from volcanoes are very hot and often destroy everything in their path. When Mount St. Helens in Washington State erupted in 1980, the temperature of the ash and gases reached about 800°C (1470°F)! The blast blew down trees as far as 25 kilometers (about 15 mi) from the volcano. At least 60 people died because of this volcanic explosion. The clouds of ash and gases were so thick that some of these people died because they couldn't breathe.

In 1983 Colo volcano on the Indonesian island of Una Una erupted. Scientists there had warned people of the possible danger. All of the 7000 people who lived in the area left their homes and went to safe places.

Deadly Volcanic Eruptions		
Year	Volcano	Fatalities
1792	Unzen, Japan	About 14,500 people lost their lives, mainly from the tsunami (wave) caused by the eruption.
1815	Tambora, Indonesia	About 92,000 people died, mainly from starvation.
1902	Mount Pelée, Martinique	About 28,000 people lost their lives, mainly because of the ash cloud.
1980	Mount St. Helens, Washington	About 60 people were killed. Scientists had predicted the eruption and warned people to leave.
1991	Mount Pinatubo, Philippines	More than 700 people lost their lives, mainly from the heavy fall of ash.

◀ An explosion of ash, rock, and gases from a volcano often kills everything in its path. These trees were flattened by the eruption of Mount St. Helens in 1980.

When the volcano erupted, houses, crops, livestock, and nearly everything else in the area were destroyed. But no people died.

✔ **What are some harmful effects of volcanoes?**

Summary

A volcano is a mountain that forms when melted rock called lava flows out onto Earth's surface. Most volcanoes form along plate edges. Volcanic eruptions add crust to the Earth and can be harmful. Lava flows can make soils rich in minerals that help crops grow.

Review

1. What are the three kinds of volcanoes?
2. What is a magma chamber?
3. How can volcanic eruptions be harmful?
4. **Critical Thinking** Compare magma and lava.
5. **Test Prep** What is the name of the rocky tube in a volcano through which magma travels?
   - **A** magma chamber
   - **B** vent
   - **C** crater
   - **D** lava

LINKS

MATH LINK

Ordering Volcanoes Look at the chart on page C22. It lists eruptions in the order in which they happened. List the volcanoes in another type of order. Use library reference materials to find other volcanic eruptions to add to your chart.

WRITING LINK

Informative Writing — Description Write an article that describes the journey of the rock that erupts to form a volcano. Begin with the colliding of the plates. End with lava erupting from the volcano. Be sure to include the effects of the volcano on the land and its people.

SOCIAL STUDIES LINK

Locate on a Map Use library reference materials to find out the ten most recent major volcano eruptions. Highlight the location of each on a copy of a world map. Write the name of the continent on which each volcano is located.

TECHNOLOGY LINK

Learn more about volcano eruptions by visiting this Internet site.
www.scilinks.org/harcourt

SCILINKS
THE WORLD'S A CLICK AWAY

DANTE,
Robot Volcano Explorer

Suppose you're a scientist who wants to explore a volcano. You want to know about the air and gases inside the volcano and about the kinds of rock and ash. You think the harsh environment is similar to what people might experience on another planet. There's only one problem—real danger. In 1993, eight scientists died trying to get samples. You don't want to risk your life.

Dante II climbing down into Mt. Spurr

ROBOT EXPLORERS

Luckily, there's a solution to your problem. It's *Dante* (DAHN•tay), a walking robot designed to explore volcanoes. *Dante* was named for an Italian writer who wrote about an imaginary trip to the Underworld. In January 1993 *Dante* tried to explore an Antarctic volcano. But wires that sent information from the robot to the scientists broke. *Dante* had to be hauled out.

DANTE II

The designers of *Dante* returned to the Field Robotics Center at Carnegie Mellon University in Pittsburgh. Using what they learned from *Dante,* they built a new robot, *Dante II.* In August 1994 *Dante II* entered the crater of Mount Spurr, a volcano in Alaska. *Dante II* sent images to scientists about 130 kilometers (80 mi) away. Using a laser to scan the surroundings, *Dante II* made 3-D maps. It also had a video camera. For a week the robot explored the crater and analyzed the gases.

Dante II had a snowshoe on each of its eight legs. It was designed to move on its own, following preset directions. But it could also be controlled by the scientists far away.

A NEAR DISASTER

A week of warm weather melted about 2 meters (6 ft) of snow. This caused problems when *Dante II* tried to climb out of the volcano crater. The snowshoes on its legs were no longer useful, and the robot fell. Engineers tried to lift *Dante II* using a helicopter, but a cable broke. Finally, two people had to hike into the crater. They put the robot into a sling, hanging from a helicopter.

DANTE'S FUTURE

Dante II now travels around the country as part of a science exhibit. Its designers are working on improved robots. Their goal is to use similar robots to explore distant planets.

Think About It

1. How might an Antarctic volcano be like a planet other than Earth?
2. Why do you think *Dante II* had eight legs?

WEB LINK:
For Science and Technology updates, visit the Harcourt Internet site.
www.harcourtschool.com

Careers | **Field Geology Technician**

What They Do
Field geology technicians set up, use, and repair geology equipment. The equipment is used for measuring rocks, minerals, volcanoes, and other parts of Earth's

surface. The technicians work both in the laboratory and outdoors. They measure, calculate, and record results. They also communicate conclusions. They work with scientists and help them, often using computers, robots, and other machines.

Education and Training To be a field geology technician, you need at least two years of training. You might go to a community college or a technical institute. Some field geology technicians have a college degree in geology.

Hiroo Kanamori

SEISMOLOGIST

"I have many fond memories of pondering over some curious problems, coming up with some rough ideas, and finally solving them to my satisfaction."

Dr. Hiroo Kanamori (hee•roh•oh kahn•ah•moh•ree) studies earthquakes and teaches at the California Institute of Technology, or Caltech. He began studying earthquakes in Japan at Tokyo University. Later, he came to this country to study and decided to stay.

Kanamori tries to find out what causes earthquakes and how to reduce their effect on society. He has developed ways to analyze data from earthquakes that happened long ago. The data is from before modern earthquake science tools were made or used. For example, he studied the 1923 earthquake in Tokyo.

The motion, forces, and energy of California earthquakes are of special interest to Kanamori. His work has helped reduce earthquake hazards.

1923 earthquake damage in Tokyo

For example, people can better prepare for an earthquake if they understand earthquakes better. They can also design stronger buildings that can survive earthquakes. Kanamori is pleased to see his work used to make people safer.

Kanamori has published several articles on earthquakes and on Earth's structure. He says he has been lucky to work with many good people, both in Japan and in the United States.

THINK ABOUT IT

1. In what way does Dr. Kanamori share credit for his work?

2. What kinds of things would a person have to know to study earthquakes?

Moving Magma

How does toothpaste in a tube move like magma in a volcano?

Materials

- paper towel
- half-full tube of toothpaste, with cap

Procedure

1 Place the paper towel on the table. Be sure the cap to the toothpaste is on the tube loosely. Do <u>not</u> screw it on tight.

2 Squeeze the tube of toothpaste from the bottom. Continue squeezing until the toothpaste has risen to the top of the tube.

3 Continue squeezing the tube as the toothpaste spills onto the sides of the tube.

4 Observe the toothpaste as it hardens after rising out of the tube.

Draw Conclusions

How is the movement of the toothpaste similar to the movement of magma? How is the hardened toothpaste outside the tube like lava?

Making Seismic Waves

How does movement of Earth's plates make waves in Earth?

Materials

- 9 in. × 13 in. cake pan
- apron
- safety goggles
- water
- food coloring
- spoon
- clay

Procedure

1 **CAUTION** **Put on your apron and safety goggles.** Fill the pan with about $\frac{1}{2}$ in. of water. Color the water with a few drops of food coloring. Use the spoon to mix the color.

2 Form the clay into two long, square-sided blocks. Place the two blocks of clay in the water. Push the blocks together so that they are sticking to one another.

3 Quickly slide the two blocks of clay along each other in opposite directions.

4 Observe what happens to the water around the two blocks of clay.

Draw Conclusions

What happens if you move the blocks more slowly? Describe how this model is similar to moving plates in an earthquake.

Vocabulary Review

Use the terms below to complete the sentences. The page numbers in ( ) tell you where to look in the chapter if you need help.

crust (C6)   seismograph (C14)

mantle (C6)   volcano (C18)

core (C6)   lava (C18)

plates (C8)   magma (C18)

earthquake (C12)   vent (C18)

fault (C12)   magma chamber (C19)

focus (C13)   crater (C20)

epicenter (C13)

1. An underground holding pool for hot magma is called a ____.

2. Scientists use a ____ to measure earthquake waves.

3. A vibration of Earth's crust is an ____.

4. A large basin that can form at the top of a volcano is a ____.

5. Most of the magma from a volcano comes up through a long, narrow, rocky tube called a ____.

6. ____ is melted rock that flows out onto Earth's surface.

7. If you somehow dug down to Earth's center, the first two layers you would pass through are the ____ and ____.

8. Hot, melted rock that is underground is called ____.

9. The deepest layer of Earth is the ____.

10. The point on Earth's surface that is directly above an earthquake's focus is the ____.

11. Earth's crust and upper mantle are broken into several ____.

12. A mountain that forms from lava is a ____.

13. The ____ of an earthquake is the point underground where the movement of the earthquake first takes place.

14. A break in the crust along which rocks move is a ____.

Connect Concepts

Use the terms in the Word Bank to complete the concept map.

crust
earthquakes
inner core
mantle
volcanoes
plates

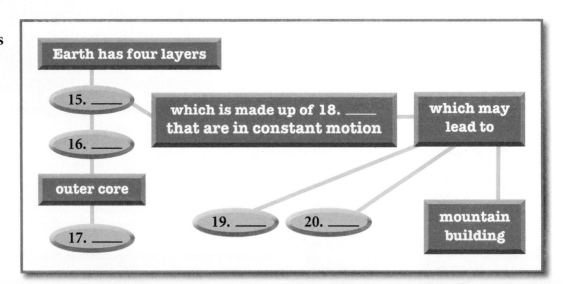

Earth has four layers

15. ____

which is made up of 18. ____ that are in constant motion

which may lead to

16. ____

outer core

19. ____   20. ____

mountain building

17. ____

Check Understanding

Write the letter of the best choice.

21. When a volcano collapses into itself at its top, it forms a —
    A crater
    B magma chamber
    C plate
    D vent

22. The plates of Earth's crust and mantle can **NOT** move —
    F toward each other
    G away from each other
    H very slowly
    J very quickly

23. The layer of Earth that is the hottest is the —
    A mantle
    B inner core
    C outer core
    D crust

24. _____ are mountains made of lava layers that alternate with layers of cinders.
    F Cinder cones
    G Shield volcanoes
    H Composite volcanoes
    J Crater volcanoes

25. Volcanoes can be useful to people because volcanoes —
    A add minerals to the soil
    B spread ash
    C send out lava and gases that are very hot
    D cause huge waves

Critical Thinking

26. What happens to Earth's crust and mantle during an earthquake? How is this reaction of Earth's crust similar to what happens when a volcano erupts?

27. Scientists sometimes put seismographs on a volcano to help them predict when the volcano will erupt. Why do you think a seismograph might be useful in this situation?

Process Skills Review

28. Why is **making models** a useful way to study volcanic eruptions?

29. Suppose you are pumping up a bicycle tire. What would you observe happening to the tire as you pumped air into it? **Infer** what would happen if you pumped too much air into the tire.

30. How could **measuring** be useful as you pump up the bicycle tire?

Performance Assessment

Plate Model

Use clay to make models of two of Earth's plates. Move the clay to show how plates might behave during an earthquake. Now use the clay to show two ways plates can form volcanoes.

Rocks and Minerals

Rocks and minerals are all around you. The ground you walk on every day is made of rocks and minerals. They are in the soil. They are the gems that sparkle in jewelry. The Earth itself is made mostly of rocks and minerals.

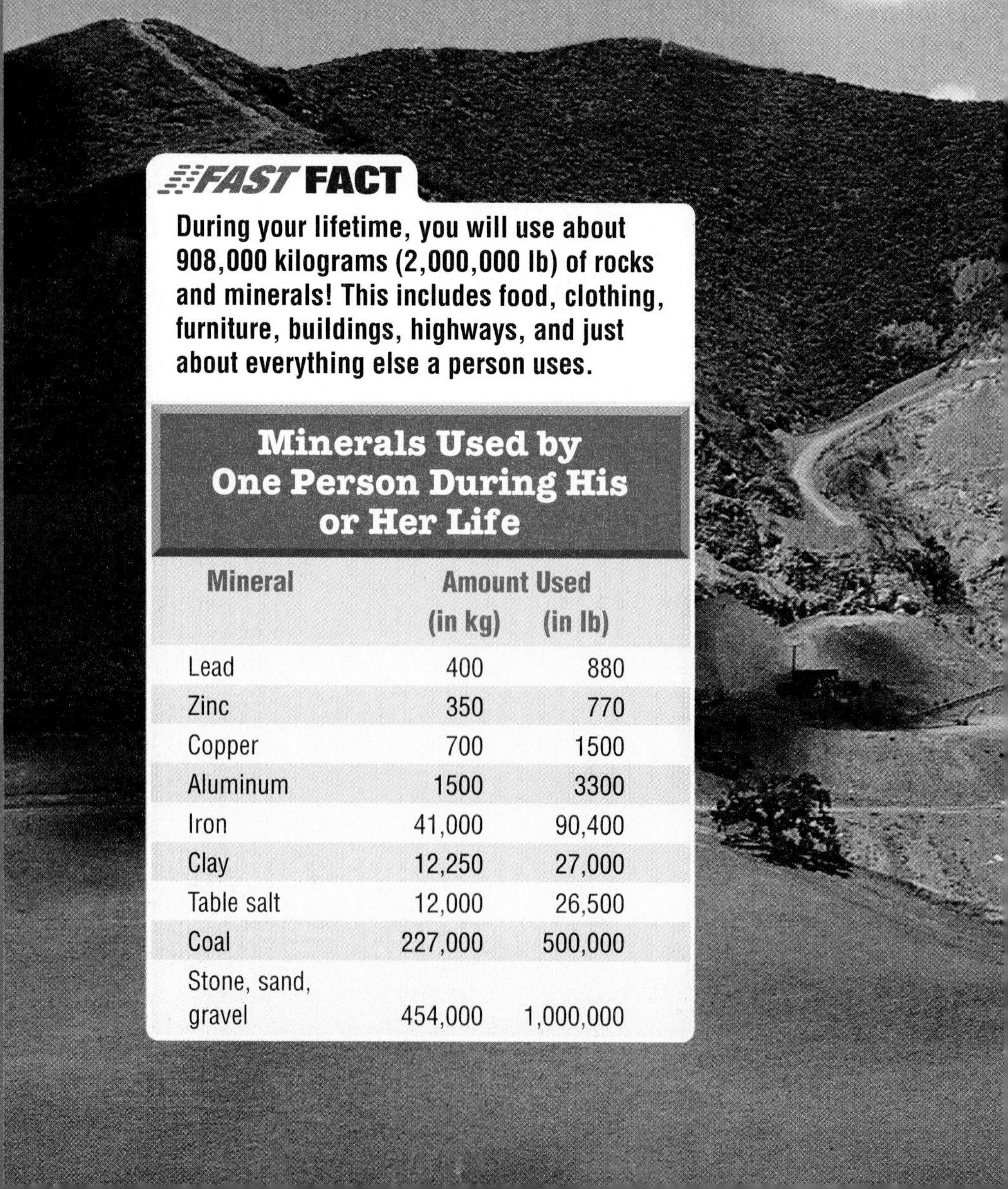

FAST FACT

During your lifetime, you will use about 908,000 kilograms (2,000,000 lb) of rocks and minerals! This includes food, clothing, furniture, buildings, highways, and just about everything else a person uses.

Minerals Used by One Person During His or Her Life

Mineral	Amount Used (in kg)	Amount Used (in lb)
Lead	400	880
Zinc	350	770
Copper	700	1500
Aluminum	1500	3300
Iron	41,000	90,400
Clay	12,250	27,000
Table salt	12,000	26,500
Coal	227,000	500,000
Stone, sand, gravel	454,000	1,000,000

Vocabulary Preview

mineral
streak
hardness
luster
rock
igneous rock
sedimentary rock
metamorphic rock
erosion
weathering
rock cycle

All the gold known in the world would fit in a cube measuring about 18 meters (60 ft) on each side! But a little bit goes a long way. Twenty-eight grams (1 oz) of gold can be flattened into a thin sheet covering about 28 square meters (300 sq ft). That's enough to cover one-fourth of a tennis court!

These pictures show equal weights of gold and salt. In ancient times, salt was so precious that it was traded ounce for ounce for gold! If you worked hard and you were "worth your salt," you were paid a "salary." This word meant "money for buying salt"!

This gravel quarry provides gravel for roads and buildings.

LESSON 1

What Are Minerals?

In this lesson, you can . . .

 INVESTIGATE mineral properties.

 LEARN ABOUT how minerals form and how we use them.

 LINK to math, writing, social studies, and technology.

Mineral Properties

Activity Purpose Chalk leaves a mark on a chalkboard because the board is harder than the chalk. Hardness is a property, or characteristic, of minerals, such as the calcite (KAL•syt) that makes up chalk. In this investigation you will **observe** that a mineral can be scratched by some things but not by other things. You will also test other mineral properties and then **classify** minerals by their properties.

Materials

- 6 labeled mineral samples
- hand lens
- streak plate
- copper penny
- steel nail

Activity Procedure

1 Copy the chart shown on page C33.

2 Use the hand lens to **observe** each mineral. Describe the color of each sample. **Record** your observations in the chart. (Picture A)

3 Use each mineral to draw a line across the streak plate. (Picture B) What color is the streak each made? **Record** your observations.

4 **CAUTION** **Use caution with the nail, it is sharp.** Test the hardness of each mineral by using your fingernail, the copper penny, and the steel nail. Try to scratch each mineral with each of these items. Then try to scratch each sample with each of the other minerals. **Record** your observations in the chart.

◀ A mineral can be different colors. Tourmaline (TOOR•muh•lin) can be pink, purple, green, black, or the mix of colors called watermelon, shown here. Tourmaline is often used in jewelry.

C32

Picture A

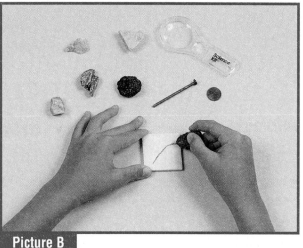

Picture B

Mineral Sample	Color of the Mineral Sample	Color of the Mineral's Streak	Things That Scratch the Mineral
A			
B			
C			
D			
E			
F			

5 **Classify** the minerals based on each property you tested: color, streak, and hardness. Make labels that list all three properties for each mineral.

Draw Conclusions

1. How are the minerals you tested different from each other?

2. Which of the minerals you tested is the hardest? Explain your choice.

3. **Scientists at Work** Scientists **classify** things so it is easier to study them. How do you think scientists classify minerals?

Investigate Further Obtain five other unknown mineral samples. Determine the hardness, color, and streak of each. **Classify** all of the mineral samples after testing the new samples.

Process Skill Tip

When you **classify** things, you put them into groups based on ways they are alike. Organizing things in this way can make it easier to learn about them. Often, you can classify the same group of objects in many ways.

Minerals

How Some Minerals Form

FIND OUT

- what minerals are
- how to identify minerals
- how minerals are used

VOCABULARY

mineral
streak
luster
hardness

To be a mineral, a material must have certain features. A **mineral** (MIN•er•uhl) is always a solid material with particles arranged in a repeating pattern. This pattern is called a crystal (KRIST•uhl). Almost all minerals are made from material that was never alive. Also, true minerals form only in nature. They are not made in a laboratory.

Minerals form in many ways. Some minerals, such as diamond, form in Earth's mantle. There, high heat and pressure change carbon into hard, sparkling crystals called diamond. Diamonds have many uses. Some are cut and shaped to make jewelry. Most are used on cutting tools such as drills and saws.

Other minerals, such as calcite, can form at or near Earth's surface. Some calcite forms in the ocean when calcium, oxygen, and carbon combine in sea water. Some ocean animals form calcite shells or other body parts. Calcite also forms as water evaporates in limestone caves.

Water also plays a role in forming other minerals. Galena crystals form when hot, mineral-rich water moves slowly through cracks in Earth's crust, mixing with other minerals before it cools and evaporates.

▲ Calcite is a mineral found in chalk.

✔ **What are some features a material must have to be called a mineral?**

◄ This shiny mineral is galena (guh•LEE•nuh), which is made of lead and sulfur. Galena crystals often form cubes.

The first compass needles were made from a mineral called magnetite. Magnetite is magnetic, as shown by the nail stuck to the sample. ▼

Mica is a mineral that splits easily into thin, clear sheets. ▼

Some Mineral Properties

You saw in the investigation that one property of a mineral is streak. **Streak** is the color of the powder left behind when you rub a mineral against a white tile called a streak plate. Usually the streak is the same color as the mineral. Chalcopyrite (chal•koh•PY•ryt), however, looks like shiny gold but has a black streak.

Luster (LUHS•tuhr) describes the way the surface of a mineral reflects light. Some minerals look shiny, like aluminum foil looks. These minerals have a *metallic* luster. Others look dull or dark. These minerals have a *nonmetallic* luster. The sparkling appearance of a diamond is known as a *brilliant* luster.

Hardness is a mineral's ability to resist being scratched. Mohs' hardness scale, shown at the right, lists minerals that have hardnesses from 1 to 10. A mineral with a higher number on the scale can scratch a mineral with a lower number.

✔ **Which minerals on Mohs' hardness scale can be scratched by quartz?**

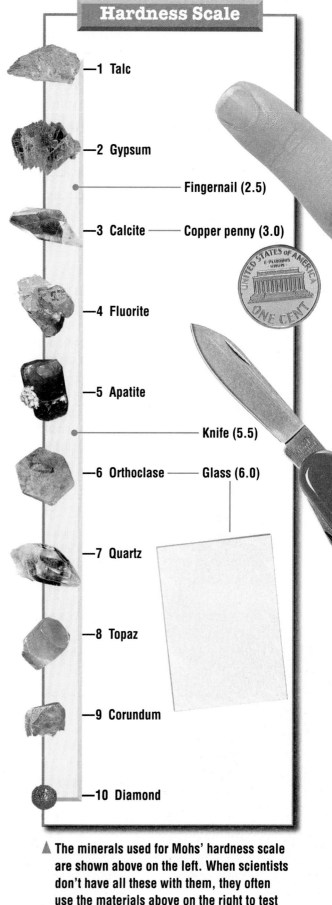

Hardness Scale

- —1 Talc
- —2 Gypsum
- Fingernail (2.5)
- —3 Calcite —— Copper penny (3.0)
- —4 Fluorite
- —5 Apatite
- Knife (5.5)
- —6 Orthoclase —— Glass (6.0)
- —7 Quartz
- —8 Topaz
- —9 Corundum
- —10 Diamond

▲ The minerals used for Mohs' hardness scale are shown above on the left. When scientists don't have all these with them, they often use the materials above on the right to test for hardness.

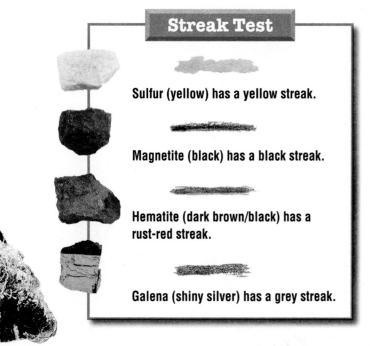

Streak Test

Sulfur (yellow) has a yellow streak.

Magnetite (black) has a black streak.

Hematite (dark brown/black) has a rust-red streak.

Galena (shiny silver) has a grey streak.

How We Use Minerals

Some minerals can be used in nearly the same form they have in nature. They don't need much refining, or processing to remove other materials. For example, silver and copper can be used to make musical instruments, electric wire, and jewelry. Gypsum can be used to make plaster and wallboard. Graphite is used in pencils. Halite, or table salt, can be used to flavor and preserve foods.

Pure silver is a very soft metal. It has a hardness of about 2 on the Mohs' hardness scale. Because it is so soft, it can be shaped easily. It also can be mixed with other metals to make beautiful jewelry or to cover musical instruments, such as this fluegelhorn.

Hematite is a mineral made of iron and oxygen. It has a hardness of 5 to 6.5 on the Mohs' hardness scale. Hematite is an important source of the iron used to make steel. Steel beams are used to make tall buildings strong.

Diamond is the hardest natural substance found on Earth. It has a hardness of 10 on Mohs' hardness scale. Some diamonds are used to make beautiful jewelry. Diamonds that are not good enough for jewelry are used on drills that dig deep into Earth's crust. The small cylinders all along the edges of this drill are industrial diamonds. They're hidden under the silver paint.

Some minerals are not useful in their natural form. They must be refined to be useful. The mineral cuprite (KOOP•ryt) is made of copper and oxygen. After cuprite is refined, the copper is used in making pennies, pots and pans, and water pipes.

✓ **What are five uses of minerals?**

Summary

Some minerals form in Earth's mantle, and others form at or near Earth's surface. Minerals can be identified by their properties. Some mineral properties are streak, hardness, and luster. People use minerals in many ways.

Review

1. List three features a material must have to be a mineral.
2. What is mineral hardness?
3. Name six ways people use minerals.
4. **Critical Thinking** You have a sample of an unknown mineral. It can scratch fluorite but not quartz. What is its approximate hardness?
5. **Test Prep** Which of the following minerals is the hardest?
   A diamond
   B apatite
   C topaz
   D talc

LINKS

MATH LINK

Measure the Mass Collect six different mineral samples that are all about the same size. Use a balance to find the mass of each sample. Record each value in a table. Explain why minerals that are about the same size may have very different masses.

WRITING LINK

Expressive Writing—Poem A birthstone is the gem that stands for a particular month. Find a list of the birthstones for all the months, and make a poster about them. Draw a color picture of each gem next to its name. Write a poem for a family member about your birthday month and birthstone.

SOCIAL STUDIES LINK

Go West! Find out why so many Americans in the mid-1800s risked their lives riding west in covered wagons or sailing around Cape Horn to get to California. Make a map of the routes they took. Add pictures of what they did in California.

TECHNOLOGY LINK

Learn more about the mineral gold by viewing *Gold Mining* on the **Harcourt Science Newsroom Video.**

What Are Rocks?

In this lesson, you can . . .

INVESTIGATE
different kinds of rocks.

LEARN ABOUT
how rocks form.

LINK to math, writing, physical education, and technology.

INVESTIGATE

Identifying Rocks

Activity Purpose Have you ever helped make chocolate chip cookies? If so, you know that you put ingredients in a bowl, mix them, spoon the mixture onto a cookie sheet, and then bake it in an oven. The heat in the oven causes the ingredients to change and stick together to form something new— cookies. Some rocks form in a similar way. In this investigation you will **observe** some rocks and **classify** them by the ways they formed.

Materials

- 5 labeled rock samples
- hand lens
- dropper
- vinegar
- safety goggles
- paper plate
- paper towels

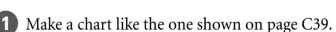

CAUTION

Activity Procedure

1. Make a chart like the one shown on page C39.

2. Use the hand lens to **observe** each rock. What color or colors is each rock? **Record** your observations in your chart.

◀ Wind-blown sand and rain carved away bits of rock to form this arch in Arches National Park, Utah.

Rock Sample	Color	Texture	Picture	Bubbles When Vinegar Added
1				
2				
3				
4				
5				

3 Can you see any grains, or small pieces, making up the rock? Are the grains very small, or are they large? Are they rounded, or do they have sharp edges? Do the grains fit together like puzzle pieces? Or are they just next to one another? **Record** your observations under *Texture* in your chart. Draw a picture of each rock in the *Picture* column.

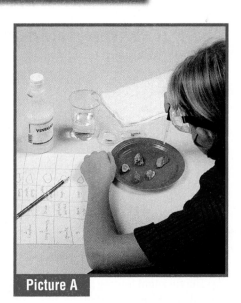

Picture A

4 **CAUTION** **Put on your safety goggles.** Vinegar bubbles when it is dropped on the mineral calcite. Put the rock samples on the paper plate. Use the dropper to put a few drops of vinegar on each rock. **Observe** what happens. **Record** your findings. (Picture A)

5 **Classify** your rocks into two groups based on how the rocks are alike.

Draw Conclusions

1. What properties did you use to **classify** your rocks?

2. How does your classification system **compare** with those of two other students?

3. **Scientists at Work** One way scientists **classify** rocks is by how they formed. Choose one rock and explain how you think it might have formed.

Investigate Further Take a walk around your school or neighborhood. Using your **observations**, list at least three ways people use rocks.

Process Skill Tip

Classifying is a way to study a large number of objects. You **classify** by grouping things, based on how they are alike. For rocks, their size, shape, color, and what has happened to them are all things that can be alike.

Types of Rocks

Igneous Rocks

FIND OUT

- how rocks form
- how people use rocks

VOCABULARY

rock
igneous rock
weathering
erosion
sedimentary rock
metamorphic rock

Earth is made mostly of rocks. A **rock** is material made up of one or more minerals. But unlike minerals, rocks are not crystals. Like minerals, some rocks form at or near Earth's surface. Others form deep in the crust or in Earth's middle layer, the mantle. There are many different kinds of rocks. But they all can be classified into three groups based on how they formed.

Rocks that form when melted rock hardens are called **igneous** (IG•nee•uhs) **rocks**. In Chapter 1 you learned that lava is melted rock that reaches Earth's surface through a volcano. Lava cools and hardens before large mineral crystals have time to form. Rocks formed from lava have small mineral pieces and are called *fine-grained*. Usually their mineral crystals can be seen only with a microscope.

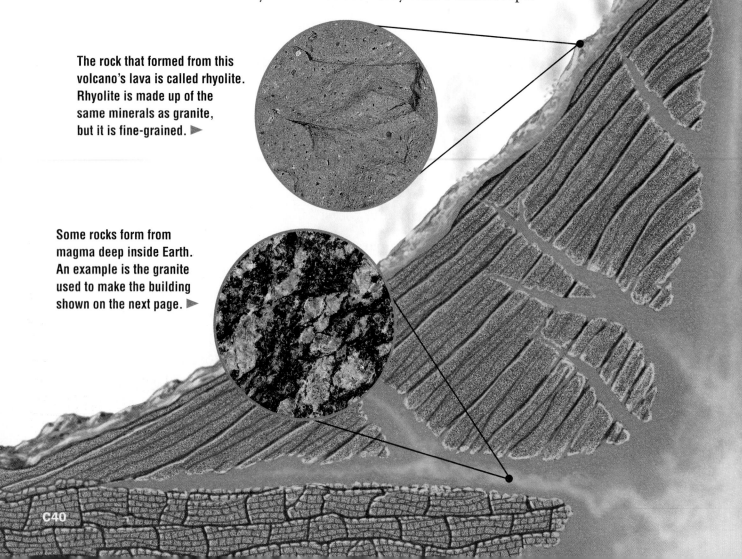

The rock that formed from this volcano's lava is called rhyolite. Rhyolite is made up of the same minerals as granite, but it is fine-grained. ▶

Some rocks form from magma deep inside Earth. An example is the granite used to make the building shown on the next page. ▶

▲ Basalt

▲ Gabbro

▲ Pumice

▲ Obsidian

Melted rock that stays below Earth's surface is called magma (MAG•muh). Magma cools and hardens slowly. Its minerals can form large grains that are easy to see. Igneous rocks formed from slowly cooling magma are called *coarse-grained*.

Basalt (buh•SALT) is the most common igneous rock that forms from lava at Earth's surface. Basalt is a dark, greenish-black rock made up mostly of the minerals feldspar (FELD•spar) and pyroxene (py•RAHKS•een). Gabbro (GAB•roh) is an igneous rock that is also made up mostly of these two minerals. But gabbro has larger mineral grains than basalt. That's because gabbro forms inside Earth instead of at Earth's surface.

Pumice (PUHM•ihs) is another igneous rock. The tiny holes in pumice are caused by gases escaping from the lava as it cools. Pumice feels rough and scratchy. Obsidian (uhb•SID•ee•uhn) also forms from lava. The lava cools so quickly that the rock looks like black glass. When obsidian breaks, sharp edges form.

Granite is a common igneous rock that forms when magma cools slowly beneath Earth's surface. Most granite is made up of large grains of feldspar, quartz, and mica (MY•kuh). These mineral grains are joined together tightly, making granite a strong rock that lasts for a long time.

✔ **What are igneous rocks?**

◀ Granite is an igneous rock often used for building. Brookings Hall at Washington University in St. Louis is made of unpolished pink granite blocks.

Sedimentary Rocks

Rocks are broken down into smaller pieces by **weathering** (WETH•er•ing). Weathering is caused by many things. At Earth's surface the actions of wind, water, ice, and plant roots cause weathering.

After rocks are weathered into small pieces, blowing winds, flowing water, gravity, or slow-moving glaciers often move the pieces to other places. The movement of weathered rock pieces from one place to another is **erosion** (ee•ROH•zhuhn).

When erosion is caused by water, over time the rock pieces drop to the bottoms of streams, rivers, or lakes. The material that is dropped is called *sediment*. Over a long time, layers of sediments can form **sedimentary** (sed•uh•MEN•ter•ee) **rock** as they are squeezed and stuck together.

Most sediments are dropped by moving water when it slows down, such as when a river or stream enters a lake. The largest pieces of weathered rock are dropped first. Conglomerate (kuhn•GLAHM•er•it) is a type of sedimentary rock that can form from these larger pieces. The pieces in a conglomerate can be as big as boulders or as small as peas. In a conglomerate, the pieces are round and smooth. Most conglomerates form in shallow water.

Smaller sediments are carried farther by the water and dropped later. Siltstone is one type of rock made up of smaller sediments.

Limestone is a fine-grained sedimentary rock. It is made up mostly of the mineral calcite. Most limestone forms in oceans, sometimes from seashells. A few kinds of limestone form in lakes.

Many sedimentary rocks form in bodies of water like this stream. Sedimentary rocks may contain fossils. This happens when shells, bones, or other remains of once-living organisms are buried in sediment layers.

▲ Conglomerate

▲ Limestone

▲ Sandstone

▲ Shale

Sandstone is another kind of sedimentary rock. Sandstones, as you might guess from their name, are made up of bits of rocks and minerals the size of sand grains. Nearly all sandstones are made up mostly of the mineral quartz.

Some sandstones are fine-grained. They feel smooth when you touch them. Other sandstones are coarse-grained. They feel rough against your skin. Sandstones can form in water or on land.

Shale is a fine-grained sedimentary rock made of very small sediments. The sediments in most shales are so small that you can see them only with a strong hand lens. Some shale sediments are so small that you can see them only with a microscope.

✓ **What processes help form sedimentary rocks?**

THE INSIDE STORY

Crossbedding

1. Many sandstones are *crossbedded.* Crossbeds begin to form when wind blows sand grains in one direction for a long time. The grains pile up until the piles become so steep that sand begins to drop off the top edge. These sand piles, or dunes, will become the first rock layer.

2. Over time, more sand covers the first layer. This new sand keeps the first layer from moving. Sand blown by the wind keeps filling the gaps between dunes.

3. When the wind changes direction, the next sand layer is put down at a different angle. As the wind keeps changing direction, new layers are put down at different angles. The rock layers that form from the sand layers will show these changes in wind direction.

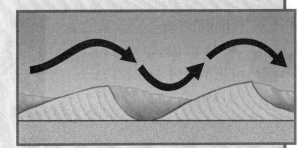

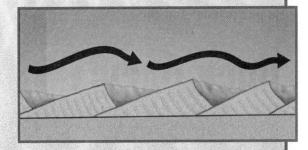

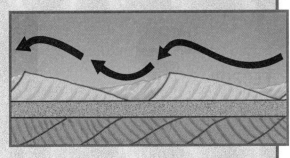

Metamorphic Rocks

High heat and great pressure can change the texture of rock—the way it looks and feels. They can also change the form of the minerals that make up the rock. These changed rocks are called **metamorphic** (met•uh•MAWR•fik) **rocks**. Metamorphic rocks can form from any kind of rock— sedimentary, igneous, or even other metamorphic rocks.

Some metamorphic rocks form when mountains are built up. Schist (SHIST) and gneiss (NYS) are two examples. Schist has wavy lines. It splits easily into layers. Gneiss forms when schist is heated and squeezed more. Gneiss often has bands of light and dark minerals.

Marble is another metamorphic rock. Marble forms when limestone is squeezed and heated. Artists often use marble to make statues. It also is used in buildings.

Slate is a metamorphic rock that forms when shale is under great pressure. Like shale, slate has layers. In the past, people used slate to make chalkboards for schools. Slate tiles are sometimes used to cover roofs.

Quartzite forms from sandstone when heat melts the sand grains together. Quartzite usually has a milky color. Other minerals in the sandstone can give quartzite a gray or pink color.

✓ **How do metamorphic rocks form?**

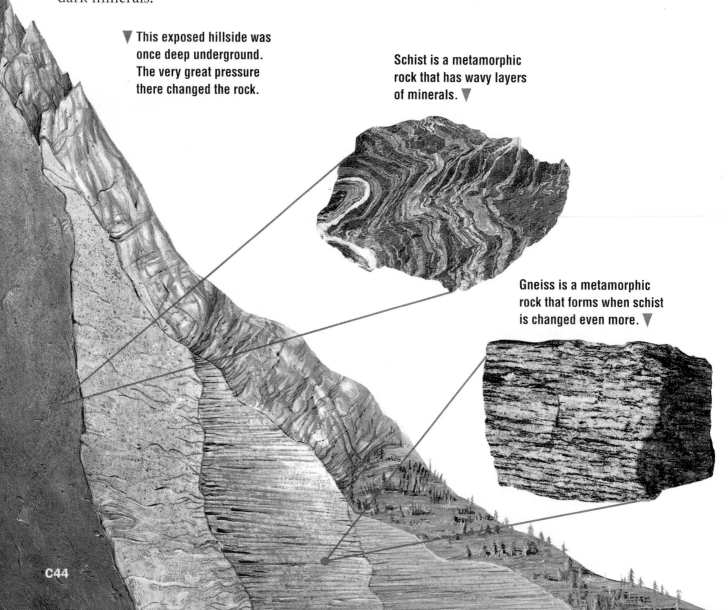

▼ This exposed hillside was once deep underground. The very great pressure there changed the rock.

Schist is a metamorphic rock that has wavy layers of minerals. ▼

Gneiss is a metamorphic rock that forms when schist is changed even more. ▼

Slate is a metamorphic rock that can be split into thin sheets. Slate pieces are used to cover roofs on houses.

Summary

Rocks are made up of one or more minerals. Rocks are classified by the way they form. Igneous rocks form when magma or lava cools and hardens. Sedimentary rocks are usually made of pieces of rock that have been squeezed and stuck together. Metamorphic rocks form when heat and pressure change rocks.

Review

1. What are rocks?

2. How are rocks classified?

3. In which type of rock are fossils found?

4. **Critical Thinking** You find a rock that is made of small grains. How can you tell whether it is igneous or sedimentary?

5. **Test Prep** Which kind of rock is granite?

   A igneous

   B metamorphic

   C layered

   D sedimentary

LINKS

MATH LINK

Make a Graph A lake has three rivers flowing into it. Each river deposits 1 centimeter of sediment in one year. How deep will the sediments be after 10 years? If the lake is a meter deep, when will it be completely filled by sediment?

WRITING LINK

Informative Writing—Narration Use library reference materials to find out about the Navajo Sandstone crossbeds. Then write a story for your teacher describing the area while the crossbeds were forming.

PHYSICAL EDUCATION LINK

Rock Climbing Use library reference materials to find out the equipment needed for safe rock climbing. Make a list of safety rules for the sport of rock climbing. Tell how rock types affect climbing rules.

TECHNOLOGY LINK

Learn more about rock types by visiting this Internet site.
www.scilinks.org/harcourt

What Is the Rock Cycle?

In this lesson, you can . . .

INVESTIGATE how rocks can change.

LEARN ABOUT ways in which rocks change.

LINK to math, writing, technology, and other areas.

INVESTIGATE

The Rock Cycle

Activity Purpose Do you recycle aluminum cans? After the recycling truck takes away the cans, they go through many changes before they become new products. In this investigation you will **make a model** to show how Earth's natural processes can change rocks.

Materials

- small objects—pieces of aquarium gravel, fake jewels, and a few pennies
- 3 pieces of modeling clay, each a different color
- 2 aluminum pie pans

Activity Procedure

1 The small objects stand for minerals. Press the "minerals" into the three pieces of clay. Each color of clay with its objects stands for a different igneous rock.

2 Now suppose that wind and water are weathering and eroding the "rocks." To **model** this process, break one rock into pieces (sediments) and drop the pieces into one of the pie pans (a lake). (Picture A)

◀ Giant's Causeway in Ireland began to form when lava quickly cooled and shrank to form basalt. Over many years, water and ice weathered the rock to form these spectacular, six-sided columns.

Picture A

Picture B

3 Drop pieces from the second rock on top of the first rock layer. Then drop pieces of the third rock on top of the second layer. Press the layers together by using the bottom of the empty pie pan. What kind of rock have you made?

4 Squeeze the "sedimentary rock" between your hands to warm it up. What causes the rock to change? Which kind of rock is it now? (Picture B)

Draw Conclusions

1. How did the igneous "rocks" change in this investigation?

2. What might weathering and erosion do to a metamorphic rock?

3. **Scientists at Work** Scientists often **make a model** to help them understand processes that occur in nature. What process did your hands represent in Step 4 of the activity?

Investigate Further Tell how you could change this model to show igneous rocks that formed from magma and igneous rocks that formed from lava.

Process Skill Tip

If you **make a model**, you can often understand a natural process that is hard to observe. Because rocks change over a long time, it's hard to see the changes happening.

How Rocks Change

Processes That Cause Change

Rocks are always changing. However, the changes usually happen so slowly that you would never notice them. It can take thousands of years for a rock to weather and erode. It can take many more years for the eroded pieces to be changed into sedimentary rock.

You learned in Lesson 2 that high heat and pressure can change rocks. Sometimes the rocks get hot enough to melt completely. When this melted rock cools and hardens, it has changed from metamorphic to igneous. It usually takes many years for rock to be buried deep enough inside Earth to melt.

A rock can begin as one type and be changed many times. You made a model of these changes in the investigation. Instead of a few minutes, however, changes can take many thousands of years. Some part of the first rock, however, will still be there after each change.

✔ **How does weathering affect rock?**

Follow the blue arrows to learn about the changes that might happen to one rock. ▼

◄ Basalt forms when lava quickly cools and hardens at Earth's surface. Basalt is the most common igneous rock on Earth.

Wind or rain carries the weathered pieces of basalt to the river. The river carries the pieces downstream. As they move, they bump into one another. Jagged edges are slowly rounded off. ▼

Tree roots weather the basalt by growing into the rock and breaking it into pieces. Freezing and thawing and rain also weather the rock. ▶

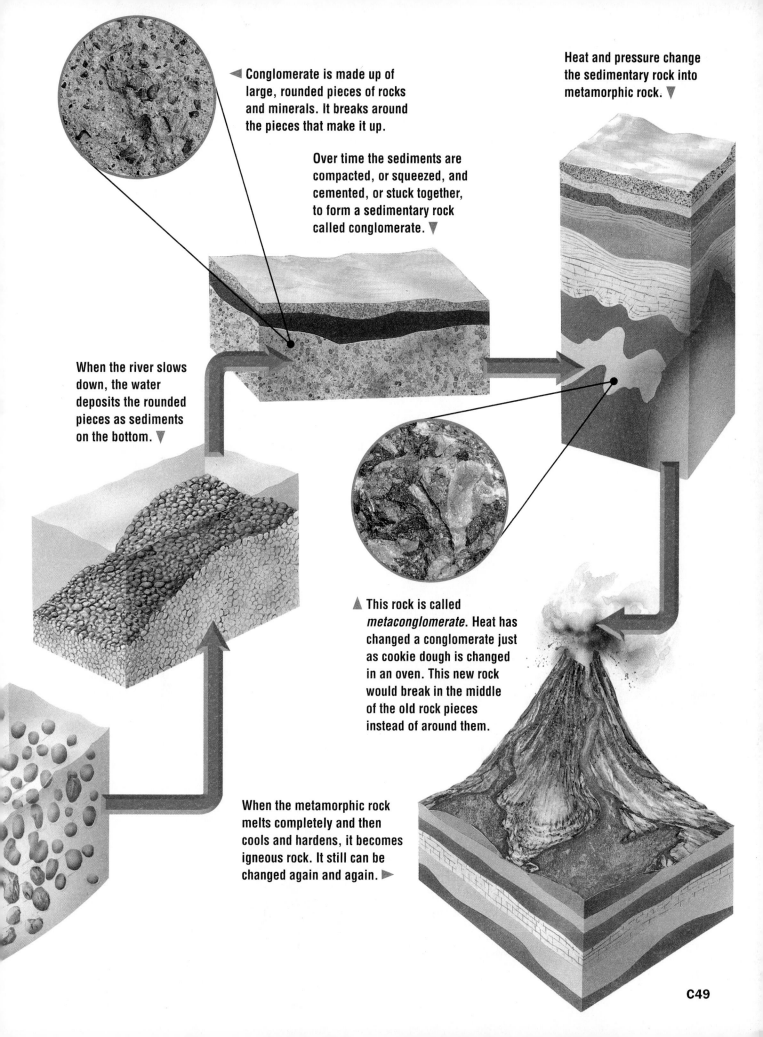

◀ Conglomerate is made up of large, rounded pieces of rocks and minerals. It breaks around the pieces that make it up.

Heat and pressure change the sedimentary rock into metamorphic rock. ▼

Over time the sediments are compacted, or squeezed, and cemented, or stuck together, to form a sedimentary rock called conglomerate. ▼

When the river slows down, the water deposits the rounded pieces as sediments on the bottom. ▼

▲ This rock is called *metaconglomerate*. Heat has changed a conglomerate just as cookie dough is changed in an oven. This new rock would break in the middle of the old rock pieces instead of around them.

When the metamorphic rock melts completely and then cools and hardens, it becomes igneous rock. It still can be changed again and again. ▶

The Rock Cycle

The diagram below and on the next page shows the never-ending rock changes that are called the **rock cycle**. Notice that many arrows lead out from each rock type. This shows that there is more than one path through the rock cycle.

As rocks move through the rock cycle, the materials that make them up are used over and over. Look at the diagram. Try to find where rocks are squeezed. Also notice where sticking together might take place, where rocks melt, and where rocks are under heat and pressure. As you study the diagram, remember that all these processes take a very long time.

✓ **How can a metamorphic rock be changed into a different metamorphic rock?**

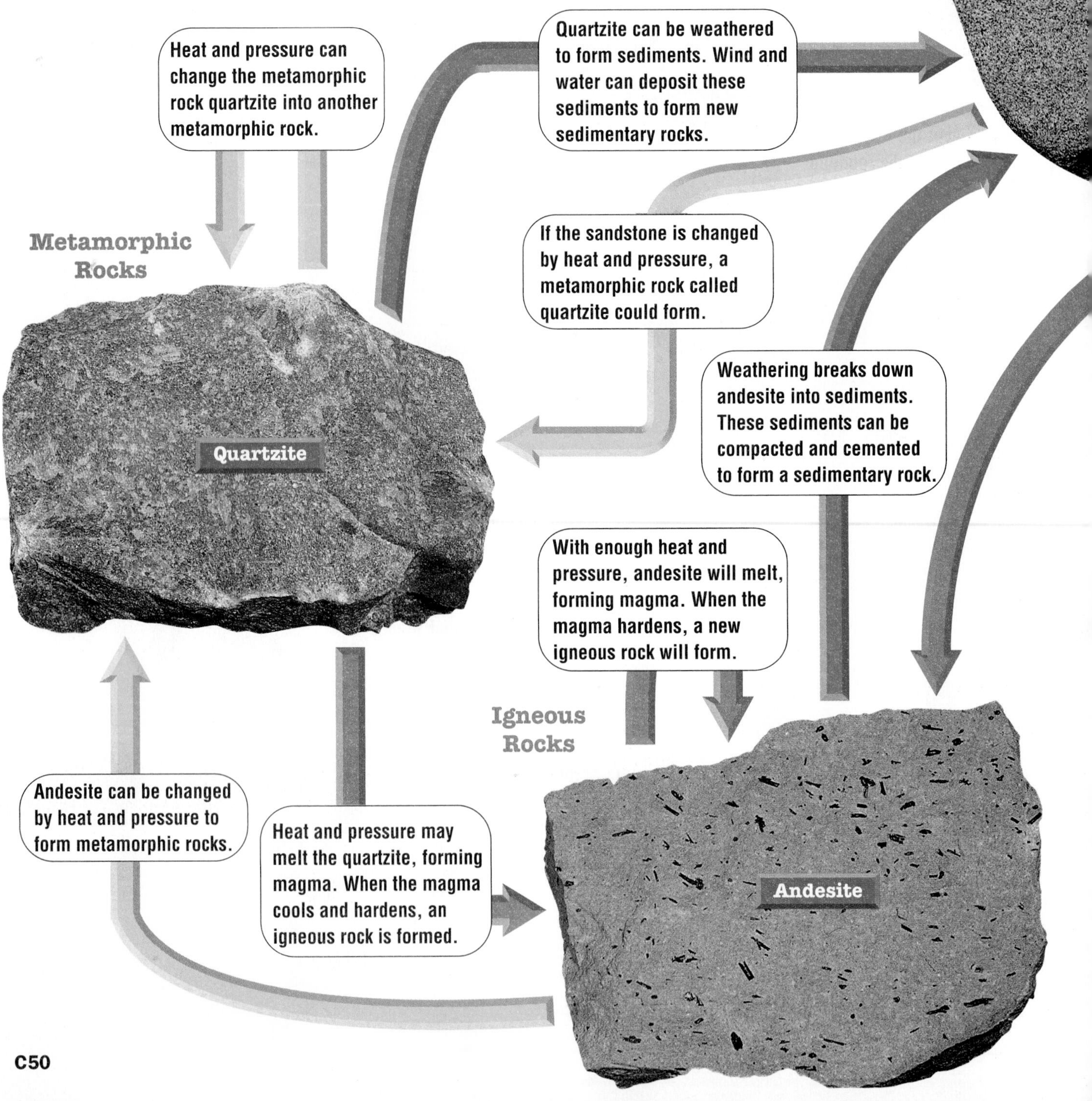

Heat and pressure can change the metamorphic rock quartzite into another metamorphic rock.

Quartzite can be weathered to form sediments. Wind and water can deposit these sediments to form new sedimentary rocks.

Metamorphic Rocks

If the sandstone is changed by heat and pressure, a metamorphic rock called quartzite could form.

Weathering breaks down andesite into sediments. These sediments can be compacted and cemented to form a sedimentary rock.

Quartzite

With enough heat and pressure, andesite will melt, forming magma. When the magma hardens, a new igneous rock will form.

Igneous Rocks

Andesite can be changed by heat and pressure to form metamorphic rocks.

Heat and pressure may melt the quartzite, forming magma. When the magma cools and hardens, an igneous rock is formed.

Andesite

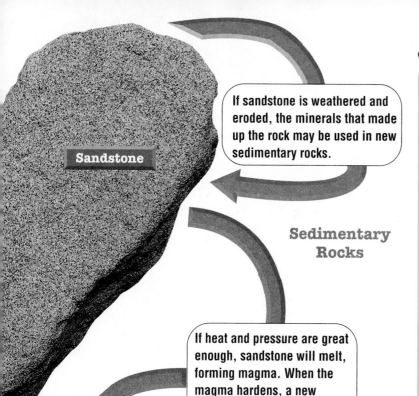

Sandstone

If sandstone is weathered and eroded, the minerals that made up the rock may be used in new sedimentary rocks.

Sedimentary Rocks

If heat and pressure are great enough, sandstone will melt, forming magma. When the magma hardens, a new igneous rock will form.

Summary

Rocks change from one kind to another in the rock cycle. Some of the processes in the rock cycle are weathering, erosion, melting, compaction, and cementation.

Review

1. What is the rock cycle?
2. What part do volcanoes play in the rock cycle?
3. What is one thing that can change a rock to metamorphic rock?
4. **Critical Thinking** How might a sandstone change into another sandstone?
5. **Test Prep** What starts the change from an igneous rock to a sedimentary rock?
   A heat
   B pressure
   C melting
   D weathering

LINKS

MATH LINK

How Long Did It Take? A layer of sedimentary rock is 5 meters thick. The layer was laid down at the rate of 1 centimeter per year. How many years did it take to form?

WRITING LINK

Narrative Writing—Story For a younger child, tell about the "life" of a rock from the rock's point of view. Tell where the rock has been. Tell where it will go. Make sure the rock has been changed into each type of rock at least once.

SOCIAL STUDIES LINK

Building Materials Use library references to find out why some types of rocks are most often used as building materials in your city. Make a model or poster to show what you learned.

LITERATURE LINK

Everybody Needs a Rock Read the book *Everybody Needs a Rock* by Byrd Baylor. Make a list of rules to follow to find your own special rock.

TECHNOLOGY LINK

Visit the Harcourt Learning Site for related links, activities, and resources.
www.harcourtschool.com

WELCOME TO
THE
LEARNING
SITE

DIAMOND COATINGS

Perhaps you've seen a ring that holds a diamond—a sparkling natural mineral. But did you know that diamonds can be made? These artificial diamonds aren't made for jewelry but for use by scientists and in factories.

ARTIFICIAL DIAMONDS

In nature, diamonds form when carbon is kept at very high pressures and temperatures. It may take millions of years for the diamonds to reach Earth's surface. To make artificial diamonds, scientists imitate the natural process. They use enormous pressures and temperatures to make diamonds in a much shorter time than in nature. However, these diamonds are usually plain-looking and very small. These artificial diamonds have been made since the 1950s.

CVD

Now a new, easier way to make artificial diamonds has been found. It takes high temperature but not high pressure. The new method uses simple hydrocarbons (HY•droh•kar•buhnz). These are materials made of the elements hydrogen and carbon.

Scientists heat these materials to very high temperatures. At these temperatures the materials become gases. When the gases cool, they form a thin layer of diamond crystals. This process is called chemical vapor deposition, or CVD. The thin layers of hard diamond crystals are used to protect softer materials.

A thin coating of artificial diamond can protect metal parts. Examples are airplane wings and parts of automobile engines. The coating makes the parts last longer. A thin diamond coating also lowers friction and improves speed. Perhaps someday golf clubs and racing boats will have diamond coatings.

◀ **This microscope photograph shows a diamond crystal growing on a metal surface.**

Researchers also have removed the wire after it was coated. This leaves behind a very small, hollow diamond tube. These tubes might be used as fiber optic wires for computers, or they could be very fine needles for use by doctors and surgeons.

Think About It

1. Why would people want to make artificial diamonds?
2. Why is chemical vapor deposition useful?

WEB LINK:
For Science and Technology updates, visit the Harcourt Internet site.
www.harcourtschool.com

SEND ME A WIRE

A group of scientists in England is working to develop diamond-coated wires and fibers. The coating adds very little weight but makes the coated materials much stronger. For example, the metal tungsten (TUHNG•stuhn) is too heavy to use as wire for some jobs. But a thin, lightweight wire coated with diamond would work as well as a thicker, heavier, uncoated wire.

Careers   Organic Chemist

What They Do
Organic chemists work with materials containing the element carbon, such as hydrocarbons. These materials include plastics as well as animal and vegetable matter. Organic chemists develop new products or test them. Some organic chemists teach high school or college chemistry.

Education and Training   Organic chemists have at least a four-year college degree. Most have a master's degree or a Ph.D.

Mack Gipson, Jr.

STRUCTURAL GEOLOGIST

Dr. Mack Gipson grew up on a farm in South Carolina. He helped with farm work and was interested in nature. In junior high, he read a book about Earth and began to wonder how rocks were formed and what caused Earth's layers.

After finishing college with degrees in science and mathematics, Gipson became a high school teacher. He was drafted into the U.S. Army and trained as a radio technician. While he was with the army in Germany, he decided to go back to school and study geology. He decided he wanted to work outdoors as a geologist rather than spend all day indoors teaching.

One of Dr. Gipson's jobs in college was to test core samples. A core sample shows layers of soil and rock from underground. To get a core sample, a long metal tube is drilled into the ground.

Builders test core samples to make sure the ground can withstand the weight of a building or road. Gipson tested core samples for the building of runways at O'Hare International Airport in Chicago. He also studied rock layers near coal mines in Illinois.

After graduating from the University of Chicago, Dr. Mack Gipson stayed to help study samples of rock and clay from the ocean floor. This study helped scientists learn about how the oceans have changed over time.

Dr. Gipson founded the Department of Geological Sciences at Virginia State University. In addition to teaching, he has done studies for the National Aeronautics and Space Administration (NASA). He studied pictures of pyramidlike mountains on Mars. He concluded that the pictures show extinct volcanoes eroded by the wind.

THINK ABOUT IT

1. How might studying a core sample show how much weight the ground could safely support?
2. What skills do you think are needed to study worlds far from Earth?

Geologists studying core samples

Growing Crystals

How are minerals left behind by evaporation?

Materials

- plastic gloves
- safety goggles
- apron
- 1 tablespoon of laundry bluing
- 1 tablespoon of water
- 1 tablespoon of ammonia
- 1 tablespoon of table salt
- plastic cup
- spoon
- sponge
- plastic bowl
- food coloring

Procedure

CAUTION Be sure to wear gloves, safety goggles, and an apron.

1 Mix the bluing, water, ammonia, and salt in the plastic cup. Stir gently until the salt has dissolved.

2 Place the sponge in the bowl. Pour the mixture over the sponge. Throw away the cup.

3 Sprinkle 4 drops of food coloring over the sponge. Wait one day.

Draw Conclusions

Observe the sponge. Does it change? What is forming?

Weathering Rock

How can you model weathering by using chalk?

Materials

- 2 pieces of chalk
- plastic jar with lid
- water
- strainer

Procedure

1 Break each piece of chalk into about three pieces. Put all the chalk pieces except one into the jar.

2 Pour water into the jar until the chalk is covered. Put the lid on the jar. Make sure it is tightly sealed. Shake the jar for about 5 minutes to "weather" the chalk.

3 Pour the water through the strainer to get the chalk pieces.

Draw Conclusions

Compare the strained pieces to the chalk that was left out. What happened? Why? Compare this model to real rocks, weathering, and erosion. How are they alike? How are they different?

Vocabulary Review

Use the terms below to complete the sentences. The page numbers in ( ) tell you where to look in the chapter if you need help.

mineral (C34)   **sedimentary rock** (C42)
streak (C35)   **metamorphic rock** (C44)
hardness (C35)   **erosion** (C40)
luster (C35)   **weathering** (C42)
rock (C40)   **rock cycle** (C50)
igneous rock (C40)

1. The effects of ice, wind, and rain on rocks are called _____.

2. A natural, nonliving, solid material that has particles in a repeating pattern is a _____.

3. A _____ is made up of one or more minerals.

4. Limestone is a form of _____.

5. The _____ is the repeating of changes from one kind of rock to another over time.

6. _____ carries away pieces of weathered rock to other places.

7. A _____ is a rock changed by heat and pressure.

8. Melted rock cools and hardens to form _____.

9. The color of the powder left behind when you rub a mineral on a white porcelain plate is called the mineral's _____.

10. _____ is a mineral property that describes the way light reflects from the mineral's surface.

11. A mineral's ability to resist being scratched is its _____.

Connect Concepts

Fill in the blanks with the correct terms from the Word Bank.

color   **luster**   **Mohs' hardness scale**
hardness   **streak**

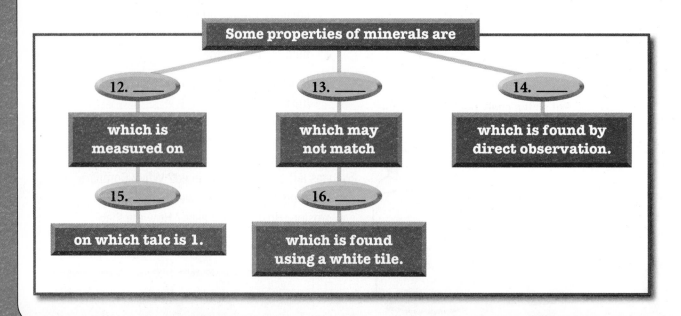

Some properties of minerals are

12. _____ which is measured on 15. _____ on which talc is 1.

13. _____ which may not match 16. _____ which is found using a white tile.

14. _____ which is found by direct observation.

Check Understanding

Write the letter of the best choice.

17. A rock forms in layers of small pieces. It is a ____ rock.
    A sedimentary   C igneous
    B mineral   D metamorphic

18. Mohs' hardness scale is used to identify a mineral's —
    F color   H streak
    G luster   J hardness

19. If you describe a mineral as being shiny, you are describing the property of —
    A streak   C hardness
    B luster   D color

20. A rock that has been changed by pressure and heat is called a ____ rock.
    F sedimentary
    G metamorphic
    H igneous
    J metallic

21. When wind or water breaks a rock into smaller pieces, the process is called —
    A weathering   C igneous
    B hardness   D schist

22. Which of the following minerals is the hardest on Mohs' hardness scale?
    F talc   H diamond
    G gypsum   J quartz

23. Rocks change over time from one type to another. This process is called —
    A type changing
    B the rock cycle
    C erosion
    D melting

24. Particles in minerals form regular patterns called —
    F crystals   H conglomerates
    G layers   J shells

Process Skills Review

25. Based on the **model** you made of the rock cycle, what might happen to the "rock" if you made it hot enough to melt?

26. Why do scientists **classify** minerals?

27. How do scientists **classify** rocks?

Critical Thinking

28. How can a metamorphic rock be changed into an igneous rock?

29. Describe the path of a rock through the rock cycle.

Performance Assessment

Mineral Tests

Work with a partner. Use the hand lens to take a closer look at five mineral samples. Make a chart showing all the properties of each mineral. Tell how you tested for each property.

Chapter 3

Fossils

The history of life on Earth is buried under your feet. You might find clues left behind in a back yard by someone who lived in the house years ago. If you know where to look, you might even find clues left behind millions of years ago by dinosaurs.

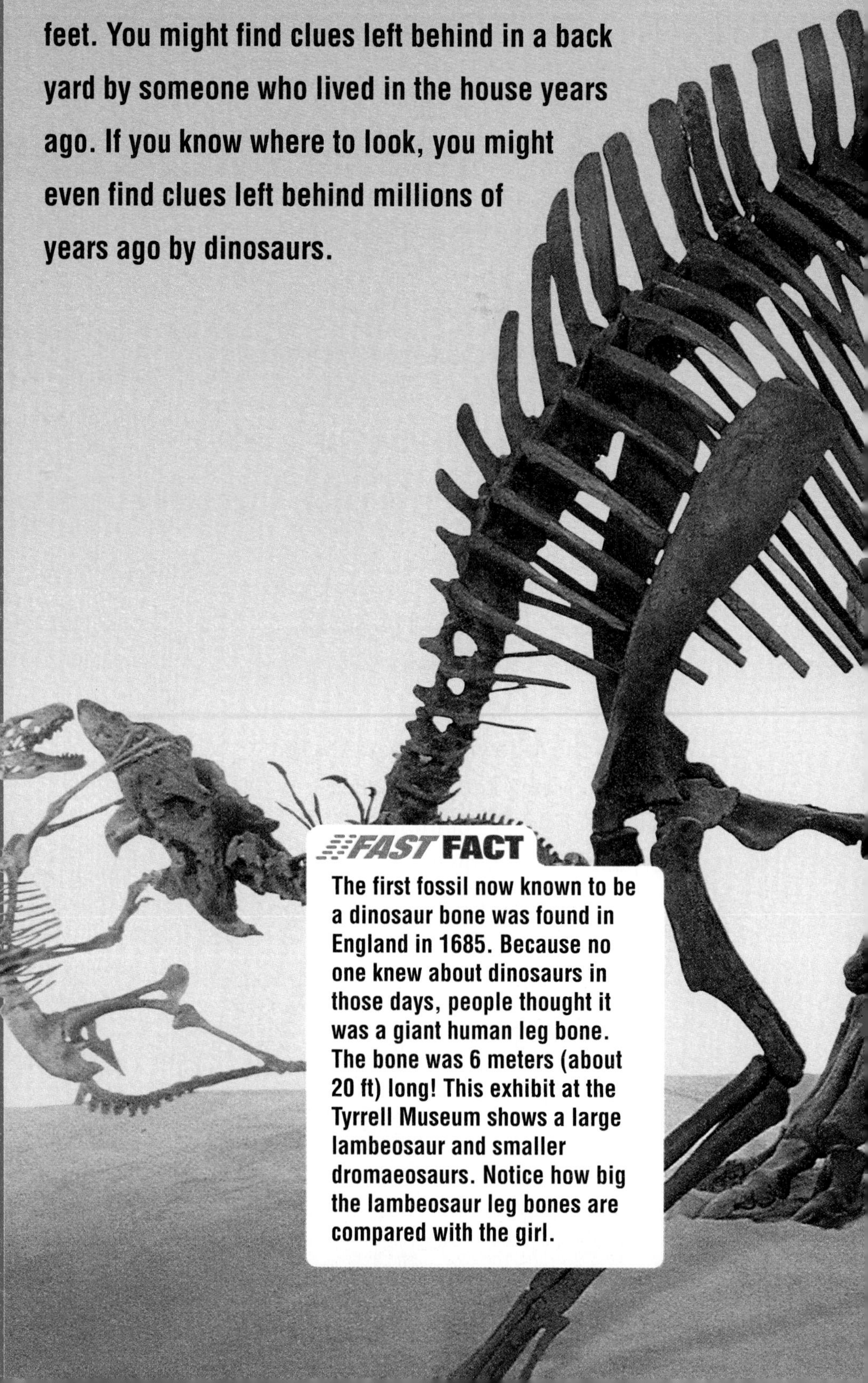

FAST FACT

The first fossil now known to be a dinosaur bone was found in England in 1685. Because no one knew about dinosaurs in those days, people thought it was a giant human leg bone. The bone was 6 meters (about 20 ft) long! This exhibit at the Tyrrell Museum shows a large lambeosaur and smaller dromaeosaurs. Notice how big the lambeosaur leg bones are compared with the girl.

Vocabulary Preview

fossil
trace fossil
mold
cast

Ammonoids (AM•uh•noydz) are a type of shellfish that lived long ago. The largest found so far was dug up in the Westphalia region of Germany. Its spiral shell is almost 2 meters (about $6\frac{1}{2}$ ft) across.

The first dinosaur footprints discovered in North America were found in Connecticut by Pliny Moody, a 12-year-old farm boy!

How Do Fossils Form?

In this lesson, you can . . .

 INVESTIGATE how animal parts can be preserved as a fossil.

 LEARN ABOUT ways in which some fossils form.

 LINK to math, writing, art, and technology.

 **INVESTIGATE**

Making a Fossil

Activity Purpose When a living thing dies, its soft parts quickly rot away. The hard parts, such as bones or woody stems, take much longer to decay, or rot away. Long ago some of these hard parts were buried and became fossils. In this activity you will **make a model** of the hard and soft parts of an "animal." Then you will **observe** how parts of your model "decay."

Materials
- 8 sugar cubes
- glue gun, low temperature
- strainer
- sink or large bowl
- warm water

 CAUTION

Activity Procedure

1 Glue together four sugar cubes to make one 2 × 2 layer. **CAUTION** **The tip of the glue gun is hot.** Make a second 2 × 2 layer with the other four cubes. (Picture A) Let the layers dry for five minutes.

2 Spread glue on top of one layer, and place the second layer on top of it. Let the glue dry overnight.

◀ This is a fossil ammonoid (AM•uhn•oyd). Ammonoids had hard shells and lived in ancient oceans.

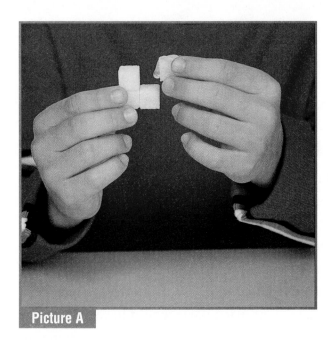

Picture A

Picture B

3 Put the two-layered structure in the strainer. Put the strainer in the sink or over a bowl. (Picture B) Pour warm water over the structure and **observe** what happens.

4 What happens to the sugar? Does anything happen to the dried glue?

Draw Conclusions

1. In your model what parts of a plant or an animal did the sugar cubes stand for? What parts of a plant or an animal did the dried glue stand for?

2. In your model, what process did the warm water stand for?

3. **Scientists at Work** Scientists often **make inferences** based on their observations. What can you infer about how fossils form, based on what you learned in the investigation?

Investigate Further With an adult's permission, bury a cooked chicken leg about 15 cm deep in the ground outdoors. After a couple of weeks, put on rubber gloves and goggles, and dig up the chicken leg. **Observe** how it has changed. What happened to the soft parts of the chicken leg? Did the hard parts change?

Process Skill Tip

When you don't know enough to be sure why something happens, you may infer an explanation. When you **infer**, you use what you already know to explain your observations. When more information is available, you might find out whether your inference is right or wrong.

Fossil Formation

How Fossils Form

Some rocks hold clues to life on Earth long ago. These clues, called **fossils**, are found most often in sedimentary rocks. This is because most fossils formed when a dead plant or animal was buried quickly by sediments. As with your model in the investigation, the soft parts of the plant or animal decayed, or rotted away. The hard parts took longer to decay. They were preserved, or saved, by being buried. Unburied parts would have been eaten or destroyed by weather. As the sediments hardened, the remains became trapped in rock and formed a fossil.

Fossils also can form in other ways. Not all fossils are parts of once-living things. Some fossils are traces, such as footprints, left by living things. Sometimes the shape of a plant or an animal is left as a hollow in a rock. The hollow left behind is a fossil. If minerals fill the hollow, the new rock they form is also a fossil.

✔ **How do most fossils form?**

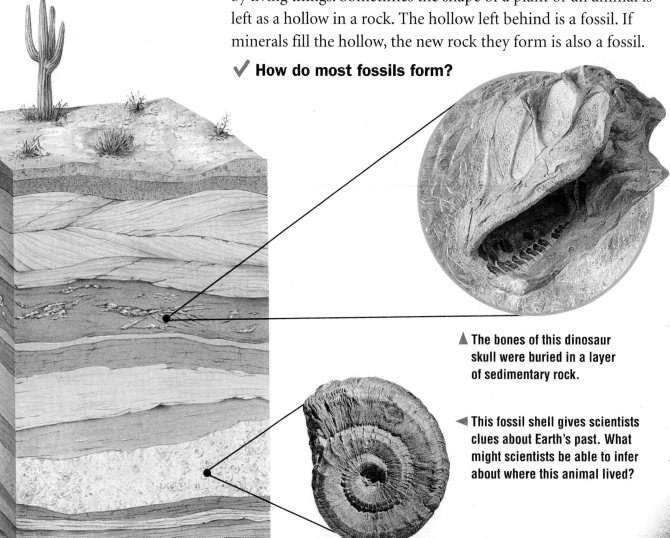

▲ The bones of this dinosaur skull were buried in a layer of sedimentary rock.

◀ This fossil shell gives scientists clues about Earth's past. What might scientists be able to infer about where this animal lived?

Trace Fossils

Wood, bones, teeth, and
shells aren't the only things that
become fossils. Some fossils show
changes long-dead animals made in their
surroundings. These are **trace fossils**.
Tracks, burrows, droppings, and worm holes
are some examples of trace fossils. These
types of fossils give scientists clues about
animals. They tell how an animal might
have moved. They show how big or small it
might have been. They also show what it
might have eaten. The photographs on this
page show different types of trace fossils.

✔ **What is a trace fossil?**

▲ Fossilized tracks give clues about an animal's
size and how it moved. The dinosaur track
above is found in limestone near Glen Rose,
Texas. It is many years old. The tracks above
left were made recently in sand by a living bird.
How might they become a fossil?

Scientists can learn a lot about what
an animal ate by looking at coprolites
(KAHP•roh•lyts). Coprolites are animal
droppings that have become fossils. ▶

◀ A worm made this burrow, or tunnel,
as it hunted for food in soft sediment.
When the sediment was buried and
hardened into rock, the burrow
was preserved.

Other Types of Fossils

Usually, the parts of living things that make up fossils are changed as rock forms. For example, fossil molds and casts form after the parts are destroyed. A **mold** is an imprint made by the outside of a dead plant or animal. A mold forms when water slowly washes animal or plant remains out of rock. The space left in the rock layer matches the shape of the once-living thing. Sometimes sediments or minerals fill a mold and form a **cast**. The cast has the same outside shape as the original living thing.

Sometimes chemical and physical changes take place as remains become fossils. Heat and pressure may destroy most of the buried remains. Only a thin film, or sheet, of black carbon is left. This type of fossil is called a carbon film.

Some fossils form when minerals slowly take the place of original, once-living material. Fossils that form in this way are called *petrified* (PET•trih•fyd) fossils. *Petri-* means "stone." The trees in Petrified Forest National Park became

◄ Fossil molds and casts give clues about the outside of the once-living thing.

fossils in this way. Their wood was replaced by the mineral quartz.

A whole plant or animal, including soft parts, can become a fossil. Sometimes insects were trapped in the sticky sap of trees. When the sap hardened, the whole insect was preserved. Large animals such as woolly mammoths have also been trapped and preserved in glacier ice.

Tar pits have also preserved once-living things. Animals got stuck when they tried to walk through the sticky tar. Plants and plant parts were blown or fell into the tar and got stuck. Many animal fossils have been found in the La Brea (luh BRAY•uh) tar pits in Los Angeles, California. They include deer, elephants, horses, birds, and saber-toothed tigers.

✔ **How were whole plants or animals preserved as fossils?**

◄ A carbon film forms when heat and pressure force out most of the materials that made up a once-living thing. Only a thin sheet of carbon is left. What kind of organism is this a fossil of?

Millions of years ago, this dragonfly got stuck in sap from a pine tree. Later the sap hardened to form a clear yellow material called *amber.* ▶

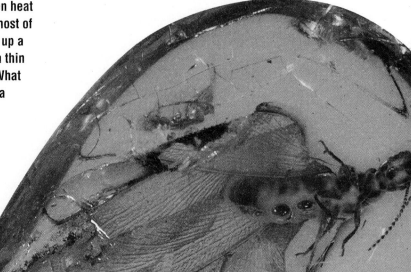

▲ Petrified Forest National Park in Arizona has many petrified logs like this one. The fossils began forming when water containing minerals soaked into fallen trees. As the wood slowly rotted away, minerals took its place.

Summary

Fossils are the remains of living things that lived on Earth long ago. Fossils are usually made of the hard parts of plants and animals. But they can form in several other ways. For example, trace fossils, such as tracks, burrows, and droppings, give clues about what animals did.

Review

1. What are fossils?
2. How does a carbon film form?
3. How does a petrified fossil form?
4. **Critical Thinking** Compare and contrast trace fossils and mold fossils.
5. **Test Prep** Which of the following forms when a fossil mold is filled?
   - **A** fossil cast
   - **B** petrified fossil
   - **C** carbon film
   - **D** tar pit

LINKS

MATH LINK

How Old? Many cities bury their trash in big holes called landfills. The trash often forms layers like those in sedimentary rock. If you dig a hole in a city landfill and find a newspaper dated 1900, what do you think is the age of that layer of the landfill? Design a graph that you could use to show the age of several landfill layers.

WRITING LINK

Narrative Writing—Story Find out how the Badlands of South Dakota formed. Then write a story for a classmate. Tell about a fourth grader hunting fossils in the Badlands. Be sure to give a detailed description of the setting of the story.

ART LINK

Lost-Wax Casting Ask an art teacher or use library resources to find out about the lost-wax casting method. With the help of an adult, try it. How is it like what happens when fossil casts and molds form?

TECHNOLOGY LINK

Learn more about finding fossils by investigating *Digging Up Dinosaurs* on **Harcourt Science Explorations CD-ROM.**

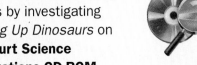

What Can We Learn from Fossils?

In this lesson, you can . . .

INVESTIGATE how scientists decide which events happened first.

LEARN ABOUT when certain living things appeared on Earth.

LINK to math, writing, physical education, and technology.

INVESTIGATE

Sets of Animal Tracks

Activity Purpose Have you and your friends ever made footprints in snow or mud? If you then looked at the crisscrossing tracks, could you tell which were made first? In this investigation your group will **make a model** of several sets of tracks. You'll then share the model with another group of students. They will try to figure out the order in which the tracks were made.

Materials

- poster board
- markers, crayons, and colored pencils
- animal footprint stamps
- ink pad

Activity Procedure

1 On the poster board, draw a picture of an area where animal tracks are found. The picture might show a riverbank or a sandy beach. (Picture A)

2 Each person in your group should choose a different animal. Mark these animals' tracks on the poster board. Use the ink pad and stamps, or any of the other items. Make sure that some sets of tracks go over other sets. Keep a record of which animal made tracks first, second, third, and so on. (Picture B)

◀ This fossil is the skull of a protoceratops. Some pieces were missing, so scientists had to infer the shape of part of the skull.

Picture A

Picture B

3 When your group has finished making tracks, trade poster boards with another group. Try to figure out the order in which the other group's tracks were made. **Record** your conclusions in an ordered list. Give reasons for the order you chose. **Compare** your conclusions with the written record of the other group's track order.

Draw Conclusions

1. Did all the animals move in the same way? If not, how could you tell the kind of animal from the tracks it made?

2. How did your group decide which tracks were made first?

3. **Scientists at Work** Scientists can **infer** relationships among rock layers and the fossils they contain. They do this after carefully **observing** the rocks and fossils. What observations led you to infer the order in which the footprints were made?

Investigate Further Get a potato. Using a plastic knife, carefully carve the potato into an animal track stamp. Use an ink pad and the stamp to make some tracks on a sheet of paper. Have a classmate **infer** from the tracks how the "animal" moves. Does it slither? Does it walk on two legs or four legs? Or does the animal jump or fly to get from place to place?

Process Skill Tip

Observations and inferences are not the same. When you **observe**, you use your senses to see, touch, hear, smell, or taste an object. When you **infer**, you form an opinion. To do this, you use what you know about the object or situation.

Fossil Clues to the Past

How Living Things Have Changed

Fossils are like snapshots of the past. They are preserved evidence of how long-dead living things may have looked. Fossil evidence also can suggest how living things may have changed over time. Look at the pictures on this page. As you can see, some living things, like the ginkgo tree, have changed very little over time. Other living things have changed a lot during Earth's history. For example, archaeopteryx (ar•kee•AHP•ter•iks) was a chicken-sized reptile that lived on Earth millions of years ago. It was probably related to birds that live today. It had feathers and was shaped like a bird. Some scientists hypothesize that it could fly because its wings were like those of birds alive today. But like other reptiles, it had claws, a long tail, and teeth.

The archaeopteryx was a reptile that had some of a bird's features. ▼

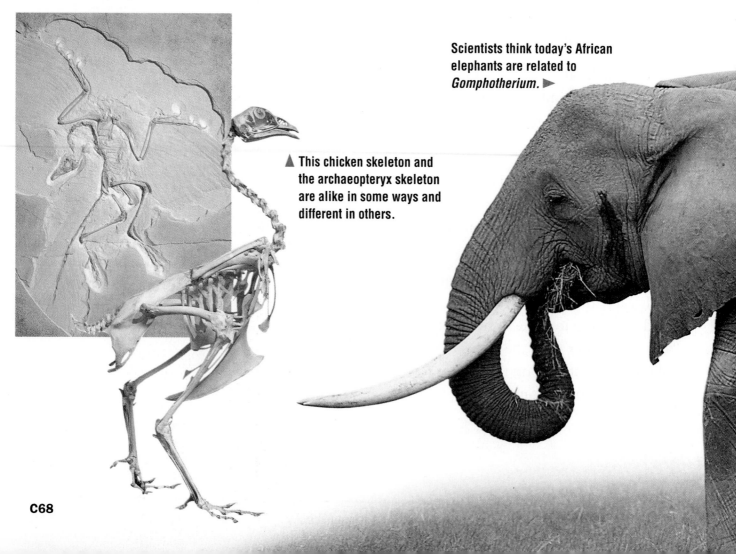

Scientists think today's African elephants are related to *Gomphotherium*. ▶

▲ This chicken skeleton and the archaeopteryx skeleton are alike in some ways and different in others.

Elephants, too, have changed over time as their environments changed. Some animal types that were like elephants died out. Other types changed slowly over a long time. Woolly mammoths lived during the long, cold Ice Age. Glaciers (GLAY•shurz), or huge sheets of ice, covered large parts of North America, Europe, and Asia during the Ice Age. Mammoths died out soon after it ended. Another elephant-like animal, *Gomphotherium* (gahm•foh•THEER•ee•uhm), was able to live. Scientists think today's African elephant is related to it.

✔ **How do scientists know that living things have changed over time?**

▲ Ginkgoes belong to a family of trees that lived about 175 to 200 million years ago. Does the ginkgo leaf of today look different from the ginkgo fossil?

Gomphotherium's tusks and long curling trunk were like those of elephants alive today. ▼

Thick hair and big curling tusks helped woolly mammoths live during the Ice Age. Even though mammoths looked much like elephants today, for some reason they died out when the climate changed. ▼

▲ Most fossils are found in sedimentary rocks. Getting fossils out of rocks can take a long time. People have to be careful not to break the fossils.

The Importance of Fossils

Fossils are important for many reasons. They tell us what living things were like in the past and how they have changed over a very long time. They also tell us what Earth was like long ago. For example, if we find rocks that have fossil shells, we know the rocks formed in or near water. Probably long ago the area where the rocks were found was under water. If rocks have fossil ferns, then the rocks probably formed in a swampy area.

Scientists can infer from fossils how an animal moved. As you saw in the investigation, fossil footprints can show how an animal walked. Bones also can show this. For example, the dinosaur in the pictures at the right had four legs. The front legs were much shorter, so the animal probably walked on only two legs.

▲ The bones of this dinosaur were found at a place like the one above. Scientists put the bones together like a jigsaw puzzle. The skeleton stands the way the animal probably stood when it was alive.

▲ Artists often work with scientists to plan and make museum displays. They use both imagination and science facts to make models that seem to be alive.

If a fossil mold shows the animal's soft parts, scientists can tell more about how the animal looked. They can tell if it had skin, fur, feathers, or scales. More often, though, scientists infer how animals looked. To do this, they look at similar animals that are alive now.

✔ **Why are fossils important?**

THE INSIDE STORY

Animatronic Dinosaur

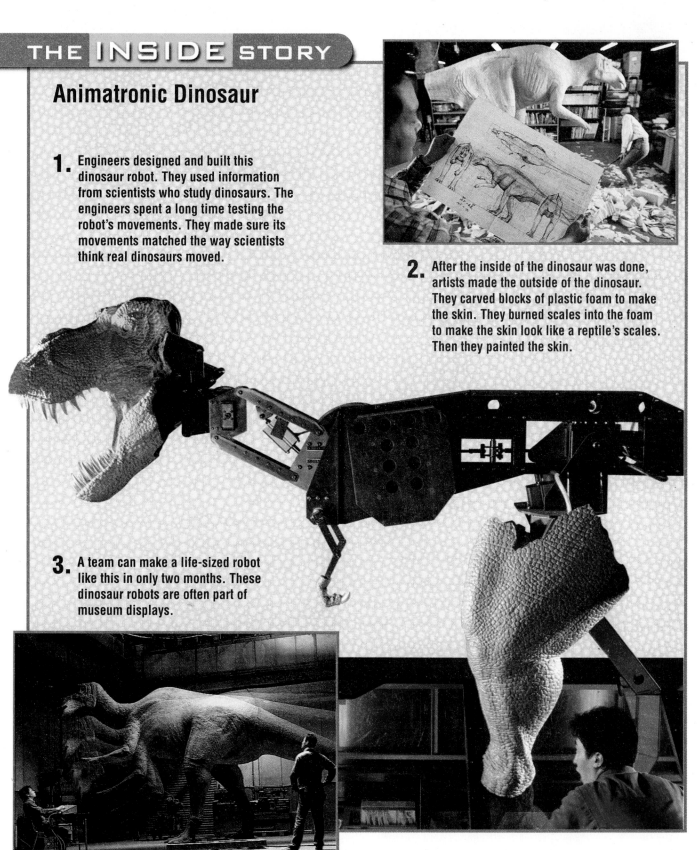

1. Engineers designed and built this dinosaur robot. They used information from scientists who study dinosaurs. The engineers spent a long time testing the robot's movements. They made sure its movements matched the way scientists think real dinosaurs moved.

2. After the inside of the dinosaur was done, artists made the outside of the dinosaur. They carved blocks of plastic foam to make the skin. They burned scales into the foam to make the skin look like a reptile's scales. Then they painted the skin.

3. A team can make a life-sized robot like this in only two months. These dinosaur robots are often part of museum displays.

◀ Magnolia blossom

The Ages of Rocks and Fossils

Scientists study rocks and fossils to find out how old the fossils are. Recall that some rocks form in layers. Each layer is newer than the one below it. Scientists study the order of these layers and compare the layers in different places. They can't tell exactly how old a layer is this way. However, they can tell whether a rock or fossil is older or younger than the layers above and below it.

Scientists find the age of rocks in another way. Some rocks have particles that decay, or break down over time, to form different particles. Many igneous rocks are like this. Scientists can compare the amounts of the original particles and the new particles that form to find out the age of the rock.

✔ **What are two ways scientists can find out the age of a rock?**

Fern in limestone ▼

Scientists uncover many fossils as they examine and find the age of rock layers. The fossils on these pages show the diversity of living things during Earth's past.

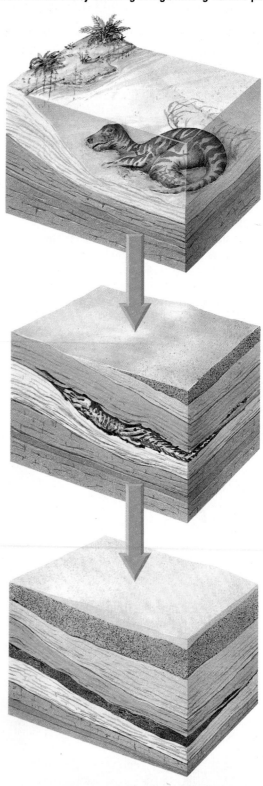

▲ The oldest rocks are usually at the bottom of the "stack." The rock beds, or layers, at the top are younger. Sometimes, however, movement in Earth's crust can twist stacks of layers or turn them over.

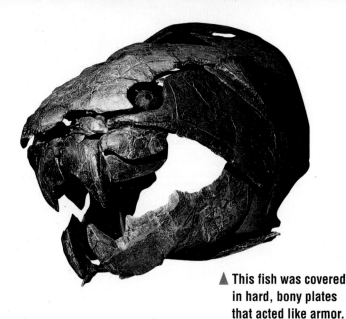

▲ This fish was covered in hard, bony plates that acted like armor.

Summary

Fossils tell us about living things of the past, how living things have changed over time, and how Earth has changed. Fossils are evidence of the diversity of life that existed on Earth in the past.

Review

1. What is an example of a living thing that has changed little over time?

2. How was a gomphotherium like an African elephant?

3. How are layers of sedimentary rocks useful in finding out the age of fossils?

4. **Critical Thinking** Suppose scientists find a fossil like an archaeopteryx, but it does not have teeth or a tail. Would this support the hypothesis that archaeopteryx is related to birds that are alive now? Explain.

5. **Test Prep** Suppose you observe several layers of rock that have been exposed by road work. The oldest rock is probably —

   A   in the top layer
   B   in the middle layer
   C   in the bottom layer
   D   just below the top layer

LINKS

MATH LINK

Ammonoids, such as the one shown on page C59, were like squid except ammonoids had shells. Use reference materials to find the sizes of squid living now. Compare them with the ammonoid. Which animal is largest? What is the difference in size?

WRITING LINK

Informative Writing—Description
Suppose you are hiking near a cliff. Suddenly you see something that looks like a large bone trapped in the rock. Describe for your teacher the animal whose fossil you found. Tell how you think it lived and how the fossil formed.

PHYSICAL EDUCATION LINK

Animal Movements With a partner, make a list of 10 different animals. Make sure that some of your choices move in different ways. Take the list outside and find an area of dry sand or dirt that will show tracks. Choose an animal from the list. Have your partner look away while you move the way the animal moves. Then have your partner guess the animal just by looking at the tracks.

TECHNOLOGY LINK

Learn more about recent fossil discoveries by viewing *Dinosaur Egg* on the **Harcourt Science Newsroom Video**.

BURIED IN TIME

Have you ever collected fossils? If you have, you are following a very old tradition. One of the Roman emperors had a fossil collection in his home. Some ancient Greek scientists found fossils of sea animals on mountains. The scientists reasoned that the mountains must have been underwater at some time. One of these scientists, Theophrastus (thee•uh•FRAS•tuhs), wrote a book about fossils.

Early Fossil Discoveries

The word *fossil* was first used in the 1500s. Georgius Agricola (JAWR•jee•uhs uh•GRIK•uh•luh) used it to refer to anything that was dug up. He thought fossils were just oddly shaped stones. He didn't realize that fossils were parts of things that once were alive.

Soon after Agricola, a German scientist, Konrad von Gesner, classified fossils into 15 different types. In the late 1500s a teacher named Bernard Palissy (pah•lee•SEE) showed fossils to his students as part of his science lectures. He was the first person to understand that fossils are remains of once-living organisms.

The first major discovery of dinosaur bones happened in England during the early 1800s. Around this time Georges Cuvier (ZHAWRZH koo•VYAY) began studying fossils. He identified some fossil remains as those of a giant salamander. Cuvier thought that fossils were remains of long-dead plants and animals. He also thought that sudden, violent natural events, such as volcanic eruptions and earthquakes, had destroyed the organisms that became the fossils. Other scientists disagreed with this idea. They thought fossils were remains of animal types that still lived in unknown places on Earth.

The History of Fossils

Theophrastus 300 B.C.
Theophrastus writes a book on fossils.

Cuvier 1825 A.D.
Georges Cuvier suggests fossils are parts of extinct animals.

300 B.C.   1500 A.D.   1600 A.D.   1700 A.D.   1800 A.D.

Gesner about 1500 A.D.
Agricola first uses the word *fossil.* Konrad von Gesner classifies fossils. Bernard Palissy uses fossils in his lectures.

Owen 1842 A.D.
Richard Owen first uses term *dinosaur.*

Fossils—Ages Old

During the 1940s scientists began using radioactive materials to judge the age of rocks in which fossils were found. One element that is naturally radioactive is called potassium-40, or K-40. It is found in many rocks. K-40 decays very slowly. As it decays, it changes into different elements. By comparing the amount of K-40 left to the amounts of those different elements, scientists can judge the age of the rock.

What Fossils Tell Us

When scientists first collected fossils, they tried to figure out what the ancient animals looked like. After putting together animal skeletons, they inferred what their body coverings looked like and how the animals lived. Sometimes scientists made mistakes. For example, they thought that *Tyrannosaurus rex* stood up straight and dragged its tail.

Scientists now think it stood as shown on page C70. Scientists are still doing this kind of study today.

New discoveries are also being made as the same bones are examined again with new tools. For example, scientists in New Mexico hypothesize that one type of duck-bill dinosaur made sounds like those of a musical instrument called a bassoon. Their hypothesis is based on computer models of the dinosaur's skull and CT scans, a special kind of X-ray picture. All these discoveries help us better understand what fossils can tell us.

Think About It

1. How did scientists who studied fossils build on what was already known?
2. Suppose you found a bone buried in your backyard and thought it might be a fossil. What would you do to find out?

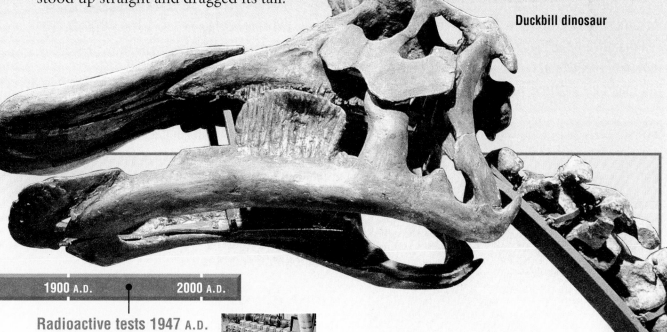

Duckbill dinosaur

1900 A.D.   2000 A.D.

Radioactive tests 1947 A.D.
Scientists use radioactive elements to judge age of fossils.

Lisa D. White
MICROPALEONTOLOGIST

When she was young, Lisa White visited the California Academy of Sciences, near where she lived. She was most interested in the geology exhibits. In college, White was again drawn toward geology. During summers, she worked for the U.S. Geological Survey. The people there encouraged her fascination with climate change and geologic time. As a result, she became a paleontologist (pay•lee•uhn•TAHL•uh•jist), a scientist who studies fossils and Earth's past.

Dr. White became part of the Ocean Drilling Program, an international team of scientists, engineers, and technicians. The program makes six ocean cruises a year. Each cruise lasts about two months. The specially equipped ship is the only ship of its kind in the world.

The goal of the program is to find out about Earth's history. A special drill on the ship brings up core samples, or narrow tubes, of rock and sediment from the ocean floor. Each $9\frac{1}{2}$-meter (about 30-ft) long core is cut in half lengthwise. One-half of the core is preserved, much as

Ocean Drilling Program's ship

books are stored in a library. The other half of the core is analyzed on the ship.

White studies the tiny fossils, or microfossils, of diatoms in the core samples. She tries to find the age of the fossils in each sample.

Dr. Lisa White now teaches at San Francisco State University. She grew up in that city, and is glad to be teaching at the school she once attended. She enjoys sharing her research experiences with students in her geology and oceanography classes.

THINK ABOUT IT

1. Why would collecting samples from the ocean floor be a good way to study fossils?

2. Why do you think Dr. White studies microfossils in core samples, and not fossils of large animals?

Cast and Mold

How can you make a mold and a cast of a seashell?

Materials

- seashell
- petroleum jelly
- clay
- plastic bowl
- paper cup
- white glue

Procedure

❶ Coat the ridges of the seashell with a thin layer of petroleum jelly. Press the seashell into the clay. Remove the seashell carefully from the clay. Place the clay with the imprint of the seashell in the plastic bowl.

❷ Drizzle white glue in the shell imprint. Fill it completely.

❸ Let the glue harden. When it has hardened completely, separate it from the clay.

Draw Conclusions

Which is the cast of your seashell? The mold?

Reconstructing the Past

How can you reconstruct past events using a word "fossil"?

Materials

- unlined paper
- pencil
- ruler
- scissors

Procedure

❶ Write a paragraph that tells about a past event. The paragraph should be at least three sentences long. Leave a blank space between each line you write.

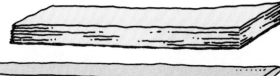

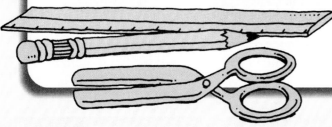

❷ Cut the paragraph into square-edged pieces. Each piece should have one or two words written on it. The pieces are the "bones" of this "fossil."

❸ Remove two or three bones, and put them in a safe place.

❹ Mix up the rest of the bones, and exchange them with a partner.

❺ Try to figure out what your partner's paragraph says. Check your guess with your partner.

Draw Conclusions

How did the missing bones affect Step 5? How is this puzzle like what scientists do with fossils?

Chapter ③ Review and Test Preparation

Vocabulary Review

Use the terms below to complete the sentences. The page numbers in ( ) tell you where to look in the chapter if you need help.

fossil (C62)

trace fossil (C63)

mold (C64)

cast (C64)

1. A _____ is a clue to the activity of an animal that lived long ago.

2. A _____ is a clue, preserved in rock, about life in the distant past.

3. A fossil imprint left by a plant or animal is called a _____.

4. If minerals fill a mold fossil and then harden, a _____ forms.

Connect Concepts

Use the terms in the Word Bank to complete the concept map.

buried	carbon film	cast	rock layers
fossils	mold	petrified	

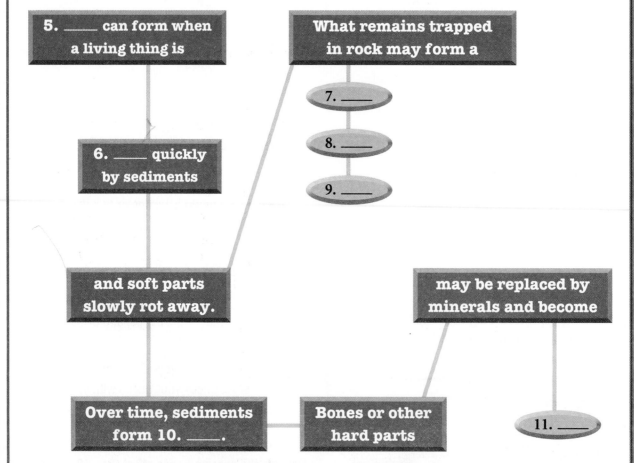

5. _____ can form when a living thing is

6. _____ quickly by sediments

7. _____

8. _____

9. _____

What remains trapped in rock may form a

and soft parts slowly rot away.

may be replaced by minerals and become

Over time, sediments form 10. _____.

Bones or other hard parts

11. _____

Check Understanding

Write the letter of the best choice.

12. The most likely place to find a fossil is
    ____ rock.
    A sedimentary
    B volcanic
    C igneous
    D metamorphic

13. A fossilized dinosaur footprint is an
    example of —
    F a cast
    G a trace fossil
    H a mold
    J index fossils

14. When woody material in a tree is
    replaced with minerals, the tree
    becomes —
    A petrified
    B a trace fossil
    C carbon film
    D amber

15. Which of the following features of
    Archaeopteryx is **NOT** like a reptile?
    F scales
    G wings
    H claws
    J long tail

Critical Thinking

16. What could you infer about an animal
    from a fossil of its jawbone?

17. Would you be likely to find a fossil in
    igneous rock? Explain.

18. Explain why some animals and plants
    became fossils and others did not.

Process Skills Review

19. Can you **infer** from the picture which
    rock layer is the oldest? Explain.

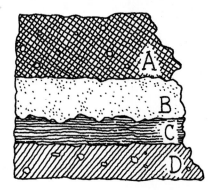

20. You find a fossil trilobite in a rock layer.
    You know when trilobites lived. What
    can you **infer** about other fossils in the
    same rock layer? Explain.

Performance Assessment

Fossil Search

You and a partner should each find five
small objects in the classroom. Without
your partner watching, make an imprint of
part or all of each object in its own ball of
soft clay. Return the objects to the classroom. Then ask your partner to find the
object that matches each clay imprint. How
is this like a fossil mold? If the imprint were
filled with another
material that
hardened, what
kind of fossil
would that
stand for?

C79

Unit Project Wrap Up

Here are some ideas for ways to wrap up your unit project.

Make a Book

Use index cards to make a book about your collection. Use one card for each sample. Draw a picture or attach a photo of the sample, identify it, and add information you have gathered.

Landscape with Rocks

Get permission to landscape a small outdoor area with your rocks. Use the rocks along with living and other nonliving things to make a landscape design that you like. Identify each rock with a label.

Display at a Science Fair

Display your earth-sample collection in a school science fair. Make maps, charts, or tables to help communicate what you learned.

Investigate Further

How could you make your project better? What other questions do you have about Earth's surface? Plan ways to find answers to your questions. Use the Science Handbook on pages R2-R9 for help.

Patterns on Earth and in Space

UNIT D

EARTH SCIENCE

Patterns on Earth and in Space

Unit Project

Weather Station

Make a weather station for your classroom. Make instruments to help you measure the weather. Use charts and tables to record changes in the weather. Prepare a weather report each day, and predict the weather for the following day. Be sure to support your prediction with data you've collected. Then compare your prediction with the actual weather.

Chapter 1

Weather Conditions

Everyone talks about the weather, but weather forecasters get paid to talk about it. Many people depend on weather forecasts to plan their day. Sometimes forecasts of severe weather can even save lives.

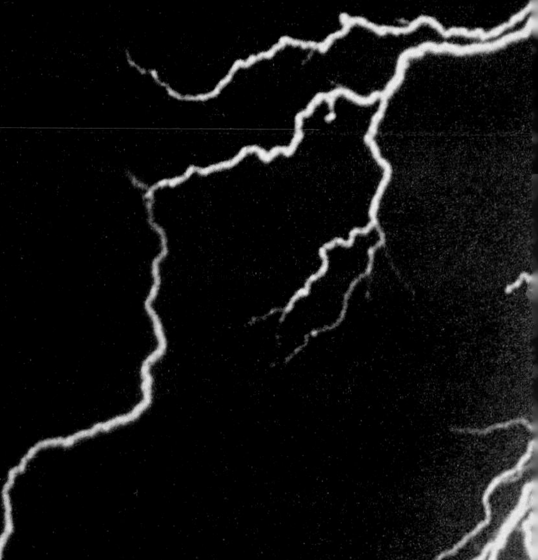

Vocabulary Preview

atmosphere
air pressure
troposphere
stratosphere
greenhouse effect
air mass
front
barometer
humidity
anemometer

FAST FACT

Right now, 2000 thunderstorms are happening around the Earth. While you are reading this sentence, lightning will strike the Earth about 500 times!

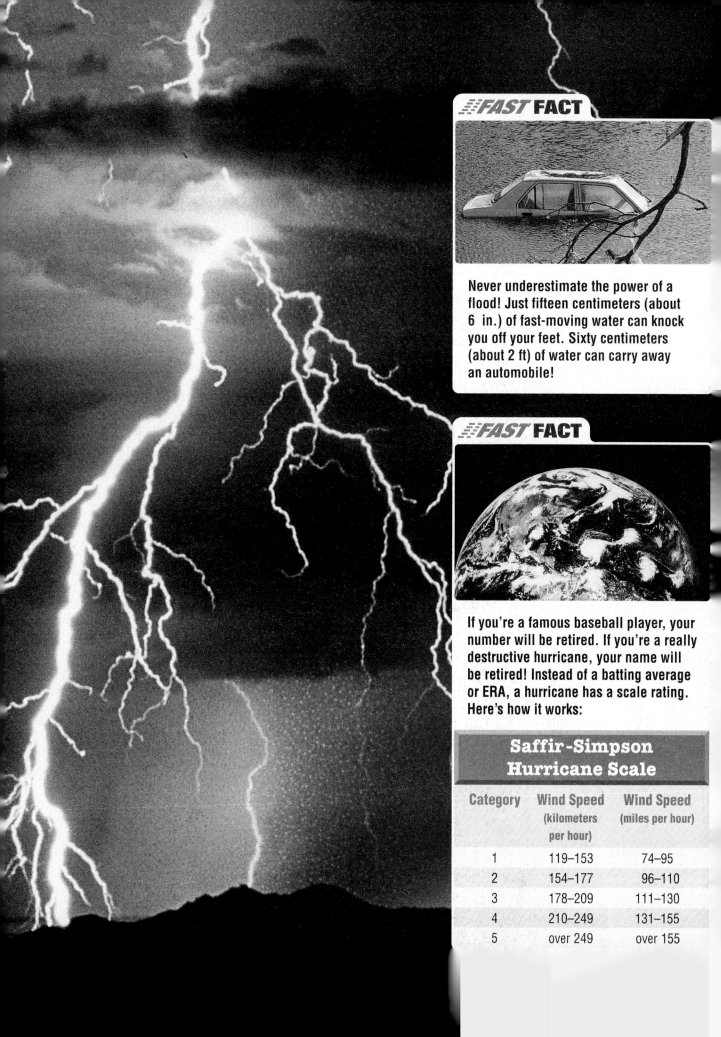

Never underestimate the power of a flood! Just fifteen centimeters (about 6 in.) of fast-moving water can knock you off your feet. Sixty centimeters (about 2 ft) of water can carry away an automobile!

If you're a famous baseball player, your number will be retired. If you're a really destructive hurricane, your name will be retired! Instead of a batting average or ERA, a hurricane has a scale rating. Here's how it works:

Saffir-Simpson Hurricane Scale

Category	Wind Speed (kilometers per hour)	Wind Speed (miles per hour)
1	119–153	74–95
2	154–177	96–110
3	178–209	111–130
4	210–249	131–155
5	over 249	over 155

1

What Makes Up Earth's Atmosphere?

In this lesson, you can . . .

 INVESTIGATE a property of air.

 LEARN ABOUT Earth's atmosphere.

 LINK to math, writing, art, and technology.

A Property of Air

Activity Purpose Everything around you is matter. Matter is anything that takes up space and has weight. In this investigation you will **observe** a property of air. Then you will **infer** whether air is matter.

Materials

- metric ruler
- piece of string about 80 cm long
- scissors
- 2 round balloons (same size)
- safety goggles
- straight pin

CAUTION

Activity Procedure

1 Work with a partner. Use the scissors to carefully cut the string into three equal pieces. **CAUTION** **Be careful when using scissors.**

2 Tie one piece of the string to the middle of the ruler.

◀ Oxygen is part of the air you breathe. High on a mountain the particles of air are far apart. The climber can't get enough oxygen from the air. He needs extra oxygen from a tank to keep his body working properly.

3 Blow up the balloons so they are about the same size. Seal the balloons. Then tie a piece of string around the neck of each balloon.

4 Tie a balloon to each end of the ruler. Hold the middle string up so that the ruler hangs from it. Move the strings so that the ruler is balanced. (Picture A)

5 **CAUTION** **Put on your safety goggles.** Use the straight pin to pop one of the balloons. **Observe** what happens to the ruler.

Picture A

Draw Conclusions

1. Explain how this investigation shows that air takes up space.

2. Describe what happened when one balloon was popped. What property of air caused what you **observed?**

3. **Scientists at Work** Scientists often **infer** conclusions when the answer to a question is not clear or can't be **observed** directly. Your breath is invisible, but you observed how it made the balloons and the ruler behave. Even though you can't see air, what can you infer about whether or not air is matter? Explain.

Investigate Further The air around you presses on you and everything else on Earth. This property of air, called air pressure, is a result of air's weight. When more air is packed into a small space, air pressure increases. You can feel air pressure for yourself. Hold your hands around a partly filled balloon while your partner blows it up. Describe what happens. Then **infer** which property of air helps keep the tires of a car inflated.

Process Skill Tip

Observations and inferences are different things. An **observation** is made with your senses. An **inference** is an opinion based on what you have observed and what you know about a situation.

Earth's Atmosphere

The Air You Breathe

You can live for a few days without water and for many days without food. But you can live only a few minutes without air. Nearly all living things need air to carry out their life processes. The layer of air that surrounds our planet is called the **atmosphere** (AT•muhs•feer). When compared to the size of Earth, the atmosphere looks like a very thin blanket surrounding the entire planet.

The atmosphere wasn't always as it is today. It formed millions of years ago as gases from erupting volcanoes collected around the planet. This mixture of gases would have poisoned you if you had breathed it. But bacteria and other living things used gases in this early atmosphere. They released new gases as they carried out their life processes. Over time, the gas mixture changed slowly to become the atmosphere Earth has now.

The atmosphere now is made up of billions and billions of gas particles. Almost four-fifths of these gas particles are nitrogen. Oxygen, a gas that your body uses in its life processes, makes up about one-fifth of the atmosphere. Other gases, including carbon dioxide and water vapor, make up the rest of the atmosphere.

Although you can't see all of it, a thin blanket of air called the atmosphere surrounds Earth. ▼

Plants use carbon dioxide during the process of photosynthesis. Plants give off oxygen as photosynthesis occurs. Carbon dioxide also absorbs heat energy from the sun and from Earth's surface. This helps keep the planet warm.

Like carbon dioxide, water vapor can absorb heat energy. The amount of water vapor in the air varies from place to place. Air over bodies of water usually contains more water vapor than air over land. High in the air, water vapor condenses to form clouds.

Air has certain properties. As you saw in the investigation, air takes up space and has weight. All the particles of air pressing down on the surface cause **air pressure** (PRESH•er). Air pressure changes as you go higher in the atmosphere. The picture shows what a column of air might look like. At the surface of Earth, air particles are close together. The higher you go in the atmosphere, the farther apart the air particles are. So the air pressure is less as you go higher in the atmosphere.

✔ What is the atmosphere?

1 Air particles in the upper atmosphere have the least weight pressing on them. The particles are far apart. Air in this part of the atmosphere is much less dense than air lower in Earth's atmosphere.

2 Air near the middle of the atmosphere has more weight pressing down on it. So it is denser than air higher above Earth.

3 The weight of the entire column of air presses down on the air particles closest to Earth, forcing them close together. This makes air densest at Earth's surface. Air pressure is greatest where air is densest.

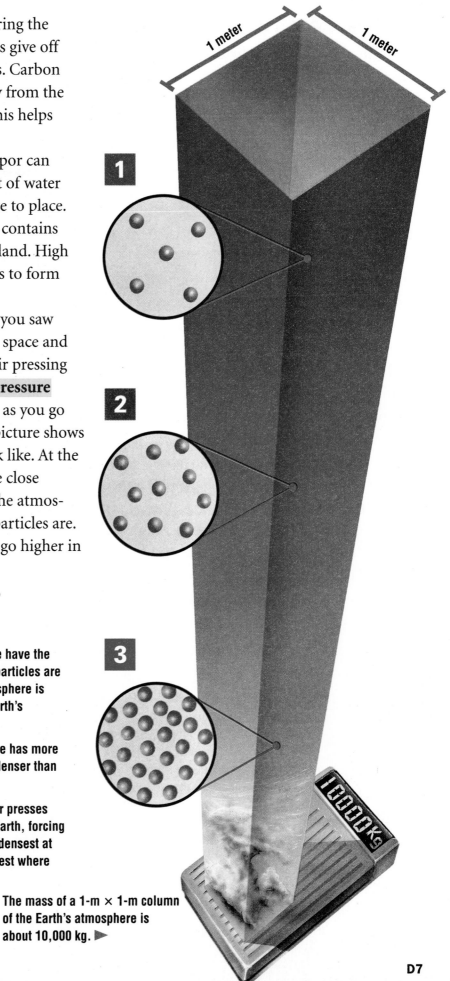

The mass of a 1-m × 1-m column of the Earth's atmosphere is about 10,000 kg. ▶

D7

Atmosphere Layers

Earth's atmosphere is divided into four layers. The layer closest to Earth is the **troposphere** (TROH•poh•sfeer). We live in the troposphere and breathe its air. Almost all weather happens in this layer. In the troposphere, air temperature decreases as you go higher.

Some airplanes that travel long distances fly in the **stratosphere** (STRAT•uh•sfeer) to be above most bad weather. The stratosphere contains most of the atmosphere's ozone, a kind of oxygen. The ozone protects living things from the sun's harmful rays. Temperatures in the stratosphere increase with height.

In the mesosphere (MES•oh•sfeer), air temperature decreases with height. In fact, the mesosphere is the coldest layer of the atmosphere. The thermosphere (THER•moh•sfeer) is the hot, outermost layer of air. In the thermosphere, temperature increases quickly with height. Temperatures high in the thermosphere can reach thousands of degrees Celsius.

✔ **What are the four layers of the atmosphere?**

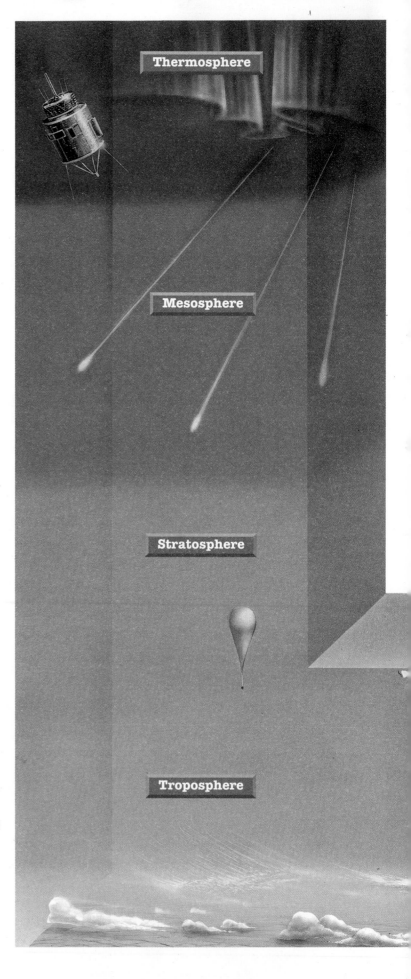

Earth's atmosphere is divided into four layers based on changes in air temperature. Each layer blends into the next. The thermosphere fades into outer space, where there is no air at all. ▶

Summary

The thin blanket of air that surrounds Earth is called the atmosphere. Earth's atmosphere is divided into four layers based on changes in temperature. The layers, starting with the one closest to Earth, are the troposphere, stratosphere, mesosphere, and thermosphere.

Review

1. What is the atmosphere?
2. How does air pressure change with height?
3. How is the atmosphere divided?
4. **Critical Thinking** Compare and contrast the stratosphere and the mesosphere.
5. **Test Prep** In which layer of the atmosphere does most weather occur?
   A troposphere
   B stratosphere
   C mesosphere
   D thermosphere

LINKS

MATH LINK

Atmospheric Temperatures In the troposphere the air temperature drops about $6\frac{1}{2}$°C for every 1 kilometer increase in height. If the troposphere is about 10 kilometers thick and the air temperature at the ground is 30°C, what is the temperature at a height of 2 kilometers?

WRITING LINK

Informative Writing—Description Pretend that you are falling from space toward Earth. For your teacher, write a story describing what you see and feel as you go through each layer of the atmosphere.

ART LINK

Atmosphere Layers Paint a picture showing the atmosphere as you would see it from space. Label the layers.

TECHNOLOGY LINK

Learn more about Earth's atmosphere and weather by visiting this Internet site.
www.scilinks.org/harcourt

LESSON 2

How Do Air Masses Affect Weather?

In this lesson, you can . . .

INVESTIGATE wind speed.

LEARN ABOUT what causes weather.

LINK to math, writing, health, and technology.

Wind, which is air in motion, keeps these kites fluttering in the sky.

Wind Speed

Activity Purpose Have you ever flown a kite? A strong wind makes the kite flutter and soar through the air. A gentle breeze is usually not enough to keep the kite flying. What is wind? Wind is air in motion. In this investigation you will make an instrument to **measure** wind speed.

Materials

- sheet of construction paper
- tape
- hole punch
- 4 gummed reinforcements
- glue
- piece of yarn about 20 cm long
- strips of tissue paper, about 1 cm wide and 20 cm long

Activity Procedure

1. Form a cylinder with the sheet of construction paper. Tape the edge of the paper to keep the cylinder from opening.

2. Use the hole punch to make two holes at one end of the cylinder. Punch them on opposite sides of the cylinder and about 3 cm from the end. Put two gummed reinforcements on each hole, one on the inside and one on the outside. (Picture A)

3. Thread the yarn through the holes, and tie it tightly to form a handle loop.

Wind Scale			
Speed (km/h)	Description	Objects Affected	Windsock Position
0	no breeze	no movement of wind	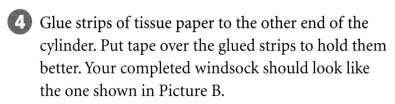
6–19	light breeze	leaves rustle, wind vanes move, wind felt on face	
20–38	moderate breeze	dust and paper blow, small branches sway	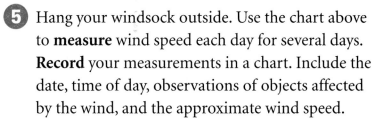
39–49	strong breeze	umbrellas hard to open, large branches sway	

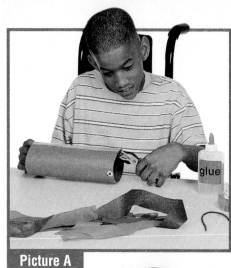

Picture A

Picture B

4. Glue strips of tissue paper to the other end of the cylinder. Put tape over the glued strips to hold them better. Your completed windsock should look like the one shown in Picture B.

5. Hang your windsock outside. Use the chart above to **measure** wind speed each day for several days. **Record** your measurements in a chart. Include the date, time of day, observations of objects affected by the wind, and the approximate wind speed.

Draw Conclusions

1. How fast was the weakest wind you **measured**? How fast was the strongest wind?

2. How did you determine the speed of the wind?

3. **Scientists at Work** *Light*, *moderate*, and *strong* are adjectives describing wind speed. Scientists often use number **measurements** to describe things because, in science, numbers are more exact than words. What is the wind speed measurement in kilometers per hour if the wind is making large tree branches sway?

Investigate Further Use a magnetic compass to determine which way is north from your windsock. **Measure** both wind speed and direction each day for a week. **Record** your data in a chart.

Process Skill Tip

The use of standard **measurements** allows people to communicate precisely. Telling someone there is a gentle breeze is not as exact as saying the wind is blowing at 8 km/h.

Air and Weather

Air and the Sun

FIND OUT

- how the sun affects weather
- what makes an air mass

VOCABULARY

greenhouse effect
air mass
front

Have you ever watched a weather report on television? If so, you know that temperature, air pressure, and wind are some of the things reported. You also know that these weather conditions change every day. But do you know why?

Weather begins with the sun, which provides energy for making weather. But the amount of the sun's energy reaching Earth is not the same everywhere. More energy reaches the equator than the poles. This uneven heating is part of what causes air to move and what makes weather.

Most of the sun's energy never reaches Earth. It is lost in space. Of the tiny fraction of the sun's energy that does reach Earth, about three-tenths is reflected out into space. Another three-tenths warms the air. The other four-tenths warms the land and oceans. The atmosphere traps this heat much like the glass of a greenhouse. Without this **greenhouse effect**, Earth would reflect most of the sun's energy back into space and Earth's surface would be too cold to support life.

✔ **How does the atmosphere work like a greenhouse?**

▲ Have you ever seen ripples like these above a paved road on a hot day? The air just above the hot pavement is also hot. Light travels differently through hot air. That's why the view is blurry.

Sunlight passes through the atmosphere and warms Earth's surface. The greenhouse effect keeps most of the heat from escaping back into space. ▼

Not to scale

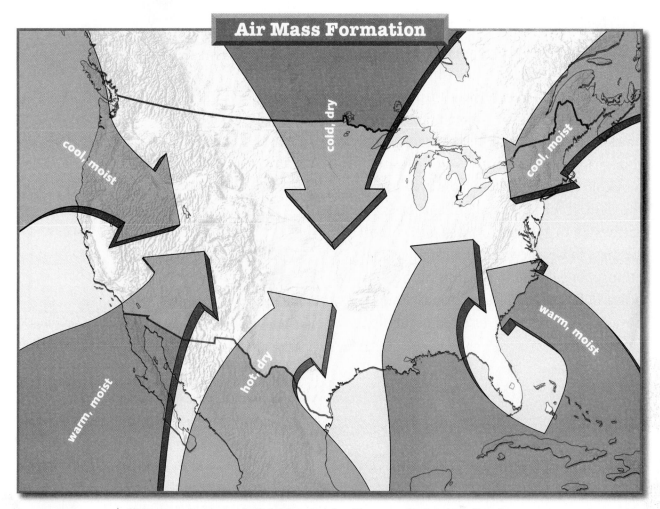

Air Mass Formation

cool, moist

cold, dry

cool, moist

warm, moist

hot, dry

warm, moist

▲ Air masses form over both land and water. The map shows where the air masses that affect North America form. Cool air masses are in blue colors. Warm air masses are in red colors.

Air Masses

If you could see the air around Earth from outer space, you would see large clumps of it forming, moving over Earth's surface, and slowly changing. These huge bodies of air, which can cover thousands of kilometers, are called air masses.

Like air heated by a hot road, an **air mass** has the same general properties as the land or water over which it forms. Two properties—moisture content and temperature—are used to describe air masses. Moist air masses form over water. Air masses that form over land are generally dry. Air masses that form near Earth's poles are cold. Air masses that form in the tropics, or areas near the equator, are warm.

The map shows air masses forming and moving over the North American continent. You can see a polar air mass bringing cold, dry air from the north into the United States. You can also see warm, moist air coming in from the south as part of tropical air masses.

✔ **What is an air mass?**

Air Masses Meet

Look again at the map on page D13. What do you think happens when different air masses meet? When two air masses meet, they usually don't mix. Instead they form a border called a **front**. Most of what you think of as weather happens along fronts.

A cold front is shown on the map just to the right. It forms when a cold air mass catches up to a warm air mass. The colder air mass forces the warmer air up into the atmosphere. As the warm air is pushed upward, it cools and forms clouds. Rain develops. Thunderstorms often occur along a cold front.

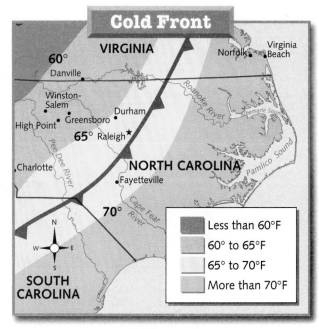

Cold Front

VIRGINIA
60°
Danville
Winston-Salem
High Point • Greensboro • Durham
65° Raleigh ★
Charlotte
NORTH CAROLINA
• Fayetteville
70°
Cape Fear River
Pee Dee River
Roanoke River
Albemarle Sound
Pamlico Sound
Norfolk • Virginia Beach
SOUTH CAROLINA

▨	Less than 60°F
▨	60° to 65°F
□	65° to 70°F
▨	More than 70°F

▲ A line with triangles is the symbol for a cold front. The air is colder behind a cold front than ahead of it. The triangles point in the direction of movement. In which direction is this front moving?

THE INSIDE STORY

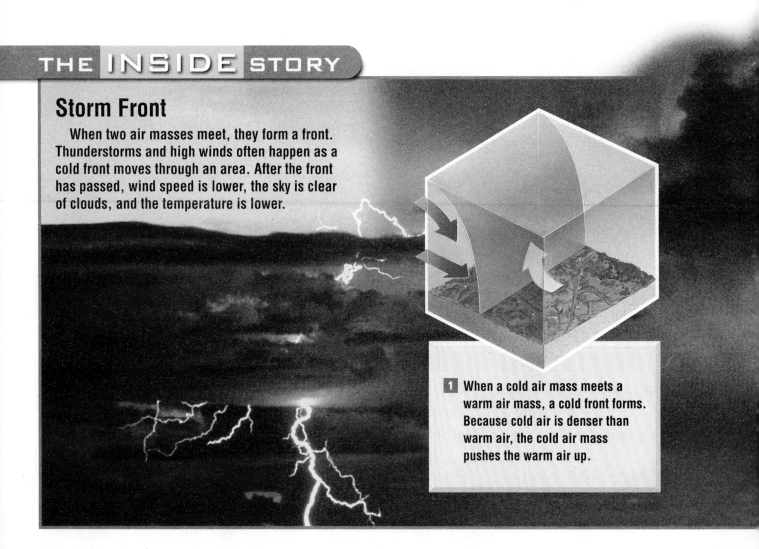

Storm Front

When two air masses meet, they form a front. Thunderstorms and high winds often happen as a cold front moves through an area. After the front has passed, wind speed is lower, the sky is clear of clouds, and the temperature is lower.

1 When a cold air mass meets a warm air mass, a cold front forms. Because cold air is denser than warm air, the cold air mass pushes the warm air up.

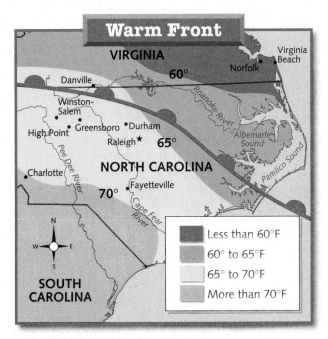

Warm Front

VIRGINIA

Virginia Beach

Norfolk

60°

Danville

Winston-Salem

High Point • Greensboro • Durham

Raleigh ★ 65°

Roanoke River

Albemarle Sound

Pamlico Sound

NORTH CAROLINA

Charlotte

Fayetteville

Pee Dee River

70°

Cape Fear River

N W E S

SOUTH CAROLINA

Less than 60°F
60° to 65°F
65° to 70°F
More than 70°F

▲ A line with half-circles is the symbol for a warm front. The half-circles point in the direction the front is moving. The air is warmer behind this front than ahead of it.

A warm front forms when a warm air mass catches up to a cold air mass. The warm air slides up over the colder, denser air. Clouds form, sometimes many miles ahead of where the front is moving along the ground. Steady rain or snow may fall as the front approaches and passes. Then the sky becomes clear of clouds and the temperature becomes higher.

Sometimes a front stops moving. Such a front is called a stationary front. A stationary front can stay in one place for several days. The constant fall of snow or rain along a stationary front can leave behind many inches of snow or cause a flood.

✔ **What is a front?**

2 As the warm air is forced up, it cools. It can no longer have as much water vapor. The extra water vapor begins to form clouds.

3 Dense, puffy clouds with flat bottoms form along cold fronts. Sometimes these clouds are called thunderheads. They often produce lightning, thunder, and lots of rain in a short time.

Air Masses Move

You can see air masses moving from place to place by watching how weather forms and changes. In the investigation you built a device to measure wind speed. Wind speed often increases as a front approaches. Wind direction also changes.

Air pressure also changes as air masses move over an area. As a front moves closer, air pressure drops. Air pressure rises as the front moves over the area.

Temperature, too, changes as a front moves over an area. Warmer air is brought into a region by a warm front. Likewise, the temperature goes down when a cold front moves over an area.

✔ **How does air pressure change as a front moves toward and then over an area?**

▲ The wind direction on each side of this cold front is shown by the arrows.

◀ The arrow of a weather vane points to the direction from which the wind is blowing.

▲ The same cold front has moved and changed shape. The wind direction changes with the shape of the front.

Summary

The sun provides the energy to make weather. The atmosphere traps heat near Earth's surface much as a greenhouse does. Air masses form over continents and oceans. When two air masses meet, they form a front. Fronts are the areas where most weather happens.

Review

1. What is the greenhouse effect?
2. What is a weather front?
3. How does a cold front form?
4. **Critical Thinking** Why are weather forecasts sometimes incorrect?
5. **Test Prep** What kind of front forms when a warm air mass catches up to a cold air mass?

   A a warm front   **C** a rain front

   B a cold front   **D** a hot front

LINKS

MATH LINK

Make a Rain Gauge Rain is usually measured in inches. Find out what a rain gauge is. Make one, and use it to measure daily rainfall for two weeks. Make a table to organize your data. Check your measurements against those shown in a newspaper or on TV.

WRITING LINK

Expressive Writing—Poem Use what you've learned in this chapter so far. For a third-grade student, write a short poem about weather. Use these words in your poem: *air mass, cold front, warm front, rain*, and *clouds*.

HEALTH LINK

Severe-Weather Safety Find out what types of severe weather most often affect your area. Find out how to be prepared for severe weather. Also find out what to do to stay safe during severe weather. Write a safety checklist, and share it with your family.

TECHNOLOGY LINK

Learn more about forecasting severe weather by viewing *Tornado Tracking* on the **Harcourt Science Newsroom Video.**

LESSON 3

How Is Weather Predicted?

In this lesson, you can . . .

 INVESTIGATE how to measure air pressure.

 LEARN ABOUT weather prediction.

 LINK to math, writing, drama, and technology.

Air Pressure

Activity Purpose You've learned that air pressure is the force with which the atmosphere presses down on Earth. You've also learned that air pressure changes as weather changes. In this investigation you will make a barometer, an instrument to **measure** air pressure.

Materials
- safety goggles
- scissors
- large, round balloon
- plastic jar
- large rubber band
- tape
- wooden craft stick
- small index card
- ruler

CAUTION

Activity Procedure

1. **CAUTION** **Put on your safety goggles. Be careful when using scissors.** Use the scissors to carefully cut the neck off the balloon.

2. Have your partner hold the jar while you stretch the balloon over the open end. Make sure the balloon fits snugly over the jar. Secure the balloon with the rubber band.

3. Tape the craft stick to the top of the balloon as shown. Make sure that more than half of the craft stick stretches out from the edge of the jar. (Picture A)

◄ Rain falls from clouds when water droplets in the clouds become big and heavy.

Picture A

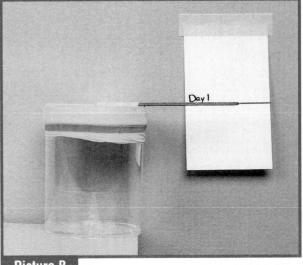

Picture B

4 On the blank side of the index card, use a pencil and a ruler to make a thin line. Label the line *Day 1*. Tape the card to a wall. Make sure the line is at the same height as the wooden stick on your barometer. (Picture B)

5 At the same time each day for a week, **measure** relative air pressure by marking the position of the wooden stick on the index card. Write the correct day next to each reading.

Draw Conclusions

1. Describe how air pressure changed during the time that you were **measuring** it.

2. What might have caused your barometer to show little or no change during the time you were taking **measurements?**

3. **Scientists at Work** Meteorologists are scientists who use instruments to **measure** weather data. How did your barometer measure air pressure?

Investigate Further Use your air pressure **measurements** and information from daily weather reports to **predict** the weather in your area for the next few days.

Process Skill Tip

When you compare data to a standard, you are **measuring**. Careful measurements can help you make inferences or draw conclusions about your data.

Weather Prediction

Measuring Weather

FIND OUT

- about instruments used to measure weather conditions

- how to read weather maps

VOCABULARY

barometer
humidity
anemometer

Meteorologists (mee•tee•uhr•AHL•uh•jihsts) are scientists who study and measure weather conditions. Some of these conditions are air temperature, air pressure, and wind speed and direction. Meteorologists have developed tools for measuring each of these weather conditions.

When you want to know if it's hot or cold outside, you look at a thermometer or listen to a weather report. Thermometers measure the temperature of air. In the investigation, you measured another property of the atmosphere, air pressure. Air pressure is measured with an instrument called a **barometer** (buh•RAHM•uht•er). In one type of barometer, air presses down on the instrument, causing a needle to move. The needle points to a number that tells how much the air is pressing down. In other words, the instrument measures the weight of the air above it. You learned in Lesson 2 that the particles of air are closer together in a cold air mass than in a warm air mass. Most cold air masses are denser and so have higher air pressure than warm air masses.

This weather instrument is a rotating-drum barometer. It continuously records changes in air pressure. ▼

Earth's land surfaces heat faster than its bodies of water. So the air above land is usually warmer. That means it is also less dense. ▼

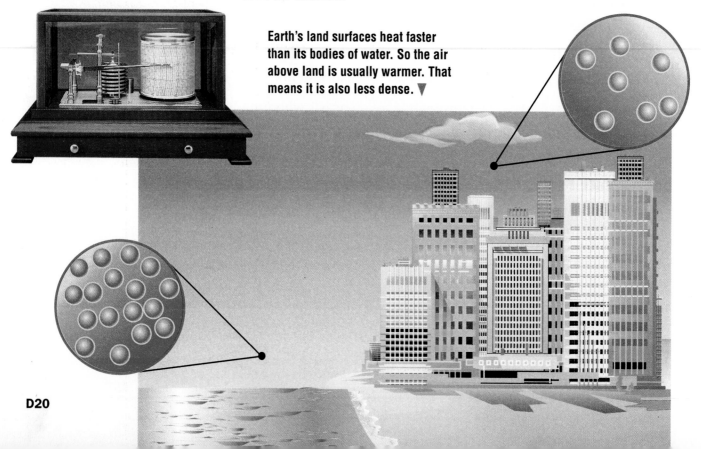

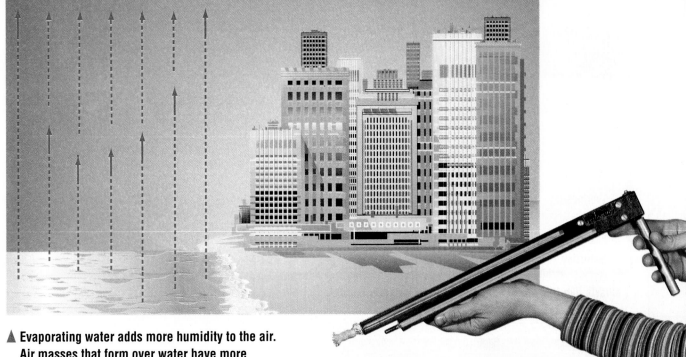

▲ Evaporating water adds more humidity to the air. Air masses that form over water have more moisture than those that form over land.

▲ A sling psychrometer (sy•KRAHM•uht•uhr) measures moisture in the air. The bulb of one thermometer is covered with a wet cloth. Then both thermometers are whirled in the air. The drier the air, the faster the water on the cloth evaporates (ee•VAP•uh•raytz), or dries up. This evaporation cools the cloth-covered thermometer. The temperatures of the wet and dry thermometers are compared to find the humidity.

Another characteristic of weather you can measure is **humidity** (hyoo•MID•uh•tee), or the amount of water vapor in the air. Humidity depends on several things. The area over which an air mass forms affects its humidity. For example, air masses that form over bodies of water have more moisture than air masses that form over land.

Temperature also affects how much moisture can be in the air. Warm air can have more water vapor than cool air. This is why water drops form on the outside of a glass of cold water during a warm day. Air near the glass cools. The air can no longer have as much water. The water vapor comes out of the air, forming drops.

In the investigation in Lesson 2, you made a windsock. With it you estimated the speed and direction of the wind. Meteorologists measure wind speed by using an instrument called an **anemometer** (an•uh•MAHM•uht•er). They find wind direction by using a weather vane or windsock.

✔ **What affects the humidity of air?**

◀ This is a type of anemometer that also includes a weather vane. Wind speed is measured by counting how many complete turns the cups make in one minute. Usually, a machine counts the turns.

D21

Daily Temperature Data for Weather City, Any State

	Daily High/ Daily Low (°F)	Record High/ Record Low (°F)	Daily Average Temperature (°F)
Sunday	89/72	101/44	81
Monday	90/74	100/50	82
Tuesday	85/65	99/42	75
Wednesday	88/69	103/40	79
Thursday	92/70	98/41	81
Friday	75/60	99/45	68
Saturday	79/62	102/44	71

▲ Charts like this are used to record daily weather conditions.

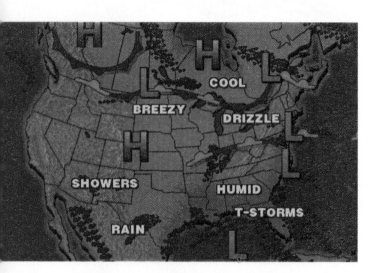

▲ Symbols on a weather map stand for fronts and weather conditions.

▲ A satellite photograph shows the positions of clouds and fronts. This satellite photograph matches the weather map above.

Mapping and Charting Weather

By watching and measuring weather conditions, scientists can keep track of moving air masses. Scientists record their measurements on charts and maps. Then they analyze the data to predict weather.

A weather map can be big or small. Large maps show how the weather differs across a country. Small maps show weather changes across a state or a smaller area. Satellite pictures and maps often show clouds and weather for a large part of Earth.

A weather map uses symbols to show weather conditions. Long lines marked with half-circles or triangles stand for fronts. Words or symbols describe the weather in an area. For example, small dashes may stand for rain, and small stars may stand for snow. Symbols also may show the type of clouds that are in the area.

✓ **How do weather charts and maps help scientists predict the weather?**

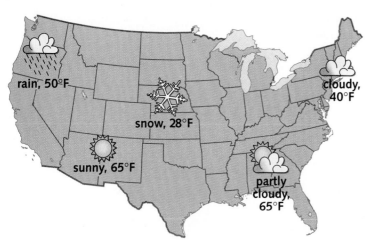

rain, 50°F

snow, 28°F

sunny, 65°F

cloudy, 40°F

partly cloudy, 65°F

▲ Simple weather maps like this are often printed in daily newspapers. What are the temperature and the weather in Nebraska?

Summary

Meteorologists are scientists who study and measure weather conditions. These conditions include air pressure, air temperature, humidity, and wind speed and direction. By measuring and studying weather conditions, meteorologists are able to predict the weather.

Review

1. What is an anemometer?

2. What factors affect humidity?

3. What are two tools that meteorologists use to study and predict the weather?

4. **Critical Thinking** An air mass forms over Alaska. Describe what you think the temperature and humidity of this air mass will be like.

5. **Test Prep** Which instrument is used to measure air pressure?
   A thermometer
   B weather vane
   C anemometer
   D barometer

LINKS

MATH LINK

Temperature Differences Make a chart like the one on page D22. In it, list the daily high and low temperatures of your area for one week. Find how much the temperature changed each day.

WRITING LINK

Expressive Writing—Friendly Letter Suppose you have a pen pal who lives in an area of the country very different from your area. Write a letter to your pen pal. Describe how the weather in your area changes when a cold front moves through.

DRAMA LINK

Be a Weather Forecaster Make a weather map showing imaginary weather conditions for your state. Present your forecast to the rest of the class. Make your presentation more interesting by using props.

TECHNOLOGY LINK

Learn more about tools for measuring weather conditions by joining a *Tornado Chase* on **Harcourt Science Explorations CD-ROM.**

Red Sprites, Blue Jets, and E.L.U.E.S.

Suppose you saw something completely new. How would you describe it? That was the challenge facing some airplane pilots and scientists. They tried to name unusual flashes they saw in the sky by calling them "upward lightning," "flames," and even "giant glowing doughnuts"!

Sprites, Jets, and ELUES

In 1989 scientists began trying to show that these light flashes are real. A videotape showed the unusual flashes during a thunderstorm. Nearly 20 were photographed during the early 1990s using video cameras that could work with very little light.

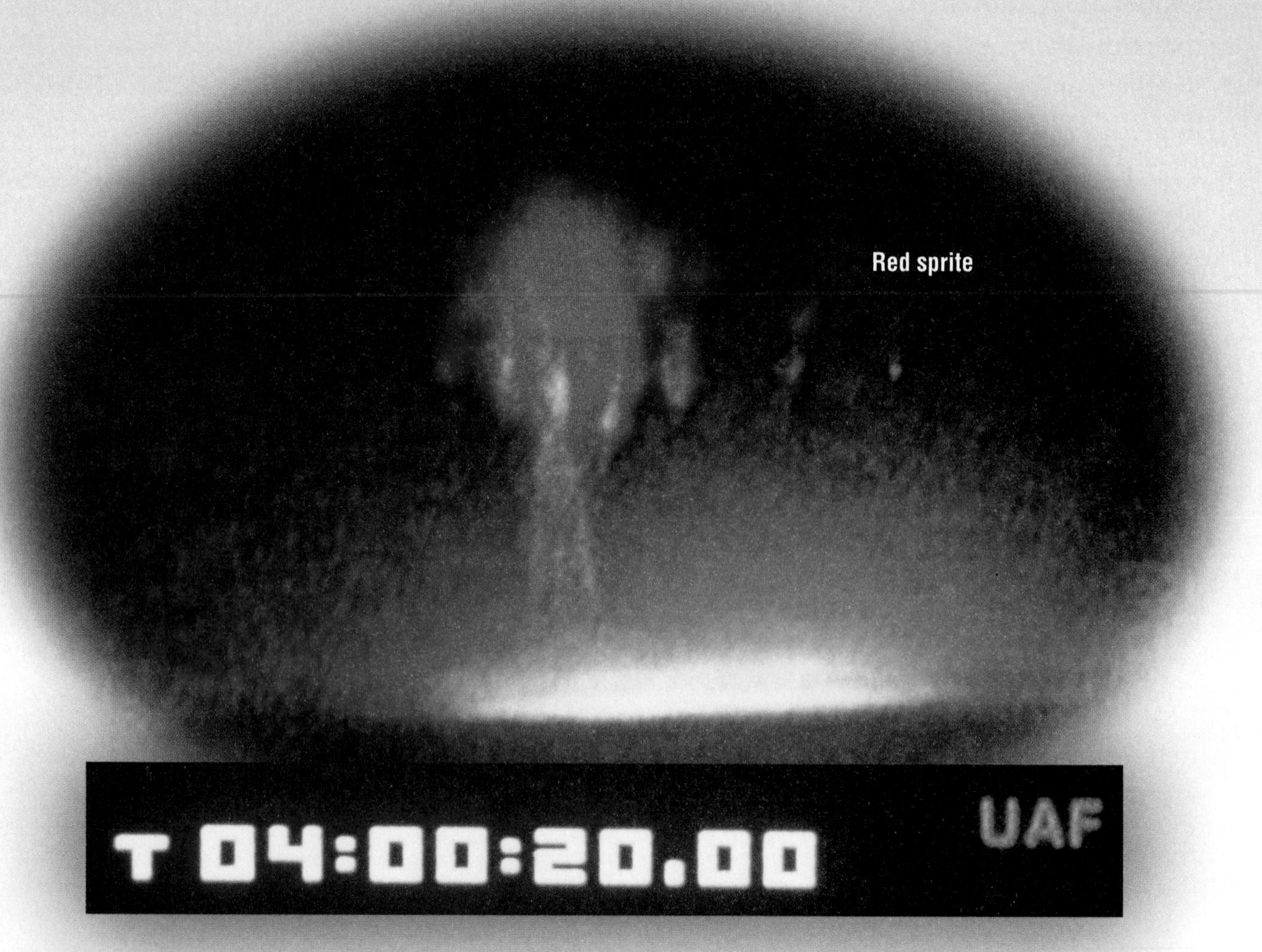

Red sprite

T 04:00:20.00   UAF

At least three types of flashes were identified. The scientists finally decided to name them sprites, jets, and ELVES.

ELVES stands for "*e*missions of *l*ight and *v*ery-low-frequency perturbations from *e*lectromagnetic-pulse *s*ources". You can see why the term is abbreviated. ELVES are very dim, quick red flashes. They move outward like ripples on a pond.

Sprites are red and seem to move in groups. They appear above a thunderstorm system, 65–75 kilometers (about 40–47 mi) above the ground. They have a "head" and strands coming down from the head. Sprites can occur over both sea and land.

Blue jets were once described as rocket lightning. Not until 1994 did weather scientists show, by using color video, that these glowing streaks are blue. Blue jets occur lower in the atmosphere than red sprites do, at 40–50 kilometers (about 25–30 mi) above the ground. Blue jets travel around 100 kilometers (about 62 mi) per second.

People in airplanes and on mountains could see blue jets and red sprites because the people were above storms. No one had ever seen ELVES because they last only a thousandth of a second. This is far too little time for the human eye to see. In 1990, videos taken from the space shuttle did show ELVES. Five more years passed before a second video of ELVES was made.

Finding Sprites, Jets, and ELVES

There are several reasons why it took so long to discover these unusual lights:

- They occur only above thunderstorms, so clouds usually block the view from the ground.

- They are dim and can be seen only after the eyes have adjusted to the dark. That adjustment is spoiled by bright lightning.
- Sprites last only about 3 ten-thousandths of a second (0.0003 second).
- Only about 1 in 100 lightning strikes produces these lights.

It took careful observation to find out that sprites, jets, and ELVES are real.

Think About It

1. What do you think scientists thought of the early reports of sprites and jets, before the videotapes?
2. Why do scientists use low-light video cameras to take pictures of sprites, jets, and ELVES?

WEB LINK:
For Science and Technology updates, visit the Harcourt Internet site.
www.harcourtschool.com

Careers **Meteorologist**

What They Do
Meteorologists study the atmosphere and the changes that produce different kinds of weather. Meteorologists may work for business or government. They may also research new uses for computer programs in the study of weather.

Education and Training   Someone who wants to be a meteorologist must study science in college. Many meteorologists get further training in weather research and technology after college.

Denise Stephenson-Hawk

ATMOSPHERIC SCIENTIST

Dr. Denise Stephenson-Hawk always loved school and was especially good in math. She skipped her senior year in high school and entered Spelman College. While there, she received a scholarship to a summer program at the National Aeronautics and Space Administration (NASA). She worked on a project to test panels for the space shuttle to make sure the panels would withstand the high temperatures they experience upon reentry into Earth's atmosphere. Stephenson-Hawk was so excited by what she learned about the atmosphere that she decided to apply her math skills to the study of atmospheric science.

Stephenson-Hawk's first job was at AT&T Bell Laboratories. There she made computer models to learn how sound travels in the ocean. After teaching mathematical modeling at Spelman College, Stephenson-Hawk moved to Clark Atlanta University in Georgia. There she works as a senior research scientist and associate professor of physics.

Stephenson-Hawk is also a member of the Climate Analysis Center (CAC) at the National Oceanic and Atmospheric Administration (NOAA). The CAC uses computer models to analyze and predict climate changes that happen in a short time. Stephenson-Hawk's special project has been building computer models of the effects of El Niño, a series of events set off by warmer-than-normal surface-water temperatures in the Pacific Ocean. Stephenson-Hawk and the other scientists working on this project are trying to more accurately predict the impact of El Niño so that people can better prepare for unusual weather.

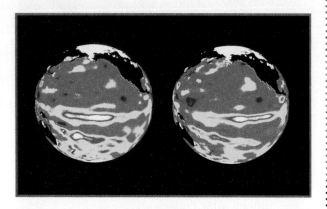

El Niño water temperature maps

THINK ABOUT IT

1. Why else might scientists be interested in studying El Niño?

2. Why do you think atmospheric scientists use computer models?

Relative Wind Speed

What is a way to measure relative wind speed?

Materials
- pattern (TR p.107)
- cardboard
- scissors
- permanent marker
- plastic straw
- long pencil
- masking tape
- paper fastener
- small paper cup

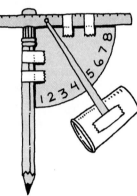

Procedure
1. **CAUTION** Be careful when using scissors. Trace the pattern pieces onto the cardboard and cut them out. Add the scale markings.

2. Cut a hole for the pencil in the middle of the straw. Push the pencil eraser into the hole. Tape the straw and pencil to the corner of the cardboard wedge.

3. Use the fastener to attach the cardboard strip. Tape the cup to the strip.

4. Push the pencil point into the ground in an open, windy area. Observe and record relative wind speed twice a day for one week. Use the table on page D11 to help you match gauge readings to actual wind speeds.

Draw Conclusions
How did the gauge help you measure wind speed?

Weather Fronts

How can water model a weather front?

Materials
- tall, clear jar
- hot and cold tap water
- pitcher
- food coloring
- thermometer

Procedure
1. Fill the jar halfway with cold water.

2. Fill the pitcher with hot water. Add 10 drops of food coloring.

3. Tilt the jar of cold water. Then slowly trickle the hot water down the inside of the jar. Slowly put the jar upright. Observe what happens in the jar.

4. Use the thermometer to measure the temperature of the hot water in the jar. Carefully move the thermometer down to measure the cold water in the jar. Can you find the front by using the thermometer?

Draw Conclusions
How did the hot water and cold water interact? How were they like air masses?

Chapter **1** Review and Test Preparation

Vocabulary Review

Use the terms below to complete the sentences. The page numbers in ( ) tell you where to look in the chapter if you need help.

atmosphere (D6)
air pressure (D7)
troposphere (D8)
stratosphere (D8)
greenhouse effect (D12)
air mass (D13)
front (D14)
barometer (D20)
humidity (D21)
anemometer (D21)

1. The _____ is the thin layer of air that surrounds Earth.

2. The amount of water vapor in the air is called _____.

3. The warming caused when air traps some of the sun's energy is the _____.

4. _____ is the force with which the atmosphere presses down on Earth.

5. In the atmosphere, the _____ is the layer in which most weather occurs.

6. An _____ is a large body of air, and it forms and moves over land or water.

7. An instrument that measures air pressure is a _____.

8. A _____ forms when two air masses meet.

9. In the atmosphere, the layer that contains a lot of ozone is the _____.

10. An instrument that measures wind speed is an _____.

Connect Concepts

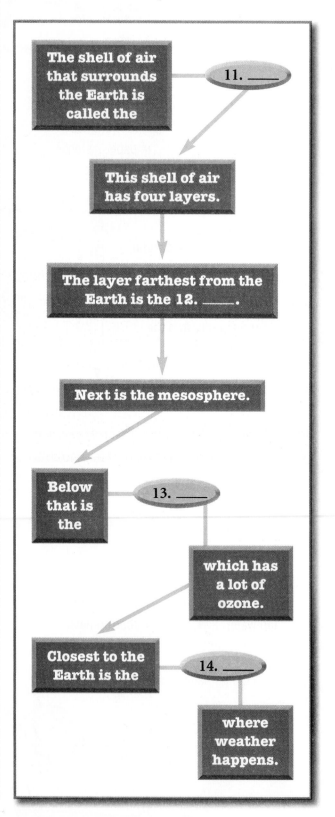

The shell of air that surrounds the Earth is called the

11. _____

This shell of air has four layers.

The layer farthest from the Earth is the 12. _____.

Next is the mesosphere.

Below that is the

13. _____

which has a lot of ozone.

Closest to the Earth is the

14. _____

where weather happens.

Check Understanding

Write the letter of the best choice.

15. As you get higher in the atmosphere, the space between air particles —

    A decreases

    B doesn't change

    C increases

    D masses

16. Energy from the _____ is trapped by gases in the air, causing the greenhouse effect.

    F Earth   H barometer

    G sun   J stratosphere

17. An air mass that forms over tropical waters would be —

    A warm and moist

    B cold and moist

    C cold and dry

    D warm and dry

18. A _____ front forms when two air masses meet and don't move.

    F cold   H stationary

    G warm   J pressure

19. _____ air can have more water vapor than _____ air.

    A Warm, cold

    B Dense, less dense

    C Cold, warm

    D Thermosphere, mesosphere

Critical Thinking

20. Why do mountain climbers use oxygen tanks?

21. You hear on a weather report that a cold front is coming. What weather changes can you expect?

22. Suppose you watch the weather report each day for five days. Each day the average temperature is the same and the air pressure doesn't change. What could be happening?

Process Skills Review

23. Remember the first investigation in this chapter. What did you **observe** that allowed you to **infer** that air is matter?

24. How is a **measurement** of wind speed different from a word description of wind speed?

25. Suppose you will **measure** weather conditions over the next five days. What equipment will help you measure? Make a table to record your data. Include units of measure.

Performance Assessment

Weather Maps

With a partner, study the three maps your teacher gives you. Tell how the weather has changed in the map area over the past three days. Then predict what the weather will be for the next two days. Explain the reasons for your prediction.

Chapter 2

Water in the Oceans

Nearly three-fourths of Earth is covered with a great ocean of salt water. It is a moving body of water and full of life. Its currents bring warm temperatures to otherwise cold areas. Its depths hide great mountain ranges. And its nutrient-rich waters are home to all sorts of living things.

Vocabulary Preview

water cycle
evaporation
condensation
precipitation
wave
storm surge
tide
deep ocean current
surface current

⠿FAST FACT

The oceans of the Earth are vast and deep. If Earth were a smooth ball with no mountains or valleys at all, it would be completely covered with water to a depth of more than 2 kilometers (about $1\frac{1}{4}$ mi).

FAST FACT

Mount Everest

The deepest spot in the ocean is in the Mariana Trench in the Pacific—11,000 meters (about 36,000 ft) below sea level. If Mount Everest, Earth's highest mountain, were dropped into that spot, it would be covered with about $1\frac{1}{2}$ kilometers (about 1 mi) of water!

FAST FACT

The Pacific Ocean holds about half of Earth's ocean water, and it covers nearly a third of Earth's surface. Here's how three oceans compare:

Ocean Sizes

Ocean	Size (square kilometers)	Size (square miles)
Pacific	181,000,000	70,000,000
Atlantic	94,000,000	36,000,000
Indian	74,000,000	29,000,000

What Role Do Oceans Play in the Water Cycle?

In this lesson, you can . . .

INVESTIGATE how to get fresh water from salt water.

LEARN ABOUT Earth's ocean water.

LINK to math, writing, social studies, and technology.

◄ Buoys float but are held in place by anchors. They mark paths where the water is deep enough for ships.

INVESTIGATE

Getting Fresh Water from Salt Water

Activity Purpose If you've ever been splashed in the face by an ocean wave, you know that sea water is salty. The salt in ocean water stings your eyes, leaves a crusty white coating on your skin when it dries, and tastes like the salt you put on food. In this investigation you'll evaporate artificial ocean water to find out what is left behind. From your **observations** you will **infer** how you can get fresh water from salt water.

Materials

- container of very warm water
- salt
- spoon
- cotton swabs
- large clear bowl
- small glass jar
- plastic wrap
- large rubber band
- piece of modeling clay
- masking tape

CAUTION

Activity Procedure

1 Stir two spoonfuls of salt into the container of very warm water. Put one end of a clean cotton swab into this mixture. Taste the mixture by touching the swab to your tongue. **Record** your observations. **CAUTION** **Don't share swabs. Don't put a swab that has touched your mouth back into any substance. Never taste anything in an investigation or experiment unless you are told to do so.**

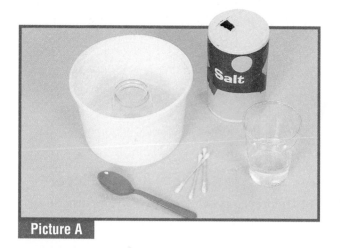

Picture A

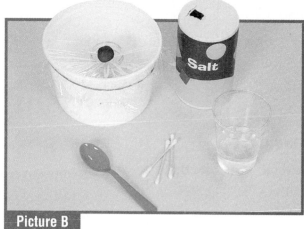

Picture B

2 Pour the salt water into the large bowl. Put the jar in the center of the bowl of salt water. (Picture A)

3 Put the plastic wrap over the top of the bowl. The wrap should not touch the top of the jar inside the bowl. Put a large rubber band around the bowl to hold the wrap in place.

4 Form the clay into a small ball. Put the ball on top of the plastic wrap right over the jar. Make sure the plastic wrap doesn't touch the jar. (Picture B)

5 On the outside of the bowl, use tape to mark the level of the salt water. Place the bowl in a sunny spot for one day.

6 After one day, remove the plastic wrap and the clay ball. Use clean swabs to taste the water in the jar and in the bowl. **Record** your **observations.**

Draw Conclusions

1. What did you **observe** by using your sense of taste?

2. What do you **infer** happened to the salt water as it sat in the sun?

3. **Scientists at Work** The movement of water from the Earth's surface, through the atmosphere, and back to Earth's surface is called the water cycle. From what you **observed,** what can you **infer** about the ocean's role in the water cycle?

Investigate Further Put the plastic wrap and the clay back on the large bowl. Leave the bowl in the sun for several days, until all the water in the large bowl is gone. **Observe** the bowl and the jar. What can you **conclude** about ocean water?

Process Skill Tip

Observing and inferring are different things. You **observe** with your senses. You **infer**, or form an opinion, based on what you have observed and what you know about a situation.

Ocean Water

The Water Cycle

Oceans cover more of Earth's surface than dry land does. About three-fourths of the Earth is covered by water. Almost all of that water is ocean water. Even though ocean water is salty, it provides a large amount of Earth's fresh water. Earth's water is always being recycled. As the model in the investigation showed, heat from the the sun causes fresh water to evaporate (ee•VAP•uh•rayt) from the oceans, leaving the salt behind. This evaporated water condenses to form clouds. Fresh water falls from the clouds to Earth's surface as rain. This constant recycling of water is called the **water cycle**. During the cycle, water changes from a liquid to a gas and back to a liquid. The diagram on these pages shows how the water cycle works. It includes the parts played by the sun, the water, the air, and the land.

✔ **What is the water cycle?**

FIND OUT

- about processes that make up the water cycle
- why ocean water is salty

VOCABULARY

water cycle
evaporation
condensation
precipitation

The sun warms the ocean, causing the water particles to move faster and faster. After a while, they have enough energy to leave the water and enter the air as water vapor. This is evaporation, the process by which a liquid changes to a gas. ▼

A cloud forms when water vapor condenses high in the atmosphere. Condensation (kahn•duhn•SAY•shuhn) happens when the water vapor rises, cools, and changes from a gas to liquid water. These drops of water in a cloud are so small that they stay up in the air.

Water vapor from an ocean can be carried a long way through the atmosphere. Water that evaporates from the Gulf of Mexico may fall back to Earth's surface far away in North Carolina.

In the cloud, some water drops bump into others and stick together. The drops get bigger. When they get too large to stay up in the air, they fall to Earth as rain, snow, sleet, or hail. Some of this **precipitation** (pree•sip•uh•TAY•shuhn) collects in lakes, rivers, and other bodies of water. Some precipitation soaks into the ground to become groundwater. Some falls directly back into the ocean.

What Is in Ocean Water

Ocean water is a mixture of water and many dissolved solids. Most of these solids are salts. Sodium chloride is the most common salt in ocean water. You probably know this substance by another name—table salt.

Where do you think the salts and other solids in the ocean come from? Most of the salts and other substances in the ocean come from the land. As rivers, streams, and runoff flow over the land, they slowly break down the rocks that make it up. Over time, flowing water carries substances from the rocks to the ocean.

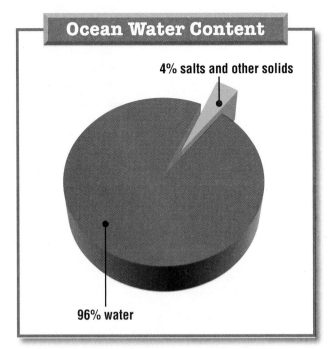

Ocean Water Content

4% salts and other solids

96% water

▲ Ocean water is made up of almost the same substances everywhere on Earth. Ocean water is about 96 percent water and 4 percent salts and other dissolved solids.

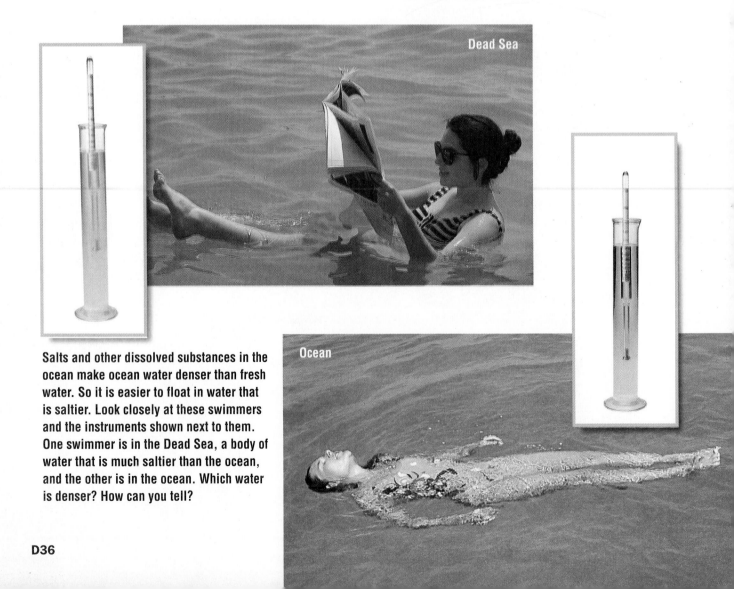

Dead Sea

Ocean

Salts and other dissolved substances in the ocean make ocean water denser than fresh water. So it is easier to float in water that is saltier. Look closely at these swimmers and the instruments shown next to them. One swimmer is in the Dead Sea, a body of water that is much saltier than the ocean, and the other is in the ocean. Which water is denser? How can you tell?

Near places where rivers empty into the ocean, the ocean water is less salty than it is farther from the shore. This is because the fresh water mixes with the salt water. Ocean water is a little saltier near the equator, where it is hot and water evaporates faster. And ocean water is a little less salty near the North and South Poles, where it is colder and water evaporates more slowly.

✔ **What is in ocean water?**

Summary

The waters of the ocean provide fresh water for Earth through the water cycle. As water moves through this cycle, it changes from a liquid to a gas and back to a liquid through the processes of evaporation and condensation. The water returns to Earth as precipitation. Sodium chloride is the most common salt in the ocean. The salts and other substances dissolved in ocean water make it denser than fresh water.

Review

1. What is the water cycle?
2. Explain how water changes from a liquid to a gas and back to a liquid in the water cycle.
3. What factors affect the saltiness or density of ocean water?
4. **Critical Thinking** How could you make salt water denser?
5. **Test Prep** Which of these processes occurs when a gas changes to a liquid?
   - A evaporation
   - B condensation
   - C precipitation
   - D salinity

LINKS

MATH LINK

Compare Fresh Water and Salt Water Use library reference materials to find out more about the amounts of fresh water and salt water on Earth. Draw a large square on a sheet of paper, and divide it into fourths. Color the squares to show the amounts of land and ocean. Stack pennies or checkers on the squares to stand for the amounts of fresh water and salt water.

WRITING LINK

Narrative Writing—Story Suppose you are sailing alone around the world. For your teacher, write down some of your thoughts that describe the ocean and what it is like to have nothing but water all around you.

SOCIAL STUDIES LINK

El Niño Find out what El Niño is. Locate on a world map the places where this condition occurs. Write a report that explains what causes this situation and how it affected weather and crops around the world in 1998.

TECHNOLOGY LINK

Learn more about Earth's water systems by visiting the National Air and Space Museum Internet site.
www.si.edu/harcourt/science

Smithsonian Institution®

2

What Are the Motions of Oceans?

In this lesson, you can . . .

 INVESTIGATE water currents.

 LEARN ABOUT the ways ocean water moves.

 LINK to math, writing, social studies, and technology.

INVESTIGATE

Water Currents

Activity Purpose If you've ever gone swimming in the ocean, you've probably felt waves crash against your body. You may also have felt water moving against you below the surface. This movement below the water's surface is a *current*. In this investigation you'll **make a model** and **infer** one way currents form.

Materials
- clear, medium-sized bowl
- warm tap water
- colored ice cube
- clock

Activity Procedure

1 Put the bowl on a flat surface. Carefully fill the bowl three-quarters full of warm tap water.

2 Let the water stand undisturbed for 10 minutes.

◀ Ocean water moves in many ways. Both the rising water and the waves are washing away this sand castle.

3 Without stirring the warm water or making a splash, gently place the colored ice cube in the middle of the bowl. (Picture A)

4 **Observe** for 10 minutes what happens as the ice cube melts. Every 2 minutes, make a simple drawing of the bowl to **record** your observations.

Draw Conclusions

1. Describe what you **observed** as the ice cube melted in the bowl of warm water.

2. In your **model**, what does the bowl of water stand for? What does the ice cube stand for?

Picture A

3. Since the liquid in the bowl and the ice cube were both water, what can you **infer** about the cause of what happened in the bowl?

4. **Scientists at Work** In Chapter 1, you learned that cold air is denser than warm air. The same is true for water. Using this information and what you **observed** in the investigation, explain one way ocean currents form.

Investigate Further Mix up two batches of salt water. Use twice as much salt in one batch as in the other. Use the water to **model** another kind of ocean current. Fill a clear bowl three-fourths full with the less salty water. Add a few drops of food coloring to the saltier water. Along the side of the bowl, slowly pour the colored, saltier water into the clear, less salty water. Describe your **observations. Make a hypothesis** to explain what you observed. What **prediction** can you make based on the hypothesis? How could you test the prediction?

> **Process Skill Tip**
>
> People make models to help them **observe** things in nature that are too small, too big, or too hard to see or understand. By observing a model, you can infer how things work.

Ocean Movements

FIND OUT

- about ocean waves and currents
- what causes tides

VOCABULARY

wave
storm surge
tide
surface current
deep ocean current

Waves

If you've ever been in the path of a wave in the ocean, in a lake, or in a wave pool, you know that even big waves don't move you either forward or back. You bob up and down, but you're still in about the same place after the wave passes. This is because a **wave** is the up-and-down movement of the water particles that make it up.

Water waves are caused by the wind. As wind blows over the water's surface, it pulls on the water particles. This causes small bumps, or ripples, of water to form. As the wind continues to blow, the ripples keep growing. Over time they become waves.

The height of a wave depends on three things: the strength of the wind, the amount of time the wind blows, and the size of the area over which the wind blows. Strong, gusty winds blowing

Waves drop and take away bits of rock and sand grains from a beach as they break on a rocky shore. ▶

Waves like these are caused by the wind. Waves break, or give up their energy, as they move onto the shore. ▼

▲ Waves erode a shore as the water carries sediment back toward the sea. What might happen to these houses if erosion continues?

over an area of many square kilometers can cause a very large wave called a **storm surge** to form. Storm surges often occur during hurricanes and can cause a lot of damage along a shore.

Waves change the shore in different ways. When waves break on a beach, water carries sand and other sediments as it flows back into the ocean. This carrying away of sediments is called *erosion*. Erosion along a shore causes beaches to become smaller. As waves give up their energy, they also deposit, or drop, sediments. This process is called

deposition (dep•uh•ZISH•uhn). When waves deposit sediments near shore, a beach gets bigger.

The photograph at the bottom of this page shows a harbor during a hurricane. You probably know that a hurricane is a severe storm that has strong winds and a lot of rain. Storm surges during hurricanes cause erosion and deposition along a shore. Whole beaches can be washed away.

✔ **How do water waves change a shoreline?**

This is a harbor during a hurricane. Storm surges during hurricanes can be as high as 10 meters (more than 30 ft). ▼

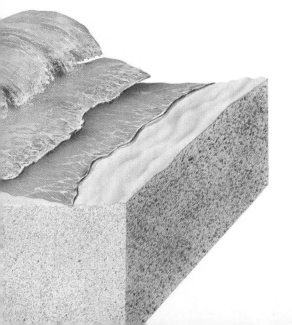

D41

Tides

If you watched a beach for 12 hours, you would probably notice that the waves don't always reach the same place. This is because of another type of ocean water motion called tides. **Tides** are the daily change in the local water level of the ocean.

At *high tide* much of the beach is covered by water. At *low tide* waves break farther away from shore. Less of the beach is under water. Every day most shorelines have two high tides and two low tides. High tide and low tide are usually a little more than six hours apart.

Tides are caused by gravity. *Gravity* is a force that causes all objects to be pulled toward all other objects. The force of gravity between two objects depends on two things: the sizes of the objects and the distance between them. Big objects have a greater pull than small objects. Objects that are closer together have a greater pull on one another than objects farther apart do.

Even though the moon is much smaller than the sun, the pull of the moon's gravity on Earth is the main cause of ocean tides. This is because the moon is much closer to Earth than the sun is.

▲ This photograph shows low tide in a harbor on the Bay of Fundy in Nova Scotia, Canada.

▲ This is the same harbor on the Bay of Fundy during high tide. Compare the positions of the ships with their positions in the photograph above.

◀ A tide pool is a small body of water on the shore. Parts of it may be out of the water during low tide. Sea animals such as starfish, crabs, and sea anemones (uh•NEM•uh•neez) live in these pools.

The moon pulls on everything on Earth. As the moon pulls on ocean water, the water forms a bulge that always faces the moon. Another water bulge forms on the side of Earth farthest from the moon, where the moon's pull is weakest. As Earth rotates, the bulges stay in the same places. High tide occurs as a point on Earth moves through a bulge. The water level rises on the shore. Low tide occurs as a point on Earth moves between the bulges. The water level on the shore gets lower.

At certain times each month, tides are very high or very low. Read The Inside Story to find out why.

✔ **What are tides?**

The Moon and Tides

Not to scale

Not to scale

Even though the moon's pull on the oceans is greater than the sun's pull, the sun still affects tides. The pictures show how.

1 When the sun, Earth, and moon form a right angle, the bulge of water that forms high tides is smaller than usual. This causes *neap tides*, or only a small difference between high and low tides. Neap tides occur when the moon is in its first-quarter phase or in its third-quarter phase.

2 When the sun, moon, and Earth are in a straight line, the bulge of water that forms high tides is bigger than usual. This causes *spring tides*, or higher high tides and lower low tides. Two spring tides occur every month, when the moon is in its new-moon and full-moon phases.

D43

Currents

Currents are rivers of water that flow in the ocean. A **surface current** forms when steady winds blow over the surface of the ocean. In the Northern Hemisphere, surface currents flow in a clockwise direction. In the Southern Hemisphere, surface currents flow in a counterclockwise direction.

Deep ocean currents form because of density differences in ocean water. You made a model of deep ocean currents in the investigation. The density of ocean water depends on two things—the amount of salt in the water and the temperature of the water. The more salt there is in water, the denser it will be. Cold ocean water also is

Scientists have mapped the paths of surface currents and deep ocean currents in the oceans. ▼

Cold water flows underneath warm water, forming a deep ocean current. The cold water can flow for great distances along the ocean floor. The green arrows on the globe show deep ocean currents.▼

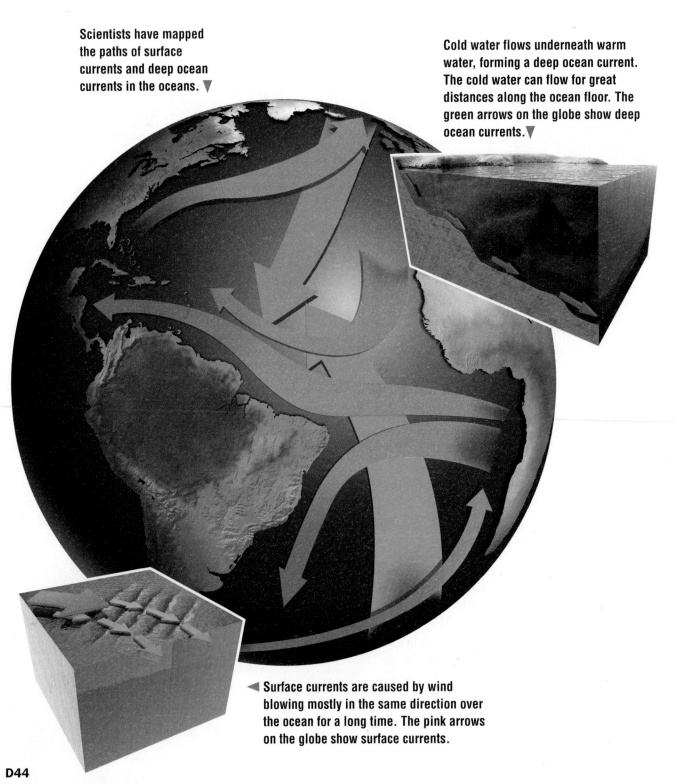

◀ Surface currents are caused by wind blowing mostly in the same direction over the ocean for a long time. The pink arrows on the globe show surface currents.

denser than warm ocean water. Deep ocean currents form when dense, cold water meets less dense water. The denser water flows under the less dense water, forcing the less dense water to rise.

✓ **What causes deep ocean currents?**

Summary

Ocean waves form as wind blows over the water's surface. Strong, gusty winds over a large area can cause a large wave called a storm surge. Tides are the rise and fall of ocean water caused by the pull of gravity between Earth, the moon, and the sun. Surface currents are caused by the blowing of steady winds. Deep ocean currents are caused by differences in saltiness or water temperature.

Review

1. How does an object floating in water move as a wave passes it?
2. What causes tides?
3. Why does the moon have a greater effect on tides than the sun has?
4. **Critical Thinking** Compare and contrast surface currents in the Northern and Southern Hemispheres.
5. **Test Prep** Which is caused by density differences?
   - A surface currents
   - B ocean waves
   - C deep ocean currents
   - D ocean tides

LINKS

MATH LINK

Rising Sea Level Scientists estimate that sea level rose 10 to 15 centimeters between the years 1900 and 1998. They estimate that it will rise another 30 centimeters before 2025. What will the average yearly rate of sea level rise be for the years 1998 to 2025?

WRITING LINK

Informative Writing—Description Suppose you are a creature that lives in a tide pool. For a younger student, write a short description that explains how your life changes when the tide comes in and goes out.

SOCIAL STUDIES LINK

Trade Routes Find out about the triangle trade route that existed in colonial times in the United States. Mark this route on a copy of a world map, and explain how ocean currents and wind patterns made this route possible.

TECHNOLOGY LINK

Learn more about new ways to explore deep in the ocean by viewing *Robot Submarine* on the **Harcourt Science Newsroom Video.**

CNN Turner Le@rning

Deep Flight II

Deep Flight II is a submersible, or sub, that is being developed to explore the ocean depths. It will carry a pilot and will go to the deepest part of the ocean, the Mariana Trench. This trench in the Pacific Ocean is 11,275 meters (almost 7 mi) deep. From that depth, it would take more than 25 Empire State Buildings stacked on top of each other to reach the surface.

Exploring the Deep Ocean

Only one mission with people has ever gone to the Mariana Trench. In 1960 two men in a bathyscaph (BATH•uh•skaf) called the *Trieste* (tree•EST) went down for 20 minutes. The ship had none of the video cameras or computers we have today. And the *Trieste* could only go straight down and come straight back up.

Graham Hawkes, an engineer, and his business partner, Sylvia Earle, have been working to make deep-ocean subs, such as *Deep Flight II*. Scientists want better subs to learn more about the ocean. The subs will help them investigate ocean-floor geology as well as deep-ocean plants and animals. Subs, however, can't meet all research

Graham Hawkes in a museum model of *Deep Flight I*

needs. Robot, or remote-controlled, subs are often better for dangerous or long trips.

Built for Speed and Comfort

The time needed to go so deep is a problem, so Hawkes is designing a craft that "flies" through water like an airplane. It should reach the ocean floor in 90 minutes.

Another problem is the high pressure. The sub must support the weight of a column of water 11,275 meters high, so the hull of *Deep Flight II* is being built of strong, new ceramic materials. These materials are lighter than steel and won't break under high pressure. The ship will also protect its crew from the near-freezing cold of the ocean water.

Hawkes is using shapes from nature for the design of *Deep Flight II*. Its smooth body and wings look like parts of dolphins, whales, and birds, as well as aircraft. It can skim forward below the ocean's surface or dive down into the depths. It can even do spins and rolls like a stunt airplane.

Deep Flight II has an unusual feature. The pilot is strapped face down in a form-fitting body pan. He or she can see out through a cone-shaped window at the front. Hawkes explains that this is a natural swimming position, so it feels right to the pilot.

If the first voyage of *Deep Flight II* is a success, Hawkes and Earle may soon be designing and building more deep-sea subs.

Think About It

1. How will the pilot of *Deep Flight II* be like an astronaut landing on the moon?
2. Why do you think most of the ocean remains unexplored?

 WEB LINK:
For Science and Technology updates, visit the Harcourt Internet site.
www.harcourtschool.com

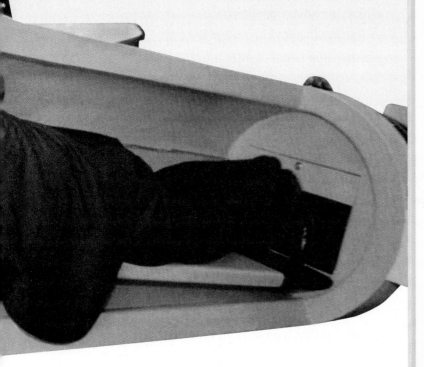

Careers	Scuba Support Crew

What They Do

People working on a scuba support crew prepare equipment for diving. They make sure that everything needed for a dive *works.* The scuba support crew stays on land or in a boat  while the diver goes under water. The crew communicates with the diver and takes care of any emergencies.

Education and Training Scuba support crew members must have emergency medical training and a Divemaster certificate from the Professional Association of Diving Instructors.

D47

Rachel Carson

MARINE BIOLOGIST

"Science is part of the reality of living: it is the what, the how, and the why of everything in our experience."

Although Rachel Carson did not actually visit the ocean until she was 22 years old and a college graduate, she had been fascinated by it all her life.

Everything in nature thrilled Carson—flowers and birds, trees and rivers, animals and insects. She surprised many people at her college by changing from an English major to a biology major. At the time, science was seen as a career for men. No one expected her to do well.

Carson used both biology and writing in her work. She taught college classes after she graduated. Another of her early jobs was with the U.S. Bureau of Fisheries, writing scripts for radio broadcasts about life under the sea. She eventually moved up in the Bureau to become editor-in-chief of publications.

Carson was encouraged to write articles, which eventually were printed in one book, *Under the Sea-Wind.* Carson wrote other books

about the sea, including *The Sea Around Us*, which became a best-seller.

Carson is best known for her book *Silent Spring.* She began it after a friend who had a bird sanctuary wrote a letter. Her friend wrote Carson that pesticides had killed all the birds at the sanctuary. It took Carson several years to collect information and write the book. She closely studied the dangers of DDT, a chemical used to kill insects. *Silent Spring* tells what a spring would be like without new life.

THINK ABOUT IT

1. Why was it important that Carson spend so much time collecting information for *Silent Spring*?

2. Why might it have been important that Carson had already published several books before writing *Silent Spring*?

Spiny sea urchins

Measuring Density

What are the relative densities of different solutions?

Materials

- unsharpened pencil with eraser
- tall, narrow glass or jar
- permanent marker
- safety goggles
- thumbtack
- water
- salt
- spoon

Procedure

1. **CAUTION** **Put on your goggles.** Carefully push the thumbtack completely into the eraser.

2. Fill the glass three-fourths full of tap water. Place the pencil, eraser end first, into the water. When it floats up on its own, grab the pencil at the point where it meets the surface of the water. Use the permanent marker to mark this point.

3. Add four spoonfuls of salt to the water. Stir until the salt dissolves. Place the pencil in the water, and mark it as you did in Step 2.

Draw Conclusions

Explain your observations in Steps 2 and 3.

Making Waves

How does a wave move?

Materials

- safety goggles
- heavy washer
- 2-m length of rope

Procedure

1. **CAUTION** **Put on your goggles.** String the washer onto the rope. It should fit loosely.

2. Work with a partner. Each of you should hold one end of the rope. It should hang loosely with the washer in the center of the rope. The rope should not be stretched between you and your partner.

3. Shake one end of the rope by moving your arm while your partner holds the other end still. Observe the movement of the washer on the rope. Compare this movement to the movement of objects floating in ocean water.

Draw Conclusions

How did the washer move? How is the movement of the rope like the movement of a wave?

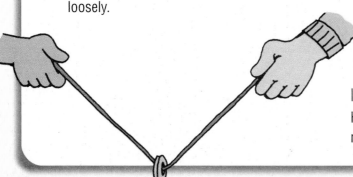

Vocabulary Review

Use the terms below to complete the sentences. The page numbers in ( ) tell you where to look in the chapter if you need help.

evaporation (D34)   **storm surge** (D40)

water cycle (D34)   **tides** (D42)

condensation (D35)   **surface current** (D44)

precipitation (D35)   **deep ocean**

wave (D40)   **current** (D44)

1. A large wave caused by strong winds is called a ____.

2. ____ is a process that changes a liquid to a gas.

3. A gas changes to a liquid by a process called ____.

4. Blowing winds form a ____, a river of water in the ocean.

5. Water vapor, clouds, rain, and the ocean are parts of the ____.

6. Neap and spring ____ are examples of changes in ocean level caused by the pull of the sun, moon, and Earth.

7. ____ is any form of water that falls from clouds.

8. A ____ forms when cold, dense ocean water meets and flows beneath warmer ocean waters.

9. The up-and-down motion of water is called a ____.

Connect Concepts

The diagram below shows how water moves from the land and oceans to the atmosphere and back again. Label each section of the diagram, and write a title for it.

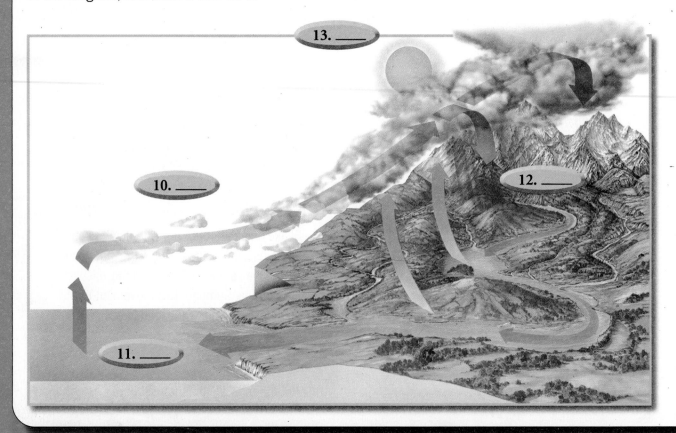

13. ____

10. ____

12. ____

11. ____

Check Understanding

Write the letter of the best choice.

14. The _____ provides the energy for the water cycle.
    A moon   C atmosphere
    B sun   D ocean wave

15. Ocean water is a mixture of water and many —
    F gases   H liquids
    G salts   J fluids

16. Wind causes an up-and-down movement of ocean water, called a —
    A deep ocean current
    B tide
    C surface current
    D wave

17. Waves change a shoreline by erosion and —
    F condensation
    G precipitation
    H deposition
    J evaporation

18. The pull of _____ on Earth is the main reason for tides.
    A the moon
    B winds
    C the sun
    D currents

Critical Thinking

19. Would it be easier to float in the Great Salt Lake or in Lake Michigan? Explain your answer.

20. What do you think would happen to tides if the moon's gravity had a stronger pull than it does now?

Process Skills Review

21. Suppose there is a heavy rainstorm far out over the ocean. What can you **infer** about the density of the ocean water at the surface in that area right after the storm?

22. You **observe** clouds forming on a bright, sunny day. What can you **infer** is happening in the atmosphere? What may happen later in the day?

Performance Assessment

Currents

Completely fill a plastic cup with hot water. Add three or four drops of food coloring to the water. Cover the cup with plastic wrap. Hold the wrap in place with a rubber band.

Put the cup inside a bowl. Fill the bowl with cold water until it is almost full. There should be 2–3 cm of water over the cup. Use a pencil to poke a hole in the plastic wrap. Observe what happens. Explain what is happening inside the bowl. How could you make the same thing happen using salt water instead of hot water?

Chapter 3

Vocabulary Preview

solar system
star
planet
asteroid
comet
orbit
axis
inner planet
outer planet
gas giant
telescope
space probe
constellation

Planets and Other Objects in Space

From Earth you can study objects in space by just stepping outside on a clear night. Most of the objects you will see are stars, which are very, very distant suns. A few of the objects you will see are planets. Some are a little like Earth, and some are amazingly different.

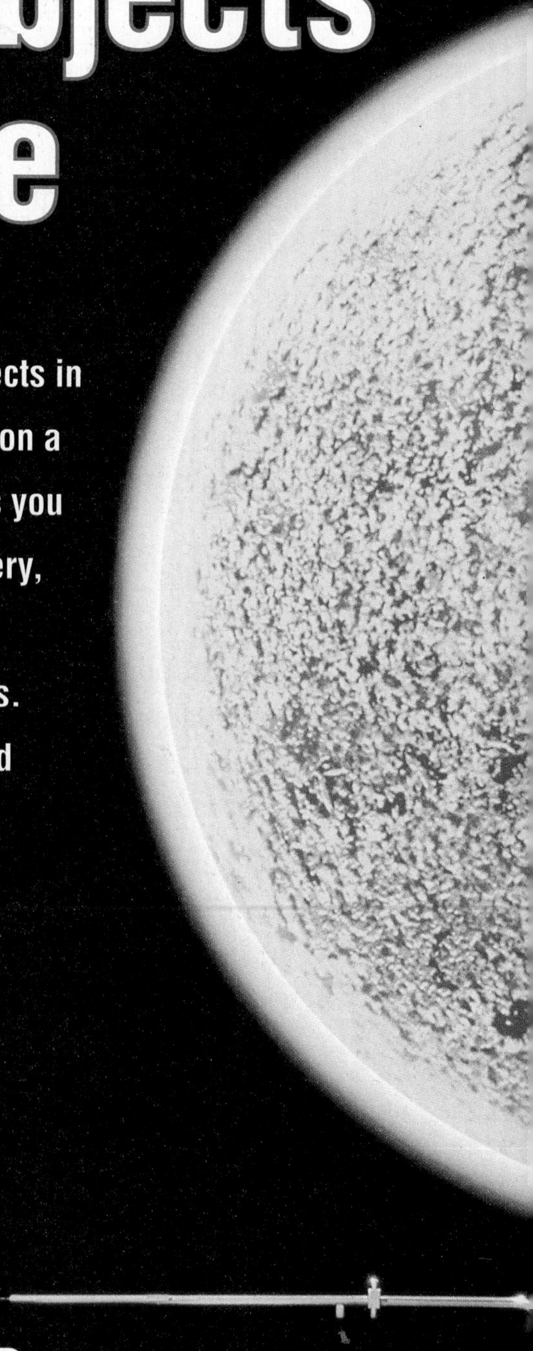

FAST FACT

The sun is about 150,000,000 kilometers (93 million mi) from the Earth. It would take you about 193 years to travel this distance in a car at highway speed!

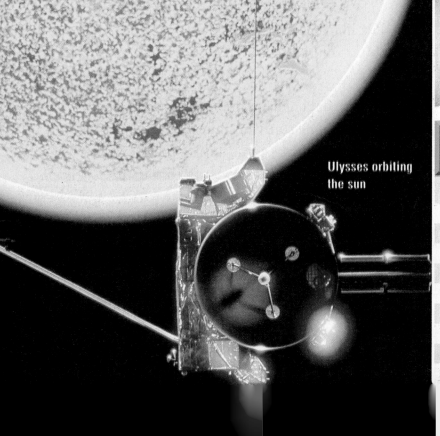

Ulysses orbiting
the sun

About 500,000 craters can be seen on the moon through telescopes on Earth. It would take you more than 400 hours to count them all. And this doesn't include the craters on the far side of the moon!

FAST FACT

Like most of the planets, Earth has seasons because it is tilted on its axis. But no planet is tilted like Uranus. Uranus is tilted so far that it is tipped over on its side! This gives Uranus a winter that lasts about 21 years!

Sun   Mercury   Earth   Uranus   Pluto

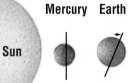

How the Tilts of the Planets Compare

Planet	Degrees of Tilt
Mercury	0
Venus	177
Earth	23
Mars	25
Jupiter	3
Saturn	25
Uranus	98
Neptune	28
Pluto	122

How Do Objects Move in the Solar System?

In this lesson, you can . . .

INVESTIGATE the ways planets move.

LEARN ABOUT our solar system.

LINK to math, writing, art, and technology.

Planet Movement

Activity Purpose Even though you can't feel it, Earth moves through space at nearly 30 kilometers (about 19 mi) per second. At this speed, our planet moves around the sun almost 100 times as fast as most jet planes cruise. You can't make anything move that quickly. So, in this investigation you'll **make a model** that shows how the planets in our solar system move.

Materials

- index cards
- scissors
- black marker

Activity Procedure

1 Label one of the cards *Sun.* Label each of the other cards with the name of one of the planets shown in the chart on the next page.

2 Put all of the cards face down on a table and shuffle them. Have each person choose one card.

3 Use the data table to find out which planet is closest to the sun. Continue **analyzing the data** and **ordering** the cards until you have all the planets in the correct order from the sun.

◄ This is Stonehenge, an ancient rock structure located in Britain. Stonehenge may have been used to study and predict the movement of Earth around the sun.

Planets and Distances from Sun			
Planet	Average Distance from the Sun (millions of km)	Planet	Average Distance from the Sun (millions of km)
Earth	150	Pluto	5900
Jupiter	778	Saturn	1429
Mars	228	Uranus	2871
Mercury	58	Venus	108
Neptune	4500		

4 In a gym or outside on a playground, line up in the order you determined in Step 3. (Picture A)

5 If you have a planet card, slowly turn around as you walk at a normal pace around the sun. Be sure to stay in your own path. Do not cross paths with other planets. After everyone has gone around the sun once, **record** your **observations** of the planets and their movements.

Picture A

Draw Conclusions

1. The sun and the planets that move around it are called the solar system. What is the order of the planets, starting with the one closest to the sun?

2. What did you **observe** about the motion of the planets?

3. **Scientists at Work** Why did you need to **make a model** to study how planets move around the sun?

Investigate Further Look again at the distances listed in the data table. How could you change your model to make it more accurate?

Our Solar System

The Sun

In the investigation you made a model of our solar system. A **solar system** is a group of objects in space that move around a central star. Our sun is a **star**, a burning sphere (SFEER) of gases. This enormous fiery ball is more than 1 million kilometers (about 621,000 mi) in diameter. The sun is the largest object in our solar system. It is larger than the rest of the objects in the solar system put together.

The sun puts out a lot of energy in all directions. In fact, it is the source of almost all the energy in our solar system. Some of this energy reaches Earth as light, and some reaches it as heat.

Two features of the sun's surface are shown on this page. The dark areas, called *sunspots*, are cooler than the rest of the sun's surface and don't give off as much light. The red streams and loops of gases that shoot out from the sun are called *prominences* (PRAHM•ih•nuhn•suhs). These hot fountains often begin near a sunspot. They can be thousands of kilometers high and just as wide. Sunspots and prominences usually last for only a few days. Some can last for a few months.

✔ **What is the largest object in our solar system?**

FIND OUT

- **about the star we know as the sun**
- **the ways objects move in our solar system**

VOCABULARY

solar system
star
planet
asteroid
comet
orbit
axis

The sun is the largest object in our solar system. The next largest object, Jupiter, is small compared to the sun. Earth is even smaller. ▼

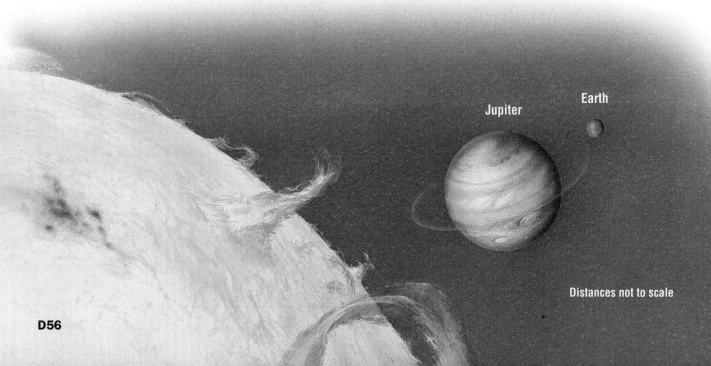

Jupiter

Earth

Distances not to scale

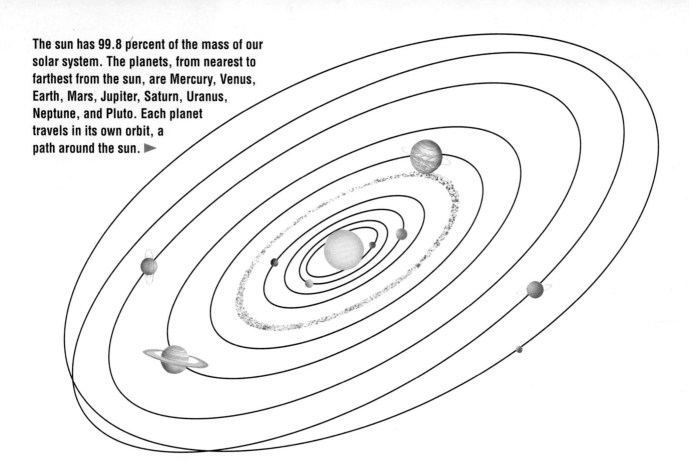

The sun has 99.8 percent of the mass of our solar system. The planets, from nearest to farthest from the sun, are Mercury, Venus, Earth, Mars, Jupiter, Saturn, Uranus, Neptune, and Pluto. Each planet travels in its own orbit, a path around the sun. ▶

Other Objects in Our Solar System

As you saw in the investigation, our solar system is made up of the sun and nine planets. It also includes moons around the planets, and asteroids and comets.

A **planet**, such as Earth and its eight neighbors, is a large object that moves around a star. Most planets in our solar system also have at least one natural satellite (SA•tuhl•yt), or object that moves around it. These satellites are called *moons*. Earth and Pluto each have only one moon. Jupiter and Saturn, on the other hand, each have many moons.

Asteroids and comets are other objects that move around the sun. **Asteroids** are small and rocky. Most of them are scattered in a large area between the orbit paths of Mars and Jupiter. Some scientists hypothesize that these asteroids are pieces of a planet that never formed. All the asteroids put together would make an object less than half the size of Earth's moon.

A **comet** is a small mass of dust and ice that orbits the sun in a long, oval-shaped path. When a comet's orbit takes it close to the sun, some of the ice on the comet's surface changes to water vapor and streams out to form a long, glowing tail.

✔ **Name the objects in our solar system.**

◀ As a comet orbits the sun, its tail always points away from the sun. Comet Hale-Bopp passed near Earth in April 1997. Its orbit is so big that it will not be seen from Earth again for 2380 years.

Paths Around the Sun

In the investigation, student "planets" moved around a "sun." An object *revolves* as it moves around another object. The path of an object as it revolves is called an **orbit**. The time for one complete orbit by a planet around the sun is its *year*. The orbits of the planets are not circles. Instead, they are a little bit elliptical, or oval, in shape.

Have you ever watched ice skaters spin? You may have noticed that as they bring their arms closer to their bodies, they spin faster. When they hold their arms out, they spin more slowly. The motion of the planets in their orbits is a little like the motion of a spinning ice skater. Planets with orbits closer to the sun move faster around the sun than those with orbits that are farther away.

✔ **Where in our solar system are the planets that orbit fastest?**

▲ As Earth *revolves* around the sun, it also spins, or *rotates,* around an imaginary line. This imaginary line, which runs through both poles of a planet, is called an **axis** (AK•sis).

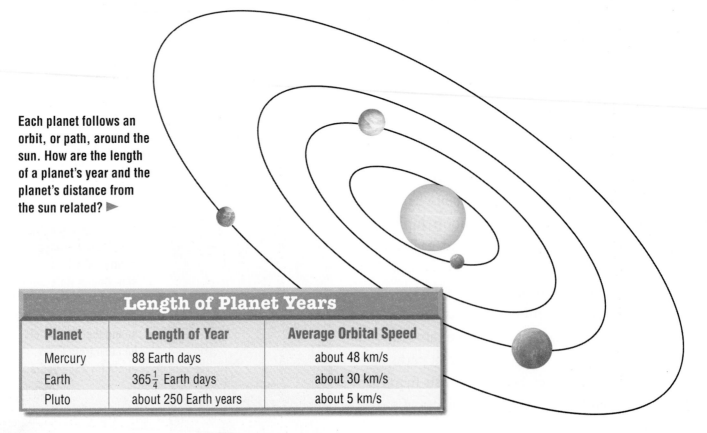

Each planet follows an orbit, or path, around the sun. How are the length of a planet's year and the planet's distance from the sun related? ▶

Length of Planet Years		
Planet	**Length of Year**	**Average Orbital Speed**
Mercury	88 Earth days	about 48 km/s
Earth	$365\frac{1}{4}$ Earth days	about 30 km/s
Pluto	about 250 Earth years	about 5 km/s

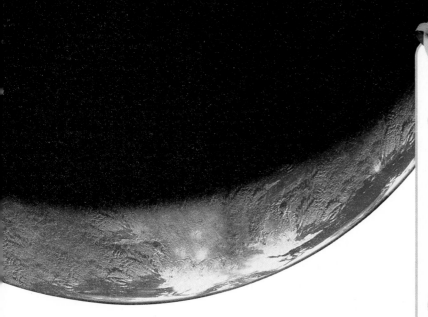

▲ Earth's rotation on its axis causes day and night. The side of Earth that faces the sun has day. At the same time, the opposite side of Earth has night.

Summary

Our solar system is made up of the sun, nine planets and their moons, asteroids, and comets. Each planet revolves in an elliptical orbit around the sun and rotates on its own axis.

Review

1. What is the sun?
2. In what way are the planets, comets, and asteroids alike?
3. How does a planet's distance from the sun affect its orbit speed?
4. **Critical Thinking** What might happen if the number of sunspots got much larger?
5. **Test Prep** What provides most of the heat and light to our solar system?
   A the comet Hale-Bopp
   B asteroids
   C the sun
   D Jupiter

LINKS

MATH LINK

The Size of the Sun The sun's diameter is about 1,392,000 km. About 109 Earths or 9 Jupiters would fit side by side across the sun. Use this information to figure out how many Earths would fit across Jupiter.

WRITING LINK

Expressive Writing—Poem Think about all the things you have learned about our solar system. Write a poem for your family describing how things move in our solar system or what makes up the solar system.

ART LINK

Drawing an Ellipse Tie the ends of a piece of string together to make a loop. Put the loop around two pushpins stuck several inches apart in a thick piece of cardboard. Place the point of a pencil inside the loop so the pencil touches the string. Keep the string tight as you draw around the pushpins. The shape you have drawn is an ellipse. What happens to the shape drawn if you move the pins closer together? Try it.

TECHNOLOGY LINK

Learn more about how asteroids move around the sun by visiting the National Air and Space Museum Internet site.
www.si.edu/harcourt/science

 Smithsonian Institution®

What Are the Planets Like?

In this lesson, you can . . .

INVESTIGATE distances between planets.

LEARN ABOUT the planets in our solar system.

LINK to math, writing, technology, and other areas.

INVESTIGATE

Distances Between Planets

Activity Purpose If you've ever used a map, you know what a scale model is. A scale model is a way to compare large distances in a smaller space. In this investigation you will **use measurements** to **make a scale model** that shows the distances between planets in our solar system.

Materials

- piece of string about 4 m long
- meterstick
- 9 different-colored markers

Activity Procedure

1 Copy the chart shown on the next page.

2 At one end of the string, tie three or four knots at the same point to make one large knot. This large knot will stand for the sun in your model.

3 In the solar system, distances are often measured in astronomical units (AU). One AU equals the average distance from Earth to the sun. In your model, 1 AU will equal 10 cm. Use your meterstick to accurately measure 1 AU from the sun on your model. This point stands for Earth's distance from the sun. Use one of the markers to mark this point on the string. Note in your chart which color you used. (Picture A)

◀ Europa (you•ROH•puh) is one of Jupiter's many moons. This natural satellite has a diameter of 3100 kilometers (about 1925 mi) and takes about $3\frac{1}{2}$ Earth days to orbit Jupiter.

Planet	Average Distance from the Sun (km)	Average Distance from the Sun (AU)	Scale Distance (cm)	Marker Color	Planet's Diameter (km)
Mercury	58 million	$\frac{4}{10}$	4		4876
Venus	108 million	$\frac{7}{10}$	7		12,104
Earth	150 million	1			12,756
Mars	228 million	2			6794
Jupiter	778 million	5			142,984
Saturn	1429 million	10			120,536
Uranus	2871 million	19			51,118
Neptune	4500 million	30			49,532
Pluto	5900 million	39			2274

4 Complete the Scale Distance column of the chart. Then measure and mark the position of each planet on the string. Use a different color for each planet, and **record** in your table the colors you used.

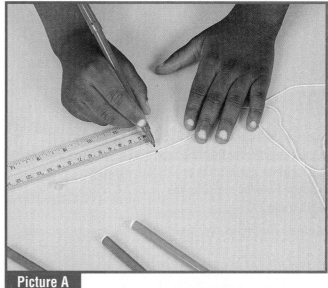

Picture A

Draw Conclusions

1. In your **model**, how far from the sun is Mercury? How far away is Pluto?

2. What advantages can you think of for using AU to measure distances inside the solar system?

3. **Scientists at Work** Explain how it helped to **make a scale model** instead of trying to show actual distances between planets.

Investigate Further You can use a calculator to help make other scale models. The chart gives the actual diameters of the planets. Use this scale: Earth's diameter = 1 cm. Find the scale diameters of the other planets by dividing their actual diameters by Earth's diameter. Make a scale drawing showing the diameter of each planet.

Process Skill Tip

Models are made to study objects or events that are too small or too large to observe directly. A **scale model** shows large objects or areas in smaller sizes so that they can be more easily studied.

The Planets

The Inner Planets

The area of the asteroid belt can be thought of as a dividing line between two groups of planets, the inner and outer planets. The **inner planets**—Mercury, Venus, Earth, and Mars—lie between the sun and the asteroid belt. Like the asteroids, the inner planets are rocky and dense. Unlike the asteroids, these planets are large and, except for Mercury, have atmospheres.

Mercury, the planet closest to the sun, is about the size of Earth's moon. Mercury, which is covered with craters, even looks like the moon. Very small amounts of some gases are present on Mercury, but there aren't enough of them to form an atmosphere.

Venus, the second planet from the sun, is about the same size as Earth. But Venus is very different from Earth. Venus is dry and has a thick atmosphere that traps heat. The temperature at the surface is about 475°C (887°F). The thick atmosphere presses down on Venus with a weight 100 times that of Earth's atmosphere. Also, Venus spins on its axis in a direction opposite from that of Earth's rotation.

FIND OUT

- about the planets in our solar system
- how moons and rings may have formed

VOCABULARY

inner planets
outer planets
gas giants

This drawing shows the planets in the correct order from the sun but not at the correct size or distance from the sun. Can you explain why? ▼

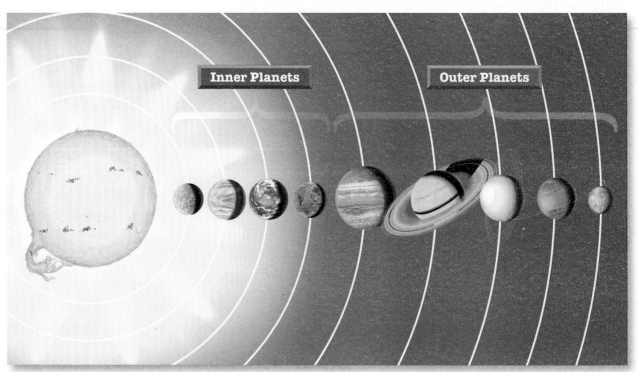

Mercury has a diameter of 4876 kilometers (about 3031 mi) and is 58 million kilometers (about 36 million mi) from the sun. This inner planet has no moons and takes about 59 Earth days to make one rotation, or turn once on its axis. Mercury orbits the sun in about 88 Earth days.

Venus has a diameter of 12,104 kilometers (about 7517 mi) and is 108 million kilometers (about 67 million mi) from the sun. This inner planet has no natural satellites. It takes Venus about 243 Earth days to make one rotation and 225 Earth days to orbit the sun.

Earth, the third planet from the sun, is the largest of the inner planets. It has one natural satellite, the moon. Earth is the only planet that has liquid water. It is also the only known planet that supports life. Earth's atmosphere absorbs and reflects the right amount of solar energy to keep the planet at the correct temperature for living things such as humans to survive.

Mars, the fourth planet from the sun, is sometimes called the Red Planet because its soil is a dark reddish brown. Mars has two moons and the largest volcano in the solar system—Olympus Mons (oh•LIHM•puhs MAHNS). Space probes have shown us that nothing lives on Mars. Dust storms can last for months and affect the whole planet. Although no liquid water has been found on Mars, it is believed that liquid water once existed there. This is because probes and satellites have found deep valleys and sedimentary rocks. These features probably were formed by flowing water.

✔ **List the inner planets in order from the sun.**

Earth has a diameter of 12,756 kilometers (about 7922 mi). Our planet is 150 million kilometers (about 93 million mi) from the sun. Earth has one moon and takes almost 24 hours to complete one rotation on its axis. It takes about 365 days to orbit the sun.

Not to scale

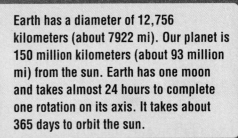

Mars has a diameter of 6794 kilometers (about 4230 mi) and is 228 million kilometers (about 142 million mi) from the sun. This inner planet has two moons. Mars completes a rotation in about 24.5 hours. Mars takes about 687 Earth days to complete one orbit around the sun.

The Outer Planets

On the other side of the asteroid belt are the **outer planets**—Jupiter, Saturn, Uranus, Neptune, and Pluto. Four of these planets— Jupiter, Saturn, Uranus, and Neptune—are large spheres made up mostly of gases. Because of this, these planets are often called the **gas giants**.

Jupiter is the largest planet in our solar system. A thin ring that is hard to see surrounds it. At least 16 moons orbit around it. Jupiter's atmosphere is very active. Its energy causes a circular storm known as the Great Red Spot. This weather, which is a lot like a hurricane, has lasted more than 300 years. It is so big around that three Earths would fit inside it.

Saturn is a gas giant known for its rings. Space probes have found that other planets also have rings. But Saturn's are so wide and so bright that they can be seen from Earth through a small telescope. Saturn has at least 18 named moons.

Not to scale

Uranus (YOOR•uh•nuhs), the seventh planet from the sun, is the most distant planet you can see without using a telescope. Uranus, a blue-green ball of gas and liquid, has at least 15 moons as well as faint rings around it.

Neptune, the farthest away of the gas giants, has at least eight moons and a faint ring. It also has circular storms, but none have lasted as long as the Great Red Spot on Jupiter.

In the investigation you saw that *Pluto* is the planet farthest from the sun. If you completed the Investigate Further, you also learned that Pluto is the smallest planet. From Pluto's surface the sun looks like a very bright star. Little heat or light reaches Pluto or its one moon. Unlike the other outer planets, Pluto is not a gas giant. Instead, Pluto has a rocky surface that is probably covered by frozen gases.

✔ **Which planets are gas giants?**

Uranus has a diameter of 51,118 kilometers (about 31,700 mi). This planet is 2870 million kilometers (1782 million mi) from the sun. Uranus makes one rotation in 17 hours and one orbit around the sun in about 84 Earth years.

Pluto has a diameter of 2274 kilometers (about 1366 mi) and is 5900 million kilometers (about 3664 million mi) from the sun. It takes Pluto about 7 days to complete one rotation and 249 Earth years to complete one revolution.

Neptune has a diameter of 49,532 kilometers (about 30,740 mi) and is 4500 million kilometers (about 2795 million mi) from the sun. Neptune completes one rotation in a little more than 16 hours and one revolution in about 165 Earth years.

▲ The rings around Saturn are made up of dust, ice crystals, and small bits of rock coated with frozen water. The rings are about 270,000 kilometers (about 167,700 mi) across but only about 10 kilometers (about 6 mi) thick.

▲ Titan, Saturn's largest moon, has a diameter of 5150 kilometers (about 3200 mi). Titan has no clouds in its atmosphere and is very cold.

Io (EYE•oh) is a moon of Jupiter. Io has a diameter of 3630 kilometers (about 2254 mi) and has several active volcanoes on its surface. The volcanoes are the big orange patches. ▶

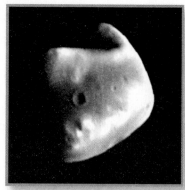

▲ Deimos (DY•muhs) is one of the two Martian moons. It has many craters and an uneven shape. It is about 14 kilometers (9 mi) in diameter.

Moons and Rings

Every planet except Mercury and Venus has at least one natural satellite, or *moon*. Earth's moon is round and rocky, and it has many craters. Others, like the two moons of Mars or the outer moons of Jupiter, are small and rocky and have uneven shapes. Jupiter and Mars orbit near the asteroid belt. So, their moons may be asteroids pulled in by the planets' gravity. The large moons of Jupiter and Saturn are almost like small planets. Io, one of Jupiter's larger moons, has active volcanoes. Titan (TYT•uhn), one of Saturn's moons, has a dense atmosphere that glows red-orange.

Besides having moons, each of the gas giants has a system of rings. These rings are made of tiny bits of dust, ice crystals, and small pieces of rock. Saturn's rings may have formed as a moon was pulled apart by gravity because it got too close to the planet.

✔ **What are planet rings made of?**

▲ Phobos (FOH•buhs) is the other moon that orbits Mars. Like Deimos, it is a small, rocky object. Its diameter is about 22 kilometers (14 mi). Phobos makes three trips around its planet each Martian day.

Summary

The inner planets—Mercury, Venus, Earth, and Mars—are small and rocky. Four of the five outer planets are gas giants. They are Jupiter, Saturn, Uranus, and Neptune. The outer planet that is farthest from the sun is Pluto, another rocky planet. Most of the planets have at least one moon. The gas giants also have rings.

Review

1. Name the inner planets, starting with the planet closest to the sun.
2. What can be thought of as the dividing line between the inner planets and the outer planets?
3. Which planets have no moons?
4. **Critical Thinking** Compare and contrast Venus and Earth.
5. **Test Prep** The outer planet that is **NOT** a gas giant is —
   A Jupiter
   B Saturn
   C Neptune
   D Pluto

LINKS

MATH LINK

Graphing Planet Data Make a bar graph showing the diameter of each planet. Use data from the table on page D61 and a computer program such as *Graph Links*.

WRITING LINK

Persuasive Writing—Opinion Suppose you are a real-estate agent trying to get adults to move to the planet of your choice. Write a newspaper ad pointing out all the benefits of living on your chosen planet.

ART LINK

View of a Planet Paint or draw a realistic landscape of the surface of another planet. Or paint the view of the planet as it would be seen from one of its moons.

LITERATURE LINK

The Wonderful Flight to the Mushroom Planet Read this book by Eleanor Cameron to find out what happens when two boys go on an adventure in space. Compare the planet with Earth.

TECHNOLOGY LINK

Learn more about planets and other objects in space by visiting this Internet site.

www.scilinks.org/harcourt

SCI LINKS
THE WORLD'S A CLICK AWAY

How Do People Study the Solar System?

In this lesson, you can . . .

 INVESTIGATE how to make a telescope.

 LEARN ABOUT how people study objects in space.

 LINK to math, writing, social studies, and technology.

 **INVESTIGATE**

Telescopes

Activity Purpose Have you ever looked up into the sky at night and wished you could see some of the objects more clearly? Because distances in space are so great, scientists need to use instruments to study what is beyond Earth's atmosphere. In this investigation you will make a simple telescope and use it to **observe** some objects in space.

Materials

- small piece of modeling clay
- 1 thin (eyepiece) lens
- small-diameter cardboard tube
- 1 thick (objective) lens
- large-diameter cardboard tube

CAUTION

Activity Procedure

1. Press small pieces of clay to the outside of the thin lens. Then put the lens in one end of the small tube. Use enough clay to hold the lens in place, keeping the lens as straight as possible. Be careful not to smear the middle of the lens with clay. (Picture A)

2. Repeat Step 1 using the thick lens and large tube.

◄ This vehicle is the moon rover. Astronauts used it to travel over the surface of Earth's only natural satellite, the moon.

Picture A

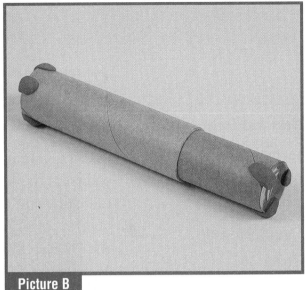

Picture B

3 Slide the open end of the small tube into the larger tube. You have just made a telescope. (Picture B)

4 Hold your telescope up, and look through one lens. Then turn the telescope around, and look through the other lens. **CAUTION Never look directly at the sun.** Slide the small tube in and out of the large tube until what you see is in focus, or not blurry. How do objects appear through each lens? **Record** your **observations.**

Draw Conclusions

1. What did you **observe** as you looked through each lens?

2. Using your observations, **infer** which lens you should look through to **observe** the stars. Explain your answer.

3. **Scientists at Work** Astronomers (uh•STRAWN•uh•merz) are scientists who study objects in space. Some astronomers use large telescopes with many parts to **observe** objects in space. How would your telescope make observing objects in the night sky easier?

Investigate Further Use your telescope to observe the moon at night. Make a list of the details you can see using your telescope that you can't see using only your eyes.

Process Skill Tip

When you **observe** an object, you use your senses to notice details about it. Using an instrument such as a telescope helps you observe objects that are too far away to be seen clearly using only your eyes.

Space Exploration

Telescopes

Using nothing more than your eyes, you can see most of the planets in the solar system. But what if you want to see them as more than just points of light in the sky? What if you want to see objects in space that are even farther away than the visible planets? Or what if you want to see smaller objects such as moons? To do any of these things, you need to use a telescope. A **telescope** is a device people use to observe distant objects.

Two very different types of telescopes are used to observe objects in space: *radio telescopes* and *optical telescopes*, or telescopes that use light. There are also two types of optical telescopes. A refracting telescope, which is what you made in the investigation, uses lenses to magnify an object, or make it appear larger. A reflecting telescope uses a curved mirror to magnify an object. Most large telescopes used today are reflecting telescopes.

FIND OUT

- about telescopes
- about missions into space

VOCABULARY

telescope
space probe

Even without using a telescope, you can see dark areas, bright areas, and craters on the moon. ▼

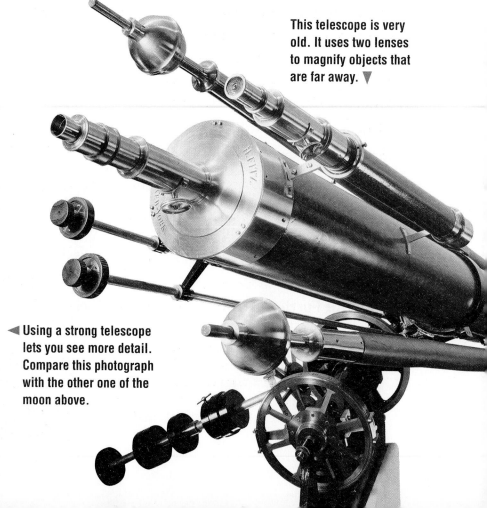

This telescope is very old. It uses two lenses to magnify objects that are far away. ▼

◄ Using a strong telescope lets you see more detail. Compare this photograph with the other one of the moon above.

▲ The large mirror of the Keck telescope is made up of many smaller mirrors. They work together to gather light and magnify images of objects in space.

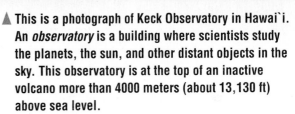

▲ This is a photograph of Keck Observatory in Hawai`i. An *observatory* is a building where scientists study the planets, the sun, and other distant objects in the sky. This observatory is at the top of an inactive volcano more than 4000 meters (about 13,130 ft) above sea level.

Telescopes that scientists use are much larger than the one you made in the investigation. Besides being large, telescopes that are used to study space objects are powerful. Many of them have cameras that constantly take pictures of space. Computers keep the telescopes pointed at the same place in the sky. This allows the powerful lenses and mirrors to collect more light so they can produce brighter and clearer pictures. Astronomers then study the pictures to find out about space objects.

Earth's atmosphere limits what optical telescopes can "see." Moving air causes the "twinkling" of stars. It also blurs pictures taken using optical telescopes. This is why observatories that use optical telescopes are often located high on mountains.

Scientists have found that stars and other objects in space give off more than just light energy that we can see. Radio telescopes work the way optical telescopes do. But instead of collecting and focusing light, they collect and focus invisible radio waves. Moving air, clouds, and poor weather don't affect radio waves. Computers process the data collected by radio telescopes. The computers then make "pictures" that astronomers can study.

A radio telescope collects radio waves with a large, bowl-shaped antenna. Scientists study images formed by these waves to learn about the objects that gave them off. This radio telescope is in Arecibo (ar•uh•SEE•boh), Puerto Rico. ▶

The telescopes you have seen so far in this chapter are Earth-based, or located on Earth's surface. Scientists have also built telescopes for use in space. These telescopes don't have any problems caused by the atmosphere. The Inside Story shows the parts of the most famous space-based telescope, the Hubble Space Telescope.

✓ **What is a telescope?**

HUBBLE SPACE TELESCOPE

The Hubble Space Telescope, or HST, is a reflecting telescope. Its mirror, which has a diameter of 240 cm (about 94 in.), can "see" details ten times as clearly as telescopes on Earth.

The HST uses sunlight as its energy source. The instrument's solar panels change sunlight into electricity. Each panel is about $2\frac{1}{2}$ meters (about 8 ft) wide and 13 meters (about 42 ft) long.

The main cover tube of the HST protects the telescope as well as other instruments used to study space.

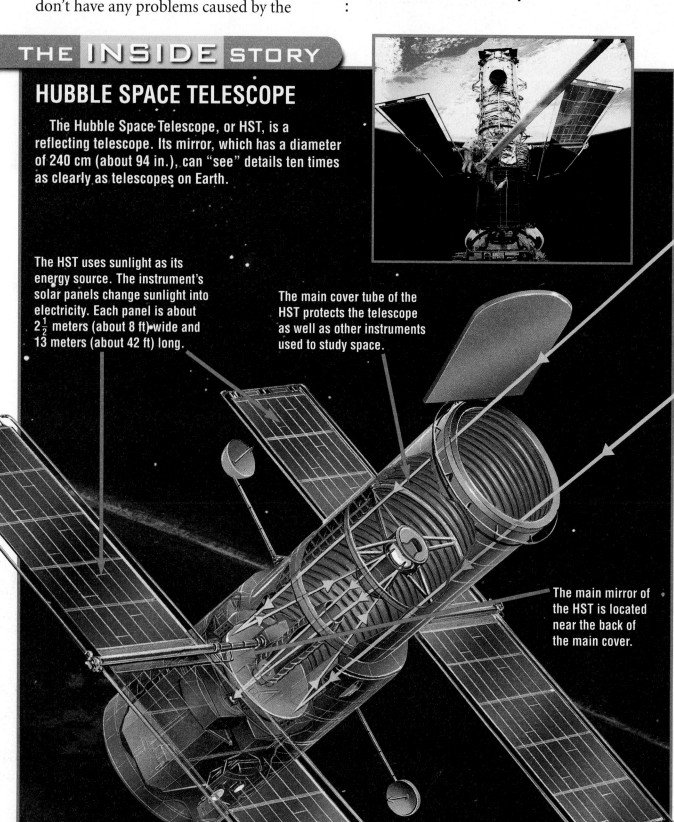

The main mirror of the HST is located near the back of the main cover.

▲ During some of the Apollo missions, astronauts explored our moon's surface. This spacecraft allowed astronauts to land on the moon. Later they could blast off and return to the main part of their ship, which was circling the moon.

Mir was a Russian *space station* in orbit above Earth. Aboard *Mir*, astronauts and scientists from many countries worked for months at a time. They experimented to find out how conditions in space affect things and people. ▼

Crewed Missions

Another way to learn about space is to actually go there. Trips that people take into space are called *crewed missions.* Crewed missions are useful because people can actually find out for themselves what it is like to live and work in space.

The first person to be sent into space was a Russian, Yuri Gagarin, in 1961. Since then, astronauts from many countries have made trips into space. One of the most famous missions was carried out on *Apollo 11,* which was launched by the United States on July 16, 1969. On this mission Neil Armstrong and Edwin "Buzz" Aldrin spent two hours exploring the moon's surface. The United States sent five more crewed missions to the moon before the Apollo program ended in 1972.

Today the United States uses the space shuttle to carry crews, materials, and satellites to and from space. Astronauts on the shuttles do experiments, launch and get back satellites, and repair instruments.

✓ **What is a crewed space mission?**

Astronauts aboard the U.S. space shuttles also do experiments. These astronauts are working in Space Lab, which rides in the cargo area of a space shuttle. ▼

D73

Space Probes

We have learned much of what we know about the solar system by using space probes. **Space probes** are vehicles that carry cameras, instruments, and other tools. Probes are sent to explore places that are too dangerous or too far away for people to visit. Probes gather data and send it back to Earth for study. The pictures of Mars and Callisto were sent to Earth by probes millions of kilometers away in space.

Some probes have fly-by missions. That is, they fly by the object to be studied but do not land. As they pass the object, they gather data, including pictures. Other probes land on the surfaces of planets. These probes take pictures, collect and analyze rock samples, test for the presence of substances such as water, and collect other data.

✔ **What is a space probe?**

▲ Information about this moon of Jupiter, Callisto, was gathered as the space probe *Galileo* flew past it.

Sojourner is a probe that was used to study the surface of Mars. *Sojourner* took thousands of photos of the surface as it gathered information about the Red Planet. ▼

▲ The space probe *Galileo* was sent to Jupiter in 1989. Instruments launched from *Galileo* measured the sizes of particles that make up the clouds of Jupiter and the amounts of hydrogen and helium in Jupiter's atmosphere.

▲ *Voyager 2*, launched in 1977, flew by Jupiter in 1979, Saturn in 1981, and Uranus in 1986. The probe then headed on to Neptune.

Summary

A telescope is a device people use to observe distant objects. A refracting telescope uses lenses, and a reflecting telescope uses mirrors to magnify an object. Radio telescopes collect and focus radio waves. The Hubble Space Telescope is an optical telescope in orbit around Earth. Crewed missions and space probes are other ways to study objects in space.

Review

1. What are two types of telescopes?
2. What limits the things an Earth-based optical telescope can "see"?
3. What kind of work do astronauts on a crewed space mission do?
4. **Critical Thinking** What are the advantages of sending crewed missions instead of probes into space? The disadvantages?
5. **Test Prep** An instrument that uses lenses to magnify distant objects is a —
   A radio telescope
   B refracting telescope
   C reflecting telescope
   D space station

LINKS

MATH LINK

Faster than a Speeding Rocket When Earth and Jupiter are closest together, they are about 630 million km apart. *Voyager 2* took two years to reach Jupiter. About how far did it travel each year?

WRITING LINK

Informative Writing—Description Suppose you are an astronaut who will take part in the next space-shuttle mission. Find out about a typical day on the space shuttle. Then write a composition for a friend describing a typical day of your mission.

SOCIAL STUDIES LINK

International Space Station Find out which countries are building parts of the International Space Station. Locate each country on a map or globe. Make a chart that lists the name of each country, its continent, and which parts of the space station it is building.

TECHNOLOGY LINK

To learn more about pictures from space watch *Hubble Images* on the **Harcourt Science Newsroom Video.**

CNN. Turner Le@rning

LESSON 4

What Are Constellations?

In this lesson, you can . . .

 INVESTIGATE how to make a constellation box.

 LEARN ABOUT star patterns called constellations.

 LINK to math, writing, literature, and technology.

Constellations

Activity Purpose On a clear night, away from city lights, the sky is filled with twinkling stars. Some of these stars form patterns in the sky. Ancient people named these patterns after the objects or persons the patterns reminded them of. In this investigation you will **make a mode**l to show a pattern made by stars in the sky.

Materials

- safety goggles
- scissors
- shoe box with lid
- penlight
- black construction paper
- straight pin
- thin, wooden skewer
- masking tape

CAUTION

Activity Procedure

1. **CAUTION** **Put on your safety goggles.** Use the scissors to carefully cut a rectangle about 10 cm by 6 cm from one end of the box.

2. At the other end of the box, trace the diameter of the penlight's head. Use the scissors to carefully cut out the circle.

3. Cut two or three rectangles from the black construction paper. Make sure they are a little larger than the rectangular opening in the shoe box.

4. Use the pin and the wooden skewer to carefully make small holes in the construction paper. Make a different pattern on each rectangle. (Picture A)

◀ This instrument is called a *sextant* (SEKS•tuhnt). It was commonly used by sailors hundreds of years ago. By measuring the position of the sun above the horizon, you can find out your exact location on the ocean.

D76

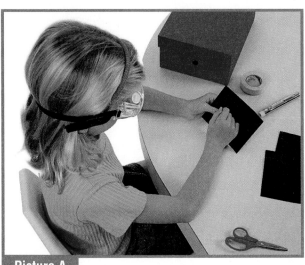
Picture A

Picture B

5. Put the head of the penlight into the circular opening in the shoe box. Hold the penlight in place with masking tape. Put the lid on the box.

6. Put one of your rectangles over the opening at the other end of the box. Tape it in place. (Picture B)

7. Darken the room. Hold the box about 0.5 m from a white wall, and turn on the penlight. **Record** your **observations** of your star pattern and those of your classmates.

8. Work with a partner to find a pattern of stars that looks like an object or person. Name your pattern, and make up a story about it.

Draw Conclusions

1. What did the star patterns look like?

2. Could you find a group of "stars" that looked like the shape of an object or person? These patterns found among the stars are called constellations. Describe your constellation.

3. **Scientists at Work** Not all stars are the same distance from Earth. Also, not all stars shine with the same brightness. Think about your **model**. What do you think the larger holes stand for? What do the smaller holes stand for?

Investigate Further Again, project your star pattern on the wall, this time with the lights on. How does what you see in the light **compare** with what you saw in the dark? **Infer** why you can't see most stars during the day.

> **Process Skill Tip**
>
> Scientists often use models to study objects or events that they can't directly observe. **Making models** of space objects makes it much easier to study the objects and the relationships among them.

D77

Constellations

Patterns of Stars

If you look into the night sky, you'll notice that many of the brightest stars form patterns much like those you made and projected on the wall in the investigation. Each pattern or group of stars in the sky is called a **constellation** (kahn•stuh•LAY•shuhn).

The people of many ancient cultures around the world saw constellations as outlines of objects, mythological (MITH•uh•lahj•ih•kuhl) characters, or animals. Those people made up stories to explain how the object, character, or animal came to be in the night sky.

Orion, one of the brightest constellations, is an example of a mythological character. In ancient Greek myths, Orion was a hunter who annoyed the gods by bragging all the time. When they got tired of him, the gods sent a scorpion to bite and kill him. Afterward, they felt sorry for Orion and placed him in the sky.

✔ **What is a constellation?**

FIND OUT

- about constellations
- how constellations seem to change their positions during the year

VOCABULARY

constellation

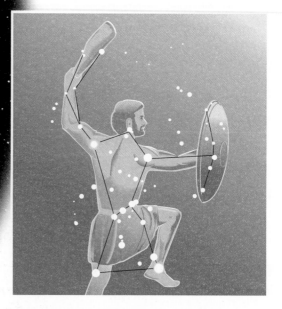

◄ If you think about the legend, you can see Orion in this group of stars.

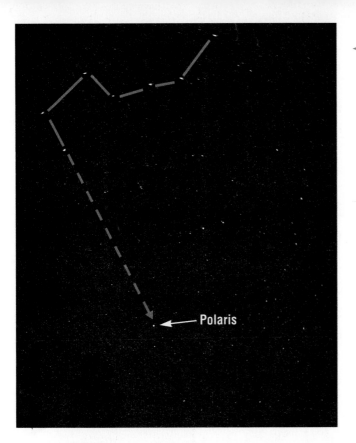

← Polaris

◄ The Big Dipper is an easy constellation to find. Then you can use it to find Polaris. Use the "pointer stars" in the end of the dipper's bowl, and follow them to Polaris. Polaris marks the end of the Little Dipper's handle.

Stars as Tools for Navigation

Because Earth rotates on its axis, most constellations appear to rise in the east and set in the west during the night. As Earth revolves around the sun, most constellations seem to appear in different positions in the sky. However, if you look toward the northern sky, you will see a group of stars that are visible all night, all year long. Instead of appearing to rise and set, these stars seem to circle Earth's North Pole each night. They are called circumpolar (sir•kuhm•POH•ler) stars. Polaris (poh•LAR•ihs), the North Star, is located almost directly above the North Pole. This star appears in the same place all night long, every night of the year.

If you are in the Northern Hemisphere and can find Polaris in the night sky, you can find which direction is north. And if you know where north is, you can find your way when you are traveling. Sailors used stars such as Polaris to navigate, or find their way on the ocean. Besides knowing which direction is north, sailors can look at other stars and tell how far east or west they have traveled.

It's not as easy to find your way if you are in the Southern Hemisphere. There is no star above the South Pole. Instead, travelers look for the smallest constellation in the sky—the Southern Cross. The long side of this circumpolar constellation of four bright stars and several dimmer ones points toward the South Pole.

✔ **Why is Polaris called the North Star?**

The Southern Cross is used to locate south in the Southern Hemisphere. It is not directly over the South Pole, but it is near it. There is no bright star called the "South" Star. ▶

Stars as Calendars

As Earth revolves around the sun, the constellations that rise and set appear to rise a little earlier in the east each evening. This means that as the seasons change, we see different constellations in the night sky. For example, in the Northern Hemisphere, Orion is high in the night sky during the winter, while the constellation Scorpio is visible only in summer.

Ancient people used these seasonal changes of star patterns as calendars. Some historians think that ancient people watched constellations to decide when to plant and harvest their crops. Seeing Leo and Virgo in the night sky, for example, may have told them that the last frosts of the year had happened and that it was now safe to plant. This is not very different from a farmer today using a paper calendar to count days.

✔ **How did ancient people use the seasonal appearance of certain constellations?**

▲ Although constellations near the poles are always visible and never rise or set, their positions do change with the seasons. This is the North Polar sky in summer.

▲ This is the same section of sky as above at the same time of night, but in winter. All the stars and constellations are still here, but their positions appear to have rotated.

This half of a star chart shows the positions of the constellations in the sky from February to August. To use a chart like this one, face north. Hold the chart so the current month is at the top. Then once you find the Big Dipper and Polaris, it is easy to find other constellations. ▶

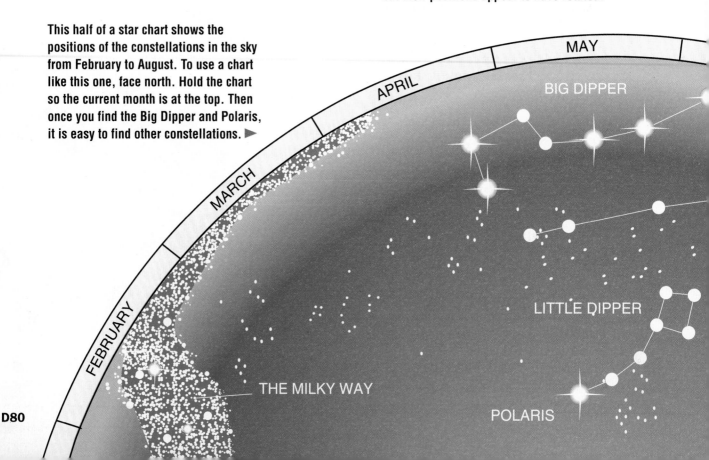

MAY

APRIL

MARCH

FEBRUARY

BIG DIPPER

LITTLE DIPPER

THE MILKY WAY

POLARIS

Summary

In the sky, stars form patterns called constellations. Circumpolar constellations appear to circle the poles. Stars and constellations can be used for navigation. Ancient people may have used seasonal constellations as calendars.

Review

1. What is a constellation?

2. How do circumpolar stars differ from other stars?

3. Describe how to locate the North Star.

4. **Critical Thinking** If you were lost in Australia on a clear night, explain how you could find your way.

5. **Test Prep** A constellation that is seen high in the night sky at only certain times of the year is —

   A circumpolar
   B seasonal
   C mythical
   D navigational

LINKS

MATH LINK

Distances in Space Find out about two units used to measure distances in space: the astronomical unit, or AU, and the light-year. Tell when each of these units of measurement is used.

WRITING LINK

Informative Writing—Narration Choose a constellation, and find out the story behind it. Write a story for a younger child explaining a myth that ancient people told about your constellation.

LITERATURE LINK

The Ultimate Guide to the Sky Go to your library, and check out this book by John Mosley. On a clear night, work with an adult family member to locate and identify some of the constellations described in this book. Note that star viewing is best done away from city lights and between 9 P.M. and 10 P.M.

TECHNOLOGY LINK

Visit the Harcourt Learning Site for related links, activities, and resources.
www.harcourtschool.com

WELCOME TO
THE LEARNING SITE

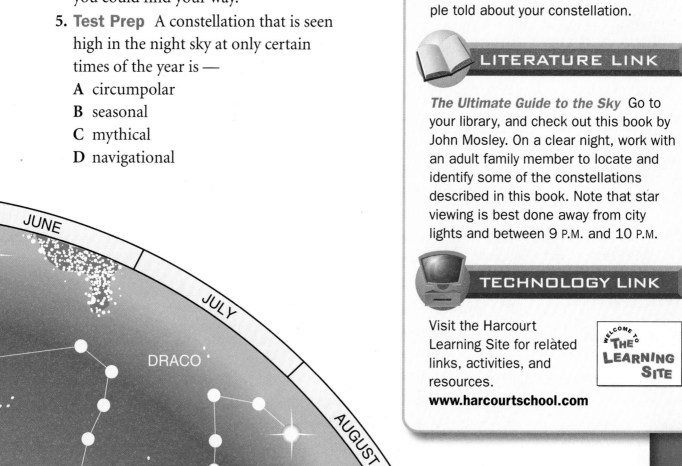

JUNE

JULY

AUGUST

DRACO

Discovering the Planets

Five of the nine planets in our solar system can be seen using just your eyes. These five—Mercury, Venus, Mars, Jupiter, and Saturn—were all known to astronomers before 1700. These early astronomers named the planets for gods and goddesses of Roman mythology.

Galileo and the Telescope

The invention of the telescope made astronomy a more complex science. Galileo, an Italian scientist and inventor who lived from 1564 to 1642, was the first person to use a telescope to view the stars and planets. Compared to telescopes now, his telescope wasn't very powerful. It magnified, or enlarged the view, only about 20 or 30 times. However, using just that weak telescope, Galileo was the first person to observe mountains on the moon, sunspots, and the phases of Venus. In 1610 Galileo was the first to see moons around Jupiter. His observations of planets and moons showed that not all bodies in space circled Earth, as many people at that time believed.

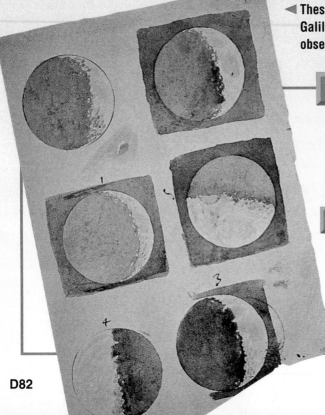

◀ These ink drawings are how Galileo recorded his telescope observations of Earth's moon.

The History of Planet Discoveries

Uranus 1781
Uranus discovered

| 1600 A.D. | | 1700 A.D. |

Jupiter 1610
Jupiter's moons discovered

Discovering Uranus

Other scientists slowly improved on Galileo's telescope design. William Herschel, a British astronomer, discovered Uranus, the seventh planet from the sun. He used a telescope that his sister, Caroline, helped him build. On the night of March 13, 1781, Herschel saw something that he knew was not a star. He first thought it was a comet. Over time he mapped the orbit of the object and realized it was a planet, which was later named Uranus. For a long time, others had a hard time seeing what Herschel had seen, because their telescopes weren't as good.

Using Math to Find New Planets

Two astronomers, the English John C. Adams and the French Urbain Leverrier (oor•BAN luh•vair•YAY), found the location of the eighth planet at about the same time. They did not see the planet themselves. Using mathematics, they predicted its location. Then they sent their predictions to other scientists.

Adams sent his prediction to the Astronomer Royal of England, who paid little attention to it. Leverrier sent his prediction to the Urania (oo•RAHN•ee•uh) Observatory in Berlin, Germany. The director there, Johann Galle (YOH•hahn GAH•luh), and his assistant used Leverrier's research and found Neptune on September 23, 1846.

Pluto was also discovered through mathematics. In 1905 American astronomer Percival Lowell noticed that something seemed to be affecting the orbits of Uranus and Neptune. He hypothesized that a ninth planet was the cause. He searched unsuccessfully for it until his death in 1916.

In 1930 Pluto appeared as a small dot on three photographs Clyde Tombaugh took at Lowell Observatory, which was built by Percival Lowell.

Think About It

1. How have improvements in technology helped astronomers?
2. How did scientists Urbain Leverrier and Johann Galle work together?

Ganymede, one of Jupiter's moons

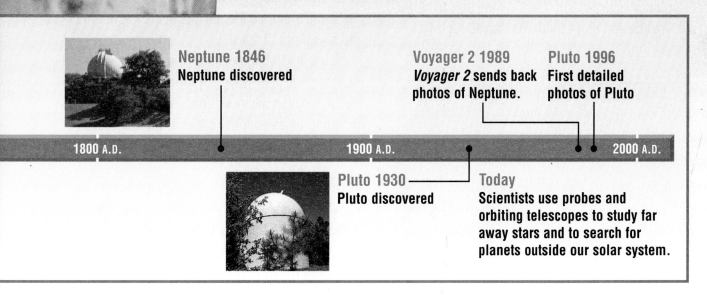

Neptune 1846
Neptune discovered

Voyager 2 1989
Voyager 2 sends back photos of Neptune.

Pluto 1996
First detailed photos of Pluto

1800 A.D.   1900 A.D.   2000 A.D.

Pluto 1930
Pluto discovered

Today
Scientists use probes and orbiting telescopes to study far away stars and to search for planets outside our solar system.

Clyde Tombaugh

ASTRONOMER, INVENTOR

"I think the driving thing was curiosity about the universe. That fascinated me. I didn't think anything about being famous or anything like that, I was just interested in the concepts involved."

Working on a farm in Kansas taught Clyde Tombaugh to be persistent and creative with materials at hand. He was always interested in astronomy. His uncle and father had a telescope, which they gave him when he was 9 years old. By the time Tombaugh was 20, he decided to build his own telescope. He used part of a dairy machine for the base and part of his father's 1910 Buick.

Later, Tombaugh's uncle asked Tombaugh to build a telescope for him. Tombaugh also built a better telescope for him. With that homemade telescope, he observed Mars and Jupiter. He drew what he saw and sent his sketches to the Lowell Observatory in Flagstaff, Arizona. The scientists at the observatory were impressed by Tombaugh's drawings. They invited him to come to Arizona and work there. He stayed for 14 years.

Tombaugh in 1995 with his first telescope

On February 18, 1930, Tombaugh discovered the planet Pluto. Other scientists had predicted its existence, but he was the first to locate it in the sky. During his life, he discovered asteroids and hundreds of stars.

After completing college, Tombaugh taught navigation to U.S. Navy personnel during World War II. He also designed many new instruments, including an astronomy camera. He taught at New Mexico State University for nearly 20 years.

THINK ABOUT IT

1. What have you read about Tombaugh that leads you to think he is resourceful?

2. How was Tombaugh's discovery of Pluto related to work by other scientists?

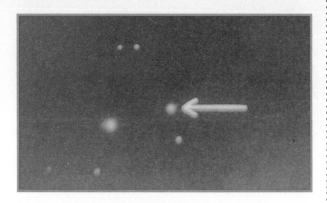

Telescope photo of Pluto, 1930

Sundial

How can you make an instrument that uses the sun to tell time?

Materials
- small ball of clay
- short pencil
- cardboard, about 15 cm x 20 cm

Procedure

1. Use the lump of clay to stand the short pencil in the center of the cardboard. Make sure the sharpened end of the pencil is up.

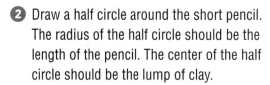

2. Draw a half circle around the short pencil. The radius of the half circle should be the length of the pencil. The center of the half circle should be the lump of clay.

3. Put your sundial on a windowsill that gets sun all day. Each hour, trace the shadow of the pencil on the cardboard. Mark the time at the end of each line. Do this for six hours.

4. On the next sunny day, use your sundial to tell time.

Draw Conclusions

How does your sundial use Earth's movement to tell time?

Moving Constellations

How do the positions of the constellations change?

Materials
- ruler

Procedure

1. Observe the Big Dipper and the Little Dipper twice each night. One time should be in the early evening. The second time should be at least one hour later.

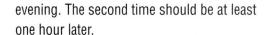

2. Find something to use as a reference, such as the top of a fence or tree. Hold the ruler at arm's length, and measure the distance from the reference point to the constellations. Record your observations as drawings.

3. Repeat Steps 1 and 2 at the same time each night for four weeks. Remember to put the dates on your drawings.

Draw Conclusions

How did the constellations change their positions? What caused the changes?

Chapter 3 Review and Test Preparation

Vocabulary Review

Use the terms below to complete the sentences. The page numbers in ( ) tell you where to look in the chapter if you need help.

solar system (D56) **inner planets** (D62)

star (D56) **outer planets** (D64)

planet (D57) **gas giants** (D64)

asteroid (D57) **telescope** (D70)

comet (D57) **space probe** (D74)

orbit (D58) **constellation** (D78)

axis (D58)

1. A _____ is a group of planets and their moons that orbit a central star.

2. Venus is a _____ that revolves around the sun.

3. An _____ is an imaginary line around which a planet rotates, or spins.

4. A group of stars that forms a pattern in the night sky is called a _____.

5. The four planets nearest the sun are called the _____.

6. An _____ is a rocky object that orbits the sun in a path between Mars and Jupiter.

7. A _____ is a vehicle sent into space in order to explore places too dangerous or too far away for people to visit.

8. The path a planet takes around the sun is its _____.

9. A _____ is a burning ball of gases.

10. Neptune is one of the four _____.

11. A _____ is an instrument used to observe distant objects.

12. A _____ is a space object made of ice, dust, and gases.

13. The five planets on the outer side of the asteroid belt are called the _____.

Connect Concepts

List the planets, and classify them as to their position in the solar system. Be sure to list them in the correct order from the sun.

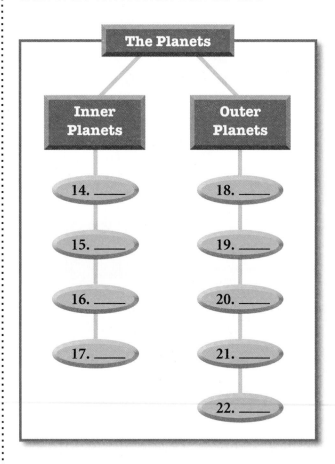

Check Understanding

Write the letter of the best choice.

23. The sun provides _____ of the energy to the solar system.

    A most   **C** none

    B little   **D** some

24. An imaginary line that runs through both poles of a planet is its —

    F star   **H** comet

    G orbit   **J** axis

25. _____ is the outer planet that is **NOT** a gas giant.

A Saturn   C Uranus

B Pluto   D Jupiter

26. _____ has a ring.

F Jupiter   H Earth

G Pluto   J Venus

27. This type of telescope never has problems seeing through Earth's atmosphere. It uses lenses to enlarge an object.

A Earth-based telescope

B reflecting telescope

C refracting telescope

D space-based telescope

28. Trips that people take into space are called —

F crewed missions

G uncrewed missions

H space probes

J observatories

29. Constellations that appear to circle the poles are called _____ constellations.

A seasonal   C planet

B circumpolar   D star

Critical Thinking

30. Why do you think some stars in constellations look brighter than others?

31. Most asteroids are in the asteroid belt between the orbits of Mars and Jupiter. But some asteroids have "escaped" and have long, oval-shaped orbits like those of the comets. How do you think these asteroids escaped the asteroid belt?

Process Skills Review

32. In Lesson 1 you **made a model** showing how planets rotate on their axes and revolve around the sun. How would you make a model to show the motions of Jupiter and its many moons?

33. In Lesson 2 you **made a model** to show the distances between the planets. What activity of planets would be modeled by cars racing around a racetrack?

34. In Lesson 3 you made a telescope to **observe** the night sky. Why did you need a telescope for this? What would you see if you didn't use a telescope?

35. In Lesson 4 you **made a model** of star patterns. Do you think you could model actual constellations by using this method? How might this kind of model be useful?

Performance Assessment

Model Solar System

With a partner, draw a model of an imaginary solar system. Include one star, five planets, and two comets. Also include at least one more object that would be found in a solar system. Compare your model solar system with the one we live in.

Unit Project Wrap Up

Here are some ideas for ways to wrap up your unit project.

Produce a Weather Program

Videotape your daily weather reports and forecasts, and play the tapes for the school.

Write Guidelines

Write directions that tell how to use your weather instruments. Include information about why and how each instrument works.

Make a Chart

For a week, evaluate how accurately the weather was forecast by professional meteorologists. Make a chart to organize your data.

Investigate Further

How could you make your project better? What other questions do you have? Plan ways to find answers to your questions. Use the Science Handbook on pages R2-R9 for help.

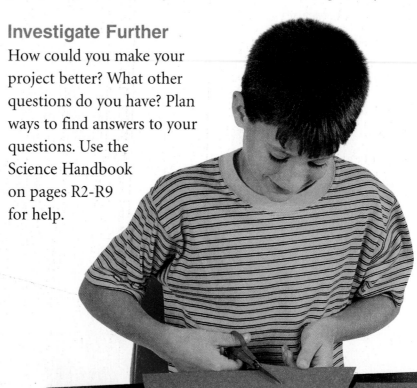

Matter and Energy

P H Y S I C A L   S C I E N C E

Matter and Energy

Unit Project | ## Energy-Efficient Home

Make a model of a house. Use the model to test how well different kinds of materials insulate for sound and heat. Find ads for insulation, and insulate your house in ways that you think are most efficient. Then test the different materials.

Chapter 1

Physical Properties of Matter

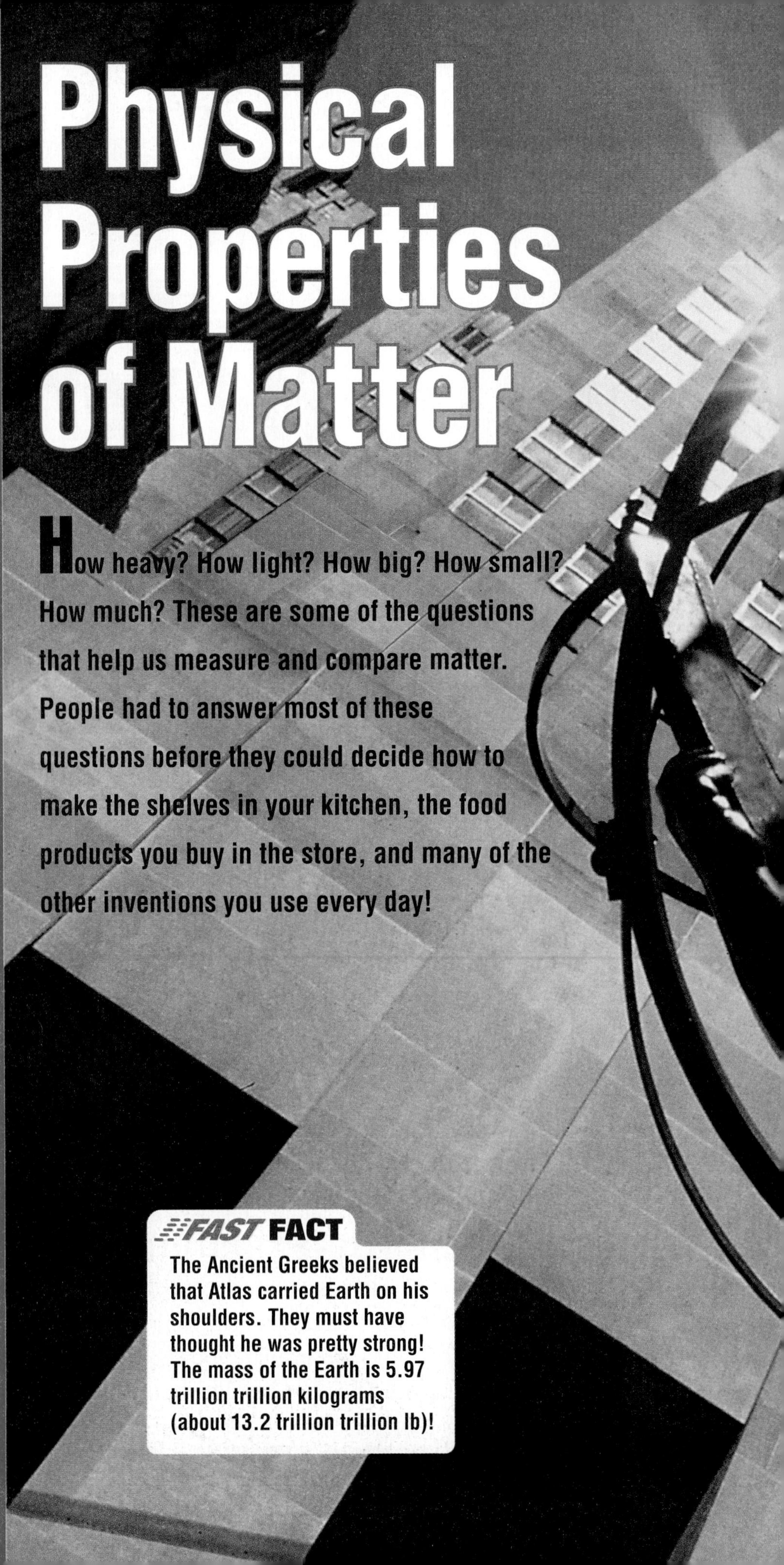

How heavy? How light? How big? How small? How much? These are some of the questions that help us measure and compare matter. People had to answer most of these questions before they could decide how to make the shelves in your kitchen, the food products you buy in the store, and many of the other inventions you use every day!

Vocabulary Preview

matter
mass
solid
liquid
gas
volume
density
solution
dissolve
solubility
buoyancy

FAST FACT

The Ancient Greeks believed that Atlas carried Earth on his shoulders. They must have thought he was pretty strong! The mass of the Earth is 5.97 trillion trillion kilograms (about 13.2 trillion trillion lb)!

If all the ice in the world melted (a volume of 60 million cubic kilometers or 14.3 million cubic miles), the oceans would rise 55–80 meters (180–262 ft or 18–27 stories)! In New York City's harbor, the entire Statue of Liberty would be under water except for her crown and torch!

Which is denser, gold or lead? To figure out how dense a material is, scientists compare an object's density to the density of water. Water has a density of 1 g/cubic centimeter. How dense are some other common materials?

Densities

Materials	Density (g/cm³)
Aluminum	2.7
Copper	9.0
Gold	19.3
Ice	0.9
Iron	7.9
Lead	11.4
Mercury	13.6

Atlas Statue in New York City

What Are Three States of Matter?

In this lesson, you can . . .

INVESTIGATE a physical property of matter.

LEARN ABOUT solids, liquids, and gases.

LINK to math, writing, technology, and other areas.

INVESTIGATE

Physical Properties of Matter

Activity Purpose You can't see it. Often you can't even feel it. But air is all around you. In this investigation you will **observe** one way air behaves and you will **infer** a property of matter.

Materials
- plastic bag
- plastic drinking straw
- book

Activity Procedure

1. Wrap the opening of the plastic bag tightly around the straw. Use your fingers to hold the bag in place. (Picture A)

2. Blow into the straw. **Observe** what happens to the bag.

◀ After a while this horse carving made of ice will melt into a puddle of water. How are the carving and a puddle alike? How are they different?

Picture A

Picture B

3 Empty the bag. Now place a book on the bag. Again wrap the opening of the bag tightly around the straw and use your fingers to hold the bag in place. (Picture B)

4 **Predict** what will happen when you blow into the straw. Blow into it and **observe** what happens to the book.

Draw Conclusions

1. What happened to the bag when you blew air into it? What happened to the book?

2. What property of air caused the effects you observed in Steps 2 and 4?

3. **Scientists at Work** Scientists **draw conclusions** after they think carefully about observations and other data they have collected. What data supports your answer to Question 2 above?

Investigate Further In a sink, place a filled 1-L bottle on an empty plastic bag. Use a tube connected to a faucet to slowly fill the bag with water. What happens to the bottle when the bag fills with water? What property of water do you **observe**?

E5

States of Matter

Solids

One way you know about the world around you is from your sense of touch. A tree trunk stops your finger. Water changes its shape as you poke your finger into it. You feel the moving air of a breeze. By touch you know that wood, water, and air have different properties. Yet they are all matter. Everything in the universe that has mass and takes up space is classified as **matter**.

In the investigation you saw that air takes up space. Matter also has mass. **Mass** is the amount of matter something contains. A large, heavy object such as an elephant has a lot of mass. A small, light maple leaf has much less mass. Even though an elephant and a leaf are very different, each is an example of matter.

All matter is made up of small bits called *particles*. The particles are so small that they can be seen only with the strongest microscopes. These tiny particles are always moving quickly.

The arrangements of particles give matter properties. Each arrangement is called a *state of matter*. A door key is an example of matter in the solid state. When you touch a door key, it stops your finger. A **solid** is matter that has a definite shape and takes up a definite amount of space. The particles in a solid are close together, like neat and even stacks of tiny balls. Each particle moves back and forth around one point. This arrangement of particles gives a solid its definite shape.

✔ **How are particles arranged in a solid?**

FIND OUT

- how particles are arranged in matter
- how three states of matter are different

VOCABULARY

matter
mass
solid
liquid
gas

This old key is a solid. It keeps its shape when you put it into a lock. ▶

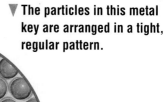
▼ The particles in this metal key are arranged in a tight, regular pattern.

Liquids

A frozen ice cube keeps its shape. But when you heat the ice cube in a pan, the ice becomes liquid water. The water changes shape and fills the bottom of the pan. If you spill the water onto a table, the water will spread out to cover the tabletop. The water still takes up the same amount of space as in the pan. It just has a new shape. A **liquid** is matter that takes the shape of its container and takes up a definite amount of space.

When matter is a liquid, its particles slip and slide around each other. The particles don't keep the same neighbors, as particles in a solid do. They move from place to place. But they still stay close to each other.

As the particles in a liquid move, they bump into the walls of their container. The solid walls of the container don't change shape. The particles of the liquid can't move past the walls, and the liquid particles stay close together. So, the liquid takes the shape of its container.

If you pour a liquid from one container into another, the amount of matter in the liquid stays the same. The amount of space the liquid takes up also stays the same.

✔ **Why does a liquid have the same shape as its container?**

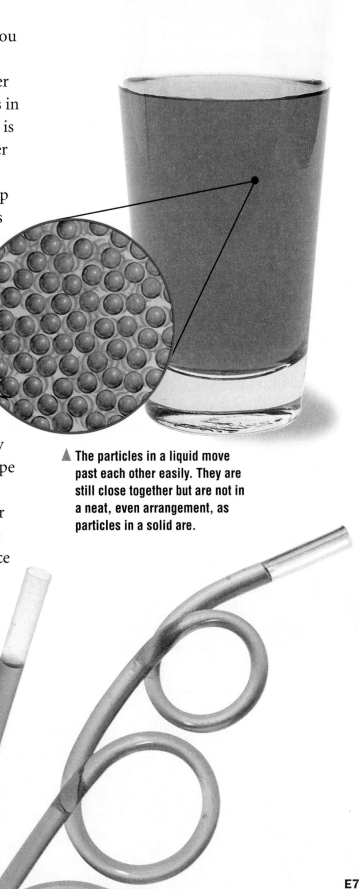

▲ The particles in a liquid move past each other easily. They are still close together but are not in a neat, even arrangement, as particles in a solid are.

As these straws show, a liquid always takes the shape of its container. ▶

E7

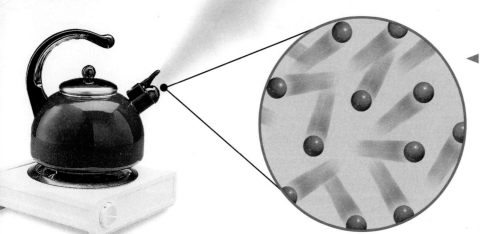

Water vapor is a gas that you can't see. Its particles fly out the whistling teakettle spout. Some particles cool and clump together to form tiny water drops. The drops are the white mist that you can see.

Gases

A **gas** is matter that has no definite shape and takes up no definite amount of space. Like particles in liquids, the particles in gases are not arranged in any pattern. Unlike particles in liquids, however, particles in gases don't stay close together. This is because particles in gases are moving much faster than particles in liquids.

The amount of space a gas takes up depends on the amount of space inside its container. A gas always fills the container it is in. If the container is open, the gas particles move out.

Most matter can change state from a solid to a liquid to a gas. You can see this when you leave an ice cube in a pan on a hot stove. In a few minutes, the cube changes from a solid to a liquid. Minutes later the liquid is gone—the water has become a gas called *water vapor*. The gas particles have moved off in all directions.

Heating matter makes particles move faster. When ice is heated, some particles begin to move fast enough to break away from their neighbors. As the regular arrangement of particles breaks down, the ice melts. Heated particles of liquid water move faster and faster. After a while they move fast enough to bounce away from each other. The liquid boils, or changes quickly into a gas.

✔ **How does heating matter change its state?**

◀ A lot of air is squeezed into the tank carried by this diver. The tank valve is open. Particles of gases move out of the tank as the diver breathes in.

▲ A gas completely fills this balloon. The gas particles push out against the balloon's sides.

Summary

Matter takes up space. Matter is made up of particles. Particles in solid matter stay close together and move back and forth around one point. Particles in liquid matter stay close together but move past each other. Particles in a gas are spread far apart.

Review

1. What are three states of matter?
2. Which state of matter keeps its shape?
3. Which states of matter take the shapes of their containers?
4. **Critical Thinking** How can matter be changed from a liquid to a solid?
5. **Test Prep** Which sentence describes a liquid?

   A Particles slide past each other.

   B Particles stay near their neighbors.

   C Particles are arranged in a pattern.

   D Particles bounce away from each other.

 # LINKS

 ### MATH LINK

Liquid Mercury Mercury is a metal that becomes a solid at 39° *below* 0°C. It becomes a gas at 357° *above* 0°C. What is the total number of degrees Celsius at which mercury is a liquid?

 ### WRITING LINK

Narrative Writing—Story Suppose that you are a particle in a solid that melts and then becomes a gas. Write a story for your teacher about your experiences.

 ### HEALTH LINK

States of Matter in the Body Find out which organ in the body is a liquid. Name some of the organs that bring a gas into the body. Plan and make a model of one body system that uses a liquid or a gas.

 ### ART LINK

Using Matter in Art Find and describe in your own words one example each of a work of art that uses a solid, a liquid, and a gas.

 ### TECHNOLOGY LINK

Visit the Harcourt Learning Site for related links, activities, and resources.

www.harcourtschool.com

How Can Matter Be Measured and Compared?

In this lesson, you can . . .

 INVESTIGATE the densities of some types of matter.

 LEARN ABOUT measuring and comparing matter.

 LINK to math, writing, health, and technology.

Density

Activity Purpose Some objects have more matter packed into a smaller space than other objects. In this investigation you will **measure** the mass of raisins and of breakfast cereal. Then you will **compare** their masses and the amounts of space they take up.

Materials

- 3 identical plastic cups
- raisins
- breakfast cereal
- pan balance

Activity Procedure

1 Fill one cup with raisins. Make sure the raisins fill the cup all the way to the top. (Picture A)

2 Fill another cup with cereal. Make sure the cereal fills the cup all the way to the top.

3 **Observe** the amount of space taken up by the raisins and the cereal.

◄ A gold coin as small as a dime has more mass than a quarter.

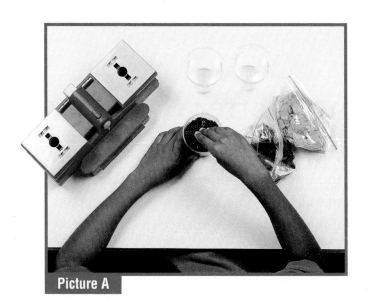
Picture A

Picture B

4 Adjust the balance so the pans are level. Place one cup on each pan. **Observe** what happens. (Picture B)

5 Fill the third cup with a mixture of raisins and cereal. **Predict** how the mass of the cup of raisins and cereal will compare with the masses of the cup of raisins and the cup of cereal. Use the pan balance to check your predictions.

Draw Conclusions

1. **Compare** the amount of space taken up by the raisins with the space taken up by the cereal.

2. Which has more mass, the cup of raisins or the cup of cereal? Explain your answer.

3. Which cup has more matter packed into it? Explain your answer.

4. **Scientists at Work** It is important to know the starting place when you measure. What would happen if you **measured** without making the balance pans equal? Explain your answer.

Investigate Further Write step-by-step directions to **compare** the masses of any two materials and the space they take up. Exchange sets of directions with a classmate. Test the directions and suggest revisions.

Process Skill Tip

A balance **measures** by comparing two masses. To make sure the comparison is accurate, you must make both sides of the balance equal before you measure. This is what you did in Step 4.

Measuring Matter

Measuring Mass

FIND OUT

- about mass and volume and how to measure them

- a way to use measurements of mass and volume to describe density

VOCABULARY

volume

density

When the pans of a balance are level, the pieces of matter on the two pans have the same mass. These cotton balls have the same mass as the wood block. ▼

You can compare the amount of matter in two objects by measuring the mass of each. The object with more mass has the greater amount of matter. Mass is measured in units called grams and kilograms (KIL•uh•gramz). Half a kilogram, or $\frac{1}{2}$ kg, is about the same mass as four sticks of margarine. A medium-sized paper clip has a mass of about 1 gram, or 1 g.

One way to compare two masses is by using a pan balance. Put an object in each pan. When the pans of the balance are level, the matter in the two pans has the same mass. In the investigation, you used a pan balance to find out that a cup of raisins has more mass than a cup of cereal.

If you know the mass of the matter in one pan, you can find the mass of the matter in the other pan. This is one way scientists measure mass. They have objects with masses that are known—for example, 50 grams, 200 grams, and 1 kilogram. These objects are known as *standard masses*. Scientists put an object whose mass they don't know in one pan and put standard masses in the other pan. Then they add or remove standard masses until the two pans balance. The total of the standard masses equals the mass of the object.

✔ **Name one way you can measure mass.**

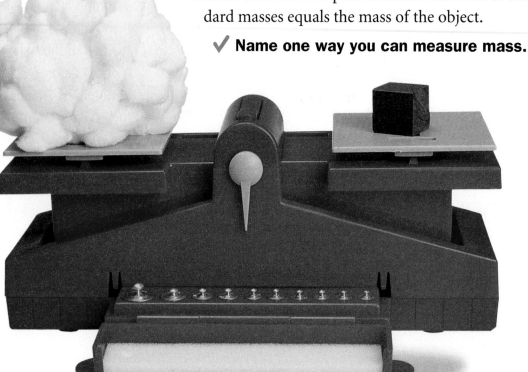

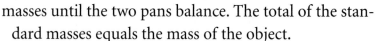

It is easy to measure the volume of a liquid by using this container marked in milliliters, or mL. This container is called a beaker, and it has about 400 mL of red liquid.

Volume

Matter has mass and takes up space. The amount of space that matter takes up is called its **volume** (VAHL•yoom). You can measure the amount of space a solid or liquid takes up. You also can measure a container such as a box and calculate its volume. Volume often is measured in cubic centimeters. A *cubic centimeter* is the space taken up by a cube that has each side equal to 1 centimeter. A cubic centimeter is the same as a milliliter.

Cooks use measuring cups and measuring spoons to find the volume of ingredients for a recipe. Scientists measure volume with a beaker or a graduate, a tall cylinder with measuring marks on the side.

A solid keeps its shape, so it is easy to see that its volume stays the same. A liquid changes shape to match its container. But it does not change its volume. A gas has no definite volume. However, the mass of a gas sample doesn't change when the volume of the gas changes.

✔ **What is volume?**

▲ You can find the volume of odd-shaped solid objects, such as these marbles, by sinking them in water. They push away some of the water, and the water level rises. The change in water level gives the volume of the solids.

▲ The level in this graduate changed from 50 mL to 57 mL when the marbles were added. Therefore, the volume of the marbles is 57 mL − 50 mL = 7 mL.

To find the volume of a box, first measure its height, width, and length. Then multiply the three numbers together. This box is about 6 cm thick, 20 cm wide, and 30 cm tall. Its volume is 6 cm × 20 cm × 30 cm = 3600 cubic centimeters. ▶

Density

Some matter takes up a large space but has a small mass. A balloon filled with gas may take up 10,000 cubic centimeters. But it may have such a small mass that it floats in the air. Other matter takes up very little space and has a large mass. A brick is smaller than the balloon, but it has much more mass.

The property of matter that compares the amount of matter to the space taken up is called **density** (DEN•suh•tee). The gas in a balloon has a low density. The density of a brick is much higher.

You can find the density of an object by dividing the mass of the object by its volume. For example, an apple may have a mass of 200 grams and a volume of 200 cubic centimeters. Its density is 200 grams ÷ 200 cubic centimeters, or 1 gram per cubic centimeter.

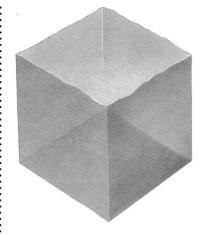

◀ One cubic centimeter of water has a mass of 1 gram. The density of water is 1 gram per cubic centimeter.

In the investigation you saw that cereal is less dense than raisins. You also found that a mixture of cereal and raisins is denser than cereal and less dense than raisins. Whenever you mix two kinds of matter, the density of the mixture is between the densities of the two separate materials.

✔ **Which material in the table has the greatest density?**

Density of Some Common Materials		
Materials	Density (g per cubic centimeter)	Relative Size of 1-kg Disk
Pine	0.40	
Motor oil	0.90	
Plastic (HDPE)	0.96	
Lead	11.30	

◀ The disks show the volume needed to make up one kilogram of each material. Notice how the size of the disks compares to the density of the materials.

Summary

All matter has mass and volume. Mass is the amount of matter in an object. The space that matter takes up is called volume. Density compares the amount of matter in an object to the amount of space it takes up. You can find the density of an object by dividing its mass by its volume.

Review

1. What is one way to measure mass?
2. What word is used to describe the amount of space that matter takes up?
3. What property of matter compares the amount of matter to the space that the matter takes up?
4. **Critical Thinking** You are shopping for cereal. How does estimating density help you find a good buy?
5. **Test Prep** If a black ball is denser than a white ball of the same size, the black ball has —
   A less volume
   B more volume
   C more matter taking up the same space
   D less matter taking up the same space

LINKS

MATH LINK

Compare Volumes Use a pan balance and three cups to measure 100 g, 200 g, and 300 g of water. Use a beaker or a graduate to measure and compare the volumes of water.

WRITING LINK

Informative Writing—Narration You are making a short video for younger students. It will show how to measure volume and mass. Decide what you will show. Then, write a script to explain what you are showing.

HEALTH LINK

Your Density Find out how to measure and compare the mass of a person's muscles and body fat. Make a comic strip that shows how this is done.

TECHNOLOGY LINK

Learn more about measuring matter by visiting this Internet site.
www.scilinks.org/harcourt

LESSON 3

What Are Some Useful Properties of Matter?

In this lesson, you can . . .

 INVESTIGATE what happens to some solids in water.

 LEARN ABOUT ways to group kinds of matter.

 LINK to math, writing, technology, and other areas.

Floating and Sinking

Activity Purpose Some solids sink in liquid water, and others float. But even solids that sink can be made to float. In this investigation you will see what happens to two solid materials when they are placed in water. Then you will make boats from the materials. You will **infer** some of the things that affect floating and sinking.

Materials

- plastic shoe box
- water
- sheet of aluminum foil
- modeling clay

Activity Procedure

1 Fill the plastic shoe box halfway with water.

2 Take a sheet of aluminum foil about 10 cm long and 10 cm wide. Squeeze it tightly into a ball. Before placing the ball in the shoe box, **predict** whether it will sink or float. Test your prediction and **record** your **observations.**

3 Take a thin piece of modeling clay about 10 cm long and 10 cm wide. Squeeze it tightly into a ball. Place the ball in the shoe box. **Observe** whether it sinks or floats.

◀ This sailing ship is made to float, but its black metal anchor is made to sink.

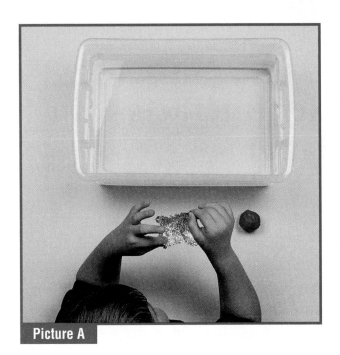

Picture A

Picture B

4 Uncurl the foil. Use it to make a boat. (Picture A) Before placing the boat on the water, **predict** whether it will sink or float. Test your prediction and **record** your **observations.**

5 Make a boat out of the modeling clay. Before placing the boat on the water, **predict** whether it will sink or float. Test your prediction and **record** your **observations.** (Picture B)

Draw Conclusions

1. Which objects floated? Which objects sank?

2. Which do you think has the greater density, the ball of aluminum foil or the ball of modeling clay? Explain.

3. **Scientists at Work** Scientists often look at two situations in which everything is the same except for one property. What property was the same in Step 3 as in Step 5? What property was different in Step 3 and Step 5? What can you **infer** about how that difference changed the results?

Investigate Further Poke a hole of the same size in the bottom of each boat. Put both boats in the water. What happens?

> **Process Skill Tip**
>
> Usually in an investigation, only one property is changed at a time. This makes it easier to **infer** the causes of the results. This is called controlling variables.

How Water Interacts with Other Matter

Water and Sugar

If you put a spoonful of solid sugar into a glass of liquid water and stir, what happens? The sugar seems to disappear. The glass still contains a clear liquid. Where did the sugar go?

The answer is that the sugar and the water formed a kind of mixture called a solution. A **solution** (suh•LOO•shuhn) is a mixture in which the particles of different kinds of matter are mixed evenly with each other. In this case the sugar particles mixed with the water particles. You can't see the sugar, but you can tell it is there because the solution tastes sweet. Another way to show that the sugar is still there is to let the water evaporate, or dry up. After all the water is gone, solid sugar will be left at the bottom of the glass.

FIND OUT

• how solids dissolve in water
• why objects float or sink

VOCABULARY

solution
dissolve
solubility
buoyancy

When you mix sugar and water, they form a solution. What is happening to the sugar as you stir the water? ▼

Dissolving

1 When a lump of sugar dissolves in water, water particles pull sugar particles away from the solid sugar.

2 Moving water particles spread sugar particles to all parts of the solution.

3 After a while all the sugar particles are pulled away by water particles. The sugar is completely dissolved. It can't be seen because the particles are too small and spread out.

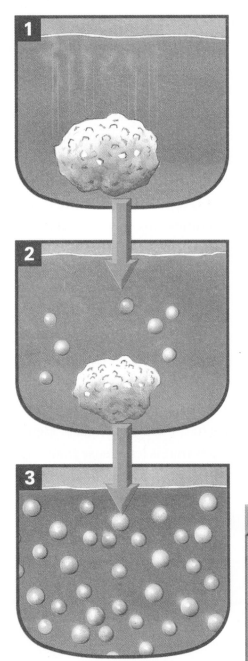

When one material forms a solution with another material, we say it **dissolves** (dih•ZAHLVZ). As sugar dissolves in water, particles of solid sugar are pulled away from each other by water particles. The water particles bump into and move the sugar. Very quickly the sugar particles spread to all parts of the solution. You can no longer see the sugar because the very small sugar particles are mixed evenly with the water particles.

If you add more and more sugar to a glass of water, at some point the sugar particles can't mix evenly with the water particles. The extra sugar doesn't dissolve. When you stop stirring, the extra sugar falls to the bottom of the glass.

Some solids dissolve in water. Other solids do not. Try stirring sand into water. While you are stirring, the sand mixes with the water but does not dissolve. When you stop stirring, the sand falls to the bottom of the jar. **Solubility** (sahl•yoo•BIL•uh•tee) is a measure of the amount of a material that will dissolve in another material. The solubility of sand in water is zero. No amount of sand dissolves in water.

✔ **What happens to a solid when it forms a solution with water?**

Solubility in Water		
Material	Volume of Water (mL)	Mass of Materials That Can Be Dissolved in Water at 25°C (g)
Sugar	100	105
Salt	100	36
Baking soda	100	7
Sand	100	0

Floating and Sinking

If you put a coin, such as a penny, into water, it doesn't dissolve. It sinks. A chip of wood doesn't dissolve in water, either. It floats. The ability of matter to float in a liquid or gas is called **buoyancy** (BOY•uhn•see).

A solid object denser than water sinks in water. Lead is more than 11 times as dense as water, so a lead fishing weight rapidly sinks. A solid object less dense than water floats in water. Pine wood is about half as dense as water. So a plank of pine floats.

▲ Most humans have a density that is a little less than 1 gram per cubic centimeter, so they float in water.

If you tied several pine planks together to form a raft, the raft would float because it is made of a material that is less dense than water.

Liquids can also float or sink. Have you ever seen rainbow streaks on puddles on a road or sidewalk? Motor oil floating on the water causes the streaks. The oil floats because it is less dense than water.

Some liquids sink in water. Maple syrup is mostly a sugar solution. It is denser than pure water. Maple syrup sinks to the bottom when you pour it into a glass of water.

Gases can also sink or float. All the gases in the air you breathe are much less dense than liquid water. When you blow through a drinking straw into water, air bubbles are pushed up, or buoyed up, by the water. They rise to the top of the glass. Helium is another gas that is less dense than air. When you fill a balloon with helium, it is buoyed up by the air and rises.

◄ A scuba diver wears a belt or vest with dense pieces of lead. This makes the diver's density about the same as that of water. With the belt on, the diver can swim up or down easily.

The density of the cup and air is less than water so the cup floats.

Most rocks sink. But pumice (PUHM•is) is a kind of rock that contains a lot of air, so pumice floats.

Diet soft drink is less dense than water, so a can of diet soft drink floats. A can of regular soft drink sinks.

Most wood floats, but most metal sinks.

Remember from Lesson 2 that you can change the density of a material by mixing it with material that has a different density.

Air is not very dense. A good way to lower the density of an object is to add air to it. If you add enough air, the object will become less dense than water. Then it will float. Clay is denser than water. In the investigation you got clay to float by making it into a boat. A boat contains air. The sides and bottom of a boat keep water out and hold air in. The clay boat floated because it contained a lot of air. Even a heavy metal boat will float if it contains enough air.

Most human bodies are a little less dense than water. So, most people float on water. Scuba divers don't want to float or sink. If they floated, they would have to swim hard to stay under water. If they sank, they would have to swim hard to get back to the water's surface. Scuba divers control their buoyancy by wearing a belt or vest loaded with dense lead pieces. While wearing the lead weights, a diver has about the same density as water.

✔ What is buoyancy?

Each liquid layer in this beaker has a different density. The densest layer is liquid mercury on the bottom. Even a steel bolt floats on mercury. The less dense materials float on the more dense materials. ▶

Floating Transportation

Humans use machines to control buoyancy and to move from place to place. Submarines, hot-air balloons, and blimps all use buoyancy to help move people. Hot-air balloons are buoyed up by air, so they rise. This is because hot air is less dense than cool air. Blimps are big, football-shaped balloons. They are filled with helium, a gas that is less dense than air. Submarines control their density to float and to sink in the water.

✔ **How is buoyancy used for travel?**

THE INSIDE STORY

How Submarines Work

Submarines can float on top of the ocean or dive down and travel deep under water. They do this by adding or removing water to control their density.

1. When a submarine floats on the surface of the water, it is like any other metal boat. It is filled with enough air to make it float.

2. Tanks inside the submarine have air in them when the submarine is at the surface. To make the submarine float just below the surface, some of the air is taken out and the tanks are partly filled with water. The combination of the submarine, the water, and the air has about the same density as water.

3. The submarine can dive to the bottom by squeezing air in its tanks into smaller tanks. Because the air's volume is now smaller, its density is greater. The original tanks are then filled with water. This makes the metal submarine denser than water. To allow the submarine to return to the surface, water is pumped out of the tanks. Air is allowed to expand back into them. The submarine becomes less dense than water. It is buoyed up and rises to the surface.

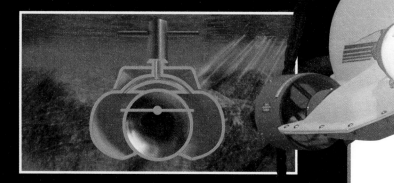

Summary

Solutions are mixtures in which the particles are mixed evenly. Some matter dissolves in water and some does not. Matter that is less dense than water floats on water. Buoyancy can be controlled by changing density.

Review

1. What changes happen to sugar when it dissolves in water? What stays the same?

2. What happens when you add more of a material to water than the water will dissolve?

3. How can you float a piece of solid material that is denser than water?

4. **Critical Thinking** What could you do to make an object float in air?

5. **Test Prep** Any material that floats in water —
   A is denser than water
   B has the same density as water
   C is less dense than water
   D is made of metal

LINKS

MATH LINK

Solubility The greatest amount of sugar you can dissolve in 100 milliliters of water is 105 grams. How much sugar can you dissolve in 1000 milliliters of water?

WRITING LINK

Informative Writing—Explanation Find out what the ancient Greek scientist Archimedes discovered about density. Write an explanation of what you learn for a younger student.

PHYSICAL EDUCATION LINK

Floating and Swimming Find out what survival floating is. Use a model to demonstrate it for your class, or make a poster that explains it.

LITERATURE LINK

Submarine Predictions Read *20,000 Leagues Under the Sea* to find out what French science-fiction writer Jules Verne predicted about the modern submarine.

TECHNOLOGY LINK

Learn more about physical properties of matter by viewing *Peep Science* on the **Harcourt Science Newsroom Video.**

Plastics You Can Eat

Plastics are artificial materials, or substances that are made by people. They can be shaped into different objects, such as bottles, chairs, or notebook covers. There are hundreds of different plastics, each with its own properties. One new type has an unusual property for a plastic. It dissolves in a special way, so it can be eaten!

Why Would Anyone Want to Eat Plastic?

You wouldn't want to eat regular plastic. It could be harmful. But the people who

The two inventors of edible plastic

invented plastic that can be eaten weren't thinking about making it edible. Two students were trying to make green slime in their high-school laboratory for a Halloween trick. But something went wrong. There was a small explosion. Green slime flew everywhere, covering the laboratory floor, ceiling, and walls. The students cleaned up the mess before anyone found out. But they missed a little bit of slime that landed in a jar.

The next day, their teacher found the green slime in the jar. It was stuck to a glass stirring rod. It looked like a lollipop. It even looked edible, and it really was.

Plastic Coated Medicine

It turned out that the green slime dissolves in the saliva in your mouth, but it doesn't dissolve in just water. This makes it perfect as a coating for pills. It protects the medicine in the pills from moisture in the air, but still is digested easily in the stomach. Other pill coatings take in moisture from the air. This can make the medicine less effective.

Green slime works well for coating medicine that can be absorbed in the stomach. But some medicines, such as the insulin needed by people who have diabetes, are destroyed by the digestive juices in the stomach. For that reason, these medicines are usually given as shots instead of pills. But no one likes to get shots.

Another Edible Plastic

Scientists have invented another kind of edible plastic that won't dissolve in the mouth, the stomach, or even the small intestine. Medicine that has been coated with this plastic gets all the way to the large

intestine. There, the plastic absorbs water and gets larger. Tiny holes in the plastic open up as that happens. The medicine gets out through the holes, and the patient gets the medicine without getting a shot.

Think About It

1. What other uses can you think of for edible plastic?

2. Do you know of any other medicines that can't be swallowed that edible plastic could be used for?

WEB LINK:
For Science and Technology updates, visit the Harcourt Internet site.
www.harcourtschool.com

Careers   Industrial Engineer

What They Do
Industrial engineers design and build machines for factories. They solve problems to help people make things and put things together easily and quickly. For example,  they might design the machines to make pills and coat them with plastic. They also might decide what shapes work best for plastic or metal car parts.

Education and Training   Industrial engineers need a college degree. They may be licensed as a professional engineer by the state they live in. For that, they will need four years of experience and a passing grade on a state test.

Shirley Ann Jackson

PHYSICIST

As a little girl in Washington, D.C., Shirley Jackson collected live hornets, bumblebees, and wasps to study. She kept the animals in old mayonnaise jars under the back porch. She also studied fungi and molds around her home. Her father helped her with these science projects. She won first place at a science fair with an experiment on how different environments affect the growth of bacteria.

Jackson graduated first in her class at Roosevelt High School. She won scholarships for college and decided to go to the Massachusetts Institute of Technology (MIT). She became the first African-American woman to receive a doctoral degree, or advanced degree, from MIT.

In 1995, President Clinton nominated her to the five-member U.S. Nuclear Regulatory Commission (NRC). She is now chairperson of that group. NRC makes sure nuclear reactors and radioactive materials are used safely. Dr. Jackson is also chairperson of the International Nuclear Regulators' Association. This group is made up of representatives from eight countries.

In 1998, Jackson was inducted into the National Women's Hall of Fame. She was included because of her work in education, science, and public policy.

THINK ABOUT IT

1. What areas of science first interested Jackson when she was young? What area of science most interests her now?

2. What skills and talents do you think a person needs to work for NRC?

◀ This is a view downward into the core of a nuclear reactor.

Liquid Layers

How does density help you predict which liquids float?

Materials

- 3 clear plastic cups
- water
- corn oil
- maple syrup

Material	Density
water	1 g/mL
corn oil	< 1 g/mL
maple syrup	> 1 g/mL

Procedure

1. Fill one cup about one-fourth full of water.

2. Repeat Step 1 for the corn oil and for the maple syrup.

3. Slowly pour the maple syrup down the inside of the cup containing water. Observe what happens.

4. Predict what will happen when you pour the corn oil into the same cup. Slowly pour the corn oil down the side of the cup. Observe what happens.

Draw Conclusions

What can you conclude about the buoyancy of these liquids?

Solubility

How can you determine solubility?

Materials

- safety goggles
- rubber gloves
- 200-mL beaker
- water
- balance
- 40 g alum
- small scrap of paper
- stirring stick

Procedure

1. Put on the goggles and gloves.

2. Fill the beaker to the 100-mL mark with cold tap water.

3. Measure 25 g of alum on the paper. Use the paper to pour the alum into the water.

4. Stir until the alum dissolves.

5. Measure 1 g of alum, and add it to the beaker. Stir. Observe the solution.

6. Repeat Step 5 until no more alum will dissolve.

Draw Conclusions

What is the solubility of alum?

Chapter 1 Review and Test Preparation

Vocabulary Review

Use the terms below to complete the sentences. The page numbers in ( ) tell you where to look in the chapter if you need help.

matter (E6)　　　　　**density** (E14)

mass (E6)　　　　　**solution** (E18)

solid (E6)　　　　　**dissolve** (E19)

liquid (E7)　　　　　**solubility** (E19)

gas (E8)　　　　　**buoyancy** (E20)

volume (E13)

1. The _____ of a solid cube is the amount of space it takes up.

2. In a _____, the particles are far away from each other and move quickly.

3. You can't see a solid when you _____ it, because its particles become separated by water particles.

4. If the particles of matter move back and forth around one point, the matter is in the _____ state.

5. The amount of matter in an object is its _____.

6. _____ is a measure of whether an object floats or sinks in a gas or liquid.

7. When matter is in the _____ state, its particles can slip and slide past each other.

8. When the particles of a mixture are evenly mixed and can't be seen, the mixture is a _____.

9. Air and pine wood each have a _____ that is less than that of water.

10. _____ is a measure of the amount of a material that will dissolve in another material.

11. _____ is anything that takes up space and has mass.

Connect Concepts

Some of the substances and objects mentioned in the chapter are listed in the Word Bank. In the table below, list each substance or object under each of its properties. Use each item as often as necessary.

air　　　　**lead weight**　　　　**water vapor**　　　　**brick**

wood　　　　**sugar cube**　　　　**ice**　　　　**water**

Properties of Matter		
Dissolves in Water	**Floats in Water**	**Density About 1 g/mL**
12. _____	13. _____	15. _____
	14. _____	
Takes Shape of Container	**Sinks in Water**	**Has No Definite Volume**
16. _____	19. _____	21. _____
17. _____	20. _____	22. _____
18. _____		

Check Understanding

Write the letter of the best choice.

23. A boat made from matter that is denser than water can float on water if it is filled with enough —

    A water
    B air
    C salt
    D salt water

24. When two materials are mixed, the _____ of the mixture is between those of the separate materials.

    F mass
    G volume
    H density
    J state

25. Which of the following properties of sugar does **NOT** change when sugar dissolves in water?

    A color
    B shape
    C texture
    D taste

26. The volume of a _____ depends on the size of its container.

    F liquid
    G solid
    H gas
    J solution

27. A _____ has a definite shape.

    A solid
    B sugar-water solution
    C gas
    D liquid

Critical Thinking

28. Compare the relationships between particles in ice, water, and water vapor.

29. When a solid dissolves completely in water, what happens to the particles that made up the solid?

Process Skills Review

30. You measure the temperature of four pans of boiling water. Your measurements are 99°C, 100°C, 100°C, and 101°C. What **conclusion** can you **draw** about the temperature at which water boils? Explain your answer.

31. You use the same pan balance to **measure** the mass of a rock on two days. Your measurement is larger on the second day. The rock hasn't changed. How do you explain the difference in measurements?

32. You take a sip from a glass of clear water, and it tastes salty. What can you **infer** about what is in the glass?

Performance Assessment

Maximum Float

Use a piece of aluminum foil to make a shape that will float in water. Experiment to find the boat shape that will support the largest number of pennies. Explain the reasons you changed the boat's shape.

Heat— Energy on the Move

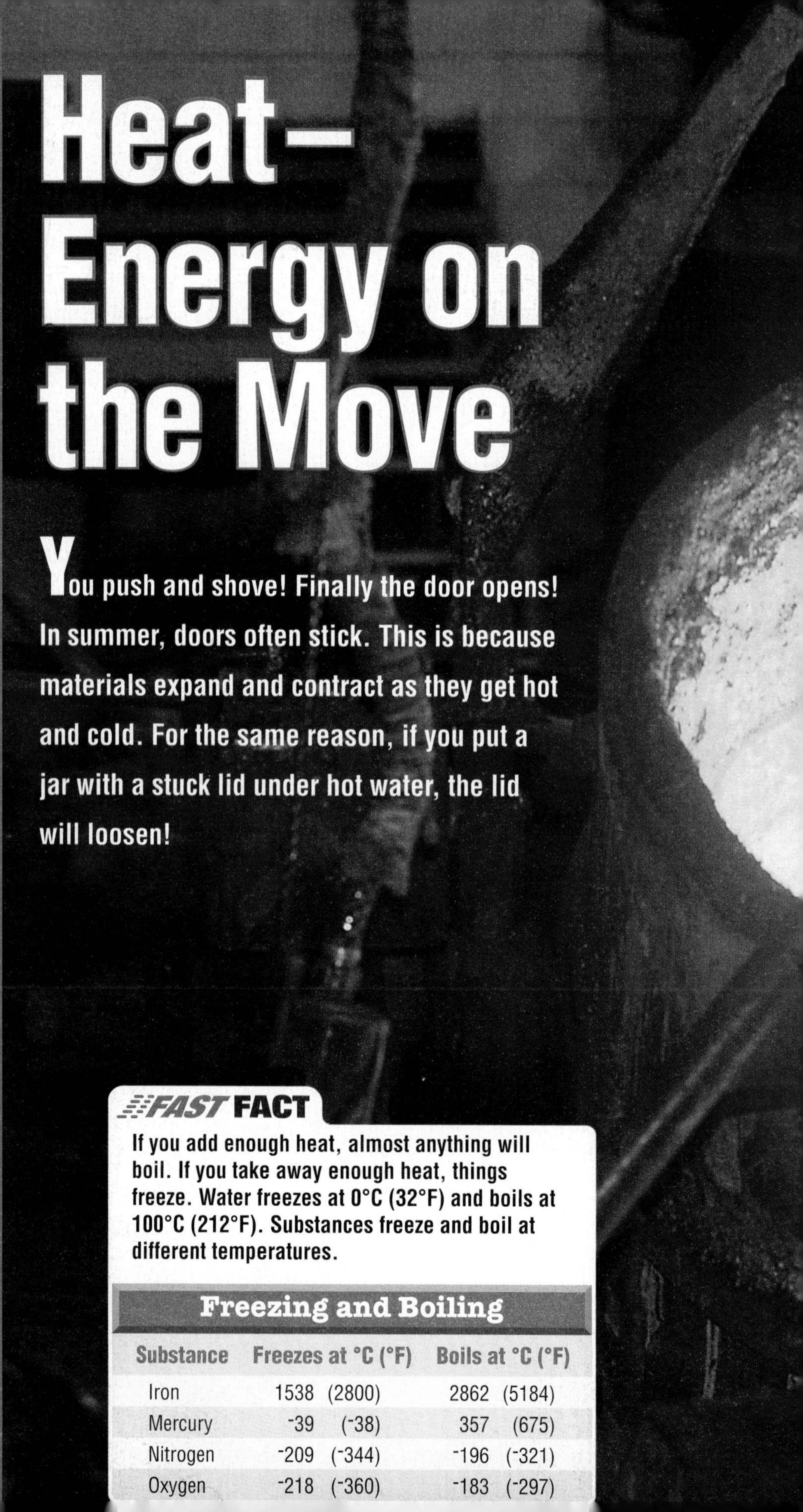

You push and shove! Finally the door opens! In summer, doors often stick. This is because materials expand and contract as they get hot and cold. For the same reason, if you put a jar with a stuck lid under hot water, the lid will loosen!

Vocabulary Preview

energy
thermal energy
temperature
heat
conduction
convection
radiation
infrared radiation
fuel
solar energy

FAST FACT

If you add enough heat, almost anything will boil. If you take away enough heat, things freeze. Water freezes at 0°C (32°F) and boils at 100°C (212°F). Substances freeze and boil at different temperatures.

Freezing and Boiling		
Substance	Freezes at °C (°F)	Boils at °C (°F)
Iron	1538 (2800)	2862 (5184)
Mercury	-39 (-38)	357 (675)
Nitrogen	-209 (-344)	-196 (-321)
Oxygen	-218 (-360)	-183 (-297)

Molten iron

When a light bulb is on, the temperature of the glowing wire inside is a sizzling 2500°C (about 4500°F). That's why the outside of a light bulb gets hot while the bulb is on. The empty space around the wire keeps the bulb from melting and the wire from burning up.

The temperature of a lightning bolt is estimated to be 30,000°C (54,000°F)! If people could harness the energy from a single lightning bolt, they could light up an average-size town for a year.

LESSON 1

How Does Heat Affect Matter?

In this lesson, you can . . .

INVESTIGATE how heat affects air in a balloon.

LEARN ABOUT thermal energy.

LINK to math, writing, social studies, and technology.

Changes in a Heated Balloon

Activity Purpose Have you ever wondered why a hot-air balloon rises? Or how a thermometer measures temperature? The answers have something in common—a property of matter. In this investigation you will **measure** changes in a balloon as it is heated. Then you'll **infer** what caused the changes.

Materials

- desk lamp
- bulb
- safety goggles
- 3 rubber balloons
- balloon clamps
- ruler

CAUTION

Activity Procedure

1 Turn on the lamp, and let the light bulb get warm.

2 **CAUTION** **Put on your safety goggles.** Blow up a rubber balloon just enough to stretch it. Clamp the end.

3 **Measure** the length of the balloon with the ruler. **Record** the measurement. (Picture A)

4 Carefully hold the balloon by its clamped end about 3 cm above the lamp. Hold it there for two minutes. (Picture B) **CAUTION** **The light bulb is hot. Do not touch it with your hands or with the balloon. Observe** what happens to the balloon. **Record** your observations.

◄ Icicles form when water melts, flows, and freezes again.

Picture A

Picture B

5. **Measure** the length of the balloon while it is still over the lamp. **Record** the measurement.

6. Repeat Steps 2 through 5 using a new balloon each time.

Draw Conclusions

1. What did you **observe** as you warmed the balloons?

2. **Compare** the lengths of the heated balloons with the lengths of the unheated balloons.

3. What can you **infer** happened to the air inside the balloons as you heated it?

4. **Scientists at Work** Scientists often **measure** several times to make sure the measurements are accurate. In this investigation you measured the lengths of three different balloons. Were the measurements all the same? Explain.

Investigate Further Fill a balloon with water that is at room temperature. Put the balloon on a desk and **measure** its length. Heat the balloon by putting it in a bowl of hot tap water for 15 minutes. Take the balloon out of the bowl and measure its length. **Compare** these lengths with those you measured with the air-filled balloons in the investigation.

Matter and Energy

Thermal Energy

Have you ever thrown a ball? Pushed a grocery cart? Run in a race? All these activities need energy. **Energy** is the ability to cause a change. In each of these cases, the thing that changed was the position of an object. You threw the ball from one place to another. You pushed the grocery cart through the store. You moved yourself along the racetrack. Moving anything from one place to another takes energy.

The particles in matter are always moving from one place to another. The particles in a solid jiggle back and forth like balls on a spring. The particles in a liquid slide past each other. The particles in a gas move quickly in many directions. All of this movement requires energy. The energy of the motion of particles in matter is called **thermal energy**. The word *thermal* means "heat." We feel the thermal energy of the particles in matter as heat.

✔ **What is thermal energy?**

FIND OUT

- what thermal energy is
- the difference between thermal energy and temperature

VOCABULARY

energy
thermal energy
temperature

Water boils when its particles are moving so fast that many begin to fly away from its surface. This happens when the water's temperature is 100°C (212°F). ▼

When liquid water freezes, its particles settle into an arrangement as a solid. This happens when the temperature of the water is 0°C (32°F). The ice cubes and lemonade are at 0°C. ▼

E34

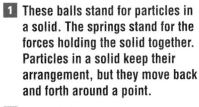

1 These balls stand for particles in a solid. The springs stand for the forces holding the solid together. Particles in a solid keep their arrangement, but they move back and forth around a point.

2 When you add thermal energy, the particles move faster. The solid gets hotter.

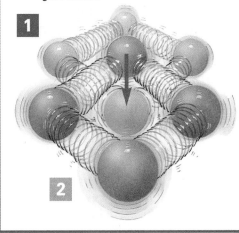

▲ The water in this cup is the same temperature as the nearly boiling water in the hot spring. But the water in the spring has more thermal energy because it has more water and, therefore, more moving particles of matter.

Temperature

Most people think that temperature is a measure of heat. Actually, **temperature** is a measure of the average energy of motion of the particles in matter. At 50°F (about 10°C) the particles in the air move more slowly than they do at 80°F (about 27°C). They have less thermal energy.

In the investigation you heated a balloon and observed how its volume changed. You can measure temperature by observing how the volume of a liquid changes as it is heated or cooled. One kind of thermometer has liquid in a narrow tube. When the liquid gets hotter, its volume changes and it moves up the tube. When it gets colder, it moves back down the tube.

✓ **What does temperature measure?**

Temperature and Thermal Energy

Two pieces of matter can be at the same temperature but not have the same amount of thermal energy. Temperature measures the *average* amount of motion of the particles in a piece of matter. Thermal energy is the *total* energy of motion of the particles in a piece of matter. More matter equals more particles. More particles equals more energy of motion.

When a drop of cold water falls into a hot pan or skillet, the water boils away in a second or two. Its particles speed up and fly off. Little thermal energy is needed to warm the drop to 100°C (212°F). A pan full of cold water has many more particles. It takes much more thermal energy to boil the water.

✓ **What is the difference between temperature and thermal energy?**

Adding Thermal Energy

When thermal energy is added to matter, the particles in the matter move faster. Below 0°C (32°F) water is solid ice. The particles move back and forth around one point. As you add thermal energy, the particles move faster and faster. At 0°C (32°F) the particles begin to move past and around each other. The ice melts.

After ice melts, adding energy causes the particles of liquid water to move faster and faster. The temperature of the liquid water rises. After a while, particles begin to fly away from the water's surface. The water boils, or rapidly becomes a gas.

✔ **What happens to matter when you add thermal energy?**

Water vapor in the air loses energy to the cold air outside the window. First, it becomes small water droplets on the glass. Then, it becomes a solid and forms these ice crystals. ▼

▲ When thermal energy is added to frozen water, the water slowly changes from a solid to a liquid and then from a liquid to a gas. When thermal energy is removed from water vapor, this process is reversed.

Summary

Energy is the ability to cause change. Energy is needed to move something from one place to another. The total energy of motion of the particles in matter is thermal energy. Temperature is a measure of the average motion of these particles. Adding thermal energy causes the particles of matter to move faster. More matter equals more particles. More particles mean more total thermal energy.

Review

1. What does temperature measure?

2. If all particles in a metal spoon start moving faster, how has the spoon's temperature changed?

3. When you add thermal energy to matter, what happens?

4. **Critical Thinking** The water in two glasses has the same average energy of motion. One glass holds 250 mL, and one holds 400 mL. Which glass of water has more thermal energy? Why?

5. **Test Prep** The particles in two pieces of chocolate have the same average energy of motion. One piece has more mass than the other. Which piece is at a higher temperature?

   A the piece with more mass

   B the piece with less mass

   C the piece with more thermal energy

   D They are the same temperature.

LINKS

MATH LINK

Thermometers On a Fahrenheit temperature scale, water freezes at 32°F and boils at 212°F. How many Fahrenheit degrees are between the two temperatures? Now think about the boiling and freezing temperatures in Celsius degrees. Are degrees Celsius bigger or smaller units of measure than degrees Fahrenheit?

WRITING LINK

Expressive Writing—Poem Write a poem for your family that describes a hot day and a cold day. You could describe how your neighborhood looks, things people do, and how you feel.

SOCIAL STUDIES LINK

Early Thermometers Find out who invented the first thermometers and temperature scales and how the thermometers worked. Make a time line that shows what you learned.

TECHNOLOGY LINK

Visit the Harcourt Learning Site for related links, activities, and resources.
www.harcourtschool.com

WELCOME TO THE LEARNING SITE

LESSON 2

How Can Thermal Energy Be Transferred?

In this lesson, you can . . .

 INVESTIGATE one way thermal energy is transferred.

 LEARN ABOUT the three ways thermal energy is transferred.

 LINK to math, writing, art, and technology.

Hot Air

Activity Purpose Have you ever watched a hawk soaring high in the sky? The hawk rides on air that is moving up. But what makes the air move up? In this investigation you will **observe** the effects of air moving up and **infer** why the air is moving up.

Materials

- sheet of construction paper
- scissors
- straight pin
- 20-cm piece of thread
- desk lamp
- bulb

Activity Procedure

1 **CAUTION** **Be careful when using scissors.** Cut out a spiral strip about 2 cm wide from the sheet of construction paper. (Picture A)

2 **CAUTION** **Be careful with the pin.** With the pin, carefully make a small hole through the center of the paper spiral. Tie the thread through the hole.

◀ A glass blower uses a tube to blow air into hot glass. The long tube keeps heat from the glass away from his face. How can you tell the glass is hot?

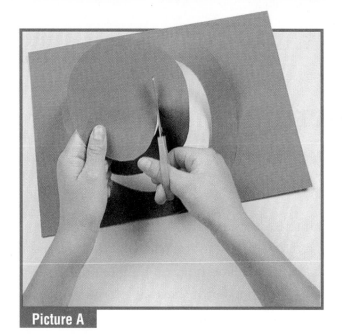

Picture A

Picture B

3 Hold the spiral above your head by the thread. Blow upward on it. **Observe** the spiral.

4 Carefully hold the spiral a few centimeters above the unlighted desk lamp. **Observe** the spiral.

5 Turn on the desk lamp. Let the bulb warm up for a few minutes.

6 Carefully hold the spiral a few centimeters above the lighted desk lamp. **Observe** the spiral. (Picture B)

Draw Conclusions

1. What did you **observe** in Steps 3, 4, and 6?

2. What caused the result you **observed** in Step 3?

3. What was different about Steps 4 and 6?

4. **Scientists at Work** Scientists often **infer** from **observations** a cause that they can't see directly. What do you think caused the result you observed in Step 6?

Investigate Further Hold the spiral a few centimeters away from the side of the lighted desk lamp. **Observe** the spiral. What can you **infer** from your observation?

> **Process Skill Tip**
>
> You need to **observe** what an object does in different situations before you can **infer** the causes of what it does.

How Thermal Energy Is Transferred

Heat

FIND OUT

- what heat is
- three ways thermal energy is transferred

VOCABULARY

heat
conduction
convection
radiation
infrared radiation

When you touch an icicle, some of the thermal energy in your hand is transferred, or moved, to the icicle. Your hand gets colder. The icicle gets warmer. If you hold on long enough, the icicle melts completely. This transfer of thermal energy from one piece of matter to another is called **heat**.

Thermal energy is transferred naturally from hot matter to cold matter. When you walk in warm sand, some of the thermal energy from the sand moves to your feet. The soles of your feet get warmer. When your lips touch a cold can of soft drink, thermal energy is transferred from your lips to the can. Your lips lose thermal energy and get cooler. The can gains thermal energy and gets warmer.

Thermal energy is transferred in three ways—conduction, convection, and radiation. You will learn more about these processes on the next pages.

✔ **What is heat?**

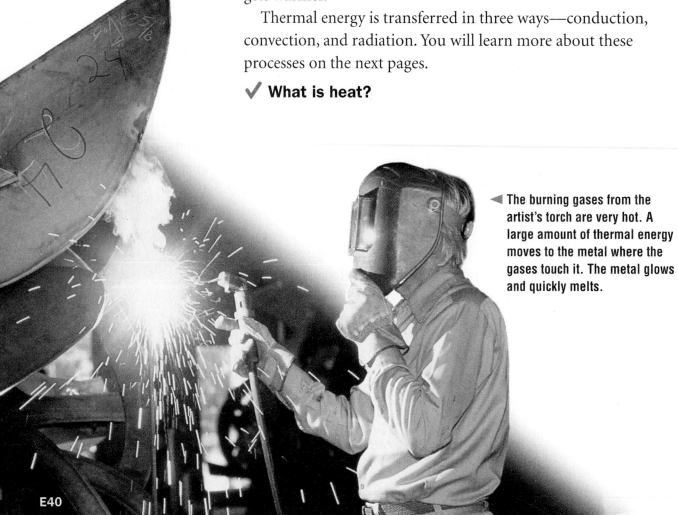

◀ The burning gases from the artist's torch are very hot. A large amount of thermal energy moves to the metal where the gases touch it. The metal glows and quickly melts.

Conduction

You can tell if tap water is hot by touching the metal faucet it is running through. This works because the hot particles of water bump into the particles of the faucet and transfer some of their thermal energy. Soon the particles of the faucet have the same temperature as the particles of water. The transfer of thermal energy by particles of matter bumping into each other is called **conduction** (kuhn•DUHK•shuhn).

Thermal energy moves from an electric stove burner to a metal pot by conduction. Conduction happens every time you grab something hot or cold. Conduction can cause a painful burn from a hot pan.

Some kinds of matter don't conduct thermal energy well. A plastic-foam cup full of cocoa does not conduct well. The plastic foam's particles take a long time to speed up when the particles of hot cocoa bump

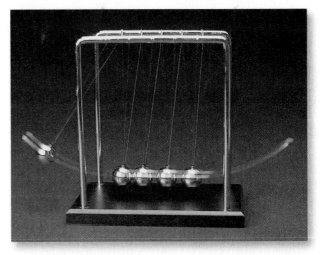

▲ A moving ball transfers motion energy when it bumps into its neighbor. A particle in matter transfers motion energy when it bumps into a nearby particle.

into them. Materials that don't conduct thermal energy well are called *insulators*. Materials that easily conduct thermal energy are called *conductors*. Most metals are good conductors.

✔ **What is conduction?**

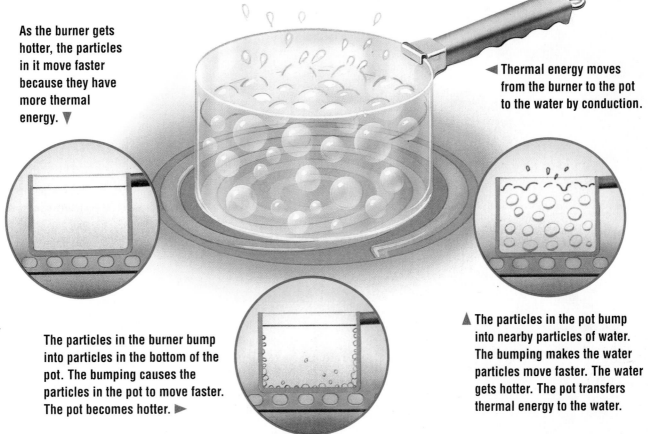

As the burner gets hotter, the particles in it move faster because they have more thermal energy. ▼

◄ Thermal energy moves from the burner to the pot to the water by conduction.

The particles in the burner bump into particles in the bottom of the pot. The bumping causes the particles in the pot to move faster. The pot becomes hotter. ▶

▲ The particles in the pot bump into nearby particles of water. The bumping makes the water particles move faster. The water gets hotter. The pot transfers thermal energy to the water.

E41

Convection

Unlike particles in solids, particles in liquids and gases move from one place to another. A large group of hot particles can move and transfer thermal energy. This type of energy transfer in a liquid or a gas is called **convection** (kuhn•VEK•shuhn).

In the investigation you held a paper spiral above a lighted bulb. The heated air above the light bulb moved enough to cause the spiral to twirl. Convection caused that movement.

As the air near a hot object gets hot, it takes up more space, or expands. You saw a balloon expand in the investigation on pages E32–E33. Because the hot air is less dense, it is forced up by the cooler, denser air around it.

As the hot air is forced up, it warms the air around it. The hot air cools. Its density increases, and it sinks. This process can repeat. The air can move in a circle—warming, being pushed up, cooling, sinking, and then warming again. This pattern of movement is called a *convection current*.

✔ **What is convection?**

The air above the stove gets warm. Cool air pushes in and forces the warm air up. The warm air moves through the room and transfers energy to the things around it.

◀ As cooler air pushes up air warmed by a campfire, sparks, smoke, and soot are pushed up also.

The warm air slowly cools and sinks to the floor.

Cool air moves toward the stove and forces up the warm air near the stove. Then the cool air is heated. This cycle of convection currents transfers thermal energy from the stove to the rest of the room.

A Hot-Air Balloon

1 A hot-air balloon is a large empty sack that is placed with its opening above a burner. The burner heats the air. The density of the heated air decreases. It is pushed up into the balloon by cooler air. The balloon soon fills with warm air.

2 Convection keeps air inside the balloon hot. As the warm air is forced upward by the cooler air below, it cools. The cooled air sinks and is warmed again by the burner.

3 The density of the warm air inside the balloon is less than the density of the cooler air outside the balloon. The balloon filled with hot air is pushed up. When the balloon is floating, the push of the cool air upward equals the weight of the filled balloon and its passengers.

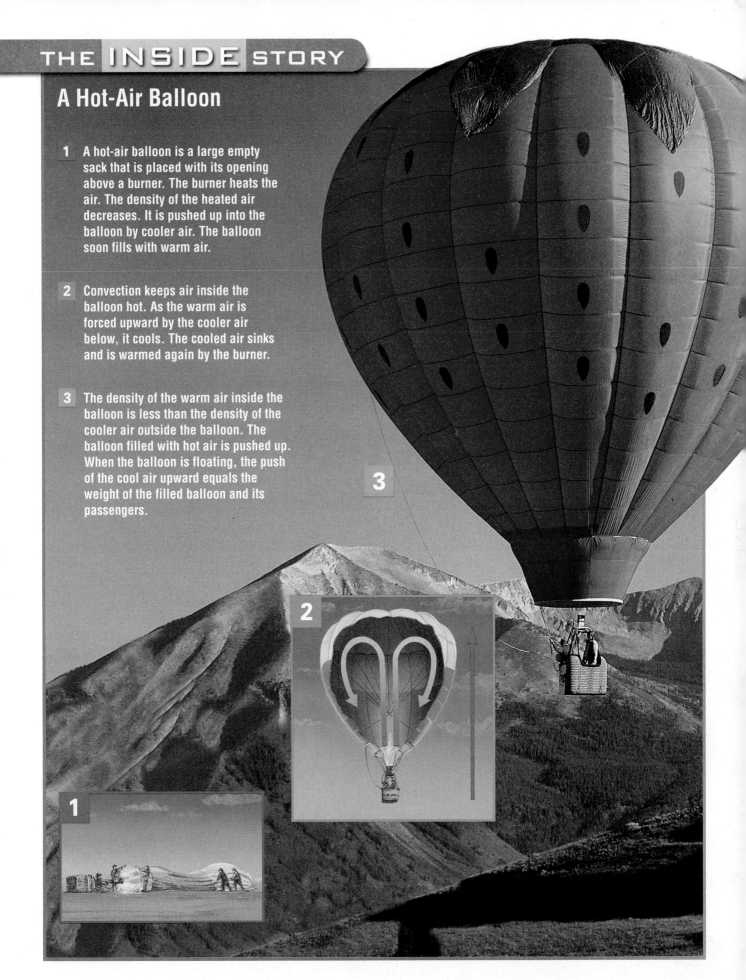

Radiation

The sun produces great amounts of thermal energy. But there's no matter between Earth and the sun to which it can transfer that energy. So energy can't reach Earth by conduction or convection. The sun transfers bundles of energy that can move through matter and empty space. Bundles of energy that move through matter and empty space are called **radiation** (ray•dee•AY•shuhn).

You sense some bundles of energy with your eyes. This radiation is visible light. You sense other bundles of energy with your skin. These bundles of energy are transferring heat. Bundles of energy that transfer heat are called **infrared** (in•fruh•RED) **radiation**. Outside on a sunny day, your skin feels warm because of infrared radiation from the sun.

Some things can transfer thermal energy by conduction, convection, and radiation at the same time. For example, the air above a campfire is warmed by convection. This hot air quickly warms your hands by conduction. You can warm your hands around the sides of a campfire, too. But it is radiation, not hot air, that is warming them.

✔ **How is thermal energy transferred from the sun?**

▼ A gila (HEE•luh) monster warms its body by moving to a sunny place where its skin absorbs infrared radiation.

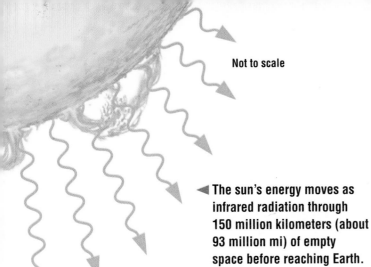

Not to scale

 The sun's energy moves as infrared radiation through 150 million kilometers (about 93 million mi) of empty space before reaching Earth.

Summary

Heat is the transfer of thermal energy from one piece of matter to another. Thermal energy naturally moves from warm matter to cool matter. Conduction and convection need moving particles of matter to transfer thermal energy. Thermal energy is transferred as infrared radiation through matter and empty space.

Review

1. Which type of thermal-energy transfer requires moving liquids and gases?

2. How is thermal energy transferred through empty space?

3. How is thermal energy transferred when particles are touching?

4. **Critical Thinking** Which type of thermal-energy transfer is prevented when a baker uses a potholder to remove hot cookie sheets from an oven?

5. **Test Prep** What property must be different between two pieces of matter for thermal energy to be transferred between them?
   A density
   B mass
   C temperature
   D volume

LINKS

MATH LINK

Figuring Cooling The ability of air conditioners to cool air is rated in British thermal units (Btus). It takes about 12,000 Btus to cool a room that measures 500 square feet. How many Btus are needed to cool a room with 100 square feet of floor space?

WRITING LINK

Persuasive Writing—Business Letter Imagine that you are selling a furnace for a house to a homeowner. Write a letter describing the furnace and giving reasons for the homeowner to buy it.

ART LINK

Icons A "don't walk" sign that shows a walking person inside a circle with a slanted line across it is an icon. So is a smiley face. Design icons that show (1) heating by conduction, (2) heating by convection, and (3) heating by radiation.

TECHNOLOGY LINK

Learn more about how thermal energy is used to shape glass by viewing *Glass Blowing* on the **Harcourt Science Newsroom Video.**

CNN
Turner
Le@rning

How Is Thermal Energy Produced and Used?

In this lesson, you can . . .

INVESTIGATE temperatures in a solar cooker.

LEARN ABOUT ways to produce and use thermal energy.

LINK to math, writing, literature, and technology.

INVESTIGATE

Temperatures in a Solar Cooker

Activity Purpose You know that heat from a campfire can cook hot dogs. Heat from the sun can cook them, too. A solar cooker uses a mirror to reflect, or bounce, infrared radiation from the sun to the food. In this activity you will make a mirror to reflect infrared radiation onto a thermometer. You will then **gather, record, display,** and **interpret data** about the temperatures in the cooker.

Materials

- 2 sheets of graph paper
- shoe-box lid
- aluminum foil
- tape
- thermometer
- clock or watch
- scissors
- poster board
- glue
- string

Activity Procedure

1. Label the two sheets of graph paper like the one shown on page E47.

2. Tape a piece of foil into the shoe-box lid. Place the thermometer in the lid. (Picture A)

3. Place the lid in sunlight. **Record** the temperature immediately. Then record the temperature each minute for 10 minutes.

4. In the shade, remove the thermometer from the shoe-box lid.

◄ Most people like pizza best when it is crisp and fresh from the oven. This pizza oven burns wood to produce thermal energy for baking. In what other ways is thermal energy produced and used?

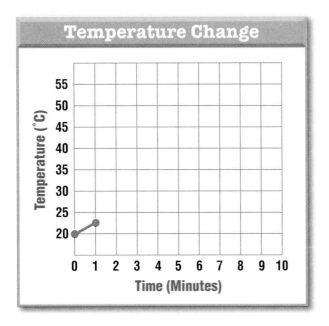

Temperature Change

Picture A

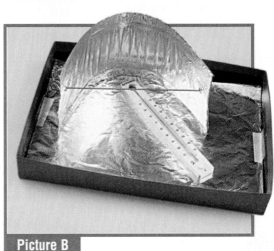

Picture B

5 Cut a rectangle of poster board 10 cm by 30 cm. Glue foil to one side. Let the glue dry for 10 minutes.

6 **CAUTION** **Be careful when using scissors.** Use scissors to punch a hole about 2 cm from each end of the rectangle. Make a curved reflector by drawing the poster board ends toward each other with string until they are about 20 cm apart. Tie the string.

7 Put the curved reflector in the shoe-box lid. Put the thermometer in the center of the curve. Repeat Step 3. (Picture B)

8 Make a line graph of the measurements in Step 3. Make another line graph of the measurements in Step 7.

Draw Conclusions

1. Describe the temperature changes shown on each graph.

2. **Compare** the temperature changes shown on the two graphs.

3. **Infer** what may have caused the differences in the temperatures on the two graphs.

4. **Scientists at Work** How does **displaying the data** in a graph help you **interpret** what happened to the temperature in Steps 3 and 7?

Process Skill Tip

When scientists **interpret data** in graphs, they look at the slants of the lines on the graphs. In your graphs a line with a steep slant means a fast change in temperature. A line with a less steep slant means a slower temperature change.

Using Thermal Energy

Burning Fuel

FIND OUT

- ways to produce thermal energy
- uses of the sun's energy
- examples of wasted thermal energy

VOCABULARY

fuel
solar energy

When something burns, it gets hot. Burning releases thermal energy. Many homes are heated by furnaces that burn oil or natural gas. Some cooking stoves burn natural gas. Any material that can burn is called a **fuel**. Wood was the first fuel people used, and it is still used today. Wood contains a substance called carbon. When wood burns, the carbon combines with oxygen from the air. Together they form a new substance called carbon dioxide. As the wood burns, energy stored in the wood is released as thermal energy and light.

Many fuels contain carbon. Coal is mainly carbon. Fuel oil and natural gas both contain carbon. Much of the thermal energy people use today comes from burning fuels that contain carbon.

✔ **What happens when a fuel burns?**

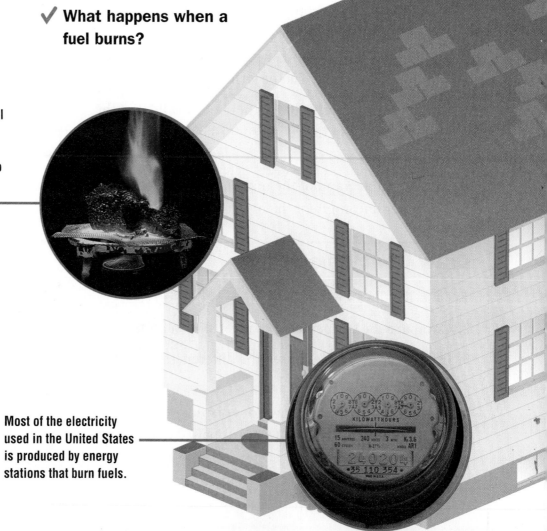

Burning coal releases thermal energy. In some houses the energy is used to warm air directly. In others it is used to heat water in radiators. Like the burner below the coal, a gas stove burns natural gas. The thermal energy released from the flame is used for cooking and baking.

Most of the electricity used in the United States is produced by energy stations that burn fuels.

Solar Energy

The energy given off by the sun is called **solar energy**. People use solar energy to heat water. They put solar panels on top of their roofs. The panels absorb infrared radiation from the sun. The radiation heats water flowing through the panels. The hot water can be used for washing. Solar energy also heats some homes and businesses.

Solar energy can also be used to cook. A solar cooker gathers infrared radiation from the sun and reflects it onto food. You know this works because you measured temperature change in a solar cooker in the investigation.

The sun is the source of most energy on Earth. Even the thermal energy in fossil fuels, such as coal and oil, came from the sun. These fuels have stored energy from plants and animals that lived long ago. The plants used the sun's energy to make food by photosynthesis. The animals got their energy by eating plants or other animals.

✔ **What is solar energy?**

Rooftop solar panels like these are used to heat water.

An electric water heater contains a tank of water. Under the tank is an electric heating coil.

▲ These mirrors focus the sun's thermal energy on a target. The thermal energy gathered in the target is used to produce electricity.

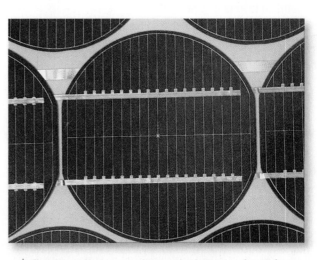

▲ Small appliances such as calculators and watches often use solar cells to supply electricity. Solar cells can also keep batteries charged.

Waste Heat

Using fuel for energy has a side effect. It often makes thermal energy that no one wants or needs. This unneeded thermal energy is called *waste heat*. For example, a campfire produces thermal energy even if the campers need it only for light. Even a campfire used for warmth sends most of its thermal energy straight up, where it is not useful to campers.

Common light sources such as candles and bulbs also make waste heat. So do car engines, electric energy stations, computers, and people. Almost any time energy is produced or used, thermal energy is a part of the process. Much of that thermal energy is not useful, and it can even be harmful. It must be gotten rid of. For example, cars have radiators to carry thermal energy that is not needed away from the engine.

✔ **What is waste heat?**

▲ Light bulbs give off both light and heat. But most of the thermal energy from light bulbs in your home is waste heat.

A candle produces less light than a light bulb but can produce more thermal energy. Most of the thermal energy from candles is not used. ▶

Electric energy stations can't change all thermal energy from fuel into electricity. There is always some waste heat produced. One way to remove this waste heat is to let it heat water. The hot water then cools in towers or ponds. ▼

Fans and radiators carry waste heat away from a car engine. If either the fan or the radiator stops working, the engine soon overheats and stops working as well. ▼

Radiator

▲ Large, very fast computers need special cooling systems such as this one to get rid of waste heat from wiring and circuits.

Summary

Much of the thermal energy used by people today comes from burning fuels that contain carbon. Energy given off by the sun is called solar energy. Solar energy can be used to heat homes and businesses, heat water, and cook food. Most processes that use energy also produce thermal energy. If this thermal energy isn't useful, it is waste heat.

Review

1. What is a fuel?
2. What happens when a fuel burns?
3. What do we call energy given off by the sun?
4. **Critical Thinking** What happens to most waste heat?
5. **Test Prep** Which of the following removes waste heat?
   A car radiator
   B solar cell
   C stove burner
   D windmill

LINKS

MATH LINK

Waste Heat A water heater produces a total of 500 Btus of thermal energy each hour. Only 400 Btus go to heat water. How much waste heat is produced per hour? How much waste heat is produced in a 24-hour day?

WRITING LINK

Persuasive Writing—Opinion A new kind of light bulb, called a compact fluorescent bulb, produces less waste heat than an incandescent light bulb. Write an ad telling consumers why you think they should use this new bulb.

LITERATURE LINK

A Cold Time in the North In Jack London's short story "To Build a Fire," a man lost in the wilderness has a lot of trouble getting thermal energy. Read the story and suggest other ways the man might have kept warm.

TECHNOLOGY LINK

Learn more about fossil fuels and thermal energy by visiting this Internet site.

www.scilinks.org/harcourt

Refrigerants

Hot weather and high humidity can be unpleasant. For some people, such as older people or those with lung diseases, heat can even be dangerous. Their bodies don't work well enough to stay cool. They need to be kept cool by air conditioning.

Air Conditioning

You already know that when thermal energy moves from one place to another, the place it moves *to* gets hotter. The place it moves *from* gets colder. That's part of what makes air conditioners work.

An air conditioner is a machine that uses energy to move heat in the opposite direction from where it would flow on its own. An air conditioner moves heat from inside a house to the outdoors, where it's hotter. To do this, an air conditioner uses a material called a *refrigerant* (ree•FRIJ•er•uhnt).

In an air conditioner, liquid refrigerant is pumped under pressure through tubes. In the part of the air conditioner that is inside

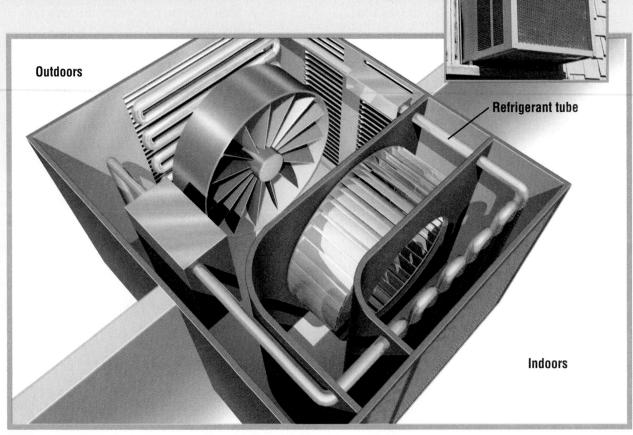

Outdoors

Refrigerant tube

Indoors

the house, the refrigerant gets thermal energy from the air. This causes it to boil. The refrigerant, which is now a gas, is pumped to the part of the air conditioner that is outside the house. There the gas is squeezed and changed back to a liquid. It must lose thermal energy to do this. The thermal energy moves to the outside air.

The first refrigerant used was ammonia (uh•MOHN•yuh). It's still used for large refrigerators in factories. It has an unpleasant smell, however, and it is a poison. Leaks of ammonia, common in the first air conditioners, can cause breathing problems for any people nearby. The second refrigerant used was methyl chloride (METH•uhl KLOR•eyed). But when methyl chloride leaked into the air, it exploded.

Freon

Freon (FREE•ahn) is a colorless, tasteless, odorless gas that doesn't explode and does not make people ill. It also boils at a temperature that works best for refrigerants. So when Thomas Midgley discovered Freon, he thought he'd found the perfect refrigerant.

Freon made home air conditioners and modern refrigerators possible. From its discovery in the 1930s until the 1990s, Freon was almost the only refrigerant used. In the 1970s, however, scientists discovered that Freon and similar refrigerants harm Earth's protective ozone layer. So the use of Freon as a refrigerant was banned in the United States. Scientists started looking for other materials to use.

Old and New Refrigerants

Ammonia and other "old" refrigerants may be used to replace Freon in refrigerators and home air conditioners. New

machines use less ammonia and are sealed more tightly. Other substances that are like Freon but are less damaging are being developed. However, none of these materials work very well in cars, where refrigerants sometimes must both heat and cool the air. Scientists at the University of Illinois are testing ordinary carbon dioxide gas as a refrigerant for cars. So, some of the gas that you breathe out may end up cooling you off!

Think About It

1. Why do you think refrigerant leaks were so common in early air conditioners?
2. Where does the thermal energy that leaves an air-conditioned home go?

WEB LINK:
For Science and Technology updates, visit the Harcourt Internet site.
www.harcourtschool.com

Careers   HVAC Technician

What They Do
HVAC (heating, ventilation, and air conditioning) technicians install, repair, and maintain heating and cooling systems. These systems may be in buildings, vehicles, or machinery such as the refrigerator in your home.

Education and Training   Most HVAC technicians need a high-school education that includes math, electricity, and technical drawing. Most employers prefer technicians to have also finished either a two-year apprenticeship or a technical program.

Frederick McKinley Jones

INVENTOR

Frederick Jones was an orphan by the age of nine and quit school after sixth grade. He was sent to live with a Catholic priest in Kentucky. As an older teenager, he moved to Minnesota and began a job fixing farm machinery. He studied electricity and mechanical engineering when he wasn't working.

Jones served in World War I. When he came back from the war, he built a radio transmitter in his town. He also invented machine parts so that movies with sound could be run on small projectors. During the early 1930s, he heard a man who owned trucks telling his boss that a whole shipment of chicken had spoiled because of the heat. Jones began to design a refrigeration unit for trucks.

Earlier ways to keep trucks cold took up too much room. Most also fell apart quickly because of being shaken during travel. Jones built his first refrigeration unit by using odds and ends of machine parts. It was small, shake-proof, and lightweight. But it was made to go beneath the truck and broke down often because mud and dirt from roads got inside.

Modern refrigerated truck

After a time, Jones designed and made a unit that went on top of a truck. He and his boss formed a partnership to build the trucks. Jones was vice-president of the company.

The refrigerated trucks could ship more than food. During World War II, Jones's invention saved lives. Because the units were portable, badly needed blood and medicine could be shipped safely to battlefields.

Jones continued to work on his inventions. He eventually received more than 60 patents. More than 40 of them were for refrigeration products.

THINK ABOUT IT

1. What were some design problems that Jones solved to make a working truck-refrigerator?
2. What foods do you eat that might be shipped in a refrigerated truck?

Compare Conductors

Which material conducts thermal energy fastest?

Materials

- 3 thermometers
- warm tap water
- tape
- jar
- plastic, wood, and metal spoons of about the same size

Procedure

1. Carefully tape the bulb of a thermometer to the handle of each spoon.

2. Fill the jar with warm tap water to a level that will cover only the bottoms of the spoons. Carefully place the spoons in the jar.

3. Measure and record the temperature of each spoon every minute for 5 minutes.

Draw Conclusions

Which spoon conducted thermal energy most quickly? How do you know?

Thermal Energy

How do different amounts of water affect melting?

Materials

- warm tap water
- 2 jars, 1 large and 1 small
- 4 ice cubes that are the same size
- clock or watch

Procedure

1. Fill each container almost full with warm tap water.

2. Put two ice cubes in each container.

3. Measure the time it takes for each pair of cubes to melt completely.

Draw Conclusions

Did one pair melt faster than the other pair? Why were the times different?

Chapter 2 Review and Test Preparation

Vocabulary Review

Use the terms below to complete the sentences. The page numbers in ( ) tell you where to look in the chapter if you need help.

energy (E34)
thermal energy (E34)
temperature (E35)
heat (E40)
conduction (E41)
convection (E42)
radiation (E44)
infrared radiation (E44)
fuel (E48)
solar energy (E49)

1. _____ is the transfer of thermal energy.

2. The ability to cause a change is _____.

3. A material that is burned to produce thermal energy is _____.

4. _____ is a measure of the average energy of motion of particles in matter.

5. The total energy of motion of particles of matter is _____.

6. _____ is the transfer of heat by particles bumping into each other.

7. Radiation that transfers heat is called _____.

8. _____ is bundles of energy that can travel through empty space.

9. Energy given off by the sun is called _____.

10. _____ is the heat transfer that can occur only in a liquid or gas.

Connect Concepts

Fill in the blanks in the diagram below to correctly describe some of the main concepts of this chapter.

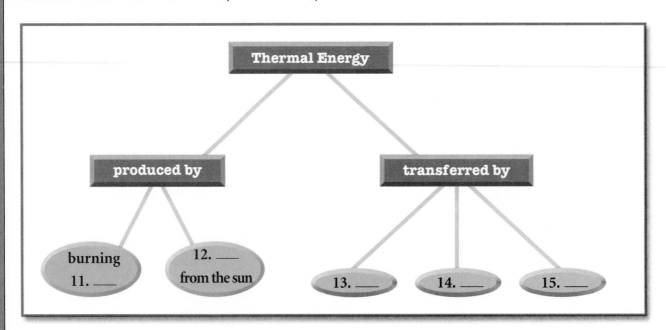

Check Understanding

Write the letter of the best choice.

16. Most thermometers work because matter ____ when it is heated.
    A disappears
    B collects radiation
    C expands
    D loses mass

17. A thermometer measures the ____ energy of motion of particles of matter.
    F total   H solar
    G long-term   J average

18. Two pieces of the same kind of matter have the same temperature. The one with the larger mass has more —
    A conduction
    B thermal energy
    C convection
    D solar energy

19. When thermal energy moves from one piece of matter to another, the transfer is called —
    F solar energy H temperature
    G heat   J fuel

20. Thermal energy can be transferred by conduction from one piece of matter to another only if the two pieces are —
    A liquids   C solids
    B touching   D fuel

21. Convection takes place only in liquids and —
    F gases   H solids
    G energies   J states

22. Thermal energy that travels from the sun to Earth is being transferred by —
    A conduction   C convection
    B fuel   D radiation

Critical Thinking

23. You put a pot of water on the burner of an electric stove and turn the burner on high heat. The water soon boils. Describe how the heat from the stove gets to the water in the pot.

24. A solar panel on a roof collects solar energy to warm water for a house. Describe how the heat is transferred from the sun to the panel, and then from the panel to the water.

Process Skills Review

25. What property of particles of matter do you **measure** with a thermometer?

26. Suppose a thermometer is hanging from a thread inside a jar completely empty of gases or liquids. You **infer** that infrared radiation is falling on the thermometer. What observation would lead you to this inference? Explain.

27. A line graph has the temperature scale on the left and the time scale on the bottom. If the line is level, what can you conclude by **interpreting** the temperature **data** shown?

Performance Assessment

Temperature Balance

Your teacher will give you a thermometer, a straw, a full glass of warm water, a full glass of cool water, and an empty glass. Your goal is to use the materials to end up with a glass that is half full of water that is about room temperature. You can't wait for the two full glasses to cool and warm naturally. Explain what you did and why it worked.

Sound

Have you ever heard nothing at all? Probably not. Even in a space suit while orbiting Earth, you can still hear the sound of your blood flowing and your heart beating!

Vocabulary Preview

sound
compression
sound wave
loudness
pitch
speed of sound
echo
sonic boom

⫶⫶FAST FACT

Bats don't use their eyes to catch prey. They use their ears! Bats send out high-pitched squeaks and clicks that bounce off objects. The returning echoes direct them to their prey. Using echoes, some bats can find an insect as thin as a human hair in total darkness!

Every type of animal has a different hearing and voice range. When the Canadian Pacific Railroad switched to air-driven horns, large numbers of female moose were killed by trains. Biologists determined that the low-pitched horns sounded like the calls of male moose! Changing the pitch of the horns has greatly reduced the number of moose on the tracks.

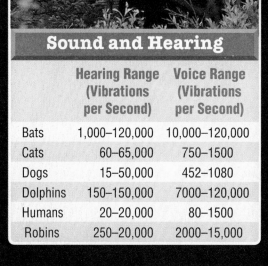

Sound and Hearing

	Hearing Range (Vibrations per Second)	Voice Range (Vibrations per Second)
Bats	1,000–120,000	10,000–120,000
Cats	60–65,000	750–1500
Dogs	15–50,000	452–1080
Dolphins	150–150,000	7000–120,000
Humans	20–20,000	80–1500
Robins	250–20,000	2000–15,000

FAST FACT

SUMATRA

Jakarta

JAVA

When a volcano on the island of Krakatau, Indonesia, erupted in 1883, it made the loudest natural sound ever observed. Heard 4500 km (2796 mi) away, the eruption was so strong that it blew the island apart!

LESSON 1

What Is Sound?

In this lesson, you can . . .

INVESTIGATE making and hearing sounds.

LEARN ABOUT the way sound travels.

LINK to math, writing, social studies, and technology.

Sound from a Ruler

Activity Purpose Sit still a moment and listen. What do you hear? People talking, car horns honking, dogs barking, the refrigerator humming? We hear different kinds of sounds all day long. In this investigation you will **observe** how a sound is made. You will also observe some ways to change sound.

Materials
- plastic ruler

Activity Procedure

1 Place the ruler on a tabletop. Let 15 to 20 cm stick out over the edge of the table.

2 Hold the ruler tightly against the tabletop with one hand. Use the thumb of your other hand to flick, or strum, the free end of the ruler. (Picture A)

3 **Observe** the ruler with your eyes. **Record** your observations.

4 Repeat Step 2. **Observe** the ruler with your ears. **Record** your observations.

◄ Hitting cymbals together produces a loud sound that can be heard over that of an entire band or orchestra.

Picture A

Picture B

5. Flick the ruler harder. **Observe** the results. **Record** your observations.

6. Change the length of the ruler sticking over the edge of the table, and repeat Steps 2 through 5. **Observe** the results. **Record** your observations. (Picture B)

Draw Conclusions

1. What did you **observe** in Step 3?

2. What did you **observe** in Step 4?

3. **Make a hypothesis** to explain what you **observed** in Steps 3 and 4. How could you test your explanation?

4. **Scientists at Work** When scientists want to learn more about an experiment, they change one part of it and **observe** the effect. What did you change in Step 6? What effect did you observe?

Investigate Further Place one ear on the tabletop. Cover the other ear with your hand. Have a partner repeat Steps 1 and 2. What do you **observe?**

> **Process Skill Tip**
>
> When people use the word *observe*, they usually think of seeing. But you can use all your senses to **observe.** In this investigation you also used your sense of hearing to observe the effects of the movements of the ruler.

Characteristics of Sound

Vibrations

FIND OUT

• causes of sounds

• how sound travels

• how your ears help you hear

VOCABULARY

sound

compression

sound wave

Strumming a guitar string, snapping a ruler, or humming a note—all of these actions make sounds. Each of them also starts a back-and-forth movement called a *vibration* (vy•BRAY•shuhn). **Sound** is a series of vibrations that you can hear. You can't see vibrations of particles in air. But you can watch or feel the vibrations of objects that make sounds. In the investigation you saw the ruler vibrate after you snapped it. After you strum a guitar string, it vibrates for a while and slowly stops. You hear the guitar note start and then slowly fade away. When you hum a note, you can feel the vibrations of your larynx (LAIR•inks), or voice box, by putting your fingers on the outside of your throat.

✔ **What is sound?**

As the ruler vibrates, the particles in air are pushed closer together. The areas where air is pushed together are called compressions (kuhm•PRESH•uhnz). ▶

When one end of the ruler is snapped, it vibrates, or moves back and forth. The ruler pushes against the air around it. ▼

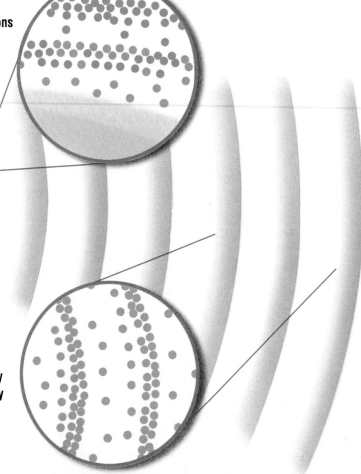

Each compression moves away from the ruler, in the same way that ripples move away from a pebble thrown into a pond. ▶

Traveling Waves

The vibrations of the guitar string, the ruler, and your voice box push and then pull on the particles of air around them. As they push, they increase the pressure in the air. The area where air is pushed together is called a **compression**. As the vibrations pull, they decrease the pressure in the air. This results in alternating areas of high and low pressure in the air. **Sound waves** are quickly moving areas of high and low pressure. All sound is carried through matter as sound waves.

Sound waves move out in all directions from a vibrating object. You can hear something making sound all around you, above you, and below you. As the sound waves move away from their source, their energy is spread over a larger area. So the farther you are from the source of a sound, the softer the sound is.

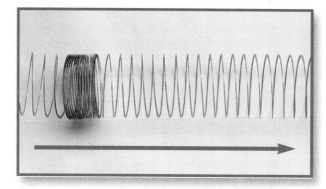

▲ A wave travels through this spring toy just as a sound wave travels through the air. The places where the springs are close together are like compressions, or areas of high pressure, in the air. The places where the springs are far apart are like areas of low pressure in the air.

Most of the sound we hear travels through the air. In the investigation you found that sound waves travel through other materials, too. Sound waves can move through each state of matter.

✔ **In what direction do sound waves travel?**

1 Each instrument in a marching band makes a sound by vibrating something. For example, the head of a bass drum vibrates when it is hit. The vibrations cause sound waves in the air. The audience watching and listening to the parade hears the drumbeat.

2 Sound waves can also travel through liquids. These underwater swimmers could hear the band play if it marched by the pool.

3 Someone behind a closed door could hear the band, too, because sound waves can also travel through solids.

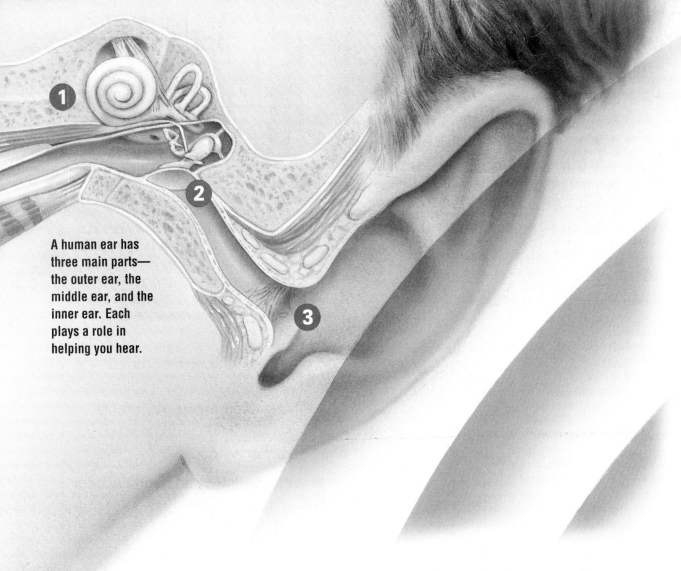

A human ear has three main parts—the outer ear, the middle ear, and the inner ear. Each plays a role in helping you hear.

1 The inner ear is a snail-shaped tube filled with liquid. Tiny hairs on the inside are connected to nerves. Sounds move the hairs, which then send signals along nerves to the brain. Your brain figures out the signal, and you hear a sound.

2 The middle ear is made up of three tiny bones that connect the outer ear to the inner ear. The three bones are called the hammer, the anvil, and the stirrup because of their shapes.

3 The outer ear is like a funnel. It collects sounds and guides them to the eardrum.

Hearing Sounds

We hear sound when sound waves reach our ears. Our ears take in the sound waves and turn them into signals that go to our brains. Our brains figure out these signals and tell us what the sound is.

The first part of the ear that a sound wave hits is the outer ear. The outer ear is like a funnel that collects sound waves and guides them to the eardrum.

The eardrum is made of thin material that bends easily. It is about 1 centimeter ($\frac{1}{2}$ in.) across. It works like the top of a drum. The eardrum vibrates when sound waves hit it. As the eardrum moves back and forth, it moves a tiny bone at the outside end of the middle ear.

The middle ear is about the size of the tip of your little finger. In it, vibrations pass through three tiny bones. The bones connect the eardrum to the inner ear.

The inner ear is shaped like a snail. It is filled with liquid. The walls of the inner ear are lined with tiny hairs. These hairs are connected to nerves.

The third bone of the middle ear vibrates one end of the inner ear. These vibrations cause waves in the liquid. The waves move the tiny hairs. This causes nerve cells to send signals to your brain. Your brain interprets the signals as sounds.

✔ **Which part of the ear connects it to the outside world?**

Summary

Sound is made by vibrating objects. The vibrations travel through matter as areas of high and low pressure called sound waves. Sound waves move through the three parts of the ear. You sense the vibrations as sound.

Review

1. What is sound?
2. What are sound waves?
3. Which part of the ear is connected to nerves that send signals to the brain?
4. **Critical Thinking** Sometimes you can hear and feel the rumble of a passing truck. What are you feeling?
5. **Test Prep** The middle ear contains —
   A liquid
   B the eardrum
   C three bones
   D hairs

LINKS

MATH LINK

Music Scales Some music scale notes can be found by shortening the length of a string to a fraction. For example, if the base pitch is played on a length of 1, an *octave* (AHK•tiv) higher would be played on a length of $\frac{1}{2}$. What would be the length of the second octave higher? The third octave?

WRITING LINK

Informative Writing—Description Suppose that you are a sound wave traveling through someone's ear. Write a description for your classmates of what happens to you as you move from the outer ear to the inner ear.

SOCIAL STUDIES LINK

Flutes and Drums In many countries traditional music is played on flutelike and drumlike instruments. Choose a country. Find pictures of these types of musical instruments from that country. Make a map showing the location of the country. Add labeled pictures of the instruments.

TECHNOLOGY LINK

Learn more about early recorders by visiting the Jerome and Dorothy Lemelson Center for Invention and Innovation Internet site.
www.si.edu/harcourt/science

Smithsonian Institution®

LESSON 2

Why Do Sounds Differ?

In this lesson, you can . . .

INVESTIGATE making different sounds.

LEARN ABOUT differences in sounds.

LINK to math, writing, music, and technology.

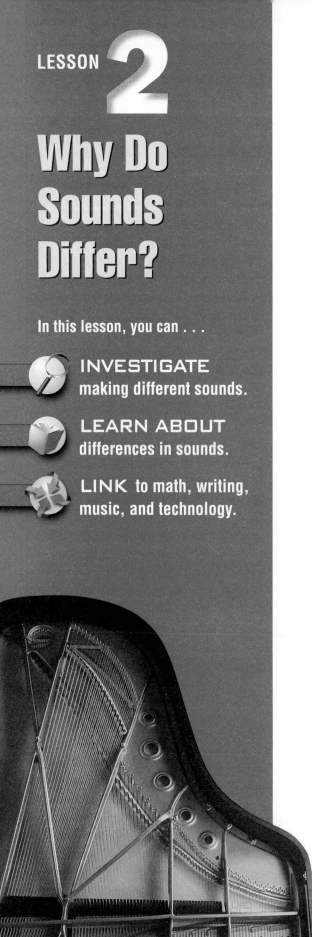

Making Different Sounds

Activity Purpose If you pluck a guitar string, you hear a sound. If you pluck another guitar string, you hear a different sound. How are the sounds different? What causes the difference? In this activity you will **observe** sounds made by a vibrating rubber band. You will **compare** observations and **infer** what causes differences in sounds.

Materials

- safety goggles
- foam cup
- long rubber band
- paper clip
- ruler
- masking tape

CAUTION

Activity Procedure

1 **CAUTION** **Put on the safety goggles.** With a pencil, punch a small hole in the bottom of the cup. Thread the rubber band through the paper clip. Put the paper clip inside the cup, and pull the rubber band through the hole. (Picture A)

2 Turn the cup upside down on a table. Stand the ruler on the table next to it, with the 1-cm mark at the top. Tape one side of the cup to the ruler. Pull the rubber band over the top of the ruler, and tape it to the back. (Picture B)

◄ The word *piano* is short for *pianoforte* (pee•ah•noh•FOR•tay). *Piano* is the Italian word for "soft." *Forte* is the Italian word for "loud." Why do you think this instrument is called a pianoforte?

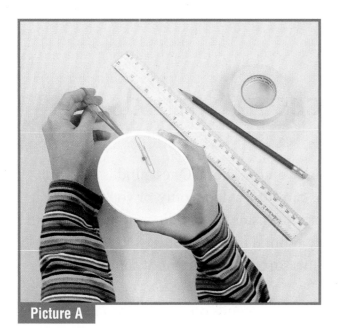

Picture A

Picture B

3 Pull the rubber band to one side and let it go. **Observe** the sound. **Record** your observations.

4 Repeat Step 3, but this time pull the rubber band farther. **Observe** the sound. **Record** your observations.

5 With one finger, hold the rubber band down to the ruler at the 4-cm mark. Pluck the rubber band. **Observe** the sound. **Record** your observations.

6 Repeat Step 5, but this time hold the rubber band down at the 6-cm mark. Then do this at the 8-cm mark. **Observe** the sounds. **Record** your observations.

Draw Conclusions

1. **Compare** the sounds you observed in Steps 3 and 4.

2. **Compare** the sounds you observed in Steps 5 and 6.

3. When was the vibrating part of the rubber band the shortest?

4. **Scientists at Work** Scientists use their observations to help them **infer** the causes of different things. Use your observations from Steps 5 and 6 to infer what caused the differences in the sounds.

Investigate Further Try moving your finger up and down the ruler as you pull on the rubber band. Can you play a scale? Can you play a tune? What other ways can you investigate sounds made by the rubber band?

Process Skill Tip

Scientists use their observations to **infer** the causes of their results. In this investigation your observations helped you infer the causes of different sounds.

Differences in Sounds

Loudness

FIND OUT

- the difference between loud and soft sounds

- the difference between high and low sounds

VOCABULARY

loudness

pitch

You can whisper and you can shout. One sound is soft, and the other is loud. You can close a door softly, or you can bang it shut so hard that everyone inside the building can hear. You can hear how loud or soft a sound is. This property is called loudness. **Loudness** is a measure of the amount of sound energy reaching your ears.

The loudness of a sound depends on how far the vibrating object is moving as it goes back and forth. In the investigation the sound was louder when you pulled the rubber band farther. You added more energy to the rubber band by stretching it more. In the same way, if you hit a drum harder or slam a door harder, you make a louder sound.

✔ **What does loudness measure?**

A bluebird's song is pretty, but it is not loud. The close together, curved, thin blue lines stand for soft, high sounds. ▶

◀ Noise from a jackhammer is much louder than a bluebird's song. It's so loud that it will injure your ears if you don't protect them. The far apart, curved, thick blue lines stand for loud, low sounds.

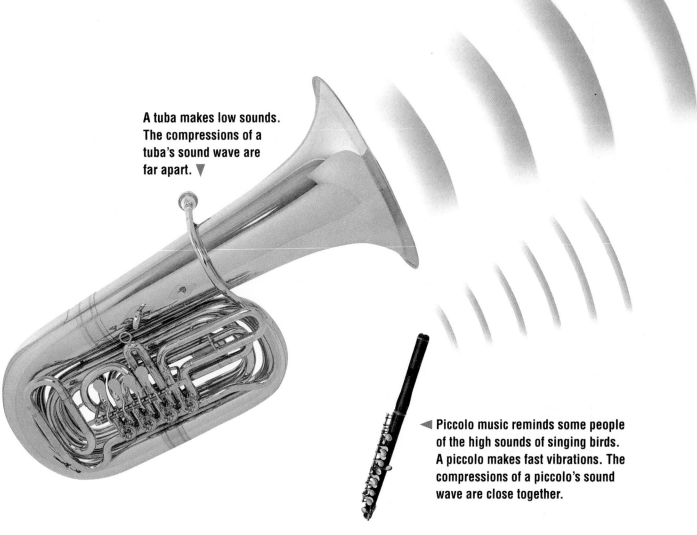

A tuba makes low sounds. The compressions of a tuba's sound wave are far apart. ▼

◄ Piccolo music reminds some people of the high sounds of singing birds. A piccolo makes fast vibrations. The compressions of a piccolo's sound wave are close together.

Pitch

You can make loud sounds and soft sounds. You can also make high sounds and low sounds. When you growl like a dog, you are making a low sound. When you squeak like a mouse, you are making a high sound.

A sound's **pitch** is a measure of how high or low it is. Pitch depends on how fast the source of the sound is vibrating. The faster the vibrations, the higher the pitch.

You can change how fast a string or rubber band vibrates by changing its length. In the investigation, when you made the vibrating part of the rubber band shorter, it vibrated faster. The sound it made got higher in pitch.

✔ **What does the pitch of a sound depend on?**

The keys at the right-hand end of a piano make high sounds. The keys to the left make lower sounds. The lowest note on a modern piano vibrates about $27\frac{1}{2}$ times a second. The highest note on a piano vibrates about 4224 times a second. Humans can hear sounds from about 20 to about 20,000 vibrations a second. ▶

Changing Pitch

Many musical instruments can be played at different pitches by changing the length of certain parts. A guitar or violin player puts his or her fingers down on the strings in different places. This changes the lengths of the vibrating strings. As a result, the violin or guitar plays different pitches.

Another way to make a different pitch is to change the thickness of the material that vibrates. A thin string vibrates faster than a thick string. Low-pitched guitar and piano strings have wire wrapped around them to make them thicker.

✔ **Name two ways you can change the pitch of a vibrating object.**

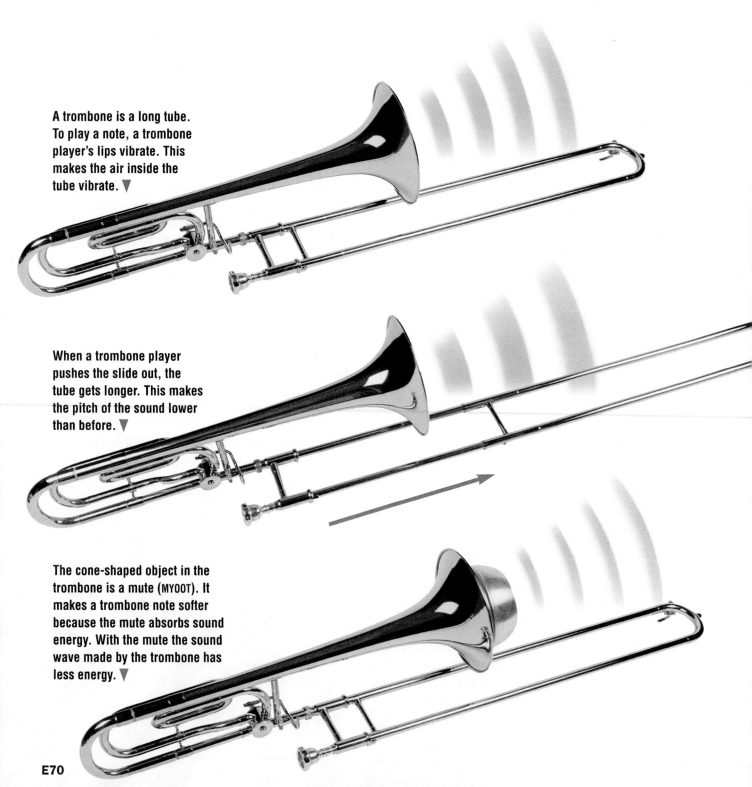

A trombone is a long tube. To play a note, a trombone player's lips vibrate. This makes the air inside the tube vibrate. ▼

When a trombone player pushes the slide out, the tube gets longer. This makes the pitch of the sound lower than before. ▼

The cone-shaped object in the trombone is a mute (MYOOT). It makes a trombone note softer because the mute absorbs sound energy. With the mute the sound wave made by the trombone has less energy. ▼

A voiceprint is an electronic "picture" of a voice. It shows the changing pitch and loudness of the voice as a person speaks. ▼

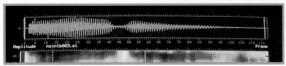

Summary

Loudness is a measure of the sound energy reaching your ears. It depends on the size of the vibrations. Pitch is a measure of how high or low a sound is. Pitch depends on how fast an object vibrates. You can change pitch by changing the length or the thickness of a vibrating object.

Review

1. What is the loudness of a sound?

2. What is the pitch of a sound?

3. What happens to sound as it gets farther away from the object making the sound?

4. **Critical Thinking** How do you think the finger holes on the side of a piccolo control the pitch of its sound?

5. **Test Prep** If you put your finger down on a guitar string to make the string shorter, the sound the string makes will get —

   A lower   **C** louder

   B higher   **D** softer

LINKS

MATH LINK

Calculate the Difference in Pitch The highest note on a piano vibrates 4224 times a second. The lowest note on a piano vibrates $27\frac{1}{2}$ times a second. What is the difference between these two pitches?

WRITING LINK

Informative Writing—Description Sit still and listen for one minute. Time yourself. As you're listening, make a list of every sound you hear. Then write a paragraph for your teacher describing all the sounds. Be sure to include loudness and pitch in your descriptions.

MUSIC LINK

High and Low Two of the families of instruments in an orchestra are the brass instruments and the woodwind instruments. Find out the names of the instruments in each of these families. Then find out the highest and lowest pitches each instrument family can play.

TECHNOLOGY LINK

Learn more about how scientists and engineers are using sound energy by viewing *Sound Wave Energy* on the **Harcourt Science Newsroom Video.**

LESSON 3

How Do Sound Waves Travel?

In this lesson, you can . . .

INVESTIGATE ways sound is reflected.

LEARN ABOUT how sound waves travel.

LINK to math, writing, health, and technology.

Hearing Sounds

Activity Purpose Have you ever made a sound and heard it come back to you? In this investigation you will **gather and record data** while making a sound and listening to find out if it comes back to you.

Materials
- large metal spoon
- metal pot
- red crayon

Activity Procedure

1 Find a playing field with a scoreboard or building at one end. Use a pencil to make a drawing of the playing field.

2 Walk out onto the playing field. Bang the spoon against the pot once. Wait and **observe** whether or not the sound comes back to you. (Picture A)

3 Use a pencil to **record** on your drawing where you are on the playing field and which way you are facing. (Picture B)

4 Keep moving to new locations on the field and banging the pot until you hear the sound come back to you.

◀ When the space shuttle reenters the atmosphere and coasts toward a landing, it is traveling much faster than the speed of sound.

5 **Record** on your drawing where you are on the playing field and which way you are facing each time you bang the pot. Use the red crayon to mark the places where the sound came back to you.

6 Move forward and back. Move from side to side. Each time you move, bang the pot once and wait to see whether or not the sound comes back to you.

7 **Record** on your drawing where you are on the playing field and which way you are facing each time you bang the pot. Use the red crayon to mark the places where the sound came back to you. Make sure your drawing shows at least 20 different positions.

Picture A

Draw Conclusions

1. Look at your drawing. How many different positions did you show? At how many different places did the sound come back to you?

2. Look at all the places marked in red on your drawing. Do they have anything in common?

Picture B

3. **Scientists at Work** Each mark that you made on your drawing was a piece of data. When scientists do investigations, they **gather and record** as much **data** as they can. All the data helps them draw conclusions. How could you gather more data in an organized way?

Investigate Further Move to each of the places on the field where you heard the sound come back to you. Blow a whistle loudly in each place. Does the sound come back to you? Why do you think it did or didn't?

> **Process Skill Tip**
>
> Scientists often use drawings when they **gather and record data**. Their drawings help them see patterns in the information they gather. They use the patterns to help them draw conclusions.

How Sound Travels

Speed

VOCABULARY

speed of sound
echo
sonic boom

Have you ever been to a baseball game and watched a batter hit a home run? If you were sitting all the way across the ballpark, you saw the batter hit the ball a split second before you heard the crack of the bat. This is because sound waves take more time to move through the air than light does. Even so, it took less than a second for the sound wave to travel from the bat to your ears.

The speed at which a sound wave travels is called the **speed of sound**. Sound waves move at different speeds through different materials. In dry, cool air, sound waves travel 340 meters (about 1115 ft) per second. The speed of sound traveling through steel is 5200 meters (about 17,070 ft) per second.

In hard, solid materials, sound waves move very fast. This is because the particles in solids are close together and bump into each other often. The particles in liquids don't bump into each other as often as particles in solids do. So vibrations take longer to move through liquids. Sound moves more slowly through liquids than through most solids.

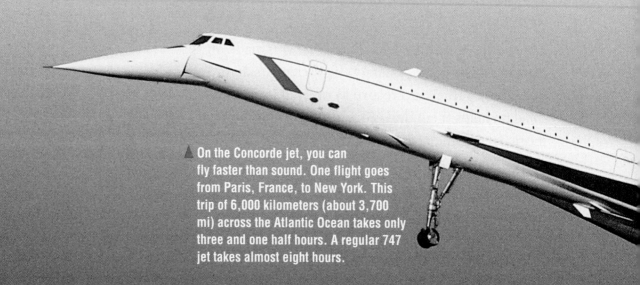

On the Concorde jet, you can fly faster than sound. One flight goes from Paris, France, to New York. This trip of 6,000 kilometers (about 3,700 mi) across the Atlantic Ocean takes only three and one half hours. A regular 747 jet takes almost eight hours.

Sound moves even more slowly in gases. The particles in gases are far apart. They don't bump into each other often, so vibrations take longer to move through gases.

Sound travels through moving particles. If there are no particles, there can be no sound. We hear sounds mostly through air. In outer space there is no air for sound waves to travel through. If you were in a spacesuit outside the space shuttle, no one inside the shuttle could hear you shout. You could talk back and forth only by using a radio.

✓ **What does the speed of sound measure?**

1 In air, sound travels about 1 mile in 5 seconds. You can use this to find the distance to a thunderstorm. Light travels so fast that you see a lightning bolt almost as it happens. Start the stopwatch when you see the flash, and wait to hear the thunder.

2 When you hear the thunder, you stop the stopwatch. It reads 10 seconds.
10 sec ÷ 5 sec/1 mi = 2 mi
The storm is about 2 miles away.

Sound waves travel at different speeds in different materials. The arrangement of particles in materials affects how the waves move. ▼

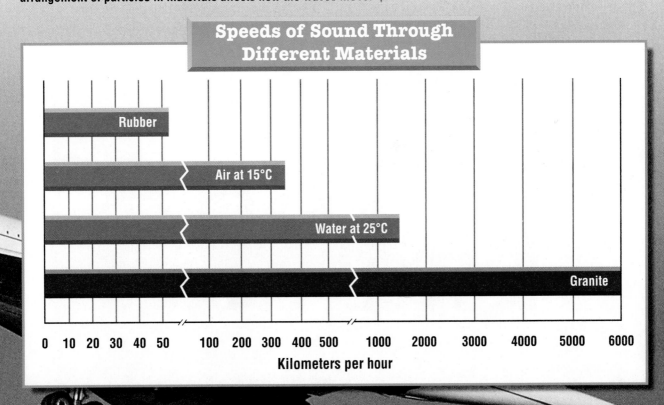

Speeds of Sound Through Different Materials

Rubber

Air at 15°C

Water at 25°C

Granite

0 10 20 30 40 50   100   200 300 400 500   1000   2000   3000   4000   5000   6000

Kilometers per hour

Reflection

A mirror shows you a clear image. The light that bounces, or reflects, from the mirror looks like the light that hit the mirror. That's because a mirror has a very smooth surface.

Sound waves also reflect from surfaces. A sound reflection is called an **echo**. Sound waves reflected from smooth, hard surfaces sound like the original sound. In the investigation, you heard an echo when you faced the scoreboard or building and hit the pot with the spoon.

You can see your reflection in a smooth pond just as you see it in a mirror. But if the surface of the pond ripples, your reflection gets broken up. You can no longer see yourself clearly. The same thing happens when sound waves reflect off rough, uneven surfaces. Each sound wave hits a different part of the bumpy surface and is reflected in a different direction. A line of trees or a rough rock wall doesn't reflect clear echoes.

✔ **What is an echo?**

THE INSIDE STORY

"Seeing" with Sound

Dolphins see with their eyes. They also "see" underwater by using echoes. Dolphins use sound to find their way around rocks and other things in their way. They also use sound to find food such as small fish and squid.

1 Dolphins make sounds that have high pitches. The sounds are called clicks. Scientists aren't sure how dolphins make the clicks. The click sound waves travel through the water.

2 The click sound waves reflect off the rocks and fish. Some echoes return to the dolphin.

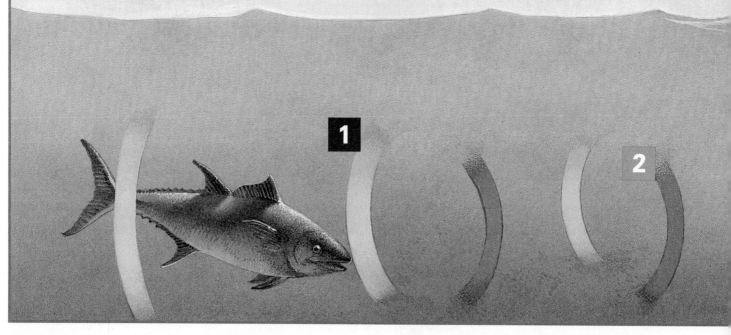

E76

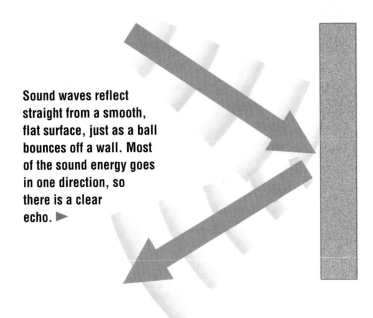

Sound waves reflect straight from a smooth, flat surface, just as a ball bounces off a wall. Most of the sound energy goes in one direction, so there is a clear echo. ▶

When sound waves hit a rough, uneven surface, they are reflected in many different directions. The sound energy is spread out, so there is no clear echo. ▶

3 Dolphins have an organ called a melon on the top of their heads. It senses the echoes of the clicks. The melon absorbs the sound and helps the dolphin avoid rocks and find its food.

Sonic Booms

Jet airplanes move fast. Some airplanes can fly faster than sound. Powerful jet engines produce loud sounds. What happens to these sounds when the plane is moving faster than they are?

An airplane traveling faster than sound makes sound waves that move away in all directions. But the airplane is moving faster than the sound waves moving away in front of it. When the plane catches up to these sound waves, they are squeezed closer together. All the energy of the sound waves becomes one strong wave. This strong wave is called a shock wave. You can hear this shock wave as a loud "boom-boom." People call the double boom a **sonic boom**. Any object moving faster than sound makes such a shock wave. You hear the "crack" of a rifle shot because the bullet is moving faster than sound.

A plane is always making sound waves. So if it is flying faster than sound, its sonic boom travels with it, just as the plane's shadow does.

▲ The supersonic Concorde jet is allowed to fly faster than sound only over the ocean or deserts. Because of this, most of the time people don't hear its sonic booms.

Suppose you and 20 of your friends were to stand in a line down the length of a football field. You stand on a goal line. Each of your friends stands on a different yard line. Coming from the direction nearest you, an airplane flies down the field going faster than sound. You will be the first to hear its sonic boom. Then, one by one, each of your friends will hear it. Finally, the person standing on the far goal line will hear it.

✔ **What is a sonic boom?**

A sonic boom is a large, quick air pressure increase followed by a large quick decrease. Then the pressure returns to normal. ▶

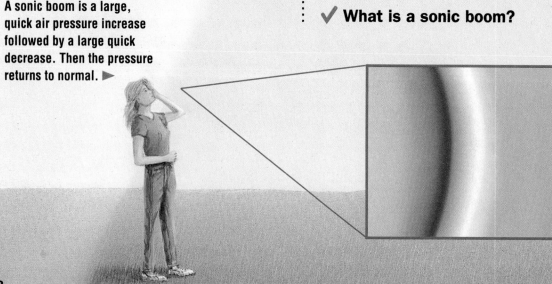

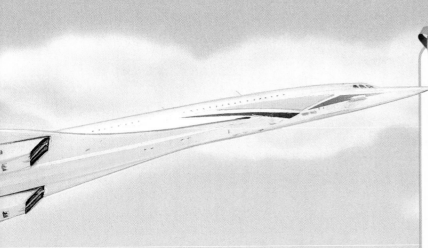

Summary

Sound waves travel at different speeds through different materials. They travel fastest through hard, solid materials. Sound waves reflect from smooth, hard surfaces. An echo is a sound reflection. Objects traveling faster than the speed of sound cause shock waves that we hear as sonic booms.

Review

1. What does the speed of sound measure?
2. Why is there no sound in outer space?
3. Where does the energy of a sonic boom come from?
4. **Critical Thinking** Why don't you hear echoes in a forest?
5. **Test Prep** In which material would sound waves probably travel the fastest?
   A cotton
   B milk
   C iron
   D oxygen

LINKS

MATH LINK

Sound Comparison The speed of sound in air is 340 meters per second. In water it is 1497 meters per second. About how many times as fast is the speed of sound in water as in air?

WRITING LINK

Informative Writing—Narration Suppose you are at home and a thunderstorm is going on outside. By watching the lightning and listening to the thunder, you track the storm. Write a story for a younger child telling what you see and hear, and where the storm is going.

HEALTH LINK

Ultrasound Doctors use ultrasound in medical tests. Find out what ultrasound is and how it works. Then find out about some of the tests it's used for. Make a poster or display to show what you learned.

TECHNOLOGY LINK

Learn more about sound wave differences by exploring *Waves of Music* on **Harcourt Science Explorations CD-ROM.**

Active Noise Control

Sound can be beautiful, as some music is. Sound can give information, as in the case of warning bells or someone speaking to tell you how to fix your bicycle. But sometimes sound is just noise.

Noise

Some noise is unwanted sound. It upsets people and makes them angry. Think of how listening to a jackhammer or a chain-saw outside your window all day long would make you feel. A sound that one person thinks is pleasantly loud may be an unwanted noise to another person. Still, any loud sound, whether or not you like it, can cause permanent damage to your ears.

Noise Reduction

Most ways of reducing noise involve absorbing sound or spreading out sound energy. For example, inside a car muffler, sound waves bounce off many walls and

dividers. Each bounce takes a little energy out of the sound wave. As a result, the car makes less noise. Rugs, curtains, and ceiling tiles work in much the same way. All these ways of reducing noise are *passive*—they don't need energy to make them work.

For several years now, scientists have been working on a process called active noise control (ANC). ANC makes sounds to cancel out noise. It does this by making sound waves that are the exact opposite of the noise waves. Where a noise wave has a compression, the ANC wave doesn't. When the two waves meet, their areas of high and low pressure cancel each other out.

An ANC system is made up of microphones to pick up the noise, a computer to analyze the noise, and speakers to make the sound waves that cancel other sounds.

ANC works best indoors on noise that repeats, for example inside airplanes and cars, where you might hear the sound of tires on the road or propellers turning. ANC headphones for use in helicopters are one success story. They allow the person wearing them to hear people talking and warning sirens, but they cancel out the low-pitched sounds from the rotor blades.

Other Uses for ANC

What works for noise may also work for other unwanted vibrations. ANC technology might help prevent or lessen earthquake damage. When a building begins to shake, opposing vibrations made by an ANC system could help stop the shaking.

Another way ANC ideas could be used is to reduce vibrations while making lenses for cameras and telescopes. For example, it's important that lenses be as smooth as possible to give a clear image. Most lenses now are ground by a robot using a grinding tool. The tool vibrates, so the surface of the lens isn't completely smooth. A person must do the final polishing. This adds time and cost. If the grinder did not vibrate, no human polisher would be needed. This would lower the cost of lenses.

Think About It

1. Why do you think ANC works best indoors?

2. Do you think ANC could be used to block out noise from your neighbor's stereo?

WEB LINK:
For Science and Technology updates, visit the Harcourt Internet site.
www.harcourtschool.com

Careers Acoustical Engineer

What They Do
Acoustics
(uh•KOOS•tiks) is the science of sound. Acoustical engineers analyze sounds and design ways to control sound. They work with industries to control noise, and they help design buildings such as hospitals that need quiet. They also help design buildings that have special sound needs, such as concert halls.

Education and Training   To be an acoustical engineer, you must have at least a bachelor's degree in engineering. Some acoustical engineers study physics and then engineering. Engineers who have the letters *PE* after their names have passed state tests to prove they have the knowledge needed to be professional engineers.

Amar Gopal Bose

SOUND ENGINEER

To celebrate finishing his college research, Amar Bose treated himself to a new sound system. But he didn't like the way the speakers sounded. He began to study acoustics (uh·KOOS·tiks), the science of sound, so he could build better speakers.

The speaker in a stereo system changes electric signals to vibrations. The vibrations create sound waves. Most sound systems need two speakers to play sounds correctly. One speaker makes high sounds, and one makes low sounds. Each speaker is usually put into a wooden box. The size and shape of the box affect how the speaker sounds.

Bose graduated from the Massachusetts Institute of Technology (MIT) and went to Delhi, India, to teach at the National Physics Laboratory. He later returned to teach at MIT. During this time, he continued experimenting with sound. Starting in 1959, Bose received a number of patents for designs of sound systems, including loudspeakers. Five years later, Bose started his own company with a former student.

At the beginning, Bose wasn't paid a salary and he worked at night after teaching classes at MIT. Now, his company is successful and has more than 2,500 workers.

Bose still listens to music. He took violin lessons when he was younger but decided to study science instead. When he has time, he listens to classical music, including classical music of India.

THINK ABOUT IT

1. The speaker that handles low-pitched sounds is called a woofer. The speaker that handles high-pitched sounds is called a tweeter. Why might this be so?

2. With an adult's permission, look at a sound system in your school, home, or family car. What size and shape are the speakers? How do they sound?

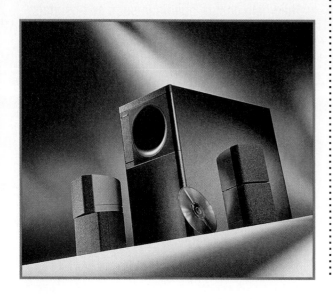

Sounds of Water Glasses

How do water glasses make sounds with different pitches?

Materials

- 4 or 5 identical water glasses
- water
- metal spoon

Procedure

1. Put a different amount of water in each glass.

2. Predict which glass will have the highest pitch and which will have the lowest pitch.

3. Tap each glass lightly with the back of the spoon and listen.

Draw Conclusions

Were your predictions correct? What relationship did you observe between pitch and water level?

Sounds and Matter

Can you hear sounds through a solid, a liquid, and a gas?

Materials

- tuning fork
- board eraser
- metric ruler
- balloon
- water

Procedure

1. **Listen to a sound through a gas.** Hold the tuning fork about 20 cm from one ear. Strike the fork with the eraser.

2. **Listen to a sound through a solid.** Place one ear on a desk. Cover your other ear with your hand. Have a partner strike the tuning fork with the eraser, and hold the base of the tuning fork against the desktop about 20 cm from your ear.

3. **Listen to a sound through a liquid.** Fill the balloon with water until it is about 20 cm long. Place one end of the balloon against your ear. Cover your other ear with your hand. Have your partner strike the tuning fork and hold its base against the opposite end of the balloon.

Draw Conclusions

Was the tuning fork loudest when you heard it through the air, through the water, or through the desk? Explain.

Vocabulary Review

Use the terms below to complete the sentences. The numbers in ( ) tell you where to look in the chapter if you need help.

sounds (E62)   **pitch** (E69)

sound waves (E63)   **speed of sound** (E74)

compression (E63)   **echo** (E76)

loudness (E68)   **sonic boom** (E78)

1. The _____ of a sound describes how high or low a sound is.

2. Moving areas of high and low pressure that carry sound are _____.

3. Vibrations that you hear are _____.

4. The amount of sound energy reaching your ears is _____.

5. A reflection of sound is an _____.

6. How fast sound moves is the _____.

7. The sound of a shock wave produced by an object moving faster than the speed of sound is a _____.

8. A _____ is a place where particles are squeezed closer together by a sound wave.

Connect Concepts

Use the terms in the Word Bank to complete the diagram.

pitch   **sound wave**   **sound**   **echo**

loudness   **vibrates**   **reflect**

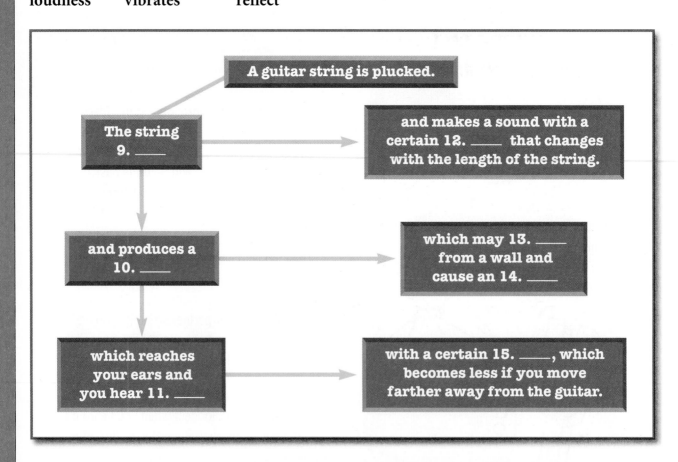

A guitar string is plucked.

The string 9. _____

and makes a sound with a certain 12. _____ that changes with the length of the string.

and produces a 10. _____

which may 13. _____ from a wall and cause an 14. _____.

which reaches your ears and you hear 11. _____

with a certain 15. _____, which becomes less if you move farther away from the guitar.

Check Understanding

Write the letter of the best choice.

16. Sound waves cannot travel through —
    - A a solid
    - B gases
    - C empty space
    - D liquids

17. What we hear as pitch is related mostly to —
    - F reflection
    - G how far away the source of the sound is
    - H the speed of sound
    - J how fast the source of the sound is moving back and forth

18. You can make the sound louder if you pluck a guitar string by —
    - A moving the string farther before letting go
    - B stopping the string when it starts to move
    - C shortening the string
    - D lengthening the string

19. A sound wave has areas called _____ where particles are squeezed together.
    - F echoes
    - G compressions
    - H sonic booms
    - J pitches

20. A _____ reflects sound best.
    - A hard, smooth surface
    - B rough, uneven surface
    - C soft, white wall
    - D very hot gas

21. You are more likely to hear an echo when standing —
    - F close to a short wall
    - G facing a tall, smooth wall
    - H in a large, open field
    - J in a very small room

22. A _____ is the sound you hear when something is moving faster than the speed of sound.
    - A vibration
    - B pitch wave
    - C high pitch
    - D sonic boom

Critical Thinking

23. Explain how the vibrations you cause by hitting a drum move from the drum to your brain, where they are interpreted as sound.

24. How does a sonic boom form?

Process Skills Review

25. What features would you use to describe a sound that you **observed**?

26. What is the difference between **observing** a vibration and **inferring** how the vibration affects air particles?

27. Why do scientists sometimes use drawings to **record** the **data** they **gather**?

Performance Assessment

Sound Vibrations

Strike a tuning fork. After you hear the sound of the fork, place its base on a tabletop. Observe and report what happens. Explain your observations in terms of vibrations and sound waves. You may use a drawing as part of your explanation.

Electricity and Magnetism

Snap! Crackle! Pop! Your socks crackle and spark when you separate them from your freshly dried sweater! This kind of electricity is called static electricity. You can become charged with static electricity just by dragging your feet when you walk across carpet. Then *ZAP!* you'll get a "charge" out of opening the next door you come to!

Vocabulary Preview

charge
static electricity
electric field
electric current
circuit
electric cell
conductor
insulator
resistor
series circuit
parallel circuit
magnet
magnetic pole
magnetic field
electromagnet

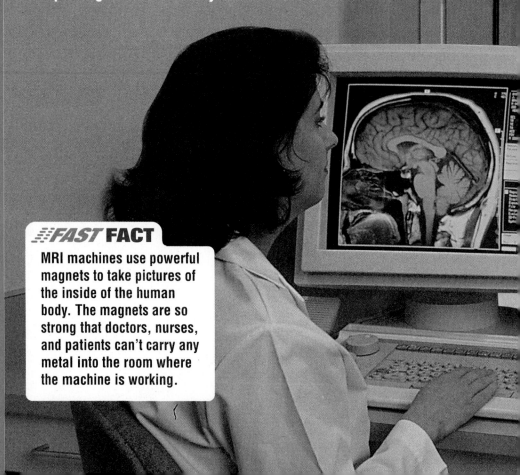

FAST FACT

MRI machines use powerful magnets to take pictures of the inside of the human body. The magnets are so strong that doctors, nurses, and patients can't carry any metal into the room where the machine is working.

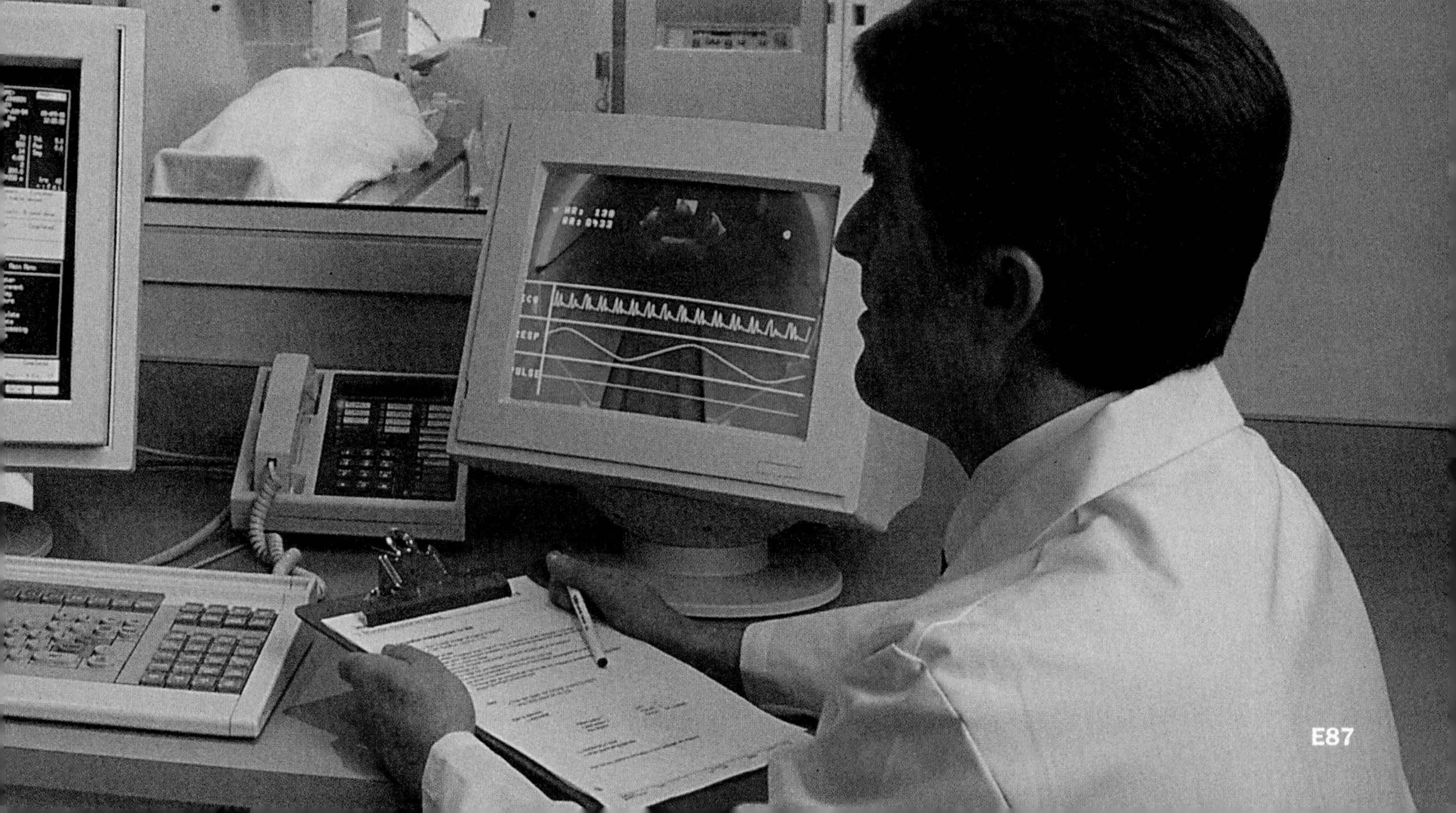

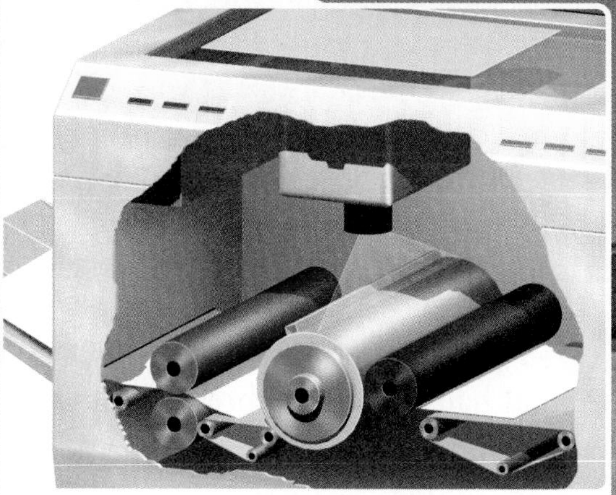

Photocopiers make images by using static electricity! A large charged drum inside a photocopier pulls powdered ink to it. The ink goes to wherever dark spots on the original are reflected on the drum. The powder pattern is put on a piece of paper. Then the paper is heated and the ink melts, making a permanent copy.

Electricity use is measured in kilowatt-hours. Every home has a meter that measures how many kilowatt-hours have been used. A 60-watt light bulb uses 0.06 kilowatt-hours in one hour. Here's a list of the number of kilowatt-hours different appliances use in an hour:

Electricity Use

Appliance	Kilowatt-Hours Used in One Hour
Color television	0.23
Toaster	1.2
Hair dryer	1.5
Microwave oven	1.5
Clothes dryer	4.0
Refrigerator/freezer	5.0–7.0

LESSON 1

What Is Static Electricity?

In this lesson, you can . . .

INVESTIGATE rubbing balloons with different materials.

LEARN ABOUT causes of static electricity.

LINK to math, writing, health, and technology.

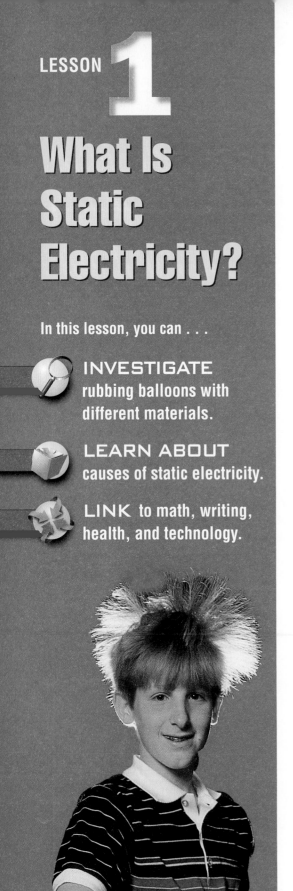

◀ It's not the wind that's making this boy's hair stand on end. It's static electricity. You may be surprised to learn what else static electricity can do.

Balloons Rubbed with Different Materials

Activity Purpose Have you ever opened a package that had something breakable inside? There may have been little foam pieces in the box, and you may have noticed the strange way they acted. They jumped away from each other but stuck to almost everything else. You can make balloons act this way, too. In this investigation you will rub balloons with different materials. Then you'll **compare** your **observations** to **infer** why the balloons behaved the way they did.

Materials

- two small, round balloons
- string
- tape
- scrap of silk cloth
- scrap of wool cloth
- paper towel
- plastic wrap

Activity Procedure

1 Blow up the balloons, and tie them closed. Use string and tape to hang one balloon from a shelf or table.

2 Rub the silk all over each balloon. Slowly bring the free balloon near the hanging balloon. **Observe** the hanging balloon. **Record** your observations. (Picture A)

Picture A

Picture B

3 Again rub the silk all over the hanging balloon. Move the silk away. Then slowly bring the silk close to the balloon. **Observe** the hanging balloon, and **record** your observations. (Picture B)

4 Repeat Steps 2 and 3 separately with the wool, a paper towel, and plastic wrap. **Record** your **observations.**

5 Rub the silk all over the hanging balloon. Rub the wool all over the free balloon. Slowly bring the free balloon near the hanging balloon. **Observe** the hanging balloon. **Record** your observations.

Draw Conclusions

1. **Compare** your observations of the two balloons in Step 2 with your observations of a balloon and the material it was rubbed with in Steps 3 and 4.

2. **Compare** your observations of the hanging balloon in Step 2 with your observations of it in Step 5.

3. **Scientists at Work** Which of your observations support the **inference** that a force acted on the balloons and materials? Explain your answer.

Investigate Further When you rubbed the balloons, you caused a charge to build up. Like charges repel. Opposite charges attract. Review your results for each trial. Tell whether the balloons or material had like charges or opposite charges.

Process Skill Tip

A force is a push or a pull. You can **infer** a force between two objects by observing whether the objects are pulled toward each other or pushed away from each other.

Static Electricity

Two Kinds of Charge

Remember that matter is made of particles that have mass and volume. Particles of matter also have a property called *electric charge*. A particle can have a positive (+) charge, a negative (−) charge, or no charge at all.

Matter in an object normally has equal numbers of positive and negative particles. It is *neutral*. Rubbing two objects together, however, can move negative particles from one object to the other. In the investigation, rubbing made the number of positive charges different from the number of negative charges. Charge is a measure of the extra positive or negative particles that an object has. Rubbing gave one object an overall *positive charge*, and it gave the other an overall *negative charge*.

The charge that stays on an object is called static electricity (STAT•ik ee•lek•TRIS•ih•tee). *Static* means "not moving." Even though the charges moved to get there, they stay on the charged object.

✔ **What are the two types of charges?**

FIND OUT

- about a property of matter called charge
- how charges move from one piece of matter to another
- how electric fields cause forces

VOCABULARY

charge
static electricity
electric field

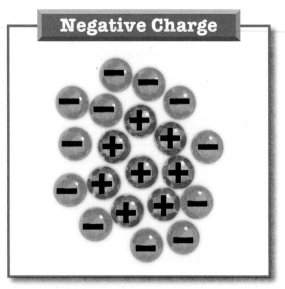

▲ A single positive charge is labeled +. A single negative charge is labeled −. When an object has more positive charges than negative charges, its overall charge is positive.

▲ If an object has more negative charges than positive charges, its overall charge is negative. How many extra negative charges are shown here?

Separating Charges

Most of the time, you, a balloon, and a doorknob have neither an overall negative charge nor an overall positive charge. You and the objects are neutral. To see the effects of forces between charges, you must separate negative charges from positive charges.

Only the negative charges move. When you rubbed the balloons, only the negative particles were pulled away. Combing dry hair is another example of separating charges. As you comb, the teeth of the comb rub negative charges from your hair. The comb gets extra negative charges, so it has an overall negative charge. Your hair loses some negative charges. It now has an overall positive charge.

✔ **Which kind of charge moves to make a static charge?**

As clothes tumble in a dryer, different fabrics rub against each other. Negative charges move from one piece of clothing to another. When this happens the clothes stick together. ▼

▲ If you hold a piece of wool next to a balloon, nothing happens. So you know that neither the wool nor the balloon is charged. The numbers of positive and negative charges on the balloon are equal. The charges are also equal on the wool. Both items have a neutral charge.

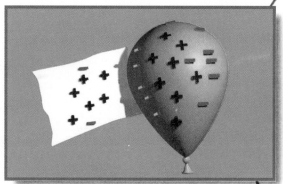

▲ Rubbing wool on a balloon separates charges. Negative charges move from the wool to the balloon. The balloon now has more negative charges than positive charges. The balloon is negatively charged. The wool loses negative charges. Now it has more positive charges than negative charges. It is positively charged.

E91

Electric Forces

In the investigation you saw how a charged balloon pushed or pulled another charged balloon. The push or pull between objects with different charges is an *electric force*. The electric force causes two objects with opposite charges to *attract*, or pull, each other. The electric force also causes two objects with like charges to *repel* (rih•PEL), or push away from, each other.

The space where electric forces occur around an object is called an **electric field**. The electric field of a positive charge attracts a nearby negative charge. The electric field of a positive charge repels a nearby positive charge.

In diagrams, arrows are used to show an electric field. They point the way one positive charge would be pulled by the field. The pictures here show the electric fields of two pairs of balloons. One pair has opposite charges. The other pair has the same charges.

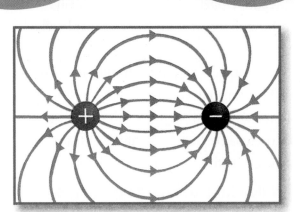

▲ One balloon has a positive charge. The other has a negative charge. Their electric fields form a closed pattern of field lines. Balloons with opposite charges attract each other.

✔ **What is an electric field?**

Both balloons have negative charges. Their electric fields do not form a closed pattern of field lines. Balloons with the same type of charge repel each other.

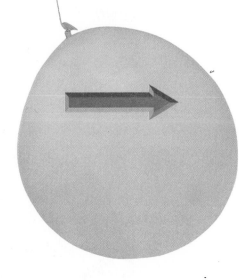

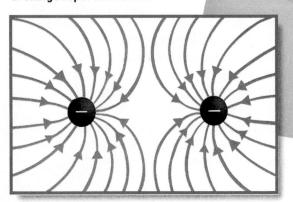

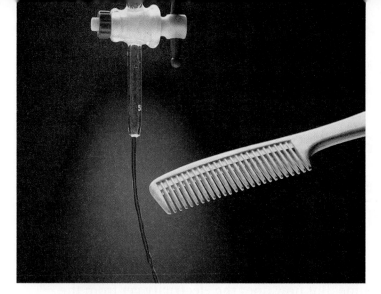

▲ After you comb your hair, your comb has a negative charge. Its electric field repels the negative particles in the stream of water. Negative particles are pushed to the opposite side of the stream. That leaves extra positive charges on the side near the comb. The stream bends toward the comb.

Summary

Objects become electrically charged when they gain or lose negative charges. A charge causes an electric field. The electric fields of charged objects interact to produce electric forces. Objects with like charges repel each other. Objects with unlike charges attract each other.

Review

1. What is static electricity?
2. What is charge?
3. What is an electric field?
4. **Critical Thinking** How can you make a piece of rubber that has an overall positive charge neutral again?
5. **Test Prep** A plastic ruler can get a positive charge by —
   A gaining a single negative charge
   B losing a single negative charge
   C gaining a single positive charge
   D losing a single positive charge

LINKS

MATH LINK

Charge Count The two pictures on page E90 show charges. How many single negative charges must each object gain or lose to become neutral? Use numbers and math symbols to show how you found your answer.

WRITING LINK

Informative Writing—Description Suppose you are a balloon. Write a paragraph for a classmate describing what happens to you as you gain a negative charge from a piece of wool.

HEALTH LINK

Lightning Safety Lightning is a big movement of charged particles. It can kill people and animals, and it can start fires. Find out the safety rules you should follow during a thunderstorm. Make a poster illustrating the rules.

TECHNOLOGY LINK

Learn more about early use of electricity by visiting the National Museum of American History Internet site.
www.si.edu/harcourt/science

 Smithsonian Institution®

What Is an Electric Current?

In this lesson, you can . . .

 INVESTIGATE using a battery to light a bulb.

 LEARN ABOUT electric current.

 LINK to math, writing, social studies, and technology.

 **INVESTIGATE**

Making a Bulb Light Up

Activity Purpose Can a flashlight work without batteries? You would be right if you said *no*. The batteries produce the electricity that makes the bulb shine. But how does the electricity get from the batteries to the bulb? You can **plan and conduct a simple investigation** to find out how materials need to be arranged to make a bulb light.

Materials

- D-cell battery
- insulated electrical wire
- miniature light bulb
- masking tape

Activity Procedure

1. Make a chart like the one shown on the next page. You will use it to **record** your **observations**.

2. **Predict** a way to arrange the materials you have been given so that the bulb lights up. Make a drawing to **record** your prediction. (Picture A)

3. Test your prediction. **Record** whether or not the bulb lights up. (Picture B)

◀ The lights of a Ferris wheel shine in the night as the wheel goes round and round. The electricity that makes the bulbs glow and moves the wheel also goes round and round.

Picture A

Picture B

Predictions and Observations

Arrangement of Bulb, Battery, and Wire	Drawing	Observations

4 Continue to work with the bulb, the battery, and the wire. Try different arrangements to get the bulb to light. **Record** the results of each try.

Draw Conclusions

1. What did you **observe** about the arrangement of materials when the bulb lighted?

2. What did you **observe** about the arrangement of materials when the bulb did NOT light?

3. **Scientists at Work** To find out more about bulbs and batteries, you could **plan and conduct an investigation** of your own. To do that, you need to decide the following: What question do you want to answer? What materials will you need? How will you use the materials? What will you observe?

Investigate Further **Plan and conduct your investigation.**

Electric Currents

Moving Charges

You know that a static charge stays on an object. But even a static charge will move if it has a path to follow. The snap and crackle of a static electric shock are the result of a moving charge.

Have you ever gotten a small electric shock from touching a doorknob? Here's how it happens. Walking on a carpet rubs negative charges off the carpet and onto your feet. The charges spread out on your body. Your whole body becomes negatively charged. When you touch the doorknob, all the extra negative charges move at once from your hand to the doorknob. You get a small "zap." The static, or unmoving charge, has become a *current*, or moving charge. A flow of electric charges is called an **electric current**.

In the investigation you arranged a wire, a bulb, and a battery to make a path in which negative charges could flow. A path that is made for an electric current is called a **circuit** (SER•kit). The battery was an important part of the circuit you made. A battery is an **electric cell**, which supplies energy to move charges through a circuit.

✔ **What does an electric current need in order to flow?**

FIND OUT

• how electric charges can move

• ways different materials control electric current

• differences between series and parallel circuits

VOCABULARY

electric current
circuit
electric cell
conductor
insulator
resistor
series circuit
parallel circuit

◀ An electric current in a circuit moves like a bike wheel. When you pedal, you give energy of motion to the whole wheel at once. When you connect a circuit, a battery moves energy to all parts of the circuit at the same time.

◀ Use your finger to trace the path of the current through each part of the circuit. What do you notice?

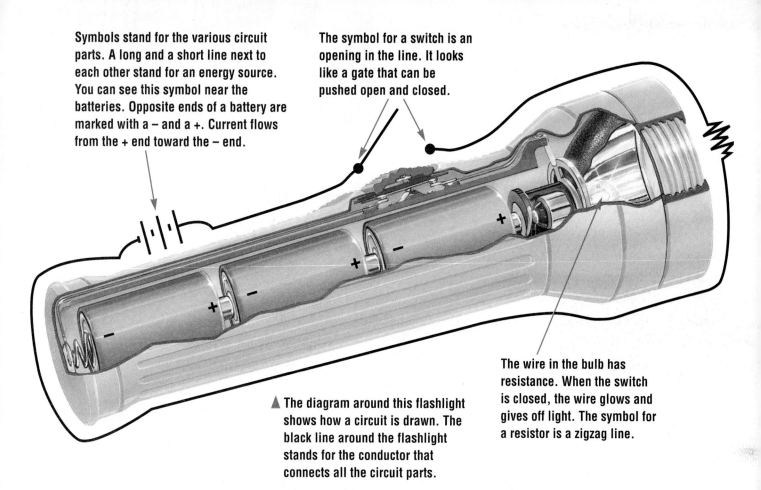

Symbols stand for the various circuit parts. A long and a short line next to each other stand for an energy source. You can see this symbol near the batteries. Opposite ends of a battery are marked with a − and a +. Current flows from the + end toward the − end.

The symbol for a switch is an opening in the line. It looks like a gate that can be pushed open and closed.

The diagram around this flashlight shows how a circuit is drawn. The black line around the flashlight stands for the conductor that connects all the circuit parts.

The wire in the bulb has resistance. When the switch is closed, the wire glows and gives off light. The symbol for a resistor is a zigzag line.

Controlling Current

A circuit with a battery, bulb, and wires contains different materials such as copper and plastic. You can classify these materials by the way they control the flow of charges through them.

A **conductor** is a material that current can pass through easily. Most metals are good conductors of electric current. Electric wires are made of metal, often copper. The base of a light bulb is made of metal because it must conduct an electric current.

A material that current cannot pass through easily is called an **insulator** (IN•suh•layt•er). The black band between the metal tip and the screw-in part of a light bulb is an insulator. A plastic covering insulated the wire you used in the investigation. Plastic keeps the metal of the wire from touching other metal.

A flashlight has a switch to turn it on and off. A *switch* uses conductors and insulators to make and break a circuit. When the switch is on, two conductors touch. When they touch, the path is complete. Current flows through the circuit. When the switch is off, air separates the two conductors, breaking the path. No current can flow.

Some materials cut down, or resist, the flow of charges. A material that resists but doesn't stop the flow of current is called a **resistor** (rih•ZIS•ter). A flashlight bulb contains a tiny coil of metal. The coil is a resistor. As charges move through the resistor, they transfer thermal energy to it. The metal becomes hot. The glowing coil transfers some of its thermal energy to the air as radiation. It gives off light.

✔ **What does a switch do in a circuit?**

Series and Parallel Circuits

When you turn on a flashlight, there is one path for the current to follow through the circuit. A circuit that has only one path for the current is called a **series circuit**. The pictures below show a series circuit. Note that the current runs from the battery to one bulb, then to the next bulb, and then back to the battery. What happens if you remove one bulb or a bulb burns out? The single path is broken. No current moves through the circuit. The second bulb will go out.

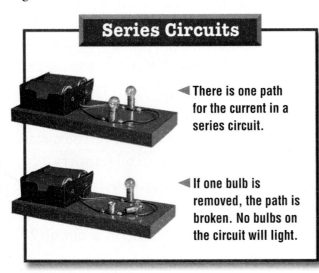

Series Circuits

◄ There is one path for the current in a series circuit.

◄ If one bulb is removed, the path is broken. No bulbs on the circuit will light.

Parallel Circuits

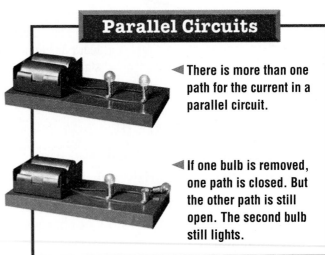

◄ There is more than one path for the current in a parallel circuit.

◄ If one bulb is removed, one path is closed. But the other path is still open. The second bulb still lights.

A **parallel** (PAIR•uh•lel) **circuit** has more than one path for current to travel. With your finger, trace the path of the current in the parallel circuit shown above. Part of the current moves through each path of the circuit. What happens when a bulb is removed from this circuit? The current still moves through the other path. The second bulb stays lit. If one bulb in a parallel circuit burns out, the other bulbs will stay on.

✔ **Which type of circuit has more than one path for current?**

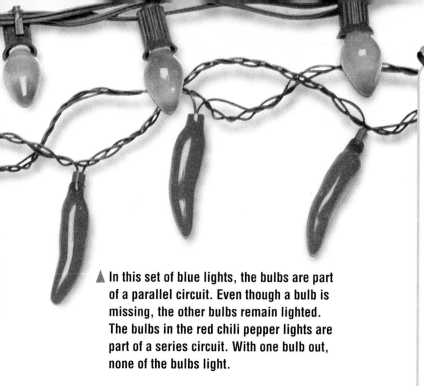

▲ In this set of blue lights, the bulbs are part of a parallel circuit. Even though a bulb is missing, the other bulbs remain lighted. The bulbs in the red chili pepper lights are part of a series circuit. With one bulb out, none of the bulbs light.

Summary

Electric current is a flow of charges through a path called a circuit. A material in a circuit can be classified as a conductor, an insulator, or a resistor. If a circuit has one path for current, it is a series circuit. A parallel circuit has more than one path for current.

Review

1. What is an electric current?

2. Describe what has to be in place for a circuit to work.

3. Contrast conductors and insulators.

4. **Critical Thinking** Most wall outlets in your home have places for two plugs. Infer which type of circuit an outlet is part of. How do you know?

5. **Test Prep** What supplies energy in an electric circuit?

   A conductors

   B electric cells

   C resistors

   D switches

LINKS

MATH LINK

Current Costs Electric energy is measured in a unit called a kilowatt-hour, or kWh. Suppose a utility company charges 10 cents for each kWh of energy. A family uses 900 kWh of energy a month. How much does the energy cost?

WRITING LINK

Informative Writing—Compare and Contrast Write a paragraph for a younger student explaining why it would be easier to decorate a home with strings of lights in a parallel circuit instead of strings of lights in a series circuit.

SOCIAL STUDIES LINK

Inventing the Light Bulb The invention of the first practical electric light bulb is a good example of not giving up. Research the story of the light bulb's invention. When was it invented? Who invented it? How many materials were tried and set aside before a light bulb that worked well was made?

TECHNOLOGY LINK

Learn more about controlling large circuits by viewing *L.A. Traffic Control* on the **Harcourt Science Newsroom Video.**

INVESTIGATE

What Is a Magnet?

In this lesson, you can . . .

 INVESTIGATE how a compass works.

 LEARN ABOUT the ways magnets interact.

 LINK to math, writing, social studies, and technology.

A Compass

Activity Purpose If you are like most people, you have papers stuck with magnets to your refrigerator. A *magnet* is an object that attracts certain materials, mainly iron and steel. The material in your refrigerator magnet attracts the steel in your refrigerator door. The attraction is strong enough that it works through paper. In this investigation you will make your own magnet and, based on your **observations, infer** how a compass works.

Materials

- safety goggles
- small bar magnet
- small objects made of iron or steel, such as paper clips
- large sewing needle or straight pin (4–5 cm long)
- small piece of cork
- glue
- cup of water

CAUTION

Activity Procedure

1 **CAUTION** **Put on your safety goggles.** Hold the bar magnet near a paper clip. **Observe** what happens. Now hold the needle near the paper clip. Observe what happens.

2 **CAUTION** **Be careful with sharp objects.** Hold the needle by its eye and drag its entire length over the magnet 20 times, always in the same direction. (Picture A)

◀ The compass is an important tool that helps sailors find their way across the oceans.

Picture A

Picture B

3. Repeat Step 1. **Observe** what happens.

4. Hold the needle on top of the cork. Then check to be sure that the needle will be parallel to the surface of the water when the cork floats. Glue the needle to the top of the cork. (Picture B)

5. Move the bar magnet at least a meter from the cup. Float the cork in the water. **Observe** what happens to the needle.

6. Carefully and slowly turn the cup. **Observe** what happens to the needle.

7. Hold one end of the bar magnet near the cup. **Observe** what happens to the needle. Switch magnet ends. What happens?

Draw Conclusions

1. Describe what happened when you floated the cork with the needle in water. What happened when you turned the cup?

2. What happened when you brought the bar magnet near the floating needle?

3. **Scientists at Work** What **hypothesis** can you make based on your observations of the needle? What predictions can you make by using your hypothesis?

Investigate Further **Plan and carry out a simple investigation** to test one of your predictions from Question 3, above.

Process Skill Tip

When you **hypothesize**, you carefully explain all your observations. A hypothesis is more detailed than an inference. Unlike an inference, a hypothesis can be used to make predictions that you can test.

Magnets

Two Poles

FIND OUT

- about magnetic poles
- how magnetic fields cause magnetic forces
- how to use Earth's magnetic field to find directions

VOCABULARY

magnet
magnetic pole
magnetic field

In the investigation you made a needle into a magnet. You could tell it was a magnet because it attracted metal paper clips, just as other magnets do. A **magnet** is an object that attracts certain materials, usually objects made of iron or steel. A needle isn't a natural magnet. You changed it into a magnet by dragging it along the bar magnet.

A magnet has two ends called **magnetic poles**, or just *poles* for short. A magnet's pull is strongest at the poles. If a bar magnet can swing freely, one end, called the *north-seeking pole*, will always point north. The opposite end, called the *south-seeking pole*, will always point south. A magnet's north-seeking pole is usually marked *N*. Its south-seeking pole is marked *S*.

✔ **What is each end of a magnet called?**

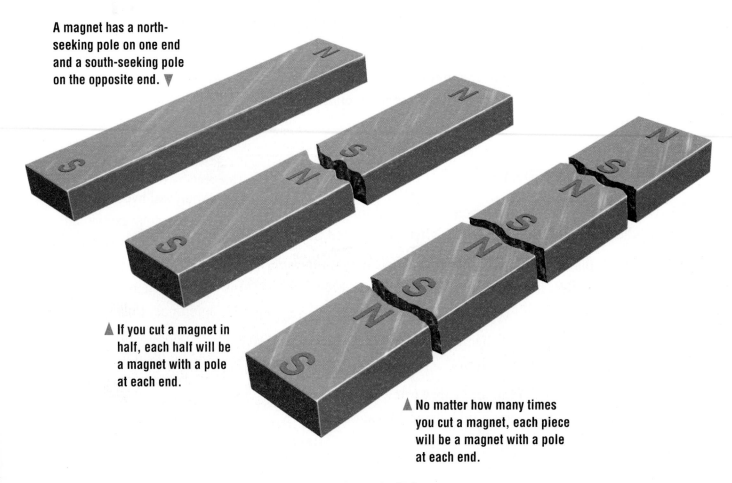

A magnet has a north-seeking pole on one end and a south-seeking pole on the opposite end. ▼

▲ If you cut a magnet in half, each half will be a magnet with a pole at each end.

▲ No matter how many times you cut a magnet, each piece will be a magnet with a pole at each end.

Magnetic Forces

If you've ever played with magnets, you've probably felt them pull toward each other. At other times they seem to push away from each other. The forces you felt are magnetic forces caused by magnetic fields.

A **magnetic field** is the space all around a magnet where the force of the magnet can act. You can't see the field. However, a magnet can move iron filings into lines. The pattern made by the iron filings shows the shape of the magnet's field.

Forces between magnet poles are like forces between electric charges. Opposite magnetic poles attract, and like poles repel. If the N pole of one magnet is held toward the S pole of another magnet, their fields form a closed pattern. This closed pattern of lines shows a force that pulls the magnets together.

If two magnets are held with their N poles near each other, their magnetic fields form an open pattern of lines. Just as with electric charges, this pattern shows a force that pushes the magnets away from each other.

✔ **Where is the pull of a magnet strongest?**

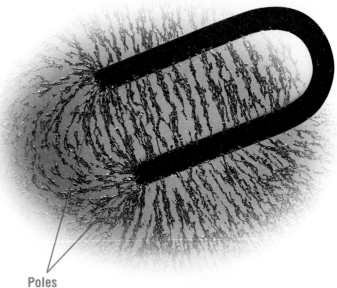

Poles

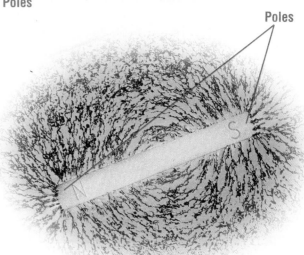

Poles

▲ The shape of a magnetic field depends on the shape of the magnet. The bunching of iron filings on the end of a magnet shows that the magnetic force is strongest at a magnet's poles.

▲ Opposite poles of two magnets attract. The pattern of iron filings is closed. This shows a magnetic force that attracts, or pulls, the magnets together.

▲ Like poles of two magnets repel. The field lines are open, showing lines of force that push the magnets apart.

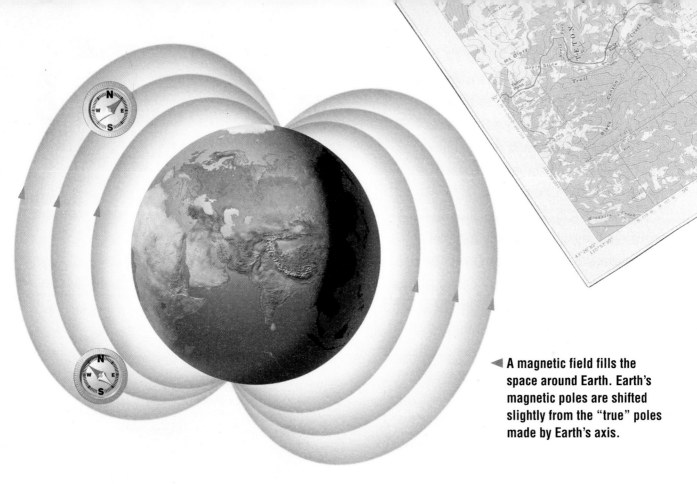

◀ A magnetic field fills the space around Earth. Earth's magnetic poles are shifted slightly from the "true" poles made by Earth's axis.

Compasses

The north-seeking and south-seeking property of magnets is useful. For hundreds of years, people have used magnets to find direction. The first magnets used were made of a heavy natural material called *lodestone*. Today geologists know this material as the mineral magnetite.

A compass today uses a lightweight magnetic needle that is free to turn. This is much like the needle you made into a magnet in the investigation. A compass needle points along an imaginary line connecting the North and South Poles. This is because Earth is like a giant magnet.

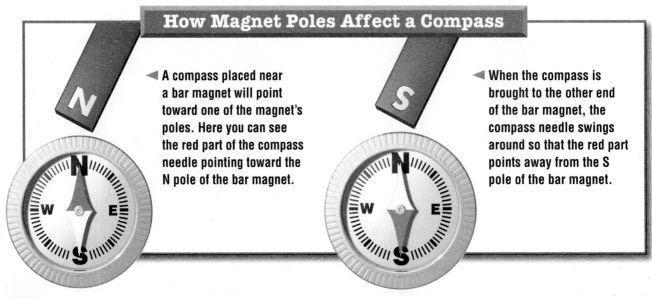

How Magnet Poles Affect a Compass

◀ A compass placed near a bar magnet will point toward one of the magnet's poles. Here you can see the red part of the compass needle pointing toward the N pole of the bar magnet.

◀ When the compass is brought to the other end of the bar magnet, the compass needle swings around so that the red part points away from the S pole of the bar magnet.

◀ When there are no landmarks you know, a map and a compass can help you find your way.

The field lines of Earth's magnetic field come together close to the planet's North and South Poles. This pattern is like the one shown by the iron filings around the bar magnet on page E103. Indeed, Earth's magnetic field is like the field of a giant bar magnet.

✔ **How does a compass work?**

Summary

Magnets are objects that attract materials such as iron. Every magnet has two magnetic poles. Magnetic forces are caused by the interaction of magnetic fields. Earth's magnetic field is like the field of a bar magnet. A compass needle interacts with Earth's magnetic field.

Review

1. How can you find the poles of a magnet?
2. What is a magnetic field?
3. Which type of magnet has a field that is about the same shape as Earth's magnetic field?
4. **Critical Thinking** Describe the field lines formed if the south poles of two magnets are brought close together.
5. **Test Prep** How many poles does a magnet have?

   A none

   B one

   C two

   D four

LINKS

MATH LINK

Magnet Strengths Decide on a way to measure the strength of different bar magnets or different magnet shapes. Test some magnets. Then use a computer program such as *Graph Links* to make a bar graph to show what you measured.

WRITING LINK

Informative Writing—How-to Write a paragraph telling a classmate how to use a compass to find the direction in which he or she is traveling.

SOCIAL STUDIES LINK

Earth's Moving Magnetic Poles Earth's north magnetic pole is constantly moving. Find out how the pole's location is shown on topographical (tahp•uh•GRAF•ih•kuhl) maps, which show the land's surface features, and on navigational charts. Find the current location of the north magnetic pole on a globe. Measure the distance between the true North Pole and the magnetic north pole.

TECHNOLOGY LINK

Learn more about Earth's magnetic field by visiting the National Air and Space Museum Internet site.
www.si.edu/harcourt/science

Smithsonian Institution®

LESSON 4

What Is an Electro- magnet?

In this lesson, you can . . .

INVESTIGATE the magnetic field around a wire that carries current.

LEARN ABOUT uses of electromagnets.

LINK to math, writing, language arts, and technology.

Strong magnetic forces lift this train slightly from the tracks and push it forward. ▽

INVESTIGATE

How Magnets and Electricity Can Interact

Activity Purpose The pictures at the bottom of page E104 show how a bar magnet affects a nearby compass. Have you ever tried this yourself? In this investigation you will **observe** how a bar magnet affects a compass needle. You'll **compare** it with the way a current in a wire affects a compass needle. You can then **infer** some things about electricity moving through wires.

Materials

- bar magnet
- small compass
- sheet of cardboard
- tape
- insulated wire, about 30 cm long, with stripped ends
- D-cell battery

Activity Procedure

1. Try several positions of the magnet and compass. **Record** your **observations** of how the magnet affects the compass needle.

2. Place the compass flat on the cardboard so the needle is lined up with north. Tape the middle third of the insulated wire onto the cardboard in a north-south line.

3. Tape one end of the wire to the flat end of a D-cell battery. Tape the battery to the cardboard. (Picture A)

4. Without moving the cardboard, put the compass on the taped-down part of the wire.

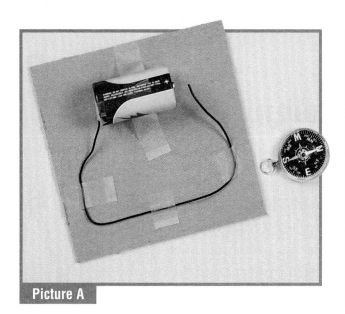

Picture A

Picture B

5) Touch the free end of the wire to the (+) end of the battery for a few seconds. (Picture B) **Observe** the compass needle. Repeat this step several more times. **Record** your observations.

6) Carefully remove the taped wire. Place the compass underneath the wire so that both line up along a north-south line. **Predict** what will happen if you repeat Step 5.

7) Repeat Step 5. **Record** your observations.

Draw Conclusions

1. **Compare** your observations in Step 5 with those in Step 7. Was your prediction accurate? Explain.

2. Using what you know about compasses in magnetic fields, what can you **infer** about currents in wires?

3. **Scientists at Work** Just as you predicted what would happen in Step 7, scientists often **predict** the outcome of an experiment based on their observations and inferences. Based on your observations, what would you predict will happen in this experiment if the current is made to move in the opposite direction?

Investigate Further Test your **prediction**. Remove the battery from the cardboard. Turn it so that its ends are pointing in the opposite direction. Attach the wire again. **Record** your **observations**.

> ### Process Skill Tip
>
> When you **predict**, you tell what you expect to happen. A prediction is based on patterns of observations. If you think you know the cause of an event, you can predict when it will happen again. Predictions aren't always correct.

Electromagnets

Currents Make Magnets

In the past, scientists wondered if electric charge and magnetism were related. They knew that charged objects and magnets both produce a force that can pull or push without touching. The discovery that an electric current can turn a compass needle proved that the two forces are related.

A current in a wire produces a magnetic field around the wire. You saw evidence of this in the investigation. The magnetic field produced by current moved the compass needle.

If you could see them, the field lines around a wire that carries current would look different from those around a bar magnet. They circle around the wire instead of looping out from the wire ends. A compass needle moves to point along magnetic field lines. So, it moves to point at right angles to the wire.

FIND OUT

- how electricity and magnetism are related
- ways to change the strength of an electromagnet
- uses of motors and generators

VOCABULARY

electromagnet

When current flows in the wire, it produces a circular magnetic field. The compass needle lines up with the field lines by turning at right angles to the wire. ▶

When the switch is open, current no longer flows and the magnetic field goes away. The compass needle swings back to its original position. ▶

This coil of wire is carrying an electric current. Iron filings show the shape of the magnetic field inside the coil. The lines of filings are closest together where the field is strongest. ▶

Compared with bar magnets, current-carrying wires produce weak magnetic fields. But there's a way to put a lot of wire in one place. When a current-carrying wire is coiled, the fields of the loops overlap. The strengths of the fields add up. The more loops you put together, the stronger the field gets.

The fields produced by many wire coils add up to make a field like that of a bar magnet. Iron filings line up along the middle of the coil. Outside the coil, the magnetic field lines loop out from one open end and back to the other.

Alone, a coil of wire easily bends. To make it stiffer and easier to use, the coil is wrapped around a solid material called a *core*. This arrangement of wire wrapped around a core is called an **electromagnet** (ee•LEK•troh•mag•nit). An electromagnet is a temporary magnet. There is a magnetic field only when there is an electric current in the wire.

If the core of an electromagnet is made of iron, the core also becomes a magnet when there is current in the wire. This makes the electromagnet stronger.

✔ **Why is an electromagnet a temporary magnet?**

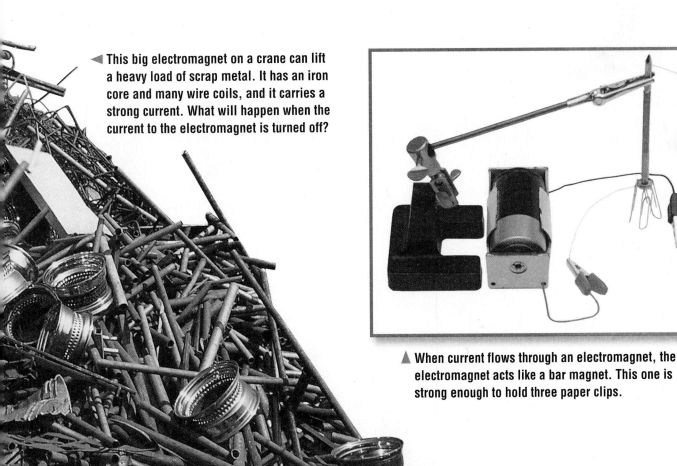

◀ This big electromagnet on a crane can lift a heavy load of scrap metal. It has an iron core and many wire coils, and it carries a strong current. What will happen when the current to the electromagnet is turned off?

▲ When current flows through an electromagnet, the electromagnet acts like a bar magnet. This one is strong enough to hold three paper clips.

Controlling Electromagnets

A magnet and an electromagnet have one main difference. An electromagnet is a temporary magnet. You can turn it on and off with a switch. A bar magnet is a permanent magnet. It doesn't have an *off* switch. Electromagnets are a useful tool because you can control them. You can learn how one is used in The Inside Story.

Turning an electromagnet on and off is one way to control it. You can also control the strength of an electromagnet. One way to do this is to add or remove coils of wire. The more coils an electromagnet has, the stronger it is.

The amount of current also affects the strength of an electromagnet. The more current that is flowing, the stronger the electromagnet is.

Electromagnets today are made to use large amounts of current to lift large amounts of weight. Smaller and weaker ones are also made. Small electromagnets work out of sight inside computer disk drives, video players, television screens, and other electronic devices.

✓ **What is the main difference between a bar magnet and an electromagnet?**

THE INSIDE STORY

Alarm Bell

The bells used in fire alarms, doorbells, and telephones work because electromagnets can be turned off and on very quickly. The picture and diagram on the right show you how an electric bell works.

1. When the bell is turned on, current flows in the electromagnet. The electromagnet pulls the long iron rod into the coils.

2. The hammer is connected to the rod. It moves and strikes the bell, making a sound.

3. The strip of metal with the hammer acts like a switch. As the hammer moves to strike the bell, the switch opens. No current flows in the circuit. The electromagnet is turned off. The hammer returns to its original position.

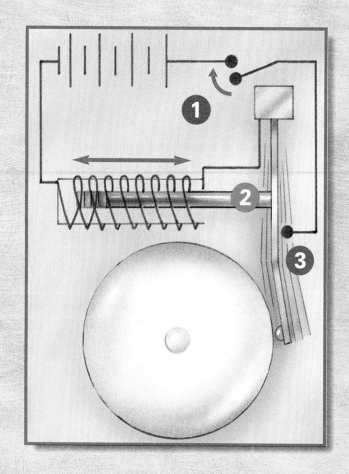

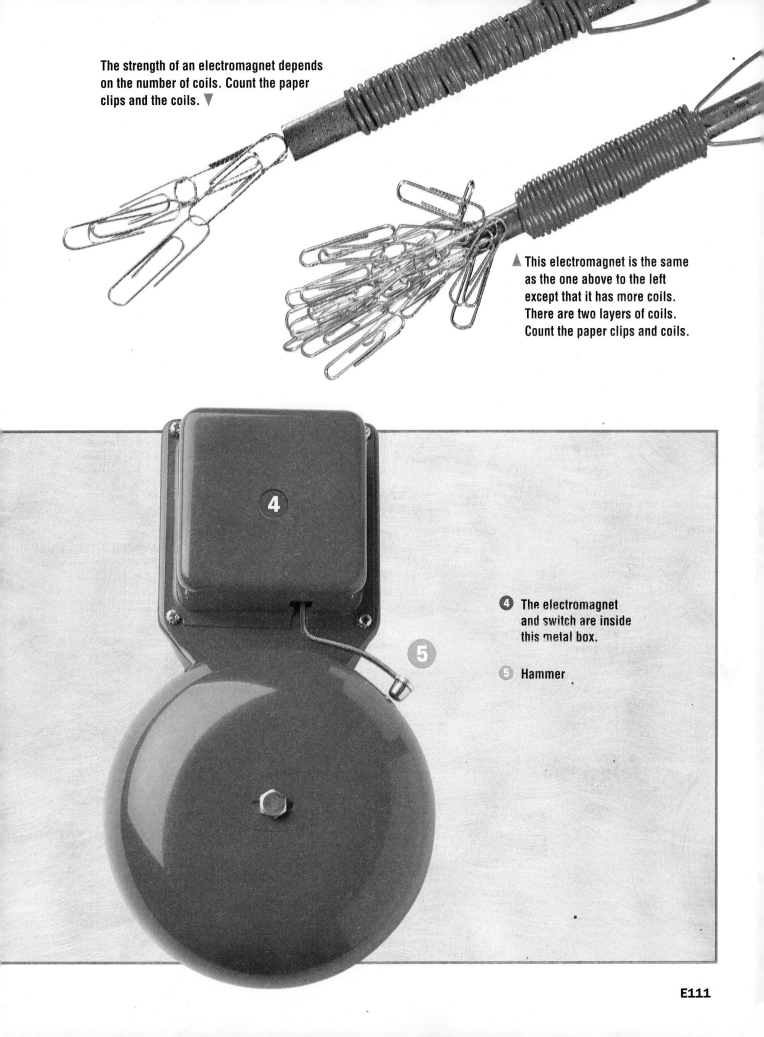

The strength of an electromagnet depends on the number of coils. Count the paper clips and the coils. ▼

▲ This electromagnet is the same as the one above to the left except that it has more coils. There are two layers of coils. Count the paper clips and coils.

④ The electromagnet and switch are inside this metal box.

⑤ Hammer

Motors and Generators

If electricity can produce a magnetic field, can a magnetic field produce electricity? Yes! If you move a coil of wire near a magnet, current flows in the wire. Current flows as long as the wire is moving through magnetic field lines. This is how an electric generator works.

A coil of wire, a magnet, and electricity can also be used to cause motion. That's how an electric motor works. The coil of an electromagnet is pushed and pulled by the poles of other magnets. The coil turns. This turning motion is used in machines such as kitchen appliances, toys, and tools.

✔ **What things do generators and motors have in common?**

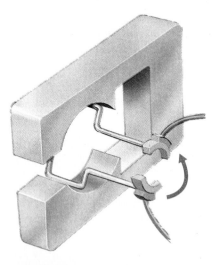

▲ One simple electric motor contains an electromagnet and a permanent magnet. When the motor is on, the direction of current is changed in a pattern. As it changes, the coil is pushed and then pulled by the permanent magnet. The coil turns.

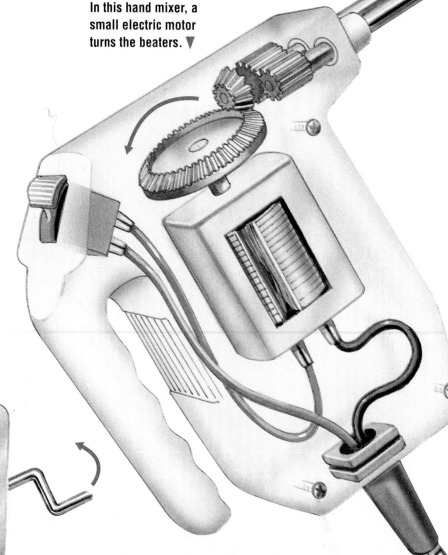

In this hand mixer, a small electric motor turns the beaters. ▼

◄ A small, simple generator uses a hand crank to turn a magnet around a loop of wire. Generators that supply electric power for homes and factories are much bigger, about the size of a bus. They usually use steam or water power to turn a coil.

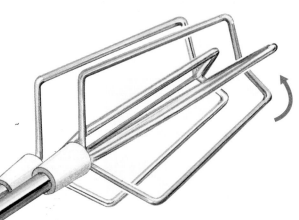

Summary

Wires carrying an electric current become magnets. An electromagnet is a core wrapped with wires that carry current. The ends of the electromagnet coil are its poles. An electromagnet is magnetic only when there is a current in the wire. Generators use electromagnets to produce current from motion. Motors use electromagnets to produce motion from current.

Review

1. What do magnets and electric charges have in common?
2. Name two ways that you can make an electromagnet stronger.
3. What is a motor?
4. **Critical Thinking** Why is it useful to have a magnet that can be turned on and off?
5. **Test Prep** The ends of an electromagnet that are useful are called —
   A cores
   B loops
   C poles
   D wires

LINKS

MATH LINK

Strength of an Electromagnet An electromagnet with 10 loops of wire can pick up 5 paper clips. With 20 loops it can pick up 10 paper clips. Predict how many paper clips the electromagnet can pick up if it has 40 loops. Write a procedure to find out how many paper clips this electromagnet can pick up if you know the number of loops of wire.

WRITING LINK

Informative Writing—Description Think of an appliance in your home that has an electric motor. Write a description for a younger child, telling what the appliance does. If there were no electric motors, how would you do what the appliance does?

LANGUAGE ARTS LINK

Making Words The word *electromagnet* was made by joining two words. What are they? Research these two words to find out where they came from and how old they are. Why do you think this word is used to describe the device you learned about in this lesson?

TECHNOLOGY LINK

Visit the Harcourt Learning Site for related links, activities, and resources.
www.harcourtschool.com

WELCOME TO
THE
LEARNING
SITE

Discovering Electromagnetism

Have you used a computer today? Answered the telephone or the doorbell? Watched television? These are just a few examples of everyday machines that work because of electromagnetism.

The First Discoveries

The early Greeks were the first people to observe and describe static electricity. They noticed that rubbing amber, a yellowish gemstone, with a cloth caused the amber to attract bits of straw or feathers. The Greek word for amber is *elektron*. Our words *electron* and *electricity* come from this Greek word.

The Greeks were also the first to observe and describe magnetism. Thales (THAY•leez), a Greek philosopher, lived in a town called Magnesia. Some of the rocks near his town seemed to pull at the shepherds' walking sticks, which had iron tips. Thales noted that the rocks also pulled toward each other and toward all iron objects that were close to them. These rocks were magnetite, a natural magnet. Later, people in Europe called this natural magnet *lodestone* (LOHD•stohn), which means *leading stone*.

The Chinese may have been the first to use magnets as compasses. Sailors and other travelers found that lodestone always turns to point along a north-south line. Compasses could be made by putting a thin piece of lodestone on a piece of wood floating in

Amber and feathers

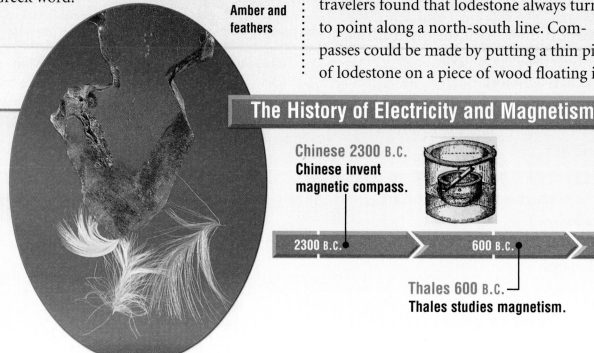

The History of Electricity and Magnetism

Chinese 2300 B.C.
Chinese invent magnetic compass.

2300 B.C.   600 B.C.

Thales 600 B.C.
Thales studies magnetism.

water. Later, lodestone was used to magnetize iron compass needles.

Learning More About Electricity

In the 1700s scientists began experimenting with electricity and magnetism, which they thought might be related. One scientist, Alessandro Volta (ah•leh•SAHN•droh VOHL•tah), discovered that he could make electricity by using pieces of two different metals. He made the first battery, which he called a voltaic (vohl•TAY•ik) pile. Using this battery moved electricity steadily through a conductor, such as a salt solution, instead of giving off the electricity all at once, like a lightning bolt or a spark caused by static electricity.

The key to understanding the connection between electricity and magnetism came from a chance observation. While giving a demonstration for a class, Hans Oersted (HAHNZ ER•stuhd) noticed that when he put a compass over a wire carrying electricity, the compass needle moved. He went on to prove that an electric current always produces a magnetic field.

Other scientists built on Oersted's discovery. Michael Faraday invented a generator, a machine that produces electricity. The generator makes electricity from a moving magnet and a coil of wire.

James Clerk Maxwell also studied Oersted's work. Maxwell hypothesized that electric and magnetic fields work together to make radiant energy, or light. About 20 years after Maxwell's experiments, Heinrich (HYN•rik) Hertz proved Maxwell was right.

Superconductors

In 1911 Dutch scientist Heike Onnes (HY•kuh AW•nuhs) discovered superconductors. At very low temperatures, near ⁻273°C (⁻459°F), these metals or mixtures of metals conduct electrical current without any resistance. Superconductors are part of MRI machines, which are used by doctors to make images of the inside of the human body. In the late 1990s, trains that float above their tracks using superconducting magnets were being built and tested in Japan!

Think About It

1. How did observation and curiosity help Oersted?
2. How has the research of Thales, Volta, Faraday, and others affected your life?

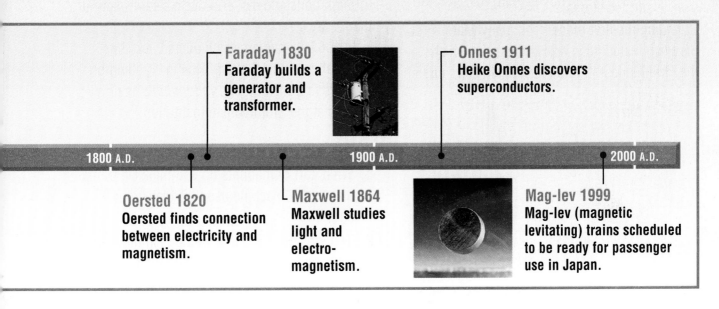

Faraday 1830
Faraday builds a generator and transformer.

Onnes 1911
Heike Onnes discovers superconductors.

1800 A.D.   1900 A.D.   2000 A.D.

Oersted 1820
Oersted finds connection between electricity and magnetism.

Maxwell 1864
Maxwell studies light and electromagnetism.

Mag-lev 1999
Mag-lev (magnetic levitating) trains scheduled to be ready for passenger use in Japan.

Raymond V. Damadian

INVENTOR

"I think the thing that matters is not so much what you are doing but the spirit in which you are doing it."

Dr. Damadian and *Indomitable*

Dr. Raymond Damadian had many interests besides science as he was growing up. He was an accomplished violinist by the time he was eight. He attended The Juilliard School of Music before becoming a doctor. He also was a professional tennis player.

Dr. Damadian and his co-workers invented the magnetic resonance imaging machine (MRI). An MRI machine uses very strong magnets to take pictures of the inside of the body. When certain atoms are in a strong magnetic field, they can be made to put out radio waves. Healthy cells and cancerous cells give off different radio waves. This allows doctors to detect cancer.

Damadian spent eight years building the first MRI machine, which he named *Indomitable.* The project had little money. He and the others working with him often had to buy equipment at electronics surplus stores.

Testing the first model took many years. First, the team tested mice who had cancer. Finally, they tried to test it on Damadian himself, but he

was too big for the machine! They found a smaller man to test the machine, and produced the first human body MRI scan in 1977.

MRI has many good qualities. It is safer than many other tests. No surgery is needed. A patient gets no dangerous radiation. MRI "sees" through bone and can produce a clearer picture than X rays.

In 1989 Damadian was inducted into the National Inventors Hall of Fame in Washington, D.C. His first MRI model, *Indomitable*, is now housed at the Smithsonian Institution.

THINK ABOUT IT

1. What sort of magnets do you think Dr. Damadian's MRI machine used? Explain your answer.

2. Why do you think new methods in medicine must be tested on animals and then on humans?

MRI machine

Make an Electroscope

How can you use an electroscope to measure a charge?

Materials

- scissors
- cardboard
- small glass jar
- stiff, thin wire
- tape
- thin gum-wrapper foil
- aluminum foil
- plastic pen
- scrap of silk

Procedure

1. Cut a disk from the cardboard to cover the mouth of the jar. Bend one end of the wire at a right angle, and push it through the cardboard disk. Tape the wire in place.

2. Fold the gum-wrapper foil in half. Tape it over the bent end of the wire. Put the wire into the jar, and tape the disk in place.

3. Crumple a piece of aluminum foil into a ball. Place the ball on the top of the wire.

4. Rub the plastic pen with the silk.

5. Hold the pen close to the aluminum-foil ball. Test other charged items by holding them near the ball.

Draw Conclusions

Explain what happened to the gum-wrapper foil.

Make a Generator

How can you use a magnet to produce a current?

Materials

- bar magnet
- tape
- cardboard
- compass
- insulated wire, 100 cm with ends stripped

Procedure

1. Wrap 20 loops of the wire loosely around the bar magnet. Twist the stripped ends of the wire tightly together.

2. Tape a length of the unlooped section of wire to the cardboard. Tape the compass over the wire so the needle lines up with the wire.

3. Move the magnet back and forth inside the loops of wire. Observe what happens to the compass needle.

Draw Conclusions

Describe how the compass needle behaves. Explain why this happened.

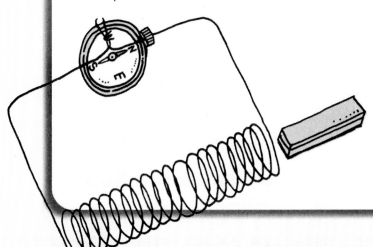

Vocabulary Review

Use the terms below to complete the sentences. The page numbers in ( ) tell you where to look in the chapter if you need help.

charge (E90)
static electricity (E90)
electric fields (E92)
electric current (E96)
circuit (E96)
electric cell (E96)
conductor (E97)
insulator (E97)

resistor (E97)
series circuit (E98)
parallel circuit (E98)
magnet (E102)
magnetic pole (E102)
magnetic fields (E103)
electromagnet (E109)

1. A pathway for current is called a ____.

2. ____ and ____ are similar because they are both areas where forces can act without objects touching.

3. Current passes easily through a ____ but doesn't pass easily through an ____.

4. A core wrapped in a wire that is carrying current is called an ____.

5. A measure of the extra charges that are on an object is called ____.

6. A material that resists the flow of current is called a ____.

7. An ____ is a flow of charges.

8. In a ____, taking out one light does not turn off the whole circuit.

9. The charge that stays on an object is called ____.

10. A ____ attracts objects made of iron or steel.

11. A ____ has only one path for the current.

12. Energy to move current through a circuit is supplied by an ____.

13. A ____ is where a magnet's pull is strongest.

Connect Concepts

Use the terms in the Word Bank to complete the concept map.

poles
negative
charges
attract
north
repel
positive
south

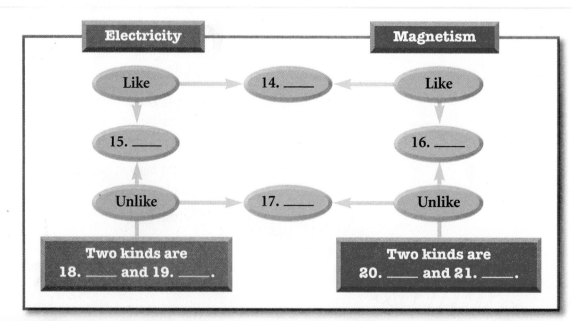

Electricity — Magnetism

Like → 14. ____ ← Like

15. ____ — 16. ____

Unlike → 17. ____ ← Unlike

Two kinds are
18. ____ and 19. ____.

Two kinds are
20. ____ and 21. ____.

Check Understanding

Write the letter of the best choice.

22. An object has a ____ charge if it has extra positive charges.

   A large   **C** negative

   B neutral   **D** positive

23. If the electric fields of two charged objects form a closed pattern of field lines, the objects are ____ charged.

   F negatively   **H** neutrally

   G positively   **J** oppositely

24. If one bulb is removed from a series circuit, the other bulbs will —

   A dim   **C** flicker

   G get brighter   **D** go out

25. The strip of material that glows in a light bulb is —

   F a charge   **H** a conductor

   G an insulator **J** a resistor

26. A device that produces motion energy from electrical energy is —

   A a compass   **C** an electromagnet

   B a generator   **D** a motor

Critical Thinking

27. Look at the circuit below. What will happen to each bulb if Switch 1 is off and Switch 2 is on?

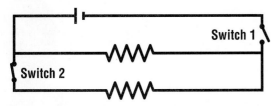

28. Why will chalk dust sprinkled on a plastic sheet placed over a bar magnet **NOT** show the shape of the magnetic field?

Process Skills Review

29. You **observe** that the north pole and south pole of two magnets attract each other when there is a piece of paper between them. What can you **infer** about magnetic fields and paper?

30. **Plan a simple investigation** to show the results of wrapping more coils of wire around a magnet. Be sure to include a description of the observations you would make and the conclusions you might draw. Use the following materials: a battery, a long piece of insulated copper wire with the ends stripped, an iron nail, a pile of paper clips.

31. You observe in the investigation you planned for Question 30 that the magnet picks up 5 paper clips with 10 coils of wire, 10 paper clips with 20 coils of wire, and 15 with 30 coils of wire. What would you **predict** will happen when you test the electromagnet with 40 coils of wire? How could you test your prediction?

Performance Assessment

Make a Circuit

Make a diagram of a parallel circuit with wires, three light bulbs, and two batteries. Show where to put a switch to turn all the lights off and on. Explain why you chose that switch location. Build and test the circuit.

Unit Project Wrap Up

Here are some ideas for ways to wrap up your unit project.

Write an Advertising Campaign

Make a series of ads that tell how energy-efficient your house is. Be sure you have evidence for your claims.

Display at a Science Fair

Display your model house in a school science fair. Prepare a written report describing the procedure you used and your results. You may want to add examples of energy-saving products to your display.

Build a Generator

Plan and install a device that will generate energy for your house. Show others how your device works.

Investigate Further

How could you make your project better? What other questions do you have about matter and energy? Plan ways to find answers to your questions. Use the Science Handbook on pages R2-R9 for help.

Forces and Motion

UNIT F

PHYSICAL SCIENCE

Forces and Motion

Unit Project

Simple Machine Models

Build a working model of each simple machine. Good materials to use are spools, string, craft sticks, wood, cardboard, paper, and tape. Make a diagram of each simple machine, and label the parts. Display the diagram with the simple machine.

Chapter 1

Vocabulary Preview

position
motion
frame of reference
relative motion
speed
force
newton
acceleration
gravity
weight
friction

Motion—Forces at Work

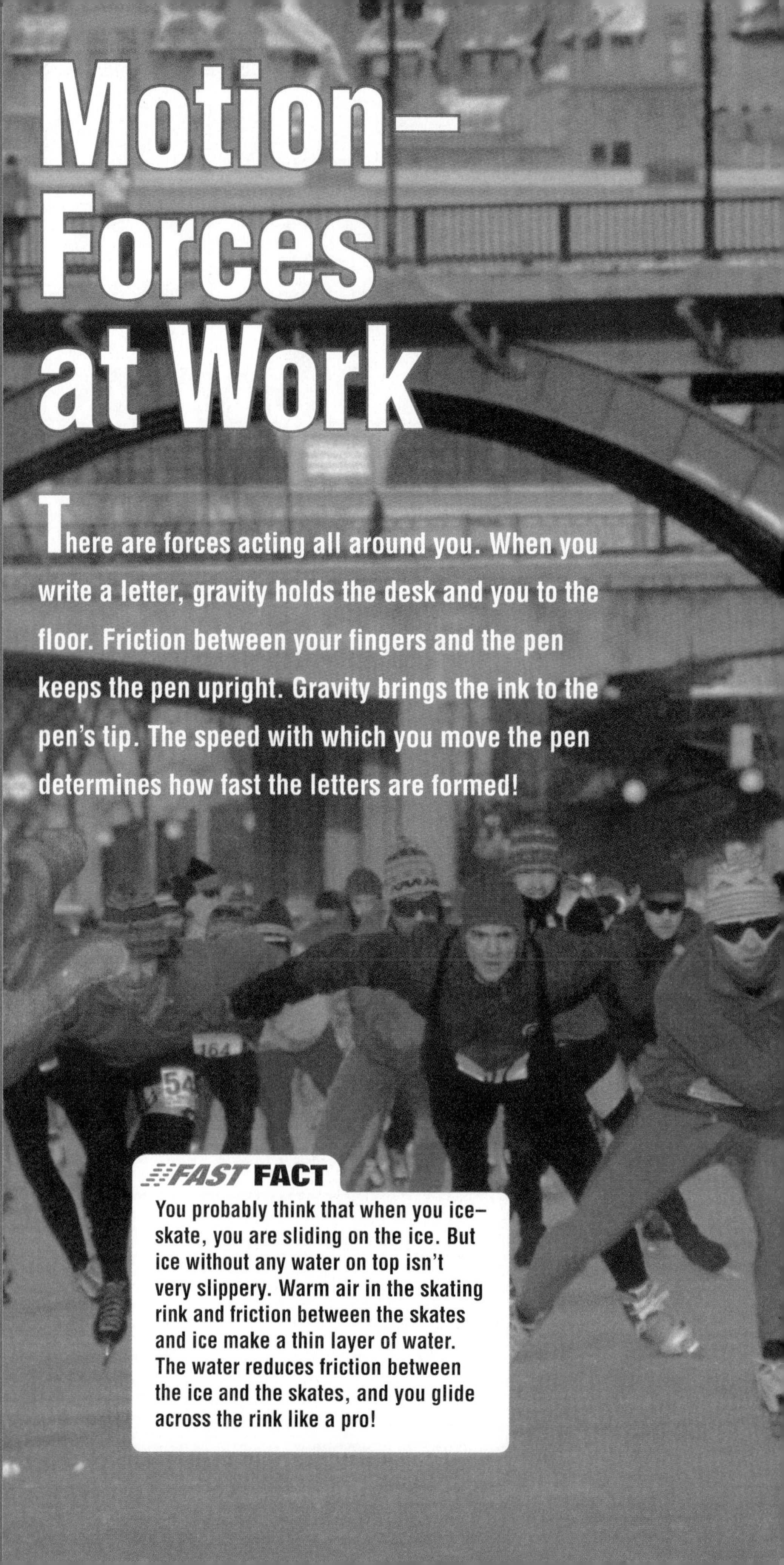

There are forces acting all around you. When you write a letter, gravity holds the desk and you to the floor. Friction between your fingers and the pen keeps the pen upright. Gravity brings the ink to the pen's tip. The speed with which you move the pen determines how fast the letters are formed!

FAST FACT

You probably think that when you ice-skate, you are sliding on the ice. But ice without any water on top isn't very slippery. Warm air in the skating rink and friction between the skates and ice make a thin layer of water. The water reduces friction between the ice and the skates, and you glide across the rink like a pro!

On the bottoms of their feet geckos have hairs that increase friction. These hairs let the lizards grip very smooth surfaces, even glass!

Friction slows a car when a driver brakes. It takes about 1.5 seconds for an alert driver to react to an emergency. It takes even longer to stop the car after the driver brakes. This table shows how far a car travels while a driver is reacting and braking and the total distance it takes to stop.

Car Braking

Speed (mi/hr)	A Reaction Distance (ft)	B Braking Distance (ft)	Total Stopping Distance [A+B]
20	44	25	69
30	66	57	123
40	88	101	189
50	110	158	268
60	132	227	359
70	154	310	464

What Is Motion?

In this lesson, you can . . .

INVESTIGATE giving directions.

LEARN ABOUT motion and speed.

LINK to math, writing, language arts, and technology.

INVESTIGATE

Giving Directions

Activity Purpose When you give directions to get to a place, you tell someone when to turn and where to move. So, giving directions is a way to describe movement and position. For example, you might tell a new neighbor how to get to the grocery store, or you might tell a visiting family member how to find the school office. In this investigation you will write directions to get to a place you have chosen in your school.

Materials
- paper
- pencil

Activity Procedure

1 Choose a place in the school, such as a water fountain or an exit door. A person going there should have to make several turns. Tell your teacher the place you chose.

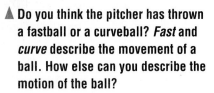

▲ Do you think the pitcher has thrown a fastball or a curveball? *Fast* and *curve* describe the movement of a ball. How else can you describe the motion of the ball?

2 After your teacher has approved your place, start walking to it. As you walk, **record** where and how you are moving. For example, you might include the distance you walk, about how long it takes for each part of the trip, where you turn, and any landmarks you use to tell where you are. (Picture A)

3 Go back to your classroom. On a separate sheet of paper, write directions to the place you chose. Use your notes to add details about time, distance, and position. Don't name the place on the directions page. Give the directions to a classmate and ask him or her to follow them. (Picture B)

4 When your partner comes back, talk about any problems he or she had with your directions. Underline the parts of the directions that caused the problems.

5 Walk with your partner as he or she follows the directions again. Decide together how to make the directions clearer. **Record** the reasons for any changes.

6 Switch roles with your partner and repeat Steps 1–6.

Picture A

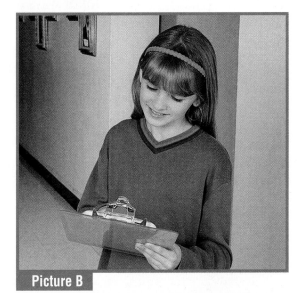
Picture B

Draw Conclusions

1. How did your partner know where to start following the directions?

2. How did your partner know how far to walk, which direction to walk, and where to turn?

3. **Scientists at Work** Directions **communicate** the way to get from one place to another. **Compare** your directions to the procedure of an experiment.

Investigate Further Using your notes and directions, draw a map showing the way to the place you chose. Trade maps with a new partner. Is the map easier to use than written directions? Explain your answer.

Process Skill Tip

Often scientists repeat experiments that were done by others. So, it is important to **communicate** clearly all the parts of an experiment. These parts include how to do the experiment, the data collected, and the results and conclusions.

Motion

Changing Places

FIND OUT

- ways to describe motion
- what speed measures
- how to calculate speed

VOCABULARY

position
motion
frame of reference
relative motion
speed

In a race the position of the runner on the track changes from moment to moment. The race will be won by the person who moves, or changes position, fastest. ▼

How do you tell someone where you are? Are you behind a desk? Under a light? Are you 2 meters (about 6 ft) to the left of the bookshelf? Each of these describes a certain place, or **position**. In the investigation, you chose a certain place. Then you wrote directions to tell someone how to move to get there, or how to change position. Good directions gave your partner a lot of ways to know his or her positions along the way and to find the next position.

As your partner followed your directions, he or she was in motion. **Motion** is any change of position. Your partner started in one position, moved to another, and kept changing position until he or she reached the final position—the place you chose. The photo below shows runners in motion around a track.

✔ **How do you know a runner is in motion?**

Point of View

Look around you. Are you moving? You probably would say that you're not. You don't sense any change in your position. You answer questions about your motion by checking, or referring to, the things around you. Together, all the things around you that you can sense and use to describe motion make up your **frame of reference**.

You know that Earth is rotating on its axis and revolving around the sun. So, even when you sit at your desk, you actually *are* moving. But you can't sense that movement. You can't tell you are moving by using your frame of reference—the classroom and what you can sense from your seat.

Suppose an astronaut is watching your school from space far away from Earth. His or her answer about your movement on Earth will be different because the frame of reference is different. From space, the astronaut sees Earth rotate. Motion that is described based on a frame of reference

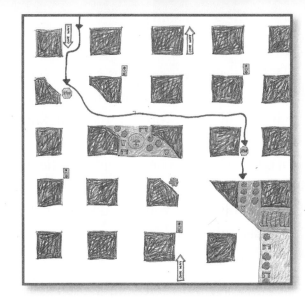

▲ To describe your position, you need a frame of reference. On a map you find your position by looking for landmarks or street names. How would you give directions to the park shown on the map? How would you check your position if you were following the directions?

is called **relative motion**. When you're sitting at your desk, your movement relative to the classroom is nothing. But your movement relative to the astronaut in space is very fast.

✔ **What is a frame of reference?**

▲ Jim watches Sarah and Rosa ride by on their bicycles. His frame of reference is what he sees by standing still on the sidewalk. Relative to him, the two girls are moving and the buildings and street are not moving.

Rosa's frame of reference is what she sees from her bike. Relative to Rosa, Sarah is not moving because the two girls are riding at the same speed. To Rosa, the buildings and street seem to be speeding by. Jim and Rosa describe Rosa's motion differently because they have different frames of reference. ▼

Speed

Did you ever hear someone say that his or her house was only a five-minute bike ride from school? When you hear that, you know that the house and school are not too far apart. But what if someone said, "My house is only a five-minute spaceship ride away from school?" Then you would know that the house and school were very far apart. Why? You know that a spacecraft travels a lot faster than a bike. So it could go a lot farther in five minutes than a bike could.

Speed is one way to describe how fast something is moving. **Speed** is a measure of an object's change in position during a unit of time. For example, a racing swimmer has a speed of 1 meter (about 3 ft) per second. From these two numbers, you know the swimmer is moving a distance of 1 meter (about 3 ft) during each second. So during 3 seconds, he or she will travel 3 meters (about 9 ft).

To find a swimmer's speed, you need two measurements. One measurement is change in position, or distance moved. Remember, you can't describe motion without a frame of reference. So you would measure how far the swimmer traveled from the end of the pool.

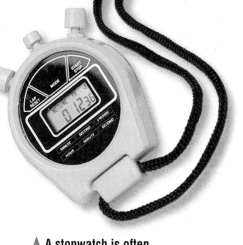

▲ A stopwatch is often used to measure time during track and swimming events.

How Fast Can You Go?

Activity	Distance (km)	Time (h)	Speed (km/h)
Flying in a jet plane	1000	1	1000
Riding in a car	240	3	80
Riding a bike	30	2	15
Walking	3	1	3

In a race each swimmer goes the same distance. The one who goes that distance in the least amount of time wins the race. That person has the greatest speed. ▼

In some track and swimming events, distance is measured in meters.

The other measurement needed is time. You would start timing as the swimmer left the edge of the pool. The swimmer's speed is the distance moved divided by the time it took to move that distance. The table on page F8 shows how distance, time, and speed are related.

✓ **What is speed?**

Summary

Motion is any change from one position to another. A frame of reference is a point of view from which to describe motion. The same motion can look different from different frames of reference. Motion described from one frame of reference is called relative motion. Speed is a measure of motion. Speed describes the distance an object travels in a unit of time.

Review

1. What is position?
2. What is motion?
3. What is relative motion?
4. **Critical Thinking** Give two different frames of reference from which to describe a roller-coaster ride.
5. **Test Preparation** What is the speed of a cat that runs 6 meters in 3 seconds?

   A $\frac{1}{2}$ meter per second

   B 2 meters per second

   C 3 meters per second

   D 9 meters per second

LINKS

MATH LINK

Leaping Leopard and Swaying Sloth Use reference books to find the speeds of different land animals. Use a computer program such as *Graph Links* to make a bar graph of the speeds of some of the faster ones and some of the slower ones.

WRITING LINK

Expressive Writing—Poem Write a poem for your teacher. Describe the motion of running horses as you pass them while riding a passenger train.

LANGUAGE ARTS LINK

Moving Words Make a set of cards for matching. On one group of cards, write words describing motion, such as *fluttering, twirling,* and *dangling.* On another set of cards, write the names of different objects, such as *dog, leaf,* and *kite.* Turn the cards face down, and choose a card from each set. Turn the two cards face up. Write a sentence using the two words. Read your sentence to the class.

TECHNOLOGY LINK

Visit the Harcourt Learning Site for related links, activities, and resources.

www.harcourtschool.com

WELCOME TO
THE
LEARNING
SITE

What Effects Do Forces Have on Objects?

In this lesson, you can . . .

INVESTIGATE forces measured by spring scales.

LEARN ABOUT forces acting on objects.

LINK to math, writing, physical education, and technology.

INVESTIGATE

Pairs of Forces Acting on Objects

Activity Purpose When you push a bicycle or a grocery cart, you expect it to move. But what happens if two people pull a grocery cart in opposite directions? What happens if they pull in the same direction? In this investigation you will **plan and conduct an investigation** to learn how pulling in two directions at the same time moves a toy car.

Materials

- safety goggles
- toy car
- 2 pieces of string, each 1 m long
- 2 spring scales
- ruler

Activity Procedure

1 **CAUTION** Wear safety goggles to protect your eyes. The spring scale hooks or string may slip loose and fly up. Work with a partner. Tie the ends of each string to the toy car. Pull on the string to make sure it won't come off easily. Attach a spring scale to each loop of string.

◀ This rock climber has strong arm and leg muscles that pull and push him up the rock face.

Picture A

2 With a partner, try different ways and directions of pulling on the spring scales attached to the toy car. (Picture A)

3 **Plan a simple investigation.** Your goal is to **describe** how the toy car moves when two spring scales pull it at the same time. Plan to include a chart and a diagram to **record** your data and **observations.**

4 With your partner, carry out the investigation you planned.

Draw Conclusions

1. How did pulling in different directions affect the toy car?

2. How did pulling in the same direction affect the toy car?

3. **Scientists at Work** Scientists use what they know to help them **plan and conduct investigations**. What knowledge did you use to help you plan and conduct this investigation?

Investigate Further What would happen if you attached a third piece of string and another spring scale to the car? **Plan and conduct an investigation** to find out. Can you find a way to have three people pull without moving the car? Explain your answer.

> **Process Skill Tip**
>
> To **plan and conduct an investigation**, scientists must first ask a good question. Then they must decide what they will observe or measure, what they will change, and what they will keep the same.

Forces

FIND OUT

- what a force is
- how an object moves when no force is acting on it
- how forces are added and subtracted

VOCABULARY

force
acceleration
newton

Pushes and Pulls

Think of all the times in a day you push or pull on something. You may push open doors, pull on your dog's leash, or push a pencil across paper. In the investigation you pulled a toy car. Every time you push or pull something, you use a force. A **force** is a push or a pull. When you throw a ball, the force of your muscles moves your arm to push the ball into the air. When you pick up a book, the force of your muscles moves your arm to pull the book off the desk.

You're not the only source of forces. Other forces are pushing and pulling things all around you. The force put out by a car's engine turns the wheels to push the car down the road. The force of the wind pushes flags and tree branches, making them flap and rustle. The force of a magnet pulls it to a refrigerator door.

✔ **What is a force?**

◀ This archer pulls on the bowstring. When she lets go, the string will push the arrow away from the bow and toward the target.

Starting Motion

Many of the things around you are probably motionless, or not moving. The books on your desk are motionless. So are the pictures on the wall. Objects stay in place unless a force starts them moving. If something is moving, you know that a force started it moving.

How a force affects an object depends on the object's mass. An object with more mass is affected less. Suppose you push with equal force on a toy car and a wagon filled with books. When you stop pushing, the toy car will be moving much faster than the wagon.

The force needed to start an object moving also depends on other forces that are acting on the object. Suppose your coat is fastened closed with Velcro. In that case the force needed to open your coat must be more than the force of the Velcro that's holding it closed.

▲ You have to pull to keep a sled moving uphill. If you stop pulling, the weight of the sled will pull it back down.

Once an object is moving, it moves until a force stops it. Sometimes it's easy to see where the stopping force comes from, such as when a soccer goalie stops a kicked ball. At other times, the stopping force is harder to name. You know that even if no other player stops a kicked soccer ball, the ball will stop rolling at some time. You can't see what stops the ball. It's a force called *friction* (FRIK•shuhn).

✔ What do you have to do to start motion?

◄ It's easy to start an empty grocery cart moving at a walking speed. After the cart is full, you must push it much harder to start it moving at a walking speed.

Changing direction is another kind of change in motion. It always takes a force to change the direction an object is moving. To turn, this in-line skater changes the angle of her skates. The skates push sideways to the left against the ground, and she skates around the curve. ▼

▲ When you stop, you change your motion. You slow down until you are not moving. It always takes a force to change motion. This in-line skater uses the force of the brake against the ground to make herself stop.

Changing Motion

It takes a force to start motion. Starting is a change from no motion to some motion. A force is needed to change motion in other ways, too. Speeding up, slowing down, turning, and stopping all are motion changes that need a force.

If you've ridden a bicycle on a smooth, level surface, you know that you can coast. Once you start moving, you can keep going for a while without pedaling. But to speed up, you have to pedal. The force of your feet pushing on the pedals speeds up the bicycle. To slow down or stop, you squeeze, or put force on, the brake handles.

Suppose you are riding a bicycle and want to turn left. You turn the handlebars to the left. The front wheel pushes sideways against the pavement and the bicycle moves left. If you were riding on icy pavement, turning would be harder. The front wheel couldn't push sideways against the pavement without slipping.

Starting and slowing to a stop are examples of changing speed. Turning is an example of changing direction. Starting, slowing, and turning are all accelerations. An **acceleration** (ak•sel•er•AY•shuhn) is any change in the speed or the direction of an object's motion. It always takes a force to cause an acceleration.

✔ **What is needed to make an object change its motion?**

Changing Speed

A larger force causes a larger acceleration. This means that the harder you push something, the more quickly it speeds up. When you pedal your bicycle harder, it goes faster. If you squeeze harder on the brake handles, you will stop faster.

Pushing for a longer time also causes a larger acceleration. If you get on a bicycle and pedal hard for 2 seconds, you will be moving slowly. If you pedal just as hard for 20 seconds, you will be moving much faster.

✔ **What is needed to give an object a greater acceleration?**

At the start of a race, the push of the bobsled team starts the bobsled moving. The push of the team increases the speed of the sled from 0 to 15 kilometers (about 10 mi) per hour.

Force accelerating bobsled

◀ As the bobsled slides down the curving course, its weight accelerates it bit by bit. The longer the bobsled moves down the hill, the faster it goes. The sled's final speed may be 145 kilometers (about 90 mi) per hour or more.

▲ Both dogs are pulling with the same force. The forces on the rope are balanced. There is no acceleration, and the rope doesn't move. The arrows stand for the forces. When you put them side by side, you can see they are balanced.

Adding Forces

Suppose you push on a box from one side and your friend pushes on it from the opposite side. What happens? If your friend pushes just as hard as you do, the box won't move. The forces are balanced. When all forces acting on an object are balanced, the motion of an object does not change. It does not accelerate.

If you push harder than your friend pushes, the box will move toward your friend. But if your friend pushes harder than you do, the box will move toward you.

When forces on an object are in opposite directions, you subtract the smaller force from the larger force. The force that remains will accelerate the object.

When two forces on an object are in the same direction, they add together. The force that results is in the same direction as the two forces and is larger than either of them. The photo below shows how forces can add together to move a piano easily.

✔ **What happens to an object when the forces acting on it are balanced?**

◀ When three people push together, the piano moves easily. Their forces add together to make one larger force. The arrows show how the three forces add together.

Measuring Forces

You used spring scales in the investigation to help you observe the effects of two forces on a toy car. The numbers on the spring scale showed you the size of the force in units called newtons. The **newton** is the metric, or Système International (SI), unit of force. It's abbreviated as *N*. A newton is a small amount of force. It's about as much force as you need to lift a medium-sized apple.

A spring scale can show how accelerating an object depends on the object's mass. Suppose you hook a spring scale to an empty wagon. Then you take two steps to pull the wagon up to your walking speed. As you pull, the scale reads 10 N. Next, you put your dog in the wagon. Again, you take two steps to pull the wagon up to walking speed. This time the scale reads 20 N. Putting the dog in the wagon added mass. Because of the added mass, it took a larger force to accelerate the wagon to the same speed in the same amount of time.

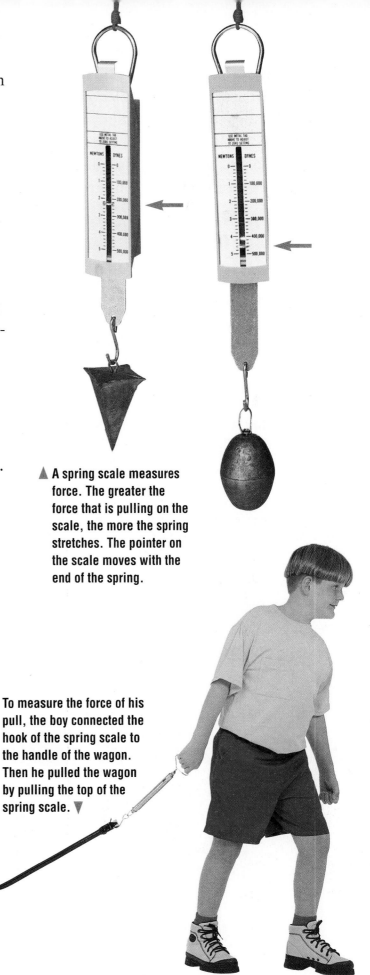

▲ A spring scale measures force. The greater the force that is pulling on the scale, the more the spring stretches. The pointer on the scale moves with the end of the spring.

To measure the force of his pull, the boy connected the hook of the spring scale to the handle of the wagon. Then he pulled the wagon by pulling the top of the spring scale. ▼

As its name suggests, a spring scale has a spring in it. When you pull on the scale, you stretch the spring. The pointer on the scale moves as you pull. To measure the force you are using, you have to be able to lift or pull on the spring scale. Holding the scale and pushing won't give you a reading on the scale.

Other kinds of scales also measure forces. You've probably seen a bathroom scale or the scale at a grocery store checkout lane.

✔ **What does the stretch of a spring scale measure?**

THE INSIDE STORY

Two Scales

These are two other kinds of scales. They also measure force, but they work differently from a simple spring scale.

This is a dial spring scale. Dial spring scales are often found in the produce sections of grocery stores. The push of an object placed in the pan stretches a spring that has a gear attached to it. As the gear moves down, it causes a needle to turn. The tip of the needle points to the amount of force with which the object pushes on the pan. ▶

◀ In this electronic scale, the force of the food placed on the pan pushes a rod on the bottom of the pan into a magnet. An electric current in the coil around the rod makes an electromagnet. Like poles of the magnet and electromagnet interact. The two forces balance exactly when the pan is lifted to its original position. When the pan stops moving, the number you see shows the force of the food on the pan.

▲ Scales can also be very large. This scale measures the weight of trucks full of gravel and asphalt.

Summary

A force is a push or a pull. Starting, stopping, slowing down, and turning are all changes in motion, or kinds of acceleration. An object does not accelerate unless a force acts on it. Forces can add together, subtract, or balance each other. When all the forces on an object are balanced, it does not accelerate. Forces are measured in newtons (N).

Review

1. What is a force?
2. What is the name of the unit of force?
3. What is acceleration?
4. **Critical Thinking** What happens to a door if you push on one side and someone else pushes with the same amount of force on the other side?
5. **Test Preparation** What happens when you are riding your bicycle on a smooth, level surface and you stop pedaling?
   A You stop right away.
   B You go faster.
   C You slowly slow down.
   D You turn to the right.

LINKS

MATH LINK

Piano Movers Two students are pushing on a piano. One student can push with a force of 30 newtons. The other can push with a force of 50 newtons. What is the greatest force they can use to push on the piano? What is the smallest force that they can put on the piano if they both push hard?

WRITING LINK

Expressive Writing—Song Lyrics Choose a tune you know. Then write words to go with that tune. The words should describe for a younger child ways to use forces to move an elephant from the zoo to your house. You might want to include a verse about what you will do with the elephant once you get it home.

PHYSICAL EDUCATION LINK

Sports and Motion Make a list of at least five different sports. Then make a chart to identify objects that change motion while each sport is being played.

TECHNOLOGY LINK

Learn more about forces and accelerations by viewing *Coaster Physics* on the **Harcourt Science Newsroom Video.**

LESSON 3

What Are Some Forces in Nature?

In this lesson, you can . . .

INVESTIGATE
forces on a sliding box.

LEARN ABOUT
four different types
of forces.

LINK to math, writing,
art, and technology.

Forces on a Sliding Box

Activity Purpose Have you ever slipped on a patch of ice? To make ice on a sidewalk less slippery, you can put sand on it. In this investigation you will **measure** the force that you need to slide a box across several different materials. You will **order** the measurements and use them to **compare** the materials.

Materials

- shoe box
- spring scale
- books

Activity Procedure

1. Make a table to **record** your **observations.**

2. Put the hook of the spring scale through the two openings on the end of the box. Place several books in the box. (Picture A)

3. Use the spring scale to slowly drag the box across the top of a desk or table. Be sure to pull with the spring scale straight out from the side of the box. Practice this step several times until you can pull the box at a steady, slow speed. (Picture B)

◀ The force of gravity is pulling this snowboarder down the hill. The force of friction is holding him back. But the snowboard is made to slide on the snow with as little friction as possible. So its speed is quite fast.

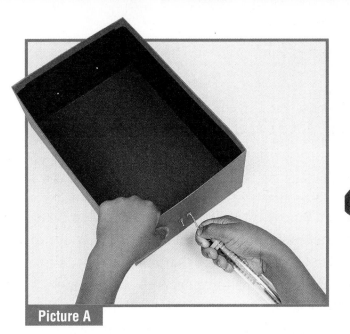
Picture A

Picture B

4 When you are ready, **measure** the force of your pull as you drag the box. **Record** the force measurement and the surface on which you dragged the box. **Observe** the texture of the surface.

5 Repeat Steps 3 and 4, dragging the box across other surfaces, such as the classroom floor, carpet, tile, and cement. **Predict** the force needed to drag the box on each surface.

Draw Conclusions

1. Make a new table. In this table, list the forces you used in order from the smallest to the largest. What was the least amount of force you used?

2. In your new table, write the name of each surface next to the force you used on it. On which surface did you use the greatest amount of force?

3. How did a surface affect the force needed to drag the shoe box across it?

4. **Scientists at Work** After scientists gather data, they often put it in some kind of **order** to help them understand their results. How did putting your data in order help you in this investigation?

Investigate Further **Predict** how much force it would take to pull the shoe box across a patch of ice. If possible, find a place, and test your prediction.

> **Process Skill Tip**
>
> When scientists measure many things in the same way, they usually put the data in **order.** Often they start with the smallest measurement and end with the largest. This helps them compare data and makes any patterns easier to see.

Kinds of Force

Gravity

FIND OUT

- what gravity is
- what holds atoms together
- how friction slows down motion

VOCABULARY

gravity
weight
friction

If you pick up a rock and then drop it, it will fall to the ground. The rock can't move by itself. A force is needed to move it. The force that pulls things toward Earth is called gravity. **Gravity** (GRAV•ih•tee) is a force that pulls all objects toward each other. The size of the force depends on the mass of the objects and how far apart they are. The pull between objects that have a large mass is stronger than the pull between objects that have a small mass. For example, the mass of Earth is large, so its pull on you is strong. But you have much less mass than Earth has, so the pull of your gravity on other objects is much too small to notice.

The greater the distance between objects, the weaker the pull of gravity is. The pull of gravity is strong between Earth and everything near its surface, including you. Space satellites orbit far from Earth. The pull between Earth and a satellite orbiting over one place on Earth's equator is small. It is only about $\frac{2}{100}$ of what the pull would be at Earth's surface.

✔ **What is gravity?**

The force of gravity between the sun and Earth pulls them toward each other. The pull between Earth and the sun holds Earth in its orbit around the sun. ▼

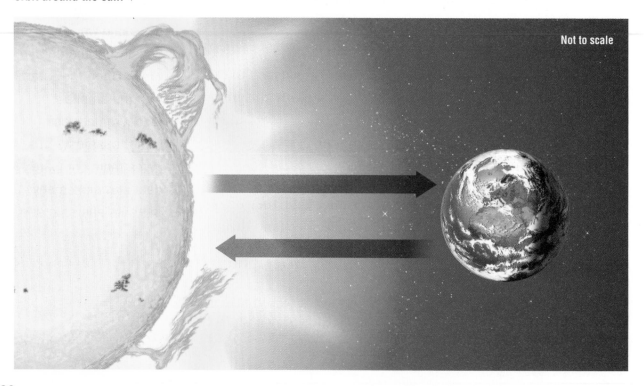

Not to scale

The girl's weight is a measure of the force of gravity between Earth and the girl. ▼

Weight on Planets in Our Solar System	
Planet	**Weight**
Mercury	102 N (23 lb)
Venus	245 N (54 lb)
Earth	270 N (60 lb)
Mars	102 N (23 lb)
Jupiter	638 N (142 lb)
Saturn	247 N (55 lb)
Uranus	240 N (53 lb)
Neptune	304 N (68 lb)
Pluto	18 N (4 lb)

◄ This arrow stands for the girl's weight on Earth.

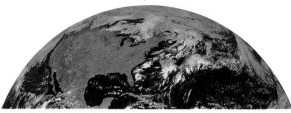

The force of gravity between Mars and the girl is about one-third the force of gravity between Earth and the girl. On Mars her weight would be about one-third her weight on Earth. ►

Weight

How many times have you had your weight measured? You probably know what your weight is now. **Weight** is a measure of the force of gravity on an object. Your weight is a measure of the force of gravity between you and Earth.

If you go to a place where the force of gravity is different, your weight will be different, too. The force of gravity on the moon is less than on Earth. That's mostly because the moon has less mass than Earth. The moon's gravity is about one-sixth of Earth's gravity. So on the moon your weight would be one-sixth of your weight on Earth. The force of gravity near Jupiter is much larger than it is near Earth. On Jupiter your weight would be more than twice what it is on Earth.

✔ **Why would you weigh less on the moon than you do on Earth?**

Atoms

Gravity and friction are forces that affect objects you can see. There are also other forces that affect much, much smaller objects. All matter is made of tiny particles called *atoms* (AT•uhms). In some kinds of matter, the atoms are combined with each other. In other kinds of matter, the atoms are separate.

Atoms are made up of even smaller particles called *protons* (PROH•tahns), *neutrons* (NOO•trahns), and *electrons*. The number of protons in an atom determines the kind of matter it is. For example, atoms of helium gas have 2 protons. Iron atoms have 26 protons. Protons and neutrons are held tightly together in an atom's nucleus. The nucleus is at the center of the atom. Protons have a positive electric charge. Neutrons have no charge.

The electrons in an atom move around the nucleus but are far away from it. The area where the electrons move is called an *electron cloud*. Electrons have a negative charge. Electricity results from moving electrons.

✔ **What are the three kinds of particles that make up an atom?**

This is a model of an atom. The nucleus, or center, of a helium atom has two protons and two neutrons. The electron cloud around the atom has two electrons. ▼

Forces Inside Atoms

You will remember that opposite electric charges attract each other and that like charges repel each other. These pulls and pushes are called *electromagnetic* (ih•lek•troh•mag•NET•ik) *forces*. Electromagnetic forces are what cause electricity. They are also the reason magnets and electromagnets work.

Electromagnetic forces also help hold the particles in an atom together. Electrons moving around the nucleus are held in the electron cloud by the pull of protons in the nucleus. But electrons also push each other away. So, the electrons of an atom are as far from each other as possible.

Protons also push each other away. They are held tightly in the nucleus by another force called the *strong nuclear force*. This force is larger than the electromagnetic force pushing the protons apart. However, it pulls hard only on things that are very close together, such as particles in the nucleus.

✔ **What is the strong nuclear force?**

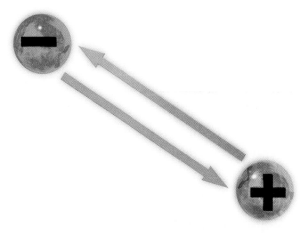

▲ The negative charge of an electron is attracted by, or pulled toward, the positive charge of a proton.

In some large atoms, the nucleus can split to form smaller atoms. If such a nucleus takes in an extra neutron, the strong nuclear force can no longer hold the nucleus together. ▼

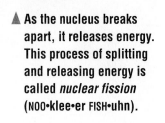

▲ As the nucleus breaks apart, it releases energy. This process of splitting and releasing energy is called *nuclear fission* (NOO•klee•er FISH•uhn).

Friction

In the investigation you pulled a shoe box filled with books across a desktop. As you were pulling the shoe box forward, another force was pulling it back. That force was friction. **Friction** (FRIK•shuhn) is a force that keeps objects that are touching each other from sliding past each other easily. As you observed in the investigation, the rougher a surface is, the more friction it has.

Sometimes friction is useful. Without friction, walking on a sidewalk would be like slipping on perfectly smooth ice. Friction also can stop motion. When you use a bicycle brake, pieces of rubber rub against the wheel rims. The friction between the rubber and the rims slows and stops the wheels. The harder you squeeze, the faster the bicycle stops.

Often people want to make the force of friction smaller. Friction can wear away machine parts that rub against each other. To reduce friction, people put oil on the machine parts to make them more slippery. This is why car engines need oil.

✔ **What is friction?**

When the wheel of this grinder touches the sculpture, it drags away little pieces of metal. Some of the energy from the grinder makes the metal red-hot. ▼

▲ An in-line skater pushes the heel stop of the skate against the ground to slow down or stop. Friction reduces the skater's speed.

▲ The friction caused by the brake rubbing against the bicycle wheel stops the wheel.

Summary

Forces in nature include gravity, electromagnetic forces, the strong nuclear force, and friction. Gravity keeps you on Earth. The electromagnetic force and the strong nuclear force keep atoms together. Friction is a force that keeps things from sliding past each other easily.

Review

1. What are the three types of particles that make up an atom?
2. Between what types of particles does the strong nuclear force act?
3. What is the force between two objects that keeps one object from sliding past the other easily?
4. **Critical Thinking** Where do you think the pull of gravity is stronger—at the surface of Earth or at the surface of the sun? Explain.
5. **Test Preparation** The direction of the force of friction on a book sliding to the right on a table is —
   A down
   B to the left
   C to the right
   D up

LINKS

MATH LINK

Moon Weight A rock that weighs 18 newtons on Earth weighs 3 newtons on the moon. What would a rock that weighs 12 newtons on Earth weigh on the moon?

WRITING LINK

Expressive Writing—Friendly Letter Suppose you are an astronaut who has landed on a planet that has a force of gravity two times as strong as Earth has. Write a letter to a friend on Earth, describing how it feels to walk and to lift tools.

ART LINK

See the Force Look at the things around you. Choose one object and then think of the different forces that are acting on it. Make a drawing, painting, or sculpture that shows the object and all the forces acting on it.

TECHNOLOGY LINK

Learn about friction, gravity, and motion by investigating *Build a Model Race Car* on **Harcourt Science Explorations CD-ROM.**

High-Speed Human Powered Vehicles

Engineers who develop high-tech bicycles work with forces, accelerations, and friction every day. Their job is to build Human Powered Vehicles (HPVs) that are as fast and as easy to ride as possible.

What's the big idea?

Most people in the United States who ride bikes do it for fun, not because they need them for transportation. When you want to travel long distances quickly, you often go in a car. But teams of scientists and engineers who work on HPVs have developed bikes that can go even faster than some cars.

How fast are they?

One of the best-known HPVs is called the Cheetah. It was built by a team of college students at the University of California. In 1992, scientists recorded the Cheetah traveling as fast as 112 kilometers (70 mi) per hour. The fastest that most regular bikes can go is 40–48 kilometers (25–30 mi) per hour.

The fastest HPV that has been built so far is the Ultimate Bike. Because its engineers understood ideas such as friction, force, and weight, they were able to design a bike that can reach speeds as fast as 332.64 kilometers (206.7 mi) per hour. The Ultimate Bike is made from the same

Cheetah

HUMAN POWERED VEHICLE

Wind resistance can greatly reduce bicycle speed. That's why these HPVs have the pedals in front of the rider. The rider sits close to the ground, so less of his or her body is hit by the wind. See if you can feel the wind resistance the next time you ride a bicycle. What can you do safely to reduce this resistance?

You probably won't see HPVs like these in a bike store soon. But the problems HPV scientists and engineers are solving may make ordinary bicycles faster and easier to ride.

Think About It

1. How could an HPV be useful to the average person?
2. In addition to that of an engineer, what are some jobs where ideas like acceleration, force, and friction are important?

WEB LINK:
For Science and Technology updates, visit the Harcourt Internet site.
www.harcourtschool.com

super-lightweight material used in jet planes. But even though it weighs only about $4\frac{1}{2}$ kilograms (about 10 pounds), the Ultimate Bike is stronger than any bike made from metal.

How do they work?

You've probably noticed from the photos that these bikes don't look like the bikes you see in your neighborhood. That's because they need to be built differently to reach such high speeds. For example, most HPVs have a gear system that's different from the one on regular bikes. The front crank that is turned by the pedals is much bigger than the crank on most bikes. This allows small movements of the pedals to make the wheels turn a large distance quickly.

Careers | Bicycle Mechanic

What They Do
Bicycle mechanics usually work for bike shops or sporting goods stores. They repair broken bikes and build new ones. HPVs like the Cheetah and the Ultimate Bike need mechanics to keep them running.

Education and Training Most bike shops will train their workers to be mechanics. Some high schools offer bike repair classes.

Ellen Ochoa

ASTRONAUT

"Only you put limitations on yourself about what you can achieve, so don't be afraid to reach for the stars."

Ellen Ochoa puts no limitations on herself. She became the first Hispanic woman in space. Chosen in 1990 by the National Aeronautics and Space Administration, Ochoa was a mission specialist on the 9-day-long *Discovery* mission in April 1993. On this mission she studied the sun and Earth's atmosphere to find out how the sun affects Earth's climate. She also flew on an 11-day mission in November 1994. She has spent almost 500 hours in space.

The most challenging part of space travel is remembering details. Every astronaut is trained to run all shuttle systems, such as computer, communication, air and water, and other equipment. All astronauts learn about the experiments and other jobs that are part of a shuttle mission. Ochoa says that astronauts must work very hard in space, because they have little time.

Ochoa dreams of helping to build a space station. She thinks it is needed for human exploration in space to advance. For two years, she directed all Astronaut Office support for the International Space Station program.

Ochoa believes that education is key to success in life. She learned this from her mother. Ochoa believes students, especially girls, should study math and science. Another role model for Ochoa was Sally Ride, the first American woman in space. "Sally made it possible for anyone to become an astronaut," Ochoa has said. Ride was in space when Ochoa was in college and first thinking of becoming an astronaut.

THINK ABOUT IT

1. How could studying math and science be helpful to you?

2. Who in your life has taught you that education is important?

Model of International Space Station

Observing Motion

How does motion result from changing position?

Materials

- pad of small self-stick notes
- ruler
- pencil

Procedure

➊ Hold the pad so that the sticky band is across the top. On the first note, draw a dot 1 cm from the bottom of the pad and 1 mm from the left side. Lift the note, but do not remove it from the pad.

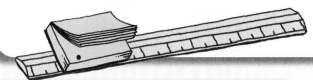

➋ On the second note, draw a dot 1 cm from the bottom and 2 mm from the left side.

➌ On separate notes, continue drawing dots, each one 1 mm to the right of the previous one until the last dot is at the right side. Remove any notes that were not used.

➍ Hold the note pad by the top, and flip the pages with your thumb. Observe the dots.

Draw Conclusions

How do the dots show a change in position over time? What happens if you flip the pages faster?

Marbles on a Ramp

Which marbles go faster?

Materials

- masking tape
- 2 metersticks
- books
- meter tape or ruler
- 10 marbles
- stopwatch

Procedure

➊ Tape the two metersticks together at a right-angle as shown. Prop up one end of the metersticks with books to make a ramp.

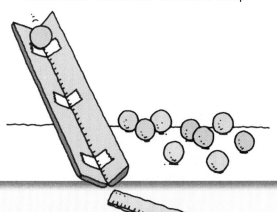

➋ Put the meter tape on the floor with the zero mark at the low end of the ramp. Make a table for your data, with columns labeled *Starting Position* and *Time*.

➌ Roll the marbles down the ramp one at a time. Start the marbles from different positions on the ramp. In your table, record the starting position for each marble.

➍ Use the stopwatch to measure the time it takes the marble to travel the length of the meter tape. Record the time in your table.

Draw Conclusions

What force pulled the marbles down the ramp? Which height made the speed of the marbles the fastest as they left the ramp? The slowest?

Vocabulary Review

Use the terms below to complete the sentences. The page numbers in ( ) tell you where to look in the chapter if you need help.

position (F6)   **newton** (F14)

motion (F6)   **acceleration** (F17)

frame of reference (F7)   **gravity** (F22)

relative motion (F7)   **weight** (F23)

speed (F8)   **friction** (F26)

force (F12)

1. The force that pulls all objects together is called ____.

2. Meters per second is a unit of ____, or the distance an object travels in a unit of time.

3. A certain place is called ____.

4. A ____ is a push or a pull.

5. A unit called a ____ is used to measure pulls and pushes.

6. ____ is a change in position.

7. Your ____ is the measure of the force of gravity on you.

8. A ____ is a point of view from which to describe motion.

9. Stopping your bike is an example of an ____.

10. Motion described from a frame of reference is called ____.

11. ____ is a force that keeps objects that are touching each other from sliding past each other easily.

Connect Concepts

Match the following effects with their causes.

Cause	Effect
12. Gravity	a. acceleration
13. Objects sliding past each other	b. pushes and pulls between electrons and protons
14. Unbalanced force on object	c. friction
15. No force on moving object	d. pulls any two objects toward each other
16. Balanced forces on object at rest	e. change in object's position
17. Strong nuclear force	f. no change in object's speed
18. Electromagnetic force	g. no movement of object
19. Weight	h. keeps protons and neutrons in the nucleus of an atom
20. Motion	i. a spring scale moves

Check Understanding

Write the letter of the best choice.

21. If you are standing in an elevator that is moving up at a steady speed of 1 meter per second, your motion relative to the elevator is at a speed of —

    A 0 meters per second
    B 1 meter per second down
    C 1 meter per second up
    D 2 meters per second up

22. Each of the following is an example of acceleration **EXCEPT** —

    F resting
    G starting
    H stopping
    J turning

23. The ____ pulls the moon toward Earth.

    A electric force
    B friction
    C force of gravity
    D strong nuclear force

24. Electrons are held in atoms by —

    F electromagnetic force
    G friction
    H gravity
    J the strong nuclear force

Critical Thinking

25. Suppose you are riding in a car and you pass a truck going in the same direction you are. You can easily read the words printed on the side of the truck. But then the same truck passes you going the same speed in the opposite direction. This time the words are hard to read. Why?

26. Your push on a hockey puck moving toward you stops it. What will the same push do to a hockey puck moving away from you?

27. A monkey that weighs 270 newtons is hanging from the branch of a tree. What is the size and direction of the monkey's force on the tree branch?

Process Skills Review

28. A student measured the force needed to pull a wagon across a wood floor, a heavy rug, and grass. He decided to **communicate** the results with a bar graph. The three bars on the graph each had the same width but different heights. What did the height of a bar show?

29. Look at the data in the table on page F23. How is the data **ordered**? Think of another possible order, and put the data in that order. Explain the new order.

30. A student decided to find out if a change in speed changes the force of friction. Help her **plan an investigation** to find this out. Include tips she could use as she **conducts** the **investigation**.

Performance Assessment

Force Drawing

Use a spring scale to measure the force needed to pull a book across a desktop at a steady speed. Identify and give the direction of three forces on the book as it slides. Make and label a drawing to show the forces.

Vocabulary Preview

simple machine
lever
fulcrum
effort force
work
pulley
wheel and axle
inclined plane
screw
wedge

Simple Machines

In an old comedy movie, movers try to get a piano into a fifth-floor apartment. First the piano rolls down a truck ramp and on down a hill. Then they use pulleys to lift the piano into the apartment through a window, and the piano crashes back to the ground. What makes all this comedy possible? Acting talent and simple machines!

FAST FACT

With a long enough lever your weight could lift almost any object! In fact, with a lever 12,264,000 meters long you could lift the Empire State Building!

Lever Lengths

Object One Meter from Fulcrum	Mass of Object (kg)	Your Distance from Fulcrum (m)
Student	27	1
Adult	68	2.5
30 Friends	810	30
Elephant	4995	185
Whale	129,600	4800
Empire State Building	331,128,000	12,264,000

The first computer was designed by Charles Babbage in 1832. It was to be entirely mechanical and would use more than a thousand levers!

Can you guess what kind of machine was first called a wooden ox or a gliding horse? This useful machine, made up of two levers connected by a wheel, lets one person carry a load that would normally require two. The machine was invented around A.D. 200 by the Chinese. It's a wheelbarrow!

This drawbridge is a large lever. The weight of the bridge is balanced by the large concrete blocks at the top on the right.

1

How Does a Lever Help Us Do Work?

In this lesson, you can . . .

 INVESTIGATE how one kind of lever works.

 LEARN ABOUT how levers help us do work.

 LINK to math, writing, music, and technology.

Experimenting with a Lever

Activity Purpose You may have played on a seesaw, or teeter-totter. A seesaw is a type of lever. A *lever* is a bar that turns around a point that doesn't move. In a seesaw the board is the bar and the center pipe is the point that doesn't move. A person sits near each end of the board. Each person takes a turn lifting a weight (the other person) at the other end of the board. As the people take turns using their legs and weight to lift each other, the board goes up and down. But what if the weight you were trying to lift were in the middle of the lever instead of at the end? In this investigation you will **observe** and **measure** to find out what happens.

Materials

- 2 wooden rulers
- 2 identical rubber bands, long
- safety goggles

Activity Procedure

1 **CAUTION** **Put on your safety goggles.** Put a rubber band 2 cm from each end of the ruler. One band should be at the 2-cm mark, and the other should be at the 28-cm mark.

◀ A boat oar is a lever—a type of simple machine made up of a bar and a point around which the bar moves. The wood oar is the bar. It moves around a point, called an oarlock, on the side of the boat.

Positions and Rubber Band Lengths

Finger Position	Observations	Length of Rubber Band on 2-cm Mark	Length of Rubber Band on 28-cm Mark
15-cm mark			
17-cm mark			
19-cm mark			
21-cm mark			

2 Have a partner lift the ruler by holding the rubber bands. Place your index finger at the 15-cm mark, and press down just enough to stretch the rubber bands. Your partner should lift hard enough on both rubber bands to keep the ruler level. (Picture A)

3 Have a third person **measure** the lengths of the two bands. **Record** your **observations** and measurements in a chart like the one above.

4 Move your finger to the 17-cm mark. Your partner should keep the ruler level. Again **measure** the length of the rubber bands, and **record** your **observations** and measurements.

5 Repeat Step 4, this time with your finger at the 19-cm mark and then the 21-cm mark.

Picture A

Draw Conclusions

1. Describe what happened to the ruler each time you moved your finger away from the center of it.

2. **Compare** the ruler and rubber bands to a seesaw. What was the ruler? What were the forces of the rubber bands?

3. **Scientists at Work** Look at the **measurements** you recorded. How do they support your other observations? Is there a pattern?

Investigate Further For the same ruler setup, **predict** what will happen if you put your finger on the 9-cm mark. Try it and see if your prediction is correct.

Process Skill Tip

Measuring is one type of observation. Measurements can sometimes more clearly show a pattern. They also are a good way to communicate to other people what you observed.

F37

Levers

FIND OUT

- what a simple machine is
- how a lever works
- what *work* means in science

VOCABULARY

simple machine
lever
fulcrum
effort force
work

Parts of a Lever

You may picture a machine, such as a washing machine or a sewing machine, as a device that has many parts. But these machines are built from smaller parts that are also machines. The basic machines that make up other machines are called **simple machines**. There are six simple machines. They are the lever, pulley, wheel and axle, inclined plane, screw, and wedge. All these machines help us move things by changing the size of the force applied, the direction of the force, or both at once.

One simple machine is the lever. As you saw in the investigation, a **lever** is made up of a bar that turns around a fixed point. The fixed point, or one that doesn't move, is called the **fulcrum** (FUHL•krem).

When you push or pull a lever, you put a force, called the **effort force**, on one part of the bar. This force causes the lever to turn around the fulcrum. The other end of the lever moves. The resulting force on that end is what you use to move a load, or do work. In the investigation, the length of each stretched rubber band showed the force on each end of the lever.

✔ **What are the parts of a lever?**

If both the performer's feet are the same distance away from the fulcrum, it's easy for him to stay balanced. ▶

This diagram shows how the performer is balancing on the lever. The blue arrow stands for the effort force, the red arrow is the resulting force, and the small dot is the fulcrum. The effort and resulting forces are balanced, so the lever doesn't move. ▼

Effort force

Resulting force

These pictures show the different types of levers.

This opener uses the outer rim of the can as the fulcrum. Your hand supplies the effort force. The resulting force is put out by the end under the lid. The resulting force is larger than the effort force.

Effort force

Resulting force

Fulcrum

Fulcrum

Effort force

Resulting force

A broom is a lever. Your upper hand is the fulcrum and your lower hand supplies the effort force. The resulting force is put out at the bristles of the broom. It takes more force to move the broom, but the bristle end moves much faster and farther than your hand. ▶

Effort force

Resulting force

Fulcrum

A wheelbarrow is a lever. It uses a wheel as a fulcrum. The pull up on the handles is the effort force. The resulting force is put out by the bottom of the wheelbarrow and lifts the flowers. This kind of lever also reduces the force you need to move something.

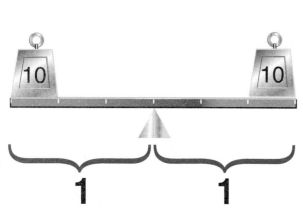

▲ A lever is often compared to a seesaw. If the weights are the same and the distances from the fulcrum are the same, the seesaw balances.

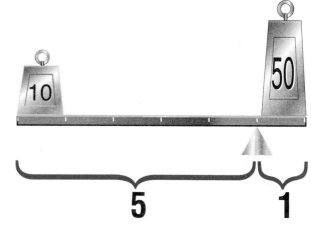

▲ Changing the position of the fulcrum changes the balance of the lever. Now a small effort force makes a larger resulting force. The distance from the fulcrum to the 10-newton weight is five times larger than the distance from the fulcrum to the 50-newton weight.

▲ The balanced lever above has the fulcrum in the center. If you move one end of the branch down, the other end moves up the same distance. An effort force of 10 newtons lifts a rock weighing 10 newtons.

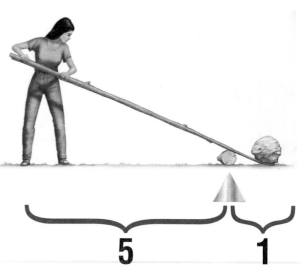

▲ When this lever moves, the long end travels five times farther down than the short end travels up. To lift a 50-newton rock would take an effort force of only 10 newtons. But you have to push five times farther down than the rock is lifted up.

Levers and Forces

The kind of lever shown above changes the direction of the force applied to it. A force down on one side pushes the other side up. On a seesaw the weight of a person on the high end pushes that end down. This lifts the person sitting on the other end.

When the fulcrum of this kind of lever is not in the middle of the bar, a light weight on the long side can balance a heavy weight on the short side.

On a seesaw you can balance a heavier person if the fulcrum is closer to him or her. Your smaller weight is on the long side of the lever. It balances the larger weight on the other end.

✓ **How does a lever change the force applied to it?**

Levers in Tools

Many hand tools are levers. A pry bar is a lever that has a long handle and a short end for prying. A small force on the handle becomes a much greater force on the prying end. Sewing scissors have long, wedge-shaped blades and short handles. The fulcrum is the bolt in the middle. A large movement of the handles causes a small movement of the blades close to the bolt. Fingernail scissors have long handles and short blades. They make it easier to cut hard fingernails.

✔ **Name three tools that include levers.**

Pliers (PLY•erz) are formed by two levers that are connected at a fulcrum. A small squeeze on the long handles makes a much greater force at the tips. ▼

Fulcrum

Resulting force

Effort force

THE INSIDE STORY

Piano Keys

A piano makes a sound when the part called a hammer hits a string that then vibrates. The force on a piano key moves through a series of levers to cause the string to be hit. Here's how it works.

❶ Pushing a piano key down lifts up the other end of a long lever (Lever 1). The direction of the effort force on the key is changed.

❷ Lever 1 pushes up on Lever 2. The direction of the force stays the same, but Lever 2 moves farther than Lever 1. This is because of the location of the fulcrum of Lever 2.

❸ Lever 2 pushes up on Lever 3. A padded hammer is on the end of Lever 3. Again, because of the position of its fulcrum, Lever 3 increases the distance the hammer moves. The hammer moves up fast and strikes the string. Then the hammer is caught as it bounces off the string, before it hits the string again.

❹ A pianist moves each finger only a small distance—about 1 centimeter (less than $\frac{1}{2}$ in.)—to produce a strong hit on a piano string.

Work

Machines are used to do work. You may think that as you read this sentence, you are doing work, but a scientist would say you're not. In science, the word *work* has a special meaning. **Work** is done on an object when a force moves the object through a distance. The force and motion must be in the same direction. By this definition, thinking isn't work. Just holding a book isn't doing work on the book. But lifting a book is doing work on the book. Carrying a basketball isn't doing work on the basketball. This is because the force holding the ball up and its motion aren't in the same direction. Shooting the basketball, however, is doing work on the ball.

Levers help you do work. You could pick up a heavy rock using just your arms, or you could use a lever to help you. Either way you do the same amount of work.

To find the work done on an object, multiply the force used to move the object by the distance the object moves.

Work = Force × distance

Here's the work done to lift a 10-newton rock 2 meters.

Work = 10 N × 2 m

Work = 20 N-m (newton-meters)

✔ **In science, when is work done?**

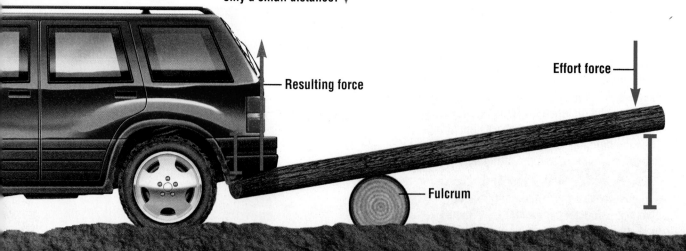

In this type of lever, the amount of work done is about the same on either side of the fulcrum. It takes only a small force to push down the long end, but that end moves through a large distance. On the short end, a large force pushes up, but that end moves only a small distance. ▼

Resulting force

Effort force

Fulcrum

◀ At work or at play? You may think that the adult dressed in black is working and the students are playing. Look again, but this time use a scientist's definition of *work.* The supervisor isn't moving any objects. So she isn't doing any work on anything. The students to the right, on the other hand, are applying forces to lift a ball. So they are actually doing work on the ball.

Summary

The basic machines that make up all other machines are simple machines. A lever is a simple machine that changes the direction or size of a force. Work is done on an object when a force moves an object through a distance.

Review

1. What are the parts of a lever?
2. How does a pry bar help you do work?
3. What is work?
4. **Critical Thinking** Why do you think it is important that the bar of a lever not bend?
5. **Test Prep** An example of a lever is a —
   A wheelbarrow
   B wedge
   C screw
   D wrench

LINKS

MATH LINK

Measuring Force Measure and compare the lengths of the effort force and resulting force arrows shown with the wheelbarrow on page F39. Which arrow is longer? About how many times as long is it? Which force is greater—the effort force or resulting force? How many times as great?

WRITING LINK

Informative Writing—Description
Some apes, including chimpanzees and orangutans, use levers. Other animals, including crows and sea otters, also use very simple tools. Find an example of how an animal uses a tool. Write an article describing how the animal uses the tool to help meet its needs.

MUSIC LINK

Instrument Keys Many musical instruments use keys, including almost all the woodwinds and many of the brasses. As with piano keys, the keys on these instruments are levers. Choose an instrument and find out how the keys work the levers. What do the levers do?

TECHNOLOGY LINK

Learn more about levers and other simple machines by visiting this Internet site.
www.scilinks.org/harcourt

LESSON 2

How Do a Pulley and a Wheel and Axle Help Us Do Work?

In this lesson, you can . . .

INVESTIGATE how pulleys work.

LEARN ABOUT pulleys and about wheels and axles.

LINK to math, writing, physical education, and technology.

INVESTIGATE

How a Pulley Works

Activity Purpose Have you ever seen someone raise or lower the flag? Together the rope and wheel on the flagpole make up a pulley (PUHL•ee). Like a lever, a pulley can change the direction of a force. Can a pulley change forces in other ways as levers do? In this investigation you'll **compare** forces to find out.

Materials

- 2 broom handles
- strong rope, 6 m or longer

CAUTION

Activity Procedure

1 Firmly tie one end of the rope to the center of one of the broom handles. This will be Handle 1.

2 Have two people face each other and stand about 30 cm apart. Have one person hold Handle 1. His or her hands should be about 40 cm apart—20 cm on either side of the rope. Have the other person hold the other broom handle (Handle 2) in the same way. (Picture A)

3 Loop the rope around Handle 2 and back over Handle 1. (Picture B)

◀ A pasta maker includes a simple machine— a wheel and axle. As you turn the crank (the wheel), it turns a post (the axle) inside the machine. Blades connected to the axle cut the pasta to the width you want.

4. Stand behind the person holding Handle 1. Have your partners try to hold the broom handles apart while you slowly pull on the free end of the rope. **CAUTION** Don't let **fingers get caught between the handles.** **Observe** and **record** what happens.

5. Repeat Steps 3 and 4. This time, loop the rope back around Handles 1 and 2 again. (Picture C) **Observe** and **record** what happens.

6. Add more loops around the broom handles. Again pull on the free end of the rope to try to bring the handles together. **Observe** and **record** what happens.

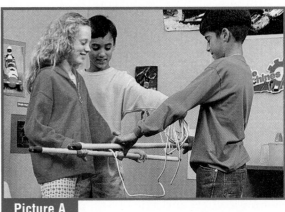
Picture A

Draw Conclusions

1. **Compare** your observations in Steps 4, 5, and 6. Which way of looping the rope made it hardest to pull the handles together? Which way made it easiest?

2. Reread the description of a pulley in the Activity Purpose. What in this investigation worked as wheels do?

3. **Scientists at Work** How did the handles and rope change your effort force? **Compare** this to how levers work. How is it like levers? How is it different?

Picture B

Investigate Further Attach a spring scale to the free end of the rope and repeat the investigation. Use one, two, three, and four loops around the broom handles. **Record** your results in a table. Then make a graph that **compares** the force needed for each number of loops.

Picture C

Process Skill Tip

Scientists often **compare** a new observation to what they know already. When you compare, you look for ways things are alike and ways they are different.

Machines That Turn

Pulleys

FIND OUT

- what fixed and movable pulleys are
- how a wheel and axle works

VOCABULARY

pulley
wheel and axle

You may have seen the wheels of pulleys on a sailboat or a flagpole. A **pulley** is made up of a rope or chain and a wheel around which the rope fits. When you pull down on one rope end, the wheel turns and the other rope end moves up. A pulley that stays in one place is called a *fixed pulley*. Fixed pulleys are often used to raise and lower something lightweight, such as a flag or a small sail, while you stay on the ground or the deck.

A fixed pulley is like a lever that has its fulcrum in the middle. Both the lever and the pulley change only the direction of the effort force. They do not change the size of the effort force.

A different kind of pulley can change the size of the effort force. This pulley is called a movable pulley because it is free to move up and down. One end of its rope is tied down. The load is hooked to the pulley. Pulling up on the rope makes both the pulley and the load rise.

Effort force

Resulting force

▲ Using a fixed pulley, a sailor on a boat deck can lift a sail to the top of the mast.

A movable pulley doesn't change the direction of the effort force. A pull up on the rope also pulls up on the load. But a movable pulley does increase the resulting force. To lift a load of 50 newtons, you need to pull up with only a 25-newton force.

As with a lever, you don't get more work out of a movable pulley than you put in. It doubles your lifting force, but you pull twice as far. To lift a load 2 meters, you must pull up 4 meters of rope.

Pulleys can be put together to make pulley systems. For example, you can use a fixed pulley with a movable pulley. The movable pulley increases your force. The fixed pulley changes the direction of your force.

Adding more movable pulleys to a system increases your force even more. Each movable pulley you add also increases the length of rope you must pull to lift a load.

✔ How does a movable pulley change your force?

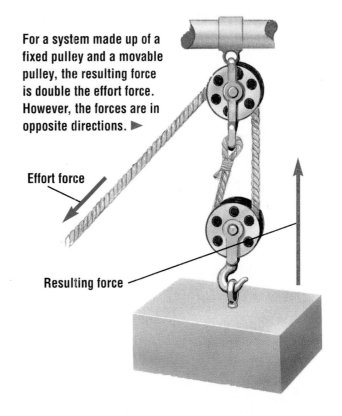

For a system made up of a fixed pulley and a movable pulley, the resulting force is double the effort force. However, the forces are in opposite directions. ▶

Effort force

Resulting force

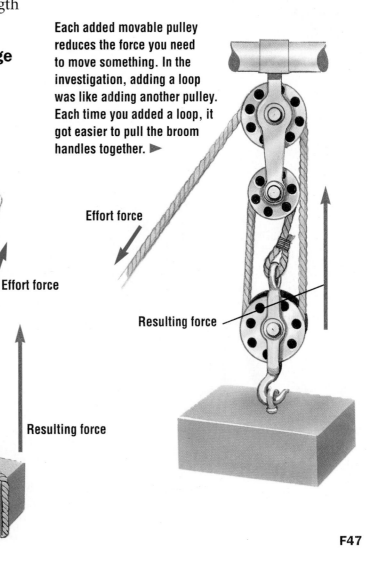

Each added movable pulley reduces the force you need to move something. In the investigation, adding a loop was like adding another pulley. Each time you added a loop, it got easier to pull the broom handles together. ▶

Effort force

Resulting force

For a single movable pulley, the resulting force is double the effort force. The resulting and effort forces are in the same direction. ▶

Effort force

Resulting force

Wheels and Axles

A wheel and axle is another simple machine that can make work seem easier. A **wheel and axle** (AKS•uhl) is made up of a large wheel attached to a smaller wheel or rod. A doorknob is part of a wheel and axle. The large round knob turns a smaller axle. The axle is what pulls in the latch to open the door. Without the large knob, it would be difficult to turn the axle. The small effort force you use to turn the knob becomes a large resulting force put out by the axle.

As with other simple machines, you can't get more work out of a wheel and axle than you put in. Effort force is made larger. But the distance the outside of the knob turns is larger than the distance the axle moves.

✓ **How does a wheel and axle make work seem easier?**

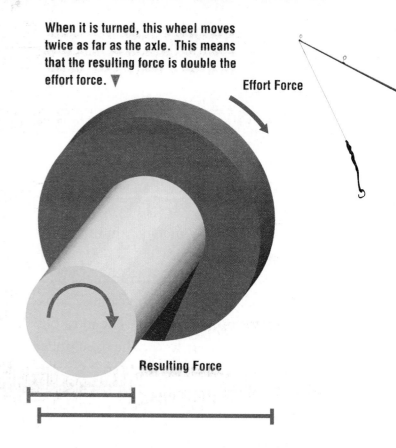

When it is turned, this wheel moves twice as far as the axle. This means that the resulting force is double the effort force. ▼

Effort Force

Resulting Force

Wheel
Axle

The wheel on this water valve is much larger than the axle. A small effort force on the large wheel makes the axle put out a large resulting force. So the valve is closed tightly but can be opened quickly in an emergency. ▶

.FIRE STATION #4.

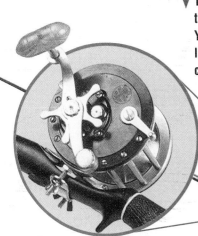

▼ The crank on this fishing reel is the wheel. The reel is the axle. Your effort force becomes a larger resulting force so you can pull in a heavy fish.

Summary

A pulley is a simple machine similar to a lever. A fixed pulley changes the direction of an effort force. A movable pulley makes the resulting force larger than the effort force. Fixed and movable pulleys can be put together to make pulley systems. A wheel and axle is a simple machine in which an effort force on a large wheel makes a larger resulting force on a smaller wheel, or axle.

Review

1. Which kind of pulley makes your effort force larger?

2. Which kind of pulley has the effort force in the opposite direction to the resulting force?

3. Does a wheel and axle change the direction of the effort force, the size of the force, or both? Explain.

4. **Critical Thinking** You want to lift a heavy box 20 meters off the ground. Describe a pulley system that could help you move the box.

5. **Test Prep** Which simple machine can **NOT** be used to increase force?

   A wheel and axle   C fixed pulley

   B lever   D movable pulley

LINKS

MATH LINK

Pulleys and Force Measure the effort force and resulting force arrows of the pulleys on pages F46–F47. Then look carefully at the pulleys and ropes. Can you find a pattern you could use to predict how a pulley or pulley system multiplies your effort force?

WRITING LINK

Persuasive Writing—Opinion Brunel's Portsmouth Pulley Works opened in 1803. It made a pulley called a block and tackle. Suppose you write advertising for this business. Find out more about a block and tackle. Then write a flyer describing the benefits of using pulleys for various tasks. Explain why the Brunel block and tackle is better than handmade pulleys.

PHYSICAL EDUCATION LINK

Gears Gears are wheels and axles. One place you can see gears is on a bicycle. Find out how bicycle gears work and how they help a person ride quickly and easily. Make and label a drawing to show what you learned.

TECHNOLOGY LINK

Learn more about amazingly small machines by viewing *Micromachines* on the **Harcourt Science Newsroom Video.**

How Do Some Other Simple Machines Help Us Do Work?

In this lesson, you can . . .

INVESTIGATE an Archimedes' screw.

LEARN ABOUT how inclined planes, screws, and wedges do work.

LINK to math, writing, technology, and other areas.

INVESTIGATE

Make an Archimedes' Screw

Activity Purpose Archimedes (ar•kuh•MEE•deez) was one of the first known scientists. He lived and worked in Greece around 250 B.C. He used science that he learned to make many inventions. One of his inventions, called the Archimedes' screw, is still used all over the world. It is a machine for lifting water. An Archimedes' screw moves water from rivers into canals for irrigation. In this investigation you will **make a model** of an Archimedes' screw and demonstrate how it works.

Materials

- round wooden pole, such as a piece of a broom handle, 20 cm long
- meterstick or metric ruler
- marker
- length of rubber or plastic hose, about 40–50 cm long
- 6 strong rubber bands
- large pan of water or sink that can be filled with water

Activity Procedure

1. Use the meterstick and marker to divide the pole into five equal sections.

2. Use a rubber band to hold the hose to one end of the pole. The band should not be so tight that it closes off the hose, but it should be tight enough to hold the hose in place.

◀ **This water-skier flies into the air off the end of a ramp, a common kind of inclined plane.**

3. Wind the hose around the pole in a spiral so that it passes over your marks. (Picture A) Use a rubber band to hold the top of the hose in place. Put two or three more bands around the hose and pole so that nothing slips. Wiggle the hose around so the ends open at right angles to the length of the pole. You have built an Archimedes' screw.

4. Put the nail end of the Archimedes' screw in the large pan or sink of water so the device rests on the head of the nail and makes a low angle with the bottom of the pan. Make sure both ends of the screw are over the pan. (Picture B) Turn the Archimedes' screw clockwise 12 times. Now turn the screw in the other direction 12 times. **Observe** what happens.

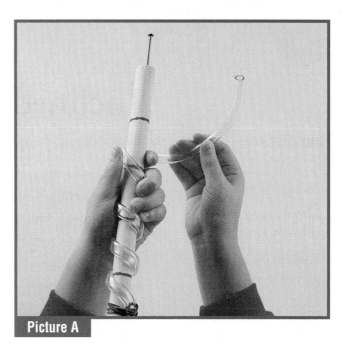

Picture A

Draw Conclusions

1. What happened when you turned the Archimedes' screw the first time? What happened the second time?

2. A screw is a type of inclined plane, a flat sloping surface. A ramp is an example of an inclined plane. Where was the inclined plane in the model you made?

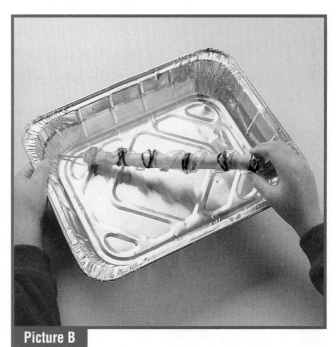

Picture B

3. **Scientists at Work** The Archimedes' screw you built is not a completely useful tool. The screw is hard to turn, and there are easier ways to move water. But it is useful as a **model.** It shows how the machine works. Why might it help to make a small model before building a full-sized machine?

Investigate Further There are many inclined planes around you. Select one day to see how many ramps and screws you can find at school and at home. Make a list of those you find. Tell how each helps people do work.

Process Skill Tip

Scientists often find it helpful to make a small **model** to study an idea or device. Then they can use what they learn from the small model to build a larger device.

Inclined-Plane Machines

Inclined Planes

FIND OUT

- how an inclined plane reduces effort
- how a screw is related to an inclined plane
- how to use inclined planes as a wedge

VOCABULARY

inclined plane
screw
wedge

To get to the top of a mountain, would you rather bicycle along a gentle slope or a steep path? You have to travel much farther on the gentle slope, but you have to use more force to pedal up the steep path. Both slopes are a kind of simple machine called an inclined plane. An **inclined plane** is a flat surface that has one end higher than the other.

An inclined plane changes an effort force into a larger resulting force. The direction of the effort force is along the plane. The resulting force lifts up on the object. When you slide a box up a ramp, you push along the ramp. The ramp pushes up on the box. The steeper the ramp, the less it changes the effort force, and the harder it is to slide the box.

▲ An inclined plane makes it easier to load and unload a truck. The inclined plane reduces the force needed to lift the objects to the height of the truck bed.

Hiking up a slope that does not rise much for the distance traveled is like going up a gentle inclined plane. You have to travel farther, but you use less force with each step.

Effort force

Resulting force

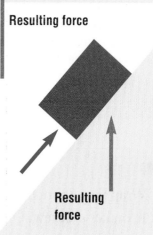

On a steep slope, your muscles must lift your body higher with each step. This is like a steep inclined plane. You move a shorter distance, but you have to use more force.

Resulting force

Effort force

As with other simple machines, you can't get more work from an inclined plane than you put into it. Remember, work is force times distance. An inclined plane is longer than it is high. The distance an object moves along the plane is more than the distance it moves up. So, even though it takes less force to move an object, you have to push it farther.

One problem with pushing something up an inclined plane is friction. When two things slide against each other, there is always friction. It's easier to push an object up a gentle slope, but it also means that friction affects the motion longer. Using a moving cart with wheels reduces friction. For example, you may have seen someone unloading stacks of boxes from a truck by using a tall rack with two wheels.

✔ **How does an inclined plane help you do work?**

This ramp is an inclined plane. People in wheelchairs can use the ramp instead of stairs. Wheelchair ramps are usually very gentle slopes. This reduces the amount of force needed to move a wheelchair up the ramps. ▼

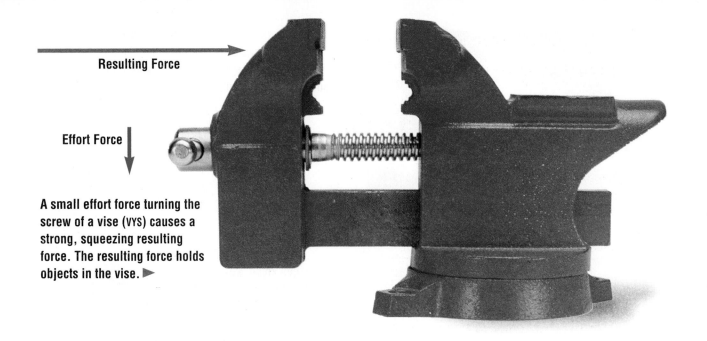

Resulting Force

Effort Force

A small effort force turning the screw of a vise (VYS) causes a strong, squeezing resulting force. The resulting force holds objects in the vise. ▶

Screws

Wrapping an inclined plane around a pole makes a **screw**. On a screw the long ramp of the inclined plane is wrapped into a space that is the same height as the inclined plane but has almost no width.

Turning a screw moves things up the spiral ramp. The Archimedes' screw you made in the investigation worked this way. Turning the Archimedes' screw pushed water to the top of its tube. The force needed to turn the screw was smaller than the force needed to lift the water straight up.

As other inclined planes do, a screw trades force for distance. The path of the water through the Archimedes' screw was longer than the height it moved up. Lifting the water with an Archimedes' screw used less force.

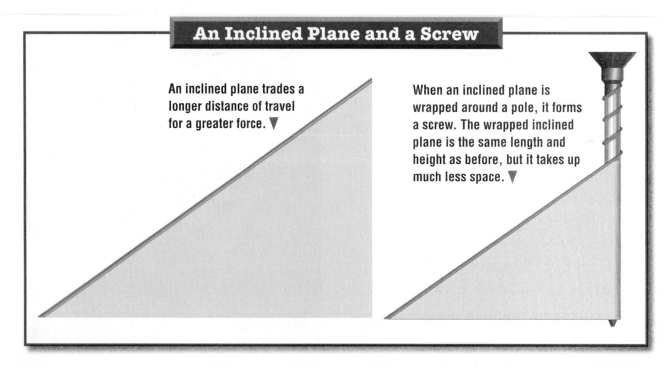

An Inclined Plane and a Screw

An inclined plane trades a longer distance of travel for a greater force. ▼

When an inclined plane is wrapped around a pole, it forms a screw. The wrapped inclined plane is the same length and height as before, but it takes up much less space. ▼

F54

Resulting Force

Effort Force

▲ This picture shows wood cut away around a screw. A small effort force turning the screw makes a large resulting force holding the wood pieces together. Also, notice how the wood touches the screw over a large area.

You have probably seen screws holding together pieces of wood or metal. Using screws in this way actually takes several simple machines. The screwdriver used to turn the screw is a wheel and axle. If you start to use a screw by pushing it into the wood, the point of the screw is acting as a wedge.

Why is using a screw better than hammering a nail? A screw takes longer to move into wood. But putting a screw into wood takes less force than putting in a nail. A nail is held in just by friction against the wood. The ridges of a screw hook and hold the wood more tightly.

✓ **How is a screw like an inclined plane?**

Holes are often dug with a kind of screw called an auger (AW•ger). The screw turns to lift dirt up and out of the ground. ▶

◀ A spiral staircase is a form of screw that makes it easier to climb from one floor to another. One advantage of a spiral staircase is that it takes up less space than a regular staircase.

Wedges

Two inclined planes placed back-to-back form a **wedge**. The main difference between a wedge and an inclined plane is how they are used. An inclined plane lifts objects. A wedge pushes things apart. An effort force down on the wide end of a wedge is changed to a much larger resulting force out from the sides of the wedge. Most blades of cutting tools such as knives, chisels, and axes are wedges. Often wedges are combined with levers to make cutting even easier.

✔ **How is a wedge related to an inclined plane?**

▲ The sharp edge of a cooking knife is a wedge. To chop vegetables, a cook may rest the point end of the knife on the cutting board. This makes the knife a combination of a wedge and a lever.

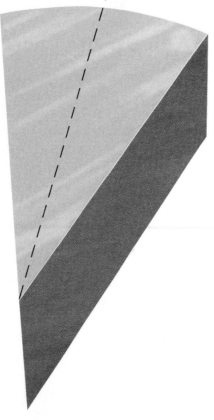

Effort force

Resulting force ←

Resulting force →

As the point of a wedge moves into a solid, the inclined planes of its sides push out. A small effort force on the wide end of the wedge is changed into a much larger resulting force out from its sides. ▶

The blade of an ax is one form of a wedge. The force of the ax down is changed into a resulting force out to the sides that splits the wood. Although chain saws are now used to cut down trees, people still use axes to split wood for fireplaces and stoves. ▶

Summary

An inclined plane is a simple machine used to move things to a different height. It takes more force to move an object up a steep inclined plane than a gently sloping one. When an inclined plane is wrapped around a pole, it becomes a screw. Two inclined planes put together form a wedge.

Review

1. How are screws and wedges related to inclined planes?

2. Name three ways screws are used.

3. Does a screw change the size of the effort force, the direction of the force, or both?

4. **Critical Thinking** How can an inclined plane help you safely lower a heavy object?

5. **Test Prep** Which simple machine is the part of scissors that pushes things apart?

   A screw
   B inclined plane
   C lever
   D wedge

LINKS

MATH LINK

The Advantage of Inclined Planes Measure and compare the effort and resulting force arrows on the top inclined plane on page F53. How many times does the inclined plane multiply your effort force?

WRITING LINK

Narrative Writing—Story Suppose you must move a piano into a second-floor apartment. Write a short story for your family, describing how you used simple machines to meet your goal.

ART LINK

A Museum and a Machine There is a famous inclined plane in the Guggenheim Museum in New York City. Find out its location and its use.

PHYSICAL EDUCATION LINK

Playing on the Planes Many sports are based on moving up or down an inclined plane. Make a list of sports that use this idea. (HINT: Look at the picture on page F50 to get started.)

TECHNOLOGY LINK

Visit the Harcourt Learning Site for related links, activities, and resources.
www.harcourtschool.com

WELCOME TO **THE LEARNING SITE**

Simple Machines and Water Transportation

Since ancient times, people have used boats to explore new areas, to ship goods from one place to another, and just to enjoy traveling. All of the early boats were moved by human muscle and a lever, either a paddle or an oar.

Floating Logs

The earliest boats were probably hollowed-out logs or rafts made of logs tied together with tree roots. Native American peoples made very fine canoes from wood, leather, and tree bark. Dugouts were another type of log boat. A large tree trunk was hollowed out by using fire, a pounding tool called a mallet, and an adz, a simple type of wedge.

Inuits use small hunting boats called kayaks (KY•aks). Kayakers use an unusual oar. It has a paddle blade at each end. This means that the fulcrum of the oar is first at one hand and then at the other as the kayaker switches the end of the oar that is in the water.

More Power

The Phoenicians (fuh•NEE•shuhnz) lived on the eastern coast of the Mediterranean Sea. They designed and built ships that were fast because they used large teams of rowers. Each side of a ship had one, two, or three long lines of rowers. Each rower had one long oar. The fulcrum of the oar was the point at which the oar went outside the ship.

The History of Water Transportation

Egyptians 3000 B.C.
Egyptians discover use of sails and learn to build ships using wooden planks.

Fulton 1807
Robert Fulton builds the first successful steamship.

3000 B.C.　1400 A.D.　1500 A.D.　1600 A.D.　1700 A.D.　1800 A.D.　1900 A.D.

Trireme 500 B.C.
Greeks build ships with sails and three lines of rowers.

Propellers 1836
Propellers to drive steamboats given patent.

Early to mid 1800s

Looking for ways to make boats faster, boat builders turned to the wind as a source of power. The Egyptians were among the first to build boats that could use either sails or human rowers.

The largest and fastest sailing ships ever were built in the mid-1800s. They were called clipper ships because they seemed to "clip off" the miles by going so fast. The large sails of a clipper ship were raised using human muscle and a pulley system called a block and tackle. Another simple machine used on clipper ships was a windlass, a type of wheel and axle. With it, a team of people could raise and lower the heavy anchor.

A Lot More Power

During the early 1800s, steam engines changed ship designs forever. Sails slowly disappeared. Newer ships were pushed by huge paddle wheels. Some had a wheel on each side, while others had a single wheel in the back.

In the late 1800s, ships slowly changed from using paddle wheels to using propellers. A propeller looks something like a fan blade. Because of their spiral shape, propellers are sometimes called screws.

As a propeller turns, it pulls a boat through the water much as a screw pulls two pieces of wood together. But it takes very big screws to move a ship. Each of the four propellers on the *Queen Mary,* a British ocean ship launched in 1934, was more than 5 meters (18 ft) across and weighed 38.5 tons!

Today 95 percent of business goods still travel from country to country on the ocean. The power source for large boats has changed from human muscles, to wind, to steam, and finally to other fuels. But simple machines are still on board as part of bigger, more complicated machines.

Think About It

1. Describe two ways simple machines helped to solve problems on a boat or ship.
2. How have more recent ship builders used what earlier people had learned about building boats and ships?

Queen Mary 1934

1900 A.D. 2000 A.D.

Today
Huge supercargo ships carry goods all over the world.

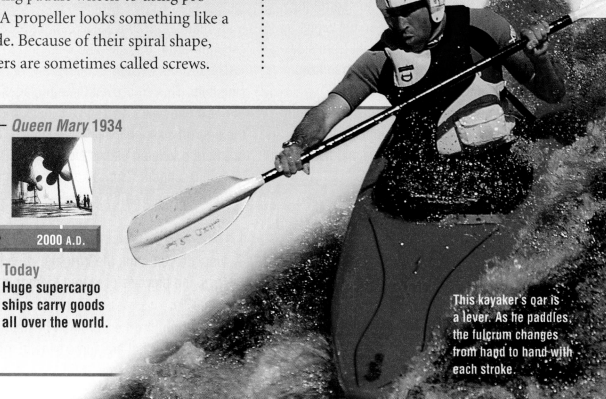

This kayaker's oar is a lever. As he paddles, the fulcrum changes from hand to hand with each stroke.

F59

Wilbur and Orville Wright

INVENTORS

Even as boys, the Wright brothers were fascinated by machines. They sold homemade mechanical toys to earn money when they were young. Orville Wright built his own printing press, and they published a weekly newspaper in Dayton, Ohio. Wilbur Wright was the editor. Later, they began to sell and to rent bicycles. Then they made bicycles in a room above the shop.

The Wright brothers became interested in flying in the 1890s. They read everything they could about how things fly. In 1899 they built their first glider.

In 1903 the two brothers built a biplane, an airplane with two levels of wings. The wings were made by covering wooden frames with cloth and then varnishing the cloth. The two wooden propellers were turned by a 12-horse-power gasoline engine built by the Wrights.

The brothers also made a way to control the plane. A "cradle" was connected to the wings by wires and pulleys. By shifting weight from side to side, the pilot could twist a wing tip to keep the plane balanced.

Orville Wright made the first successful flight on December 17, 1903. He launched the plane from an 18-meter (60-ft) rail on a sand flat. The

▲ Wilbur   ▲ Orville

plane stayed in the air about 12 seconds and flew at about 48 km/hr (30 mi/hr) for just 37 meters (120 ft). The brothers made three more trials that day. Wilbur stayed up the longest—59 seconds—and traveled 260 meters (852 ft).

The brothers preferred to work with no outside help. They improved their airplanes over the next two years. In 1908, Wilbur Wright made the first official public flights in France. The brothers predicted planes would deliver mail and carry passengers. They also hoped that airplanes might prevent a war.

THINK ABOUT IT

1. How do you think the Wrights' work with toys and bicycles prepared them to build a glider?

2. The Wright brothers worked by themselves as a team. What are some benefits of doing that? What are some problems it can cause?

Make a Screw

How are screws and inclined planes related?

Materials

- ruler
- sheet of paper
- scissors
- unsharpened pencil
- tape

Procedure

1. Draw a right triangle on the paper and cut it out. Imagine that this triangle is an inclined plane.

2. Draw a dark line along the longest edge of the triangle.

3. Tape the pencil to the back of the inclined plane.

4. Wrap the triangle around the pencil. Observe the results.

Draw Conclusions

What simple machine have you modeled? How do you know that you could move up the machine and get to the top of the pencil, just as you could move up a straight inclined plane?

Using a Wedge

How does a wedge work?

Materials

- wooden doorstop
- several books

Procedure

1. Work with a partner. Use your hands as you would use bookends, and hold the books up on a table or desk.

2. Have a partner put the narrow end of the doorstop between two of the books and gently push down.

3. Observe what happens to the books. Record your observations, including how the books felt as your partner pushed down on the doorstop.

4. Trade roles and repeat the activity.

Draw Conclusions

What did you feel as the doorstop was pushed down? What was the result of the action? What do you think will happen with a wider wedge? A narrower wedge? Try it and see.

Chapter 2 Review and Test Preparation

Vocabulary Review

Use the terms below to complete the sentences. The page numbers in ( ) tell you where to look in the chapter if you need help.

simple machine (F38)   **pulley** (F46)

lever (F38)   **wheel and axle** (F48)

fulcrum (F38)   **inclined plane** (F52)

effort force (F38)   **screw** (F54)

work (F42)   **wedge** (F56)

1. A basic device that can change the amount or the direction of force, or both at once, is a _____.

2. _____ results when a force produces a movement in the direction of the force.

3. Two inclined planes placed back-to-back form a _____.

4. A simple machine made up of a bar and a fulcrum is a _____.

5. A _____ is made up of an inclined plane wrapped around a pole.

6. To raise a heavy load, you could use a system made up of one fixed _____ and several movable ones.

7. The part of a lever around which the bar moves is the _____.

8. A large wheel connected to a smaller wheel is a _____.

9. _____ is the force that is put into a simple machine.

10. A flat surface that has one end higher than the other is an _____.

Connect Concepts

Use the Venn diagram below to classify the listed machines as either levers or inclined planes.

lever   screw   pulley   scissors
inclined plane   wedge   wheel and axle   knife

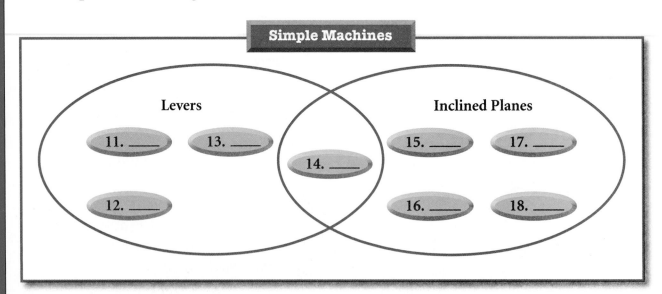

Simple Machines

Levers

11. _____   13. _____

14. _____

12. _____

Inclined Planes

15. _____   17. _____

16. _____   18. _____

Check Understanding

Write the letter of the best choice.

19. In a lever, the force that is used to move the bar is called the —
    - A effort force
    - B resulting force
    - C fulcrum
    - D machine

20. When the resulting end of a lever moves a shorter distance than the effort end, it moves with —
    - F the same force
    - G no force
    - H a smaller force
    - J a greater force

21. To use a pulley to change both force and direction, you need —
    - A one fixed pulley
    - B one movable pulley
    - C one fixed and one movable pulley
    - D two fixed pulleys

22. When you turn a doorknob, you are using —
    - F a wheel and axle
    - G a pulley
    - H a fulcrum
    - J an inclined plane

23. A wedge changes an effort force —
    - A down to a resulting force up
    - B around to a resulting force straight
    - C down to a resulting force sideways
    - D out to a resulting force in

Critical Thinking

For items 24 through 26, describe how you might use each of the following simple machines to remove a large rock from a garden plot. Tell the advantages and disadvantages of using each machine.

24. A lever
25. A pulley (or pulley system)
26. An inclined plane

Process Skills Review

27. You want to calculate the amount of work done as you move a box up a ramp. What do you need to **measure** in order to make your calculations? What tools would be useful in making these measurements?

28. You are digging and making an old-fashioned well. Decide whether to put a fixed pulley or a wheel and axle at the top of the well to raise the bucket. **Compare** these two machines. Explain which you would choose and why.

29. How could you be sure the choice you made in item 28 above is the best one without building the well?

Performance Assessment

Distance and Force

Investigate how the length of a ramp affects the force needed to move a load. Use three boards of different lengths, three books, a spring scale, and a rock. Make a table to record your data. When you have finished, make a bar graph of your data. Use it to explain what you found.

Unit Project Wrap Up

Here are some ideas for ways to wrap up your unit project.

Have a Scavenger Hunt

Place six boxes in your classroom. Label each one with the name of a simple machine. Then search for examples of simple machines. If the examples you find are small enough and can be moved, place them in the boxes. Otherwise, draw pictures of the simple machines and place the pictures in the boxes. Find at least five examples for each box.

Analyze a Bike

Spend some time looking at the parts of a bike. See how many simple machines you can identify. Describe how the simple machines work together to help the bike move.

Invent a Machine

Invent your own machine that will help you do work. Sketch the invention, and label each simple machine you used in it.

Investigate Further

How could you make your project better? What other questions do you have about simple machines? Plan ways to find answers to your questions. Use the Science Handbook on pages R2-R9 for help.

References

Planning an Investigation

When scientists observe something they want to study, they use the method of scientific inquiry to plan and conduct their study. They use science process skills as tools to help them gather, organize, analyze, and present their information. This plan will help you use scientific inquiry and process skills to work like a scientist.

Step 1—Observe and ask questions.

Which soil works best for planting marigold seeds?

- Use your senses to make observations.
- Record a question you would like to answer.

Step 2—Make a hypothesis.

My hypothesis: Marigold seeds sprout best in potting soil.

- Choose one possible answer, or hypothesis, to your question.
- Write your hypothesis in a complete sentence.
- Think about what investigation you can do to test your hypothesis.

Step 3—Plan your test.

I'll put identical seeds in three different kinds of soil.

- Write down the steps you will follow to do your test. Decide how to conduct a fair test by controlling variables.
- Decide what equipment you will need.
- Decide how you will gather and record your data.

Step 4 — Conduct your test.

I'll make sure to record my observations each day. Each flowerpot will get the same amount of water and light.

- Follow the steps you wrote.

- Observe and measure carefully.

- Record everything that happens.

- Organize your data so that you can study it carefully.

Step 5—Draw conclusions and share results.

Hmm. My hypothesis was not correct. The seeds sprouted equally well in potting soil and sandy soil. They didn't sprout at all in clay soil.

- Analyze the data you gathered.

- Make charts, graphs, or tables to show your data.

- Write a conclusion. Describe the evidence you used to determine whether your test supported your hypothesis.

- Decide whether your hypothesis was correct.

Investigate Further

I wonder if a combination of soils would work best. Maybe I'll try...

Using Science Tools

Using a Hand Lens

A hand lens magnifies objects, or makes them look larger than they are.

1. Hold the hand lens about 12 centimeters (5 in.) from your eye.

2. Bring the object toward you until it comes into focus.

Using a Thermometer

A thermometer measures the temperature of air and most liquids.

1. Place the thermometer in the liquid. Don't touch the thermometer any more than you need to. Never stir the liquid with the thermometer. If you are measuring the temperature of the air, make sure that the thermometer is not in line with a direct light source.

2. Move so that your eyes are even with the liquid in the thermometer.

3. If you are measuring a material that is not being heated or cooled, wait about two minutes for the reading to become stable, or stay the same. Find the scale line that meets the top of the liquid in the thermometer, and read the temperature.

4. If the material you are measuring is being heated or cooled, you will not be able to wait before taking your measurements. Measure as quickly as you can.

Caring for and Using a Microscope

A microscope is another tool that magnifies objects. A microscope can increase the detail you see by increasing the number of times an object is magnified.

Caring for a Microscope

- Always use two hands when you carry a microscope.
- Never touch any of the lenses of a microscope with your fingers.

Using a Microscope

1. Raise the eyepiece as far as you can by using the coarse-adjustment knob. Place your slide on the stage.

2. Always start by using the lowest power. The lowest-power lens is usually the shortest. Start with the lens in the lowest position it can go without touching the slide.

3. Look through the eyepiece, and begin adjusting it upward with the coarse-adjustment knob. When the slide is close to being in focus, use the fine-adjustment knob.

4. When you want to use a higher-power lens, first focus the slide under low power. Then, watching carefully to make sure that the lens will not hit the slide, turn the higher-power lens into place. Use only the fine-adjustment knob when looking through the higher-power lens.

You may use a Brock microscope. This is a sturdy microscope that has only one lens.

1. Place the object to be viewed on the stage.

2. Look through the eyepiece, and begin raising the tube until the object comes into focus.

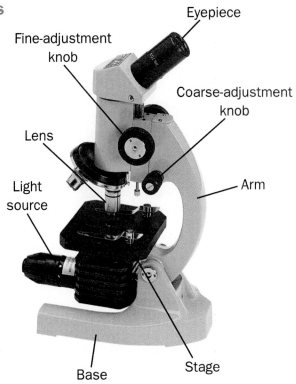

Eyepiece
Fine-adjustment knob
Coarse-adjustment knob
Lens
Arm
Light source
Base
Stage

A Light Microscope

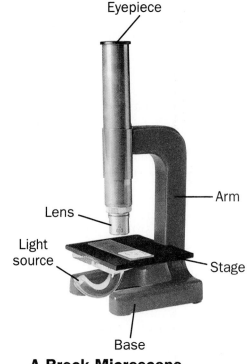

Eyepiece
Arm
Lens
Light source
Stage
Base

A Brock Microscope

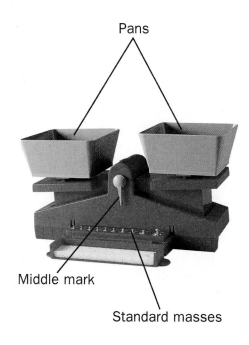

Pans

Middle mark

Standard masses

Using a Balance

Use a balance to measure an object's mass. Mass is the amount of matter an object has.

1. Look at the pointer on the base to make sure the empty pans are balanced.

2. Place the object you wish to measure in the left-hand pan.

3. Add the standard masses to the other pan. As you add masses, you should see the pointer move. When the pointer is at the middle mark, the pans are balanced.

4. Add the numbers on the masses you used. The total is the mass in grams of the object you measured.

Using a Spring Scale

Use a spring scale to measure forces such as the pull of gravity on objects. You measure weight and other forces in units called newtons (N).

Measuring the Weight of an Object

1. Hook the spring scale to the object.

2. Lift the scale and object with a smooth motion. Do not jerk them upward.

3. Wait until any motion of the spring comes to a stop. Then read the number of newtons from the scale.

Measuring the Force to Move an Object

1. With the object resting on a table, hook the spring scale to it.

2. Pull the object smoothly across the table. Do not jerk the object.

3. As you pull, read the number of newtons you are using to pull the object.

Measuring Liquids

Use a beaker, a measuring cup, or a graduate to measure liquids accurately.

1. Pour the liquid you want to measure into a measuring container. Put your measuring container on a flat surface, with the measuring scale facing you.

2. Look at the liquid through the container. Move so that your eyes are even with the surface of the liquid in the container.

3. To read the volume of the liquid, find the scale line that is even with the surface of the liquid.

4. If the surface of the liquid is not exactly even with a line, estimate the volume of the liquid. Decide which line the liquid is closer to, and use that number.

Beaker   **Graduate**

Using a Ruler or Meterstick

Use a ruler or meterstick to measure distances and to find lengths of objects.

1. Place the zero mark or end of the ruler or meterstick next to one end of the distance or object you want to measure.

2. On the ruler or meterstick, find the place next to the other end of the distance or object.

3. Look at the scale on the ruler or meterstick. This will show the distance you want or the length of the object.

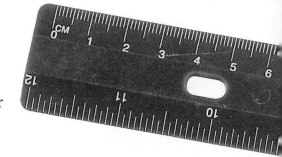

Using a Timing Device

Use a timing device such as a stopwatch to measure time.

1. Reset the stopwatch to zero.

2. When you are ready to begin timing, press *Start*.

3. As soon as you are ready to stop timing, press *Stop*.

4. The numbers on the dial or display show how many minutes, seconds, and parts of seconds have passed.

Using a Computer

A computer can help you communicate with others and can help you get information. It is a tool you can use to write reports, make graphs and charts, and do research.

Writing Reports

To write a report with a computer, use a word processing software program. After you are in the program, type your report. By using certain keys and the mouse, you can control how the words look, move words, delete or add words and copy them, check your spelling, and print your report.

Save your work to the desktop or hard disk of the computer, or to a floppy disk. You can go back to your saved work later if you want to revise it.

There are many reasons for revising your work. You may find new information to add or mistakes you want to correct. You may want to change the way you report your information because of who will read it. Computers make revising easy. You delete what you don't want, add the new parts, and then save. You can save different versions of your work if you want to.

For a science lab report, it is important to show the same kinds of information each time. With a computer, you can make a general format for a lab report, save the format, and then use it again and again.

Making Graphs and Charts

You can make a graph or chart with most word processing software programs. You can also use special software programs such as Data ToolKit or Graph Links. With Graph Links you can make pictographs and circle, bar, line, and double-line graphs.

First, decide what kind of graph or chart will best communicate your data. Sometimes it's easiest to do this by sketching your ideas on paper. Then you can decide what format and categories you need for your graph or chart. Choose that format

for the program. Then type your information. Most software programs include a tutor that gives you step-by-step directions for making a graph or chart.

Doing Research

Computers can help you find current information from all over the world through the Internet. The Internet connects thousands of computer sites that have been set up by schools, libraries, museums, and many other organizations.

Get permission from an adult before you log on to the Internet. Find out the rules for Internet use at school or at home. Then log on and go to a search engine, which will help you find what you need. Type in keywords, words that tell the subject of your search. If you get too much information that isn't exactly about the topic, make your keywords more specific. When you find the information you need, save it or print it.

Harcourt Science tells you about many Internet sites related to what you are studying. To find out about these sites, called Web sites, look for Technology Links in the lessons in this book. If you need to contact other people to help in your research, you can use e-mail. Log into your e-mail program, type the address of the person you want to reach, type your message, and send it. Be sure to have adult permission before sending or receiving e-mail.

Another way to use a computer for research is to access CD-ROMs. These are discs that look like music CDs. CD-ROMs can hold huge amounts of data, including words, still pictures, audio, and video. Encyclopedias, dictionaries, almanacs, and other sources of information are available on CD-ROMs. These computer discs are valuable resources for your research.

Measurement Systems

SI Measures (Metric)

Temperature
Ice melts at 0 degrees Celsius (°C)
Water freezes at 0°C
Water boils at 100°C

Length and Distance
1000 meters (m) = 1 kilometer (km)
100 centimeters (cm) = 1 m
10 millimeters (mm) = 1 cm

Force
1 newton (N) = 1 kilogram ×
    1 meter/second/second (kg-m/s^2)

Volume
1 cubic meter (m^3) = 1m × 1m × 1m
1 cubic centimeter (cm^3) =
    1 cm × 1 cm × 1 cm
1 liter (L) = 1000 milliliters (mL)
1 cm^3 = 1 mL

Area
1 square kilometer (km^2) =
    1 km × 1 km
1 hectare = 10 000 m^2

Mass
1000 grams (g) = 1 kilogram (kg)
1000 milligrams (mg) = 1 g

Rates (Metric and Customary)
kmh = kilometers per hour
m/s = meters per second
mph = miles per hour

Customary Measures

Volume of Fluids
8 fluid ounces (fl oz) = 1 cup (c)
2 c = 1 pint (pt)
2 pt = 1 quart (qt)
4 qt = 1 gallon (gal)

Temperature
Ice melts at 32 degrees
    Fahrenheit (°F)
Water freezes at 32°F
Water boils at 212°F

Length and Distance
12 inches (in.) = 1 foot (ft)
3 ft = 1 yard (yd)
5,280 ft = 1 mile (mi)

Weight
16 ounces (oz) = 1 pound (lb)
2,000 pounds = 1 ton (T)

Health Handbook

Good Nutrition

The Food Guide Pyramid

No one food or food group supplies everything your body needs for good health. That's why it's important to eat foods from all the food groups. The Food Guide Pyramid can help you choose healthful foods in the right amounts. By choosing more foods from the groups at the bottom of the pyramid and fewer foods from the group at the top, you will eat the foods that provide your body with energy to grow and develop.

Fats, oils, and sweets
Eat sparingly.

Meat, poultry, fish, dry beans, eggs, and nuts **2–3 servings**

Milk, yogurt, and cheese
2–3 servings

Fruits
2–4 servings

Vegetables
3–5 servings

Breads, cereals, rice, and pasta **6–11 servings**

Estimating Serving Sizes

Choosing a variety of foods is only half the story. You also need to choose the right amounts. The table below can help you estimate the number of servings you are eating of your favorite foods.

Food Group	Amount of Food in One Serving	Some Easy Ways to Estimate Serving Size
Bread, Cereal, Rice, and Pasta Group	1 ounce ready-to-eat (dry) cereal	large handful of plain cereal or a small handful of cereal with raisins and nuts
	1 slice bread, $\frac{1}{2}$ bagel	
	$\frac{1}{2}$ cup cooked pasta, rice, or cereal	ice cream scoop
Vegetable Group	1 cup of raw, leafy vegetables	about the size of a fist
	$\frac{1}{2}$ cup other vegetables, cooked or raw, chopped	
	$\frac{3}{4}$ cup vegetable juice	
	$\frac{1}{2}$ cup tomato sauce	ice cream scoop
Fruit Group	medium apple, pear, or orange	a baseball
	$\frac{1}{2}$ large banana or one medium banana	
	$\frac{1}{2}$ cup chopped or cooked fruit	
	$\frac{3}{4}$ cup of fruit juice	
Milk, Yogurt, and Cheese Group	$1\frac{1}{2}$ ounces of natural cheese	two dominoes
	2 ounces of processed cheese	$1\frac{1}{2}$ slices of packaged cheese
	1 cup of milk or yogurt	
Meat, Poultry, Fish, Dry Beans, Eggs, and Nuts Group	3 ounces of lean meat, chicken, or fish	about the size of your palm
	2 tablespoons peanut butter	
	$\frac{1}{2}$ cup of cooked dry beans	
Fats, Oils, and Sweets Group	1 teaspoon of margarine or butter	about the size of the tip of your thumb

Fight Bacteria

You probably already know to throw away food that smells bad or looks moldy. But food doesn't have to look or smell bad to make you ill. To keep your food safe and yourself from becoming ill, follow the steps outlined in the picture below. And remember—when in doubt, throw it out!

Food Safety Tips

Tips for Preparing Food

- Wash hands in warm, soapy water before preparing food. It's also a good idea to wash hands after preparing each dish.

- Defrost meat in the microwave or the refrigerator.

- Keep raw meat, poultry, fish, and their juices away from other food.

- Wash cutting boards, knives, and countertops immediately after cutting up meat, poultry, or fish. Never use the same cutting board for meats and vegetables without washing the board first.

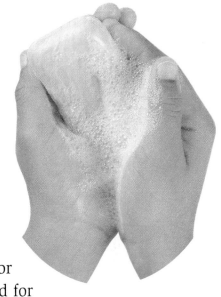

Tips for Cooking Food

- Cook all food completely, especially meat. Complete cooking kills the bacteria that can make you ill.

- Red meats should be cooked to a temperature of 160°F. Poultry should be cooked to 180°F. When done, fish flakes easily with a fork.

- Never eat food that contains raw eggs or raw egg yolks, including cookie dough.

Tips for Cleaning Up the Kitchen

- Wash all dishes, utensils, and countertops with hot, soapy water. Use a soap that kills bacteria, if possible.

- Store leftovers in small containers that will cool quickly in the refrigerator. Don't leave leftovers on the counter to cool.

Being Physically Active

Planning Your Weekly Activities

Being active every day is important for your overall health. Physical activity helps you manage stress, maintain a healthful weight, and strengthen your body systems. The Activity Pyramid, like the Food Guide Pyramid, can help you choose a variety of activities in the right amounts to keep your body strong and healthy.

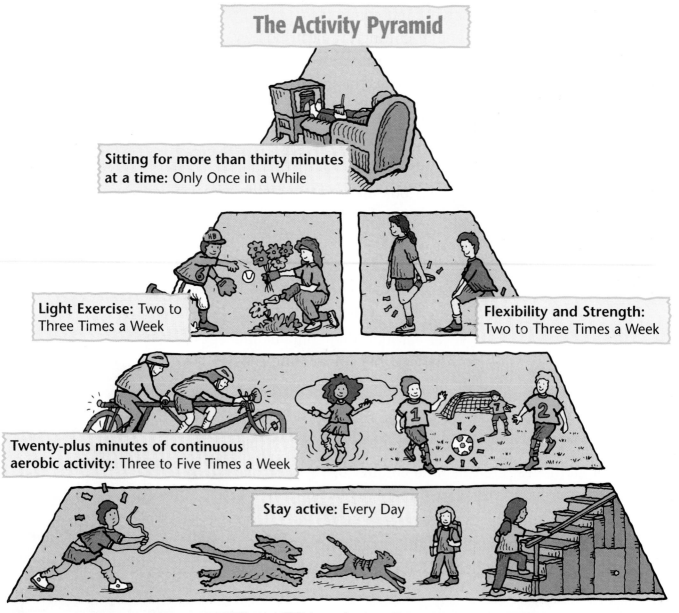

The Activity Pyramid

Sitting for more than thirty minutes at a time: Only Once in a While

Light Exercise: Two to Three Times a Week

Flexibility and Strength: Two to Three Times a Week

Twenty-plus minutes of continuous aerobic activity: Three to Five Times a Week

Stay active: Every Day

Guidelines for a Good Workout

There are three things you should do every time you are going to exercise—warm up, work out, and cool down.

Warm-Up When you warm up, your heart rate, breathing rate, and body temperature increase and more blood flows to your muscles. As your body warms up, you can move more easily. People who warm up are less stiff after exercising, and are less likely to have exercise-related injuries. Your warm-up should include five minutes of stretching, and five minutes of low-level exercise.

Workout The main part of your exercise routine should be an aerobic exercise that lasts 20 to 30 minutes. Aerobic exercises make your heart, lungs, and circulatory system stronger.

You may want to mix up the types of activities you do. This helps you work different muscles, and provides a better workout over time.

Cool-Down When you finish your aerobic exercise, you need to give your body time to cool down. Start your cool-down with three to five minutes of low-level activity. End with stretching exercises to prevent soreness and stiffness.

Using a Computer Safely

Good Posture at the Computer

Good posture is important when using the computer. To help prevent eyestrain, stress, and injuries, follow the posture tips shown below. Also remember to grasp the mouse lightly and take frequent breaks for stretching.

top of screen at or just below eye level

shoulders in line with ears and hips

neck and shoulders relaxed

arms at sides, bent as shown

wrists straight

feet flat on floor

Safety on the Internet

You can use the Internet for fun, education, research, and more. But like anything else, you should use the Internet with caution. Some people compare the Internet to a real city—not all the people there are people you want to meet and not all the places you can go are places you want to be. Just like in a real city, you have to use common sense and follow safety rules to protect yourself. Below are some easy rules to follow to help you stay safe on-line.

Rules for On-line Safety

- Talk with an adult family member to set up rules for going on-line. Decide what time of day you can go on-line, how long you can be on-line, and appropriate places you can visit. Do not access other areas or break the rules you establish.

- Don't give out information like your address, telephone number, your picture, or the name or location of your school.

- If you find any information on-line that makes you uncomfortable, or if you receive a message that is mean or makes you feel uncomfortable, tell an adult family member right away.

- Never agree to meet anyone in person. If you want to get together with someone you meet on-line, check with an adult family member first. If a meeting is approved, arrange to meet in a public place and take an adult with you.

A Safe Bike

You probably know how to ride a bike, but do you know how to make your bike as safe as possible? A safe bike is the right size for you. When you sit on your bike with the pedal in the lowest position, you should be able to rest your heel on the pedal. Your body should be 2 inches (about 5 cm) above the support bar that goes from the handlebar stem to the seat support when you are standing astride your bike with both feet flat on the ground. After checking for the right size, check your bike for the safety equipment shown below. How safe is *your* bike?

headlight

horn

white front reflector

red rear reflector

clear reflector

pedal reflectors

clear reflector

Your Bike Helmet

About 400,000 children are involved in bike-related crashes every year. That's why it's important to *always* wear your bike helmet. Wear your helmet flat on your head. Be sure it is strapped snugly so that the helmet will stay in place if you fall. If you do fall and strike your helmet on the ground, replace it, even if it doesn't look damaged. The padding inside the helmet may be crushed, which reduces the ability of the helmet to protect your head in the event of another fall. Look for the features shown here when purchasing a helmet.

approval sticker

quick-release strap

padding

hard shell

air vent

Safety on the Road

Here are some tips for safe bicycle riding.

- Check your bike every time you ride it. Is it in safe working condition?

- Ride in single file in the same direction as traffic. Never weave in and out of parked cars.

- Before you enter a street, **STOP. Look** left, then right, then left again. **Listen** for any traffic. **Think** before you go.

- Walk your bike across an intersection. **Look** left, then right, then left again. Wait for traffic to pass.

- Obey all traffic signs and signals.

- Do not ride your bike at night without an adult. Be sure to wear light-colored clothing and use reflectors and front and rear lights for night riding.

Fire Safety

Fires cause more deaths than any other type of disaster. But a fire doesn't have to be deadly if you prepare your home and follow some basic safety rules.

- Install smoke detectors outside sleeping areas and on every other floor of your home. Test the detectors once a month and change the batteries twice a year.

- Keep a fire extinguisher on each floor of your home. Check them monthly to make sure they are properly charged.

- Make a fire escape plan. Ideally, there should be two routes out of each room. Sleeping areas are most important, as most fires happen at night. Plan to use stairs only, as elevators can be dangerous in a fire.

- Pick a place outside for everyone to meet. Choose one person to go to a neighbor's home to call 911 or the fire department.

- Practice crawling low to avoid smoke.

- If your clothes catch fire, follow the three steps shown here.

1. STOP

2. DROP

3. ROLL

Earthquake Safety

An earthquake is a strong shaking or sliding of the ground. The tips below can help you and your family stay safe in an earthquake.

Before an Earthquake	During an Earthquake	After an Earthquake
• Attach tall, heavy furniture, such as bookcases, to the wall. Store the heaviest items on the lowest shelves.	• If you are outdoors, stay outdoors and move away from buildings and utility wires.	• Keep watching for falling objects as aftershocks shake the area.
• Check for fire risks. Bolt down gas appliances, and use flexible hosing and connections for both gas and water lines.	• If you are indoors, take cover under a heavy desk or table, or in a doorway. Stay away from glass doors and windows and from heavy objects that might fall.	• Check for hidden structural problems.
• Strengthen and anchor overhead light fixtures to help keep them from falling.	• If you are in a car, drive to an open area away from buildings and overpasses.	• Check for broken gas, electric, and water lines. If you smell gas, shut off the gas main. Leave the area. Report the leak.

Storm Safety

• **In a Tornado** Take cover in a sheltered area away from doors and windows. An interior hallway or basement is best. Stay in the shelter until the danger has passed.

• **In a Hurricane** Prepare for high winds by securing objects outside or bringing them indoors. Cover windows and glass with plywood. Listen to weather bulletins for instructions. If asked to evacuate, proceed to emergency shelters.

• **In a Winter Storm or Blizzard** Stock up on food that does not have to be cooked. Dress in thin layers that help trap the body's heat. Pay special attention to the head and neck. If you are caught in a vehicle, turn on the dome light to make the vehicle visible to search crews.

First Aid

For Choking . . .

The tips on the next few pages can help you provide simple first aid to others and yourself. Always tell an adult about any injuries that occur.

If someone else is choking . . .

  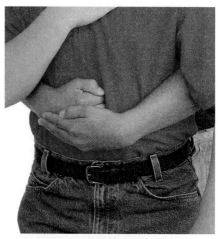

1. Recognize the Universal Choking Sign—grasping the throat with both hands. This sign means a person is choking and needs help.

2. Put your arms around his or her waist. Make a fist and put it above the person's navel. Grab your fist with your other hand.

3. Pull your hands toward yourself and give five quick, hard, upward thrusts on the choker's belly.

If you are choking when alone . . .

 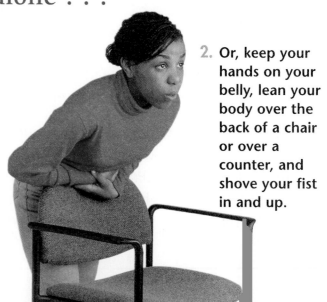

1. Make a fist and place it above your navel. Grab your fist with your other hand. Pull your hands up with a quick, hard thrust.

2. Or, keep your hands on your belly, lean your body over the back of a chair or over a counter, and shove your fist in and up.

For Bleeding . . .

If someone else is bleeding . . .

Wash your hands with soap, if possible.

Put on protective gloves, if available.

Wash small wounds with soap and water. Do *not* wash serious wounds.

Place a clean gauze pad or cloth over the wound. Press firmly for ten minutes. Don't lift the gauze during this time.

If you don't have gloves, have the injured person hold the cloth in place with his or her own hand.

If after ten minutes the bleeding has stopped, bandage the wound. If the bleeding has not stopped, continue pressing on the wound and get help.

If you are bleeding . . .

- Follow the steps shown above. You don't need gloves to touch your own blood.

- Be sure to tell an adult about your injury.

First Aid

For Nosebleeds . . .

- Sit down, and tilt your head forward. Pinch your nostrils together for at least ten minutes.

- You can also put an ice pack on the bridge of your nose.

- If your nose continues to bleed, get help from an adult.

For Burns . . .

Minor burns are called first degree burns and involve only the top layer of skin. The skin is red and dry and the burn is painful. More serious burns are called second or third degree burns. These burns involve the top and lower layers of skin. Second degree burns cause blisters, redness, swelling, and pain. Third degree burns are the most serious. The skin is gray or white and looks burned. All burns need immediate first aid.

Minor Burns

- Run cool water over the burn or soak it in cool water for at least five minutes.

- Cover the burn with a clean, dry bandage.

- Do *not* put lotion or ointment on the burn.

More Serious Burns

- Cover the burn with a cool, wet bandage or cloth. Do *not* break any blisters.

- Do *not* put lotion or ointment on the burn.

- Get help from an adult right away.

For Insect Bites and Stings . . .

▲ deer tick

- Always tell an adult about bites and stings.

- Scrape out the stinger with your fingernail.

- Wash the area with soap and water.

- Ice cubes will usually take away the pain from insect bites. A paste made from baking soda and water also helps.

- If the bite or sting is more serious and is on the arm or leg, keep the leg or arm dangling down. Apply a cold, wet cloth. Get help immediately!

- If you find a tick on your skin, remove it. Crush it between two rocks. Wash your hands right away.

- If a tick has already bitten you, do not pull it off. Cover it with oil and wait for it to let go, then remove it with tweezers. Wash the area and your hands.

For Skin Rashes from Plants . . .

▲ poison ivy

Many poisonous plants have three leaves. Remember, "Leaves of three, let them be." If you touch a poisonous plant, wash the area. Put on clean clothes and throw the dirty ones in the washer. If a rash develops, follow these tips.

- Apply calamine lotion or a baking soda and water paste. Try not to scratch. Tell an adult.

- If you get blisters, do *not* pop them. If they burst, keep the area clean and dry. Cover with a bandage.

- If your rash does not go away in two weeks or if the rash is on your face or in your eyes, see your doctor.

Sense Organs

Eyes

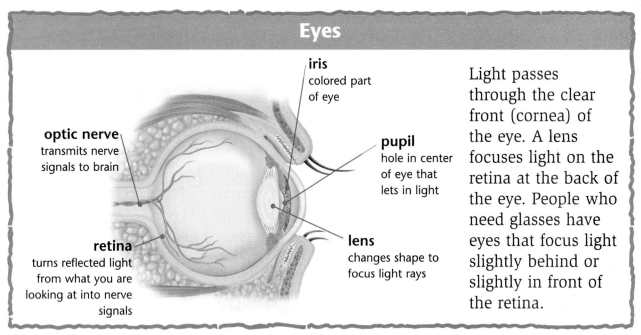

iris
colored part of eye

optic nerve
transmits nerve signals to brain

pupil
hole in center of eye that lets in light

retina
turns reflected light from what you are looking at into nerve signals

lens
changes shape to focus light rays

Light passes through the clear front (cornea) of the eye. A lens focuses light on the retina at the back of the eye. People who need glasses have eyes that focus light slightly behind or slightly in front of the retina.

Ears

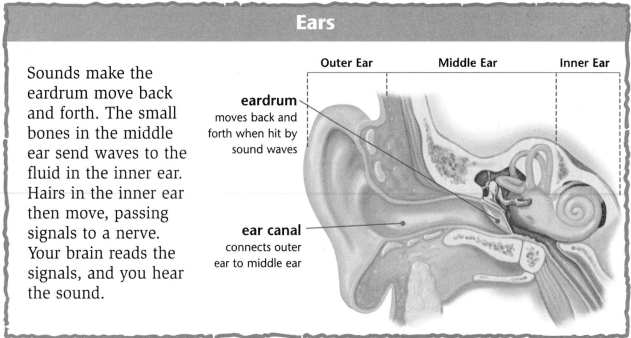

Sounds make the eardrum move back and forth. The small bones in the middle ear send waves to the fluid in the inner ear. Hairs in the inner ear then move, passing signals to a nerve. Your brain reads the signals, and you hear the sound.

Outer Ear   Middle Ear   Inner Ear

eardrum
moves back and forth when hit by sound waves

ear canal
connects outer ear to middle ear

Caring for Your Eyes and Ears

- Wear safety glasses when participating in activities where you can get hit or where a foreign object can hit an eye, such as sports and mowing grass.

- Avoid listening to very loud sounds for long periods of time. Loud sounds destroy the delicate hairs in the inner ear. You can lose your hearing little by little.

Nose

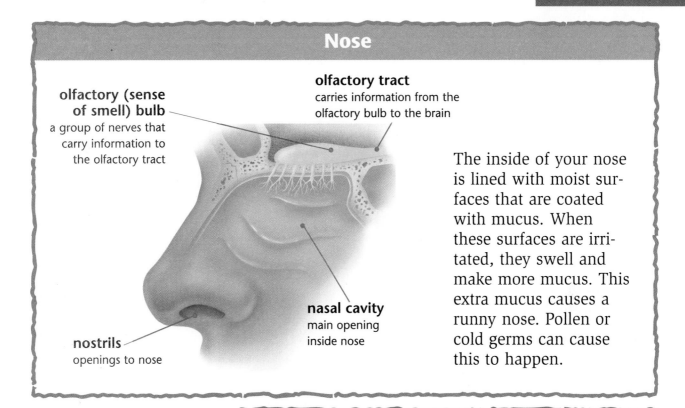

olfactory (sense of smell) bulb
a group of nerves that carry information to the olfactory tract

olfactory tract
carries information from the olfactory bulb to the brain

nostrils
openings to nose

nasal cavity
main opening inside nose

The inside of your nose is lined with moist surfaces that are coated with mucus. When these surfaces are irritated, they swell and make more mucus. This extra mucus causes a runny nose. Pollen or cold germs can cause this to happen.

Caring for Your Nose, Tongue, and Skin

- If you have a cold or allergies, don't blow your nose hard. Blowing your nose hard can force germs into your throat and ears.
- When you brush your teeth, brush your tongue too.
- Always wear sunscreen when you are in the sun.

Tongue

taste buds

Germs live on your tongue and in other parts of your mouth. Germs can harm your teeth and give you bad breath.

Skin

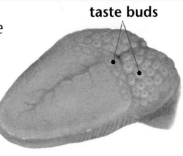

protective outer layer

strong, springy middle layer

fatty lower layer

Your skin protects your insides from the outside world. Your skin has many touch-sensitive nerves. Because your skin can feel temperature, pain, and pressure, you can avoid cuts, burns, and scrapes.

Skeletal System

Each of your bones has a particular shape and size that allow it to do a certain job. You have bones that are tiny, long, wide, flat, and even curved. The job of some bones is to protect your body parts.

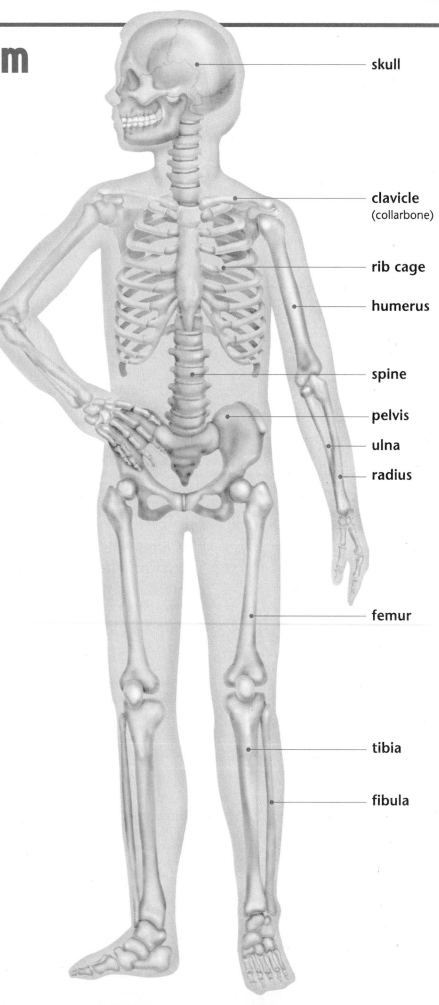

skull

clavicle
(collarbone)

rib cage

humerus

spine

pelvis

ulna

radius

femur

tibia

fibula

Spine, Skull, and Pelvis

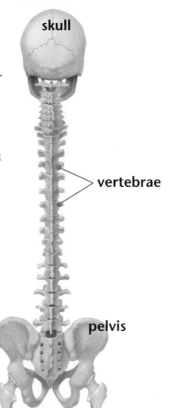

skull

vertebrae

pelvis

Spine Your spine, or backbone, is made up of small bones called vertebrae that protect your spinal cord. Each vertebra has a hole in it, like a doughnut. These bones fit together, one on top of the other, and the holes line up to form a tunnel. Cartilage disks sit like cushions between the vertebrae. Your spinal cord runs from your brain down your back inside this tunnel.

Skull The bones in your head are called your skull. Some of the bones in your skull protect your brain. The bones in your face are part of your skull too.

Pelvis Your spine connects to your hipbone, or pelvis. Your pelvis connects to your thighs. Your flexible spine, pelvis, and legs are what let you stand up straight, twist, turn, bend, and walk.

Caring for Your Skeletal System

- Calcium helps bones grow and makes them strong. Dairy products like milk, cheese, and yogurt contain calcium. Have two to three servings of dairy products every day. If you can't eat dairy products, dark green, leafy vegetables such as broccoli and collard greens or canned salmon with bones are also sources of calcium.

- Sit up straight with good posture. Sitting slumped over all the time can hurt muscles around your spine.

Activities

1. Make a stack of Life Savers® and run a string down through it. This is how your spinal cord runs through your spine.

2. Stand facing a wall. Without moving your feet, how far can you twist your body? How far can you see behind you?

3. Find the bony part of your hipbone that sticks out near your waist. Pick up one leg. Where does the thigh bone connect to your pelvis? How far is it from the bony part?

Muscular System

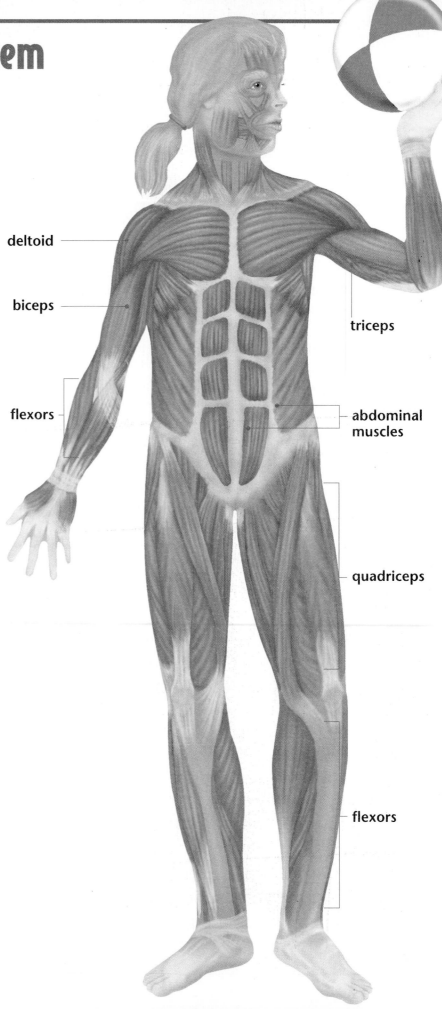

L ike your bones, each muscle in your body does a certain job. Muscles in your thumb help you hold things. Muscles in your neck help you turn your head. Your heart muscle pumps blood through your body. Small muscles control your eyes.

deltoid

biceps

flexors

triceps

abdominal muscles

quadriceps

flexors

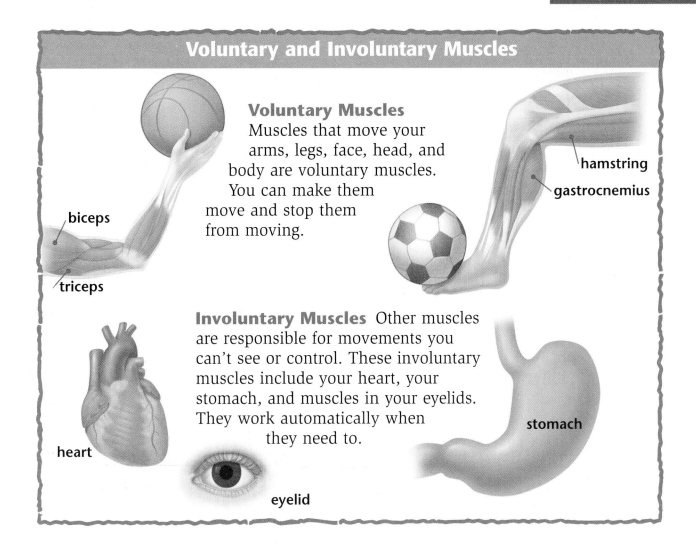

Voluntary and Involuntary Muscles

Voluntary Muscles
Muscles that move your arms, legs, face, head, and body are voluntary muscles. You can make them move and stop them from moving.

biceps

triceps

hamstring

gastrocnemius

Involuntary Muscles Other muscles are responsible for movements you can't see or control. These involuntary muscles include your heart, your stomach, and muscles in your eyelids. They work automatically when they need to.

heart

eyelid

stomach

Caring for Your Muscular System

- Exercise makes your muscles stronger and larger.
- Warming up by moving all your big muscles for five to ten minutes before you exercise helps prevent injury or pain.

Activities

1. Look into a mirror and cover one eye. Watch the pupil in the other eye. How does it change? Did you change it?

2. Try not to blink for as long as you can. What happens?

3. Without taking off your shoes, try moving each of your toes one at a time. Can you move each of them separately?

Digestive System

Food is broken down and pushed through your body by your digestive system. Your digestive system is a series of connected parts that starts with your mouth and ends with your large intestine. Each part helps your body get different nutrients from the food you eat.

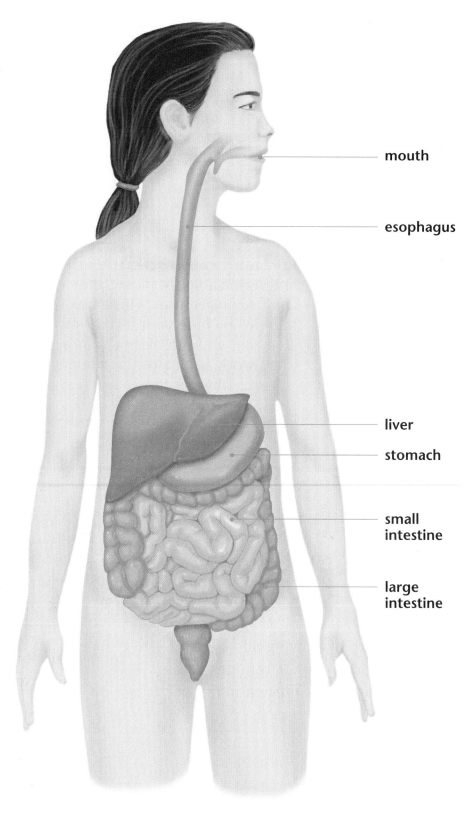

mouth

esophagus

liver

stomach

small intestine

large intestine

Small and Large Intestines

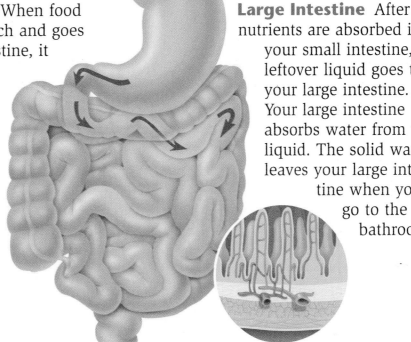

Small Intestine When food leaves your stomach and goes to your small intestine, it is a thick liquid. The walls of the small intestine are lined with many small, finger-shaped bumps. Tiny blood vessels in the bumps absorb nutrients from the liquid.

Large Intestine After nutrients are absorbed in your small intestine, the leftover liquid goes to your large intestine. Your large intestine absorbs water from the liquid. The solid waste leaves your large intestine when you go to the bathroom.

Caring for Your Digestive System

- Fiber helps your digestive system work better. Eat foods with fiber, such as fresh vegetables, beans, lentils, fruits, cereals, and breads, every day.

- Eat a balanced diet so that your body gets all the nutrients it needs.

Activities

1. Find the small and large intestines on the diagram of the digestive system. About how far is it from your belly button to where the small intestine starts?

2. On the diagram of the digestive system, trace the path that food takes through your body.

3. Draw a long line on a sheet of notebook paper. Fold the paper like an accordion. The line is like the path of food over the bumps in the small intestine.

Circulatory System

ood and oxygen
are carried by
your blood through
your circulatory
system to every cell
in your body. Blood
moves nutrients
throughout your
body, fights infec-
tion, and helps
control your body
temperature. Your
blood is mostly
made up of a watery
liquid called plasma.
It also contains three
kinds of cells.

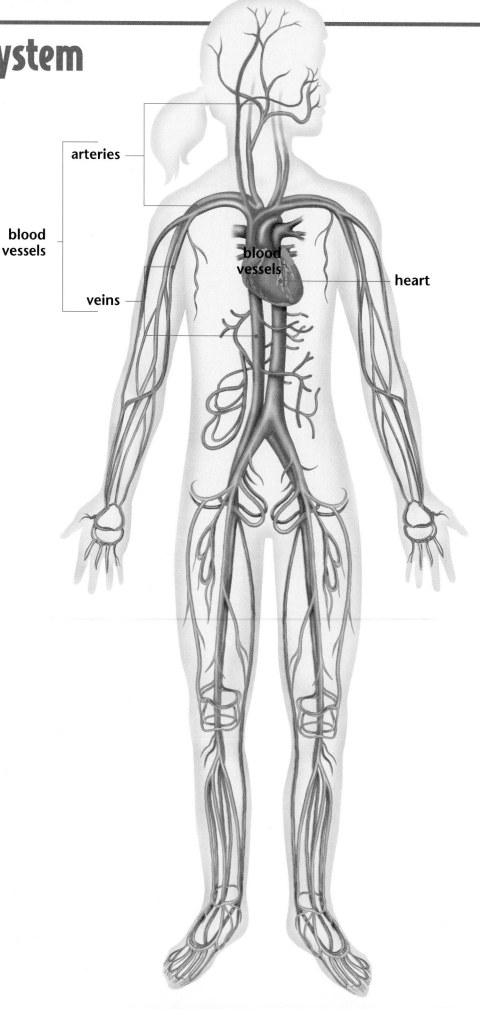

arteries

blood
vessels

veins

blood
vessels

heart

Blood Cells

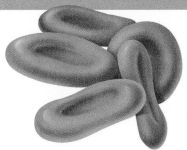

Red Blood Cells Red blood cells carry oxygen from your lungs to the rest of your body. They also carry carbon dioxide from your body back to your lungs, so you can breathe it out.

Platelets Platelets help clot your blood, which stops bleeding. Platelets clump together as soon as you get a cut. The sticky clump traps red blood cells and forms a blood clot. The blood clot hardens to make a scab and seals the cut.

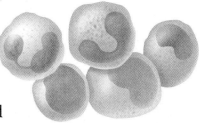

White Blood Cells When you are ill, your white blood cells come to the rescue. Some types of white blood cells identify what is making you ill. Some organize an attack. Others kill the invading germs or infected cells.

Caring for Your Circulatory System

- Never touch another person's blood.
- Don't pick scabs. If you pick a scab, you might make it bleed and the clotting process must begin again.

Activities

1. On the diagram of the circulatory system, trace the path of blood from the heart to the knee.

2. Red blood cells are medium-size and are the most common cells in your blood. White blood cells are larger and are the least common. Platelets are the smallest blood cells. Draw a picture of what a drop of blood might look like under a microscope.

Respiratory System

Your body uses its respiratory system to get oxygen from the air. Your respiratory system is made up of your nose and mouth, your trachea, your two lungs, and your diaphragm.

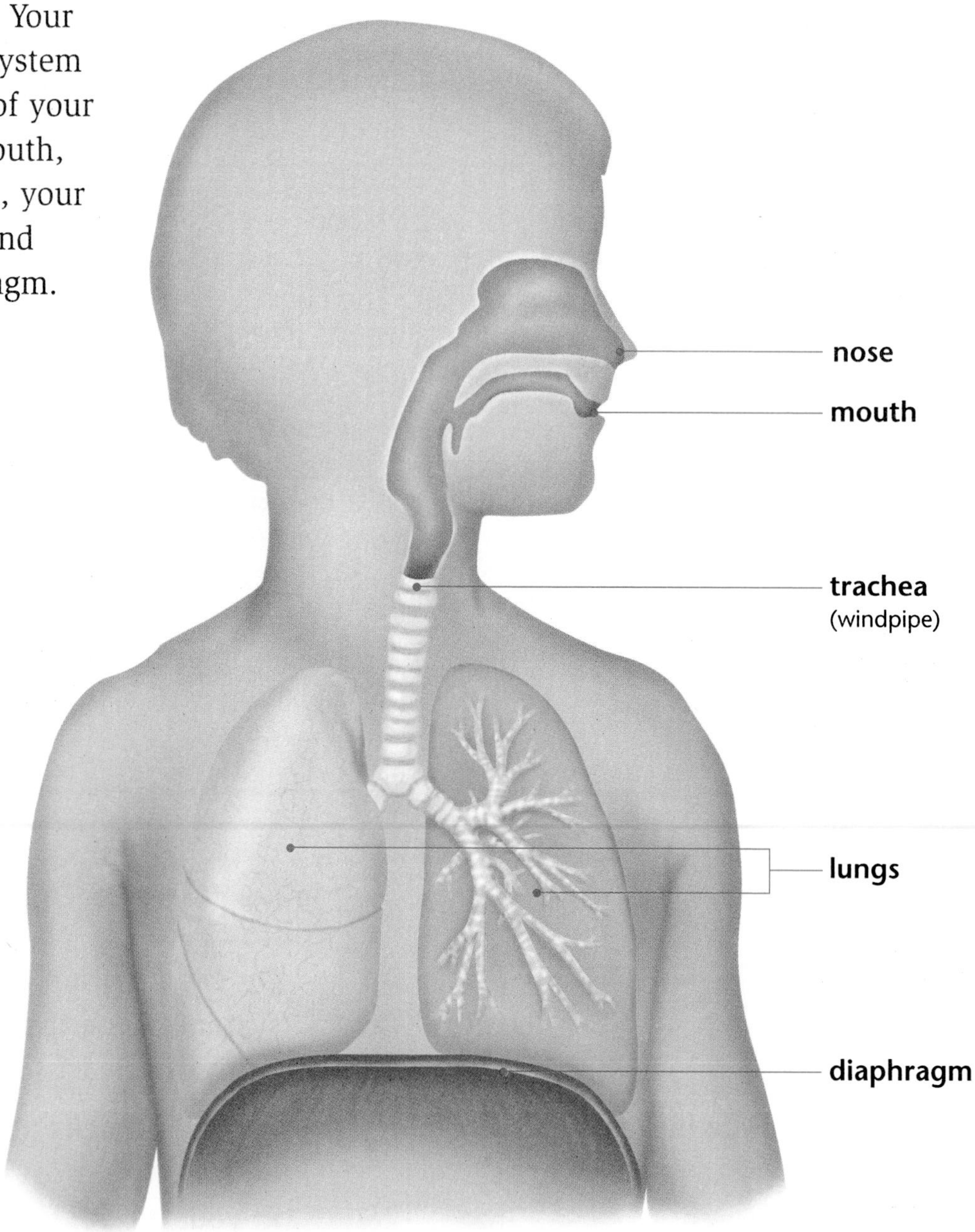

nose

mouth

trachea
(windpipe)

lungs

diaphragm

Functions of the Lungs

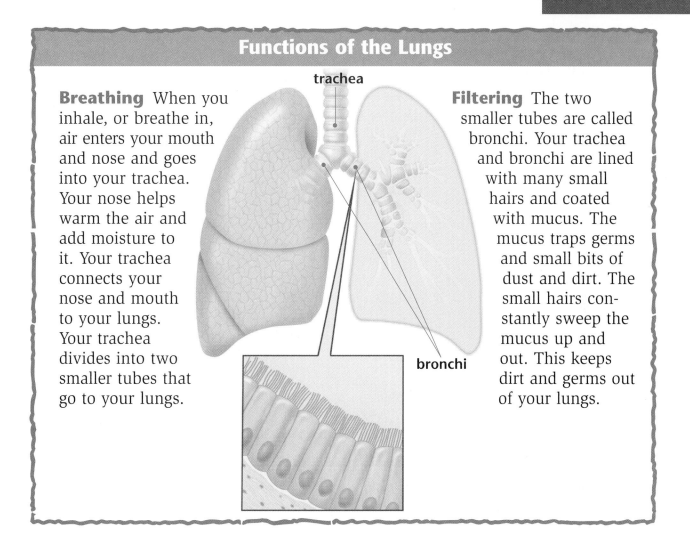

trachea

bronchi

Breathing When you inhale, or breathe in, air enters your mouth and nose and goes into your trachea. Your nose helps warm the air and add moisture to it. Your trachea connects your nose and mouth to your lungs. Your trachea divides into two smaller tubes that go to your lungs.

Filtering The two smaller tubes are called bronchi. Your trachea and bronchi are lined with many small hairs and coated with mucus. The mucus traps germs and small bits of dust and dirt. The small hairs constantly sweep the mucus up and out. This keeps dirt and germs out of your lungs.

Caring for Your Respiratory System

- Avoid smoke and other air pollution. They can paralyze the tiny hairs and cause you to become ill.
- Get plenty of exercise to keep your heart and lungs strong.

Activities

1. Take several breaths through your nose. Notice how the inside of your nose feels when you breathe in. Moisten a paper towel and take several breaths through the towel. Does your nose feel different?

2. Take a deep breath and hold it. Have someone measure your chest with a tape measure. Breathe the air out, and have someone measure your chest again. Is your chest bigger when you breathe in or when you breathe out?

Nervous System

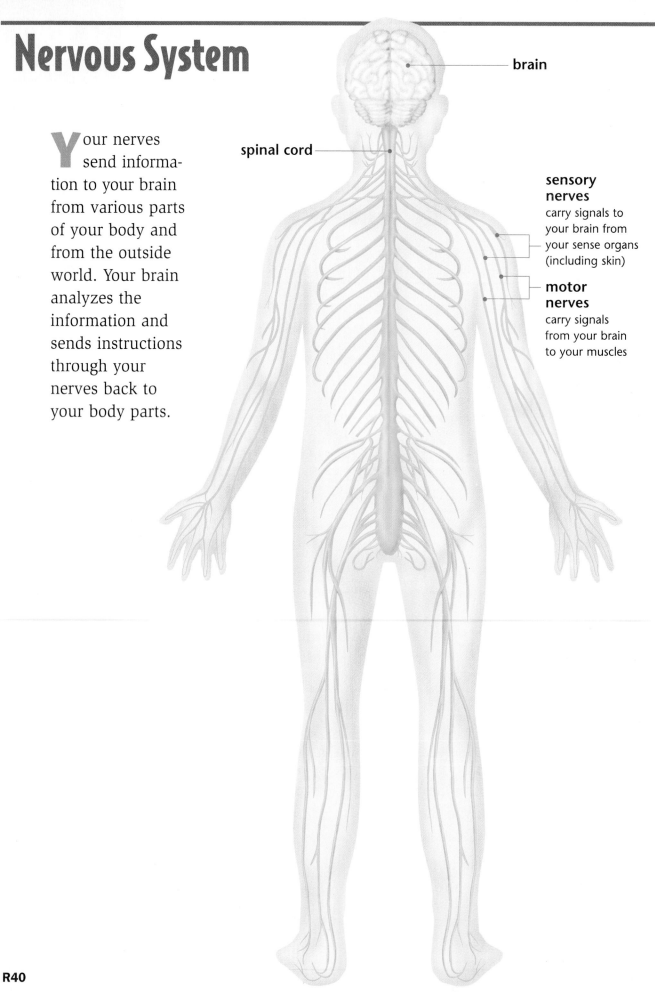

brain

spinal cord

sensory nerves
carry signals to your brain from your sense organs (including skin)

motor nerves
carry signals from your brain to your muscles

Your nerves send information to your brain from various parts of your body and from the outside world. Your brain analyzes the information and sends instructions through your nerves back to your body parts.

Messages to and from the Brain

Incoming Messages Your sensory nerves send signals to your brain from your sense organs. Every minute your brain receives millions of these signals. Your brain has to decide how to deal with each piece of information. For example, your brain might decide to deal with a barking dog nearby before it deals with a person calling to you from a distance.

Outgoing Messages Every minute, millions of nerve signals also leave your brain. Your motor nerves carry these messages. Your motor nerves connect to your muscles and tell them what to do. When you ride your bike, your brain helps you maintain balance and sends instructions to all the muscles you use to ride a bike.

Caring for Your Nervous System

- Eat a healthful, balanced diet. Your brain needs energy and nutrients to work well.

- Always wear a helmet when you ride your bike, skate, or use a skateboard.

Activities

1. Balance on one foot for as long as you can. Close your eyes and try again. Was it easier or harder the second time?

2. Pick up five pennies. Try it again wearing a glove. Why was it harder?

3. Hold a ruler at one end and dangle it just above a partner's open index finger and thumb. Drop the ruler through the gap. Where on the ruler does your partner grab? Try it several times, and then switch roles.

Glossary

This Glossary contains important science words and their definitions. Each word is respelled as it would be in a dictionary. When you see the ′ mark after a syllable, pronounce that syllable with more force than the other syllables. The page number at the end of the definition tells where to find the word in your book. The boldfaced letters in the examples in the Pronunciation Key that follows show how these letters are pronounced in the respellings after each glossary word.

PRONUNCIATION KEY

a	add, map	m	move, seem	u	up, done
ā	ace, rate	n	nice, tin	û(r)	burn, term
â(r)	care, air	ng	ring, song	yōō	fuse, few
ä	palm, father	o	odd, hot	v	vain, eve
b	bat, rub	ō	open, so	w	win, away
ch	check, catch	ô	order, jaw	y	yet, yearn
d	dog, rod	oi	oil, boy	z	zest, muse
e	end, pet	ou	pout, now	zh	vision, pleasure
ē	equal, tree	o͝o	took, full	ə	the schwa, an
f	fit, half	o͞o	pool, food		unstressed vowel
g	go, log	p	pit, stop		representing the sound
h	hope, hate	r	run, poor		spelled
i	it, give	s	see, pass		*a* in *above*
ī	ice, write	sh	sure, rush		*e* in *sicken*
j	joy, ledge	t	talk, sit		*i* in *possible*
k	cool, take	th	thin, both		*o* in *melon*
l	look, rule	t̶h̶	this, bathe		*u* in *circus*

Other symbols:

- • separates words into syllables
- ′ indicates heavier stress on a syllable
- ′ indicates light stress on a syllable

acceleration [ak•sel′ər•ā′shən] A change in the speed or direction of an object's motion **(F14)**

adaptation [ad′əp•tā′shən] A body part or behavior that helps an animal meet its needs in its environment **(A40)**

air mass [âr′mas′] A huge body of air which all has similar temperature and moisture **(D13)**

air pressure [âr′presh′ər] Particles of air pressing down on the Earth's surface **(D7)**

amphibian [am•fib′ē•ən] An animal that has moist skin and no scales **(A12)**

anemometer [an′ə•mom′ə•tər] An instrument used to measure wind speed **(D21)**

artery [är′tər•ē] A blood vessel that takes blood away from the heart **(A97)**

arthropod [är′thrə•pod] An invertebrate with legs that have several joints **(A13)**

asteroid [as′tə•roid] A small rocky object that moves around the sun **(D57)**

atmosphere [at′məs•fir] The layer of air that surrounds our planet **(D6)**

axis [ak′sis] An imaginary line which runs through both poles of a planet **(D58)**

barometer [bə•rom′ət•ər] An instrument that measures air pressure **(D20)**

brain [brān] The control center of your nervous system **(A102)**

buoyancy [boi′ən•sē] The ability of matter to float in a liquid or gas **(E20)**

camouflage [kam′ə•fläzh′] An animal's color or pattern that helps it blend in with its surroundings **(A44)**

capillary [kap′ə•ler′ē] A tiny blood vessel that allows gases and nutrients to pass from blood to cells **(A96)**

carbon dioxide [kär′bən dī•ok′sīd′] A gas breathed out by animals **(A64)**

cardiac muscle [kär′dē•ak mus′əl] A type of muscle that works the heart **(A91)**

cast [kast] A fossil formed when sediments or minerals fill a mold; it takes on the same outside shape as the living thing that shaped the mold **(C64)**

cell [sel] The basic building block of life **(A90)**

charge [chärj] A measure of the extra positive or negative particles that an object has **(E90)**

circuit [sûr′kit] A path that is made for an electric current **(E96)**

classification [klas′ə•fə•kā′shən] The grouping of things by using a set of rules **(A6)**

climate [klī′mit] The average temperature and rainfall of an area over many years **(A33, B26)**

comet [kom′it] A small mass of dust and ice that orbits the sun in a long, oval-shaped path **(D57)**

community [kə•myoō′nə•tē] All the populations that live in the same area **(B14)**

compression [kəm•presh′ən] The part of a sound wave in which air is pushed together **(E63)**

condensation [kon′dən•sā′shən] The process by which water vapor changes from a gas to liquid **(D34)**

conduction [kən•duk′shən] The transfer of thermal energy caused by particles of matter bumping into each other **(E41)**

conductor [kən•duk′tər] A material that electric current can pass through easily **(E97)**

conservation [kon′sər•vā′shən] The careful management and wise use of natural resources **(B86)**

constellation [kon′stə•lā′shən] The pattern formed by a group of stars in the sky **(D78)**

consumer [kən•soō′mər] A living thing that eats other living things for energy **(B21)**

contour plowing [kon′toōr plou′ing] Plowing around a hill to reduce erosion **(B56)**

convection [kən•vek′shən] The transfer of thermal energy by particles of a liquid or gas moving from one place to another **(E42)**

core [kôr] The dense center of Earth; a ball made mostly of two metals, iron and nickel **(C6)**

crater [krā′tər] A large basin formed at the top of a volcano when it falls in on itself **(C20)**

crust [krust] Earth's outer layer; includes the rock of the ocean floor and large areas of land **(C6)**

decomposer [dē′kəm•pōz′ər] A living thing that feeds on the wastes of plants and animals or on their remains after they die **(B21)**

deep ocean current [dēp′ ō′shən kûr′ənt] An ocean current formed when cold water flows underneath warm water **(D44)**

density [den′sə•tē] The property of matter that compares the amount of matter to the space it takes up **(E14)**

dissolve [di•zolv′] To form a solution with another material **(E19)**

diversity [di•vûr′sə•tē] Variety **(B27)**

earthquake [ûrth′ kwāk′] A vibration, or shaking, of Earth's crust **(C12)**

echo [ek′ō] A sound reflection **(E76)**

ecosystem [ek′ō•sis′təm] Groups of living things and the environment they live in **(B12)**

effort force [ef′ərt fôrs′] The force put on one part of the bar when you push or pull on a lever **(F38)**

electric cell [i·lek′trik sel′] A battery that supplies energy to move charges through a circuit **(E96)**

electric current [i·lek′trik kûr′ənt] A flow of electric charges **(E96)**

electric field [i·lek′trik fēld′] The space around an object in which electric forces occur **(E92)**

electromagnet [i·lek′trō·mag′nit] An arrangement of wire wrapped around a core, producing a temporary magnet **(E109)**

energy [en′ər·jē] The ability to cause a change **(E34)**

environment [in·vī′rən·mənt] Everything that surrounds and affects an animal, including living and nonliving things **(A32)**

epicenter [ep′i·sent′ər] The point on the surface of Earth that is right above the focus of an earthquake **(C13)**

erosion [i·rō′zhən] The process by which wind and moving water carry away bits of rock **(B43)**

esophagus [i·sof′ə·gəs] The tube that connects your mouth with your stomach **(A104)**

evaporation [ē·vap′ə·rā′shən] The process in which a liquid changes to a gas **(D34)**

fault [fôlt] A break in Earth's crust along which rocks move **(C12)**

fertile [fûr′təl] Soil that has the nutrients to grow many plants **(B50)**

fibrous roots [fī′brəs rōōts′] Long roots that grow near the surface **(A71)**

focus [fō′kəs] The point underground where the movement of an earthquake first took place **(C13)**

force [fôrs] A push or pull **(F12)**

fossil [fos′əl] A preserved clue to life on Earth long ago **(C62)**

frame of reference [frām′ uv ref′ər·əns] The things around you that you can sense and use to describe motion **(F7)**

friction [frik′shən] A force that keeps objects that are touching each other from sliding past each other easily **(F26)**

front [frunt] The border where two air masses meet **(D14)**

fuel [fyōō′əl] A material that can burn **(E48)**

fulcrum [fōōl′krəm] The fixed point, or point that doesn't move, on a lever **(F38)**

fungi [fun′jī′] Living things such as mushrooms that look like plants, but can not make their own food **(A7)**

gas [gas] The state of matter that has no definite shape and takes up no definite amount of space **(E8)**

gas giants [gas′ jī′ənts] The planets Jupiter, Saturn, Uranus, and Neptune, which are large spheres made up mostly of gases **(D64)**

genus [jē′nəs] The second-smallest name grouping used in classification **(A8)**

germinate [jûr′mə•nāt′] To sprout; said of a seed **(A76)**

gravity [grav′ə•tē] A force that pulls all objects toward each other **(F22)**

greenhouse effect [grēn′hous′ i•fekt′] The warming of Earth caused by the atmosphere trapping thermal energy from the sun **(D12)**

habitat [hab′ə•tat′] An environment that meets the needs of an organism **(B20)**

hardness [härd′nis] A mineral's ability to resist being scratched **(C35)**

heart [härt] The muscle that pumps blood through your blood vessels to all parts of your body **(A97)**

heat [hēt] The transfer of thermal energy from one piece of matter to another **(E40)**

hibernation [hī′bər•nā′shən] A period when an animal goes into a long, deep "sleep" **(A51)**

humidity [hyo͞o•mid′ə•tē] The amount of water vapor in the air **(D21)**

humus [hyo͞o′məs] The rotting plant and animal materials in topsoil **(B44)**

igneous rock [ig′nē•əs rok′] A rock that forms when completely melted rock hardens **(C40)**

inclined plane [in•klīnd′ plān′] A flat surface with one end higher than the other **(F52)**

infrared radiation [in′frə•red′ rā′dē•ā′shən] The bundles of light energy that transfer heat **(E44)**

inner planets [in′ər plan′its] The planets closest to the sun; Mercury, Venus, Earth, and Mars **(D62)**

instinct [in′stingkt] A behavior that an animal begins life with **(A48)**

insulator [in′sə•lāt′ər] A material that current cannot pass through easily **(E97)**

invertebrate [in•vûr′tə•brit] An animal without a backbone **(A13)**

kingdom [king′dəm] The largest group into which living things can be classified **(A7)**

large intestine [lärj in•tes′tən] The last part of the digestive system where water is removed from food **(A105)**

lava [lä′və] A melted rock that reaches Earth's surface **(C18)**

lever [lev′ər] A simple machine made up of a bar that turns around a fixed point **(F38)**

liquid [lik′wid] The state of matter that takes the shape of its container and takes up a definite amount of space **(E7)**

loudness [loud′nes] A measure of the amount of sound energy reaching your ear **(E68)**

lungs [lungz] The main organs of the respiratory system **(A96)**

luster [lus′tər] A way that the surface of a mineral reflects light **(C35)**

magma [mag′mə] Melted rock inside Earth **(C18)**

magma chamber [mag′mə chām′bər] An underground pool below a volcano that holds magma **(C19)**

magnet [mag′nit] An object that attracts certain materials, such as iron or steel **(E102)**

magnetic field [mag•net′ik fēld′] The space all around a magnet where the force of the magnet can act **(E102)**

magnetic pole [mag•net′ik pōl′] The end of a magnet **(E102)**

mammal [mam′əl] An animal that has hair and produces milk for its young **(A12)**

mantle [man′təl] The thickest layer of Earth; found just below the crust **(C6)**

mass [mas] The amount of matter something contains **(E6)**

matter [mat′ər] Everything in the universe that has mass and takes up space **(E6)**

metamorphic rock [met′ə•môr′fik rok′] A rock changed by heat or pressure, but not completely melted **(C44)**

metamorphosis [met′ə•môr′fə•sis] The process of change; for example, from an egg to an adult butterfly **(A36)**

migration [mī•grā′shən] The movement of a group of one type of animal from one region to another and back again **(A49)**

mimicry [mim′ik•rē] An adaptation in which an animal looks very much like another animal or an object **(A44)**

mineral [min′ər•əl] A natural, solid material with particles arranged in a repeating pattern **(C34)**

mold [mōld] A fossil imprint made by the outside of a dead plant or animal **(C64)**

mollusk [mol′əsk] An invertebrate that may or may not have a hard outer shell **(A13)**

moneran [mō•ner′ən] The kingdom of classification for organisms that have only one cell **(A7)**

motion [mō′shən] A change of position **(F6)**

nerve [nûrv] A group of neurons that carries signals from the brain to the body and from the body to the brain **(A102)**

neuron [noor′on′] A nerve cell **(A102)**

newton [noo′tən] The metric, or Système International (SI), unit of force **(F17)**

niche [nich] The role or part played by an organism in its habitat **(B21)**

nonvascular plants [non•vas′kyə•lər plants′] The plants that do not have tubes **(A20)**

nutrient [noo′trē•ənt] Substances, such as minerals, which all living things need in order to grow **(A64)**

O

orbit [ôr′bit] The path that an object such as a planet makes as it revolves around a second object **(D58)**

organ [ôr′gən] A group of tissues of different kinds working together to perform a task **(A90)**

outer planets [ou′tər plan′its] The planets farthest from the sun; Jupiter, Saturn, Uranus, Neptune, and Pluto **(D64)**

oxygen [ok′si•jən] One of the many gases in air **(A33)**

P

parallel circuit [par′ə•lel sûr′kit] A circuit that has more than one path along which current can travel **(E98)**

photosynthesis [fōt′ō•sin′thə•sis] The process by which a plant makes its own food **(A65)**

pitch [pich] A measure of how high or low a sound is **(E69)**

planet [plan′it] A large object that moves around a star **(D57)**

plate [plāt] Continent-sized slab of Earth's crust and upper mantle **(C8)**

population [pop′yə•lā′shən] A group of the same species living in the same place at the same time **(B13)**

position [pə•zish′ən] A certain place **(F6)**

precipitation [pri•sip′ə•tā′shən] Water that falls to Earth as rain, snow, sleet, or hail **(D35)**

preservation [prez′ər•vā′shən] The protection of an area **(B88)**

producer [prə•doos′ər] Living things such as plants that produce their own food **(B21)**

protist [prō′tist] The kingdom of classification for organisms that have only one cell and also have a nucleus or cell control center **(A7)**

pulley [pool′ē] A simple machine made up of a rope or chain and a wheel around which the rope fits **(F46)**

R

radiation [rā′dē•ā′shən] The bundles of energy that move through matter and through empty space **(E44)**

reclamation [rek′lə•mā′shən] The repairing of some of the damage done to an ecosystem **(B81)**

relative motion [rel′ə•tiv mō′shən] A motion that is described based on a frame of reference **(F7)**

reptile [rep′təl] An animal that has dry, scaly skin **(A12)**

resistance force [ri•zis′təns fôrs′] The force put out by the other end of the bar on a lever; the force that does work for you **(F38)**

resistor [ri•zis′tər] A material that resists the flow of current but doesn't stop it **(E97)**

rock [rok] A material made up of one or more minerals **(C40)**

rock cycle [rok′ sī′kəl] The slow, never-ending process of rock changes **(C50)**

salinity [sə•lin′ə•tē] The amount of salt in water **(B28)**

screw [skro͞o] An inclined plane wrapped around a pole **(F54)**

sedimentary rock [sed′ə•men′tər•ē rok′] A rock formed by layers of sediments squeezed and stuck together over a long time **(C42)**

seismograph [sīz′mə•graf′] An instrument that records earthquake waves **(C14)**

series circuit [sir′ēz sûr′kit] A circuit that has only one path for current **(E98)**

shelter [shel′tər] A place where an animal is protected from other animals or from the weather **(A35)**

simple machine [sim′pəl mə•shēn′] One of the basic machines that make up other machines **(F38)**

small intestine [smôl′ in•tes′tən] A long tube of muscle where most food is digested **(A104)**

smooth muscle [smo͞oth′ mus′əl] A type of muscle found in the walls of some organs such as the stomach, intestines, blood vessels, and bladder **(A92)**

soil conservation [soil′ kon′sər•vā′shən] The saving of soil **(B56)**

solar energy [sō′lər en′ər•jē] The energy given off by the sun **(E49)**

solar system [sō′lər sis′təm] A group of objects in space that move around a central star **(D56)**

solid [sol′id] The state of matter that has a definite shape and takes up a definite amount of space **(E6)**

solubility [sol′yə•bil′ə•tē] A measure of the amount of a material that will dissolve in another material **(E19)**

solution [sə•lo͞o′shən] A mixture in which the particles of different kinds of matter are mixed evenly with each other and particles do not settle out **(E18)**

sonic boom [son′ik bo͞om′] A shock wave of compressed sound waves produced by an object moving faster than sound **(E78)**

sound [sound] A series of vibrations that you can hear **(E62)**

sound wave [sound′ wāv′] A moving pattern of high and low pressure that you can hear **(E63)**

space probe [spās′ prōb′] A space vehicle that carries cameras, instruments, and other research tools **(D74)**

species [spē′shēz] The smallest name grouping used in classification **(A8)**

speed [spēd] A measure of an object's change in position during a unit of time; for example, 10 meters per second **(F8)**

speed of sound [spēd′ uv sound′] The speed at which a sound wave travels through a given material **(E74)**

spinal cord [spī′nəl kôrd′] The tube of nerves that runs through your spine, or backbone **(A102)**

spore [spôr] A tiny cell that ferns and fungi use to reproduce **(A77)**

stability [stə•bil′ə•tē] The condition that exists when the changes in a system over time cancel each other out **(B8)**

star [stär] A huge, burning sphere of gases; for example, the sun **(D56)**

static electricity [stat′ik ē′lek•tris′i•tē] An electric charge that stays on an object **(E90)**

stomach [stum′ək] A bag made up of smooth muscles that mixes food with digestive juices **(A104)**

storm surge [stôrm′ sûrj′] A very large wave caused by high winds over a large area of ocean **(D41)**

stratosphere [strat′ə•sfir′] The layer of atmosphere that contains ozone and is located above the troposphere **(D8)**

streak [strēk] The color of the powder left behind when you rub a mineral against a white tile called a streak plate **(C35)**

striated muscle [strī′āt•ed mus′əl] A muscle with light and dark stripes; a muscle you can control by thinking **(A92)**

strip cropping [strip′ krop′ing] The practice of planting one or more crops between rows of other crops to control erosion **(B56)**

succession [sək•sesh′ən] The process that gradually changes an existing ecosystem into another ecosystem **(B70)**

surface current [sûr′fis kûr′ənt] An ocean current formed when steady winds blow over the surface of the ocean **(D44)**

symmetry [sim′ə•trē] The condition in which each feature on one half of an object has a matching feature on the other half **(A70)**

system [sis′təm] A group of parts that work together as a unit **(B6)**

taproot [tap′rōot′] A plant's single main root that goes deep into the soil **(A71)**

telescope [tel′ə•skōp′] A device people use to observe distant objects with their eyes **(D70)**

temperature [tem′pər•ə•chər] A measure of the average energy of motion of the particles in matter **(E35)**

terracing [ter′əs•ing] A farming method used on steep hillsides to control erosion **(B56)**

thermal energy [thûr′məl en′ər•jē] The energy of the motion of particles in matter **(E34)**

tide [tīd] The daily changes in the local water level of the ocean **(D42)**

tissue [tish′o͞o] A group of cells of the same type **(A90)**

trace fossil [trās′ fos′əl] A fossil that shows changes that long-dead animals made in their surroundings **(C63)**

transpiration [tran′spə•rā′shən] The giving off of water vapor by plants **(A70)**

troposphere [trō′pə•sfir′] The layer of atmosphere closest to Earth **(D8)**

tuber [to͞o′bər] A swollen underground stem **(A78)**

vascular plant [vas′kyə•lər plant′] A plant that has tubes **(A18)**

vein [vān] A large blood vessel that returns blood to the heart **(A97)**

vent [vent] The rocky tube in a volcano through which magma rises toward the surface **(C18)**

vertebrate [vûr′tə•brit] An animal with a backbone **(A12)**

volcano [vol•kā′nō] A mountain that forms when red-hot melted rock flows through a crack onto Earth's surface **(C18)**

volume [vol′yəm] The amount of space that matter takes up **(E13)**

water cycle [wôt′ər sī′kəl] The constant recycling of water on Earth **(D34)**

wave [wāv] The up-and-down movement of water **(D40)**

weathering [we𝑡ħ′ər•ing] The process by which rocks are broken down into smaller pieces **(B43, C42)**

wedge [wej] A machine made up of two inclined planes placed back-to-back **(F56)**

weight [wāt] A measure of the force of gravity upon an object **(F23)**

wheel and axle [hwēl′ and ak′səl] A simple machine made up of a large wheel attached to a smaller wheel or rod **(F48)**

work [wûrk] That which is done on an object when a force moves the object through a distance **(F42)**

L

 M

Uranus, D65, D82, D83
  seasons of, D53
U.S. Bureau of Fisheries, D48
U.S. Geological Survey, C76
U.S. Nuclear Regulatory
  Commission (NRC), E26
U.S. Soil Conservation
  Service, B61

Valves, heart, A98
Vascular plants, A18–19
Veins, human, A97, A98, R36
Vent, ocean floor, C18
Venus, D62–63
Venus' flytrap, A72
Vertebrae, A11, A12, R31
Veterans Administration
  Hospital, Bronx, A108
Vibrations, E62
  reduction, E81
Viceroy butterfly, A44
Vines, A66
Virgo, D80
Virtual reality, B32
Vitamins, A81
Voiceprint, E71
Voice range, of selected
  animals, E59
Volcanic eruptions (chart), C22
Volcanoes, B73, C8, C16
  destruction by, C22
  formation of, C18
  Iceland, C3
  as land builders, C20–21
  types of, C19
Volta, Alessandro, E115
Volume, E13
Voluntary muscles, R33
Voyager 2, D75, D83
Vulture, A32

Walking stick, A44–45
Warm front, D15
Washington University, C41
Waste(s), B79
Waste heat, E50
Water
  animal need for, A35
  solubility in (chart), E19
Water cycle, D34–35
Water heater, E49
Waterlily, A66
Waterspider, A6
Water transportation, history
  of, F58–59
Water vapor, D6–7, D21, D34,
  E8, E36
Waves, ocean, D40–41
Waves, sound, E63
Weather
  and air, D12–17
  mapping and charting,
    D22–23
  measuring, D20–21
  predicting, D20–23
Weathering, B43, C42, C48
Weather map, D22–23
Weather symbols, D14, D15,
  D16–17, D22–23
Weather vane, D16
Web, spider's, B18
Wedge, F38, F56–57
Weight, F23
  on planets, F23
Whales, A33
  stomach of, A87
Wheel and axle, F38, F48–49,
  F59
Wheelbarrow
  as compound machine, F34
  as lever, F39
Wheelchair ramp, as inclined
  plane, F53
White, Lisa D., C76
White blood cells, R37
Wild orchids, A68

Wind, and ocean waves, D40
Windloss, F59
Windsock, D10, D11
Wizard Island, OR, C20
Wonderful Flight to the
  Mushroom Planet, The
  (Cameron), D67
Wooly mammoth, C69
Work, F42
Workout, guidelines for, R17
Worms, A13
Wright, Wilbur and Orville, F60

Yalow, Rosalyn, A108
Yard system, B6–8
Yard water cycle, B6
Year, planet, D58
Yellowstone National Park, B72

Researchers; C41 (b) Martha McBride/Unicorn Stock Photos; C41 (tl) Dr. E.R. Degginger,FPSA/Color-Pic.; C41 (tr) Breck P. Kent/Earth Scenes; C41 (tcr) Robert Pettit/Dembinsky Photo Associates; C41 (tcl) Dr. E.R. Degginger/Color-Pic; C42 Dr. E.R. Degginger/Color-Pic; C43 (tl) Dr. E.R. Degginger/Color-Pic; C43 (tr) Dr. E.R. Degginger/Color-Pic; C43 (bg) David Bassett/Tony Stone Images; C43 (tcl)Dr. E.R. Degginger/Color-Pic; C43 (tcr)Dr. E.R. Degginger, FPSA/Color-Pic; C44 (t) G. R. Roberts Photo Library; C44 (b) Dr. E.R. Degginger/Color-Pic; C44-C45(ti) Dr. E.R. Degginger/Color-Pic; C45 (t) Dr. E.R. Degginger/Color-Pic; C46 Tom Till/Auscape; C48 Dr. E.R. Degginger/Color-Pic; C49 (t) Dr. E.R. Degginger/Color-Pic; C49 (b) Dr. E.R. Degginger/Color-Pic; C50 (l) Dr. E.R. Degginger,FPSA/Color-Pic.; C50 (r) Dr. E.R. Degginger/Color-Pic; C50-C51(t) Dr. E.R. Degginger/Color-Pic; C52-C53James P. Blair & Victor Boswell/NGS Image Collection; C53Mark Richards/PhotoEdit; C54 (t) Photo Courtesy of Mrs. Alma G. Gipson; C54 (b) Stuart McCall/Tony Stone Images; C58-C59 Gerd Ludwig/Woodfin Camp & Associates; C59 (t) The Westthalian Museum of Natural History.; C59 (b) James Martin/Tony Stone Images; C60 Murray Alcosser/The Image Bank; C62 (t) Beth Davidow/Visuals Unlimited; C62 (b) The Natural History Museum, London; C62-C63(b) William E. Ferguson; C63 (c) The Natural History Museum, London; C63 (tl) Dr. P. Evans/Bruce Coleman Collection; C63 (tr) David J. Sams/Tony Stone Images; C64 (l) William E. Ferguson; C64-C65(t) Bob Burch/Bruce Coleman, Inc.; C64 (t) Jane Burton/Bruce Coleman, Inc.; C64-C65(b) Dr. E. R. Degginger/Bruce Coleman, Inc.; C65 (t) Dr. E. R. Degginger/Bruce Coleman, Inc.; C66 The Natural History Museum, London; C68 (l) The Natural History Museum, London; C68-C69(bg) Mark J. Thomas/Dembinsky Photo Associates; C68 (li) William E. Ferguson; C69 (t) Runk/Schoenberger/Grant Heilman Photography; C70 (t) Phil Schofield/Tony Stone Images; C70 (c) Phil Degginger/Bruce Coleman, Inc.; C71 (c) Louis Psihoyos/Matrix International, Inc.; C71 (ti) Louie Psihoyos/Matrix International, Inc.; C71 (bi) Louie Psihoyos/Matrix International, Inc.; C72 (t) Ted Clutter/Photo Researchers; C72 (b) J. C. Carton/Bruce Coleman, Inc.; C73 William E. Ferguson; C74 (b) The Granger Collection, New York; C74 (tl) Alinari/Art Resource, NY; C74 (tr) The Granger Collection, New York; C75 (t) Bill Bachman/Photo Researchers; C75 (b) James King-Holmes/Science Photo Library/Photo Researchers; C76 (t) San Francisco State University/Department of Geosciences; C76 (b) AP/Wide World Photos.

Unit D

D2-D3 Waren Faidley/International Stock Photography; D3 (t) Bob Abraham/The Stock Market; D3 (b) NRSC Ltd/Science Photo Library/Photo Researchers; D4 Keren Su/Stock Boston; D6 Space Frontiers-TCL/Masterfile; D10 Bruce Watkins/Earth Scenes; D12 Peter Menzel/Stock Boston; D14-D15C. O'Rear/Westlight; D16 (b) Bill Binzen/The Stock Market; D18 J. Taposchaner/FPG International; D20 Sam Ogden/Science Photo Library/Photo Researchers; D21 (t) Breck P. Kent/Earth Scenes; D21 (b) B. Daemmrich/The Image Works; D22 © 1998 Accu Weather; D22 © 1998 Accu Weather D46-D47Ben Margot/AP Photo/Wide World Photos; ; D24 Geophysical Institute, University of Alaska, Fairbanks/NASA; D25 Pat Lanza/Bruce Coleman, Inc.; D26 (t) Clark Atlanta University; D26 (b) NASA/Science Photo Library/Photo Researchers; D30-D31Warren Bolster/Tony Stone Images; D31 (t) Warren Morgan/Corbis; D31 (b) Tom Van Sant, Geosphere Project/Planetary Visions/Science Photo Library/Photo; D32 Philip A. Savoie/Bruce Coleman, Inc.; D36 (tr) A. Ramey/Stock Boston; D36 ((bl)) Richard Gaul/FPG International; D38 John Lel/Stock Boston; D40 Dr. E.R. Degginger/Photo Researchers; D41 (t) Fredrik Bodin/Stock Boston; D41 (b) Peter Miller/Photo Researchers; D42 (t) Francois Gohier/Photo Researchers; D42 (c) Francois Gohier/Photo Researchers; D42 (b) Steinhart Aquarium/Tom McHugh/Photo Researchers; D47 Thomas Ives/The Stock Market; D48 (t) Erich Hartmann/Magnum Photos; D48 (b) Ron Sefton/Bruce Coleman, Inc.; D52-D53Ton Kinsbergen/ESA/Science Photo Library/Photo Researchers; D54 Tom Till; D57 Frank Zullo/Photo Researchers, Inc.; D58-D59 M. Agliolo/Photo Researchers, Inc.; D60 NASA; D63 U.S. Geological Survey/Science Photo Library/Photo Researchers; D63 (b) David Crisp and the WFPC2 Science Team (Jet Propulsion Laboratory/California Institute of Technology); D63 (ct) NASA; D63 (cb) National Oceanic and Atmospheric Administration; D64 NASA; D64-D65Erich Karkoschka (University of Arizona Lunar & Planetary Lab) and NASA; D65 (r) Dr. R. Albrecht, ESA/ESO Space Telescope European Coordinating Facility; NASA; D65 (c) Lawrence Sromovsky (University of Wisconsin - Madison), NASA; D66 NASA; D66 NASA; D66 NASA, D67 NASA; D68 NASA; D70 (r) Michael Freeman; D70 (tl) David Nunuk/Science Photo Library/Photo Researchers; D70 ((bl)) Omikron Collection/Photo Researchers; D71 (t) Simon Fraser/Science Photo Library/Photo Researchers; D71 (b) Robert Frerck/Tony Stone Images; D71 (ti) Roger Ressmeyer/Corbis; D72 NASA; D73 NASA; D73 NASA; D73 NASA; D74 NASA; D74 NASA; D74 NASA; D75 NASA; D76 Michael Holford; D78 John Sandford/Science Photo Library/Photo Researchers; D79 (t) Jerry Schad/Photo Researchers; D79 (b) John Sanford/Science Photo Library/Photo Researchers D82 (l) The Granger Collection, New York; D82 (r) Jean-Loup Charmet; D82-D83 (bg) NASA; D83 (l) Sylvester Allred/Visuals Unlimited; D83 (r) Mark E. Gibson/Dembinsky Photo Associates; D84 (t) J. Kelly Beatty/Sky Publishing Corporation; D84 (b) Science VU/Visuals Unlimited.

Unit E

E2-E3Jon Riley/Tony Stone Images; E3 (l) Dr. E.R. Degginger/Color-Pic; E3 (r) Dr. E.R. Degginger/Color-Pic; E4 Superstock; E6 Michael Denora/Liaison International; E8(b) Bob Abraham/The Stock Market; E10 Robert P. Carr/Bruce Coleman, Inc.; E14-E15(b) Richard H. Hansen/Photo Researchers; E16 Tony Stone Images; E20 (t) Kathy Ferguson/PhotoEdit; E20 (b) Doug Perrine/Innerspace Visions; E20 (bi) Felicia Martinez/PhotoEdit; E21 (b) Chip Clark; E22-E23Richard Pasley/Stock Boston; E24 Courtesy of J. G.'s Edible Plastic; E25 David R. Frazier; E26 (t) United States Nuclear Regulatory Commission; E26 (b) Tom Carroll/Phototake; E30-E31Ray Ellis/Photo Researchers; E31 (t) Peter Steiner/The Stock Market; E31 (b) Murray & Assoc./The Stock Market; E32 Craig Tuttle/The Stock Market; E35 (t) Jim Zipp/Photo Researchers; E36 Ted Horowitz/The Stock Market; E40 D. Nabokov/Gamma Liaison; E42 (b) L. West/Bruce Coleman, Inc.; E42 (i)Jonathan Wright/Bruce Coleman, Inc.; E43Gary Milburn/Tom Stack

& Associates; E44 (b) Jeff Foott/Bruce Coleman, Inc.; E48 (t) Craig Hammell/The Stock Market; E48 (b) Russell D. Curtis/Photo Researchers; E49 (tl) Stu Rosner/Stock, Boston; E49 (tr) John Mead/Science Photo Library/Photo Researchers; E49 (br) John Cancalosi/Stock, Boston; E50 (b) David Falconer & Associates; E50 (bi) Montes De Oca & Associates; E50 (tr) Telegraph Colour Library/FPG International; E50 (cr) Charles D. Winters/Photo Researchers; E51 Paul Shambroom/Science Source/Photo Researchers; E53 Danny Daniels/The Picture Cube; E54 (t) Minnesota Historical Society; E54 (b) Peter Vadnai/The Stock Market; E58-E59Stephen Dalton/Photo Researchers; E59 Carl R. Sams, II/Peter Arnold, Inc.; E60 A. Ramey/PhotoEdit; E63 (li) Michelle Bridwell/PhotoEdit; E63 (ri) Peter Langone/International Stock Photography; E63 (b) Summer Productions; E66 Randy Duchaine/The Stock Market; E68 (l) David Barnes/Tony Stone Images; E68 (r) Jim Zipp/Photo Researchers; E71 (b) Hank Morgan/Science Source/Photo Researchers; E72 Stocktrek/Frank Rossotto/The Stock Market; E74 Brian Parker/Tom Stack & Associates; E80 Bruce Forster/Tony Stone Images; E81 Russ Berger Design Group; E82 (t) Bose Corporation; E82 (b) Bose/Lisa Borman Associates; E86-E87Pete Saloutos/The Stock Market; E82 (t) Bose Corporation; E82 (b) Bose/Lisa Borman Associates; E86-E87 Pete Saloutos/The Stock Market; E88 Doug Martin/Photo Researchers; E93 Charles D. Winters/Photo Researchers; E94 Cosmo Condina/Tony Stone Images; E100 National Maritime Museum Picture Library; E103 (tr) Richard Megna/Fundamental Photographs; E103 ((bl)) Richard Megna/Fundamental Photographs; E103 (br) Richard Megna/Fundamental Photographs; E103 (cr) Richard Megna/Fundamental Photographs; E104-E105 (t) Phil Degginger/Color-Pic; E106 Gamma Tokyo/Liaison International; E108-E109 Spencer Grant/PhotoEdit; E109 (t) Tom Pantages; E109 (br) Tom Pantages; E111 (t) Phil Degginger/Color Pic; E111 (c) Phil Degginger/Color Pic; E111 (b) Bruno Joachin/Liaison International; E111 (bg) W. Cody/Corbis Westlight; E114 (r) Corbis-Bettmann; E114 (l) Phil Degginger/Color-Pic; E114 (t) William E. Ferguson; E115 (b) Phil Degginger/Color-Pic; E116 (t) Fonar Corporation; E116 (b) Jean Miele/The Stock Market.

Unit F

F2-F3 PictureQuest ; F3 (tc) Dwight R. Kuhn; F3 (br) Tony Freeman/PhotoEdit; F3 (li) Dwight R. Kuhn; F4 (bl)David R. Frazier; F6 (b) Mark E. Gibson; F8 (b)Bob Daemmrich/Stock Boston; F10 (b) Miro Vintoniv/Stock Boston; F12 (bl) Jean-Marc Barey/Agence Vandystadt/PhotoResearchers; F13 (tr) Daniel MacDonald/The Stock Shop; F15 (tl) Bernard Asset/Agence Vandystadt/Photo Researchers; F15 (b) Bernard Asset/Agence Vandystadt/Photo Researchers; F16 (t) Kathi Lamm/Tony Stone Images; F20(b) William R. Sallaz/Duomo Photograpy; F23 (c)Photo Library International/ESA/Photo Researchers; F23 (cr) Photo Researchers; F26 (b)) Michael Mauney/Tony Stone Images; F28 Brian Wilson; F29 (t) PA News; F29 (b)Michael Newman/PhotoEdit; F30 (r) UPI/Corbis-Bettmann; F34-F35 (bg) Dan Porges/Bruce Coleman, Inc.; F35 (tl) The Granger Collection; F35 (tr) R. Sheridan/Ancient Art and Architecture Collection; F36 (bl)) William McCoy/Rainbow; F38(bl)Yoav Levy/Phototake/PictureQuest; F41 (tr) Michael Newman/PhotoEdit; F42(tr) David R. Frazier; F46 (bl) Mark E. Gibson; F48 (b) Jeff Dunn/Stock Boston; F50 (bl)) Tom King/Tom King, Inc.; F52 (b) Aaron Haupt/David R. Frazier; F53 (t) Dan McCoy/Rainbow; F53 (cl) David Falconer/Folio; F53(br) Michael Newman/PhotoEdit; F54(t) Superstock; F55 (r) Churchill & Klehr; F55 (bl) Staircase & Millwork Corporation, Alpharetta, GA; F56(br) Tony Freeman/PhotoEdit; F58 (l) Archive Photos; F58 (l) Alexandra Guest/John F. Coates; F58 (t) Noble Stock/International Stock Photography; F59(l) Archive Photos; F59 (br) Eric Sanford/International Stock Photography; F60(bl) Library of Congress.

Health Handbook: R23 Palm Beach Post; R27 (t) Andrew Spielman/Phototake; (c) Martha McBride/Unicorn Stock; (b) Larry West/FPG International; R28 (l) Ron Chapple/FPG; (c) Mark Scott/FPG; (b) David Lissy/Index Stock.

All other photographs by Harcourt photographers listed below, © Harcourt: Weronica Ankarorn, Bartlett Digital Photograpy, Victoria Bowen, Eric Camden, Digital Imaging Group, Charles Hodges, Ken Karp, Ken Kinzie, Ed McDonald, Sheri O'Neal, Terry Sinclair.

Art Credits

Mike Dammer A25, A57, A83, A109, B35, B63, B93, C27, C55, C77, D27, D49, D85, E27, E55, E83, E117, F31; Jean Calder A91, A92, A96 (t), A102, A103; Susan Carlson A49, D22; Daniel del Valle F7; John Downes F56 (b); John Francis B14; Lisa Frasier E48-E49, D10; George Fryer C6, C18, C19, C42, C44, B70, D20, D21, D80, F46; Geosystems A49, B20; Patrick Gnan F42, E52, E3, E87; Pedro Julio Gonzalez A14; Terry Hadler E14, E19, E41, F46, F47; Tim Hayward A8, C70, C72; Robert Hynes B26, B28, B56, Joe LeMonüer A2, A56, E59, A82; Sebastian Quigley B86, E6, E8, E22, E90, E91, E104, E108, D12, D44, D62, D63, D64, D72, F22, F24, F25; Mike Saunders A18, A19, A65, A76, C7, C48, C62, C68, B43, B44, D8, D56, D57, D58; Steve Seymour C8, C13, B7, B80, E35, E36, E43, E62, E68, E69, E70, E75, E78, E79, E92, E96, E97, D14, D15, D43, D72, F15, F41; Eberhard Reinmann A90,A92, A96 (b), A98, A104, E64; Steve Westin C12, C20, C21, C40, C43, B48, E76, E77, E102, F48, F54, F55, F56 (t)

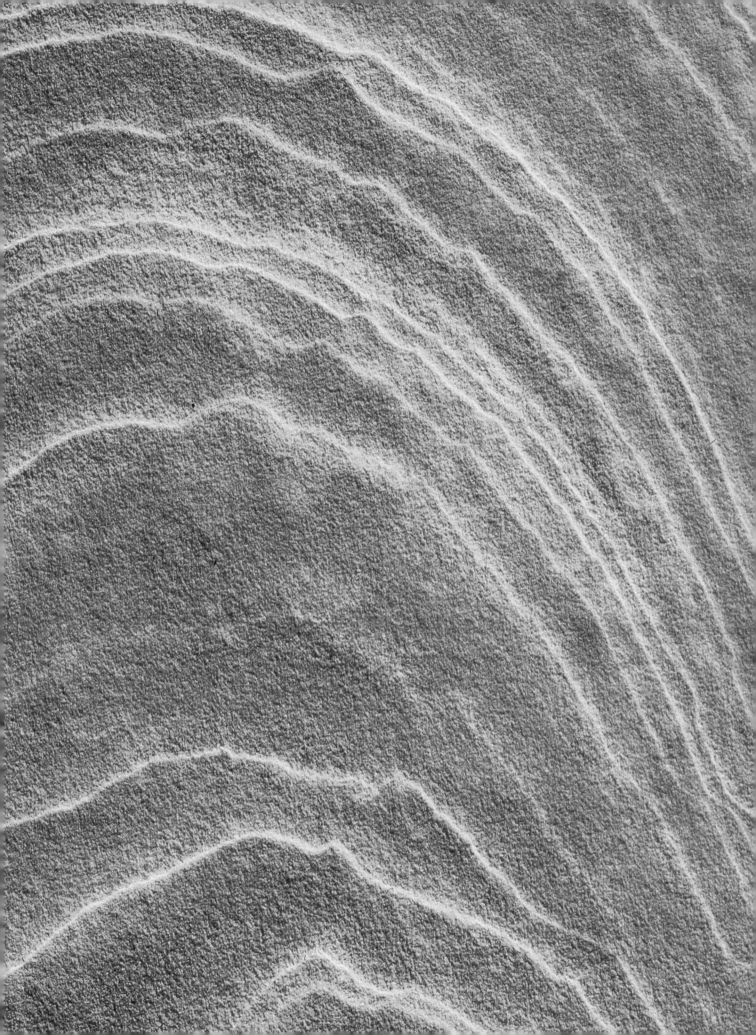

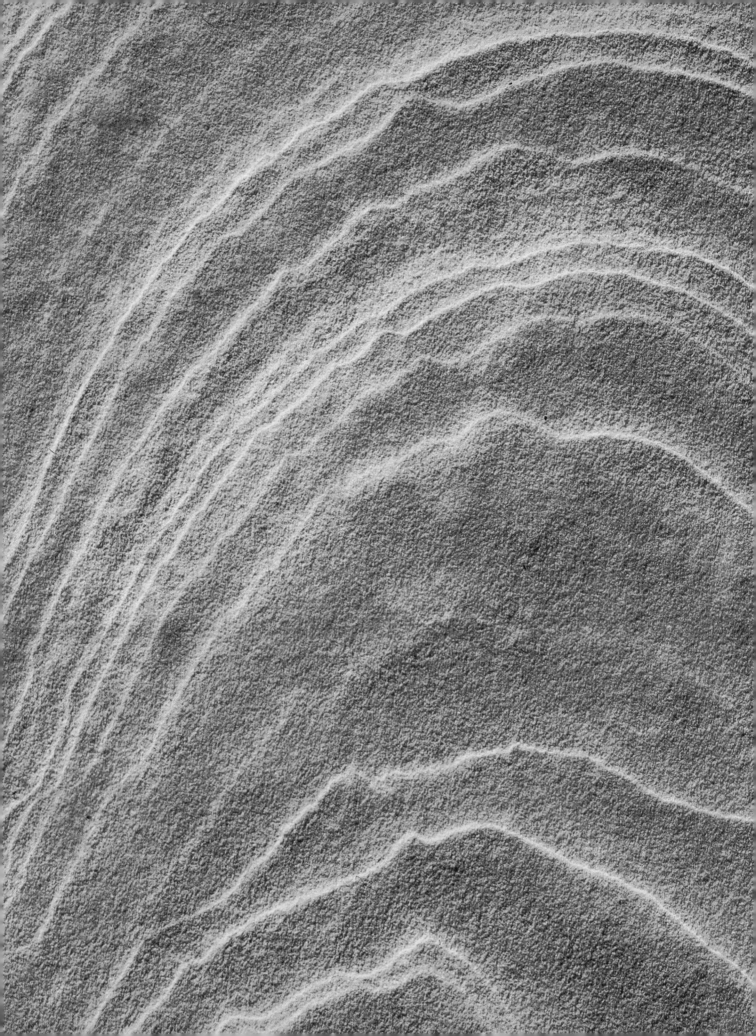